MATHEMATICS
Exploring Your World

AUTHORS

Grades K–2 Team
Herbert P. Ginsburg
Deborah B. Gustafson
Larry P. Leutzinger

Problem Solving Team
Lucille Croom
Gerald A. Goldin
Stephen Krulik
Henry O. Pollak
Jesse A. Rudnick
Dale G. Seymour

Grades 3–8 Team
Ruth I. Champagne
Carole E. Greenes
William D. McKillip
Lucy J. Orfan
Fernand J. Prevost
Bruce R. Vogeli
Marianne V. Weber

SILVER BURDETT & GINN

MORRISTOWN, NJ • NEEDHAM, MA
Atlanta, GA • Cincinnati, OH • Dallas, TX
Deerfield, IL • Menlo Park, CA

Table of Contents

Introducing . . .
MATHEMATICS Exploring Your World ix–xi

ii

The Granger Collection

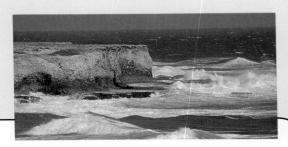

5 Geometry

6 Adding and Subtracting Fractions

PRICES *SLASHED*
50%!
Buy today
and take another
50% off!

11

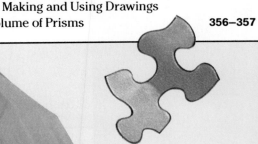

12

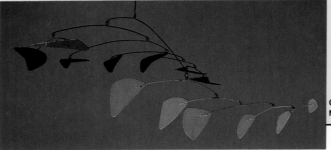

CALDER, Alexander   American, 1898–1976
National Gallery of Art, Washington.

The universal language of mathematics opens the door to a world of ideas.

MATHEMATICS
Exploring Your World

How do manufacturers of skis use mathematics?

What geometric shapes are found in nature?

What if you had to predict the number of people living in this city next year? How would you do it?

Share Your Ideas Mathematics is an important part of our world. How will you use mathematics today?

How Will You Learn Mathematics?

You will learn mathematics in several different ways. Each way will help you become a better mathematician.

Learn by Working Cooperatively with Others

Working together

What if all 2-digit numbers were reversed? What problems would you encounter until this was recognized?

In your group…

- Always contribute to the best of your ability.
- Consider all ideas carefully.
- Discuss why you agree or disagree.
- Help the group to reach agreement.

I am 13

I am 31

Learn by Making Choices

Decision-making is a part of mathematics. This symbol means you will be able to make choices to solve problems.

Do you need an exact answer or an estimate? How will you find an exact answer?

- manipulatives
- mental math
- calculator
- paper and pencil

Learn by Using Mathematics in Other Areas

Biology
What kind of symmetry does this leaf have?

Sports
Using this machine, you can burn 600 calories per hour.

Learn by Thinking in Different Ways

- **Logical thinking** is being able to piece together separate parts to find an answer.

- **Visual thinking** is being able to analyze a picture to find an answer.

- **Critical thinking** encourages questioning and searching for new possibilities.

Logical Thinking

Look at each pattern. Predict what comes next.

100, 10, 1, …

9, 16, 23, 30, …

O, T, T, F, F, …

Learn by Solving Interesting Problems

Problems can be solved with many strategies. You will decide which strategy is best: organized listing, working backward, guess and test, solving a simpler problem, or simulations.

THINK
EXPLORE
SOLVE
LOOK BACK

Was your summer vacation more than one million minutes long? Estimate.

Devise a plan to find out if you are correct. Carry out your plan.

Mathematics will enable you to explore the world in many ways. The opportunity is yours!

SUMMING UP

1 Adding and Subtracting Whole Numbers and Decimals

THEME   Sports: It's a Game of Numbers

Sharing What You Know

Ball four, strike three; 10-yard penalty, first down; 100-meter dash, 1,500-meter run—every sport has its own vocabulary, and every sport uses mathematics. "Astros Win With Three Runs in Bottom of Ninth," "15-Yard Penalty Halts 49er Drive," "Smith Takes 200-Meter Race in 21.03 Seconds" are examples of mathematics even in sports headlines. How is mathematics used in your favorite sport?

Using Language

Two legendary figures in baseball's Hall of Fame are Babe Ruth and Lou Gehrig. These sports greats have career batting averages of .342 and .340, respectively. The numerical **difference** between Ruth's and Gehrig's averages is 0.002. Two thousandths of a point is a very small number. Yet fans of Ruth or Gehrig will insist that there is a big **difference** between these two players. What other important statistics might influence these opinions? Discuss how mathematics can help to support your side of an argument.

Words to Know: difference, standard form, equivalent decimals, Associative Property, Commutative Property, Identity Property

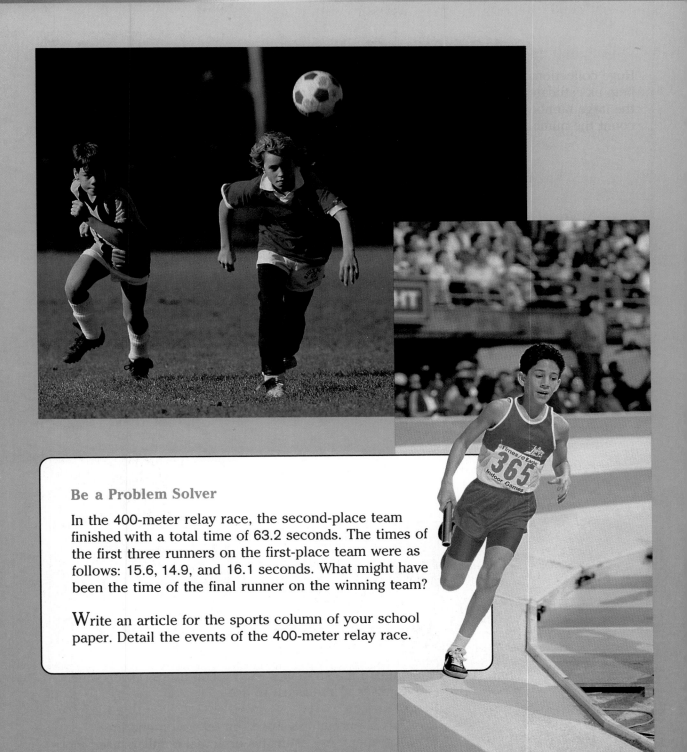

Be a Problem Solver

In the 400-meter relay race, the second-place team finished with a total time of 63.2 seconds. The times of the first three runners on the first-place team were as follows: 15.6, 14.9, and 16.1 seconds. What might have been the time of the final runner on the winning team?

Write an article for the sports column of your school paper. Detail the events of the 400-meter relay race.

Activity

A Counting Challenge

Huge collections fill our world. Mathematical skills help us estimate their size and calculate and record the large numbers needed to describe them. Can you count the number of things in each of these collections?

Working together

A. Think of ways to count or estimate the number of things on these pages. Make a list of the different ways, or strategies, that might work.

B. Decide which strategy can help you answer the following questions. Explain your answers.

Do you think there are more bees in the swarm or birds in the flock?

Do you think there are more kernels of corn or people in the stadium?

Which picture, do you think, contains the greatest number of people or objects?

Sharing Your Results

1. Compare the strategies each group used. Decide which strategies were easiest to use.

2. Think about numbers used on television and in newspapers. Are estimates or actual numbers used more often to describe large numbers of things?

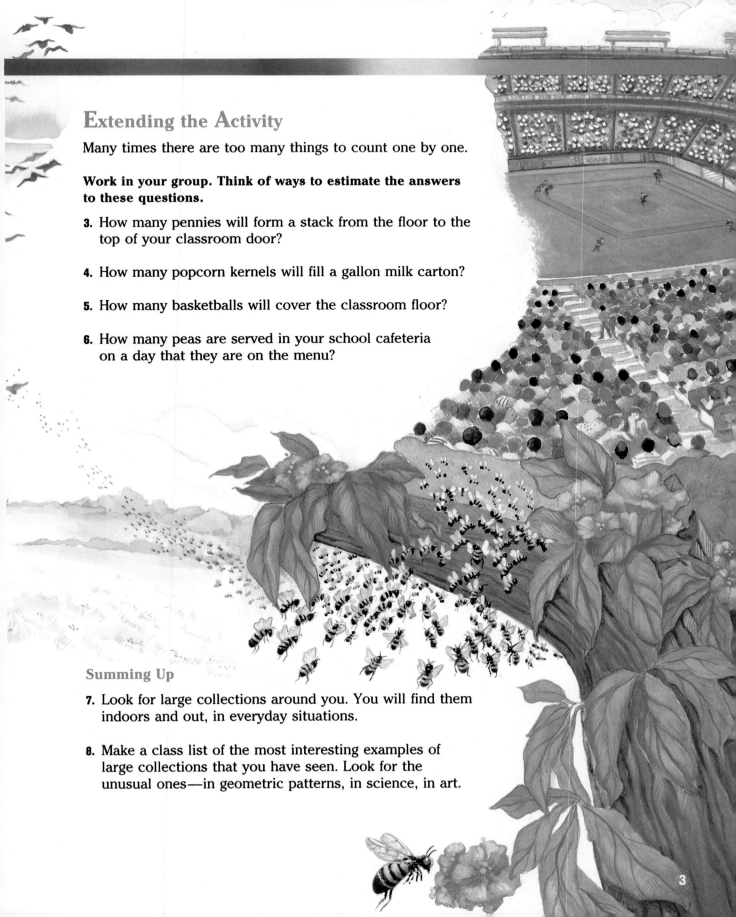

Extending the Activity

Many times there are too many things to count one by one.

Work in your group. Think of ways to estimate the answers to these questions.

3. How many pennies will form a stack from the floor to the top of your classroom door?

4. How many popcorn kernels will fill a gallon milk carton?

5. How many basketballs will cover the classroom floor?

6. How many peas are served in your school cafeteria on a day that they are on the menu?

Summing Up

7. Look for large collections around you. You will find them indoors and out, in everyday situations.

8. Make a class list of the most interesting examples of large collections that you have seen. Look for the unusual ones—in geometric patterns, in science, in art.

How big is a million? If someone gives away one thousand dollars a day, how long will it take to give away one million dollars?

Place Value

Ace McKay saw the following information in a magazine. "In a recent year, consumers spent about $17,300,000,000 on sporting goods." Ace wondered why the number had so many zeros.

The number is separated by commas into groups of three digits called periods.

This place-value chart shows the periods and the value of each digit.

Each place has a value ten times the value of the place to its right.

Trillions			Billions			Millions			Thousands			Ones		
h	t	o	h	t	o	h	t	o	h	t	o	h	t	o
10^{14}	10^{13}	10^{12}	10^{11}	10^{10}	10^9	10^8	10^7	10^6	10^5	10^4	10^3	10^2	10^1	10^0
				1	7	3	0	0	0	0	0	0	0	0

standard form	**17,300,000,000**
read	**17** billion, **300** million
write	seventeen billion, three hundred million

You can also show the value of each digit in expanded form. Here are two ways to write 17,300,000,000.

expanded form   10,000,000,000 + 7,000,000,000 + 300,000,000
         (1×10^{10}) + (7×10^9) + (3×10^8)

How should you explain to Ace what zeros mean when he writes a number?

Check Your Understanding

Read each number. Give the value of the digit 4. Then write each number in expanded form.

1. 243,100,000   **2.** 482,051,000,000   **3.** 4,006,709,000,000

Share Your Ideas   How does the value of the number 123 change when one zero is written after the digit 3? when two zeros are written? when three zeros are written?

Read each number. Give the value of the digit 4. Then write each number in expanded form.

4. 34,080,000   **5.** 29,000,406,000   **6.** 400,000,000,000,201

7. 4 billion, 356 million, 7 thousand   **8.** 36 trillion, 495 thousand, 803

Write each number in standard form.

9. $(3 \times 10^6) + (2 \times 10^3) + (5 \times 10^2) + (3 \times 10^1) + (7 \times 1)$

10. $(6 \times 10^{14}) + (4 \times 10^2) + (9 \times 10^1) + (8 \times 1)$

11. 326 million, 512 thousand, 708

12. 4 hundred million

Write each number in words.

13. 127,770,000   **14.** 200,500,006,000   **15.** 19,000,000,000,000

Give the next four numbers to continue each pattern.

16. 1, 10, 100, 1,000   **17.** 2,000, 2,100, 2,200

18. 52 million, 62 million, 72 million   **19.** 700 trillion, 70 trillion, 7 trillion

Think and Apply

20. Explain how each period in the place value chart is the same. Explain how each period is different.

21. Last year, sales at Sports World totaled seven hundred eighteen thousand dollars. Write this number in standard form.

Mathematics and History

The ancient Egyptians used the symbols shown to represent numbers.

The Egyptian number system was not a place-value system. Each symbol is repeated as many times as needed to represent a certain number.

Write the following in Egyptian numerals.

22. 24   **23.** 321   **24.** 205   **25.** 1,462   **26.** 3,023

27. What, do you think, are the advantages and disadvantages of this system? Discuss.

Explain why 25,000,000 is different from 2,500,000.

SUMMING UP

How long does it take to blink an eye?

Decimals to Millionths

This computer image shows the movement of a gymnast to a fraction of a second. Each stick figure represents a frame of 0.017 seconds.

In a decimal the fractional part of a number is written to the right of the decimal point.

The place-value chart is extended to show the value of places to the right of the ones place.

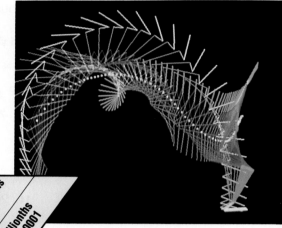

hundreds 100	tens 10	ones 1	tenths 0.1	hundredths 0.01	thousandths 0.001	ten-thousandths 0.0001	hundred-thousandths 0.00001	millionths 0.000001
100	10	1	$\frac{1}{10}$	$\frac{1}{100}$	$\frac{1}{1,000}$	$\frac{1}{10,000}$	$\frac{1}{100,000}$	$\frac{1}{1,000,000}$
		0.	0	1	7			
1	0	8.	3	0	6	0	5	4

standard form   0.017
       read   17 thousandths

standard form   108.306054
         read   108 and 306,054 millionths

You can write a decimal number in expanded form.

108.306054 = 100 + 8 + 0.3 + 0.006 + 0.00005 + 0.000004

$$= 100 + 8 + \frac{3}{10} + \frac{6}{1,000} + \frac{5}{100,000} + \frac{4}{1,000,000}$$

$$= (1 \times 100) + (8 \times 1) + (3 \times \frac{1}{10}) + (6 \times \frac{1}{1,000}) + (5 \times \frac{1}{100,000}) + (4 \times \frac{1}{1,000,000})$$

The decimal 0.5 names the fraction $\frac{5}{10}$.
The fraction $\frac{25}{100}$ names what decimal?

Check Your Understanding

Write each as a decimal in standard form.

1. $\frac{8}{100}$

2. $12\frac{135}{10,000}$

3. 38 ten-thousandths

4. 3 and 7 millionths

Share Your Ideas   How does the value of 1.3 change when zeros are written between 1 and the decimal point? between the decimal point and 3?

Write each as a decimal.

5. $\frac{6}{10}$

6. $2\frac{38}{100}$

7. $\frac{145}{10,000}$

8. $7\frac{19}{1,000}$

9. 34 millionths

10. 4 and 6 ten-thousandths

11. 5 and 24,608 millionths

12. 67 and 40 thousandths

13. 0.3 + 0.02 + 0.001 + 0.0009

14. 8 + 0.04 + 0.006 + 0.00005

15. $(3 \times \frac{1}{10,000}) + (9 \times \frac{1}{100,000}) + (4 \times \frac{1}{1,000,000})$

16. $(3 \times 100) + (5 \times \frac{1}{100})$

17. $(5 \times 10) + (2 \times \frac{1}{10}) + (7 \times \frac{1}{1,000})$

18. $(4 \times 1,000) + (3 \times 1) + (8 \times \frac{1}{1,000})$

Write each decimal in expanded form.

19. 43.5083

20. 100.005839

21. 0.0123

22. 80.06

Write each decimal in words.

23. 906.380

24. 45.396047

25. 0.00462

26. 502.05

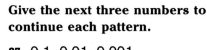

Give the next three numbers to continue each pattern.

27. 0.1, 0.01, 0.001

28. 0.12, 0.13, 0.14

29. 1.12, 1.22, 1.32

30. 0.04, 0.09, 0.14

Think and Apply

31. A sports scientist replayed 58 of the 1,000 computer frames he created of an athlete running. Write a decimal for the part of the frames the scientist replayed.

32. Of the 100 gymnasts at the meet, 34 are boys. Write a decimal for the part of the gymnasts that are girls.

33. A computer microchip works so fast that it can process information in a nanosecond. A nanosecond is 1 billionth of a second. Write the decimal in standard form.

Use the digits 0, 3, and 5 and a decimal point. Write five different numbers. Explain why the numbers are different.

SUMMING UP

Use the digits 1, 3, 6, and 8. Write the greatest and the least possible numbers.

Comparing and Ordering Whole Numbers and Decimals

Susan scored 9.85 points on her first dive and 9.8 points on her second dive. On which dive did Susan receive the better score?

You can use a number line to compare 9.85 and 9.8.

```
←——|————|————|————|————|————|————|————|————|————|————→
  9.80  9.81  9.82  9.83  9.84  9.85  9.86  9.87  9.88  9.89  9.90
```

9.8 and 9.80 are **equivalent decimals.**
They name the same number.

9.85 is at the right of 9.80 on the number line.
9.85 is greater than 9.80. 9.85 > 9.80

You can also use place value to compare the numbers.

Start at the left and compare digits in the same place-value position.

┌——same——┐
┌—same—┐
9.85 ● **9.80**

5 > 0

So 9.85 > 9.8.

When the number of decimal places in two decimals are different, annex zeros to compare.

Susan received the better score on her first dive.

List the numbers below in order from least to greatest.

23,309   23,185   23,451

To order numbers, compare them two at a time.

**23,309 > 23,185 and 23,309 < 23,451
So 23,185 < 23,309 < 23,451.**

The numbers, from least to greatest, are 23,185; 23,309; 23,451.

Check Your Understanding

Compare. Use <, >, or = for each ●.

1. 16,158 ● 17,149   **2.** 9.2 ● 9.01   **3.** 4.3 ● 4.300

Share Your Ideas   Are 4.7, 4.70, and 4.700 equivalent decimals?
Explain why or why not.

Compare. Use >, <, or = for each ●.

4. 8,917 ● 8,907
5. 15 ● 15.01
6. 43.70 ● 43.07

7. 9.98 ● 9.9800
8. 46,179 ● 4,617
9. 0.01 ● 0.001

10. 64.5 ● 65.49
11. 0.016 ● 0.16
12. 52.7 ● 52.70

13. 9.0 ● 9
14. 11.56 ● 11.563
15. 872 ● 874

16. 1.537 ● 153.7
17. 46.68 ● 56.68
18. 32,174 ● 32,740

Write in order from least to greatest.

19. 18,175; 19,175; 18,350
20. 0.5; 0.505; 0.55

21. 0.910; 0.091; 0.9
22. 654,185; 6,541,850; 651,893

23. 6; 6.01; 0.601; 6.1
24. 27.6; 27.65; 27.5; 27.62

**Write three decimals that are between the numbers in each pair.
Draw a number line and show the points for each.**

25. 2.5 and 2.6
26. 5.62 and 5.63
27. 123 and 124

28. **Look back** at **25-27**. Can you always find a decimal number between any two numbers? Explain.

Think and Apply

29. On your calculator enter any decimal number that ends with a zero at the right of the decimal point. Press any operation key. What happens to your number? Explain why.

30. Write three decimal numbers. Exchange papers with a partner. Order the numbers from least to greatest.

31. Five divers are entered in a competition. Four of the divers have had their turns. The scores are 9.8, 9.75, 9.81, and 9.79. What score must the last diver get in order to win the competition?

Logical Thinking

Solve.

32. Cindy has as many baseball cards as Larry.
Larry has as many baseball cards as Juan.
Juan has 125 baseball cards.
How many baseball cards does Cindy have?

33. If $a = b$ and $b = c$, then $a = ?$
How does this relate to **32**?

Look back at **4–18**. Write a rule in your own words for comparing two decimals.

SUMMING UP

Midchapter Review

Give the value of the digit 9. Then write each number in expanded form. pages 4–7

1. 67,900,000

2. 7.09

3. 9.65

4. 9,000,008

5. 0.916

6. 1,009,000

Write the word name for each number. pages 4–7

7. 7,000,010,005

8. 5,030,000,000,900

9. 6.008

10. 0.04

Write each number in standard form. pages 4–7

11. 7 billion, 12 million

12. 9 and 17 thousandths

13. $(6 \times 1,000) + (5 \times 10) + (7 \times 1)$

14. $(5 \times 1) + (6 \times \frac{1}{10}) + (7 \times \frac{1}{100})$

Compare. Use <, >, or = for each ⬤. pages 8–9

15. 15.099 ⬤ 15.11

16. 9,230 ⬤ 9,209

17. 12.564 ⬤ 12.56

18. 7.1498 ⬤ 7.2

19. 18 ⬤ 18.0

20. 15,008 ⬤ 15,080

Write in order from least to greatest. pages 8–9

21. 0.909; 0.090; 0.90

22. 26,057; 26,007; 2,706; 2.670

23. 8,822; 8,288; 8,282

24. 6.85; 68.5; 0.685

Solve.

25. The times for the first 3 runners of the 100-yard dash are 9.85 s, 9.625 s, and 9.6 s. What is the winning time? What is the time for the second-place runner?

26. The first marathon runner crossed the finish line in 3 h 26 min 40 s. **What if** the next 5 runners crossed the finish line in 10-second intervals. What would be the times for the next 5 runners?

Exploring Problem Solving

How Should He Train?

Stan is training for a triathlon—a race that combines biking, running, and swimming. He devised this point system to use in planning a training schedule.

Swimming 1 point per $\frac{1}{4}$ mile

Running   1 point per mile

Biking   1 point per 4 miles

Stan wants to plan a balanced program so that he earns at least 60 points each week. It is important that he practice each event at least 3 times a week. He would also like to rest 1 day each week.

Thinking Critically

Plan a training program for Stan.

When you do problem-solving lessons like this, work in a small group. Keep a written record of your work so that you can share your thinking with others.

Analyzing and Making Decisions

CHOICES **Use a calculator where appropriate.**

1. How far does Stan have to run, bike, or swim to earn a point? How many points does he want to earn in a week? Why, do you think, did he devise the point system?

2. About how many points might he want to earn by training in each event?

3. How many times each week does he wish to practice each event? How many days does he want to train during the week?

4. Will he have to train for 2 events in one day? Why? How can he do that?

5. Write Stan's schedule for the week.

Look Back Wilma is training for the triathlon with Stan. Her weakest event is biking. Write a schedule that requires Wilma to earn more points by biking.

Problem Solving Strategies

Alternate Solutions

Jackie is in training and she wants to consume at least 450 grams of carbohydrates each day. The chart below shows her diet for one day. Using the foods listed in the chart, how could Jackie add to her diet so that she consumes at least 450 grams of carbohydrates?

Meals	Foods	Carbohydrates
Breakfast	2 cups orange juice	52 grams
	1 serving oatmeal	18 grams
	2 slices toast	28 grams
	1 cup milk	11 grams
	1 grapefruit	28 grams
Lunch	2 cups chili with beans	48 grams
	1 cup milk	11 grams
	1 medium apple	21 grams
	1 serving fruit yogurt	12 grams
Dinner	1 cup milk	11 grams
	2 servings spaghetti	105 grams
	1 serving mixed salad	12 grams
	1 banana	24 grams
	1 hard roll	31 grams

Some problems can have more than one solution.

Solving the Problem

CHOICES **Use a calculator where appropriate.**

Think What do you need to find out?

Explore How many grams of carbohydrates has Jackie consumed in her diet for the day? How many more grams does she need to consume? How can you tell how many grams of carbohydrates foods have?

Solve What items might Jackie add to her diet in order to consume at least 450 grams of carbohydrates?

Look Back Does Jackie eat about the same number of carbohydrates at each meal? Explain.

Share Your Ideas

1. How might Jackie change her diet so that she eats about the same number of carbohydrates at each meal?

Practice

CHOICES **Solve. Use a calculator where appropriate.**

In baseball, a person can make an out, score a run, or be on one of 3 bases.

2. Seven people bat, and two of them make an out. How many runs could have been scored?

3. Eleven people had batted by the time three outs were made. How many runs could have been scored?

In a basketball game the following players scored field goals worth 2 points and free throws worth 1 point.

4. Jan scored 11 points. How could she have scored them?

5. Theresa scored 14 points. How could she have scored them?

Use the information in the chart to solve 6 and 7.

6. Julian wants to buy souvenirs for 3 friends. He has $10. What might he buy?

7. Milly wants to buy souvenirs for 3 friends. She has $15. What might she buy?

8. Election Day is always the first Tuesday after the first Monday in November. What are the possible dates for Election Day?

Create Your Own

Use the information about the prices of souvenirs and write a problem that can have more than one solution.

SOUVENIR STAND	
PEANUTS	$3.50
TEAM PICTURE	$4.75
AUTOGRAPHED BALL	$7.50
PROGRAM BOOK	$2.00
T-SHIRTS	$5.25

13

Add 50 + 30 in your head. Add 6 + 7 in your head. Find the sum of 56 + 37 in your head. Explain your method.

Mental Math: Using Properties

Daphney Digit is a Mathlete. She does her math work mentally by using the properties of addition and what she knows about place value.

Here is how Daphney added 48 + 35, using mental math.

$$48 + 35 = 48 + (30 + 5)$$
$$= (48 + 30) + 5$$
$$= 78 + 5$$
$$= 83$$

Identify the properties Daphney used to find the answer.

How else might you find the sum mentally?

Daphney was also able to add decimals, using mental math.

Add 6.4 + 2.8.

$6 + 2 = 8$
4 tenths + 8 tenths = 1 and 2 tenths
8 + 1 and 2 tenths = 9 and 2 tenths
$6.4 + 2.8 = 9.2$

How else might you find the sum mentally?

Addition Properties

Commutative Property

The order of the addends does not change the sum.

$$a + b = b + a$$
$$12 + 25 = 25 + 12$$

Associative Property

The way that addends are grouped does not change the sum.

$$(a + b) + c = a + (b + c)$$
$$(29 + 35) + 15 = 29 + (35 + 15)$$

Identity Property

The sum of zero and any number is that number.

$$a + 0 = a$$
$$32 + 0 = 32$$

Check Your Understanding

Find each sum mentally.

1. 46 + 39
2. 75 + 89 + 25
3. 42 + 7.9
4. 3.8 + 5.2 + 0
5. 76 + 51
6. 15.7 + 5.3

Share Your Ideas   Explain how you found your answer to 2. Identify the properties you used.

Find each sum mentally.

7. $37 + 55$

8. $280 + 460$

9. $35 + 49 + 65$

10. $117 + 523$

11. $4.5 + 3.5$

12. $10.9 + 8.4$

13. $0.17 + 0.26$

14. $1.8 + 4.9 + 7.2$

15. $26 + 0 + 59$

16. $385 + 270$

17. $74 + 591$

18. $3{,}420 + 1{,}280$

19. $51 + 45 + 29 + 55$

20. $2.3 + 6.4 + 5.7 + 8.6$

21. $35 + 20 + 0 + 15$

22. $0.035 + 0.02 + 0 + 0.015$

23. Look back at **21** and **22**. Explain how finding the answer to **21** helped you answer **22**.

Find each missing addend. Name the properties you used.

24. $(18 + 45) + 35 = 18 + (n + 35)$

25. $2.7 + 3.4 + 8.9 = 3.4 + n + 8.9$

26. $32 + n = 32$

27. $(75 + 34) + n = (75 + 25) + 34$

28. $6.5 + 0 + n = 6.5 + 2.7 + 0$

29. $(56 + n) + 41 = 56 + (39 + 41)$

Think and Apply

30. Make up a problem that is easy to solve by using a mental math strategy. Exchange problems with a partner.

Use mental math to solve each.

31. In four football games, Fred gained 125 yd, 100 yd, 75 yd, and 115 yd. What is the total gain for the four games?

32. The times for three parts of a relay race are 63 s, 57 s, and 30 s. What is the time, in minutes, for the entire relay race?

33. Derek gained 75 yd in the first half of a game. He did not play in the second half. What is his total number of yards gained for the game?

Visual Thinking

Visualization is the ability to see an image in the mind.

Visualization can help athletes improve their performances.

Visualization can help you perform computations mentally.

34. Here is an activity to test your visual memory.

- Have a partner draw a filled-in tic-tac-toe grid on a sheet of paper and cover it.

- Remove the cover and look at the grid for 1 second.

- On another piece of paper, draw what you saw.

How good is your visual memory?

Make up a problem that is so complicated to add that no mental math strategy is helpful.

SUMMING UP

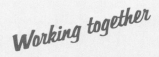

Exploring Mental Math: Addition

When mathematician Carl Friedrich Gauss was a young boy, his teacher made him add long lists of numbers to keep him busy. So he tried to find quick, easy ways to do this.

Working together

A. Devise a way to find this sum quickly and easily.

1 + 2 + 3 + 4 + 5 + 6 + 7 + 8 + 9 + 10 + 11 + 12 + 13 + 14 + 15

You may use paper and pencil, mental math, or a calculator to help you.

B. Compare your method with the way Gauss did it.

1 +	2 +	3 +	4 +	5 +	6 +	7 +	8 +	9 +	10 +	11 +	12 +	13 +	14 +	15
+15 +	14 +	13 +	12 +	11 +	10 +	9 +	8 +	7 +	6 +	5 +	4 +	3 +	2 +	1
16	16	16	16	16	16	16	16	16	16	16	16	16	16	16

$15 \times 16 = 240$ Why did he multiply by 15?

$240 \div 2 = 120$ Why did he divide by 2?

C. Find the sum of all whole numbers from 1 to 20. Work with a partner. One person should use your method. The other person should use Gauss's method. Work at the same time to see which way is quicker.

D. Exchange methods and repeat for the sum of all whole numbers from 1 to 30.

Sharing Your Results

1. How are your method and Gauss's method alike? How are they different?

2. Gauss's method can be used to add any list of consecutive whole numbers. Describe how his method works when the first number is 1.

3. How could you quickly find the sum 3 + 6 + 9 + 12 + 15 + 18 + 21 + 24 + 27 + 30? How could you use the Distributive Property and Gauss's method to help you?

Extending the Activity

Here are some other ways to add numbers quickly and easily, using mental math.

a. $164 + 197 = 164 + 200 - 3$
$\qquad\qquad\quad = 364 - 3$
$\qquad\qquad\quad = 361$

$200 - 3 = 197$

200 is easier to add mentally. Then subtract 3.

b. $3{,}995 + 957 = (3{,}995 + 5) + (957 - 5)$
$\qquad\qquad\qquad = 4{,}000 + 952$
$\qquad\qquad\qquad = 4{,}952$

What happens when you add and subtract the same number?

c. $720 + 836 = 720 + 800 + 30 + 6$
$\qquad\qquad\quad = 1{,}520 + 30 + 6$
$\qquad\qquad\quad = 1{,}550 + 6$
$\qquad\qquad\quad = 1{,}556$

Explain the method used.

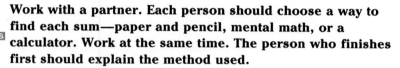

Work with a partner. Each person should choose a way to find each sum—paper and pencil, mental math, or a calculator. Work at the same time. The person who finishes first should explain the method used.

4. $872 + 968$ **5.** $3{,}650 + 2{,}998$ **6.** $796 + 1{,}247$ **7.** $2{,}397 + 1{,}475$

8. $3{,}995 + 7{,}067$ **9.** $5{,}071 + 3{,}829$ **10.** \$4.98 + \$4.98   **11.** \$15.87 + \$6.99

Summing Up

12. Which way was more frequently the quickest—paper and pencil, mental math, or a calculator? Explain.

13. Why might you choose one method over another? For example, why might you choose to solve a problem by using mental math instead of a calculator? a calculator instead of paper and pencil?

14. Could any of the ways to add by using mental math shown in **a–c** be used to subtract by using mental math? If so, how? Show an example.

How many footballs will it take to fill your classroom? Is it possible to find the exact answer? Is it realistic to find the exact answer?

Estimating Sums

Which of the numbers in these headlines do you think are estimates? Do you think most numbers in the news are estimates? Explain.

NEWS

...AYES HITS 250TH HOME RUN!

1 BILLION VIEW OLYMPICS...

NEWS

Look at the table. How would you report the total attendance at the Cosmos football games for your school newspaper?

There are many estimation strategies that you can use to estimate the sum.

COSMOS FOOTBALL

Opponent	Attendance
Stanton	408
Louisville	356
Marlboro	362

Front-end strategy

Add the front digits, and then adjust the estimate.

```
  408        408
  356        356  ⟵
+ 362      + 362  ⟵  } about 100
-----      -----
1,000      1,000 + 100 = 1,100
```

Rounding strategy

Round to the nearest hundred.

```
  408  ⟶  400
  356  ⟶  400
+ 362  ⟶  400
         -----
         1,200
```

Notice that all the amounts are close to 400. So you can also estimate the total as 3 × 400.

Both 1,100 and 1,200 are good estimates for the total attendance.

You can also use these strategies to estimate decimal sums.

Estimate 3.75 + 4.29.

Front-end

```
  3.75        3.75  ⟵
+ 4.29      + 4.29  ⟵  } about 1
-----       -----
   7         7 + 1 = 8
```

Rounding

```
nearest one    4          nearest tenth    3.8
             + 4                          + 4.3
             ---                          -----
               8                            8.1
```

Estimate. Describe your method.

1. 4,236 + 3,178
2. $7.15 + $4.54 + $6.39
3. 44,158 + 19,123 + 6,087

Share Your Ideas   When you round to estimate, you may get an overestimate or an underestimate. Explain why.

Estimate. Describe your method.

4. 43,918
    94,715
    + 9,200

5. 127,456
      2,517
    + 13,645

6. 546,834
    +115,932

7. $24.89 + $72.15

8. 6.39 + 4.25

9. $11.79 + $4.58

10. 1.93 + 5.248

11. $5.89 + $0.45 + $2.11 + $1.79

12. 0.23 + 0.009 + 0.54 + 1.89

Estimate. Then compare using < or > for each ●.

13. 7.34 + 2.9 + 25.11 ● 35

14. 327,533 + 156,132 ● 600,000

15. 8.73 + 5.25 ● 13

16. 0.24 + 0.009 + 0.398 ● 1

In which of these can you find an exact answer?
In which is only an estimate practical? Explain.

17. the votes received by your school president

18. the distance between planets

19. the capacity of your school auditorium

20. the population of Dallas, Texas

Think and Apply

21. Find an advertisement for books in a newspaper or magazine. Select several books that interest you and estimate their total cost.

22. Combine the data your class collected, and prepare a list of books you want to buy for the school library. Estimate the total cost.

When you use the front-end strategy for estimation, will you get an overestimate or an underestimate? Explain your thinking.

SUMMING UP

Add $30 + $15 mentally.
Subtract 50¢ from $45 mentally.
Find $29.50 + $15 mentally.

Adding Whole Numbers and Decimals

Sophie wants to buy skis and ski boots.
Here is how she calculated the price mentally.

$300 + $175 = $475
$475 − $.50 = $474.50

Sometimes you need paper and pencil to
complete a calculation. Find the total cost
of a toboggan, skates, and a sweater.

Align the decimal points. Use zeros to hold
places. Add as with whole numbers. Place
the decimal point in the sum.

$$
\begin{array}{r}
\$199.49 \\
43.79 \\
+\quad 50.00 \\
\hline
\$293.28
\end{array}
\qquad
\begin{array}{r}
\$200 \\
40 \\
+\quad 50 \\
\hline
\$290
\end{array}
$$

Estimate to be
sure your answer
makes sense.

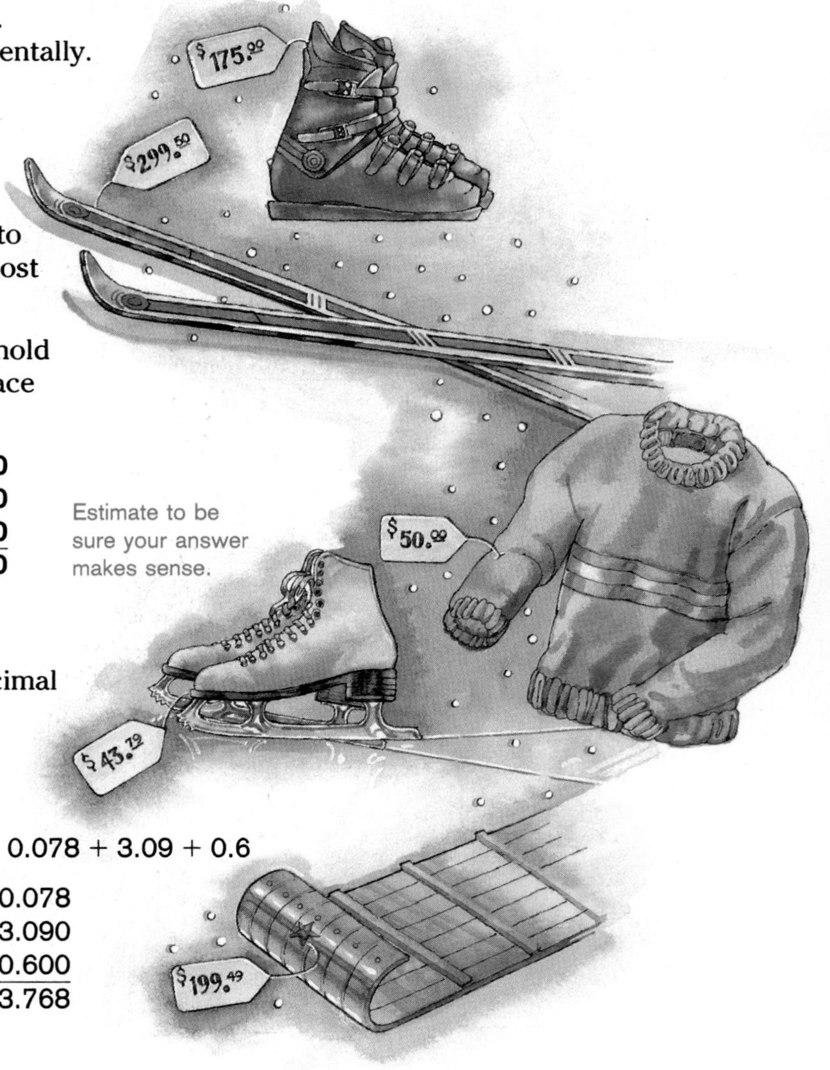

The total cost is $293.28.

Explain why it is necessary to align decimal
points when adding decimals.

More Examples

a. Add. 24 + 5.321 + 203.2

$$
\begin{array}{r}
24.000 \\
5.321 \\
+\ 203.200 \\
\hline
232.521
\end{array}
$$

b. Add. 0.078 + 3.09 + 0.6

$$
\begin{array}{r}
0.078 \\
3.090 \\
+\ 0.600 \\
\hline
3.768
\end{array}
$$

Add. Estimate to be sure your answer makes sense.

1. 934,583 + 61,742   **2.** 5.79 + 3.085   **3.** 3,298 + 47.16

Share Your Ideas   Place a decimal point in each sum. Explain your method.

4. 1.704 + 582.936 = 58464   **5.** 56.3 + 2.0184 = 583184

Add. Estimate to see if your answer makes sense.

6. 87,541 + 9,689	**7.** $234.50 + 187.95	**8.** 315.93 + 24.65	**9.** 5.67 + 38.09	**10.** 1,465.9 + 321.56

11. 15.91 6.75 + 27.08	**12.** 23,175 479,388 + 67,249	**13.** 3.986 37. + 25.902	**14.** $12.95 67.89 + 54.55	**15.** 504.6 13.7 + 0.029

16. 76.5 + 0.1609   **17.** 18.49 + 0.942   **18.** 22.1 + 0.2895

19. 78.1 + 12.975   **20.** $290 + $5.86 + $12   **21.** 0.0006 + 9.4 + 7.234

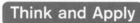

CHOICES **Solve. Use a calculator, pencil and paper, or mental math. Explain your choices.**

22. $9 + $.50 + $1.50   **23.** 0.006 + 3.4 + 12   **24.** 396 + 0.04 + 20.5

25. 6,753 + 0.87   **26.** 12.5 + 23.05 + 26.45   **27.** $27 + $352 + $.98

28. 3,609.85 + 37.987	**29.** 45. + 10.96	**30.** 5,043.007 + 11.4

31. 89.85 0.02 + 2.7	**32.** $100.25 50.99 + 33.75	**33.** $15.97 21.00 + 15.25

Think and Apply

34. Look at the pictures on page 20. Kay has $250. Can she buy ski boots and skates?

35. Which would cost more—ski boots and a toboggan or skis and a sweater?

Pretend the decimal-point key on your calculator is broken.

36. How would you add 321.73 and 43.26?

37. How would you add 321.73 and 43.261?

38. Will the same method work for both **36** and **37**?

39. How would you add 321.73 and 43.5?

Write an emergency instruction to be included in the instruction book for your calculator. Tell how to add decimals if the decimal-point key is broken.

SUMMING UP

The sports announcer reported that 10,000 fans jammed the 9,925-seat field house. Did that mean that exactly 75 people had to stand?

Estimating Differences

The table shows the seating capacity of some stadiums in the United States. About how many more seats than Riverfront Stadium does the Kingdome have?

Stadium	Seating Capacity
Texas Stadium	65,101
Riverfront Stadium	59,754
Kingdome	64,757
Astrodome	50,496

You can estimate $64,757 - 59,754$ to find the answer.

Round to the nearest ten thousand.

$$\begin{array}{r} 64,757 \longrightarrow 60,000 \\ -59,754 \longrightarrow -60,000 \\ \hline 0 \end{array}$$

Zero is not a reasonable estimate.

Round to the nearest thousand.

$$\begin{array}{r} 64,757 \longrightarrow 65,000 \\ -59,754 \longrightarrow -60,000 \\ \hline 5,000 \end{array}$$

You get a closer estimate by rounding to the nearest thousand.

The Kingdome has about 5,000 more seats than Riverfront Stadium.

Another Example

Estimate $18.32 - 4.689$.

Would rounding to the nearest ten give you a reasonable estimate? Explain.

Round to the nearest one.

$$\begin{array}{r} 18 \\ -5 \\ \hline 13 \end{array}$$

Round to the nearest tenth.

$$\begin{array}{r} 18.3 \\ -4.7 \\ \hline 13.6 \end{array}$$

Which rounding example is easier to compute mentally?

Check Your Understanding

Estimate each difference.

1. $3,178 - 1,940$

2. $23,856 - 1,985$

3. $11.89 - 5.57$

Share Your Ideas Describe how you use mental math to estimate differences.

Estimate each difference.

4. 8,245 − 3,150	**5.** 32,894 − 19,076	**6.** $34.85 − 11.45	**7.** 527,456 − 452,809	**8.** 17.54 − 6.39
9. 36.8 − 5.1	**10.** 40.295 − 18.93	**11.** 108,651 − 75,183	**12.** $199.50 − 39.99	**13.** 4.019 − 2.65

14. 24,145 − 18,170   **15.** 47.8 − 9.32   **16.** $10 − $3.75

17. 15,208 − 7,651   **18.** 2.85 − 0.5   **19.** 8.27 − 0.046

Estimate. Then compare, using < or > for each ●.

20. 2,175 − 1,466 ● 1,000   **21.** 9.27 − 4.03 ● 5

22. $19.95 − $1.09 ● $18   **23.** 347,189 − 51,260 ● 200,000

24. 6.199 − 0.04 ● 6   **25.** $20 − $5.68 ● $15

Choose all the reasonable estimates for each.

26. 6.871 − 2.15	**a.** 66	**b.** 6.6	**c.** 5	**d.** 4.9
27. $825.20 − $650.45	**a.** $100	**b.** $200	**c.** $170	**d.** $25
28. 2,361 − 1,646	**a.** 0	**b.** 800	**c.** 3,000	**d.** 1,000

Think and Apply

29. Use the table on page 22. About how many more seats does Texas Stadium have than the Astrodome?

30. Alicia is on page 37 of a 275 page novel. About how many pages does she have left to read?

31. Mark owes his brother $13.75. About how much change will he receive from a $20 bill?

32. Maria has $4. Will she be able to buy a sandwich for $1.89, fruit salad for $.79, and milk for $.89?

Common Error

33. Use estimation to explain why the answer below is not reasonable.

8.754 − 3.19 = 8.435 ←—incorrect

Look back at exercise **19**. Explain how you found your estimate. Would rounding to the nearest one give you a reasonable estimate? Explain.

SUMMING UP

Subtracting Whole Numbers and Decimals

Courtesy Historical Pictures Service, Inc.

In the first modern Olympic Games in 1896, Thomas Burke of the United States won the men's 100-meter dash with a time of 12 seconds. The first person from the U.S.S.R. to win this event was Valery Borzov, who won in 1972 with a time of 10.14 seconds. Carl Lewis of the United States won this event in 1988 with a time of 9.92 seconds. How much faster than Valery Borzov was Carl Lewis?

Estimate to predict the answer: $10.1 - 9.9 = 0.2$. You can use paper and pencil to find the exact answer.

Align the decimal points. Use zeros to hold places. Subtract as with whole numbers. Place the decimal point in the difference.

$$\begin{array}{r} 10.14 \\ -\ 9.92 \\ \hline 0.22 \end{array} \qquad \begin{array}{r} 0.22 \\ +\ 9.92 \\ \hline 10.14 \end{array}$$

You can add to check your answer.

Carl Lewis was 0.22 seconds faster than Valery Borzov.

More Examples

a. $8.06 - 8.019$

$$\begin{array}{r} 8.060 \\ -\ 8.019 \\ \hline 0.041 \end{array}$$

b. $27.098 - 6.5$

$$\begin{array}{r} 27.098 \\ -\ 6.500 \\ \hline 20.598 \end{array}$$

Check Your Understanding

Estimate. Then find each difference.

1. $18.2 - 3.199$

2. $1,456 - 983$

3. $\$329 - \$76.80$

4. $16 - 0.85$

Share Your Ideas Look back at **1–3**. Explain how you found your estimate. Was it an overestimate or an underestimate?

Estimate. Then find each difference.

5. 12,875
    − 6,459

6. $14.99
    − 7.25

7. 26.908
    − 3.507

8. 32.5
    − 7.94

9. 30,041
    − 9,785

10. 84.3
    − 0.863

11. $23 − $6.05

12. 958.502 − 37.5

13. 45 − 12.124

14. 4,800 − 56.07

Use each input number. Follow the rule, if given, to find each output number.

Rule: Subtract 3.75.

	Input	Output
15.	36.8	
16.	172	
17.	3.809	
18.	5.4	

19. Find the rule.

Input	Output
3.7	14.1
8.25	18.65
82.5	92.9
156	166.4

20. **Look back** at **19.** Describe how you found the rule.

Think and Apply

21. In the 1984 Olympics, Carl Lewis of the United States won the men's 200-meter dash with a time of 19.8 seconds. In the Olympic Games of 1988, Joe Leach of the United States won the event with a time of 19.75 seconds. What was the difference in their times?

22. Professional football games have 15-minute quarters. Two teams totaled 37.5 minutes in actual playing time. How much time was left in the game?

Look back at **21.** Would you estimate to answer the question? Explain.

Mixed Review

Write each number in expanded form.

1. 12,396

2. 100,000,006

3. 7 billion, five

4. 32 trillion

5. 0.745

6. 16 thousandths

Round each to the nearest tenth.

7. 472.091

8. 3.217

9. 86.3749

10. 109.987

11. 0.615

12. 0.95

Estimate each sum.

13. 392 + 7,864

14. 51.76 + 93.81

15. 6.78 + 296.079

16. $22.89 + $65.75

17. 37,184 + 64,179

18. 2.46 + 0.9 + 15.83

Using Problem Solving

Interview: Calculators and Baseball

Bill Dean is a senior researcher at the Baseball Hall of Fame in Cooperstown, New York. Bill collects and analyzes data, and calculates batting averages, earned run averages, fielding percentages, and other baseball statistics. "Recently a sports reporter requested the fielding records of every third baseman who had played in the last fifty years," Bill commented. "Without a calculator I couldn't have completed the report in time."

Look at the information about Charlie Comiskey, a famous baseball player, and find the ten totals for his 13-year career. Use a calculator.

Charlie Comiskey										
Year	G	AB	H	2B	3B	HR	R	RBI	BB	SO
1882	78	329	80	9	5	1	58		4	
1883	96	401	118	17	9	2	87		11	
1884	108	460	110	17	6	2	76		5	
1885	83	340	87	15	7	2	68		14	
1886	131	578	147	15	9	3	95		10	
1887	125	538	180	22	5	4	139		27	
1888	137	576	157	22	5	6	102	83	12	
1889	137	587	168	28	10	3	105	102	19	19
1890	88	377	92	11	3	0	53	59	14	17
1891	141	580	152	16	2	3	86	93	33	25
1892	141	551	125	14	6	3	61	71	32	16
1893	64	259	57	12	1	0	38	26	11	2
1894	61	220	58	8	0	0	26	33	5	5

KEY: G = games, AB = at bats, H = hits, 2B = doubles,
3B = triples, HR = homeruns, R = runs, RBI = runs batted in,
BB = base on balls(walk), SO = strike outs

Sharing Your Ideas

1. What were the lifetime totals for Charlie Comiskey?

2. How can you check your work to make sure it was accurate?

3. To find the lifetime batting average, you divide the number of hits by the number of at bats and then round the quotient to 3 decimal places. What was Charlie Comiskey's lifetime batting average?

Practice

What if a statistician wanted to compare these season totals for the National League?

National League West								
Team			Batting		Fielding		Pitching	
	Runs	2B	3B	HR	E	DP	BB	SO
Houston	654	244	32	125	130	108	523	1,160
Cincinnati	732	237	35	144	140	160	524	924
San Francisco	698	269	29	114	143	149	591	992
San Diego	656	239	25	136	137	135	607	934
Los Angeles	638	232	14	130	181	118	499	1,051
Atlanta	615	241	24	138	141	181	576	932

National League East								
Team			Batting		Fielding		Pitching	
	Runs	2B	3B	HR	E	DP	BB	SO
New York	783	261	61	148	138	145	509	1,083
Philadelphia	739	266	39	154	137	157	553	874
St. Louis	601	216	48	58	123	178	485	761
Montreal	637	255	50	110	133	132	566	1,051
Chicago	680	257	27	155	124	147	557	962
Pittsburgh	663	273	33	111	143	134	570	924

KEY: R = runs, 2B = doubles, 3B = triples, HR = homeruns,
E = errors DP = double plays, BB = base on balls(walks),
SO = strikeouts

4. Calculate the totals for the league's divisions. Compare the two divisions.

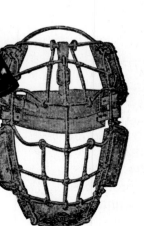

Summing Up

5. Which division led in each of the categories?

6. Why might it be important to keep totals for each year?

Courtesy National Baseball Library, Cooperstown, N.Y.

Chapter Review

Write each number in standard form. pages 4–7

1. 2 trillion, 36 million

2. 106 million, 8 thousand, 230

3. 34 and 9 ten-thousandths

4. 8 and 26 millionths

5. $(7 \times 10,000,000,000) + (4 \times 1,000,000) + (5 \times 100,000)$

6. $(4 \times 1) + (6 \times \frac{1}{10}) + (2 \times \frac{1}{100})$

Compare. Use <, >, or = for each ⬤. pages 8–9

7. 1,652 ⬤ 165.2

8. 15.7 ⬤ 15.15

9. 1.98 ⬤ 1.985

10. 7.25 ⬤ 7.250

11. 46,189 ⬤ 46,981

12. 6.6 ⬤ 6.06

Find each sum mentally. pages 14–17

13. 135 + 245

14. 1,470 + 1,998

15. 2.3 + 6.8 + 1.7

Estimate. Then find each answer. pages 18–25

16.
$$\begin{array}{r} \$175.58 \\ +\ 209.49 \\ \hline \end{array}$$

17.
$$\begin{array}{r} 32.785 \\ +\ 9.07 \\ \hline \end{array}$$

18.
$$\begin{array}{r} 6,174.5 \\ -\ 829.6 \\ \hline \end{array}$$

19.
$$\begin{array}{r} \$26.75 \\ -\ 18.68 \\ \hline \end{array}$$

20.
$$\begin{array}{r} 101.5 \\ -\ 26.01 \\ \hline \end{array}$$

21. 71.6 + 3.23 + 15

22. 198 + 2,746 + 32,471

23. $50 − $18.75

24. 17.6 − 5.387

Fill in the blanks.

25. $(5 \times 1,000) + (3 \times 100) + (6 \times 1)$ is an example of _____ form.

26. Decimals like 3.8, 3.80, and 3.800 that name the same number are _____ decimals.

27. $(18 + 47) + 13 = 18 + (47 + 13)$ is an example of the _____ Property.

Words to Know
equivalent
expanded
standard
Associative
Commutative
Identity

Solve. pages 11–13, 26–27

28. Admission for the school sports event costs $3.50 for adults and $2.00 for children. Mr. Ross paid $21.00 for admission for his group. How many adults and children attended?

29. Expenses for the Bennetts' family vacation were $984.50 for hotels, $387.95 for meals, $184 for transportation, and $84.72 for souvenirs. Estimate the total cost. Then find the exact amount.

Chapter Test

Write each in standard form.

1. 15 billion, 110 million, 408

2. 7 and 24 hundred-thousandths

3. nine trillion, two hundred million, fifty-four thousand

4. $(8 \times 10,000,000) + (6 \times 10,000) + (2 \times 1,000) + (3 \times 100)$

5. $(4 \times 10) + (1 \times 1) + (5 \times \frac{1}{100}) + (9 \times \frac{1}{1000})$

Write in order from least to greatest.

6. 37,732; 37,372; 7,753

7. 2.051; 2.05; 2.005

8. 1.75; 1; 0.9; 1.8

9. 25,897; 258,970.01; 25,896.17

Estimate each sum or difference.

10.	11.	12.	13.	14.
23,189 + 9,750	$37.95 + 18.49	3,286 − 1,641	5.28 − 3.44	$152.99 − 67.80

Add or subtract. Estimate to see if your answer makes sense.

15.	16.	17.	18.	19.
16.07 + 5.78	9.5 − 3.381	$175.49 + 380.55	128,964 + 72,098	84.361 − 6.25

20. 32.9 + 157 + 8.64

21. $160 − $42.89

22. 175,260 − 94,183

23. 2,650 + 872.9 + 57.15

Solve.

24. Andrew is training for the 200-meter dash. Yesterday he ran the dash in 31.25 seconds. He wants to run the dash in less than 28 seconds. How much time must he cut in order to reach his goal?

25. The fine for an overdue videotape at Janet's library is $1.25 for the first night and $.25 per hour for each hour after 9:00 A.M. that the tape is overdue. Janet borrowed a tape that was due on September 20. She returned it at 1:00 P.M. on September 21. What is the fine?

THINK   Using the digits 3 and 7 in any order and a decimal point, write as many numbers as possible. Then write the numbers in order from least to greatest.

Base 8 and Base 10

What is the speed limit?

67_8 means 67, *base 8*. A base 8 number uses the digits 0, 1, 2, 3, 4, 5, 6, and 7. Each place has a value 8 times the value of the place to its right.

512	64	8	1
		6	7

$67_8 = (6 \times 8) + (7 \times 1)$

$= 48 + 7$

$= 55$

The speed limit 67_8 is 55 mph in base 10.

SPEED LIMIT 67_8

How can you change 603 base 10 to a base 8 number?

$$\text{Think} \quad 512\overline{)603}^{\,1\,R\,91} \qquad 64\overline{)91}^{\,1\,R\,17} \qquad 8\overline{)17}^{\,2\,R\,1}$$

512	64	8	1
1	1	2	1

$603_{10} = 1121_8$

Write each base 10 number in base 8.

1. 158   **2.** 349   **3.** 1,213   **4.** 3,760

Write each base 8 number in base 10.

5. 712_8 **6.** 2341_8 **7.** 1056_8 **8.** 543_8

Maintaining Skills

Choose the correct answers. Write A, B, C, or D.

1. What is the value of the digit 4 in
   74,035,891?

   A 400,000   C 4,000,000

   B 40,000,000   D not given

2. What is the standard form?
   $(2 \times 10^8) + (5 \times 10^4) + (8 \times 10^2)$

   A 25,800   C 2,050,800

   B 200,050,800   D not given

3. What is 241 hundred thousandths
   written as a decimal?

   A 0.241   C 0.0241

   B 0.00241   D not given

4. What is the standard form?
   5 and 142 millionths

   A 5.000142   C 5.00142

   B 5.142   D not given

5. Compare. 12.003 ⬤ 12.030

   A <   C =

   B >   D not given

6. Order from least to greatest.
   2.905, 2.046, 2.009

   A 2.905, 2.046, 2.009

   B 2.009, 2.905, 2.046

   C 2.046, 2.009, 2.905

   D not given

7. What property is illustrated?
   $(6.5 + 8.3) + 1.7 = 6.5 + (8.3 + 1.7)$

   A Associative   C Identity

   B Commutative   D not given

8. Estimate. $85.26 + $123.87

   A $100.00   C $150.00

   B $200.00   D $90.00

9. 1,563.06 + 341.5

   A 1,597.21   C 1,804.56

   B 15,972.1   D not given

10. 0.008 + 5.6 + 7.54

    A 12.148   C 13.148

    B 8.18   D not given

11. Estimate. 16.354 − 14.22

    A 2   C 20

    B 0.1   D 30

12. 62.4 − 13.086

    A 59.324   C 51.486

    B 49.314   D not given

Solve.

13. Mr. Adams sells 3 tennis balls for $5.50
    and 3 golf balls for $3.75. Sam bought
    tennis balls and golf balls. What could
    his total bill have been?

    A $22.50   C $12.90

    B $24.75   D not given

14. Erica's basketball team was defeated by
    three points. What could the final score
    have been?

    A 50 to 30   C 42 to 29

    B 48 to 45   D not given

2 Multiplying and Dividing Whole Numbers and Decimals

THEME Automobiles in America

Sharing What You Know

Back in 1900, there were only 8,000 automobiles in the United States. Throughout this century, though, that number has increased steadily. Today, over 130 million cars are registered in the U.S. Along the way, new methods of keeping track of all these vehicles have had to be developed. Think about all the license plates in your state. Imagine if you had to keep track of all those cars! How would mathematics help you?

Using Language

To earn a driver's license, you must pass a driving test. For many people, the scariest part of the test is having to park a car. They think, "How do I know if the car will fit into the space?" Yet no one actually gets out and measures the length of the space and the length of the car. Instead, the driver relies on visual estimation. This **estimate** is a judgment based on approximation. When drivers **estimate,** they are using mathematical skills. Discuss instances when you use estimation. When do you estimate in school? at home?

Words to Know: estimate, Distributive Property, Commutative Property, Associative Property, Zero Property, Identity Property, parentheses, powers of 10

Be a Problem Solver

A small country wants to design license plates, each with just two symbols. (A symbol can be a numeral, a letter of the alphabet, or anything else from a triangle to a banana.) How could they do this? If they used only letters and numerals, how many license plates could they make?

Design your own license plate. Try and make your plate so unique that there would be little possibility of it being duplicated.

Describe how you can quickly find this sum:
25 + 32 + 25. What properties of addition
would you use?

Mental Math: Using Properties

Daphney Digit uses properties to find
products mentally.

Commutative Property	Associative Property	Identity Property
The order of the factors does not change the product.	The way the factors are grouped does not change the product.	The product of any number and 1 is that number.
$a \times b = b \times a$	$(a \times b) \times c = a \times (b \times c)$	$a \times 1 = a$ $1 \times a = a$
$25 \times 4 = 4 \times 25$ $100 = 100$	$(9 \times 4) \times 5 = 9 \times (4 \times 5)$ $36 \times 5 = 9 \times 20$ $180 = 180$	$87 \times 1 = 87$ $1 \times 87 = 87$

Zero Property	Distributive Property of Multiplication over Addition
The product of any number and 0 is 0. $a \times 0 = 0$ $0 \times a = 0$	If one factor is a sum, multiplying before adding does not change the product. $a(b + c) = (a \times b) + (a \times c)$ ↑ A number beside parentheses means multiply by the number.
$25 \times 0 = 0$ $0 \times 25 = 0$	$3(10 + 7) = (3 \times 10) + (3 \times 7)$ $= 30 + 21 = 51$

Identify the properties used to find each answer.

a. $4 \times (14 \times 25) = 4 \times (25 \times 14) = (4 \times 25) \times 14 = 100 \times 14 = 1,400$

b. $3 \times (2 \times 53) = (3 \times 2) \times 53 = 6 \times 53 = (6 \times 50) + (6 \times 3) = 300 + 18 = 318$

c. $7 \times 42 = (7 \times 40) + (7 \times 2) = 280 + 14 = 294$

Check Your Understanding

Use multiplication properties to find each product mentally.

1. 8×32

2. 3×95

3. $5 \times (34 \times 2)$

4. $53 \times (89 \times 0)$

5. 73×6

6. $4 \times 54 \times 2$

Share Your Ideas Look back at **4–6.** Explain how you
used multiplication properties to find each product.

Find each product, using mental math.

7. 3×24

8. 7×21

9. $3 \times 34 \times 2$

10. $9 \times 0 \times 29$

11. 4×32

12. 5×45

13. $25 \times 9 \times 4$

14. $4 \times 55 \times 2$

15. 4.83×1

16. $8 \times \$2.60$

17. $4 \times (7 \times 5)$

18. $(19 \times 5) \times 2$

19. $6 \times \$9.20$

20. $8 \times 76 \times 25$

21. 25×44

22. $71 \times 3(28 - 28)$

Find each missing factor. Name the property you used.

23. $0.536 \times \square = 0.536$

24. $234 \times 55 = \square \times 234$

25. $9 \times (5 \times \square) = 0$

26. $\square(2 + 8) = (7 \times 2) + (7 \times 8)$

27. $5 \times (4 \times 7) = 5 \times (7 \times \square)$

28. $(5 \times 9) \times \square = 5 \times (9 \times 2)$

29. $36 \times \square \times 22 = 0$

30. $6(3 + 9) = (\square \times 3) + (\square \times 9)$

31. $(8 \times 18) \times 3 = (18 \times \square) \times 3$

Write *true* or *false*. If true, name the property illustrated.

32. $5 + (8 \times 4) = (5 + 8) \times (5 + 4)$

33. $7 + (8 - 2) = (7 + 8) - (7 + 2)$

34. $5 + (8 + 3) = (5 + 8) + 3$

35. $(9 + 3)6 = (9 \times 6) + (3 \times 6)$

36. $9 - (7 - 2) = (9 - 7) - 2$

37. $35 \div 5 = 5 \div 35$

38. $8 \times 54 = (8 \times 50) + (8 \times 4)$

39. $5 \times 8 \times 0 = 0$

40. Is there a distributive property of multiplication over subtraction? Make a prediction. Then experiment with some examples. Analyze your results and explain your conclusion.

Write *true* or *false*. Explain your reasoning.

41. If the product of two numbers is 0, then one factor must be 0.

42. If the product of two numbers is one of the numbers, then one factor must be 1.

43. When a number is divided by itself, the quotient is that number.

44. When a number is added to 0, the sum is 0.

45. Subtraction is commutative.

46. Division is associative.

Describe how you would find the product of 7×39, using mental math.

SUMMING UP

35

Explain how to find each product.
10 × 32   100 × 32   1,000 × 32

Mental Math: Using Patterns and Powers of 10

Daphney uses mental math to multiply and divide by powers of 10. Examine the patterns. How is the number of places the decimal point is moved related to the number of zeros in the power of 10?

To multiply by a power of 10 that is greater than 1, move the decimal point to the right.

$2.58 \times 1 = 2.58$

$2.58 \times 10 = 25.8$

$2.58 \times 100 = 258.$

$2.58 \times 1,000 = 2580.$

$2.58 \times 10,000 = 25800.$

Sometimes you have to write zeros in the product.

To divide by a power of 10 that is greater than 1, move the decimal point to the left.

$235.9 \div 1 = 235.9$

$235.9 \div 10 = 23.59$

$235.9 \div 100 = 2.359$

$235.9 \div 1,000 = 0.2359$

$235.9 \div 10,000 = 0.02359$

Sometimes you have to write zeros in the quotient.

Check Your Understanding

Multiply or divide.

1. 5.8×10

2. $0.67 \times 1,000$

3. $0.35 \div 10$

4. $27 \div 1,000$

5. $421 \times 10,000$

6. $32.1 \div 100$

Share Your Ideas How is multiplying 1.32 by 1,000 like dividing 1.32 by 1,000? How is it different?

Practice

Multiply or divide.

7. 83.5×10 **8.** 853×100

9. $9.02 \div 10$ **10.** $587 \div 100$

11. $234.1 \div 1{,}000$ **12.** $5.62 \times 1{,}000$

13. $8.043 \times 10{,}000$ **14.** $0.21 \div 100$

15. $15{,}821 \div 100$ **16.** $2.3 \times 100{,}000$

17. $6.47 \div 1{,}000$ **18.** $2{,}009 \div 1{,}000$

19. $15{,}620 \times 1{,}000$ **20.** $82{,}400 \div 10{,}000$

21. $92{,}412.8 \div 100$ **22.** $274.003 \times 1{,}000$

23. $2.504 \times 1{,}000$ **24.** $327 \div 100{,}000$

25. $0.003 \div 1{,}000{,}000$ **26.** $0.945 \times 1{,}000{,}000$

Find the missing factor.

27. $74.5 \times \square = 745$ **28.** $6{,}345 \div \square = 6.345$

29. $0.704 \times \square = 70.4$ **30.** $265 \div \square = 0.0265$

31. $0.004 \times \square = 4{,}000$ **32.** $\square \times 1{,}000 = 2.354$

Solve.

33. 2,850 is 10,000 times greater than I am. What number am I?

34. I am 4.23. How many times greater am I than 0.0423?

Think and Apply

35. Ten cars and trailers were in the Mojave Seniors 100-Day Caravan. The caravan traveled 17,589.4 miles. To the nearest tenth of a mile, how many miles did the caravan average each day?

36. Visit some automobile dealerships to find the EPA fuel estimates of city and highway mileage for several car models. Use the data to estimate how much fuel is needed to drive each car 100 miles in the city; 1,000 miles on the highway.

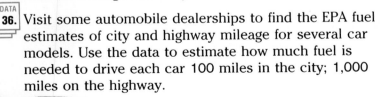

Explain why multiplying and dividing by powers of 10 can be done, using mental math.

1. $3.25 + 9.87$

2. $7.84 + 2.99$

3. $6.21 + 9.67$

4. $6.02 - 5.82$

5. $7.1 - 3.05$

6. $21.31 - 0.99$

7. $\begin{array}{r} 402.3 \\ -26.4 \\ \hline \end{array}$

8. $\begin{array}{r} 23.21 \\ 1.36 \\ +4.09 \\ \hline \end{array}$

Compare. Use >, <, or =.

9. $8.05 \;\bullet\; 8.127$

10. $9.2 \;\bullet\; 9.200$

11. $0.58 \;\bullet\; 0.098$

12. $7.2 \;\bullet\; 6.98$

13. $1.0 \;\bullet\; 1.0001$

Round 3,928.593 to each place.

14. ones

15. hundreds

16. tenths

17. hundredths

SUMMING UP

How would you round 56,520 to the nearest ten thousand?

Estimating Products

Automobiles emit an average of 3,286 tons of pollutants into the atmosphere every day. About how many tons are emitted per month?

You can round to find an estimate. There are about 30 days in a month.

3,286 rounds to	**3,000**
× 30	**× 30**
	90,000

What if 3,286 is rounded to the nearest hundred? Explain how the estimate would change.

About 90,000 tons are emitted per month.

There are many ways to round to estimate a product. Choose a way that gives a reasonable estimate for the situation.

a. Round one factor up and one factor down.

26 rounds up to	**30**
× 35 rounds down to	**× 30**
	900

Why are 26 and 35 rounded this way?

b. Round to compatible numbers.

41.3 rounds to	**40**
× 24 rounds to	**× 25**
	1,000

c. Round both factors down and then both factors up to find a range for a product.

74.8 rounds down to	**70**
× 5.7 rounds down to	**× 5**
	350

74.8 rounds up to	**80**
× 5.7 rounds up to	**× 6**
	480

The product is between 350 and 480. How do you know that the product can be no less than 350 and no greater than 480?

Check Your Understanding

Estimate.

1.	39	2.	46	3.	489	4.	52.3
	× 26		× 2.6		× 61		× 45.2

5. 6.4 × 34   **6.** 52 × 0.975   **7.** 6.3 × 10.86

Share Your Ideas   What if you rounded 73 × 6.4 to 70 × 6 to estimate? Would the estimate be an overestimate or an underestimate? Explain.

Estimate. Find a range for 8, 13, 18, and 23. Explain the method you would use to estimate 14–17.

8.	27 × 38	**9.**	53 × 22	**10.**	86 × 75

11.	231 × 41	**12.**	307 × 212

13.	9.2 × 68	**14.**	47 × 3.3	**15.**	26.8 × 57

16.	5.52 × 7.6	**17.**	0.96 × 3.85

18.	457 × 46	**19.**	35.3 × 510	**20.**	2.84 × 31.1

21.	4,018 × 240	**22.**	3.441 × 56.9

23. 2,536 × 491 **24.** 8.74 × 329 **25.** 41.11 × 48.8

26. 4.483 × 1.926 **27.** 305 × 26.4 × 7.8 **28.** 58.6 × 433 × 98.62

29. Look back at **8–12.** Predict whether your estimate is an underestimate or an overestimate. Use a calculator to verify your predictions.

Use an estimate to help select the correct product.

30. 42 × 58

   a. 246
   b. 2,436
   c. 24,366
   d. 243,606

31. 29 × 8.9

   a. 258.1
   b. 2,581.1
   c. 25,811.1
   d. 258,111.1

32. 24.2 × 61.5

   a. 14.83
   b. 148.83
   c. 1,488.3
   d. 14,883.33

Think and Apply

Decide whether an estimate is sufficient or an exact answer is necessary. For those problems for which an estimate is sufficient, do you need an overestimate or an underestimate?

33. the amount of money you need with you to pay for gas at $1.09 a gallon if the gas tank holds 12.5 gal and is 0.75 full

34. the cost of 9.6 gal of gas at $1.09 per gallon

35. the amount of change you will receive from a $20 bill when you pay for the gas

36. the distance you can go on 9.6 gal of gas if your car gets about 38 miles per gallon

Use estimation to help you create a multiplication problem for which the product is a four-digit whole number.

SUMMING UP

Which is greater—56.5 × 760 or 76 × 565? Explain.

Multiplying Whole Numbers and Decimals

It takes an average of 200 person-hours to manufacture a car in the United States. If the average worker made $18.75 an hour, how much would the labor costs be to manufacture a car?

You can multiply to solve this problem. Explain why.

Estimate the product.

$18.75	rounds to	$20
× 200		× 200
		$4,000

Is this an overestimate or an underestimate? Explain.

Find the product.

Multiply.

$18.75
×   200
375000

Place the decimal point.

$18.75 ←2 decimal places
×   200
$3,750.00 ←2 decimal places

The labor costs to manufacture a car would be $3,750.

More Examples

a.
22.6 ← 1 place
×   38
180 8
678
858.8 ← 1 place

Estimate.
20
× 40
800

b.
427
× 0.037 ← 3 places
2 989
12 81
15.799 ← 3 places

Estimate.
400
× 0.04
16

Check Your Understanding

Multiply. Estimate to be sure each answer makes sense.

1. 3.3
   × 9

2. 928
   × 0.17

3. 438
   × 57

4. $6.45
   ×   96

5. 721
   × 5.4

Share Your Ideas Explain why there are two decimal places in the product of 200 × $18.75. Why is there one decimal place in the product in example **a**? three places in the product in example **b**?

Practice

Estimate. Then multiply. Choose mental math, paper and pencil, or a calculator.

6. 3.5 × 8	**7.** 43 × 9	**8.** 0.27 × 15	**9.** 8.9 × 52	**10.** 79 × 27
11. 40 × 3.5	**12.** 0.84 × 91	**13.** 6,785 × 0.001	**14.** 405 × 0.23	**15.** 623 × 200
16. 609 × 28	**17.** 2,500 × 44	**18.** 0.356 × 93	**19.** 287 × 0.06	**20.** 59.6 × 748

21. 2.8 × 83

22. 963 × 0.0001

23. 40 × 0.874 × 25

24. 625 × 20 × 0.001

25. 637 × 0.118

26. 384 × 0.305 × 50

Look for a pattern. Then, without actually multiplying, find each product.

27. 35 × 698 = 24,430
3.5 × 698 = ☐
0.35 × 698 = ☐
35 × 0.698 = ☐

28. 745 × 289 = 215,305
745 × 2.89 = ☐
745 × 0.289 = ☐
7.45 × 289 = ☐

29. 609 × 86 = 52,374
0.609 × 86 = ☐
609 × 0.86 = ☐
6.09 × 86 = ☐

Think and Apply

30. Use this BASIC program to print the first eleven numbers of a sequence and the cumulative sum of the numbers of the sequence after each number is printed. Describe the numbers of the sequence. How are the numbers and the sums related?

```
10 FOR N = 0 TO 10
20 X = 2^N
30 SUM = SUM + X
40 PRINT "NUMBERS", "SUM"
50 PRINT X, SUM
60 NEXT N
```

Visual Thinking

Find the cost of each square.

 $.25 $.50 $.75 $1.00 $1.25

31.

32.

33.

34.

Look back at **11–15.** How did you find each product? Explain how you could use mental math to solve **11**, **13**, and **15**.

SUMMING UP

Describe how you would add 398 and 487, using mental math.

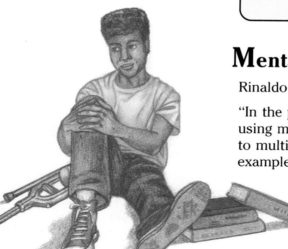

Mental Math: Multiplication

Rinaldo can multiply numbers quickly, using mental math.

"In the past, people learned ways to multiply numbers, using mental math. You can learn them, too. Here's a way to multiply numbers that are close to multiples of 100, for example, 98 × 15."

$$98 \times 15 = (100 - 2) \times 15$$
$$= (100 \times 15) - (2 \times 15)$$
$$= 1{,}500 - 30$$
$$= 1{,}470$$

What property did Rinaldo use to multiply 98 × 15?

How would you multiply these numbers mentally?

a. 32 × 25   **b.** 11 × 3.6   **c.** 38 × 42

Examine the methods shown here. How are they similar to your methods? How are they different?

a. $32 \times 25 = (8 \times 4) \times 25$
$$= 8 \times (4 \times 25)$$
$$= 8 \times 100 = 800$$

b. $11 \times 3.6 = 39.6$
    $3 + 6$

Why is the middle digit, 9, the sum of 3 and 6?

c. $38 \times 42 = (40 - 2) \times (40 + 2)$
$$= (40 - 2) \times 40 + (40 - 2) \times 2$$
$$= (40 \times 40) - (2 \times 2)$$
$$= 1{,}600 - 4 = 1{,}596$$

Check Your Understanding

Multiply, using mental math.

1. 42
    × 11

2. 36
    × 15

3. 25
    × 97

4. 4.8
    × 25

5. 50 × 198   6. 29 × 31   7. 53 × 47

Share Your Ideas What property was used in example **a** to multiply 32 × 25?

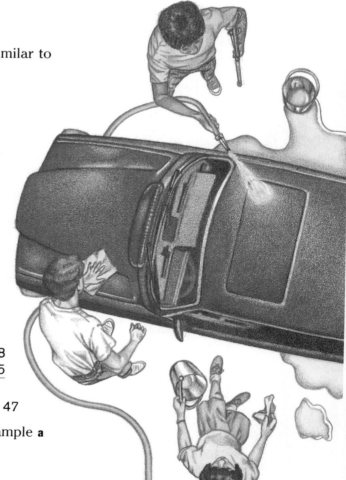

Multiply, using mental math.

8.	38 × 50	9.	61 × 11	10.	6.8 × 8	11.	18 × 35	12.	3.6 × 25

13.	199 × 43	14.	4.5 × 22	15.	398 × 17	16.	49 × 51	17.	8.1 × 11

18. $3 \times 3.7 \times 2$ 19. 45×55 20. $62 \times 25 \times 58 \times 4$

CHOICES Multiply. Choose mental math or paper and pencil.

21.	86 × 25	22.	199 × 6.4	23.	46 × 15	24.	75 × 85	25.	499 × 70

26.	68 × 51	27.	42 × 55	28.	198 × 202	29.	324.1 × 5	30.	125 × 88

31. $3,046 \times 0.0001$ 32. $3.8 \times 76 \times 3 \times 0$ 33. 999×237

34. $4 \times 0.25 \times 453$ 35. $9,998 \times 4,312$ 36. $68 \times (398 + 602) \times 5$

37. **Look back** at **13–17.** Explain how you multiplied each, using mental math. Compare your methods with those of your classmates. For which exercises was more than one method used?

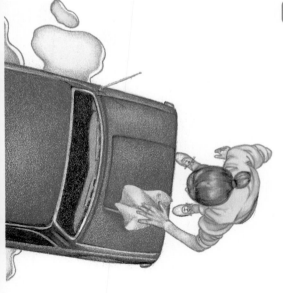

Think and Apply

Solve, using mental math. Explain your method.

38. Rinaldo's youth group ran a carwash. Rinaldo bought 25 bottles of soap at $2.99 each. How much did he pay?

39. The advertising committee made 47 posters to advertise the carwash. Marcus and Andre put up 28 posters. Pia and Nicole put up the rest. How many did they put up?

40. The youth group charged $5 to wash a car. They washed 248 cars. How much did they collect for washing the cars?

41. The youth group charged $7.50 to wash a van, large station wagon, or truck. They washed 64 of these. How much did they collect in all from the carwash?

Would you use mental math or paper and pencil to multiply 999×352? Why?

SUMMING UP

How would you estimate 2.1 × 8.9?

Multiplying Decimals

On the average, how far can Marita's new car go on the highway if the fuel tank is full?

You can multiply to solve. Explain why.

Estimate the product.

44.8	rounds to	40
× 15.4	rounds to	× 20
		800

Is this an underestimate or an overestimate? Explain.

EPA fuel estimates (mpg)
city: 35.7
highway: 44.8
fuel capacity: 15.4 gal

Find the product.

Multiply as with whole numbers.

```
   44.8
×  15.4
   1792
  2240
  448
  68992
```

Place the decimal point.

```
   44.8  } 2 decimal places
×  15.4
   17 92
  224 0
  448
  689.92  ← 2 decimal places
```

Marita's car can go 689.92 miles.

How could you use the estimate to help you place the point?

More Examples

a.
```
   30.9 } 2 places
×   2.7
   21 63
   61 8
   83.43  ← 2 places
```

Estimate.
```
   30
×   3
   90
```

b.
```
   0.121 } 5 places
×  0.02
  0.00242  ← 5 places
    ↑
Annex zeros so
there are enough places.
```

Estimate.
```
   0.1
×  0.02
  0.002
```

Place the decimal point correctly in each product.

1. 3.8 × 0.42 = 1596   **2.** 0.29 × 24.3 = 7047   **3.** 0.5 × 0.15 = 75

Multiply. Estimate to be sure each answer makes sense.

4.
```
  3.54
× 0.8
```
5.
```
  92.7
× 0.34
```
6.
```
  5.27
× 0.01
```
7. 0.511 × 1.21   **8.** 0.286 × 0.175

Share Your Ideas   How would you multiply 8.35 × 4.18 on a calculator if the decimal-point key was not working?

Practice

Place the decimal point correctly in each product.

9. $5.8 \times 9.64 = 55912$ **10.** $2.7 \times 0.505 = 13635$ **11.** $3.1 \times 4.25 = 13175$

12. $6.05 \times 0.131 = 79255$ **13.** $4.12 \times 0.003 = 1236$ **14.** $32.5 \times 0.111 = 36075$

Estimate. Then multiply. Choose mental math, paper and pencil, or a calculator. Round to the nearest cent in 25–29.

15.	**16.**	**17.**	**18.**	**19.**
0.8 × 0.5	0.7 × 0.6	0.23 × 0.5	5.4 × 0.9	6.1 × 0.8

20.	**21.**	**22.**	**23.**	**24.**
3.2 × 5.5	0.001 × 9.7	0.28 × 72	0.08 × 0.05	8.6 × 0.46

25.	**26.**	**27.**	**28.**	**29.**
$3.04 × 0.18	$4.98 × 6	$747 × 0.523	$123.50 × 0.01	$36.00 × 0.15

30. $0.05 \times 0.763 \times 0.2$ **31.** 297×30 **32.** $0.25 \times 5.68 \times 4$

33. $4.65 \times 7.8 \times 0.7$ **34.** $(3.6 \times 0.38) + (6.4 \times 0.38)$ **35.** $6.5 + 7.3 \times 0.8$

Without multiplying, answer these questions about examples a–d below. Explain your reasoning.

a.	**b.**	**c.**	**d.**
4.23 × 21.7	42.3 × 2.17	4.23 × 2.17	42.3 × 21.7

36. Which two examples have equal products?   **37.** Which example has the least product?

38. Which example has the greatest product?   **39.** How many times greater is the greatest product than the least?

Think and Apply

Solve. Decide whether an estimate is sufficient or an exact answer is necessary.

40. How far can the subcompact car go in the city on a full tank of fuel?

41. Which car can go farther on the highway on a full tank—the mid-size or the luxury?

42. Traveling at 60 mph, can the luxury car travel for 10 hours on one tank of fuel?

Money-Saver Rental Cars			
Vehicle	Fuel capacity (in gallons)	Miles per Gallon	
		Highway	City
Subcompact	12.4	44.8	31.4
Mid-size	18.6	27.2	20.5
Luxury	25.3	18.4	14.6

Is this statement always, sometimes, or never true? Explain.
• The product of two decimals is less than 1.

SUMMING UP

Midchapter Review

Multiply and divide, using mental math. pages 34-37, 42-43

1. $2 \times 28 \times 5$
2. $38.2 \times 1,000$
3. 8×23
4. 20×13
5. 48×100
6. $3 \times 8 \times 50$
7. $746 \div 1,000$
8. $25 \times 7 \times 4$
9. 9×28
10. 98×25
11. 5.63×100
12. $2,407 \div 100$
13. 39×41
14. 6×11.2
15. $3.68 \times 0.25 \times 4$
16. 11×4.5

Choose the best estimate for each. pages 38-39

17. 4.45×3.3
   a. 1.2
   b. 12
   c. 120
18. $2,255 \times 77$
   a. 1,600
   b. 16,000
   c. 160,000
19. $6,665 \times 1.12$
   a. 7,000
   b. 700
   c. 70
20. 9.54×18.6
   a. 1.8
   b. 18
   c. 180

Multiply. Estimate to be sure each answer makes sense. pages 40-45

21. 934×186
22. 3.68×0.26
23. 16×2.3
24. 198×24
25. 3×0.12
26. 0.8×0.56
27. 8.98×23
28. $18 \times 2,341$
29. 12.34×0.14
30. $0.001 \times 4,652$
31. 198×202
32. $5.4 \times 2.1 \times 0$

Choose an entry from column B to complete each sentence in column A.

A	B
33. $5(10 + 7) = (5 \times 10) + (5 \times 7)$ is an example of the _____ Property.	a. Commutative
34. The Commutative Property of Multiplication states that the order of the _____ does not change the product.	b. Distributive
	c. Identity
	d. factors
35. A number beside _____ means multiply by the number.	e. parentheses
	f. Associative
36. $54.6 \times 1 = 54.6$ illustrates the _____ Property of Multiplication.	g. power of 10
	h. multiplication
	i. addition
37. 100,000 is a _____.	j. Zero

Solve.

38. Mario's family is planning a 2-week trip. They expect to spend at least $65 a day for food and lodging. At least how much money should they set aside for the trip?

39. The sticker on Dawn's new car states that the car averages 32.6 mpg. The car has a 12.3 gal fuel tank. Can Dawn make a 375 mi trip without stopping for fuel?

Exploring Problem Solving

When Do You Stop?

The engineers at an automobile factory are testing the brakes of two cars on a roadway that is 10 miles long.

- The *braking distance* is the distance a car travels after its brake pedal is depressed.

- *Reaction time* is the time that elapses between seeing the need to stop and the application of the brakes.

- Total *stopping distance* is the braking distance plus the distance traveled during reaction time.

The table shows some of their findings.

Thinking Critically

What is the braking distance for each car at 60 mph? What is the total stopping distance when you include the reaction time?

Work in a group as you study the table to find some patterns and solve the problem.

Speed	Distance Traveled per Second	Car 1 Braking Distance	Car 2 Braking Distance
10 mph	14.6 ft	5 ft	____ ft
20 mph	29.3 ft	20 ft	32 ft
30 mph	43.9 ft	45 ft	72 ft
40 mph	58.6 ft	80 ft	128 ft
50 mph	73.3 ft	125 ft	____ ft
60 mph	88.0 ft	____ ft	____ ft

Analyzing and Making Decisions

CHOICES **Use a calculator where appropriate.**

1. Look at the data for Car 1. It is going 2 times as fast at 20 mph than at 10 mph, but it takes 4 times as long to stop. Test this relationship for 10 mph to 30 mph. Test it for 10 mph to 40 mph and 10 mph to 50 mph. What pattern do you see?

2. What do you think Car 1's braking distance is at 60 mph? Explain. Determine the missing braking distances for Car 2.

3. It usually takes a driver at least 0.75 sec to react to possible danger. Find the reaction distance (distance traveled during reaction time) for each speed. Round to the nearest whole number. What pattern do you see?

4. Find the total stopping distance for Cars 1 and 2. Make a chart for 10 mph to 60 mph for each car.

Look Back   Why might Car 2 have a different braking distance than Car 1?

Problem Solving Strategies

Too Little/Too Much Information

David and Wendy work at the Fast Service Drive-In. David earns $7.10 an hour, while Wendy, who has just started, earns $3.55 an hour. Last week they both worked 5 hours on Friday, and all day on Saturday and Sunday. Who earned more money? Exactly how much more did that person earn?

Some problems have too much information, and some have too little information. You must decide which facts are necessary to solve a problem.

Solving the Problem

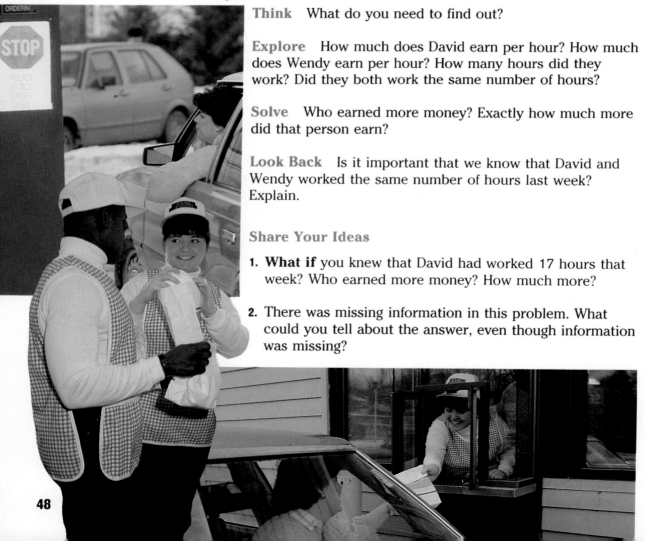

CHOICES **Use a calculator where appropriate.**

Think   What do you need to find out?

Explore   How much does David earn per hour? How much does Wendy earn per hour? How many hours did they work? Did they both work the same number of hours?

Solve   Who earned more money? Exactly how much more did that person earn?

Look Back   Is it important that we know that David and Wendy worked the same number of hours last week? Explain.

Share Your Ideas

1. **What if** you knew that David had worked 17 hours that week? Who earned more money? How much more?

2. There was missing information in this problem. What could you tell about the answer, even though information was missing?

Practice

Solve if possible. Use a calculator where appropriate.

3. Leon worked 22 hours at a carwash last week. Tom worked 30 hours. Who earned more money?

4. A carwash owner hired Janet and five other temporary workers to work 6-hour shifts at $5.78 per hour. Janet worked 3 shifts per week. What were her weekly earnings?

Last week, the Thrifty Auto Parts store sold 138 spark plugs, 42 oil filters, 27 air filters, and 53 cases of oil.

5. At this rate, how many spark plugs can the store manager expect to sell in 30 weeks?

6. How many quarts of oil were sold last week at Thrifty Auto Parts?

Mixed Strategy Review

At a swim meet the swimmer in first place earns 5 points, the one in second place earns 3 points, and the one in third place earns 1 point.

7. Alana earned a total of 11 points for her team. She competed in 3 events. How many times could Alana have finished first?

8. John swam in 5 events. In 1 event he came in fourth. How many points could he have earned?

Deven and Peggy plan to bake oat bran cookies for Family Night at school. According to the recipe, they will need 88 ounces of oat bran cereal. They can buy the small 8-ounce box of cereal for $1.89 a box. They can also buy the 18-ounce family-size box for $3.39 a box.

9. How much could it cost to purchase enough oat bran to make the cookies?

10. **What if** they only needed 44 ounces? How much could it cost?

Create Your Own

Write a problem that contains too much or too little information. Ask a partner to try to solve it and to tell you whether it has too much or too little information.

49

How would you use mental math to find each quotient?
a. 720 ÷ 80   **b.** 5,400 ÷ 90

Estimating Quotients

In 1900 most Americans worked less than 1 mile from home. In 1990, 78 million Americans drove close to a total of 729 million miles to work each day. About how far does the average commuter drive to work?

You can use compatible numbers to estimate.

729 million ÷ 78 million⟶720 million ÷ 80 million

$$\begin{array}{r} 9 \\ \text{Estimate: } 80\overline{)720} \\ \underline{720} \end{array}$$

720 and 80 are compatible numbers because 72 ÷ 8 = 9 is a basic fact.

The average commuter drives about 9 miles to work.

To estimate a quotient, you can also round the divisor.

$$6.3\overline{)4,189} \quad \text{rounds to} \quad 6\overline{)4,189}^{\,600} \quad \text{Think } 6\overline{)41}$$

Why is the actual product greater than 600 but less than 700?

Check Your Understanding

Name the compatible numbers and the basic fact that you would use to estimate each quotient.

1. $92\overline{)638}$ **2.** 5,491 ÷ 59   **3.** $82\overline{)23,641}$ **4.** $401\overline{)1,981.5}$

Estimate each quotient. Choose an appropriate method.

5. $86\overline{)8,385}$ **6.** $4.7\overline{)26,978}$ **7.** 4,192.9 ÷ 23   **8.** $853\overline{)553,597}$

Share Your Ideas   Look back at **5–8**. What methods did you use? Explain your choices.

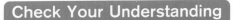

Name the compatible numbers and the basic fact you would use to estimate each quotient.

9. 29)268

10. 89)8,095

11. 2,163 ÷ 7.1

12. 1,890 ÷ 62

13. 59)3,710.5

14. 44,724 ÷ 52

15. 41)164,193

16. 38.9)126,913

Estimate each quotient. Choose an appropriate method.

17. 21)5,271

18. 63)3,843

19. 8,326 ÷ 9.2

20. 68)3,961

21. 83)269.75

22. 22,820 ÷ 28

23. 77)66,297

24. 22,553 ÷ 38

25. 18.2)152,971

26. 42)173,544

27. 567)378,189

28. 37.8)78,907.5

29. 25)$1,045.25

30. $4,721.56 ÷ 82

31. 57.4)$5,211.92

32. 98)$111,262.34

33. **Look back** at **21–24.** Predict whether your estimate is greater than or less than the actual quotient. Then use a calculator to verify your prediction.

Estimate.

34. About how many 45's are in 6,500?

35. About how many 6.2's are in 3,684.04?

36. 285,120 is about how many times greater than 704?

37. 278,949 is about how many times greater than 32.1?

Vans are used to carry small groups of commuters to and from work. Use these odometer readings to solve the problems below. The readings are in tenths of a mile.

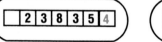

01/01/90   12/31/90

38. How many miles did the van travel in 1990?

39. There were 249 workdays in 1990. About how many miles, on the average, did the van travel each day?

40. New tires were purchased for the van on January 1, 1990. They will last about 60,000 miles. **What if** the van continues to be driven the same distance each year? Predict when a new set of tires will be needed. Name the month and the year.

Write two pairs of compatible numbers you can use to estimate 57,143 ÷ 85. Which pair gives an estimate closer to the actual quotient? How do you know?

SUMMING UP

51

Without dividing, tell which quotients are less than 10. Explain your reasoning.
a. 87)648   **b.** 92)934.6   **c.** 51)508

Dividing by Whole Numbers

Forty people in 11 cars and a truck made this historic trip in 1911. What was the average distance traveled each day?

FIRST
TRANCONTINENTAL
AUTOMOBILE TRIP
4,615.8 MILES
IN ONLY 49 DAYS!

To find an average, divide.

Decide where to place the first quotient digit.	Round the divisor, and estimate the quotient digit.	Multiply. Subtract and compare.

■
49)4,615.8   Why will the first quotient digit be in the tens place?

50   9
49)4,615.8   Think 50)461
                        5)46
                    Try 9.

9
49)4,615.8   How do you
4 41   know that 9
20   is not too large or too small?

Bring down the next digit. Continue dividing.	Place the decimal point in the quotient.	Check.

```
      94 2
49)4,615.8
  4 41
    205
    196
     9 8
     9 8
        0
```

```
      94.2
49)4,615.8
  4 41
    205
    196
     9 8
     9 8
        0
```

```
     94.2
   ×   49
    847 8
  3 768
  4,615.8
```

More Examples

```
 40      4
a. 36)18,288
   14 4
      3 8
```
38 > 36
Trial quotient is too small. Try next higher digit.

```
       508
36)18,288
   18 0
      288
      288
        0
```
28 < 36
Place 0 in the quotient and continue dividing.

```
     0.8
b. 8)6.6
   6 4
     2
```

```
    0.825
  8)6.600
  6 4
    20
    16
    40
    40
     0
```
Annex zeros and continue dividing.

Check Your Understanding

Divide. Check each answer by multiplying or by estimating.

1. 6)6.036   **2.** 28)355.6   **3.** 17)$8.33   **4.** 36)22.5   **5.** 75)49.245

Share Your Ideas Look back at example **b**. The long form for dividing was used. Explain how you would use the short form.

Practice

Estimate. Then divide. Use paper and pencil, mental math, or a calculator. Check your answers.

6. $8\overline{)24.8}$ 7. $9\overline{)\$7.11}$ 8. $7\overline{)539}$

9. $6\overline{)42.24}$ 10. $52\overline{)10.4}$ 11. $15\overline{)2,445}$

12. $45\overline{)90,454.5}$ 13. $91\overline{)13.65}$ 14. $16\overline{)3,526}$

15. $73\overline{)14.892}$ 16. $250\overline{)125}$ 17. $134\overline{)78,725}$

18. $178 \div 1,000$ 19. $8.4 \div 5$ 20. $0.6432 \div 32$

21. $5 \div 8$ 22. $7 \div 16$ 23. $2.5 \div 400$

Use patterns to find each quotient.

24. $36 \div 8 = 4.5$
$3.6 \div 8 = \square$
$0.36 \div 8 = \square$
$0.036 \div 8 = \square$

25. $425 \div 17 = 25$
$42.5 \div 17 = \square$
$4.25 \div 17 = \square$
$0.425 \div 17 = \square$

26. $80 \div 5 = 16$
$8 \div 5 = \square$
$0.8 \div 5 = \square$
$0.08 \div 5 = \square$

Without multiplying or dividing, answer these questions about examples a–c. Explain your reasoning.

a. $32\overline{)2,048}^{\,64}$ b. $32\overline{)\,?}^{\,128}$ c. $?\overline{)2,048}^{\,16}$

27. Is the dividend in **b** greater than or less than 2,048?

28. Is the divisor in **c** greater than or less than 32?

Think and Apply

HISTORIC AUTO TRIPS			
Year	Historic Importance	Time	Distance
1903	First by nonprofessional (Dr. H. N. Jackson)	63 days	5,499.9 miles
1909	First by women (Alice Ramsey and friends)	59 days	—

29. On average, how many miles a day did Dr. Jackson travel?

30. On average, how many miles a day did Alice Ramsey travel?

Write a division problem in which the quotient has three digits. Use estimation to help you.

1. $9.08 - 4.72$

2. $8.375 + 9.481$

3. $5.6 + 2.5 + 1.7$

4. $72.001 - 64.05$

5. $0.021 - 0.009$

6. $9.31 + 2.98 + 4$

7. $17 - 8.547$

Compare. Use <, >, or =.

8. $9.23 \bullet 9.099$

9. $3.7 \bullet 3.700$

10. $0.118 \bullet 0.1179$

11. $0.9998 \bullet 1.01$

12. $23.74 \bullet 24$

13. $1.101 \bullet 1.1010$

14. $34,056 \bullet 34,065$

Estimate.

15. $6.91 - 1.08$

16. $5.123 + 7.851$

17. $3.61 + 4.82$

18. $12.11 - 9.23$

19. $9 - 2.94$

20. $36.7 - 25.4$

SUMMING UP

53

Explain why 2.4 cannot be rounded to the nearest hundredth.

Rounding Quotients

Gerald will pay for his new car in 48 monthly payments. He will pay $12,259 in all, including sales tax and interest for his loan. How much will Gerald pay each month? Round to the nearest cent.

To solve this problem, you can divide. Explain why.

Divide. Annex zeros to the dividend when necessary.	Divide to one more place than the place to which you must round.	Round the quotient.

$$\begin{array}{r} \$255.39 \\ 48\overline{)\$12{,}259.00} \\ 9\,6 \\ \hline 2\,65 \\ 2\,40 \\ \hline 259 \\ 240 \\ \hline 19\,0 \\ 14\,4 \\ \hline 4\,60 \\ 4\,32 \\ \hline 28 \end{array}$$

Is $12,259 = $12,259.00? Why or why not?

$$\begin{array}{r} \$255.395 \\ 48\overline{)\$12{,}259.000} \\ 9\,6 \\ \hline 2\,65 \\ 2\,40 \\ \hline 259 \\ 240 \\ \hline 19\,0 \\ 14\,4 \\ \hline 4\,60 \\ 4\,32 \\ \hline 280 \\ 240 \\ \hline 40 \end{array}$$

←—To round to hundredths, divide to thousandths.

$255.395 rounds to $255.40.

Gerald will be paying $255.40 each month.

Another Example

Round $24.9 \div 16$ to the nearest tenth.

$$\begin{array}{r} 1.55 \\ 16\overline{)24.90} \\ 16 \\ \hline 8\,9 \\ 8\,0 \\ \hline 90 \\ 80 \\ \hline 10 \end{array}$$

rounds to —→ 1.6

←—To round to tenths, divide to hundredths.

Check Your Understanding

Divide. Round 1 and 2 to the nearest hundredth. Round 3 and 4 to the nearest thousandth. Estimate to check.

1. $6\overline{)7}$ 2. $34\overline{)\$52.10}$ 3. $18\overline{)7{,}140}$ 4. $58\overline{)123.7}$

Share Your Ideas   Explain how you determined the number of decimal places needed in each dividend in 1–4.

Estimate. Then divide. Round to the place named.

nearest tenth

5. 7)2.5

6. 8)9

7. 5.7 ÷ 20

nearest hundredth

8. 6)1.1

9. 105 ÷ 18

10. 8)1

nearest cent

11. 3)$1.52

12. $1,912 ÷ 48

13. 36)$24.62

nearest thousandth

14. 3)7

15. 3.0212 ÷ 2

16. 6,321 ÷ 92

Use a calculator to find each output.

Rule: Divide by 25.
Round to the nearest
tenth.

	Input	Output
17.	5.2	
18.	815	
19.	8.27	

Rule: Divide by 16.
Round to the nearest
thousandth.

	Input	Output
20.	14.6	
21.	27.589	
22.	1,467	

Rule: Divide by 183.
Round to the nearest
hundredth.

	Input	Output
23.	1.27	
24.	$324.78	
25.	2,340	

Without dividing, answer the following about examples a–d.
Explain your reasoning.

a. $5 ÷ 4   b. $4 ÷ 5   c. $50 ÷ 32   d. $50 ÷ 40

26. Which quotient is less than $1?

27. Which examples have equal quotients?

28. Which example has the greatest quotient?

29. Which example has the least quotient?

30. Write two division problems with quotients equal to the quotient in c.

31. Write two division problems with quotients greater than the quotient in c.

Think and Apply

32. **What if** Gerald decided to pay for the car in 36 monthly payments? He would pay a total of $11,105, including sales tax and interest for his loan. To the nearest cent, how much would he pay per month?

33. Why would the total payment be less if Gerald paid for the car in 36 months rather than in 48 months?

Describe two situations in which you would need to round a quotient.

SUMMING UP

Using a Calculator: Dividing by Decimals

Examine each pattern. Then use mental math to find each quotient.

a. $54 \div 6$
$540 \div 60$
$5,400 \div 600$

b. $35 \div 5$
$350 \div 50$
$3,500 \div 500$

c. $63 \div 9$
$630 \div 90$
$6,300 \div 900$

The second and third rows in each pattern were created by multiplying the divisor and the dividend by the same power of 10. In each pattern, what happens to the quotient?

Continue each pattern below by multiplying the divisor and the dividend by 10 until the divisor is a whole number. Then use a calculator to find each quotient.

d. $11.2\overline{)0.224}$
$112\overline{)2.24}$

e. $0.08\overline{)16}$
$0.8\overline{)160}$
$?\overline{)?}$

f. $2.584\overline{)12.5}$
$25.84\overline{)125}$
$?\overline{)?}$

Compare these examples with **a–c**. How are they alike? How are they different?

Example **g** shows how to divide by a decimal, using paper and pencil.

g. Multiply the divisor by a power of 10 to make it a whole number.

$0.8\overline{)9.6}$

Multiply the dividend by the same power of 10. Place the decimal point in the quotient.

$0.8\overline{)9.6}$

Divide.

$$\begin{array}{r} 12. \\ 0.8\overline{)9.6} \\ 8 \\ \hline 1\,6 \\ 1\,6 \\ \hline 0 \end{array}$$

Use a calculator. Find $9.6 \div 0.8$ and $96 \div 8$. Are the quotients equal? Why or why not?

Check Your Understanding

Divide. Check each answer by multiplying or by estimating. Round to the nearest hundredth.

1. $0.5\overline{)2.75}$ **2.** $0.9\overline{)31.5}$ **3.** $3.06\overline{)25.704}$ **4.** $0.024\overline{)24}$ **5.** $0.17\overline{)293}$

Share Your Ideas Look back at **3** and **4**. Why did you multiply the divisor and the dividend by 100 in **3** but by 1,000 in **4**?

Divide. Choose paper and pencil, mental math, or a
 calculator. Check your answers. Round the quotients in
14–17 to the nearest hundredth.

6. 0.2)5

7. 0.7)0.77

8. 16 ÷ 0.08

9. 0.4)0.004

10. 3.5)13.93

11. 6.5)340.6

12. 5.4 ÷ 0.009

13. 0.06)0.36

14. $9 ÷ 5.1

15. 0.16)$12.15

16. 0.3 ÷ 0.9

17. 32 ÷ 7.2

18. 0.067)1.206

19. 5.1 ÷ 3.4

20. 0.81)5,508

21. 6.2)15.996

22. 0.05)125

23. 8.9)6,213.09

24. $\frac{5,854.86}{6.6}$

25. $\frac{0.789}{0.016}$

Estimate to help select the correct quotient.

26. 6.3)354.375
   a. 0.5625
   b. 5.625
   c. 56.25

27. 26)20.41
   a. 78.5
   b. 7.85
   c. 0.785

28. 0.95)10.07
   a. 1.06
   b. 10.6
   c. 106

29. 5 ÷ 16
   a. 0.03125
   b. 0.3125
   c. 3.125

Write *true* or *false*. Explain your thinking.

30. Look back at **10.** You can multiply to check your answer.

31. Look back at **14.** You can multiply to check your answer.

Think and Apply

32. The Moller 200 has 8 rotary engines. It can rise about
75 ft in the air. **What if** it traveled 1,085 mi in 2.25 h?
How fast would it be going? [Distance ÷ time = rate
(speed)] Round to the nearest tenth.

Test Taker

You can improve your test score if you do easy problems
first. Save complicated problems until last.

Decide which problem to do first. Then solve.

33. 34.5)28.635
   a. 0.85   b. 8.5   c. 0.87   d. not given

34. 200 × 50
   a. 1,000   b. 10,000   c. 100,000   d. not given

35. 746 + 352
   a. 1,098   b. 198   c. 1,908   d. 1,018

Without dividing, select the example with the least
quotient. Explain your thinking.
   a. 5.8 ÷ 0.004   b. 5.8 ÷ 0.04   c. 5.8 ÷ 0.4

SUMMING UP

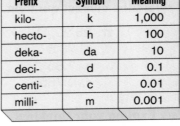

Look at the metric prefixes below. What words do you know that have these prefixes? What does each word mean?

Metric Measurement

The bucket holds 10 liters (10 L).
The hose is 20 meters (20 m) long.
The car weighs 1,000 kilograms (1,000 kg), or 1 metric ton.

How long is the hose in centimeters?

This chart shows the meaning of metric prefixes. Metric prefixes are used with *meter, liter,* and *gram* to form the names of other units of measure.

Prefix	Symbol	Meaning
kilo-	k	1,000
hecto-	h	100
deka-	da	10
deci-	d	0.1
centi-	c	0.01
milli-	m	0.001

To change from one unit to another, multiply or divide by a power of 10. Use the chart below.

To change from a larger unit to a smaller unit, multiply by a power of 10. There will be more smaller units.

$\times 10 \quad \times 10 \quad \times 10 \quad \times 10 \quad \times 10 \quad \times 10$

kilometer	hectometer	dekameter	meter	decimeter	centimeter	millimeter
kilogram	hectogram	dekagram	gram	decigram	centigram	milligram
kiloliter	hectoliter	dekaliter	liter	deciliter	centiliter	milliliter

$\div 10 \quad \div 10 \quad \div 10 \quad \div 10 \quad \div 10 \quad \div 10$

To change from a smaller unit to a larger unit, divide by a power of 10. There will be fewer larger units.

a. 3,250 mg = _____ g   **Think** Smaller unit to larger. There will be fewer units.
   3,250 ÷ 1,000 = 3.25
   3,250 mg = 3.25 g

b. 0.32 km = _____ m   **Think** Larger unit to smaller. There will be more units.
   0.32 × 1,000 = 320
   0.32 km = 320 m

Check Your Understanding

Complete.

1. 3.7 km = _____ m

2. _____ g = 9,201 mg

3. 0.92 m = _____ cm

4. 5.1 kL = _____ L

5. 172 mL = _____ L

6. _____ dam = 7.3 hm

Share Your Ideas Explain how you could use the fact 1 mg = 0.001 g to answer **2.** Explain how you could use the fact 1 kL = 1,000 L to answer **4.**

Complete.

7. 1 m = _____ cm

8. 1 _____ = 0.1 m

9. 10 g = _____ dag

10. 0.001 kL = _____ L

11. _____ mm = 1 cm

12. 1,000 _____ = 1 g

13. _____ m = 0.01 hm

14. 100 L = 1 _____

15. 1 cm = _____ m

16. 5 cm = _____ mm

17. 8 mg = 0.008 _____

18. 10,000 m = 10 _____

19. _____ hm = 1,200 m

20. 35 cm = _____ mm

21. 42 daL = 420 _____

22. _____ cm = 7.6 dm

23. 300 cg = 3 _____

24. 0.05 L = _____ cL

25. _____ m = 327 cm

26. 92.3 km = _____ m

27. 42.5 _____ = 4.25 g

28. 0.546 cL = 5.46 _____

29. 6.4 m = 6 _____ 4 _____

30. 7.06 m = 7 _____ 6 _____

Compare. Replace each ⬤ with <, >, or =.

31. 1,000 g ⬤ 1 kg

32. 1 cm ⬤ 1 mm

33. 100 mL ⬤ 1 L

34. 2.75 cm ⬤ 27.5 mm

35. 400 g ⬤ 0.4 kg

36. 200 cm ⬤ 200 dm

37. 92 L ⬤ 92,000 mL

38. 8,000 g ⬤ 8.1 kg

39. 150 cm ⬤ 1.48 m

Think and Apply

Convert the measurement in each statement to a more sensible one.

40. Rick lives 4,235,000 mm from school.

41. Drink 0.002 kL of water each day for better health.

42. This morning Yoshi ate 56,000 mg of cereal.

43. Mr. Bluehouse is 0.00177 km tall.

44. Ms. Twyma weighs 71,680 grams.

45. Nora runs the 100,000-mm dash for her high-school track team.

Logical Thinking

46. Two volumes of Shakespeare stand side by side on a bookshelf. Volume I is at the left of Volume II. The bindings are facing you. Each volume with its covers measures 4 cm thick. Each cover of each volume is 0.5 cm thick. A bookworm has eaten its way directly from the first page of Volume I to the last page of Volume II. How far has it traveled?

Describe some advantages and disadvantages of having a system of measurement based on the decimal system.

SUMMING UP

Compare. $9.50 ÷ 6 ⬬ $4.95 ÷ 3

Finding Unit Price

Which is the better buy?

To find the better buy, compare the unit prices. The **unit price** of a product is the price per unit of measure.

Estimation can help you find the better buy. Estimate the unit price of each package of spark plugs.

$$\begin{array}{r} \$1.10 \\ 8)\overline{\$8.89} \end{array} \quad \text{rounds to} \quad \begin{array}{r} \$1.10 \\ 8)\overline{\$8.80} \end{array}$$

The package of 8 spark plugs for $8.89 is the better buy, because the unit price is less.

$$\begin{array}{r} \$1.30 \\ 4)\overline{\$5.17} \end{array} \quad \text{rounds to} \quad \begin{array}{r} \$1.30 \\ 4)\overline{\$5.20} \end{array}$$

Sometimes an estimate may not be enough. You may need to find the exact answer. A calculator can help.

Which is the better buy?

$$\text{Estimate:} \quad \begin{array}{r} \$.80 \\ 5)\overline{\$3.89} \end{array} \longrightarrow \begin{array}{r} \$.80 \\ 5)\overline{\$4.00} \end{array}$$

$$\begin{array}{r} \$.80 \\ 6)\overline{\$4.63} \end{array} \longrightarrow \begin{array}{r} \$.80 \\ 6)\overline{\$4.80} \end{array}$$

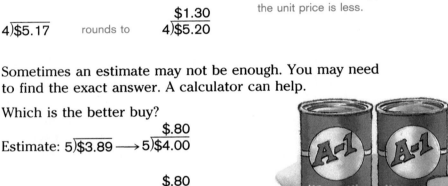

Use a calculator to get an exact answer.

$3.89 ÷ 5 = [0.778] $4.63 ÷ 6 = [0.7716666]

Which brand of motor oil is the better buy? Why?

Check Your Understanding

Find the unit price. Round up to the next greater cent.

1. 8 lb for $9.99

2. 6 cans for $3.49

3. 8 reams for $15.29

4. 10 jars for $17.99

5. 1 dozen for $1.79

6. 3 gal for $5.79

Share Your Ideas   Why would a store owner price an item at $9.99 for 5 instead of $2.00 each?

Practice

Choose mental math, paper and pencil, or a calculator. Find each unit price. Round up to the next greater cent.

7. 6 ft for $4.79

8. 3 pairs for $22

9. 10 boxes for $39

10. 3 qt for $2.16

11. 5 pairs for $4.34

12. 100 index cards for $1.79

13. 3 lb for $3.49

14. 12 oz for $6.59

15. 2 cases for $75

16. 6 lemons for $1.39

17. 5 h for $6.50

18. 3 boxes for $2.69

19. 350 sheets for $.89

20. 250 sheets for $1.16. Price per 100 sheets?

21. Look back at **7–12.** Which method did you use to solve each?

Think and Apply

For each item, predict which is the better buy. Then use paper and pencil or a calculator to find the better buy.

Item	King Auto Stores	Star Auto Parts
22. oil	**a.** 12 qt for $10.99	**b.** 6 qt for $5.99
23. brake fluid	**a.** 12 oz for $3.79	**b.** 6 oz for $1.79
24. antifreeze	**a.** 3 gal for $23.99	**b.** 2 gal for $13.99
25. carburetor cleaner	**a.** 5 cans for $6.49	**b.** 8 cans for $9.59
26. auto wax	**a.** 6 cans for $14.29	**b.** 5 cans for $12.98
27. upholstery tape	**a.** 3 rolls for $2.89	**b.** 4 rolls for $3.79

Read the details about the products. Then solve.

Monroe Oil
6 qt for $6.95
lasts up to 5,000 mi.

LITCHFIELD OIL
10 qt for only $15.95
lasts up to 10,000 mi.

WALDO TIRES
ALL SEASON TIRES
4 for $129.99!
40,000 mi. warranty

Hi Way King
All Season Tires
2 for $89.99
60,000 mi. warranty

28. Which is the better buy—Monroe Oil or Litchfield Oil? Consider price only.

29. Explain why someone might want to buy the oil with the higher unit price.

30. Which is the better buy—Waldo Tires or Hiway King Tires? Consider price only.

31. Explain why someone might want to buy the tires with the higher unit price.

Look back at **22** and **23.** Explain how you predicted the better buy.

SUMMING UP

61

Using Problem Solving

Interview: Calculators and Travel

Steve Brod is the travel manager for the American Automobile Association in Warwick, Rhode Island. "I use a calculator every time I plan a trip for an Association member," Steve reported. "I add the miles along the route with a calculator and use it to compute the estimated driving time based on an average rate of 50 mph."

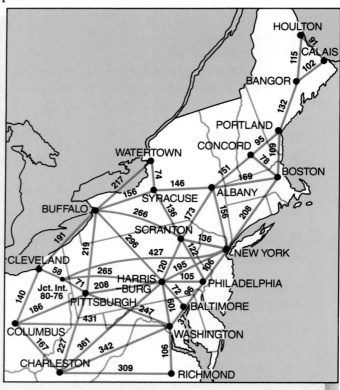

Working together

Work in a group to solve these problems. Use a calculator where appropriate.

A. Plan a trip from New York, New York, to Columbus, Ohio. List the cities along your route, the mileage between them, and the estimated driving time for each part of the trip. Then find the total mileage and the estimated driving time for the entire trip.

B. Each person in your group should list a starting point and an ending point for an imaginary trip. Then exchange trips within your group. Calculate the total mileage and estimated driving time for the trip.

C. How many hours is it safe for a person to drive in a day? Look at your planned trips and decide how long they should take.

Sharing Your Ideas

1. Compare the plans for the trip from New York to Columbus. Did different groups take different routes? If so, what were they? Why might you want to take a different route or change the driving times?

2. **What if** there is highway construction for 15 miles of your trip? The average speed for this part of the trip is only 25 mph. How would you calculate the estimated trip time now?

3. Why, do you think, was 50 mph used to get the estimated driving time?

Extending Your Thinking

4. Steve Brod reports that members often want to know how much gasoline will cost for their trips. **What if** your car gets 33 miles to the gallon and gasoline costs $1.10 a gallon? Estimate the fuel costs for the trip from New York to Columbus.

5. During a gasoline shortage, members wanted to know how far they could drive on a tank of gasoline. Car A gets 33 miles to the gallon and has a 13-gallon gasoline tank. For the trip in problem **A**, tell how far a member can drive before a refill is needed. Then tell how many times the car must be filled to complete the trip.

Summing Up

6. How were you able to tell how much gasoline would cost for the trip from New York, New York, to Columbus, Ohio? Write instructions for calculating the cost of gasoline for the trip.

7. List as many ways as you can that Steve Brod and other travel agents might use calculators in their work.

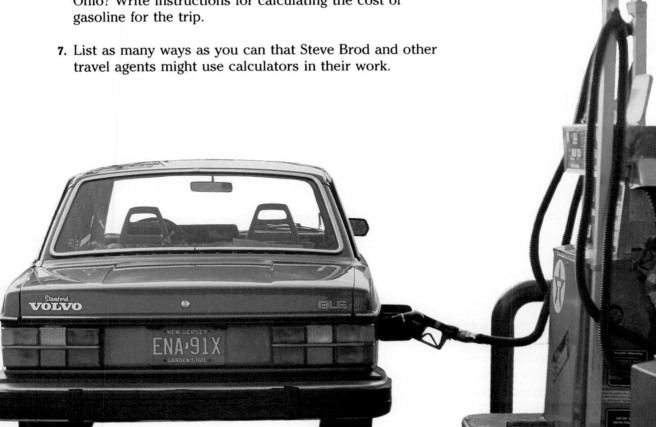

Chapter Review

Multiply or divide, using mental math. pages 34-37, 42-43

1. $3 \div 100$
2. $5 \times 1.2 \times 2$
3. $6.24 \times 1,000$
4. $36.18 \div 100$

5. 28×32
6. $25 \times 47 \times 40$
7. 8×7.5
8. $5 \times 7 \times 22$

Choose the best estimate for each. pages 38-39, 50-51

9. 935×27
   a. 2,700
   b. 27,000
10. $43\overline{)44,705}$
    a. 10,000
    b. 1,000
11. 37.7×0.4
    a. 18
    b. 1.8
12. $0.08\overline{)7.29}$
    a. 90
    b. 900

13. $18.2 \div 9.3$
    a. 0.2
    b. 2
14. 31.4×9
    a. 270
    b. 370
15. 56×75
    a. 4,000
    b. 420
16. $338\overline{)87,458}$
    a. 200
    b. 2,000

Multiply or divide. Round 20, 27, and 32 to the nearest hundredth.
Estimate to be sure each answer makes sense. pages 40-45, 52-57

17. 4.2×0.025
18. 0.9×0.021
19. $3.75 \div 5$
20. $1,533 \div 9$

21. $\begin{array}{r} 4,238 \\ \times\ \ \ 604 \\ \hline \end{array}$
22. $\begin{array}{r} 342 \\ \times\ \ 8.1 \\ \hline \end{array}$
23. $\begin{array}{r} 298 \\ \times\ 150 \\ \hline \end{array}$
24. $\begin{array}{r} 39.8 \\ \times\ 40.2 \\ \hline \end{array}$

25. $2.5\overline{)8.792}$
26. $9.9 \div 3.3$
27. $127\overline{)\$3,467}$
28. $6 \times 0.01 \times 21$

29. $6,420 \times 0.001$
30. 79×81
31. 43.6×7.95
32. $43.23 \div 28$

Complete. pages 58-59

33. $5 \text{ m} = \underline{\hspace{1cm}} \text{ mm}$
34. $\underline{\hspace{1cm}} \text{ cm} = 20 \text{ mm}$
35. $1 \text{ mg} = \underline{\hspace{1cm}} \text{ g}$

36. $2.5 \underline{\hspace{1cm}} = 250 \text{ g}$
37. $902.1 \text{ g} = \underline{\hspace{1cm}} \text{ kg}$
38. $93.2 \underline{\hspace{1cm}} = 93,200 \text{ mL}$

39. $1 \text{ cL} = \underline{\hspace{1cm}} \text{ L}$
40. $92 \text{ dam} = 9.2 \underline{\hspace{1cm}}$
41. $54.6 \text{ km} = \underline{\hspace{1cm}} \text{ m}$

Find the unit price. Round to the next greater cent if necessary. pages 60-61

42. 6 for 99¢
43. 2 for 25¢
44. 3 for $1.00
45. 7 for $2.00

46. 12 for $7.99
47. 25 for $.89
48. 9 for $.75
49. 24 for $3.68

Solve. pages 48-49, 62-63

50. It took Roger 20 minutes to drive to the Village Farmer. They were selling oranges at 3 for 69¢, grapes at $2.59 per kg, and apples at 5 for $1.00. Roger bought 1 kg of grapes and 12 apples. How much did they cost?

51. The Variety Store has pads of paper on sale for 5 for $.89. Thalea's Stationery Store sells pads for $.19 each. Which is the better buy?

Chapter Test

Choose the best estimate for each.

1. $\begin{array}{r} 502 \\ \times\ \ 23 \end{array}$

    a. 100
    b. 1,000
    c. 10,000

2. $25\overline{)3{,}087.1}$

    a. 1,000
    b. 100
    c. 10

3. $\begin{array}{r} 0.051 \\ \times\ \ \ 2.2 \end{array}$

    a. 0.01
    b. 0.1
    c. 1

Multiply or divide. Estimate to be sure each answer makes sense. Round 10 and 14 to the nearest tenth.

4. 3.25×4

5. $25 \times (9 \times 4)$

6. $2.75 \div 0.5$

7. $18 \div 10{,}000$

8. $\begin{array}{r} 5.35 \\ \times\ \ 1.2 \end{array}$

9. $\begin{array}{r} 29.1 \\ \times\ \ \ 83 \end{array}$

10. $4.7\overline{)10.36}$

11. $4.087 \times 10{,}000$

12. $84 \div 0.06$

13. $\begin{array}{r} 4{,}657 \\ \times\ \ \ 506 \end{array}$

14. $35\overline{)9{,}368}$

15. $\begin{array}{r} 398 \\ \times\ 250 \end{array}$

Complete.

16. $1 \text{ mm} = \underline{\hspace{1cm}} \text{ cm}$

17. $4.7 \underline{\hspace{1cm}} = 4{,}700 \text{ mL}$

18. $500 \text{ g} = \underline{\hspace{1cm}} \text{ kg}$

19. $7.6 \text{ m} = \underline{\hspace{1cm}} \text{ dm}$

Find each unit price. Round to the next greater cent if necessary.

20. 3 for $2.00

21. 2 for 49¢

22. 12 for $1.00

23. 4 for 59¢

Solve.

24. Robert's family toured the United States for 4 weeks. They traveled a total of 4,898 km. On the average, how many kilometers did they travel each day? Round to the nearest kilometer.

25. Salita traveled 1,026 km in 7 hours. Her car averages 10.8 km per liter of fuel. The fuel tank holds 50 liters. What was the cost of fuel for Salita's trip?

THINK Janis wants to buy some of each kind of fruit. She has $4.00 to spend. How much of each kind of fruit can she buy? Show one possibility.

apples: 3 for $.89
oranges: 4 for $.59
melons: $.89 each
peaches: 6 for $.99
grapes: $1.29 for $\frac{1}{2}$ kg

Casting Out Nines

Checking your work for reasonableness and accuracy is always a good idea. One way to check your work is to *cast out nines*.

To cast out nines for a multiplication problem, do the following.

a. Add the digits of each factor. Add the digits of the product.

$$421.8 \rightarrow 4 + 2 + 1 + 8 = 15$$
$$\underline{\times \quad 3.2} \rightarrow 3 + 2 = 5$$
$$1,349.76 \rightarrow 1 + 3 + 4 + 9 + 7 + 6 = 30$$

b. If a sum is 9, change it to 0. If a sum is greater than 9, add the digits of the sum. Continue until the sum is less than 9.

$$15 \rightarrow 1 + 5 = 6$$
$$5$$
$$30 \rightarrow 3 + 0 = 3$$

c. Multiply the sums of the factors. Cast out the nines from the result.

$$6 \times 5 = 30 \rightarrow 3 + 0 = 3$$

d. Compare the final number in **c** with the number you get from casting the nines out of the product of the problem. If they are equal, the answer to the problem is probably correct.

$$3 = 3$$

You can simplify casting out nines by looking for sums of 9 and eliminating them from the total sum.

$$4 + 2 + 1 + 8 \rightarrow 4 + 2 = 6$$
$$9$$
$$1 + 3 + 4 + 9 + 7 + 6 = 12$$
$$9$$
$$12 \rightarrow 1 + 2 = 3$$

To cast out nines to check a division problem, follow the procedure in **a** and **b** for the divisor, quotient, and dividend. Then multiply the sum for the divisor by the sum for the quotient and compare this product with the sum for the dividend.

Use casting out nines to check each problem. Correct any wrong answers.

1.
$$\begin{array}{r} 3,128 \\ \times \quad 52 \\ \hline 163,656 \end{array}$$

2.
$$\begin{array}{r} 849.1 \\ \times \quad 37 \\ \hline 31,416.7 \end{array}$$

3.
$$62\overline{)1,151.34} \quad \text{(18.57)}$$

4.
$$2.1\overline{)450.45} \quad \text{(215.3)}$$

Maintaining Skills

Choose the correct answers. Write A, B, C, or D.

1. What is the value of the digit 9 in 89,058,003,643?

   A 9,000,000 **C** 9,000,000,000

   B 90,000,000,000 **D** not given

2. What is the standard form? 23 million, 806 thousand, 411

   A 23,806,411 **C** 2,386,411

   B 23,086,411 **D** not given

3. Write 16 thousandths as a decimal.

   A 16,000 **C** 1,000.6

   B 0.16 **D** not given

4. Compare. 2.35 ⬤ 2.350

   A < **C** =

   B > **D** not given

5. What property is illustrated? 2.05 + 0 = 2.05

   A Associative **C** Identity

   B Commutative **D** not given

6. Estimate. 8.42 + 5.875

   A 4 **C** 24

   B 14 **D** not given

7. $12.96 + $142.05 + $16.25

   A $160.16 **C** $171.26

   B $170.26 **D** not given

8. 18.03
    − 5.45

   A 12.58 **C** 13.58

   B 13.42 **D** not given

9. What property is illustrated? $8 \times (62 \times 5) = (8 \times 62) \times 5$

   A Associative **C** Identity

   B Commutative **D** not given

10. 83.6 × 42

    A 501.6 **C** 3,401.2

    B 3,511.2 **D** not given

11. Estimate. 43.2 ÷ 61

    A 0.7 **C** 1

    B 7 **D** 0.07

12. 27.52 ÷ 4.3

    A 0.15625 **C** 6.4

    B 0.64 **D** not given

13. What is the unit price? 6 cans for $1.32

    A $.45 **C** $.22

    B $.18 **D** not given

Use this information to solve 14 and 15. In baseball a person can make an out, be on one of three bases, or score a run.

14. Six people batted and 2 of them made outs. What is the most runs that could have been scored?

    A 0 **C** 6

    B 2 **D** not given

15. Nine people batted, and there are no outs yet. How many runs could have been scored?

    A 9 **C** 5

    B 4 **D** not given

Number Patterns and Number Theory

THEME   Famous Mathematicians

Sharing What You Know

We're surrounded—surrounded by patterns! Pythagoras, an ancient Greek mathematician, believed that nature—including colors and the movement of the planets—was organized according to number patterns. Although many of Pythagoras' ideas were disproved, number patterns can be seen in many areas of life. For example, when certain cells divide, one cell becomes two, then two become four, then four become eight, and so on. What other patterns in nature can you think of?

Using Language

Patterns as well as sequences can be found in everyday life. The word **sequence** has many different meanings. In everyday life, we use the word **sequence** to describe any ordered series of items or events. In science, for example, the sequence that marks the stages of a butterfly's development is: egg, larva, pupa, adult. In mathematics, a **sequence** is an ordered list of numbers. The numbers 1, 2, 4, 8, 16,... form a sequence. Discuss any other examples of sequences that come to mind.

Words to Know: pattern, sequence, divisibility, base, exponent, prime, factor, prime factorization, greatest common factor, least common multiple, cubed, squared, multiple

Be a Problem Solver

Study the hexagonal pattern.

```
              * * *
    * *      * * * *
*  * * *    * * * * *
    * *      * * * *
              * * *
```

What will the next hexagonal figure in the pattern look like? How many symbols will it contain? Draw the figure. What is the pattern?

Create your own geometric pattern. Describe the sequence that you used.

BANNAKER

Look for a pattern. Then find the missing numbers.

13→9→11→7→9
16→12→14→10→?
21→17→19→?→?

Patterns and Sequences

The mathematician Leonardo of Pisa, known as Fibonacci, introduced the sequence 1, 1, 2, 3, 5, 8, 13, 21, 34, . . . in 1202. The Fibonacci sequence is found frequently in nature, for example, in the number of spirals of seeds in a sunflower.

A **sequence** is a list of numbers that follow a rule or pattern. The numbers are called *terms*.

Here are some other sequences.

> **a.** 0, 3, 6, 9, 12, 15, 18, 21, 24, 27, 30, ...
> **b.** 0, 6, 12, 18, 24, 30, 36, 42, 48, 54, 60, ...
> **c.** 0, 9, 18, 27, 36, 45, 54, 63, 72, 81, 90, ...

The rule for sequence **a** is *add 3*. The sequence is the **multiples** of 3. All multiples of 3 are **divisible** by 3. You can tell that a number is divisible by 3 if the sum of its digits is divisible by 3.

Without dividing, how do you know that a number is divisible by 2? by 5? by 10?

At the right are some rules for testing whether a number is divisible by 4, 6, 8, or 9.

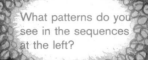
What patterns do you see in the sequences at the left?

A number is divisible by	if
4	the number formed by the last 2 digits is divisible by 4.
6	the number is even and divisible by 3.
8	the number formed by the last 3 digits is divisible by 8.
9	the sum of the digits is divisible by 9.

Check Your Understanding

Copy and complete the table. Write *yes* or *no*.

	Number	Divisible by					
		3	4	5	6	8	9
1.	765						
2.	1,464						
3.	1,080						
4.	1,073						

Share Your Ideas What numbers are all the terms of this sequence divisible by: 0, 18, 36, 54, 72, 90, 108, 126, 144, 162, 180, . . .? Use the rules for divisibility. Explain your thinking.

CHOICES Use mental math, paper and pencil, or a calculator. Copy and complete the table. Write *yes* or *no*.

	Number	Divisible by					
		3	4	5	6	8	9
5.	372						
6.	1,488						
7.	585						
8.	2,763						
9.	959						
10.	2,970						
11.	14,756						
12.	5,040						

List the first 10 multiples of each. For each exercise, tell what numbers all the multiples are divisible by.

13. 10   **14.** 8   **15.** 16   **16.** 15   **17.** 20

Use the divisibility rules to analyze.

18. What is the least three-digit number that is divisible by 3? Is it divisible by 6? by 9? How do you know?

19. What is the greatest four-digit number that is divisible by 4? Is it divisible by 2? by 8? How do you know?

20. If a number is divisible by 3 and 5, what other numbers do you know it is divisible by? Give examples to illustrate.

21. If a number is divisible by 2 and 9, what other numbers do you know it is divisible by? Give examples to illustrate.

Find the rule for each sequence. Use a calculator to help.

22. 0, 13, 26, 39, 52, . . .   **23.** 65, 59, 53, 47, 41, . . .   **24.** 1, 1, 2, 3, 5, 8, . . .

DATA
25. Examine as many different kinds of flowers as you can. Count the petals in each ring. Use the data you collect to write a petal sequence for each kind of flower. Find a rule for each sequence if you can.

Look back at **6–7.** Which methods—mental math, pencil and paper, or a calculator—did you use in each? Explain why.

SUMMING UP

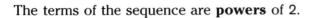

GETTING STARTED

Look for a pattern.
Then find the
missing numbers.

64→32→16→?→4
3→9→27→81→?

Patterns and Exponents

The numbers 1, 2, 4, 8, 16, 32, 64, . . . form a sequence.
What is the rule for this sequence?

The terms of the sequence are **powers** of 2.

$$2 = 2$$
$$4 = 2 \times 2$$
$$8 = 2 \times 2 \times 2$$
$$16 = 2 \times 2 \times 2 \times 2$$
$$32 = 2 \times 2 \times 2 \times 2 \times 2$$
$$64 = 2 \times 2 \times 2 \times 2 \times 2 \times 2$$

How could you use a calculator
to generate the powers of 2?

The powers of a number can also be
written using exponents.

$$2^0, 2^1, 2^2, 2^3, 2^4, 2^5, 2^6, \ldots$$

▶ The **exponent** tells how many times the
base is used as a **factor.**

$$16 = 2 \times 2 \times 2 \times 2 = 2^{4} \leftarrow \text{exponent}$$

factors   base

▶ A number (except 0) to the zero power
is always 1.

$$2^0 = 1$$

A number to the first power is always itself.

$$2^1 = 2$$

A number to the second power is **squared.**

2^2 is "two squared."

A number to the third power is **cubed.**

2^3 is "two cubed."

What is the rule for this sequence? How
would you write the sequence, using
exponents?

1, 5, 25, 125, 625, 3,125, . . .

How could you use a calculator
to help you find the rule?

Check Your Understanding

Write using exponents.

1. $8 \times 8 \times 8 \times 8$ **2.** $3 \times 3 \times 3 \times 3 \times 3$ **3.** 7×7 **4.** $1 \times 1 \times 1 \times 1 \times 1 \times 1$

Write as a product of factors. Then write in standard form.

5. 10^5 **6.** 6^2 **7.** 8^0 **8.** 5^1 **9.** 4^3

Share Your Ideas   For powers of 10, describe two things
the exponent tells. Show examples.

Select the correct answer.

10. $7 \times 7 \times 7 \times 7 \times 7 =$ _____

   a. 7^7 **b.** 7^5 **c.** 5^7

11. $121 =$ _____

   a. 2^{11} **b.** 11^{11} **c.** 11^2

12. $10 =$ _____

   a. 10^0 **b.** 10^1 **c.** 10^2

13. $64 =$ _____

   a. 8^2 **b.** 2^8 **c.** 8^8

14. $12^0 =$ _____

   a. 1 **b.** 12 **c.** 0

15. $1 =$ _____

   a. 10^1 **b.** 2^1 **c.** 1^{10}

16. $9 \times 9 \times 9 \times 9 =$ _____

   a. 4^9 **b.** 9^4 **c.** 9^9

17. $4^3 =$ _____

   a. 12 **b.** 16 **c.** 64

Write the square and the cube of each number. Use standard form.

18. 3   **19.** 5   **20.** 1   **21.** 10   **22.** 9

Write as a product of factors. Then write in standard form. Use a calculator to help.

23. 3^5 **24.** 6^3 **25.** 7^2 **26.** 10^0

27. 5^4 **28.** 4^5 **29.** 11^2 **30.** 9^1

31. 8^3 **32.** 2^8 **33.** 15^0 **34.** 12^1

35. $2^3 \times 3^2$ **36.** $4^2 \times 5^2$ **37.** $3^4 \times 4^3$ **38.** $5^3 \times 6^2$

Think and Apply

Find the rule for each sequence. Then write the sequence, using exponents.

39. 1, 3, 9, 27, 81, 243, 729, . . .

40. 1; 7; 49; 343; 2,401; 16,807; . . .

41. 1; 6; 36; 216; 1,296; 7,776; 46,656; . . .

42. 1, 1, 2, 3, 4, 9, 8, 27, 16, 81, 32, 243, . . .

43. There are 2 bugs in a jar. Every minute the number of bugs doubles. The jar is filled in half an hour. How long is it before the jar is only *half* full?

Make each sentence true. Explain your thinking.

  a. $15^2 = \square$ **b.** $5^{\square} = 625$ **c.** $\square^5 = 100{,}000$

Estimate. Then compute.

1.   75,062
    − 68,736

2.   7.45
    ×   26

3.   85.6
     7.985
   + 36.47

4. $71.8 - 36.25$

5. $25 + 134 + 66 + 75$

6. $42{,}628 \div 32$

List in order from least to greatest.

7. 0.032; 32; 0.32; 320

8. 4,126; 4,216; 4,612

9. 304; 403; 340; 430

Solve.

10. How many centimeters are there in 2.56 m?

11. How many kilograms are there in 350 g?

12. How much time has elapsed between 9:45 A.M. and 3:40 P.M.?

SUMMING UP

What number is 5.4×10^3?
What number is $362{,}000 \div 10^5$?

Scientific Notation

In the early 1800s, Ada Byron Lovelace developed the instructions for all computations, including multiplying numbers, on Charles Babbage's Analytical Engine.

Today a hand-held calculator can multiply numbers in the millions. But sometimes the product must be displayed in scientific notation, called E notation on a calculator. Scientific calculators display E notation as shown here.

$63{,}500 \times 3{,}900 =$

```
2.4765  08
```

Why could this product not be displayed in standard form on the calculator?

▶ A number in **scientific notation** is written as the product of a number between 1 and 10 and a power of 10.

$$247{,}650{,}000 = 2.4765 \times 10^8$$

Ada Byron Lovelace
Courtesy Historical
Pictures Service, Inc.

─Divide by a power of 10 to change to scientific notation.─

Standard form	Number between 1 and 10	Powers of 10	Scientific notation
7,423	7.423 ↶ 3 places	10^3	7.423×10^3
368,000	3.68000 ↶ 5 places	10^5	3.68×10^5

── Multiply by a power of 10 to change to standard form.─

If the decimal point in a number is moved 3 places to the left, what operation is being performed—multiplication or division? By what number?

Check Your Understanding

Write each in standard form.

1. 4.8×10^3

2. 5.063×10^8

3. 7.00675×10^4

Write each in scientific notation.

4. 5,062

5. 280,000

6. 45,872,000,000

Share Your Ideas Is this number displayed in E notation? Explain why or why not. If not, correct it.

```
1.036  08
```

Find each missing number.

7. $8 \times 10^{\square} = 80,000$

8. $\square \times 10^3 = 3,402$

9. $\square \times 10^6 = 7,045,400$

10. $\square = 8.35 \times 10^2$

11. $7.0602 \times 10^7 = \square$

12. $6.24 \times 10^{\square} = 624,000,000$

13. $\square = 7.9 \times 10^5$

14. $12,356,000,000 = \square \times 10^{10}$

15. $30,000,000 = 3 \times 10^{\square}$

16. $2,543,000 = 2.543 \times 10^{\square}$

Select the answer that shows the number in standard form.

17. 3.0305×10^5

   a. 30,305
   b. 303,050
   c. 3,030,500

18. 7.638×10^2

   a. 763.8
   b. 7,638
   c. 76,380

19. 5.75×10^3

   a. 57.5
   b. 575
   c. 5,750

20. 1.67×10^8

   a. 1,670,000
   b. 16,700,000
   c. 167,000,000

21. 7.3×10

   a. 0.73
   b. 73
   c. 730

22. 2.80346×10^9

   a. 28,034,600
   b. 280,346,000
   c. 2,803,460,000

Write each in scientific notation.

23. 4,000

24. 87,000

25. 23,500

26. 65 million

27. 725,800,000

28. 398 thousand

29. 42,130,000,000

30. 107,000,000

31. 188 billion

32. 756.8

33. 8,406.7

34. 64.953

35. 7.5 million

36. 37.8 million

37. 8 billion, 20 million

Find each product. Write each answer in scientific notation. Then write the answer as it would be displayed on a scientific calculator and as it is displayed on your calculator.

38. $42,000 \times 956,000$

39. $78,900 \times 102,000$

40. $329.53 \times 1,000,000$

41. $435,000 \times 9,400$

42. $23,436 \times 30,000$

43. $73,500 \times 25,800$

Write a few sentences explaining how to write a whole number in scientific notation.

SUMMING UP

Activity

Exploring Factors and Multiples

Eratosthenes lived in ancient Greece. He discovered a way to use multiples to find the factors of a number. Can you find out how he did it?

Working together

Materials: grid paper 4 squares to an inch

A. Cut a 10-square by 5-square grid from the paper. Number the squares from 1 to 50.

B. Devise a method for marking multiples. The method should allow you to identify all the multiples of a number once you have completed marking the grid. For example, you could use a different color for the multiples of each number. Mark the multiples of each number from 2 to 50.

C. The marking system tells the multiples and the factors of a number. Each person in your group should select a number between 2 and 50. Record the factors of your number by referring to the marked grid.

Sharing Your Results

Look back at the grid and the numbers you recorded.

1. If one number is a multiple of a second number, is the second a factor of the first? Explain.

2. How does the grid show factors as well as multiples?

3. Why is it not necessary to mark all the multiples of 1?

4. How many times was your number marked as a multiple?

5. Which number was marked most often? Explain why.

6. Identify three numbers that are marked only once. Are these numbers odd or even? What are the factors of each?

7. How many even numbers are marked only once? Identify them.

Extending the Activity

On a corridor at Eratosthenes Junior High there are 100 numbered lockers. They are all closed. On the first day of school, the 100 students who use those lockers decide on the following plan.

- Student #1 will open every locker.

- Student #2 will then close every second door, beginning with locker 2.

- Student #3 will then reverse (open or close) the door on every third locker, beginning with locker 3.

The process will continue until all 100 students have taken their turns. The students wish to record the number of times each door opens and closes, and whether it is open or closed at the end.

Work in your group.

8. Devise a method for modeling the students' plan. Then carry out your plan. For each locker number, record the number of times it opens and closes, and whether it is finally open or closed.

Summing Up

9. Which lockers were opened and closed most often? Of what number are these locker numbers multiples?

10. Which lockers were opened and closed least often? How many times? Can any other lockers be opened and closed the same number of times? Explain why or why not.

11. Which lockers were opened and closed only twice? Explain why.

12. Which lockers were finally open? Describe the numbers of these lockers.

13. Write a statement that tells how you could predict which lockers would be opened and closed only twice and which lockers would finally be open in a school with 1,000 lockers and 1,000 students.

Exploring Primes and Composites

▶ A whole number greater than 1 is

- **prime** if it has only two factors, 1 and itself.
- **composite** if it has more than two factors.

Look back at the grid and the locker problem on pages 78 and 79. Which of the numbers from 1 to 100 are prime? How do you know?

▶ 0 and 1 are neither prime nor composite.

There are questions about prime numbers that mathematicians have not yet answered. If you could prove or disprove just one of them, you would be famous! Try Goldbach's conjecture!

Goldbach's Conjecture

In 1742 Christian Goldbach wrote to Leonhard Euler, saying that he thought all even numbers greater than 2 could be expressed as the sum of two primes.

Working together

Work in a group of 4 to explore primes and composites.

A. List all whole numbers from 4 to 100. One person should investigate the numbers from 4 to 30; another, the numbers from 31 to 55, another, those from 56 to 79; and the fourth, those from 80 to 100.

B. Write each even number as the sum of two prime numbers.

C. Record the sums in a table.

Number	Sum of 2 primes
4	
5	
6	

Sharing Your Results

Look back at the numbers you recorded. Compare your sums with those of other groups.

1. Were there any numbers for which the groups found more than one sum? If so, which numbers were they?

2. Were there any numbers for which you could find no sum? If so, which numbers were they?

3. Would you have to examine *every* even number greater than 2 to prove Goldbach's conjecture? If so, is it *possible* to do this? Explain.

4. To disprove a conjecture you must find *counterexamples*. What is a counterexample? How many, do you think, are necessary to disprove a conjecture?

Extending the Activity

The conjectures below are related to Goldbach's conjecture.

- Every odd number greater than 5 can be expressed as the sum of three prime numbers.

- Every even number greater than 6 can be expressed as the sum of four prime numbers.

Work in your group. Each person should continue to investigate the numbers assigned on page 78.

5. Extend your table as shown below.

  a. Write each odd number greater than 5 as the sum of three primes.

  b. Write each even number greater than 6 as the sum of four primes.

Number	Sum of 2 primes	Sum of 3 primes	Sum of 4 primes
4	2 + 2		
5			
6	3 + 3		
7			

6. Were there any odd numbers that could not be written as the sum of three primes? If so, which ones?

7. Were there any even numbers that could not be written as the sum of four primes? If so, which ones?

8. If you could not use 2 as an addend, could Goldbach's conjecture or either of the two conjectures above be valid? Explain.

Summing Up

9. How is each conjecture above related to Goldbach's conjecture?

10. What if Goldbach's conjecture is found to be false? Would the two related conjectures above be false? Explain why or why not.

Midchapter Review

Tell if each number is divisible by 2, 3, 4, 5, 6, 8, or 9. pages 70–71

1. 125   **2.** 351   **3.** 864   **4.** 2,347

Write using exponents. pages 72-73

5. $6 \times 6 \times 6$ **6.** 4   **7.** $9 \times 9 \times 9 \times 9 \times 9$ **8.** 1 squared

Write 9–12 as the product of factors. Then write 9–15 in standard form. pages 72–75

9. 7^0 **10.** 9^4 **11.** 13^2 **12.** 7^3

13. 3.2×10^2 **14.** 8.061×10^5 **15.** 5.13204×10^9

Write each number in scientific notation. pages 74–75

16. 6,472   **17.** 3,720,000   **18.** 68,231,000,000

Write the first four multiples of each. Then tell what numbers are factors of all the multiples. pages 76–77

19. 7   **20.** 6   **21.** 12   **22.** 22

Identify each number as prime or composite. pages 78–79

23. 10   **24.** 17   **25.** 121   **26.** 7   **27.** 372

Select the word that best completes each sentence.

28. 4^3 is read "four _____."

29. 8 is a _____ of 2.

30. 7 is a _____ of 21.

31. In the expression 3^4, the 3 is called the _____.

32. A _____ number is a whole number greater than 1 that has only two factors, 1 and itself.

33. 12 is _____ by 3.

34. 6^2 is read "six _____."

35. In the expression 4^3, the 3 is called the _____.

a. exponent
b. factor
c. squared
d. cubed
e. prime
f. multiple
g. divisible
h. composite
i. base
j. sequence
k. conjecture

Complete each sequence. Use a calculator to help. pages 70–73

36. 1, 3, 6, 10, 15, _____, _____, _____   **37.** 1, 4, 16, 64, 256, _____, _____, _____

Exploring Problem Solving

A Famous Mathematics Problem

The number patterns shown by the X's represent part of a famous mathematical problem.

Look at the three types of arrangements at the right.

Notice these features in the rectangular pattern for 8.

- There must be at least 2 rows and 2 columns.
- All rows must contain the same number of elements.
- All columns must have the same number of elements.

Notice these features in the *in* and *out* patterns.

- Each must have an odd number of rows (3 or greater).
- The first and the last rows must be the same.
- The *in* pattern starts with a row that contains one more element than the second row. The pattern continues.
- The *out* pattern starts with a row that contains one fewer element than the second row. The pattern continues.

Thinking Critically

What numbers cannot be made into either an *in* or an *out* pattern?

Analyzing and Making Decisions

1. Try making some arrangements for numbers by using X's. Which numbers form rectangles?

2. Which numbers can make *in* patterns? *out* patterns? both *in* and *out* patterns? Which of these numbers also make rectangles?

3. Which numbers can make neither *in* nor *out* patterns? What do those numbers have in common?

Look Back   If you take a number that forms an *in* pattern and double it and then subtract 1, will the new number form a rectangle? Try doubling an *out* pattern and adding 1. Will the new number form a rectangle?

Rectangular Pattern for 8
X X X X
X X X X

In Pattern for 23
X X X X X
X X X X
X X X X X
X X X X
X X X X X

Out Pattern for 17
X X X
X X X X
X X X
X X X X
X X X

Problem Solving Strategies

Patterns

Two mathematicians were walking along the street, when one said, "René, let us see if you are a good mathematician. Look at the buildings. What number pattern is formed by the windows? What pattern would be formed by the windows of a new building at the right?"

"That is too easy, Blaise. Now I shall give you the opportunity to prove *your* ability. Tell me, without counting, how many windows would the new building have?"

What will be the pattern for the windows of the new building? How many windows will it have?

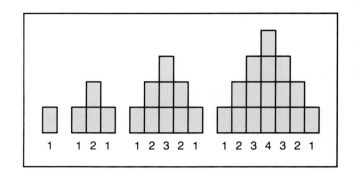

Solving the Problem

Think   What are the questions?

Explore   Examine the windows. Do you see a pattern? Explain. Can you state a rule for the pattern? How many windows are in each building?

Solve   What will be the pattern of windows for the new building? How many windows will it have?

Look Back   Find another rule for the number of windows in each building.

Share Your Ideas

1. How many different patterns and rules did your class find for the windows in the building? for the number of windows? What are the patterns and rules?

Practice

 Solve. Use a calculator where appropriate.

2. The attendance at the technology museum has been increasing each year. In the first year, 30,000 people visited the museum. In the second year, 45,000 people visited, and in the third year, 67,500 people visited. If this pattern continues, how many people will visit the museum in its fourth year?

3. In the museum cafeteria there are square tables that each seat 4 people. When 2 tables are placed end to end, 6 people can be seated. When 3 tables are placed end to end, 8 people can be seated. If 12 tables are placed end to end, how many people can be seated?

Maria, David, Chen, and Nancy all work at a museum. Maria works every day. David works every other day. Chen works every third day. Nancy works every fourth day.

4. They were all working on March 1 when they decided to go out for dinner the next time they worked together. What day did they all go to dinner?

5. Chen was sick and missed work from March 15 through March 21. Nancy agreed to substitute for him on the days that she was not scheduled to work. What days did she substitute for Chen while he was out sick?

Mixed Strategy Review

The museum made a special package of 6 posters.

6. Last Thursday the museum gave away 123 packages of posters in 8 hours. How many posters were needed for the packages?

7. Some of the posters for the package cost the museum $.53, while the others cost $.68. How much could the posters in the packages have cost the museum?

8. The price of a calendar at the museum ranges from $5.95 to $9.95. One week the museum sold 35 calendars. How much money could the museum have taken in on sales?

Create Your Own

Create a problem that makes use of numbers that form a pattern.

Write $5 \times 5 \times 5 \times 5 \times 5 \times 5$, using an exponent.

Exponents and Prime Factorization

In the 1980s, Hendrik Lenstra used a computer to test whether a number is prime or composite. A 100-digit number could be tested in seconds. Using old methods, it would have taken over 100 years to do the same thing.

How would you test a number to see if it is prime or can be factored into primes? Would you use a computer? the Sieve of Eratosthenes? some other method? If it could be factored, how would you find the prime factors?

▶ Every composite number can be written as the product of two or more prime numbers. This product is called the **prime factorization.**

The prime factorization of a number can be found by dividing by prime numbers until the quotient is prime. You can use factor trees to show the results of the divisions.

Find the prime factorization of 225.

$$225$$
$$3 \times 75$$
$$3 \times 3 \times 25$$
$$3 \times 3 \times 5 \times 5 \longleftarrow \text{Final row should be all prime numbers.}$$

How would you use divisibility rules and a calculator to help you find the prime factors of 225?

Hendrik Lenstra

Use exponents when a factor is repeated. $225 = 3^2 \times 5^2$

Check Your Understanding

Use factor trees to find the prime factorization of each number. Then write each prime factorization, using exponents.

1. 60   **2.** 81   **3.** 135   **4.** 168   **5.** 378

Share Your Ideas Look back at **1–5**. Were there different factor trees made for any of the numbers? Were there different prime factorizations written for any number? Explain why or why not. If so, give examples.

Practice

Choose paper and pencil, a calculator, or mental math to find
the prime factorization of each. Use factor trees. Write the
prime factorization, using exponents.

6. 45	**7.** 36	**8.** 125	**9.** 78	**10.** 100
11. 200	**12.** 47	**13.** 210	**14.** 176	**15.** 275
16. 256	**17.** 500	**18.** 235	**19.** 131	**20.** 1,001

Write the composite number named by each prime
factorization. Use a calculator to help.

21. $2^2 \times 7^2$

22. $3^2 \times 5 \times 11$

23. $3^3 \times 13$

24. $2^3 \times 3^4 \times 5^2$

25. 7^3

26. $5^2 \times 11^2$

27. $2^4 \times 3^2 \times 5$

28. $3^2 \times 11^2 \times 17$

Write *true* or *false*. Explain your thinking.

29. The prime factorization of 120 is $2^3 \times 3 \times 5$.

30. 141 is a prime number.

31. The prime factorization of 400 is $4^2 \times 5^2$.

32. 79 written in prime factorization is $2 \times 3 \times 13$.

33. 360 is divisible by 2, 3, 4, 5, 6, 8, 9, and 10.

34. Written in standard form, $2^4 \times 5^4$ is 10,000.

35. 9^3 equals $2^3 \times 3^2 \times 11$.

36. $2^6 \times 5^6$ equals 10^6.

Think and Apply

37. A number has two digits. Its only prime factor is 37. What is the number?

38. A number has two digits. Its only prime factors are 2, 3, and 11. What is the number?

39. A number has three digits. Its only prime factors are 3, 5, and 7. What is the least number it could be?

Visual Thinking

40. Place 5 dots in this figure so that there is no more than 1 dot in each row, column, or diagonal.

What if the only prime factors of a two-digit number are 2, 3, and 7. What could the number be? Write each possibility as a product of primes.

SUMMING UP

How many two-digit numbers are divisible by 2? by 3? by both 2 and 3? Explain your answer.

Greatest Common Factor

About 300 B.C. the Greek mathematician Euclid wrote the most famous math book ever written, *Elements*. In it he showed ways to find the greatest common factor.

▶ The **greatest common factor** (GCF) of two or more numbers is the greatest number that is a factor of each.

Here are two methods for finding the GCF. Find the GCF of 45 and 60.

a. making a list

factors of 45: 1, 3, 5, 9, 15, 45

factors of 60: 1, 2, 3, 4, 5, 6, 10, 12, 15, 20, 30, 60

The GCF is 15.

The common factors are in red.

b. using prime factorization

$45 = 3 \times 3 \times 5$

$60 = 2 \times 2 \times 3 \times 5$

$GCF = 3 \times 5 = 15$

The product of the common prime factors is the GCF. If there are no common prime factors, the GCF is 1.

The common prime factors are in red.

How are the two methods alike? How are they different? Which one do you prefer? Why?

Check Your Understanding

Find the GCF.

1. 25, 75   **2.** 12, 30   **3.** 42, 50   **4.** 24, 55   **5.** 24, 60

Share Your Ideas Which method would you prefer to use to find the GCF of 10 and 25? Why? Would you prefer a different method to find the GCF of 480 and 504? Explain why or why not.

Find the GCF.

6. 8, 28	**7.** 15, 36	**8.** 4, 26
9. 14, 35	**10.** 16, 32	**11.** 20, 40
12. 20, 50	**13.** 25, 40	**14.** 32, 48
15. 25, 36	**16.** 33, 49	**17.** 75, 100
18. 4, 8, 12	**19.** 10, 15, 30	**20.** 16, 24, 72
21. 22, 44, 55	**22.** 160, 245	**23.** 282, 375

24. Describe the method you would use to find the factors of 40. How is this method the same as the method you would use to find the prime factors of 40? How is it different?

Write _true_ or _false_. If false, explain why.

25. The only prime factors of 252 are 2, 3, and 7.

26. The GCF of 14 and 15 is 1.

27. The prime factorization of 63 is 3×21.

28. The only prime factors of a power of 10 are 2 and 5.

29. The GCF of 27 and 45 is 3.

30. If the GCF of two numbers is 1, the numbers have no common factors.

31. Every multiple of 4 is a multiple of 16.

Think and Apply

Here is another method Euclid used for finding the GCF of two numbers. Find the GCF of 45 and 60.

- Divide by the lesser number.

$$\begin{array}{r} 1 \\ 45\overline{)60} \\ \underline{45} \\ 15 \end{array}$$

- If the remainder is 0, the divisor is the GCF. If the remainder is not 0, divide the divisor by the remainder.

- Repeat until the remainder is 0. The last divisor is the GCF.

$$\begin{array}{r} 3 \\ 15\overline{)45} \\ \underline{45} \\ 0 \end{array}$$

32. Use this method to find the GCF of 36 and 56.

If the numbers for which you were finding the GCF were greater than 10,000, which method would you prefer? Why?

Mixed Review

Estimate.

1. $3.7 + 6.02 + 7.89$

2. $48.67 - 25.9$

3.
$$\begin{array}{r} 395 \\ \times\ 228 \\ \hline \end{array}$$

4. $28\overline{)\$5{,}804.83}$

5.
$$\begin{array}{r} 4{,}765 \\ 5{,}360 \\ 7{,}909 \\ +\ 11{,}264 \\ \hline \end{array}$$

Multiply or divide.

6. 31.6×100

7. $48{,}625 \div 1{,}000$

8. 0.263×10

9. $25 \times 74 \times 4$

10. $500 \times 6.8 \times 2$

Solve.

11. 65 mm = _____ cm

12. 12 km = _____ m

13. 6,000 g = _____ kg

14. 3,500 mL = _____ L

15. 250 cm = _____ m

16. 12 issues for $10.80. How much per issue?

17. 3 bars of soap for $2.19. How much per bar?

18. 4 weeks for $1,500. How much per week?

SUMMING UP

Which of these numbers are multiples of 12: 0, 6, 12, 18, 24, 30, 36, 42, 48, 54, 60? How do you know?

Least Common Multiple

Benjamin Bannaker (1731–1806) was a mathematician, astronomer, and surveyor. His *Celestial Almanac,* for which he made all the astronomical and tide calculations and weather predictions, went through 29 editions. Banneker used several methods to find the least common multiple of two numbers.

▶ The **least common multiple** (LCM) of two or more numbers is the least nonzero number that is a multiple of each.

Here are two methods for finding the LCM.
Find the LCM of 12 and 15.

a. making a list

multiples of 12: **0, 12, 24, 36, 48, 60, 72, 84, 96, 108, 120, . . .**

multiples of 15: **0, 15, 30, 45, 60, 75, 90, 105, 120, 135, . . .**

The LCM is 60.

The common multiples are in red.

b. using prime factorization

$12 = 2 \times 2 \times 3 = 2^2 \times 3$

$15 = 3 \times 5$

$LCM = 2^2 \times 3 \times 5 = 60$

The product of the highest power of each prime factor is the LCM.

The highest powers are in red.

Which method would you prefer to use to find the LCM of 8 and 12? Why? Would you prefer the same method to find the LCM of 250 and 448? Explain why or why not.

Check Your Understanding

Find the LCM.

1. 3, 4   **2.** 5, 15   **3.** 18, 24   **4.** 15, 20   **5.** 25, 50

Share Your Ideas   What if you could use a calculator to find the LCM of two numbers? Would you use one of the methods shown above? Would you use a different method? How would you use the calculator? Explain.

Practice

Find the LCM.

6. 4, 6   **7.** 4, 12   **8.** 5, 8   **9.** 12, 18

10. 8, 32   **11.** 10, 12   **12.** 16, 20   **13.** 9, 10

14. 12, 21   **15.** 25, 40   **16.** 18, 30   **17.** 24, 36

18. 2, 3, 5   **19.** 8, 12, 20   **20.** 120, 175   **21.** 36, 45, 72

 Choose mental math, paper and pencil, or a calculator to find the GCF and the LCM. Explain your choices.

22. 10, 20   **23.** 12, 16   **24.** 35, 40   **25.** 50, 100

26. 8, 9   **27.** 36, 48   **28.** 60, 180   **29.** 32, 125

Solve. There are two numbers.

30. One number is 10. The unknown number is less than 10. The GCF of the numbers is 2. Their LCM is 30. What is the unknown number?

31. One number is 8. The unknown number is less than 8. The GCF of the numbers is 1. Their LCM is 24. What is the unknown number?

32. One number is 9. The unknown number is greater than 9. The GCF of the numbers is 9. Their LCM is 36. What is the unknown number?

Think and Apply

Here is another method for finding the LCM. Find the LCM of 30 and 45.

- Find the GCF of the numbers.

$$\left. \begin{array}{l} 30 = 2 \times 3 \times 5 \\ 45 = 3^2 \times 5 \end{array} \right\} \text{GCF} = 3 \times 5 = 15$$

- Find the product of the numbers.

$$30 \times 45 = 1{,}350$$

- Divide the product by the GCF. The quotient is the LCM.

$$1{,}350 \div 15 = 90$$

33. Use this method to find the LCM of 48 and 60.

Logical Thinking

34. When the members of the Bannaker High School marching band are arranged in rows of 2, 3, or 4, there is always one person left over. But when they are arranged in rows of 5, there is no one left over. What is the least number of people in the band?

Explain the difference between the GCF and the LCM of two numbers.

SUMMING UP

89

Using Problem Solving

Venn Diagrams

A Venn diagram is often used in solving problems. This Venn diagram shows the multiples of 5 from 1 through 30 and the multiples of 3 from 1 through 30.

A. What numbers are in the circle on the left? What numbers are in the circle on the right? What numbers are in the intersection of the circles? How would you describe the numbers in the intersection?

B. Make a Venn diagram that shows the odd numbers from 1–10 and the prime numbers from 1–10.

Sharing Your Ideas

1. How did you construct your Venn diagram for **B**? What numbers are in each group? What numbers are common to both groups? Describe the numbers that are common to both groups.

2. Can you think of two groups of numbers that would not have numbers common to each group? If so, name the two groups.

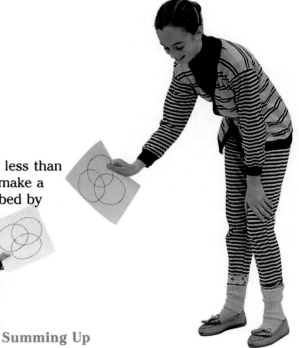

Extending Your Thinking

3. Make a Venn diagram that shows the factors of 12 and the factors of 24.

4. Below is a Venn diagram for three groups. Put the odd numbers from 1 to 15 in circle A. Put the prime numbers from 1 to 15 in circle B. Put the whole numbers from 1 to 15 in circle C. What should go in space D? space E? space F? space G?

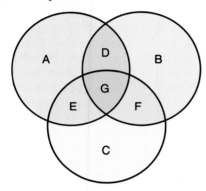

5. Describe two or three groups of numbers, all less than 24. Exchange your work with a partner, and make a Venn diagram to represent the groups described by your partner.

Summing Up

6. Was there anything special about your Venn diagram for the factors of 12 and the factors of 24? If so, what was it?

7. Look at **4.** How many areas of intersection were there when you had three groups of numbers to represent? What numbers should go in each intersection? Is it possible to not have any members in one intersection? Try to think of an example.

Chapter Review

Tell if each number is divisible by 2, 3, 4, 5, 6, 8, or 9. pages 70–71

1. 90   **2.** 143   **3.** 236   **4.** 555

Write using exponents. pages 72–73

5. 12×12 **6.** $2 \times 2 \times 2 \times 2 \times 2$ **7.** 4 cubed   **8.** $6 \times 6 \times 6 \times 6$

Write each expression in standard form. pages 72–75

9. 8^1 **10.** 3^4 **11.** 1^7 **12.** 5^3

13. 9.25×10^4 **14.** 7.61×10^1 **15.** 3.287×10^7

Write each number in scientific notation. pages 74–75

16. 3,123,600   **17.** 48 billion   **18.** 815

Write the first four multiples of each. Then tell what numbers are factors of all the multiples. pages 76–77

19. 11   **20.** 9   **21.** 15   **22.** 24

List. pages 78–79

23. the first seven prime numbers   **24.** the first seven composite numbers

Write the prime factorization of each. Use exponents. pages 84–85

25. 27   **26.** 36   **27.** 84   **28.** 500

Find the GCF and the LCM. pages 86–89

29. 2, 7   **30.** 8, 12   **31.** 10, 35   **32.** 16, 36, 48

Define. pages 84–89

33. prime factorization   **34.** greatest common factor   **35.** least common multiple

Complete each pattern. pages 81–83, 90–91

36. 4, 5, 9, 10, _____, 15, _____, _____

37. 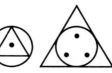 _____

Chapter Test

Tell if each number is divisible by 2, 3, 4, 6, or 9.

1. 72

2. 126

3. 321

Write using exponents.

4. $11 \times 11 \times 11 \times 11$

5. 25

6. $2 \times 2 \times 2 \times 2$

Write each expression in standard form.

7. 6^0

8. 3^4

9. 2^3

10. 7.92×10^3

11. 3.1432×10^2

12. 6.7×10^8

Express the following in scientific notation.

13. 213,000

14. 645.7

15. 12 million

Write the prime factorization of each. Use exponents.

16. 98

17. 42

18. 100

Find the GCF.

19. 12, 32

20. 18, 96

21. 11, 13

Find the LCM.

22. 3, 11

23. 15, 20

24. 6, 8

Solve.

25. Complete the pattern.   _____

THINK Rare coins are on display at the local library. The coins are mounted in 9 rows, the top row having 4 coins. The next five rows have 5, 2, 5, 4, and 5 coins. Follow the pattern. How many coins are in the last row? How many coins are on display?

Computer Link

Exploring Factors

How many factors can a
number have? Is the
number of factors
determined by the size
of the number?

AT THE
COMPUTER

Materials: Logo

A. Define the procedure FACTORS that lists all the factors
of a number input. Enter FACTORS 20. What
numbers print?

```
TO FACTORS :N                          Input a number.
MAKE "F 0
REPEAT :N [MAKE "F :F + 1          ←Type as one line.
        IF REMAINDER :N :F = 0 [PR :F]]   If the remainder is 0, the number prints.
END
```

B. What is the greatest number of factors you can find for a
number less than 100? Record your work.

C. Find a number less than 1,000 that has at least
15 factors.

Sharing Your Results

1. Does the size of a number determine the
number of its factors? Use examples
to explain.

2. Describe the method you used to find a
number that has at least 15 factors.

Extending the Activity

3. **Look back** at the numbers you recorded on page 94. Describe those that have an odd number of factors.

4. Define the procedure SUMODD that finds the sum of N odd numbers starting with 1. Enter SUMODD 2 to find 1 + 3. Then use the procedure to find the sum of the first three odd numbers; the first four odd numbers; the first five odd numbers. What pattern do you notice?

```
TO SUMODD :N
MAKE "SUM 0
MAKE "ODD 1
REPEAT :N [MAKE "SUM :SUM + :ODD
           MAKE "ODD :ODD + 2]
PRINT :SUM
END
```

Type as one line. →

N is the quantity of odd numbers to add.
Starts SUM at 0.
Starts ODD at 1.
Adds ODD to SUM each time.
Changes ODD to the next odd number.
Prints the sum of N odd numbers.

5. Predict the sum of the first eleven odd numbers. Use SUMODD to check.

6. What is an easy way to find the sum of the first 50 odd numbers without using the computer?

Summing Up

7. Explain how to find the sum of odd numbers from 1 to any number.

Magic Square

Few people would know that Ben Franklin was a mathematician in addition to being a statesman, an author, an inventor, and a scientist. The magic square below was his invention. He believed it to be "perfect in its kind."

The sum of the numbers along each column and along each row is 260. Unfortunately, the sum of the numbers along each diagonal is not 260. This makes it less than a perfect magic square. However, it has many surprising patterns. For example, the sum of the numbers along half of any row is half of 260, or 130.

Find as many patterns as you can in this magic square. Use a calculator.

52	61	4	13	20	29	36	45
14	3	62	51	46	35	30	19
53	60	5	12	21	28	37	44
11	6	59	54	43	38	27	22
55	58	7	10	23	26	39	42
9	8	57	56	41	40	25	24
50	63	2	15	18	31	34	47
16	1	64	49	48	33	32	17

Family Math

In the first three chapters of our mathematics book, we have added, subtracted, multiplied, and divided whole numbers and decimals. We have also studied number patterns and number theory.

Doubling Adds Up!

Did you ever wonder how much money you could save in 30 days if you began with one penny and doubled the amount you put in the bank each day?

Try this experiment.

- Choose a large empty jar or can from the kitchen.

- Pick an object around the house of which there are plenty. For example, use marbles, beans, or raisins. We will use beans.

- On the first day, put one bean into the jar. On the second day, put 2 beans in the jar. On the third day, 4 beans go into the jar. Continue doubling the amount each day.

Day 1	Day 2	Day 3	Day 4	Day 5
1 Bean	Double 1 Bean. $2 \times 1 = 2$	Double 2 Beans. $2 \times 2 = 4$	Double 4 Beans. $2 \times 4 = 8$	Double 8 Beans. $2 \times 8 = 16$

Do you think you can fill the jar in 30 days? Or will the jar be full before Day 30? Before you begin this experiment, have your family members guess what day they think the jar will be full.

Now work together to figure out how much money you would have if you did this experiment with pennies.

Start saving now!

Cumulative Review

Choose the correct answers. Write A, B, C, or D.

1. What is the standard form?
   5 billion, 71 million, 80 thousand

   A 5,071,080,000   C 571,080,000

   B 5,710,080,000   D not given

2. What is the standard form?
   $6 + 0.03 + 0.0007$

   A 6.0307   C 6.37

   B 6.037   D not given

3. What is the standard form?
   12 and 63 ten-thousandths

   A 12.063   C 12.0063

   B 12.6300   D not given

4. Order from least to greatest.
   3.061, 3.601, 3.61

   A 3.61, 3.061, 3.601

   B 3.061, 3.61, 3.601

   C 3.061, 3.601, 3.61

   D not given

5. What property is illustrated?
   $12 + 15 + 18 = 12 + 18 + 15$

   A Associative   C Identity

   B Commutative   D not given

6. $26.05 + 18.421 + 1.42$

   A 35.891   C 45.468

   B 21.168   D not given

7. Estimate. $8.035 - 0.902$

   A 0.7   C 20

   B 70   D 7

8. $\$52.85 - \$42.79$

   A $10.06   C $10.16

   B $10.14   D not given

9. What property is illustrated?
   $8 \times (400 + 70) = (8 \times 400) + (8 \times 70)$

   A Associative   C Identity

   B Commutative   D Distributive

10. $2,063 \times 10^2$

    A 20,630   C 206,300

    B 206.3   D not given

11. 2,796
    $\times\ \ 41$

    A 114,636   C 91,436

    B 13.980   D not given

12. 12.14×8.8

    A 96.832   C 19.424

    B 106.832   D not given

13. Estimate. $543 \div 63$

    A 0.1   C 4

    B 9   D not given

14. $135.9 \div 45$

    A 3.2   C 3.02

    B 0.32   D not given

15. $0.9 \div 2.5$

    A 0.36   C 0.032

    B 2.7   D not given

16. What is the unit price?
    7 jars for $.91

    A $.70   C $.07

    B $.13   D not given

Choose the correct answers. Write A, B, C, or D.

17. Which number is divisible by 6?

   A 330   **C** 358

   B 826   **D** not given

18. What is the standard form for 4^0?

   A 0   **C** 4

   B 1   **D** not given

19. 9.8601×10^5

   A 98,601   **C** 986,010

   B 9,860,100   **D** not given

20. What is 180,000 in scientific notation?

   A 10.8×10^4 **C** 1.08×10^5

   B 1.08×10^4 **D** not given

21. What is the prime factorization of 80?

   A $2^5 \times 5$ **C** $2^3 \times 10$

   B $2^4 \times 5$ **D** not given

22. What is the GCF of 16 and 24?

   A 2   **C** 6

   B 4   **D** not given

23. What is the LCM of 10 and 8?

   A 2   **C** 40

   B 80   **D** not given

24. What is the LCM of 6 and 5?

   A 30   **C** 60

   B 1   **D** not given

Use this information for 25 and 26.

Phil is displaying stamps in a special 10-page book. On page one he puts 25 stamps, on page two, 23 stamps, and on page three, 21 stamps.

25. If the pattern continues, how many stamps will be on page five?

   A 33   **C** 12

   B 17   **D** not given

26. How many stamps will be in the entire book?

   A 100   **C** 160

   B 125   **D** not given

Solve each problem. If there is not enough information, choose the fact that is needed.

27. Scott is researching ancient Greece. If he maintains his goal of reading 50 pages a day, how many days will it take him to read the book?

   A 5   **C** 7

   B number of pages   **D** number of days
     in book   in month

28. In 1990 Glenda and Ralph went on an archeological dig. They found a coin that dates back to 350 B.C. It weighs 24 grams. How old is the coin?

   A 1,640 years   **C** 2,340 years

   B weight of coin   **D** age of Ralph

4 Pre-Algebra: Expressions and Equations

Sharing What You Know

Look around you. What things and conditions create your school environment? The environment is all the surrounding influences, conditions, people, and things that affect your life. Discuss how mathematics might have played a role in creating your environment.

Using Language

Like the air we breathe, water is a necessary part of our environment. Did you know that water is the result of combining 2 parts hydrogen and 1 part oxygen? This can be expressed by the following **equation:** 2 parts hydrogen + 1 part oxygen = water. An **equation** is a statement that two quantities are equal. What are some other examples of equations?

Words to Know: equation, variable, expression, formula, inverse operation, solution

Be a Problem Solver

Sharing chores helps to create a pleasant home environment. In Joel's house he washes the dinner dishes twice as many days each week as Maria does, and Tony does the dishes one day a week. **What if** Joel offers to wash the dinner dishes three times as many days each week as Maria does? How would this new arrangement affect Tony's days for washing the dishes? Explain.

Describe one change that would make your community a better environment in which to live.

What do these symbols represent? What are some other symbols that are used in everyday life? H_2O

Writing Expressions

In the cold, windy environment of Antarctica penguins live near the ocean in groups of tens of thousands. In the spring newborn penguin chicks gather in small groups of about 200 for protection against predators and the harsh environment.

The expression $200 \cdot y$, or $200y$, represents the approximate number of penguin chicks in y groups. The variable y represents the number of groups of chicks.

▶ A **variable** is a symbol that represents a number in an expression or equation.

▶ An **expression** is a mathematical phrase made up of variables, numbers, and operations.

More Examples

Phrase	Expression
the sum of eight and six	$8 + 6$
five decreased by a number n	$5 - n$
three less than a number y	$y - 3$
the product of two and a number p	$2 \cdot p$ or $2p$ ←—— means $2 \times p$
a number t divided by 2	$t \div 2$ or $\frac{t}{2}$

$8 + 6$ is a numerical expression. $5 - n$ is an algebraic expression. How are the two alike? How are they different?

Check Your Understanding

Write an expression for each. Use n as the variable.

1. five more than a number
2. twelve less than a number
3. six divided by twice a number
4. ten more than a number

Write each expression in words.

5. $n \div 9$
6. $n + 5$
7. $3n - 7$

Share Your Ideas Explain why symbols are used in mathematics.

102

Write an expression for each. Use x as the variable.

8. ten more than ten times a number

9. ten times a number

10. forty less than a number

11. five more than twice a number

12. a number divided by thirty

13. a number divided by fifteen

14. the sum of twice a number and two

15. the product of a number and twelve

Write each expression in words.

16. $2x - 3$

17. $\dfrac{3a}{4}$

18. $b + 8$

19. $t - 4$

20. $\dfrac{(m + n)}{2}$

21. $8(p - 2)$

Choose the correct answer.

22. twice a number divided by four

   a. $2 \div 4$

   b. $(2 + y) \div 4$

   c. $y \div 4$

   d. $\dfrac{2y}{4}$

23. two less than five times a number

   a. $5y - 2$

   b. $5 + y - 2$

   c. $2 - 5y$

   d. $2 - (5 + y)$

Use each group of symbols to create an expression. Explain the expression in words.

24. $6, 7, \div, f$

25. $a, +, 10, 2.5$

26. Mt. Kilimanjaro is 2,476 feet higher than the highest point in Antarctica. Write an expression to represent the height of Mt. Kilimanjaro.

27. Antarctica has an area of 5,100,000 square miles. The area of Africa is 2.3 times that amount. Write an expression to represent the area of Africa.

28. An adult penguin eats 3 pounds of fish each day. Write an expression for the amount of fish an adult penguin will eat in 30 days; for the amount in n days.

29. Write an expression to represent all two-digit numbers. Let x be the digit in the tens place and y be the digit in the ones place. Explain your answer.

Joan earns $4 per hour. She works 35 hours per week. Write an expression to represent the amount of money she earns in 1 week; in 5 weeks; in n weeks.

SUMMING UP

> Are these two expressions the same? Explain.
> $3 \cdot 6 - 4$ and $3 \cdot (6 - 4)$

Order of Operations

The newspaper editor changed the meaning of the headline by using punctuation. In mathematics, using parentheses changes the order of operations.

Find the value of $6^2 - 4 \times (3 + 2)$.

▶ To find the value of an expression, follow this order:

1. Work inside the parentheses first. $6^2 - 4 \times (3 + 2) =$

2. Work with exponents. $6^2 - 4 \times (5) =$

3. Multiply and divide from left to right. $36 - 4 \times 5 =$

4. Add and subtract from left to right. $36 - 20 =$

           16

The value of the expression $6^2 - 4 \times (3 + 2)$ is 16.

When a division bar is used, follow the order of operations above and below the division bar before dividing.

More Examples

a. $6^2 - 4 \times 3 + 2 =$ ⟵ Explain how this expression is different from the one above.

$36 - 4 \times 3 + 2 =$

$36 - 12 + 2 =$

$24 + 2 =$

26

b. $\dfrac{18 \div (2 + 1)}{9 - 6} =$

$\dfrac{18 \div 3}{3} =$

$\dfrac{6}{3} =$

2

Find the value of each expression.

1. $60 \div 2 - 8$
2. $7 \times 8 - 5 \times 6$
3. $15 + 3 \times 5$
4. $\dfrac{3 + 9}{6} - 1$
5. $6 - \dfrac{8 - 3}{5}$
6. $7^2 - \dfrac{4 \times 6}{10 + 2}$

Share Your Ideas You can change the value of the expression $2 + 6 \times 3 - 1$ by using parentheses. Show the possible ways to do this. Find the value of each expression you have shown.

Find the value of each expression.

7. $7 + 49 \div 7$

8. $14 - 2 \times 5$

9. $5 + 9 \times 8$

10. $30 \div 5 - 3$

11. $30 \div (5 - 3)$

12. $6 \times 7 - 7 \times 3$

13. $\frac{20 + 5}{5} - 2$

14. $\frac{5 \times 6 + 3}{10 - 7}$

15. $3^2 + 2^3$

16. $(60 - 15) \div 3^2$

17. $63 \div 7 + 3 \times 5$

18. $(7 + 4 \times 3)^2$

Insert parentheses to make each sentence true.

19. $9 + 6 \div 3 + 2^3 = 13$

20. $20 - 7 - 5 \times 5 = 10$

21. $9 + 6 \div 3 + 2 = 3$

22. $3 + 9 \div 3 + 2 \times 5 = 14$

Use a calculator to find the value of each expression.

23. $7.5 \div (0.12 + 1.08)$

24. $16.25 - (2.5 + 3.85) \times 2.01$

25. $(1.7)^3 + (2.7)^3$

26. $(3.8)^2 - (3.2 + 0.8) \div 0.4$

Think and Apply

27. The government of Lincolntown has n committees. Three committees are studying the effects of acid rain. Twice that number of committees are studying water cleanup. Write an expression to show the number of committees left to study air pollution. Then describe the possible numbers that n could be.

28. The Lincolntown budget is $1,000,000. The town council approved $76,700 for fighting acid rain and three times that amount to purify the rivers in town. Write an expression to show how much money was left in the budget. Then find the value of the expression.

Logical Thinking

29. Use four 4's to write each number from 1 to 10. You may use any operation, decimal points, exponents, and parentheses.

Example $\quad 1 = \frac{4 + 4}{4 + 4}$ or $\frac{44}{44}$

Write an expression, using 18, 6, 3, $\div$, and x, that has a value of 1.

SUMMING UP

Write an expression for the number of days in *w* weeks.

Evaluating Expressions

The average depth of the Pacific Ocean is 653 feet deeper than 3 times the average depth of the Arctic Ocean.

Let *n* represent the average depth of the Arctic Ocean. Then $3n + 653$ represents the average depth of the Pacific Ocean.

What if the average depth of the Arctic Ocean is 4,362 feet? What would be the average depth of the Pacific Ocean?

Evaluate $3n + 653$ for $n = 4,362$.

▶ To evaluate an expression, substitute a number for the variable.

$3n + 653 = 3 \times 4,362 + 653$ Substitute 4,362 for *n*.
$ = 13,086 + 653$ Follow order of operations.
$ = 13,739$

The average depth of the Pacific Ocean would be 13,739 feet.

More Examples

Evaluate each expression for $x = 5$.

a. $6x + 7$
$6 \times 5 + 7 =$
$30 + 7 =$
37

b. $x^2 - 19$
$5^2 - 19 =$
$25 - 19 =$
6

Check Your Understanding

Evaluate. Let $a = 6$ and $b = 7$.

1. $6a$
2. $a + b$
3. $\dfrac{ab}{7}$
4. $2b - 3$
5. $ab + 8$

Share Your Ideas   In some sports games, the coach may substitute players. How is this similar to substituting values in an expression?

Evaluate each expression. Let $x = 3$ and $y = 9$.

6. $4y - 5x$

7. $y^2 + 1$

8. xy

9. xy^2

10. $2y + 2$

11. $x + y$

12. $y - x$

13. $\frac{y}{x}$

14. x^2y

15. $x^2 - y$

16. $y^2 - x$

17. x^2y^2

Write an expression. Evaluate for $t = 8$.

18. twice the sum of a number t and 3

19. nine less than twice a number t

20. twice a number t plus 4

21. twice a number t squared

Find each output.

Input	Output
n	$3(n - 4)$
22. 5	
23. 10	
24. 22	

Input	Output
e	$e^2 - 1$
25. 3	
26. 7	
27. 10	

Think and Apply

Write an expression for each. Then evaluate.

28. The greatest ocean current is 3 times that of the Gulf Stream. The Gulf Stream current is 3,167,000,000 cubic feet per second. How fast is the greatest ocean current?

29. The height of the highest wave ever recorded was 112 feet. The average depth of the Baltic Sea is just 68 feet more than the height of that wave. What is the average depth of the Baltic Sea?

Can the number 345 be represented as xyz when $x = 3$, $y = 4$, and $z = 5$? Explain why or why not.

1. 68×7.5

2. $4,230 \div 10^2$

3. $3,171 \div 3.5$

4. $8 + 9.25 + 3.5$

5. $11 - 3.89$

6. 0.683×10^3

7. $6 + 5.5 - 2.1$

8. $9.8 - 6.37$

Name the property.

9. $3 + x = x + 3$

10. $9 + (a + b) = (9 + a) + b$

11. $4(y + 2) = 4y + 8$

12. $x \cdot 1 = x$

Write the prime factorization for each.

13. 75

14. 140

15. 210

Write each in scientific notation.

16. 3,000,000

17. 71,000

18. 52,000,000

SUMMING UP

Describe the difference between a phrase and a sentence. Give examples of each.

Writing Equations

Scientists are concerned that our deserts are enlarging. The Thar Desert of India has grown 56,000 square miles in 80 years. An equation can be used to show the average number of square miles gained each year.

Pakistan

THAR DESERT

INDIA

► An **equation** is a number sentence with an equal sign.

Let x be the number of square miles the desert has enlarged in one year.

Then $80 \cdot x$, or $80x$, is the number of square miles the desert has enlarged in 80 years.

$80x = 56{,}000$ Explain in words what this equation means.

A **solution** of an equation is any value of the variable that makes the equation true.

Use 700 as a value for x.
$80 \cdot 700 = 56{,}000$ Substitute 700 in the original equation.
700 is the solution for $80 \cdot x = 56{,}000$.

The Thar Desert has grown an average of 700 square miles each year.

More Examples

Sentence	Equation
a. Twice a number increased by ten is twenty.	$2n + 10 = 20$
b. Half a dozen decreased by one is equal to five.	$\frac{1}{2}(12) - 1 = 5$

SAHARA DESERT

AFRICA

Check Your Understanding

Write an equation for each sentence.

1. A number y divided by ten is fifty.

2. Three dozen equals 36.

Write each equation in words.

3. $5 + x = 15$

4. $6x - 3 = 27$

Share Your Ideas How are expressions and equations different? How are they the same?

Write an equation for each.

5. Three times a number t is 83.

6. Nine is five less than a number p.

7. The trip was 583 mi by plane and n mi by car. The total mileage was 900 miles.

8. Roger is r years old. In 11 years he will be 25 years old.

9. Tom deposited y dollars into his account. The old balance was $124. The new balance is $150.

10. Each stamp costs $.30. Sue bought x stamps for $5.40.

Write each equation in words.

11. $x + 19 = 70$

12. $0.7a = 25$

13. $y - \$2 = \$18$

Substitute the given value for the variable in each equation. Then tell if it is a solution.

14. $n + 25 = 40$ Let $n = 15$.

15. $7t = 56$ Let $t = 5$.

16. $10b + 4 = 64$ Let $b = 6$.

17. $\frac{2n}{3} = 4$ Let $n = 6$.

18. $\frac{12}{m} = 4$ Let $m = 6$.

19. $\frac{3b}{4} + 1 = 7$ Let $b = 8$.

20. $3n - \frac{n}{2} = 20$ Let $n = 8$.

21. $\frac{1}{2}p - \frac{1}{4}p = 3$ Let $p = 10$.

Think and Apply

Write an equation for each.

22. The Sahara Desert has an area of 3,320,000 square miles. This is 0.33 of the area of Africa. Let x represent the number of square miles of Africa.

23. The normal daytime temperature of the Sahara is 83°F. Once the temperature reached 136°F. Let t represent the number of degrees the temperature rose.

Mathematics and History

(1) A quad $- C$ plano 2 in $A + A$ cub a equatur D solido.

(2) $A^2 - 2CA + A^3 = D$

Equation (1) could have been written by the French Mathematician François Viète (1540–1603). Equation (2) is the same equation, using today's symbols.

24. Which symbols are still used today? What was used as an equal sign?

25. Which equation seems easier? Why?

Is this an equation—two more than three times a number? Explain why or why not.

SUMMING UP

Midchapter Review

Write an expression for each. pages 102–103

1. a number f divided by ten

2. the sum of three fives

3. two years less than x years

4. twice Tom's height less nine

5. the product of six and seven

6. seven tenths of a number y

Find the value of each expression. pages 104–105

7. $6 \times 4 + 19$

8. $16 - 3 \times 5$

9. $3^3 - 4 \times 5$

10. $\dfrac{(3)\,(4) + 2}{7}$

11. $\dfrac{10 - 7}{2^3 + 1}$

12. $\dfrac{0.7 - 0.13}{3 \div 10}$

13. twice sixteen increased by twenty

14. five less than the product of two and nine

Evaluate. Let $x = 5$ and $y = 2$. pages 106–107

15. $3x - y$

16. $7xy$

17. $6x \div 2$

18. $\dfrac{x^2 + y}{3}$

19. $\dfrac{11x}{5}$

20. $6(x + y)$

Write an equation for each. pages 108–109

21. Two more than a number n equals eight.

22. A number n divided by 12 is equal to 228.

23. 9 less than 4 times a number n is 31.

24. The product of 6 and a number n is 54.

25. Twice a number n divided by 3 equals 8.

26. 10 more than half a number n is 11.

27. A whole pizza costs t dollars. Half the pizza costs $4.50.

28. There are b bricks. One brick measures 6 inches in length. The total length of the bricks is 138 inches.

Write a sentence to describe each word below.

29. variable

30. expression

31. equation

Solve.

32. An adult penguin eats 3 pounds of fish each day. Write an expression for the amount of fish 50 penguins will eat in n days. Evaluate the expression for $n = 7$.

33. The Bennett family is traveling to Vermont for a ski trip. Regular airfare costs $345 per person. If nonrefundable tickets are purchased, the airfare is $289 per person. How much will it cost to purchase 4 nonrefundable tickets?

Exploring Problem Solving

How Many Pairs?

An Italian mathematician, Fibonacci, used the following problem to create a model for population growth.

Suppose at the end of a rabbit season you received a pair of newborn rabbits. During a season newborn rabbits become young rabbits and young rabbits mature. Rabbits that are mature at the start of a season produce a pair of offspring.

Season	Mature Pairs	Young Pairs	Newborn Pairs	Total Pairs
1	—	—	1	1
2	—	1	—	1
3	1	—	1	2
4	1	1	1	3
5	2	1	2	5

Thinking Critically

How many pairs of rabbits will there be in 10 seasons? Is there a pattern to the population growth?

Analyzing and Making Decisions

1. The chart shows the rabbit population for 5 seasons. How long does it take a rabbit to mature? How often do mature rabbits have offspring?

2. Study the chart. How is the number of pairs of mature rabbits determined? How is the number of pairs of young rabbits determined? How is the number of pairs of newborn rabbits determined? How is the total population determined?

3. Complete the chart through 10 seasons. How many total pairs are there for each season?

4. Look at the total pairs of rabbits for each season. What pattern do you see? Write a rule for finding the total pairs for any season. Test your rule for season 11. Check the rule by completing the chart.

Look Back   What if a rabbit pair had to wait one season after having a pair of newborns before having a new pair of newborns? What would the total rabbit population be for the first 10 seasons?

Problem Solving Strategies

Multi-Stage Problems

Carol and Janis have opened a shop for recycling glass, newspaper, and aluminum. They buy glass and paper for $.02 a pound and sell it for $.10 a pound. They buy aluminum for $.50 a pound and sell it for $.75 a pound. Their total expenses per month for rent and utilities are $500.

During their first month they collected 2,800 pounds of glass, 2,220 pounds of newspaper, and 1,200 pounds of aluminum. Have they collected enough to make a profit from their business? If so, how much profit did they earn? If they did not, how much money did they lose?

Sometimes a problem has more than one part. It contains a question that must be answered before solving the problem. You then use the answer to the hidden question to solve the original problem.

Solving the Problem

 Use a calculator where appropriate.

Think What is the question? What are the facts?

Explore How much do they make per pound for glass, newspaper, and aluminum? How much money did they make by selling the glass? by selling the newspaper? by selling the aluminum?

Solve How much money did they gain or lose?

Look Back Use estimation to see if your answers make sense.

Share Your Ideas

1. **What if** they bought glass and paper for $.05 per pound? How much money would they gain or lose?

Practice

 Solve. Use a calculator where appropriate.

2. Jerod wants to buy a spotting scope for bird watching. He can buy it for $425 if he pays for it in one payment. He can also purchase it by making a down payment of $135 and then paying 12 monthly installments of $30 each. How much money does Jerod save by paying for the scope at the time of purchase?

3. The average rainfall in a state park for the month of April is 8.7 inches. This April 3.6 inches of rain fell in the first 10 days. During the next 10 days 2.5 inches of rain fell. How much more rain must fall the rest of the month so that the average rainfall is reached?

4. Joanne has 64 duplicates in her postcard collection. She was not able to trade them, so she gave 15 cards to her sister. She shared the remaining cards equally with 7 friends. How many cards did each friend receive?

5. A zoo attendant walks an injured red fox three times a day. Each walk is about 100 yards. The attendant will place the fox back in the viewing area after it has walked 5 miles. About how many days will elapse before the fox returns to the viewing area?

Mixed Strategy Review

6. Tara worked the same number of hours on Monday as she did on Tuesday. She earns $7.29 an hour. How much money did Tara earn in the two days?

Use this information to solve 7 and 8.

The firefighters at Fire Station 3 work in two groups. One group works for three 24-hour days. They are replaced by the other group, which works for three 24-hour days. This pattern continues.

7. **What if** you were in a group that started a new shift on Monday? How many Sundays would you work in 4 weeks?

8. How long would it take until you again started a new shift on Monday?

Create Your Own

Write a problem for which you must use two different operations to find the solution.

Name pairs of words that are opposites. Then name pairs of activities that are opposites.

Inverse Operations

Part of our responsibility to the environment is recycling. Recycling is the process of turning useless items into useful items. Center City has a recycling program.

The mayor of Center City was asked how many tons of newspapers had been collected today. He replied, "Double yesterday's collection and subtract 3."

Six tons of newspapers were collected yesterday. Follow the diagram to find how many tons were collected today.

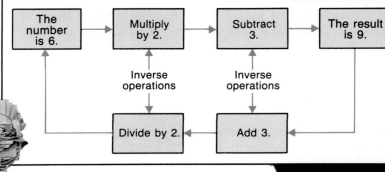

| The number is 6. | → | Multiply by 2. | → | Subtract 3. | → | The result is 9. |

Inverse operations ↕   Inverse operations ↕

| Divide by 2. | ← | Add 3. |

Suppose you know the number of tons collected today. Use inverse operations to find the number of tons collected yesterday.

▶ **Inverse operations** are operations that "undo" each other. Addition and subtraction are inverse operations. Multiplication and division are inverse operations.

Check Your Understanding

Name the inverse of each.

1. walk backwards
2. drive north
3. add 7
4. divide by 13

Share Your Ideas Think of a number. Add 4. Multiply by 6. Subtract 24. Then divide by 6. What is the result? Will the result always be the number you started with? Why? Will this work with any number?

Name the inverse of each.

5. put on shoes   **6.** close the door   **7.** light a fire   **8.** move clockwise

9. add 15   **10.** multiply by 20   **11.** subtract 9   **12.** decrease by 6

13. double a number   **14.** divide by 5   **15.** increase by 11   **16.** add 0

17. $x + 2$ **18.** $\frac{y}{3}$ **19.** $t - 32$ **20.** $16x$

For each, make a diagram like the one on page 114. Then find the missing number.

21. Start with a number t. Double the number. Subtract 1. The result is 7.

22. Start with a number y. Triple the number. Divide by 5. The result is 12.

Find the missing number.

Rule: Add 13.

	Input	Output
23.		50
24.		137
25.		1,000

Rule: Divide by 7.

	Input	Output
26.		8
27.		19
28.		100

Rule: Add 6, then divide by 5.

	Input	Output
29.		35
30.		80
31.		50

Think and Apply

32. Last week Center City collected x tons of glass to recycle. This week three times that amount was collected for a total of 12.24 tons. How many tons were collected last week? Explain how you found the answer.

33. Name an expression that has no inverse. Explain.

ENTERING

CENTER CITY

39-31-37-41 51-31-43-37 41-37-3-39-17!

Logical Thinking

39 31 37 41   51 31 43 37   41 37 3 39 17!

34. This message is in code. The code was made by taking the place that the letter holds in the alphabet, multiplying by 2, and adding 1. For example, A would be represented by $1 \times 2 + 1$ or 3. Use inverse operations to crack the code.

Give some examples of inverse operations that are used in everyday situations.

SUMMING UP

115

Activity

Exploring Equations

To solve an equation, find a value for the variable that makes the equation true.

How can you solve this equation?

3x = 24

Experiment to find out.

Working together

Materials: cups, counters

A. Model $3x = 24$ using cups and counters.

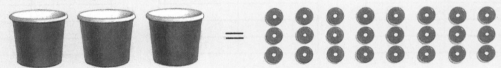

B. Experiment to find how many counters to put in each cup. The same number of counters must be on each side of the equation.

C. Devise a way to check your solution.

D. Model these equations and record their solutions.

$4x = 20$	$n + 5 = 11$	$7 = p + 1$
$n - 6 = 10$	$18 = 3n$	$8 = 2 + t$

Sharing Your Results

1. For each equation you modeled, what is true about the number of counters on each side of the equation? Explain.

2. For each equation that used more than 1 cup, what must be true about the number of counters in each cup? Explain.

3. Explain your method of solving equations.

4. What methods did you use to check your solutions?

Extending the Activity

5. Mathematicians talk about **balancing** an equation. Explain what this means.

6. a. Model the equation $n + 3 = 10$.

b. Take 3 counters from each side. Is the equation "balanced"? Why or why not?

c. Explain how the equations below show what you modeled.

$$n + 3 = 10$$
$$n + 3 - 3 = 10 - 3$$
$$n = 7$$

d. $n + 3 = 10$ is an addition equation. What operation was used to solve it? Why?

What operation would you use to solve each?

7. $3x = 18$

8. $14 + x = 20$

9. $n + 6 = 11$

10. $\frac{x}{4} = 3$

11. $5n = 20$

12. $n - 8 = 19$

13. Choose two of the equations above to model. Then solve each, using a method like the one in **c** above.

Summing Up

14. Explain how to solve a division equation, such as $n \div 3 = 8$.

15. Explain how to solve a subtraction equation, such as $n - 4 = 9$.

16. Explain how inverse operations help to solve equations.

Solving Addition and Subtraction Equations

Jungle vegetation is unique. A tropical orchid may measure 16 inches across. Yet this is 20 inches less than the measure of the world's largest flower. What is the measure of this flower? Write an equation and solve.

Heliconia Rostrata

Epidendrum SP. Orchid

Let m be the measure of the world's largest flower. Then $m - 20 = 16$.

▶ To solve a subtraction equation, add the same number to both sides of the equation.

$$m - 20 = 16 \qquad \longleftarrow \text{Use the inverse of subtracting 20.}$$
$$m - 20 + 20 = 16 + 20 \qquad \longleftarrow \text{Add 20 to both sides.}$$
$$m = 36 \qquad \longleftarrow \text{Solution}$$
$$\textbf{Check } 36 - 20 = 16 \qquad \longleftarrow \text{Replace } m \text{ with 36.}$$

The measure of the world's largest flower is 36 inches.

▶ To solve an addition equation, subtract the same number from both sides of the equation.

$$t + 19 = 44 \qquad \longleftarrow \text{Use the inverse of adding 19.}$$
$$t + 19 - 19 = 44 - 19 \qquad \longleftarrow \text{Subtract 19 from both sides.}$$
$$t = 25 \qquad \longleftarrow \text{Solution}$$
$$\textbf{Check } 25 + 19 = 44 \qquad \longleftarrow \text{Replace } t \text{ with 25.}$$

Hibiscus

St. Lucia

Check Your Understanding

Tell what should be done to both sides of the equation. Then solve and check.

1. $k + 5 = 32$ 2. $s - 18 = 90$ 3. $13 + t = 81$ 4. $r - 90 = 90$

Share Your Ideas   How are solving an addition equation and solving a subtraction equation different? How are they alike?

Write what should be done to both sides of the equation. Then solve and check.

5. $n - 10 = 3$ **6.** $x + 7 = 8$ **7.** $m - 15 = 100$

8. $47 = f - 22$ **9.** $132 = g + 14$ **10.** $40 = r - 19$

11. $23 = t - 29$ **12.** $x - 2.5 = 11$ **13.** $7.3 + y = 12.1$

14. $j + 3 + 1 = 9$ **15.** $6 + x - 2.5 = 10$ **16.** $x - 3.1 + 1 = 13.3$

Explain what was done to the first equation to get the second equation.

17. $a^2 + 3 = 28 \longrightarrow a^2 = 25$

18. $3x - 7 = 17 \longrightarrow 3x = 24$

19. $7.2 + y = 70 \longrightarrow y = 62.8$

Write an equation for each. Then solve and check.

20. A number t increased by 16 equals 90. Find t.

21. Five less than a number x is equal to 58. Find x.

Think and Apply

Write an equation. Then solve.

22. The wettest spot in the world is located in Hawaii. It receives x inches of rain each year. Last year a city in Brazil received 72 fewer inches of rain. The city in Brazil received 388 inches of rain. How many inches of rain fell in the wettest spot in the world?

23. The average number of people that live in a square mile, called the population density, for the state of Texas is 14 less than the population density for the United States. If the population density for the United States is 67 people per square mile, what is the population density for the state of Texas?

Kandy Temple

Explain how an equation is balanced by using inverse operations.

Mixed Review

1. $34 + 7.8 + 0.495$

2. $586 - 9.93$

3. $\$27.32 + \$8.87$

4. $\$50 - \$16.29$

5. $\$27.05 \div 5$

Write each number in standard form.

6. 3^5

7. $4 \times 10^5 + 2 \times 10^2$

8. 73.8×100

9. $9.44 \div 10$

10. three million thirty-three

Compare. Use >, <, or = for each ●.

11. 7.3 ● 3.7

12. 4.8 ● 0.48

13. 9.2 ● 92

14. 1.06 ● 1.1

15. 0.107 ● 0.17

Write the next 3 numbers for each pattern.

16. 0, 13, 26, . . .

17. 7, 21, 63, . . .

18. 1, 4, 9, . . .

19. 1, 10, 100, . . .

20. 7, 15, 23, . . .

Use multiplication and division to create an expression with a value of 1. Use the numbers 3, 4, and 12.

Solving Multiplication and Division Equations

Mountain environments change as the altitude increases. Chinchillas are found at altitudes up to 20,000 feet. This is twice the altitude at which bamboo grows. Up to what altitude will bamboo grow? Write an equation and solve.

Let x be the altitude at which bamboo grows.
Then $2x$ is the altitude at which chinchillas are found.

$2x = 20,000$

▶ To solve a multiplication equation, divide both sides of the equation by the same nonzero number.

$2x = 20,000$ ⟵ Use the inverse of multiplying by 2.

$\dfrac{2x}{2} = \dfrac{20,000}{2}$ ⟵ Divide both sides by 2.

$x = 10,000$ ⟵ Solution

Check $2(10,000) = 20,000$ ⟵ Replace x with 10,000.

Bamboo grows at altitudes up to 10,000 feet.

▶ To solve a division equation, multiply both sides of the equation by the same nonzero number.

$\dfrac{m}{3} = 8$ ⟵ Use the inverse of dividing by 3.

$\dfrac{m}{3} \times 3 = 8 \times 3$ ⟵ Multiply both sides by 3. Why does $\dfrac{m}{3} \times 3 = m$?

$m = 24$ ⟵ Solution

Check $\dfrac{24}{3} = 8$ ⟵ Replace m with 24.

Check Your Understanding

Tell what to do to both sides of each equation. Then solve and check.

1. $3y = 12$ **2.** $\dfrac{a}{4} = 11$ **3.** $72 = 9n$ **4.** $14 = d \div 4$

Share Your Ideas Name the number you would multiply or divide by to solve each equation. Explain why you chose that number.

$5n = 45$ $\dfrac{n}{8} = 4$

Write what to do to both sides of each equation. Then solve and check.

5. $7x = 49$

6. $8.5y = 85$

7. $t \div 3 = 11$

8. $14 = \frac{k}{6}$

9. $\frac{n}{19} = 2$

10. $15s = 75$

11. $30 = \frac{m}{6}$

12. $f \times 12 = 60$

13. $12 = \frac{d}{7}$

14. $b \div 9 = 9$

15. $\frac{c}{(8-3)} = 10$

16. $420 \div x = 7$

Solve. Use mental math, paper and pencil, or a calculator for each.

17. $10x = 370$

18. $100n = 420$

19. $9 = \frac{t}{10}$

20. $43 = \frac{s}{1,000}$

21. $6m = 2,100$

22. $\frac{m}{19} = 51$

23. $3.6r = 32.4$

24. $\frac{u}{0.24} = 11$

Write an equation. Then solve and check.

25. Twenty times a number t is 820. Find t.

26. A number b divided by 7 is 101. Find b.

Think and Apply

Write an equation and solve.

27. The mountains of Australia are 400 million years old. They are 8 times as old as the mountains of New Zealand. How old are the mountains of New Zealand?

28. Mt. Everest is 2.2 times as high as Mt. Lister in Antarctica. Mt. Everest is 29,040 feet high. How high is Mt. Lister?

Test Taker

Don't always rush into pencil and paper computation! Some equations can be solved mentally or by inspection. Solve these equations without using paper and pencil.

29. $(13)(n)(47) = 0$

30. $5.1 + 0.7t = 5.1$

31. $(10 + 4) - (8 + x) = 0$

32. $17n = 1,700$

33. $s = \frac{81 \times 93}{93 \times 81}$

34. $7 + 7 = 2x$

Explain the steps you would use to solve this equation. $\frac{1}{3}m = 4$

SUMMING UP

Formulas

Many people move to a part of the country that has a specific weather pattern. The Clark family, who enjoy skiing, chose Vermont. Burlington, Vermont, has a normal October temperature of 9°C. What is the Fahrenheit reading?

A **formula** can be used to express the relationship between Celsius and Fahrenheit temperature.

$F = 32 + 1.8C$ F is Fahrenheit degrees.
                        C is Celsius degrees.

$\quad = 32 + 1.8(9)$ Substitute 9 for C.
$\quad = 32 + 16.2$ Why multiply before adding?
$\quad = 48.2$ Solution

48.2°F is the same as 9°C.

To evaluate a formula, substitute a number for the variable.

More Examples

a. Find A if $l = 7$ and $w = 8$.

$A = l \cdot w$
$\quad = 7 \cdot 8$
$\quad = 56$

b. Find A if $s = 9$.

$A = s^2$
$\quad = 9^2$
$\quad = 81$

Check Your Understanding

Evaluate each formula.

1. $a = 7b$
Find a if $b = 19$.

2. $m = 2n - 3$
Find m if $n = 9$.

3. $s = t^2 + 1$
Find s if $t = 7$.

Write each formula in words.

4. $V = l \cdot w \cdot h$ where V is the volume, l is length, w is width, and h is height.

5. $A = s^2$ where A is area of a square, and s is length of a side.

Share Your Ideas The formula $x = 35y$ is solved for x. Rewrite the formula to solve for y. Explain your method.

Practice

Evaluate each formula for the given values. Use paper and pencil, mental math, or a calculator.

	f	$9 - f$	$= b$
6.	3	$9 - 3$	
7.	5		
8.	7		

	t	$t \div 3$	$= v$
9.	15		
10.	21		
11.	30		

	x	$2x + 7$	$= y$
12.	0		
13.	3		
14.	8		

Evaluate the formula if given.

$y = x - 13$

	x	y
15.	20	
16.	61	
17.	192	

$d = r \cdot t$

	r	t	d
18.	18	0.3	
19.	25	1.8	
20.	50	9.5	

21. Find the formula.

a	b
2	4
12	24
6	12

Think and Apply

Find each output. Use the BASIC **programs given below.**

22. $y = 4(x - 5)$

Input	Output
15	
48	
62	

```
10 INPUT "ENTER X"; X
20 Y = 4 * (X - 5)
30 PRINT "OUTPUT = "; Y
```

23. $y = x^3$

Input	Output
5	
16	
24	

```
10 INPUT "ENTER X"; X
20 Y = X^3
30 PRINT "OUTPUT = "; Y
```

DATA

24. Ten inches of snow is equivalent to 1 inch of rain. Collect data about last year's monthly rainfalls and snowfalls. Use the data you collect to determine how much rain would have fallen if it had been too warm to snow; how much snow would have fallen if it had been too cold to rain.

25. The higher the temperature, the faster crickets chirp. This can be written as $F = (n \div 4) + 40$ where F represents the temperature in degrees Fahrenheit and n represents the number of chirps per minute. What is the temperature if the crickets chirp 88 times per minute?

Visual Thinking

26. Which weather vane is different?

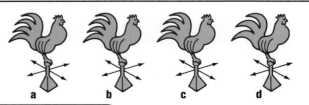

a   b   c   d

In your own words, explain what a formula is. Tell why a formula is useful.

SUMMING UP

Activity

Exploring Two-Step Equations

How can you solve these
equations? Experiment to find out.

$2x + 1 = 7$ $3x - 11 = 4$

$1 = 9 - 2x$ $10 = 4x + 2$

Working together

Materials: cups, counters

A. Model each equation using cups and counters.

 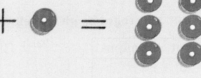 

B. Experiment to find the number of counters that must be
put into each cup. Must the same number of counters be
on each side of the equation? Explain why.

C. Record your work in a table that shows the equation and
the solution you found.

D. Model these equations and record them, along with their
solutions, in a table.

$2x + 5 = 5$ $7 - 2x = 1$

$1 + 3x = 13$ $6 = 4x + 2$

Sharing Your Results

1. Explain how you solved each equation.

2. Explain how all the equations you modeled are alike.

3. Were all your solutions whole numbers? Why? Create an
equation similar to those above, with a solution that is
not a whole number.

Extending the Activity

4. Look at your table. Choose one of the equations.

   a. Start with the variable x. Describe, step by step, in mathematical terms what is being done to x.

   b. Then work backwards. Use inverse operations to "undo" each step.

   c. Is the new answer the same as the solution listed in the table?

Example: $2x + 1 = 7$

Start with x. $\longrightarrow$ Multiply by 2. $\longrightarrow$ Add 1. $\longrightarrow$ Result is 7.

Start with result. $\longrightarrow$ Subtract 1. $\longrightarrow$ Divide by 2. $\longrightarrow$ Answer is 3.

$(7 - 1) \div 2 = 3$

5. Repeat the procedure above for each equation. Is each answer the solution of the equation? Why or why not?

Solve each equation.

6. $3x + 9 = 24$

7. $2n - 18 = 0$

8. $15 + 4t = 31$

9. $28 = 5y - 2$

10. $100 = 9x + 28$

11. $56 = 7x - 14$

12. $5n - 4 = 41$

13. $11b + 9 = 42$

Summing Up

14. How do inverse operations help to solve an equation?

15. How do you decide which inverse operation to use first in solving an equation?

16. Amaze your friends! Guess their ages. Have a friend follow these instructions.

   Add 2 to your age.
   Multiply by 3.
   Subtract 6.
   Ask for the result.

Your friend's age will be the result divided by 3. Do you think this will always work? Justify your answer. Give examples.

Using Problem Solving

Concrete Functions

One way to look at number patterns is with cubes. Look at this pattern.

When one cube is input, the resulting output is 3 cubes. Study the next two sets of cubes and try to find a rule that fits the pattern.

Input ▢ ▢▢ ▢▢▢

Output (grids)

Working together

Work with a partner and use cubes to discover a rule for building the patterns.

Materials: cubes, tiles, grid paper

A. Look at the pattern above. Use cubes and continue the pattern for 2 more terms. Complete the table to show the input of 2, 3, 4, and 5 cubes. What is the rule for the pattern? It must work for all inputs. We call this number rule or relation a **function**.

Input	1	2	3	4	5	
Output	3					

B. Decide upon a rule for a new pattern. Create the first 3 terms with cubes. Show the input and the output. Have a partner guess the next 3 outputs and the rule for the pattern. Verify the rule by using the cubes.

Sharing Your Ideas

1. How were you able to tell what the next outputs in the patterns were?

2. How were you able to determine the rule?

3. Can you determine a rule by using only one pair of inputs and outputs? Explain.

Extending Your Thinking

4. Look at this pattern.

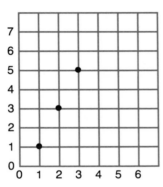

Input

Output

Find the output for inputs of 4, 5, and 6. Show your results in a chart. What is the rule for this function?

5. Make a graph for this pattern. Each pair of inputs and outputs locates a point. The inputs are on the *x*-axis (horizontal) and the outputs are on the *y*-axis (vertical). Connect the points.

6. Find a point on the line that is not on your Input–Output chart. Do the input and output for that point satisfy your rule?

7. Write a function rule. Exchange your rule with a partner. Your partner should make an Input–Output chart and graph the function on a grid.

Summing Up

8. How did the rule in **4** differ from the rule in **A** on page 126?

9. **Look back** at **7**. What did your graphs look like? Do the input and output for each point on your graph satisfy your rule? Explain.

Chapter Review

Write an expression for each. Use _x_ as the variable. pages 102–103

1. 3 less than 5 times a number

2. the sum of twice a number and 7

Find the value of each expression. pages 104–105

3. $7^2 - 5 \times 8$

4. $3 \times (5^2 + 2)$

5. $24 \div (6 \div 2)$

Evaluate each expression. Let _a_ = 2 and _b_ = 5. pages 106–107

6. $3ab - 5$

7. $a^2 + b^2$

8. $3b - 2a$

Write an equation for each. pages 108–109

9. Five times a number plus 3 is 28. Find the number.

10. Ten years ago Jack was 19. How old is he now?

Name the inverse of each. pages 114–115

11. open the book

12. subtract 41

13. divide 5

14. add 17

Solve and check. pages 118–119

15. $x + 13 = 20$

16. $y - 20 = 53$

17. $n + 123 = 456$

18. $t - 81 = 99$

Solve and check. pages 120–121

19. $3t = 27$

20. $9y = 81,000$

21. $t \div 5 = 29$

22. $\frac{a}{4} = 109$

Evaluate each formula. Let _s_ = 4. pages 122–123

23. $t = 3s - 1$

24. $t = s^2 + 7$

25. $t = 8^2 - 5s$

26. $t = 3(s - 2)$

Match.

27. variable

28. expression

29. equation

30. formula

31. inverse operations

a. a mathematical phrase

b. addition and subtraction

c. an equation that states a rule

d. a symbol representing a number

e. a number sentence with an equal sign

Solve.

32. There are _n_ nickels and 3 dimes. They are worth 85¢. How many nickels are there?

33. The geyser in Yellowstone National Park erupts to a height of 380 feet. The tallest geyser, in New Zealand, erupted 360 feet higher than 3 times the height of the one in Yellowstone. How high did the tallest one erupt? Write an equation and solve it.

Chapter Test

Write an expression. Then evaluate for $n = 8$.

1. twice the product of a number n and 9

2. the number n divided by 2 and increased by 11

3. Bob's shoe size is 2 less than Tom's shoe size. If Tom's shoe size is n, find Bob's shoe size.

4. Tara is 3 years less than twice Tom's age. If Tom's age is n, find Tara's age.

Find the value of each expression.

5. $9^2 - 5 \times 9$

6. $6 \times (7 + 8)$

7. $(5 + 9) - 3^2$

8. $16 \div (8 \div 2) + 1$

Solve and check.

9. $x + 12 = 20$

10. $23 + n = 100$

11. $x - 2 = 12$

12. $3y = 111$

13. $n \div 4 = 32$

14. $501 = 3g$

15. $45a = 135$

16. $c - 4 = 0$

Write an equation. Then solve.

17. Five more than a number is 37. Find the number.

18. Three times a number is 69. Find the number.

19. Tami's weight is 6 pounds less than the normal weight for her height and age. If Tami weighs 98 pounds, what is the normal weight?

20. The perimeter of a triangle is 51 inches. Each side is the same length. How long is one side?

Evaluate each formula for the given values.

	a	$3a + 4 = b$	
21.	3		
22.	5		

	x	$5x - 8 = y$	
23.	5		
24.	10		

Solve.

25. Each week the number of people that put out newspapers for recycling is one more than twice the number from the week before. If 10 people put out papers the first week, how many put out papers the tenth week?

THINK Last week the recycling truck collected 50 tons of glass and aluminum. There were x tons of glass. The number of tons of aluminum was 8 tons less than that of glass. How many tons of each were collected?

New Operations

Some new operations are defined below.

$$a * b = a^2 \cdot b$$

If $a = 3$ and $b = 2$, then $a * b = 3^2 \cdot 2 = 18$.

1. Use mental math to find $a * b$ if $a = 7$ and $b = 10$.

2. Use a calculator to find $a * b$ if $a = 17$ and $b = 29$.

3. Is $*$ commutative? That is, does $a * b = b * a$? Explain.

$$a \blacklozenge b = b^2 - 2ab$$

If $a = 3$ and $b = 7$, then $a \blacklozenge b = 7^2 - 2 \cdot 3 \cdot 7 = 7$.

4. Use mental math to find $a \blacklozenge b$ if $a = 1$ and $b = 5$.

5. Use a calculator to find $a \blacklozenge b$ if $a = 8$ and $b = 19$.

6. Find values for a and b so that $a \blacklozenge b = 0$.

$$a \divideontimes b = \frac{a^2 + b^2}{b - a}$$

If $a = 2$ and $b = 6$, then $a \divideontimes b = \frac{2^2 + 6^2}{6 - 2} = 10$.

7. Use mental math to find $a \divideontimes b$ if $a = 2$ and $b = 4$.

8. Use a calculator to find $a \divideontimes b$ if $a = 7$ and $b = 11$.

$$a \$ b = \text{?}$$

9. Create your own definition for $a \$ b$.

10. Give two examples for your definition.

Maintaining Skills

Choose the correct answers. Write A, B, C, or D.

1. $56.23 + 12.006 + 78.4$

   A 146.636   **C** 136.636

   B 18.413   **D** not given

2. Estimate. $\begin{array}{r} 12.006 \\ -\ 4.98 \\ \hline \end{array}$

   A 0.07   **C** 17

   B 20   **D** 7

3. What property is illustrated?
$14 \times 10 \times 6 = 14 \times 6 \times 10$

   A Associative   **C** Identity

   B Commutative   **D** not given

4. 7.45×12

   A 89.3   **C** 89.4

   B 12.25   **D** not given

5. $2.87 \div 0.82$

   A 0.035   **C** 0.285

   B 3.5   **D** not given

6. What is the unit price?
7 cans for $1.05

   A $.15   **C** $.18

   B $.65   **D** not given

7. Which number is divisible by 3?

   A 457   **C** 892

   B 2,136   **D** not given

8. What is another name for 4^3?

   A 12   **C** 64

   B 16   **D** not given

9. 2.87×10^3

   A 2,870   **C** 287

   B 28,700   **D** not given

10. What is the GCF of 35 and 21?

   A 2   **C** 5

   B 1   **D** not given

11. What is an expression for 6 less than 4 times a number x?

   A $6 - 4x$ **C** $4x - 6$

   B $4x + 6$ **D** not given

12. $3 + 36 \div 4$

   A 10   **C** 9

   B 12   **D** not given

13. Solve. $14 + n = 27$

   A 13   **C** 11

   B 41   **D** not given

Solve.

14. Steve phoned his grandmother. It costs $.90 for the first minute and $.50 for each extra minute. How much did the call cost if they talked 3 minutes?

   A $1.40   **C** $2.40

   B $1.90   **D** not given

15. Nicki cuts lawns. He charges $15.00 for small lawns and $25.00 for large lawns. He mowed two small lawns. How much did he make?

   A $40.00   **C** $30.00

   B $10.00   **D** not given

5 Geometry

THEME Plans and Designs: A-Mazing Places

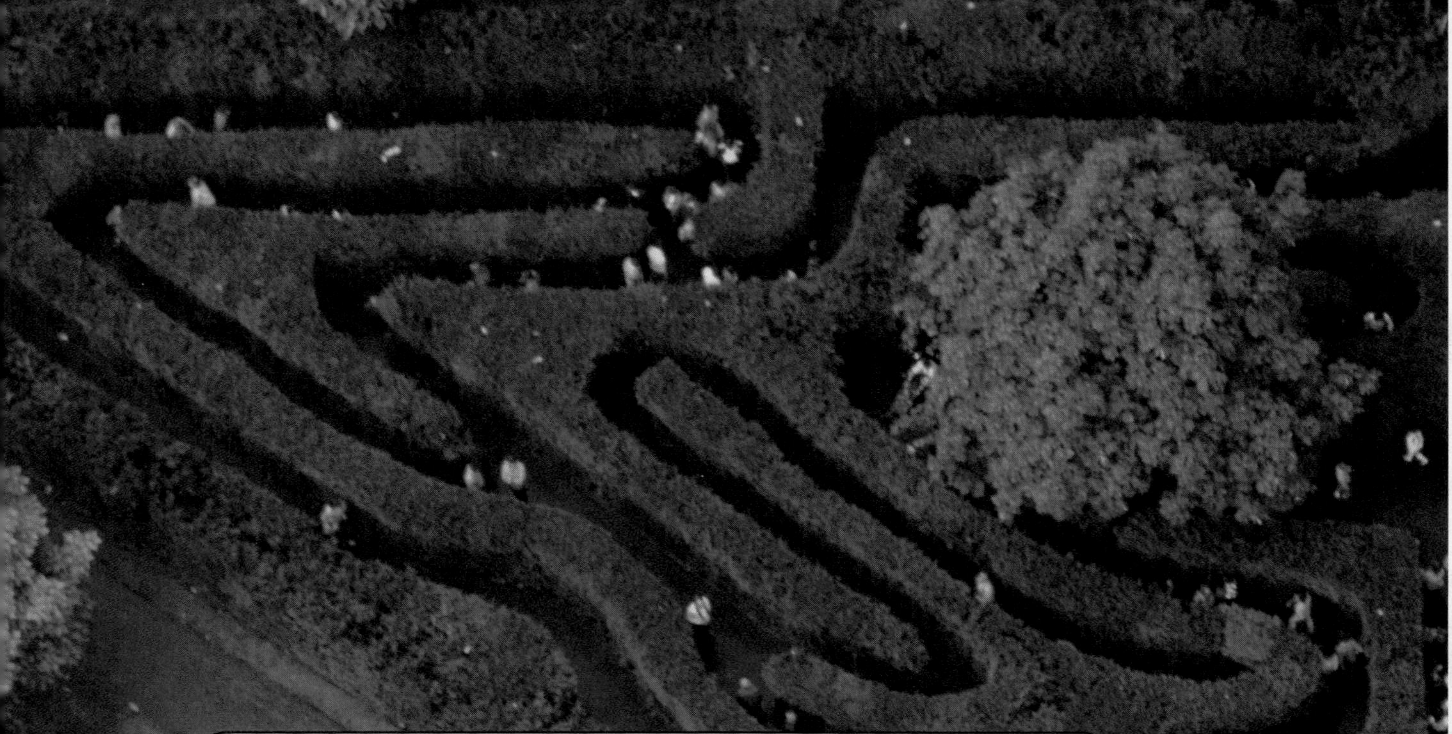

Sharing What You Know

It's fun! It's zany! It's a maze! You've done pencil-and-paper mazes before. You may even have made them with building blocks. But do you think you'd enjoy trying to find your way out of the giant maze shown here? Describe the geometric figures you see.

Using Language

Take a handful of toothpicks and design a maze on your desk. Every corner you make forms an **angle.** A **right angle** looks like this: ∟. It measures 90°. Did you use right angles in your maze? Design a maze that uses other types of angles.

Words to Know: angle, right angle, acute angle, obtuse angle, perpendicular lines, parallel lines, corresponding angles, rhombus, trapezoid

Be a Problem Solver

How many triangles can you find in this drawing?

Examine some of the structures in your town. List those structures that use triangles in their construction.

A map has lines of longitude and lines of latitude. In which direction does each kind run?

Lines

Map maker Gerhardus Mercator (1512–1594) invented a way to show the globe on a flat map. Such a map is called a Mercator projection.

On both a globe and a Mercator projection, the lines of longitude are perpendicular to the lines of latitude.

▶ Two lines that meet at a point **intersect.** Two lines that intersect to form right angles are **perpendicular lines.**

means right angle

$\overleftrightarrow{AD}$ intersects $\overleftrightarrow{BE}$ at C.
$\overleftrightarrow{AD} \perp \overleftrightarrow{BE}$

How many right angles are formed by two perpendicular lines?

On a globe the lines of longitude intersect. On a Mercator projection the lines of longitude are parallel.

▶ Two lines in the same plane that do not intersect are **parallel lines.**

Two lines *not* in the same plane that do not intersect are **skew lines.**

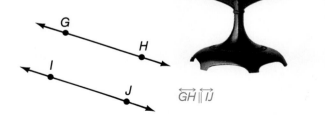

$\overleftrightarrow{GH} \| \overleftrightarrow{IJ}$

Check Your Understanding

Use the figure at the right. $\overleftrightarrow{LM} \| \overleftrightarrow{PQ}$. Write *true* or *false*. Explain your thinking.

1. $\overleftrightarrow{LM} \perp \overleftrightarrow{MQ}$

2. $\overleftrightarrow{PQ} \perp \overleftrightarrow{QL}$

3. $\overleftrightarrow{LM} \| \overleftrightarrow{LQ}$

4. $\overleftrightarrow{PQ} \perp \overleftrightarrow{QM}$

5. $\overleftrightarrow{LM}$ intersects $\overleftrightarrow{PQ}$.

6. $\angle MLQ$ is a right angle.

7. $\overleftrightarrow{LM}$ intersects $\overleftrightarrow{MQ}$ at L.

8. The measures of $\angle QML$ and $\angle MQP$ are equal.

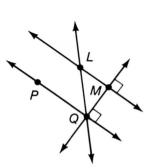

Share Your Ideas Create a model of two skew lines. How do you know they are skew?

In the figure at the right, $\overleftrightarrow{AB} \parallel \overleftrightarrow{FE}$.
Select the correct answer.

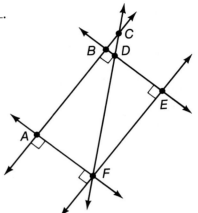

9. $\overleftrightarrow{BE} \perp$ _____

   a. $\overleftrightarrow{DF}$ **b.** $\overleftrightarrow{EF}$ **c.** $\overleftrightarrow{AF}$

10. $\overleftrightarrow{AB}$ intersects $\overleftrightarrow{DF}$ at _____.

   a. A **b.** B **c.** C

11. $\angle BAF$ measures _____.

   a. $90°$ **b.** $50°$ **c.** $30°$

12. $\overleftrightarrow{AB} \perp$ _____

   a. $\overleftrightarrow{EF}$ **b.** $\overleftrightarrow{AF}$ **c.** $\overleftrightarrow{DF}$

13. The measures of $\angle ABD$ and _____ are equal.

   a. $\angle FDE$

   b. $\angle DFE$

   c. $\angle DEF$

14. $\angle BEF$ is a(n) _____.

   a. right angle

   b. acute angle

   c. obtuse angle

Use the figure above. Write *true* or *false*.
Explain your thinking.

15. $\overleftrightarrow{AB} \perp \overleftrightarrow{DE}$

16. $\overleftrightarrow{AF} \parallel \overleftrightarrow{BC}$

17. $\overleftrightarrow{AC} \perp \overleftrightarrow{DF}$

18. $\overleftrightarrow{AB} \parallel \overleftrightarrow{FD}$

19. $\overleftrightarrow{AC}$ intersects $\overleftrightarrow{FC}$ at F.

20. $\overleftrightarrow{AB}$ is parallel to $\overleftrightarrow{FE}$ and $\overleftrightarrow{BE}$.

21. $\overleftrightarrow{AB}$ is perpendicular to $\overleftrightarrow{AF}$ and $\overleftrightarrow{BE}$.

22. $\overleftrightarrow{AF}$, $\overleftrightarrow{FE}$, and $\overleftrightarrow{CF}$ intersect at F.

23. $\overline{BD}$ and $\overrightarrow{BD}$ are the same.

24. $\overrightarrow{BD}$ and $\overrightarrow{BE}$ are the same.

25. The vertex of $\angle CDE$ is D.

26. $\angle CDE$ is an obtuse angle.

27. The endpoints of $\overleftrightarrow{BE}$ are B and E.

28. $\overline{FD}$ lies on $\overleftrightarrow{DC}$.

29. $\overleftrightarrow{AF} \parallel \overleftrightarrow{BE}$

30. The sum of the measures of $\angle BDC$ and $\angle BCD$ is $90°$.

31. **a.** Draw one point. How many lines can you draw through it?
   b. Draw two points. How many lines can you draw that pass through both?

32. Two and *only* two points are needed to *determine* a line. What is the least number of points needed to determine two perpendicular lines?

33. How many points do you need to determine two parallel lines?

34. How many points do you need to determine a plane?

Tell whether this statement is always, sometimes, or never true. Explain.
  • Intersecting lines are perpendicular.

SUMMING UP

Is the measure of ∠ABC greater than or less than 90°? How do you know?

Measuring and Estimating Angles

A draftsperson uses a protractor to measure angles on blueprints. A protractor can be used to measure and to draw angles. How would you use a protractor to draw an angle?

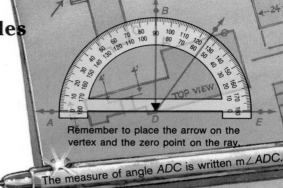

Remember to place the arrow on the vertex and the zero point on the ray.

The measure of angle ADC is written m∠ADC.

▶ Two rays with a common endpoint, called the **vertex,** form an **angle.** Angles are classified according to their measures.

▶ Two angles are **supplementary** if the sum of their measures is 180°.

∠ADC and ∠CDE are supplementary.

▶ Two angles are **complementary** if the sum of their measures is 90°.

∠BDC and ∠CDE are complementary.

ANGLES	
Type	**Definition**
Acute	< 90°
Right	90°
Obtuse	> 90° but < 180°
Straight	180°
Reflex	> 180° but < 360°

Estimate the measure of an angle by comparing it visually.

a.
– about ½ of a right angle
– about 45°

b.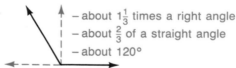
– about 1⅓ times a right angle
– about ⅔ of a straight angle
– about 120°

How would you verify each estimate?

Check Your Understanding

Classify each angle. Estimate its measure. Explain your thinking.

1.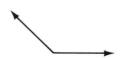

2.

3.

4. Measure each angle above.

5. Draw two angles that are complementary.

Share Your Ideas A protractor is only marked from 0° to 180°. How could you use it to measure a reflex angle?

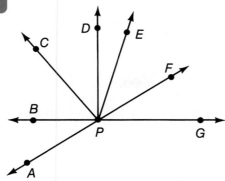

First classify each angle. Then estimate its measure. Explain your thinking.

6. ∠APB   **7.** ∠FPG   **8.** ∠BPF   **9.** ∠DPG

10. ∠APE   **11.** ∠APF   **12.** ∠EPG   **13.** ∠APG

Use the figure above.

14. Identify a pair of supplementary angles. What are their measures?

15. Identify a pair of complementary angles. What are their measures?

Draw each angle. Then classify it.

16. ∠FEG, 63°   **17.** ∠DPA, 146°

18. ∠ABC, 25° less than a right angle

19. ∠KMJ, 45° greater than a right angle

20. ∠PQR, 100° less than a straight angle

21. ∠TSV, 100° less than a right angle

22. ∠XYZ, 55° greater than a straight angle

Think and Apply

23. What if from where you are standing you have to estimate the angle between two landmarks? Describe a way to do this.

Tell whether this statement is always, sometimes, or never true. Explain.
• The supplement of an acute angle is obtuse.

1.   3,682
          5,719
      +   836

2. 17.06 − 5.783

3. 25 × 84.75 × 4

4. 3.762 ÷ 18

5.   4.783
          0.961
      + 7.045

6. 25,025 ÷ 25

7. 6,749 − 5,650

8.   3,998
      ×   5

Find the value of each.

9. $36 - 8 \times 4 + 6$

10. $72 \div 8 + 3 \times 7$

11. $3(6 - 2) + 42 \div 7$

12. $2 \times 8 \div 4 + 3^2 - 13$

Write an expression for each.

13. six more than 3 times 8

14. four times the sum of 6 and 9

15. a number n decreased by 10

16. eight less than the product of 5 and a number n

Are these two angles congruent?
Explain why or why not.

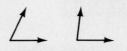

Angles and Intersecting Lines

Broadway is one of the most famous streets in the world. It cuts across other streets in New York City to form congruent angles.

is congruent to

a. $\angle 3 \cong \angle 5$

b. $\angle 1 \cong \angle 4$

c. $\angle 3$ and $\angle 4$ are supplementary angles.

Which of the facts below help you verify each of the statements above about the angles formed by Broadway and the streets it crosses?

▶ **Adjacent angles** have a common vertex and a common ray. Their interiors do not overlap. Two intersecting lines form pairs of adjacent angles that are supplementary.

▶ Two intersecting lines form pairs of **vertical angles** that are congruent.

▶ A *transversal* is a line that intersects two or more lines at different points. Two parallel lines cut by a transversal form pairs of **corresponding angles** that are congruent.

Use the facts above. Compare the measures of $\angle 2$ and $\angle 3$ on the map of Broadway. Explain your thinking.

Check Your Understanding

Classify each pair of angles as adjacent, vertical, corresponding, congruent, or supplementary.

1.   **2.**   **3.**   **4.**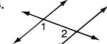

Share Your Ideas   Look back at **1–4.** Tell which angle pairs were classified in more than one category. Explain why.

Use Figure 1. $\overleftrightarrow{AB} \parallel \overleftrightarrow{CD}$

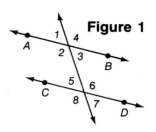

Figure 1

5. List all pairs of adjacent angles.

6. List all pairs of vertical angles.

7. List all pairs of corresponding angles.

If m∠3 = 58°, find the measure of each angle.

8. ∠2   **9.** ∠1   **10.** ∠7   **11.** ∠6   **12.** ∠5

Figure 2

Use Figure 2. $\overleftrightarrow{MN} \parallel \overleftrightarrow{PQ}$, $\overleftrightarrow{RS} \perp \overleftrightarrow{PQ}$, **and m∠1 = 70°.**
Write *true* or *false*. Explain your thinking.

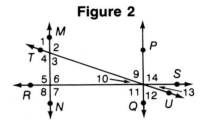

13. m∠2 = 110°   **14.** m∠3 = 90°   **15.** m∠9 = 70°

16. m∠11 = 90°   **17.** $\overleftrightarrow{RS} \perp \overleftrightarrow{MN}$ **18.** $\overleftrightarrow{TU} \parallel \overleftrightarrow{RS}$

19. ∠3 ≅ ∠9   **20.** m∠10 = 30°   **21.** m∠10 > m∠13

22. ∠1 and ∠9 are corresponding angles.   **23.** ∠9 and ∠11 are adjacent angles.

24. ∠5 and ∠6 are supplementary and congruent.   **25.** ∠9 and ∠10 are complementary angles.

26. ∠2 and ∠9 are supplementary angles.   **27.** m∠9 + m∠14 + m∠13 = 180°

Copy the figure used for 13–27. Draw $\overleftrightarrow{TP}$. $\overleftrightarrow{TP} \parallel \overleftrightarrow{RS}$

28. Describe the relationship between $\overleftrightarrow{TP}$ and $\overleftrightarrow{MN}$.

29. Describe the relationship between $\overleftrightarrow{TP}$ and $\overleftrightarrow{TU}$.

30. What is the measure of ∠PTU? Explain your thinking.

31. ∠1 ≅ ∠2. Describe the relationship between $\overleftrightarrow{WX}$, $\overleftrightarrow{YZ}$, and $\overleftrightarrow{WZ}$. Justify your answer.

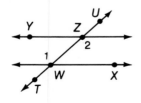

Visual Thinking

32. Visualize! Don't draw! Imagine three parallel lines 1 cm apart. Imagine three lines, 1 cm apart, perpendicular to the first three. How many squares have been formed?

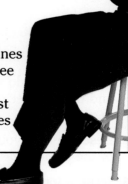

Draw two parallel lines cut by a transversal. Label a pair of vertical angles and a pair of corresponding angles. How are they alike? How are they different?

SUMMING UP

Activity

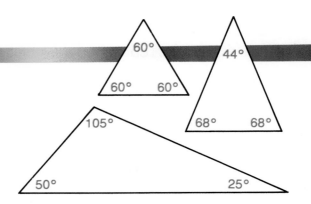

Analyzing Polygons

The sum of the angle measures of a triangle is 180°. How can you find the sum of the angle measures of other polygons?

Working together

Materials: compass, ruler, protractor, Workmat 1

A. Draw six circles. Place 4 points on one circle, 5 points on the next, 6 on the next, and so on, up to 9 points.

B. Join each point on a circle to the next point to form a polygon. Then draw all the diagonals from one vertex of each polygon.

C. Record the number of triangles you have formed. How can you use the triangles to find the sum of the angle measures of each polygon?

D. Record your data in a table like this.

A **diagonal** is a segment joining any two nonadjacent vertices of a polygon.

Polygon	Number of Sides	Number of Triangles Formed	Sum of Angle Measures
quadrilateral	4	2	
pentagon	5		
hexagon			
heptagon			
octagon			

Sharing Your Results

Look back at the numbers you recorded.

1. What pattern do you see between the number of sides and the number of triangles formed for each polygon in your table?

2. Describe how you can use this pattern to find the sum of the angle measures of any polygon.

3. Write a formula that matches your description in **2.** Use *n* for the number of sides of the polygon.

Extending the Activity

A regular polygon is a polygon with all sides congruent and all angles congruent.

Work on your own. Use the data you recorded in your table and the fact above to find the missing measures. The polygons in 4, 6, and 9 are regular.

4.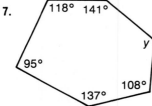

5.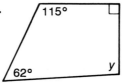

6.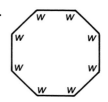

7.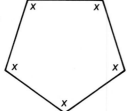

8.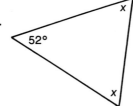

9.

Analyze each statement. Visualizing or drawing each figure may help you. Write *true* or *false*. Explain your thinking.

10. All heptagons have seven sides.

11. The sum of the angle measures of a pentagon is 560°.

12. In quadrilateral *WXYZ*, side $\overline{WX}$ is adjacent to side $\overline{YZ}$.

13. A regular quadrilateral has four right angles.

14. A polygon with angle measures 129°, 128°, 129°, 128°, 129°, 128°, and 129° is a regular heptagon.

15. A circle is a polygon.

Summing Up

16. Use a compass to draw a circle. Without changing the compass setting, use the compass to mark off equal distances around the circle. Join in order the points you have marked. Identify the polygon you have drawn. What is the measure of each angle?

Congruence

Daisy O'Farmer wanted to divide her pasture into four separate pastures of the same size and shape. She did it with fences arranged in two straight lines. Use this plan of the pasture. Make a drawing to show how she did it.

► Two polygons are congruent if they are the same size and shape. That is, two polygons are congruent if their corresponding sides and angles are congruent.

► The **corresponding parts** are the parts that match. Corresponding parts of congruent figures are congruent.

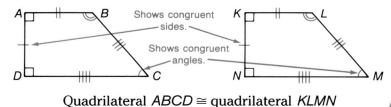

Shows congruent sides.

Shows congruent angles.

Quadrilateral *ABCD* ≅ quadrilateral *KLMN*

Congruent figures are named in the order of corresponding parts.

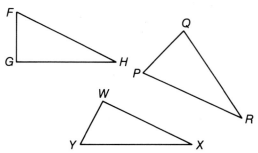

How do you know that *ABCD* ≅ *KLMN*?

If you place a tracing of *ABCD* over *KLMN*, the sides and angles will match. Trace one of Daisy's small pastures. Use your tracing to show that you have divided the large pasture into four congruent smaller ones.

Check Your Understanding

1. Name the corresponding parts of *ABCD* and *KLMN* above.

2. Think visually. Predict which two triangles at the right are congruent. Use tracing paper to check.

Share Your Ideas Draw polygon *ABCDE*. How can you draw polygon *VWXYZ* congruent to *ABCDE*?

142

Think visually. In each exercise, predict which two polygons are congruent. Use tracing paper to check.

3.

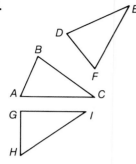

4.

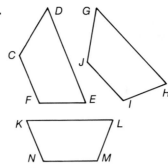

5.

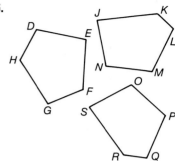

The two polygons in each exercise are congruent. Name the corresponding parts. Find the missing measures.

6.

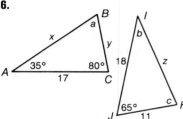

7.

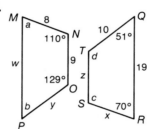

8.

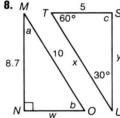

9. Find as many congruent polygons as you can.

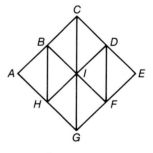

Think and Apply

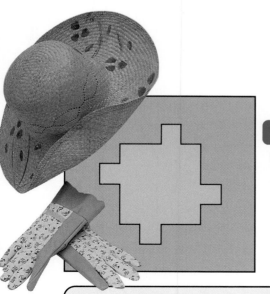

10. This is an outline of Spud McGardner's property. He is giving $\frac{1}{4}$ of his property to the wildlife refuge. He is selling $\frac{1}{4}$ to the town for a park. He is giving $\frac{1}{4}$ to his son and keeping $\frac{1}{4}$. Divide the outline into four congruent polygons to show how he can do this. Can you find other ways?

What must be true of the sides and the angles of *ABCD* and *WXYZ* if *ABCD* ≅ *ZWXY*? Draw *ABCD* and *WXYZ*.

SUMMING UP

Activity

Analyzing Triangles

How many different kinds of triangles can you create? Experiment!

Kinds of Triangles
acute—all acute angles
right—one right angle
obtuse—one obtuse angle
scalene—no congruent sides or angles
isosceles—at least two congruent sides opposite two congruent angles
equilateral—three congruent sides and three congruent angles

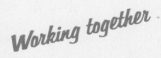

Working together

Materials: 6 straws, each at least 7 in. long, Workmat 2

A. Cut the straws so that there are three pieces 2 in. long, three pieces 3 in. long, three pieces 4 in. long, and three pieces 5 in. long.

B. Create as many different triangles as you can from the straw pieces.

C. Estimate the angle measures for each triangle you create.

D. Record your findings in a table like this.

Triangle	Length of Sides (in inches)	Type of Triangle					
		Acute	Obtuse	Right	Scalene	Isosceles	Equilateral
1. 2.	2, 2, 2	X					X

Sharing Your Results

Look back at the numbers you recorded.

1. How many different triangles did you create?

2. Identify the different types of triangles you created.

3. How many obtuse isosceles triangles did you create? What are the lengths of the sides of each?

4. Did you create an obtuse equilateral triangle? Explain why or why not.

5. Did you create a triangle with sides 2 in., 3 in., and 5 in.? Explain why or why not.

Extending the Activity

Work on your own. Use a protractor and a ruler. If possible, sketch each triangle. If it is not possible to sketch, explain why.

6. right isosceles

7. right scalene

8. right equilateral

9. acute scalene

10. an isosceles triangle with a 120° angle

11. a scalene triangle with two 30° angles

12. an equilateral triangle with a 45° angle

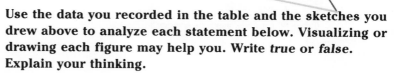

Use the data you recorded in the table and the sketches you drew above to analyze each statement below. Visualizing or drawing each figure may help you. Write *true* or *false*. Explain your thinking.

13. An equilateral triangle is an isosceles triangle.

14. An isosceles triangle is always acute.

15. An equilateral triangle is always acute.

16. No two angles of a scalene triangle are congruent.

17. A triangle with a 42° angle and a 38° angle is a right triangle.

18. It is possible to draw a triangle with sides 3 in., 4 in., and 7 in.

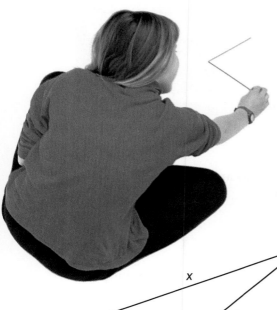

Summing Up

19. Write a statement describing a right isosceles triangle.

20. Write a statement describing how long and how short the missing length of the triangle at the left can be.

Activity

Analyzing Quadrilaterals

Is a rectangle a parallelogram?
Is a rectangle a square?

Working together

A. Examine the figures in each group below. Analyze their properties. Use the facts at the right to help.

B. Determine as many properties as you can that the figures in each group have in common.

C. Record your findings.

Facts

- A **parallelogram** has two pairs of parallel sides.

- A **rhombus** is a parallelogram with four congruent sides.

- A **trapezoid** has exactly one pair of parallel sides.

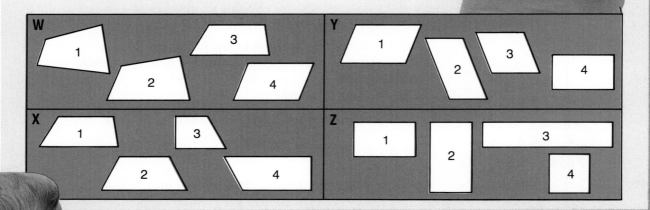

W 1 2 3 4
X 1 2 3 4
Y 1 2 3 4
Z 1 2 3 4

Sharing Your Results

Use the properties you recorded to answer 1–3.

1. What properties do the figures in each group have in common?

   a. W   **b.** X   **c.** Y   **d.** Z

2. Which groups contain each? Explain your thinking.

   a. only trapezoids   **b.** only parallelograms
   c. only rectangles   **d.** exactly one trapezoid
   e. exactly one rectangle   **f.** exactly one square

3. Which figure in **W** is congruent to a figure in **X**?
   Which figure in **Y** is congruent to a figure in **Z**?

146

Extending the Activity

Work on your own. Use a protractor and a ruler. If possible, sketch each quadrilateral. If it is not possible to sketch, explain why.

4. a parallelogram with two 45° angles

5. a square with an acute angle

6. a parallelogram with adjacent angles congruent

7. a trapezoid with the following angle measures: 45°, 65°, 120°, 130°

8. an equilateral parallelogram

9. an isosceles trapezoid

Use your analysis of the figures on page 146 and the sketches you made above to analyze each statement below. Write *true* or *false*. Explain your thinking.

10. All rectangles are parallelograms.

11. Every rhombus is a parallelogram.

12. Every parallelogram is a rhombus.

13. A rhombus always has an acute angle.

14. A parallelogram is a trapezoid.

15. A square is a regular quadrilateral.

16. The opposite angles of an isosceles trapezoid are congruent.

17. A parallelogram with one right angle is a rectangle.

Summing Up

18. Show the relationships among the following quadrilaterals: squares, parallelograms, rectangles, trapezoids, rhombuses. Use this Venn diagram. Decide where to place the name of each figure.

Midchapter Review

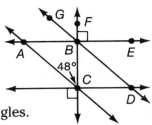

$\overleftrightarrow{AB} \parallel \overleftrightarrow{CD}$ and $\overleftrightarrow{AC} \parallel \overleftrightarrow{BD}$. Fill in each blank. pages 134–139

1. $\overleftrightarrow{AB}$ _____ $\overleftrightarrow{BC}$

2. $\angle CBG$ is a(n) _____ angle.

3. $m\angle DBC =$ _____

4. $m\angle DBE =$ _____

5. $m\angle GBF =$ _____

6. $\triangle ABC$ is a(n) _____ triangle.

7. $\angle GBA$ and _____ are vertical angles.

8. _____ and $\angle CBD$ are adjacent angles.

Use the figure above. Write *true* or *false*. pages 140–147

9. Quadrilateral $ABDC$ is a parallelogram.

10. $\triangle ABC \cong \triangle DCB$

11. The sum of the angle measures of quadrilateral $ABDC$ is 340°.

12. Two polygons are congruent if they are the same shape.

13. A regular quadrilateral is a rectangle.

14. All parallelograms are rectangles.

15. Two sides of a triangle measure 4 cm and 7 cm. The third side must be greater than 3 cm and less than 11 cm.

Copy the puzzle. Fill in the correct answers.

Across

16. an angle of 90°

17. a quadrilateral with exactly two parallel sides

19. a polygon with all sides congruent and all angles congruent

21. a pair of congruent angles formed by parallel lines and a transversal

23. two angle measures with sum 180°

25. a polygon with four sides

Down

16. a parallelogram with all sides congruent

17. a line that intersects two or more lines at different points

18. intersecting to form right angles

20. two rays with a common endpoint

22. an angle greater than 90° but less than 180°

24. never intersecting

Exploring Problem Solving

What's the Pattern?

Many repeating patterns in wallpaper, tiling, carpeting, or fabric are based on an underlying grid of triangles or quadrilaterals.

Thinking Critically

What polygons can you make by turning triangle **A** and combining the turned triangle with triangle **A**? What polygons can you make by combining triangle **A** with its mirror image? You may wish to trace and cut out several copies of triangle **A** to help you with this problem. You can also use Workmat 3.

Analyzing and Making Decisions

1. Polygons **B, C,** and **D** can be created by combining triangle **A** with itself. What type of quadrilateral is formed in each case ? How was it formed?

2. Can you find each of the three quadrilaterals in the grid below? Make a copy of the grid and shade the quadrilaterals.

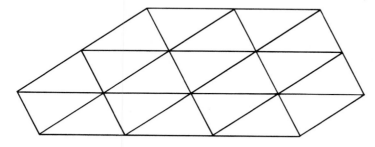

3. Do you think triangle **A** has special properties that make it possible to create polygons **B, C,** and **D**? Draw your own triangle. Form three parallelograms by following the procedure in **1.** Are the three parallelograms different? Why or why not?

Look Back **What if** you find the mirror image of triangle **A** and combine triangle **A** and its mirror image to form quadrilaterals? Can you make a hexagon, using two of the quadrilaterals? Explain.

Problem Solving Strategies

Logic

Tony, Steve, and Sherry took a true/false test. The test had three questions. One test paper had three correct answers. The other two test papers each had two correct answers and one incorrect answer. Which student had all the answers correct?

TONY	SHERRY	STEVE
1. true	1. false	1. false
2. true	2. false	2. true
3. false	3. false	3. false

To solve some problems, you must use logic. The various facts must be organized and examined. You can then draw conclusions from the facts.

Solving the Problem

Think What is the question?

Explore How many students answered all the questions correctly? How many questions did each of the other students miss?

Look at the answers to question **3** on the test. What was the answer? Look at the answers to questions **1** and **2**. If Tony answered both correctly, what score would Sherry and Steve have received? **What if** Sherry had answered them both correctly? What would the other students' scores have been? **What if** Steve had answered them both correctly? What would the other students' scores have been?

Solve Who answered each question correctly?

Look Back How do you know that your answer makes sense?

Share Your Ideas

1. **What if** the correct answer to test question **1** had been true? How would each person have had to answered the question in order to get the same score?

Practice

 Solve. Use a calculator where appropriate.

2. There are three boxes: one is empty, one contains
$1,000, and one contains $100. The statement on the
box containing $1,000 is true. The statement on the box
containing $100 is false. What does each box contain?

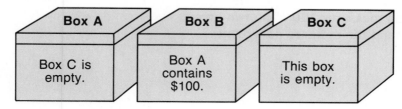

| Box A | Box B | Box C |
| Box C is empty. | Box A contains $100. | This box is empty. |

3. There are 100 marbles in a bag. The marbles are blue or
red. At least 1 marble is blue. If you select any 2
marbles, at least 1 marble is red. How many blue and
how many red marbles are in the bag?

4. Sixteen senior citizens are at a new senior citizen center.
All the men and six of the women are wearing name tags.
One man and eight of the women are playing board
games. Two of the women who are wearing name tags
are playing board games. Every senior citizen is either
wearing a name tag or playing a board game. How many
of the senior citizens attending are men?

5. The school records show that 31 students participate in
swimming and that 38 students participate in track. Of
these students, 19 are in both track and swimming. How
many students are there all together? (You may wish to
use a Venn diagram.)

Mixed Strategy Review

6. A meteorologist is tracking a storm. She finds that the
storm has moved 68 miles in 4 hours. The storm is
predicted to continue at about the same rate. How far
should the storm travel in the next 3 hours?

7. The Foxes took a trip. They drove for 4 hours at 55 miles
per hour and for 2 hours at 35 mph. How far did
they drive?

Create **Your Own**

Look at **5**. Write a
problem you can solve
using a Venn diagram.

Activity

Circles

The company emblem for OK Communications can be described as follows.

It is a circle with a radius of 2 cm. Inside the circle is a vertical diameter. Joined to the diameter are two radii. They are at the right of the diameter. The angle formed by the two radii measures 120°. The two arcs between the diameter and the radii are congruent.

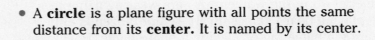

Working together

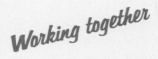

Materials: compass, protractor, straightedge

A. Decide whether you have enough information to draw the emblem. If necessary, use the definitions below to help you.

B. If you do not have enough information, explain what is needed. If you do have enough, draw the emblem.

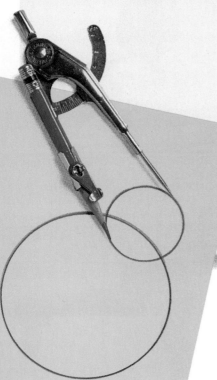

- A **circle** is a plane figure with all points the same distance from its **center.** It is named by its center.

- A **radius** of a circle is a line segment joining the center to any point on the circle. It is also the length of such a segment.

- A **chord** is a segment joining two points on the circle.

- A **diameter** is a chord that passes through the center of the circle. It is also the length of such a chord. The diameter of a circle is twice its radius.

- An **arc** is part of a circle. A **semicircle** is half a circle.

Sharing Your Results

1. Describe the emblem in your own words.

2. **What if** the angle formed by the two radii measured 180°? Would the emblem be different? Explain.

Extending the Activity

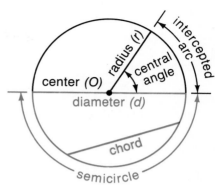

- A **central angle** is an angle with its vertex at the center of the circle.

- The measure of a central angle equals the measure of the intercepted arc.

- The arcs intercepted by congruent central angles are congruent.

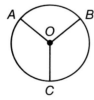

Work on your own. Use a compass, a straightedge, and a protractor, as necessary. If possible, draw each. If it is not possible to draw, explain why.

3. circle O, with horizontal diameter $\overline{MP}$ measuring 4 cm, central angle MOQ measuring 60°, and central angle POR, on the same side of $\overline{MP}$, measuring 60°

4. circle C, with vertical diameter $\overline{AB}$ measuring 3 cm, and chord $\overline{DE}$ perpendicular to $\overline{AB}$ such that $m\angle DCA = m\angle ECA = 60°$

5. two circles intersecting at two points

6. two circles intersecting at three points

7. two circles intersecting at one point

8. a circle with three radii, each 2 cm long, that form equal central angles

Describe each of these figures. Use the terms on page 152 in each description.

9.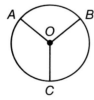

10.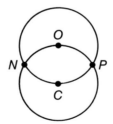

11.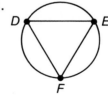

Summing Up

You are the advertising director for a company. You have to design a circular emblem for the company.

12. Decide what kind of company you work for. Then design an emblem.

13. Write a description of the emblem. Exchange descriptions with a classmate and draw each other's emblem.

Your Company

Your Name
Advertising Director

☎ (000) 123-4567

Draw the lines of symmetry for this figure. How many lines are there?

Reflections and Rotations

This garden in France was designed for the chateau at Chenonceaux. It has line and rotational symmetry.

The red line is a line of symmetry, or a line of reflection. The figure on one side of the line is a mirror image, or **reflection,** of the figure on the other side.

A figure has rotational symmetry if it can be rotated less than a full turn and the rotated figure coincides with the original one. The yellow arrow shows that if the garden is rotated a half turn around the point of symmetry, or center of **rotation,** the garden looks the same.

Identifying a reflection image

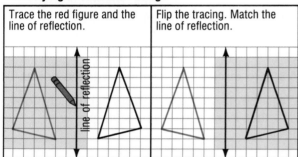

Identifying a rotation image

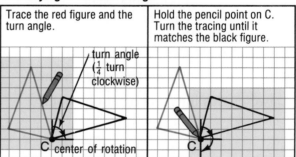

Which pairs are reflection images?

1.
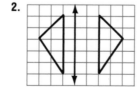

2.

3.

4. What is the turn angle for this rotation?

5. Copy the pair of figures on grid paper. Show the turn angle with an arrow.

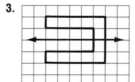
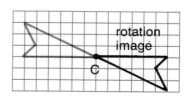

Share Your Ideas Is a figure congruent to its reflection image? to its rotation image? How do you know?

Copy each pair of figures on grid paper. Draw all lines of reflection.

6. 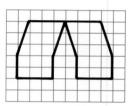 **7.** 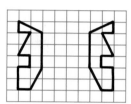 **8.** 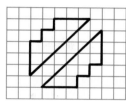 **9.**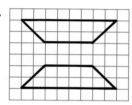

Which black figures are rotation images of the red figures?
For those that are, describe the turn angle.

10. 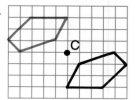 **11.** 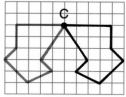 **12.** 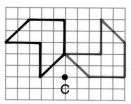 **13.**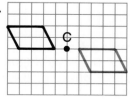

Which figures have line symmetry? How many lines of
symmetry does each have? Which have rotational symmetry?
In how many positions does each look exactly the same?

14.   **15.**   **16.**   **17.**   **18.**

19. Create your own design with one line of symmetry. Draw the line of reflection for your design.

20. Create your own design with rotational symmetry. It should have 3 positions where it looks exactly the same.

Think and Apply

Logical Thinking

21. Which figure is the same as figure A? Is it a reflection image or a rotation image?

 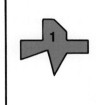 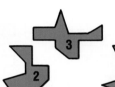 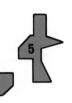

Draw a figure that has exactly one line of symmetry.
Rotate the figure one-half turn. Draw the new figure.

SUMMING UP

Is quadrilateral A congruent to quadrilateral B? How do you know?

Translations

Monique Dail designs math books. She uses this template to draw figures. She drew pentagon A. Then she slid the template to the right to draw the polygon again.

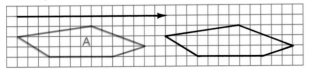

The black pentagon is the **translation,** or slide, image of the red one. The arrow shows the rule for the translation. That is, it shows the distance and the direction of the slide.

Are all the vertices of the red pentagon the same distance from the corresponding vertices of the black one? If so, what is that distance?

Identifying a translation image

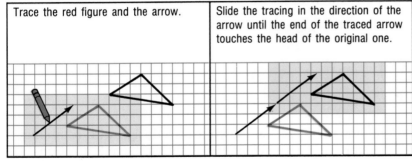

Trace the red figure and the arrow.	Slide the tracing in the direction of the arrow until the end of the traced arrow touches the head of the original one.

The arrow shows that the rule for this translation is *right 4, up 3.* What is the rule for the translation drawn by Monique?

Copy each pair of polygons on grid paper. Draw an arrow to show the distance and the direction of each slide. Then write a rule for the translation. Each black polygon is the translation image.

1.

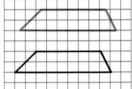

2.

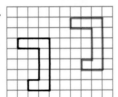

3.

Share Your Ideas Is a figure congruent to its translation image? How do you know?

**Copy each pair of polygons on grid paper. Draw an arrow and
write a rule for each. The black polygon is the translation image.**

4. 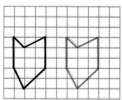 5. 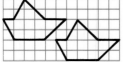 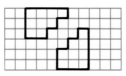 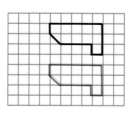 6. 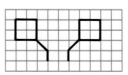 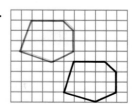 7.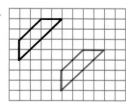

Which pairs are translation images?

8. 9. 10. 11.

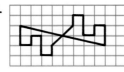   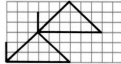

12. 13. 14. 15.

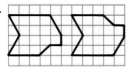

Look back at 8–15.

16. Are any pairs reflection images? If so, which ones? Justify
your answer.

17. Are any pairs rotation images? If so, which ones? Justify
your answer.

18. Are any images not the result of a single motion? If so, what
different motions were necessary? Explain your thinking.

Think and Apply

Test Taker

You will often find problems like this one on a test. It is
called an *analogy*. Read it as follows: "Translation is to
slide as rotation is to _____." The answer is *turn*.
Complete the following.

Translation : slide
as rotation : _____.

19. Circumference : circle
    as _____ : polygon.

    a. perimeter b. area c. side

20. Ruler : segment as
    protractor : _____.

    a. polygon b. angle c. degrees

What if you had to explain what a translation is to
someone who did not know? What would you say?
Write a few sentences describing a translation.

SUMMING UP

Use a dictionary to look up the meaning of the word *transformation.* How many meanings does it have? Write them.

Transformations: Drawing Images

Reflections, rotations, and translations are **transformations.** How would you draw the image of each transformation? Compare your ways with those shown below.

Detail, © 1989 M.C. Escher Heirs/
Cordon Art — Baarn — Holland, *Moths*

Drawing a reflection image

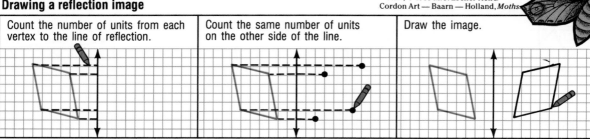

| Count the number of units from each vertex to the line of reflection. | Count the same number of units on the other side of the line. | Draw the image. |

Drawing a rotation image

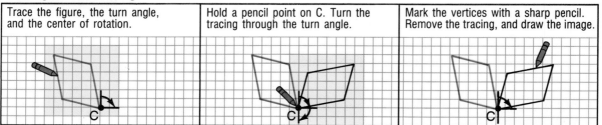

| Trace the figure, the turn angle, and the center of rotation. | Hold a pencil point on C. Turn the tracing through the turn angle. | Mark the vertices with a sharp pencil. Remove the tracing, and draw the image. |

Drawing a translation image

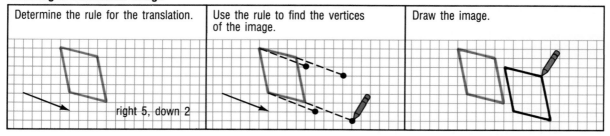

| Determine the rule for the translation. | Use the rule to find the vertices of the image. | Draw the image. |

right 5, down 2

Check Your Understanding

1. Use grid paper. Copy this polygon three times. Draw its reflection, rotation, and translation images.

Share Your Ideas   Draw the translation image of the polygon in **1** for the rule *right 12.* Explain how this image is different from the reflection image in **1**.

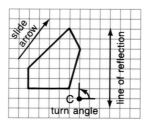

158

Copy each figure and line of reflection on grid paper. Draw each reflection image.

2.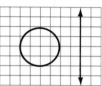

3.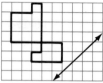

4.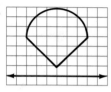

5.

Copy each figure and turn angle on grid paper. Draw each rotation image.

6.

7.

8.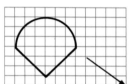

9.

Copy each figure and arrow on grid paper. Draw each translation image.

10.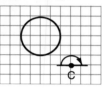

11.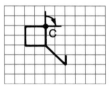

12.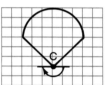

13.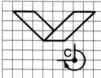

14. Draw a figure that has a reflection image and a translation image that are the same.

15. Draw a figure that has a reflection image, a rotation image, and a translation image that are the same.

© 1989 M.C. Escher Heirs/Cordon Art — Baarn — Holland, *Moths.*

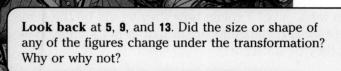

Think and Apply

This painting by M.C. Escher, called *Moths,* is made from a single shape that covers the canvas without any gaps or overlapping. The shape **tessellates** a plane. To tessellate a plane, you can move a shape, using reflections, rotations, and/or translations.

16. These are the only regular polygons that tessellate a plane. Use one to make a design that tessellates a plane. Use reflections, rotations, and/or translations.

Look back at **5**, **9**, and **13**. Did the size or shape of any of the figures change under the transformation? Why or why not?

SUMMING UP

Activity

Exploring Three-Dimensional Figures

"When I draw plans for a building, I include *directional views.*"

 front view

 side view

 top view

Can you construct a figure if you are given its front, side, and top views?

Working together

Materials: grid paper with 4 squares to an inch, scissors, cardboard, glue

A. Choose a prism at the right to investigate.

B. Use the views of the prism to make a pattern that can be folded to form the figure. Draw the pattern on grid paper.

C. Cut out the pattern. Cut out pieces of cardboard the same sizes as the faces of the prism.

D. Glue the cardboard pieces to the pattern. Fold and tape the pattern to form the prism.

rectangular prism

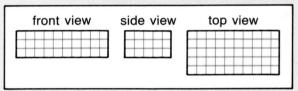

triangular prism

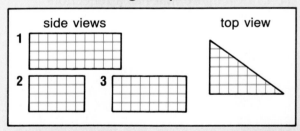

Sharing Your Results

1. Describe how you used the directional views of the prism to make the pattern for the prism.

2. Compare the two prisms. How are they alike? How are they different?

3. **What if** you had to draw the directional views and a pattern for a cube? Explain how they would be the same as those for a rectangular prism that is not a cube. How would they be different?

Extending the Activity

A three-dimensional figure whose surfaces all are flat is a **polyhedron**.

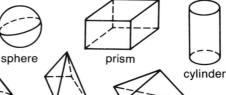
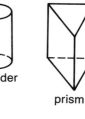

sphere

prism

cylinder

cone

pyramid

pyramid

prism

Work on your own.

4. Identify 2 three-dimensional figures that are polyhedra. How do you know they are?

5. Identify 2 three-dimensional figures that are not polyhedra. How do you know they are not?

Match each three-dimensional figure with its pattern.

6.

7.

8.

9.

a.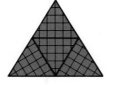

b.

c.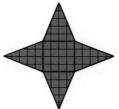

d.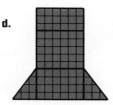

Sketch a figure that would have these directional views.

10.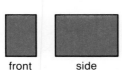

front side top

11.

front side top

12.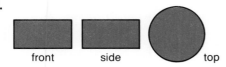

front side top

13.

front side top

Summing Up

Work in a group. Look back at your sketches for 10–13.

14. Compare the sketches made by everyone in your group. How are the sketches for each figure alike? How are they different?

15. Classify each figure.

Using Problem Solving

Tessellations

Shown here is *Pegasus,* a famous drawing by M.C. Escher. The horses are all the same size and shape.

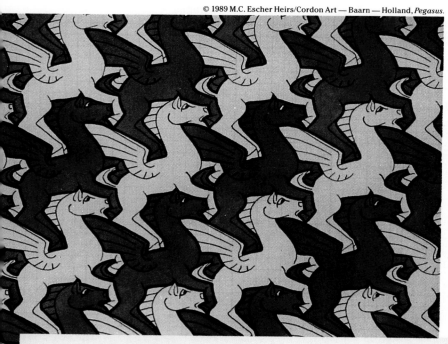

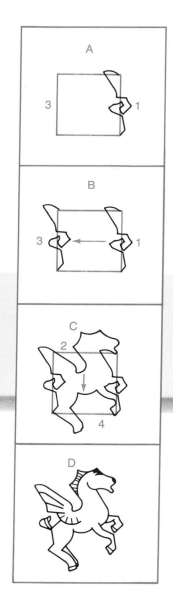

Working together

First look at these steps for the drawing of the horse. Study the squares and see if you can tell how the horse was drawn.

Sharing Your Ideas

1. Look at drawing **B**. How are the lines at areas **1** and **3** alike?

2. Look at drawing **C**. How are the lines at areas **2** and **4** alike?

3. Look at the horses in the picture above. How do they fit together? Do these figures tessellate? Explain.

162

Practice

The figures drawn on the dot paper fit together with no space in between. The figures tessellate.

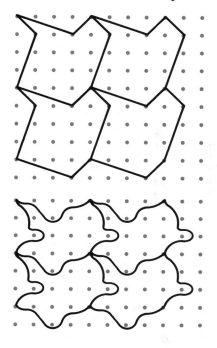

4. Use a sheet of dot paper or graph paper to make a simple tessellation like those at the right.

5. Fill in some details on your patterns to make each look like an object, person, or animal.

6. These drawings show another technique for creating patterns like Escher's.

- Modify exactly half of any side of a quadrilateral.
- Rotate that modification 180 degrees.
- Repeat the procedure on each of the other sides of the quadrilateral.

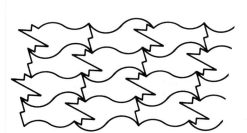

Make your own pattern by using a modified quadrilateral. You may wish to trace your shape to help you.

Summing Up

7. What difficulties did you have in making these drawings?

8. How could making a tracing of one side of the figure help you?

Chapter Review

$\overleftrightarrow{AB} \parallel \overleftrightarrow{CD}$. **Write *true* or *false*.** pages 134–139

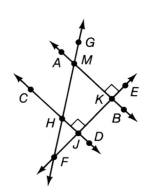

1. $\overleftrightarrow{EF} \perp \overleftrightarrow{CD}$

2. $\overleftrightarrow{AB} \parallel \overleftrightarrow{EF}$

3. $\angle CHM \cong \angle FHJ$

4. $m\angle CHM + m\angle MHD = 180°$

5. $\angle JFH$ measures about 90°.

6. $\angle MKJ$ and $\angle HJF$ are adjacent angles.

7. $\angle AMG$ and $\angle HMK$ are vertical angles.

8. $\triangle HJF$ is an obtuse triangle.

9. $\angle GMK$ and $\angle MHJ$ are corresponding angles.

Name each polygon. Then find the missing measures. pages 140–147

10.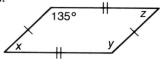

11.

12.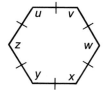

Use the figure at the right. Identify each image of K. C is the center of rotation. pages 154–159

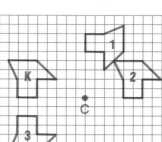

13. reflection image

14. rotation image

15. translation image

Match each definition in column A with the word it defines in column B.

A

16. a segment that joins two points on a circle

17. two angles, the sum of whose measures is 180°

18. a three-dimensional figure whose surfaces all are flat

19. a parallelogram with four congruent sides

20. an angle whose vertex is the center of a circle

B

a. radius

b. polyhedron

c. supplementary angles

d. central angle

e. rhombus

f. chord

Solve. pages 149–151, 162–163

21. Write a conclusion from these statements.
All squares are rhombuses.
RTSV is a square.

22. Draw two straight lines that divide this rhombus into four congruent polygons.

Chapter Test

$\overrightarrow{PQ} \parallel \overrightarrow{TR}$. Fill in each blank.

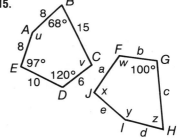

1. $\overleftrightarrow{TR} \perp$ _____

2. $\angle VSW$ is a(n) _____ angle.

3. $m\angle PWX =$ _____

4. $\overleftrightarrow{PQ}$ intersects $\overleftrightarrow{VW}$ at _____.

5. $m\angle RSZ =$ _____

6. $m\angle VSW + m\angle WSR =$ _____

7. $\angle XWY \cong$ _____

8. $\triangle VSW$ is a(n) _____ triangle.

9. $\angle VWS$ and $\angle SWQ$ are _____ angles.

10. $\angle XWY$ and $\angle YWQ$ are _____ angles.

11. The sum of the angle measures of $\triangle VWS$ is _____.

12. Two sides of a triangle measure 3 cm and 4 cm. The third side must be greater than _____ and less than _____.

The polygons in each pair are congruent. Name the polygons. Find the missing measures.

13.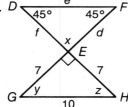

14.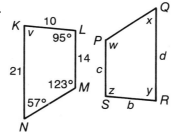

15.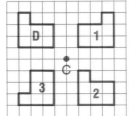

Use the figure at the right. Identify each image of D. C is the center of rotation.

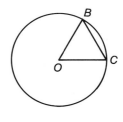

16. reflection image

17. rotation image

18. translation image

Solve.

19. Arc BC measures 60°. The diameter of circle O is 3 cm. What are the measures of the angles and the sides of $\triangle BOC$? What kind of triangle is $\triangle BOC$?

20. Write a conclusion from these statements.
All rectangles are parallelograms. $ABCD$ is a rectangle.

THINK   Move only two segments to make seven squares. The squares need not be the same size.

Parallel Lines and Parallelograms

Parallel lines are lines in the same plane that never intersect. When are line segments parallel?

AT THE COMPUTER

Materials: Logo

A. What number can you use in the `RIGHT` command to make $\overline{CD}$ parallel to $\overline{AB}$?

```
HOME
FD 50
RT 30
FD 30
RT ____
FD 50
```

B. What number can you use for the `LEFT` command to make $\overline{CD}$ parallel to $\overline{AB}$?

```
HOME
FD 50
RT 120
FD 30
LT ____
FD 50
```

C. Complete the commands to draw parallel line segments cut by a transversal. The turtle starts at A. Find the measure of each angle.

- angle $AEF =$ ____
- angle $DFG =$ ____
- angle $EFD =$ ____

```
HOME
FD 100
BK 50
RT 155
FD 70
BK 40
RT ____
FD 50
BK 100
```

D. A straight angle measures 180°. How can you use that fact to find the measure of angle CFG?

Sharing Your Results

1. Explain how you found the turns in **A** and **B** that made the line segments parallel.

2. What conjectures can you make about angles formed by parallel lines and a transversal?

Extending the Activity

3. Use the extended parallel side to find m∠ABC. What is m∠BCD? How did you find it?

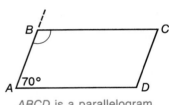

ABCD is a parallelogram.

4. Find the sum of the measures of ∠ABC and ∠DAB. Then find the sum of the measures of two other consecutive angles of a parallelogram. What seems to be true about the measures of two consecutive angles? Can you justify your conclusion, using parallel lines? Why or why not?

5. Complete the procedure PGRAM that draws a parallelogram given three inputs, SIDE 1, TURN, SIDE2. Have Logo find the number for the RIGHT turn, using the relationship you found for two consecutive angles of a parallelogram.

```
TO PGRAM :SIDE1 :TURN :SIDE2
FD :SIDE1
RT :TURN
FD :SIDE2
RT _____ - :TURN
FD :SIDE1
RT :TURN
FD :SIDE2
RT _____
END
```

6. Define the PGRAM procedure. Which figures can be drawn by using PGRAM? You may have to turn the turtle first.

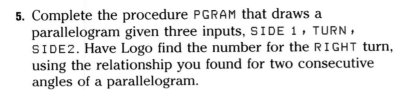

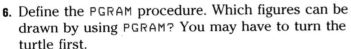

7. For each figure that cannot be drawn with the PGRAM procedure, identify the properties of the figure that differ from the properties of a parallelogram.

Summing Up

8. Explain how you can find each missing angle measure.

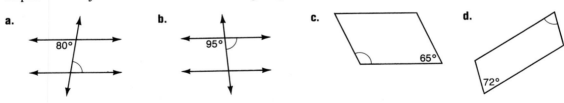

Geometric Modeling

Look at the intersections below.

a. b. c. d. e.

1. How many times can you enter each intersection and leave by an unused path?

2. Are there any intersections for which there is an unused path to reenter but no unused path by which to leave? Explain. How many paths meet at these intersections?

3. How many paths meet at each intersection you did not name in **2**?

4. What patterns do you see in the numbers you recorded in **2** and **3**? What must be true of the number of paths meeting at an intersection if you wish to have an unused path by which to leave the intersection for every unused path by which you can enter it?

The street sweeper in Miniville must clean the paths through the park every day. Is it possible to plan a route such that the sweeper never passes over any path more than once?

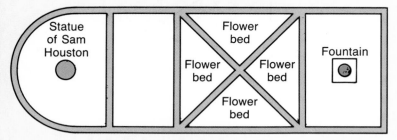

5. Use what you learned above. Classify each intersection in the park. How many are there like those in **2**? like those in **3**?

6. Do you think you can plan a route such that the sweeper passes over each path only once? Why or why not? If so, plan a route. If not, explain what is needed to do so.

Maintaining Skills

Choose the correct answers. Write A, B, C, or D.

1. 827×10^3

   A 82,700   **C** 8,270,000

   B 827,000   **D** not given

2. $169.2 \div 47$

   A 4.22   **C** 0.27

   B 3.6   **D** not given

3. What is the prime factorization of 98?

   A $2^2 \times 7$ **C** 2×7^2

   B $2 \times 3 \times 7$ **D** not given

4. What is the GCF of 25 and 32?

   A 5   **C** 4

   B 2   **D** not given

5. What is the LCM of 12 and 8?

   A 24   **C** 48

   B 12   **D** not given

6. $4^2 + 3^2$

   A 14   **C** 49

   B 25   **D** not given

7. Evaluate $26 - 2y$. Let $y = 5$.

   A 19   **C** 16

   B 1   **D** not given

8. Which equation represents 6 times a number b is 24?

   A $6b = 24$ **B** $6 + b = 24$

   C $24b = 6$ **D** not given

9. Solve $4m = 100$ for m.

   A 96   **C** 50

   B 25   **D** not given

10. What is the relationship between $\angle MQO$ and $\angle NQP$?

   A adjacent   **C** supplementary

   B congruent   **D** not given

11. What is the sum of the angle measures of a quadrilateral?

   A 180°   **C** 360°

   B 90°   **D** not given

12. What part of the circle is $\overline{AB}$?

   A diameter   **C** chord

   B arc   **D** not given

Solve.

13. Mr. Avery is a truck driver. He is permitted to drive no more than 7.5 hours a day. At an average speed of 55 mph, about how many days will it take him to travel 1,850 miles?

   A 5 days   **C** 34 days

   B 2 days   **D** not given

14. Flo either walks or bikes to and from school each day. The school is 1.3 miles from her house. Which of the following could be the distance she walks to and from school in a week?

   A 7.8 miles   **C** 15.8 miles

   B 6.5 miles   **D** not given

6 Adding and Subtracting Fractions

THEME   Careers: People on the Job

Sharing What You Know

What career field do you want to enter when you finish
school? People consider this question carefully because
whatever career they choose, they will be spending lots of
time at it. Some people work eight, twelve, even sixteen hours
a day. That's working $\frac{1}{3}, \frac{1}{2}$, or $\frac{2}{3}$ of the whole day! Think about
how you spend your day. What part of your day is spent
sleeping, eating, attending school, doing homework, talking on
the telephone, or watching TV? How can you use fractions to
describe your day?

Using Language

Do you get eight hours of sleep on a school night? Eight hours
out of a twenty-four hour day is $\frac{8}{24}$ or $\frac{1}{3}$ of a day. $\frac{8}{24}$ and $\frac{1}{3}$ are
equivalent fractions. **Equivalent** means to be equal in value
or measure. In mathematics, **equivalent fractions** are
fractions that name the same number. Think about how many
hours you spend in school. Name fractions to describe that
part of your day.

Words to Know: equivalent fractions, proper fraction, mixed
number, lowest terms, terminating decimal, repeating decimal

Be a Problem Solver

For what part of your day do you sleep? what part of a year? what part of your life? Explain your answers.

Interview someone who has a job you find interesting. Make a list of how that person uses mathematics, and perhaps fractions, on the job.

Describe what part of a 15-mile marathon has been completed at the 10-mile mark.

METRO LINE
Subway Map

MAIN ST. LOCAL

○ A Street

Fractions and Mixed Numbers

Yoshiko Hama, Middletown urban planner, has approved plans for a new subway line.

All stations on the line are $\frac{1}{4}$ mile apart.

G Street is $\frac{3}{4}$ mile from A Street.

$\frac{3}{4}$ ← numerator
  ← denominator

What station is 1 mile from A street?

○ C Street

What part of the whole Main Street Line is the distance from A Street to O Street?

○ E Street

You can classify fractions in different ways.

A **proper fraction** is one in which the numerator is less than the denominator.

$\frac{1}{5}$ and $\frac{3}{4}$ are proper fractions.

An **improper fraction** is one in which the numerator is greater than or equal to the denominator.

$\frac{7}{5}$ and $\frac{8}{8}$ are improper fractions.

○ G Street

A **mixed number** has a whole number and a fraction.

$1\frac{1}{5}$ is a mixed number.

○ I Street

You can write a mixed number or a whole number as an improper fraction.

$2\frac{1}{5} = \frac{n}{5}$ **Think** How many $\frac{1}{5}$'s in 1? in 2?

$2\frac{1}{5} \rightarrow \frac{(2 \times 5) + 1}{5} = \frac{11}{5}$

You can write an improper fraction as a mixed number or a whole number.

$$\frac{25}{6} \rightarrow 6\overline{)25} = 4\frac{1}{6}$$
$$\frac{4}{6\overline{)25}}$$
$$\underline{24}$$
$$1$$

○ K Street

Check Your Understanding

Write each as an improper fraction, a whole number, or a mixed number.

○ M Street

1. $\frac{8}{5}$ 2. $3\frac{7}{8}$ 3. $\frac{15}{9}$ 4. $\frac{26}{13}$ 5. $5\frac{7}{8}$ 6. $\frac{20}{20}$

Find the value of n to make each statement true.

7. $1 = \frac{n}{5}$ 8. $2 = \frac{n}{6}$ 9. $5\frac{3}{5} = \frac{n}{5}$ 10. $\frac{7}{7} = n$ 11. $3\frac{2}{3} = \frac{n}{3}$ 12. $1\frac{3}{10} = \frac{n}{10}$ ○ O Street

Share Your Ideas Explain how you can tell if a fraction is less than 1, equal to 1, or greater than 1.

Q Street
○

Write each as an improper fraction.

13. $3\frac{1}{2}$ 14. $5\frac{1}{3}$ 15. $2\frac{3}{8}$ 16. $1\frac{3}{5}$ 17. $9\frac{4}{5}$ 18. $2\frac{5}{7}$

19. $8\frac{2}{5}$ 20. $9\frac{1}{2}$ 21. $2\frac{3}{4}$ 22. $5\frac{1}{10}$ 23. $6\frac{1}{8}$ 24. $7\frac{2}{3}$

Write each fraction as a whole number or a mixed number.

25. $\frac{8}{4}$ 26. $\frac{9}{7}$ 27. $\frac{7}{2}$ 28. $\frac{15}{3}$ 29. $\frac{9}{9}$ 30. $\frac{12}{5}$

31. $\frac{25}{4}$ 32. $\frac{29}{7}$ 33. $\frac{33}{9}$ 34. $\frac{40}{40}$ 35. $\frac{1,000}{1,000}$ 36. $\frac{100}{20}$

Find the value of n to make each sentence true.

37. $\frac{12}{5} = 2\frac{n}{5}$ 38. $\frac{14}{3} = n\frac{2}{3}$ 39. $3 = \frac{n}{1}$ 40. $7 = \frac{7}{n}$

41. $5\frac{3}{8} = \frac{n}{8}$ 42. $\frac{9}{2} = n\frac{1}{2}$ 43. $8\frac{2}{9} = \frac{74}{n}$ 44. $5 = \frac{n}{4}$

Name each point as a mixed number and as an improper fraction.

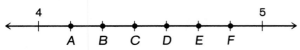

45. *A*   46. *B*   47. *C*   48. *D*   49. *E*   50. *F*

Write a fraction for each.

51. a proper fraction having only the digits 2 and 7

52. an improper fraction having only the digits 2 and 1

53. a fraction greater than 1 and less than 2, with denominator 3

54. a fraction greater than 1 and less than 2, with denominator 6

Use the Main Street Metro Line Subway map.

55. Which stop is $1\frac{1}{4}$ mi from A Street?

56. How far is M Street from A Street?

57. What stop is $\frac{5}{4}$ mi from C Street?

58. How long is the Main Street Local?

Can every mixed number be written as an improper fraction? Can every improper fraction be written as a mixed number? Explain.

SUMMING UP

Jon said, "If I multiply $\frac{1}{2} \times \frac{4}{4}$, the product must be greater than $\frac{1}{2}$." Is Jon correct?

Equivalent Fractions

Maria Morales owns an equestrian center. She keeps a chart to record parts of a stable that have been rented. This diagram shows the part of each stable that has been rented.

Morales' Stables

What part of each stable has been rented?

Do $\frac{3}{6}$, $\frac{4}{8}$, and $\frac{6}{12}$ all represent the same part of a stable?

$\frac{3}{6}$, $\frac{4}{8}$, and $\frac{6}{12}$ are **equivalent fractions.**

▶ To find equivalent fractions, multiply or divide the numerator and denominator by the same nonzero number.

$\frac{1}{2} = \frac{1 \times 4}{2 \times 4} = \frac{4}{8}$

$\frac{1}{2}$ and $\frac{4}{8}$ are equivalent.

$\frac{6}{12} = \frac{6 \div 6}{12 \div 6} = \frac{1}{2}$

$\frac{6}{12}$ and $\frac{1}{2}$ are equivalent.

▶ A fraction is in **lowest terms** when the GCF of the numerator and denominator is 1.

To find an equivalent fraction in lowest terms you can divide the numerator and denominator by the GCF.

Write $\frac{15}{60}$ in lowest terms.

$\frac{15}{60} = \frac{15 \div 15}{60 \div 15} = \frac{1}{4}$ **Think** The GCF of 15 and 60 is 15.

Sometimes it is easier to divide numerator and denominator by any common factor. Use divisibility rules to find a common factor. Continue dividing until the fraction is in lowest terms.

$\frac{15}{60} = \frac{15 \div 5}{60 \div 5} = \frac{3}{12}$ $\frac{3}{12} = \frac{3 \div 3}{12 \div 3} = \frac{1}{4}$

How do you know that $\frac{1}{4}$ is in lowest terms?

Check Your Understanding

Find each value of n.

1. $\frac{5}{6} = \frac{n}{24}$ 2. $\frac{28}{24} = \frac{7}{n}$ 3. $\frac{6}{8} = \frac{n}{32}$ 4. $2\frac{12}{16} = 2\frac{n}{4}$ 5. $\frac{3}{2} = \frac{15}{n}$

Tell if each fraction is in lowest terms.
Write yes or no.

6. $\frac{6}{9}$ 7. $\frac{2}{3}$ 8. $\frac{15}{21}$ 9. $\frac{1}{9}$ 10. $\frac{5}{4}$

Share Your Ideas List three fractions in lowest terms. Explain how you know that the fractions are in lowest terms.

174

Write three equivalent fractions for each.

11. $\frac{1}{5}$ **12.** $\frac{12}{18}$ **13.** $\frac{5}{5}$ **14.** $\frac{4}{3}$ **15.** $\frac{3}{8}$ **16.** $\frac{12}{24}$

Find each value of *n*.

17. $\frac{6}{18} = \frac{1}{n}$ **18.** $\frac{9}{15} = \frac{n}{5}$ **19.** $\frac{36}{30} = \frac{n}{5}$ **20.** $\frac{12}{40} = \frac{n}{20}$ **21.** $\frac{7}{6} = \frac{14}{n}$

22. $\frac{24}{36} = \frac{n}{6}$ **23.** $\frac{8}{20} = \frac{40}{n}$ **24.** $\frac{8}{8} = \frac{n}{16}$ **25.** $6\frac{12}{15} = 6\frac{n}{5}$ **26.** $5\frac{6}{10} = 5\frac{3}{n}$

Tell if each fraction is in lowest terms. Write *yes* or *no*.

27. $\frac{7}{10}$ **28.** $\frac{1}{8}$ **29.** $\frac{11}{33}$ **30.** $\frac{6}{5}$ **31.** $\frac{9}{9}$ **32.** $\frac{3}{4}$

33. $\frac{14}{21}$ **34.** $\frac{8}{12}$ **35.** $\frac{9}{20}$ **36.** $\frac{21}{28}$ **37.** $\frac{100}{250}$ **38.** $\frac{50}{125}$

Write each fraction in lowest terms.

39. $\frac{6}{8}$ **40.** $\frac{4}{6}$ **41.** $\frac{3}{9}$ **42.** $\frac{14}{28}$ **43.** $\frac{16}{36}$ **44.** $\frac{40}{100}$

45. $\frac{20}{25}$ **46.** $\frac{18}{24}$ **47.** $\frac{25}{75}$ **48.** $\frac{36}{48}$ **49.** $\frac{150}{250}$ **50.** $\frac{30}{300}$

Copy each number line. Label the points with fractions in lowest terms.

51.

52.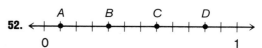

53. On Monday, Ms. Morales rode her favorite horse, Wild Racer, $1\frac{3}{4}$ mi. On Tuesday she rode $1\frac{6}{10}$ mi; on Wednesday, $1\frac{4}{5}$ mi; on Thursday, $1\frac{3}{5}$ mi. On which two days did Ms. Morales ride Wild Racer the same distance?

Multiplying or dividing numerator and denominator by the same number will change the fraction but will not change the value of the fraction. Explain.

Visual Thinking

54. Copy the circles.
In *A*, write each improper fraction.
In *B*, write each fraction that is in lowest terms. Write each fraction only once.

$\frac{9}{8}$ $\frac{12}{9}$ $\frac{3}{4}$ $\frac{5}{9}$ $\frac{12}{11}$ $\frac{4}{7}$ $\frac{20}{17}$

SUMMING UP

175

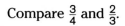

Sara said, "I'm thinking of a number that is less than 100 and is a multiple of 3, 4, and 5. What is the number?"

Comparing and Ordering Fractions

John Young, a commercial artist, is designing two magazine advertisements for Summit Bicycles. One ad covers $\frac{3}{4}$ of a page. The other covers $\frac{2}{3}$ of a page. Which is the larger advertisement?

Compare $\frac{3}{4}$ and $\frac{2}{3}$.

You can use the number line to compare fractions.

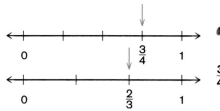

$$\frac{3}{4} > \frac{2}{3}$$

You can rename unlike fractions as like fractions to compare them.

Use the LCD to write equivalent fractions.

$$\frac{3}{4} = \frac{3 \times 3}{4 \times 3} = \frac{9}{12}$$

Think The LCD of $\frac{3}{4}$ and $\frac{2}{3}$ is 12.

$$\frac{2}{3} = \frac{2 \times 4}{3 \times 4} = \frac{8}{12}$$

Then compare the numerators.

9 > 8, so $\frac{9}{12} > \frac{8}{12}$ and

$$\frac{3}{4} > \frac{2}{3}.$$

The larger advertisement covers $\frac{3}{4}$ of the page.

Another Example

Compare $3\frac{3}{4}$, $3\frac{5}{6}$, $3\frac{2}{3}$.

Since the whole numbers are the same, compare the fractions.

$$\frac{3}{4} = \frac{9}{12} \qquad \frac{5}{6} = \frac{10}{12} \qquad \frac{2}{3} = \frac{8}{12}$$

Think The LCD of $\frac{3}{4}$, $\frac{5}{6}$, and $\frac{2}{3}$ is 12.

$$\frac{8}{12} < \frac{9}{12} < \frac{10}{12}, \text{ so } 3\frac{2}{3} < 3\frac{3}{4} < 3\frac{5}{6}$$

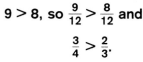

Check Your Understanding

Compare. Use >, <, or = for each .

1. $\frac{4}{5}$ ● $\frac{2}{3}$

2. $\frac{11}{16}$ ● $\frac{15}{16}$

3. $\frac{5}{8}$ ● $\frac{5}{4}$

4. $1\frac{5}{9}$ ● $1\frac{3}{5}$

5. $\frac{2}{3}$ ● $\frac{4}{6}$

Share Your Ideas Describe a method for comparing fractions with like denominators. Describe a method for comparing fractions with like numerators.

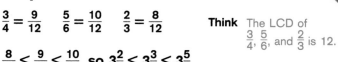

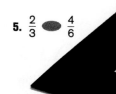

Compare. Use >, <, or = for each ⬤.

6. $\frac{3}{9}$ ⬤ $\frac{1}{3}$ **7.** $\frac{11}{3}$ ⬤ $\frac{11}{6}$ **8.** $\frac{3}{5}$ ⬤ $\frac{3}{4}$ **9.** $\frac{7}{10}$ ⬤ $\frac{3}{5}$ **10.** $\frac{9}{20}$ ⬤ $\frac{10}{20}$

11. $\frac{7}{8}$ ⬤ $\frac{4}{5}$ **12.** $1\frac{3}{8}$ ⬤ $1\frac{4}{7}$ **13.** $2\frac{3}{4}$ ⬤ $2\frac{6}{8}$ **14.** $7\frac{9}{12}$ ⬤ $7\frac{3}{5}$ **15.** $8\frac{7}{9}$ ⬤ $8\frac{2}{3}$

16. $\frac{5}{7}$ ⬤ $\frac{5}{8}$ **17.** $\frac{7}{7}$ ⬤ $\frac{12}{12}$ **18.** $\frac{2}{9}$ ⬤ $\frac{1}{6}$ **19.** $\frac{15}{3}$ ⬤ $\frac{11}{2}$ **20.** $\frac{27}{8}$ ⬤ $\frac{14}{4}$

List in order from least to greatest.

21. $\frac{1}{2}, \frac{1}{3}, \frac{1}{7}$ **22.** $\frac{3}{9}, \frac{2}{9}, \frac{5}{9}$ **23.** $\frac{8}{11}, 2, \frac{1}{3}$

24. $2\frac{3}{4}, \frac{2}{3}, 1\frac{1}{2}$ **25.** $3\frac{2}{5}, 3\frac{1}{4}, 3\frac{3}{10}$ **26.** $5\frac{13}{16}, 5\frac{3}{4}, 5\frac{5}{8}$

For each, find the value of *n* so that the fractions and mixed numbers are arranged in order from least to greatest.

27. $\frac{2}{3}, \frac{n}{4}, \frac{5}{6}$ **28.** $\frac{3}{8}, \frac{n}{16}, \frac{1}{2}$ **29.** $\frac{1}{2}, \frac{n}{5}, \frac{7}{10}$

30. $1\frac{3}{8}, 1\frac{n}{8}, 1\frac{5}{8}$ **31.** $1\frac{2}{5}, 1\frac{n}{20}, 1\frac{1}{2}$ **32.** $3\frac{2}{7}, 3\frac{n}{42}, 3\frac{1}{3}$

Think and Apply

33. Mr. Young spends $\frac{2}{5}$ of his workday designing. He spends $\frac{3}{10}$ of the day supervising other artists. On which task does he spend more time?

34. Can someone $64\frac{5}{8}$ in. tall walk through a $64\frac{9}{16}$ in. doorway without bending down? Explain.

35. Name a fraction greater than $\frac{1}{7}$ but less than $\frac{2}{7}$.

36. How many fractions are greater than $\frac{1}{2}$ but less than $\frac{3}{4}$? Explain.

Test Taker

Understanding fractions can help you become a more successful test taker. For each question, eliminate some of the incorrect choices. Then choose the correct fraction. Explain your reasoning.

37. Which fraction is greater than $\frac{3}{5}$?

   a. $\frac{1}{5}$ **b.** $\frac{3}{10}$ **c.** $\frac{7}{10}$ **d.** $\frac{1}{10}$

38. Which fraction is less than $\frac{5}{9}$?

   a. $\frac{7}{9}$ **b.** $\frac{2}{3}$ **c.** $\frac{5}{18}$ **d.** $\frac{8}{9}$

39. Which fraction is equal to $\frac{3}{4}$?

   a. $\frac{3}{8}$ **b.** $\frac{2}{4}$ **c.** $\frac{3}{7}$ **d.** $\frac{12}{16}$

Look back at exercises **21–26.** Did you find the LCD to order each group? Why or why not? If you did not use the LCD, explain the process you used.

SUMMING UP

Activity

Exploring Fractions and Decimals

Some fractions have denominators that are powers of 10. You can use place value to write these fractions as decimals.

$$\frac{7}{10} = 0.7 \leftarrow \textbf{seven tenths}$$

$$\frac{30}{100} = 0.30$$

$$\frac{12}{1,000} = 0.012$$

Other fractions also have decimal equivalents.

To find the decimal equivalent for $\frac{1}{4}$, you can write an equivalent fraction with a denominator that is a power of 10.

$$\frac{1}{4} = \frac{1 \times 25}{4 \times 25} = \frac{25}{100} = 0.25$$

Another way to find a decimal equivalent is to draw a picture.

$$\frac{1}{4} = \frac{25}{100} = 0.25$$

You can use a number line.

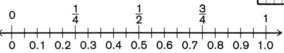

You can use a calculator to divide the numerator by the denominator.

$$\frac{1}{4} = 1 \div 4 = \boxed{0.25}$$

Can you write a decimal equivalent for any fraction?

Working together

A. Use any of the methods shown above to find the decimal equivalent for each of these fractions.

$$\frac{2}{5}, \quad \frac{3}{10}, \quad \frac{3}{8}, \quad \frac{3}{4}, \quad \frac{3}{20}, \quad \frac{5}{8}$$

B. Keep a chart to record the fractions and their decimal equivalents.

Sharing Your Results

1. Which decimal equivalents were the easiest to find? What method did you use to find them?

2. Did you draw a picture to find any of the decimal equivalents? If so, which one(s)?

3. For which fraction(s) was a calculator the best tool?

4. Can each fraction above be written as an equivalent fraction with a denominator that is a power of ten?

Extending the Activity

Work with a partner. Try to use the methods shown to write $\frac{1}{3}$ as a decimal.

5. On the number line, you can see that $\frac{1}{2}$ and 0.5 are equivalent and that $\frac{1}{4}$ and 0.25 are equivalent. Can you exactly place $\frac{1}{3}$ on the number line? Explain.

6. Can you find an equivalent fraction with a denominator that is a power of 10?

7. Use paper and pencil or a calculator to write $\frac{1}{3}$ as a decimal.

$$\frac{1}{3} = 3\overline{)\begin{array}{l} 0.33 \\ 1.00 \\ \underline{9} \\ 10 \\ \underline{9} \\ 1 \end{array}}$$

$$\frac{1}{3} = \boxed{0.3333333}$$

How is this decimal different from the decimals you found on page 178?

If you continue dividing, will the remainder ever be 0?

There is no exact decimal equivalent for $\frac{1}{3}$.

$\frac{1}{3} = 0.333...$ 0.33 is an approximation for $\frac{1}{3}$.

8. Write each of these fractions as decimals. Record the fractions and their approximations on your chart. $\frac{1}{9}$, $\frac{5}{6}$, $\frac{3}{11}$

Summing Up

9. Which method can you always use to write any fraction as a decimal?

10. Every fraction has either a decimal equivalent or a decimal approximation. Given any fraction, describe how you can tell if it has a decimal equivalent or a decimal approximation to represent it.

11. In the last lesson you learned to compare fractions. What is another method you can now use to compare fractions? Which is easier to compare—$\frac{3}{5}$ and $\frac{5}{8}$ or their decimal equivalents 0.6 and 0.625?

12. Knowing some of the equivalents is helpful. **Look back** at the charts you made. List the easy fraction-decimal equivalents and learn them.

How much is $\frac{1}{4}$ of a dollar?

How much is $\frac{1}{3}$ of a dollar?

Relating Fractions and Decimals

You can use paper and pencil or a calculator to find a decimal equivalent or approximation for any fraction.

$$\frac{2}{5} = 5)\overline{2.0}$$ with 0.4 above, $-2\,0$, remainder 0

$$\frac{2}{5} = \boxed{0.4}$$

0.4 is a **terminating decimal.**
When you divide, the remainder is 0.

$$\frac{5}{6} = 6)\overline{5.000}$$ with $0.833\ldots$ above, $-4\,8$, 20, -18, 20, -18, 20

$$\frac{5}{6} = \boxed{0.8333333}$$

0.833 . . . is a **repeating decimal.**
The remainder is never 0.
In a repeating decimal, one digit or group of digits repeats in a pattern.

$$\frac{5}{6} = 0.833 \ldots \text{ or } 0.8\overline{3}.$$ ← A bar is used to show the digit or digits that repeat.

You can use place value to write a decimal as a fraction.

a. $0.5 = \frac{5}{10} = \frac{1}{2}$

b. $3.75 = 3\frac{75}{100}$ **Think** $\frac{75}{100} = \frac{75 \div 25}{100 \div 25} = \frac{3}{4}$

  $3.75 = 3\frac{3}{4}$

c. $1.375 = 1\frac{375}{1,000}$ **Think** $\frac{375 \div 125}{1,000 \div 125} = \frac{3}{8}$

  $1.375 = 1\frac{3}{8}$

d. $0.025 = \frac{25}{1,000}$ **Think** $\frac{25}{1,000} = \frac{25 \div 25}{1,000 \div 25} = \frac{1}{40}$

  $0.025 = \frac{1}{40}$

Check Your Understanding

Write each fraction or mixed number as a decimal.
Write each decimal as a fraction or mixed number
in lowest terms.

1. $\frac{5}{8}$ **2.** $9\frac{1}{2}$ **3.** 0.48   **4.** 3.175   **5.** $\frac{8}{2}$ **6.** $1\frac{7}{8}$

Share Your Ideas   Explain how you would compare $\frac{7}{8}$ with 0.9.

Write each fraction or mixed number as a decimal. Write each decimal as a fraction or mixed number in lowest terms.

7. $\frac{4}{9}$ 8. 0.32   9. 5.025   10. $\frac{7}{10}$

11. 8.75   12. $\frac{5}{6}$ 13. $\frac{3}{8}$ 14. 0.08

15. $\frac{23}{100}$ 16. 0.125   17. 0.625   18. $3\frac{3}{5}$

19. 5.875   20. $\frac{3}{50}$ 21. $2\frac{5}{8}$ 22. 1.15

Compare. Use <, >, or = for each ●.

23. 1.2 ● $1\frac{1}{5}$ 24. $\frac{1}{4}$ ● 0.25   25. $1\frac{3}{4}$ ● 1.7

26. $\frac{5}{8}$ ● 0.55   27. $1\frac{5}{9}$ ● $1.\overline{5}$ 28. 0.6 ● $\frac{3}{5}$

List in order from least to greatest.

29. $0.\overline{5}$, 0.5, $0.0\overline{5}$ 30. 1.34, 1.3, $1.\overline{3}$ 31. 0.8, $0.\overline{8}$, $0.8\overline{1}$

Use a calculator to write each fraction as a decimal.

32. $\frac{1}{9}$ 33. $\frac{2}{9}$ 34. $\frac{3}{9}$ 35. $\frac{1}{99}$ 36. $\frac{2}{99}$

37. $\frac{3}{99}$ 38. $\frac{1}{11}$ 39. $\frac{2}{11}$ 40. $\frac{3}{11}$ 41. $\frac{4}{11}$

Look for patterns in the decimals above. Use the patterns to write a decimal for each fraction.

42. $\frac{5}{9}$ 43. $\frac{8}{9}$ 44. $\frac{7}{99}$ 45. $\frac{5}{11}$ 46. $\frac{7}{11}$

Think and Apply

47. The price of one share of a stock is shown below. How much did one share cost at the close? What was the high for the day? Write each answer as a decimal.

DATA
48. Look at the stock reports in a newspaper to find the quotations for five stocks. How did the closing price change since yesterday? Use the data you collect to determine yesterday's closing price for each stock.

STOCK	HIGH	LOW	CLOSE	CHANGE
MKJ	$64\frac{3}{8}$	$63\frac{3}{4}$	$64\frac{1}{4}$	$+1\frac{1}{8}$

Look back at **32–41**. Describe the pattern found for fractions whose denominators are 3, 9, and 11 when the fractions are converted to decimals.

SUMMING UP

Mixed Review

1. 18 × 35

2. 1,505 ÷ 35

3. 3.4 × 6.2

4. 95 ÷ 0.05

5. 127 ÷ 0.127

6. 7 + 8 × 5

7. (7 + 8) × 5

8. 7 ÷ (8 × 5)

Find n.

9. 7n = 21

10. n − 8 = 17

11. n ÷ 9 = 8

12. 8 + n = 14

Solve.

13. What are the prime factors of 42?

14. What is the GCF of 18 and 32?

15. What is the LCM of 8 and 12?

Which is greater?

16. 5^2 or 2^5

17. 3^3 or 2^4

18. 2^{10} or 10^2

Midchapter Review

Find each value of _n_. pages 172–173

1. $\dfrac{7}{2} = n\dfrac{1}{2}$

2. $3\dfrac{1}{3} = \dfrac{n}{3}$

3. $\dfrac{16}{5} = 3\dfrac{n}{5}$

4. $\dfrac{3}{4} = \dfrac{n}{100}$

5. $\dfrac{7}{8} = \dfrac{49}{n}$

6. $2\dfrac{6}{8} = 2\dfrac{3}{n}$

7. $\dfrac{4}{3} = \dfrac{n}{6}$

8. $7\dfrac{1}{4} = \dfrac{29}{n}$

Write each fraction in lowest terms. pages 174–175

9. $\dfrac{125}{175}$

10. $\dfrac{72}{81}$

11. $\dfrac{24}{36}$

12. $\dfrac{6}{9}$

13. $\dfrac{6}{8}$

14. $\dfrac{27}{36}$

15. $\dfrac{180}{210}$

16. $\dfrac{200}{600}$

17. $\dfrac{4}{10}$

18. $\dfrac{9}{18}$

Compare. Use >, <, or = for each ●. pages 176–177, 180–181

19. $\dfrac{3}{8}$ ● $\dfrac{2}{7}$

20. $\dfrac{13}{50}$ ● 0.25

21. $\dfrac{5}{9}$ ● 0.55

22. $\dfrac{1}{8}$ ● $\dfrac{1}{9}$

23. $\dfrac{21}{30}$ ● $\dfrac{7}{10}$

24. $\dfrac{6}{8}$ ● 0.75

25. $\dfrac{5}{8}$ ● 0.625

26. $\dfrac{4}{7}$ ● $\dfrac{5}{6}$

Write each fraction or mixed number as a decimal. Write each decimal as a fraction or mixed number in lowest terms. pages 178–181

27. $2\dfrac{1}{4}$

28. $\dfrac{3}{8}$

29. 0.48

30. $3.\overline{3}$

31. $6\dfrac{5}{6}$

32. 8.325

33. $\dfrac{7}{9}$

34. $1\dfrac{3}{4}$

35. $5\dfrac{7}{8}$

36. 9.8

Trace the number line. Label each point. pages 174–181

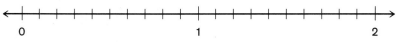

37. _A:_ $1\dfrac{7}{10}$

38. _B:_ 1.5

39. _C:_ $\dfrac{4}{5}$

40. _D:_ $1\dfrac{1}{5}$

Complete.

41. A fraction is in _____ when the GCF of the numerator and denominator is 1.

42. 0.6, 0.375, and 1.6 are examples of _____ decimals.

43. $0.\overline{3}$, 0.171717 . . ., and $0.\overline{2}$ are examples of _____ decimals.

Words to Know
mixed number lowest terms terminating repeating

Solve. Express each answer as a fraction in lowest terms and as a decimal.

44. The average number of working days in a month is 20. What part of the entire month of June is this?

45. Robert's dad travels $1\dfrac{1}{2}$ hours each way to work. What part of his day is spent commuting to and from work?

Exploring Problem Solving

How Can You Subdivide the Lot?

Four people offered to buy a plot of land if
it could be divided into four equal parts.
The plot has the shape shown in the diagram.

Thinking Critically

Try to divide the land into four equal parts.
Make diagrams to help you solve the
problem. Compare your diagrams with
those of your classmates.

Analyzing and Making Decisions

1. **What if** only three people wanted to buy
   the land? How can you divide it equally
   among them?

2. Look at how you divided the land
   among three people. Can you take a part
   from each of them to make the fourth
   piece of land? Draw a diagram to show
   how to do it.

3. Show how you would divide the land
   equally among four people. Draw
   diagrams to show two different
   ways to do it?

Look Back **What if** you wanted to divide
the land among six people? Draw a diagram
to show how it can be done. Then show
how it can be divided among eight people.

183

Problem Solving Strategies

Guess and Test

When Mabel and Jerome arrived at the restaurant they found that they had lost the lunch order. They knew that each of the 18 people had ordered either a hamburger or a slice of pizza. Pizza costs $2.00 a slice and a hamburger costs $1.70. Mabel and Jerome had collected exact amounts from everyone, totaling $33.90. What was the order?

Some problems can be solved by guessing. However, after you make a guess, you must test it. If that guess is not correct, then guess again.

Solving the Problem

 Use a calculator where appropriate.

Think   What is the question?

Explore   What are the facts?

Guess the number of pizza slices and hamburgers that they should order. Test your guess. Did you find the correct amount of money? If not, you will need to make a new guess.

What if your total was too high? Should you increase the number of pizza slices or hamburgers? If you record your work in a table, you can see how close your guess is to the correct answer.

Solve   What was the order?

Look Back   Was your first guess helpful in solving the problem? Was your second guess better than your first guess? Explain what you did and why you did it.

Share Your Ideas

1. **What if** Mabel and Jerome had collected $39.00 from 21 people? How many hamburgers and pizza slices should they have ordered?

Practice

 Solve. Use a calculator where appropriate.

2. Julia works for Allied Parcel Delivery Service. She delivered half as many packages on Tuesday as she did on Monday. Her log showed a total of 144 packages delivered during the two days. How many packages did Julia deliver each day?

3. Richard and Sandy both work in an appliance store. During a heat wave they sold a total of 16 air conditioners. Richard sold one-third as many as Sandy. How many air conditioners did each sell?

4. Leon has 11 coins worth a total of $1.19. Karen asked him for change for $1, but Leon could not give her change. What coins does Leon have?

5. Mrs. Choo and Mr. Young work in the research and development department of Pear Electronics. Mrs. Choo has worked there twice as long as Mr. Young. Four years ago she had worked there three times as long as Mr. Young. How long has each of them worked at Pear Electronics?

Mixed Strategy Review

6. Jamie was editing a new book when she noticed that the page numbers on two facing pages had been switched. The product of the two numbers was 812. What were the page numbers?

7. A mechanic, a neurologist, and an engineer live on the same block in three houses next to one another. The neurologist lives in the blue house. The red house is immediately to the right of the green house. The engineer formerly lived in the red house. The mechanic lives next door to the neurologist. Which house is in the middle?

8. Eric earns money by doing odd jobs for his neighbors. He made $\frac{1}{2}$ of his money working for Mr. Jones, $\frac{1}{3}$ of his money for Ms. Hochever, and $\frac{1}{8}$ of his money at Mr. Stein's. Are these the only places he worked? Explain.

THINK
EXPLORE
SOLVE
LOOK BACK

Create
Your Own

Write a problem in which a partner must guess and test to find the answer.

What is the decimal equivalent of all fractions equal to $\frac{1}{2}$?

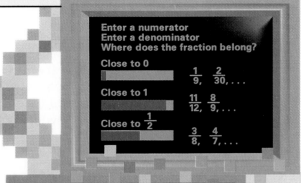

Enter a numerator
Enter a denominator
Where does the fraction belong?

Close to 0
$\frac{1}{9}$, $\frac{2}{30}$, ...

Close to 1
$\frac{11}{12}$, $\frac{8}{9}$, ...

Close to $\frac{1}{2}$
$\frac{3}{8}$, $\frac{4}{7}$, ...

Estimating with Fractions

Alexina's company creates computer software for use in classrooms. This screen of Fraction Frenzy displays a fraction and asks students to decide if the fraction is closer to 0, $\frac{1}{2}$, or 1.

How can you tell if a fraction is closer to 0, $\frac{1}{2}$, or 1?

Another screen classifies fractions.

Study the screen. Write a rule that tells how the numerators and denominators relate for fractions equal to $\frac{1}{2}$; for fractions less than $\frac{1}{2}$; for fractions greater than $\frac{1}{2}$.

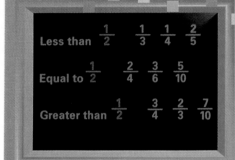

Less than $\frac{1}{2}$ $\frac{1}{3}$ $\frac{1}{4}$ $\frac{2}{5}$

Equal to $\frac{1}{2}$ $\frac{2}{4}$ $\frac{3}{6}$ $\frac{5}{10}$

Greater than $\frac{1}{2}$ $\frac{3}{4}$ $\frac{2}{3}$ $\frac{7}{10}$

You can use these ideas to estimate sums and differences.

a. $\frac{1}{2} + \frac{3}{8}$ **Think** $\frac{3}{8}$ is close to $\frac{1}{2}$.

$\frac{1}{2} + \frac{3}{8}$ is about 1.

b. $4\frac{3}{7} + \frac{1}{9}$ **Think** $\frac{3}{7}$ is close to $\frac{1}{2}$.

$\frac{1}{9}$ is close to 0.

$4\frac{3}{7} + \frac{1}{9}$ is about $4\frac{1}{2}$.

c. $5\frac{1}{8} + 4\frac{4}{5}$ **Think** $5\frac{1}{8}$ is close to 5.

$4\frac{4}{5}$ is close to 5.

The sum is about 10.

d. $\frac{3}{4} + \frac{2}{3}$ **Think** $\frac{3}{4}$ is greater than $\frac{1}{2}$.

$\frac{2}{3}$ is greater than $\frac{1}{2}$.

$\frac{3}{4} + \frac{2}{3}$ is greater than 1.

Check Your Understanding

Estimate each sum or difference.

1. $\frac{6}{7} + \frac{1}{2}$ **2.** $\frac{9}{10} - \frac{3}{8}$ **3.** $8\frac{1}{4} + 5\frac{1}{5}$ **4.** $7\frac{3}{4} - \frac{9}{10}$

5. $17\frac{1}{4} + 9\frac{2}{3}$ **6.** $6\frac{1}{2} - \frac{2}{9}$ **7.** $2\frac{11}{12} + \frac{3}{7}$ **8.** $6\frac{4}{5} - \frac{1}{2}$

Share Your Ideas   Describe some methods you can use to tell if a fraction is closer to 0, $\frac{1}{2}$, or 1.

Tell whether each fraction is less than, equal to, or greater than $\frac{1}{2}$.

9. $\frac{3}{5}$ 10. $\frac{4}{7}$ 11. $\frac{5}{10}$ 12. $\frac{3}{7}$ 13. $\frac{2}{5}$ 14. $\frac{4}{9}$

15. $\frac{3}{8}$ 16. $\frac{10}{19}$ 17. $\frac{1}{3}$ 18. $\frac{7}{8}$ 19. $\frac{4}{6}$ 20. $\frac{6}{12}$

Estimate each sum or difference.

21. $\begin{array}{r} \frac{3}{7} \\ + \frac{8}{10} \\ \hline \end{array}$ 22. $\begin{array}{r} 4\frac{3}{4} \\ + 5\frac{1}{5} \\ \hline \end{array}$ 23. $\begin{array}{r} 7\frac{2}{3} \\ - 2\frac{3}{4} \\ \hline \end{array}$ 24. $\begin{array}{r} 8\frac{7}{9} \\ - 3\frac{7}{8} \\ \hline \end{array}$ 25. $\begin{array}{r} 5\frac{8}{10} \\ - 3\frac{7}{8} \\ \hline \end{array}$

26. $\begin{array}{r} 18\frac{2}{5} \\ + 9\frac{5}{8} \\ \hline \end{array}$ 27. $\begin{array}{r} \frac{2}{9} \\ + \frac{2}{3} \\ \hline \end{array}$ 28. $\begin{array}{r} 22\frac{5}{8} \\ - 5\frac{5}{8} \\ \hline \end{array}$ 29. $\begin{array}{r} 16\frac{3}{5} \\ - \frac{7}{8} \\ \hline \end{array}$ 30. $\begin{array}{r} 25\frac{4}{5} \\ - 20\frac{2}{5} \\ \hline \end{array}$

31. $2\frac{3}{5} - 1\frac{1}{10}$ 32. $6\frac{1}{4} - 2\frac{7}{8}$ 33. $3 + 5\frac{1}{7}$ 34. $8\frac{1}{3} + 5$

Estimate to choose the correct answer.

35. $5\frac{1}{8} + 2\frac{1}{3}$

a. $8\frac{11}{4}$

b. $9\frac{11}{24}$

c. $7\frac{11}{24}$

36. $5\frac{3}{4} - 3\frac{5}{8}$

a. $2\frac{1}{8}$

b. $3\frac{1}{8}$

c. 2

37. $12\frac{1}{2} - 2\frac{1}{10}$

a. 10

b. $10\frac{2}{5}$

c. $11\frac{1}{10}$

38. $7\frac{5}{6} + 2\frac{1}{6}$

a. 10

b. 9

c. $9\frac{5}{6}$

Think and Apply

39. Try playing this fraction game with a partner.

- Take turns rolling four number cubes.

- Use the numbers on the cubes to form two fractions whose sum or difference is close to $\frac{1}{2}$.

- After both partners have a turn, compare answers. The player whose answer is closer to $\frac{1}{2}$ wins.

  If you cannot tell by estimation or mental math which answer is closer to $\frac{1}{2}$, use a calculator. Convert each fraction to a decimal. Then find the sum or difference. Round each decimal to the nearest thousandth when necessary.

Describe a situation where you might want to estimate with fractions. Explain why. Use an example.

SUMMING UP

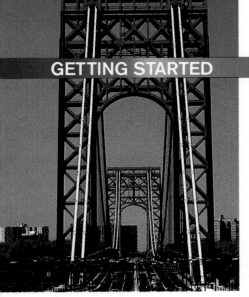

Without computing, tell which difference is closer to $\frac{1}{2}$ and which is closer to 0. Explain your thinking.

$$\frac{5}{8} - \frac{1}{6} \qquad\qquad \frac{7}{8} - \frac{5}{6}$$

Adding and Subtracting Fractions

During his career as an engineer, Othmar Ammann helped design two of the world's largest suspension bridges. The George Washington Bridge has a main span of about $\frac{2}{3}$ mile. The Verrazano Bridge has a main span of about $\frac{4}{5}$ mile. How much longer is the main span of the Verrazano Bridge than that of the George Washington Bridge?

You can draw a number line to find $\frac{4}{5} - \frac{2}{3}$.

Explain why a number line showing fifteenths is used to show the difference.

Is the difference closer to 0, $\frac{1}{2}$, or 1?

What is the difference?

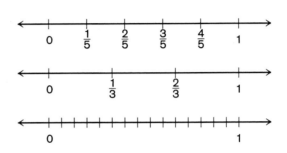

You can use the LCD to find the difference.

▶ To add or subtract fractions, first find equivalent fractions using the LCD. Then add or subtract. Write the answer in lowest terms.

$$\frac{4}{5} = \frac{4 \times 3}{5 \times 3} = \frac{12}{15} \qquad \frac{4}{5} = \frac{12}{15}$$

$$-\frac{2}{3} = \frac{2 \times 5}{3 \times 5} = \frac{10}{15} \qquad -\frac{2}{3} = \frac{10}{15}$$

$$\frac{2}{15}$$

How do you know that $\frac{2}{15}$ is in lowest terms?

The main span of the Verrazano-Narrows Bridge is about $\frac{2}{15}$ mile longer.

More Examples

a. $\frac{7}{8} + \frac{1}{4} + \frac{1}{2} =$ **Think** The LCD is 8.

$\frac{7}{8} + \frac{2}{8} + \frac{4}{8} = \frac{13}{8} = 1\frac{5}{8}$

b. $\frac{3}{5} - \frac{1}{2} =$ **Think** The LCD is 10.

$\frac{6}{10} - \frac{5}{10} = \frac{1}{10}$

Check Your Understanding

Add or subtract. Write each in lowest terms.

1. $\frac{5}{8} + \frac{1}{2}$ **2.** $\frac{2}{3} + \frac{3}{4}$ **3.** $\frac{5}{7} - \frac{1}{7}$ **4.** $\frac{1}{2} - \frac{3}{10}$ **5.** $\frac{1}{2} - \frac{4}{9}$ **6.** $\frac{7}{10} + \frac{4}{5}$

Share Your Ideas One way to find a common denominator is to multiply the two denominators. Solve this problem twice—once using this method and then using the LCD. Which way is more efficient? Explain why.

$$\frac{5}{6} + \frac{3}{8}$$

Without computing, tell if each sum or difference is closer to 0, $\frac{1}{2}$, or 1.

7. $\frac{2}{3} + \frac{1}{6}$

8. $\frac{1}{2} + \frac{5}{11}$

9. $\frac{1}{2} + \frac{1}{16}$

10. $\frac{1}{2} - \frac{5}{11}$

11. $\frac{9}{10} - \frac{1}{10}$

12. $\frac{9}{10} - \frac{8}{9}$

13. $\frac{3}{8} + \frac{3}{8}$

14. $1 - \frac{1}{12}$

Add or subtract. Write each sum or difference in lowest terms.

15. $\begin{array}{r} \frac{3}{4} \\ + \frac{3}{4} \\ \hline \end{array}$

16. $\begin{array}{r} \frac{7}{10} \\ + \frac{1}{5} \\ \hline \end{array}$

17. $\begin{array}{r} \frac{7}{12} \\ + \frac{1}{2} \\ \hline \end{array}$

18. $\begin{array}{r} \frac{4}{5} \\ + \frac{3}{4} \\ \hline \end{array}$

19. $\begin{array}{r} \frac{6}{7} \\ + \frac{1}{3} \\ \hline \end{array}$

20. $\begin{array}{r} \frac{5}{6} \\ + \frac{1}{3} \\ \hline \end{array}$

21. $\begin{array}{r} \frac{2}{3} \\ - \frac{1}{4} \\ \hline \end{array}$

22. $\begin{array}{r} \frac{7}{8} \\ - \frac{3}{8} \\ \hline \end{array}$

23. $\begin{array}{r} \frac{4}{5} \\ - \frac{2}{7} \\ \hline \end{array}$

24. $\begin{array}{r} \frac{4}{5} \\ - \frac{3}{10} \\ \hline \end{array}$

25. $\begin{array}{r} \frac{5}{6} \\ - \frac{1}{2} \\ \hline \end{array}$

26. $\begin{array}{r} \frac{2}{3} \\ - \frac{3}{8} \\ \hline \end{array}$

27. $\frac{7}{10} - \frac{3}{5}$

28. $\frac{5}{7} - \frac{1}{2}$

29. $\frac{3}{8} - \frac{1}{3}$

30. $\frac{5}{9} - \frac{1}{3}$

31. $\frac{2}{3} - \frac{1}{6}$

32. $\frac{3}{5} - \frac{1}{6}$

33. $\frac{6}{7} - \frac{3}{7}$

34. $\frac{3}{5} + \frac{2}{3}$

Solve.

35. What is the sum of $\frac{2}{9}$ and $\frac{1}{2}$?

36. What is the difference between $\frac{3}{4}$ and $\frac{2}{3}$?

37. What is the difference between $\frac{3}{7}$ and 0?

38. $\frac{3}{8}$ is how much less than $\frac{1}{2}$?

39. To get a sum of $1\frac{1}{8}$, what would you add to $\frac{3}{4}$?

40. To find a sum of $1\frac{3}{5}$, what would you add to $\frac{7}{8}$?

Think and Apply

To win at U-Know, partners trade cards one at a time until each player has a sum of 1.

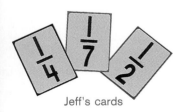

Jeff's cards

Chen's cards

41. What two cards must Jeff and Chen trade to win the game?

Explain how adding fractions is like adding measurements. For example, how is adding $1\frac{3}{4} + \frac{2}{3}$ like adding 15 in. + 3 ft?

SUMMING UP

How many cups are in 1 quart? in 2 quarts? in $2\frac{1}{2}$ quarts?

Adding Mixed Numbers

Everyone who tasted Ellen's homemade apple bread thought it was delicious. So Ellen decided to start a small business. Soon Ellen's Apple Bread was selling in five states. Look at the recipe. What if your electric mixer bowl has a $2\frac{1}{2}$ qt capacity. Can it hold the batter?

$2\frac{1}{2}$ qt = 10 c

Do you need to find the sum of all 9 ingredients? Explain.

Estimate first.

$3\frac{3}{4} + 3 + 1\frac{1}{3} + 1\frac{1}{2} \rightarrow 4 + 3 + 1 + 1\frac{1}{2} = 9\frac{1}{2}$

To find the sum, add $3\frac{3}{4} + 3 + 1\frac{1}{3} + 1\frac{1}{2}$.

▶ To add mixed numbers, first write equivalent fractions using the LCD. Add the fractions. Then add the whole numbers. Write the answer in lowest terms.

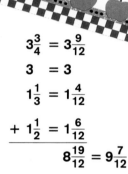

Ellen's Apple Bread

$3\frac{3}{4}$ c chopped apples
3 c flour
$1\frac{1}{3}$ c oil
$1\frac{1}{2}$ c sugar
2 eggs
2 tsp baking soda
1 tsp vanilla
$2\frac{3}{4}$ tsp cinnamon
$\frac{1}{2}$ tsp salt

Mix oil and sugar. Add flour. Combine ingredients in bowl of electric mixer. (over)

$$3\frac{3}{4} = 3\frac{9}{12}$$
$$3 \quad = 3$$
$$1\frac{1}{3} = 1\frac{4}{12}$$
$$+ \, 1\frac{1}{2} = 1\frac{6}{12}$$
$$\overline{\phantom{+ \, 1\frac{1}{2} =} \; 8\frac{19}{12} = 9\frac{7}{12}}$$

The recipe makes about $9\frac{7}{12}$ cups of batter. It will fit in a 10-cup bowl.

Check Your Understanding

Estimate. Then add. Write each sum in lowest terms.

1. $7\frac{2}{3}$
    $+ 5\frac{2}{3}$

2. $8\frac{2}{5}$
    $+ 5\frac{2}{3}$

3. 8
    $6\frac{1}{8}$
    $+ 5\frac{3}{4}$

4. $6\frac{3}{8}$
    $4\frac{1}{2}$
    $+ 5\frac{1}{8}$

5. $6\frac{5}{7}$
    $4\frac{1}{2}$
    $+ 7$

Share Your Ideas Look back at **1** and **2**. Which of the two problems required more steps? Explain why.

Estimate. Then add. Write each sum in lowest terms.

6. $8\frac{3}{4}$
  $+ 5\frac{1}{4}$

7. $9\frac{3}{10}$
  $+ 3\frac{2}{5}$

8. $9\frac{3}{10}$
  $+ 8\frac{1}{3}$

9. $5\frac{7}{10}$
  $+ 3$

10. $6\frac{4}{9}$
  $+ 5\frac{1}{3}$

11. $8\frac{3}{5}$
  $+ 7\frac{1}{2}$

12. $5\frac{8}{9}$
  $+ 5\frac{1}{3}$

13. $8\frac{9}{10}$
  $+ 9\frac{4}{5}$

14. $9\frac{1}{2}$
  $+ 5\frac{7}{8}$

15. $6\frac{3}{4}$
  $+ 7\frac{2}{3}$

16. $5\frac{3}{4}$
  $8\frac{2}{3}$
  $+ 7\frac{5}{8}$

17. $8\frac{1}{2}$
  $4\frac{3}{8}$
  $+ 6\frac{5}{6}$

18. $4\frac{7}{8}$
  $3\frac{5}{6}$
  $+ 8\frac{2}{3}$

19. $7\frac{2}{3}$
  $9\frac{5}{6}$
  $+ 6\frac{5}{9}$

20. $5\frac{2}{3}$
  $6\frac{1}{2}$
  $+ 3\frac{1}{7}$

21. $15\frac{1}{8} + 13\frac{3}{4} + 29\frac{1}{4}$

22. $23\frac{5}{7} + 4\frac{1}{2} + 11\frac{1}{2}$

23. $16\frac{3}{8} + 22\frac{3}{4} + 18\frac{1}{3}$

24. Find the sum of $8\frac{1}{2}$ and $7\frac{1}{3}$.

25. Find the sum of $9\frac{3}{5}$ and 6.

Without computing, choose the correct answer for each.

26. $2\frac{3}{4} + 5\frac{1}{2}$
  a. $7\frac{1}{4}$
  b. $8\frac{1}{4}$
  c. $7\frac{4}{6}$
  d. 8

27. $5\frac{3}{10} + 6\frac{1}{5}$
  a. $10\frac{1}{2}$
  b. $12\frac{1}{2}$
  c. $11\frac{1}{2}$
  d. $11\frac{4}{15}$

28. $6\frac{3}{7} + 2\frac{1}{3}$
  a. $8\frac{4}{10}$
  b. $8\frac{4}{7}$
  c. $9\frac{1}{3}$
  d. $8\frac{16}{21}$

29. $8\frac{3}{8} + 3\frac{5}{6}$
  a. $11\frac{5}{24}$
  b. $11\frac{8}{14}$
  c. $12\frac{5}{24}$
  d. $13\frac{5}{24}$

Think and Apply

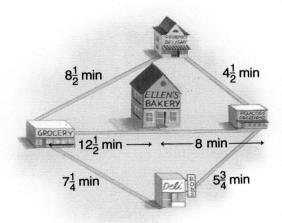

30. Dennis delivers Ellen's Natural Apple Bread from the bakery to the 4 locations on the map. The average time it takes to travel between stops is shown. Plan the route that takes the least time. How much traveling time is that?

31. **What if** the delivery truck holds only 150 loaves and each store orders 50 loaves? What is the shortest route if Dennis must return to the bakery to pick up more loaves?

Sue's punch bowl holds 6 qt. Can she serve apple punch made with $4\frac{1}{3}$ qt apple juice and $1\frac{3}{4}$ qt lemonade, or grape punch made with $4\frac{2}{3}$ qt grape juice and $1\frac{1}{4}$ qt lemonade?

SUMMING UP

If $1 = \frac{5}{5}$, then $2\frac{2}{5} = 1 + \frac{5}{5} + \frac{2}{5}$, or $1\frac{7}{5}$.
Write a similar statement for renaming $5\frac{7}{8}$ as $4\frac{15}{8}$.

Time	Reading
9:00 A.M.	0 in.
10:00 A.M.	$1\frac{3}{10}$ in.
11:00 A.M.	$3\frac{1}{2}$ in.
12:00 P.M.	$6\frac{1}{8}$ in.
1:00 P.M.	8 in.

Subtracting Mixed Numbers

During a severe tropical storm, meteorologists Dr. Issac Bar and Dr. Wendy Day took hourly readings. Between which two hours did the most rain fall?

Estimate the rainfall for each interval.

For which intervals do you need to find the exact difference? Explain why.

Subtract $3\frac{1}{2} - 1\frac{3}{10}$ to find how much rain fell between 10:00 A.M. and 11:00 A.M.

9:00 A.M.–10:00 A.M.
$1\frac{3}{10} - 0 = 1\frac{3}{10}$

10:00 A.M.–11:00 A.M.
$3\frac{1}{2} - 1\frac{3}{10} \rightarrow 3\frac{1}{2} - 1 = 2\frac{1}{2}$

11:00 A.M.–12:00 noon
$6\frac{1}{8} - 3\frac{1}{2} \rightarrow 6 - 3\frac{1}{2} = 2\frac{1}{2}$

12:00 noon–1:00 P.M.
$8 - 6\frac{1}{8} \rightarrow 8 - 6 = 2$

▶ To subtract mixed numbers, first write equivalent fractions using the LCD. Subtract the fractions. Then subtract the whole numbers.

$$3\frac{1}{2} = 3\frac{5}{10}$$
$$- 1\frac{3}{10} = 1\frac{3}{10}$$
$$\overline{\quad 2\frac{2}{10} = 2\frac{1}{5}}$$

Between 10:00 A.M. and 11:00 A.M. $2\frac{1}{5}$ in. of rain fell.

Subtract $6\frac{1}{8} - 3\frac{1}{2}$ to find how much rain fell between 11:00 A.M. and 12:00 noon.

$$6\frac{1}{8} = 6\frac{1}{8} = 5\frac{9}{8}$$

Rename if you cannot subtract.

$$- 3\frac{1}{2} = 3\frac{4}{8} = 3\frac{4}{8}$$
$$\overline{\quad\quad\quad 2\frac{5}{8}}$$

Think $6\frac{1}{8} = 5\frac{8}{8} + \frac{1}{8}$

Between 11:00 A.M. and 12:00 noon $2\frac{5}{8}$ in. of rain fell.

Compare $2\frac{1}{5}$ and $2\frac{5}{8}$.

$2\frac{5}{8} > 2\frac{1}{5}$, so the most rain fell between 11:00 A.M. and 12:00 noon.

Check Your Understanding

Estimate. Then subtract. Write each difference in lowest terms.

1. $8\frac{3}{5}$
$- 5\frac{4}{5}$

2. $9\frac{1}{2}$
$- 5\frac{3}{8}$

3. $15\frac{8}{9}$
$- 6\frac{5}{9}$

4. $7\frac{3}{8}$
$- 5\frac{3}{4}$

5. 12
$- 4\frac{2}{3}$

Share Your Ideas Look back at **5**. Explain your method. How did you rename 12?

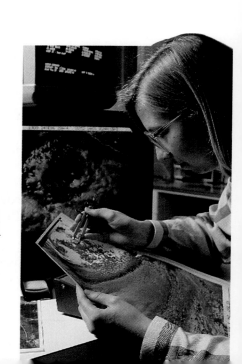

Estimate. Then subtract. Write each answer in lowest terms.

6. $5\frac{1}{4}$
   $-\ 3\frac{1}{10}$

7. $8\frac{2}{5}$
   $-\ 4\frac{1}{3}$

8. $7\frac{3}{8}$
   $-\ 2\frac{1}{4}$

9. $15\frac{5}{6}$
   $-\ 5\frac{2}{3}$

10. $11\frac{4}{9}$
    $-\ 5\frac{1}{6}$

11. $5\frac{3}{8}$
    $-\ 2\frac{5}{8}$

12. $8\frac{5}{9}$
    $-\ 2\frac{8}{9}$

13. $5\frac{2}{5}$
    $-\ \frac{4}{5}$

14. 19
    $-\ 5\frac{3}{10}$

15. 22
    $-\ 11\frac{6}{7}$

16. $8\frac{2}{5}$
    $-\ 5\frac{3}{4}$

17. $7\frac{5}{9}$
    $-\ 2\frac{2}{3}$

18. $7\frac{2}{3}$
    $-\ 3\frac{4}{5}$

19. $5\frac{1}{10}$
    $-\ \frac{3}{4}$

20. $7\frac{1}{6}$
    $-\ \frac{2}{3}$

21. $8\frac{3}{5}$
    $-\ 1\frac{3}{10}$

22. $5\frac{5}{8}$
    $-\ 2\frac{7}{8}$

23. $9\frac{2}{5}$
    $-\ 4\frac{2}{3}$

24. 15
    $-\ 7\frac{5}{8}$

25. $19\frac{2}{3}$
    $-\ 8\frac{8}{9}$

Follow the rule to find each missing number.

Rule: Subtract $\frac{2}{3}$ from the input.

	Input	Output
26.	$6\frac{1}{4}$	
27.	$\frac{7}{8}$	
28.	$5\frac{2}{3}$	

Rule: Subtract $6\frac{1}{2}$ from the input.

	Input	Output
29.	8	
30.	$12\frac{1}{4}$	
31.	$10\frac{3}{8}$	

Rule: Add $2\frac{1}{4}$ to the input.

	Input	Output
32.	11	
33.	$2\frac{1}{4}$	
34.	$3\frac{5}{6}$	

Think and Apply

Use the chart to answer each question.

35. How much more rain falls in Mobile than in Las Vegas? How much more rain falls in Houston than in Phoenix?

36. Which city had the greatest average rainfall? About how much more rain would have to fall in Houston for it to equal the average of that city?

37. **What if** the weather conditions of the U.S. changed and the average rainfall in Las Vegas increased by $20\frac{1}{2}$ in. while the average in New York decreased by $15\frac{1}{2}$ in. Which city would have more rain? How much more?

AVERAGE ANNUAL RAINFALL	
City	Rainfall (Inches)
Mobile, AL	$64\frac{2}{3}$
Phoenix, AZ	$7\frac{1}{10}$
Atlanta, GA	$48\frac{3}{5}$
Chicago, IL	$33\frac{1}{3}$
New York, NY	$42\frac{4}{5}$
Las Vegas, NV	$4\frac{2}{10}$
Houston, TX	$44\frac{3}{4}$

Complete the chain.

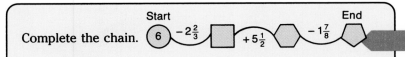

Start
6 — $-2\frac{2}{3}$ — ☐ — $+5\frac{1}{2}$ — ⬡ — $-1\frac{7}{8}$ — ⬠
End

Nina said she spent $\frac{1}{3}$ of the day sleeping, $\frac{1}{4}$ of the day in school, and $\frac{1}{2}$ of the day on other activities. Is this possible?

Adding and Subtracting Fractions and Mixed Numbers

Dr. Cartwright spends about $\frac{1}{4}$ of his workday attending to dogs, $\frac{1}{3}$ of his day with cats, and $\frac{1}{6}$ of his day with birds. What part of his workday does he spend on other matters?

Two steps are needed to solve the problem.

Add $\frac{1}{4} + \frac{1}{3} + \frac{1}{6}$. Subtract the total from 1.

$$\begin{aligned} \frac{1}{4} &= \frac{3}{12} \\ \frac{1}{3} &= \frac{4}{12} \\ + \frac{1}{6} &= \frac{2}{12} \\ \hline \frac{9}{12} &= \frac{3}{4} \end{aligned}$$

$$\begin{aligned} 1 &= \frac{4}{4} \\ - \frac{3}{4} &= \frac{3}{4} \\ \hline & \frac{1}{4} \end{aligned}$$

Explain the two steps needed to solve the problem.

Explain why the total is subtracted from 1.

Dr. Cartwright spends $\frac{1}{4}$ of his workday on other matters.

More Examples

a.
$$\begin{aligned} 5\frac{4}{5} &= 5\frac{8}{10} \\ -2\frac{7}{10} &= 2\frac{7}{10} \\ \hline & 3\frac{1}{10} \end{aligned}$$

b.
$$\begin{aligned} 9\frac{1}{5} &= 9\frac{3}{15} = 8\frac{18}{15} \\ -4\frac{1}{3} &= 4\frac{5}{15} = 4\frac{5}{15} \\ \hline & \qquad\qquad 4\frac{13}{15} \end{aligned}$$

Check Your Understanding

Add or subtract. Write each answer in lowest terms.

1. $\begin{aligned} \frac{5}{8} \\ + \frac{1}{3} \end{aligned}$

2. $\begin{aligned} \frac{7}{9} \\ - \frac{2}{3} \end{aligned}$

3. $\begin{aligned} 4\frac{2}{9} \\ - 1\frac{2}{3} \end{aligned}$

4. $\begin{aligned} 6\frac{1}{10} \\ - 5\frac{3}{4} \end{aligned}$

5. $\begin{aligned} 12\frac{1}{2} \\ 5\frac{5}{6} \\ + 2\frac{5}{9} \end{aligned}$

Share Your Ideas Look back at examples **a** and **b**. Explain how they are alike and how they are different.

Practice

Add or subtract. Write the answers in simplest form.

6.
$$\frac{5}{6}$$
$$\frac{1}{4}$$
$$+\frac{1}{2}$$

7.
$$8\frac{1}{5}$$
$$3\frac{2}{3}$$
$$+5\frac{4}{5}$$

8.
$$9\frac{3}{8}$$
$$6\frac{3}{4}$$
$$+8\frac{1}{3}$$

9. $9\frac{3}{5} - 5\frac{5}{6}$

10. $4\frac{2}{3} - 1\frac{3}{8}$

11. $\frac{3}{7} - \frac{1}{3}$

Evaluate each expression if $a = 3\frac{3}{4}$, $b = \frac{2}{3}$, and $c = 4\frac{5}{6}$.

12. $a + b$

13. $c - (a + b)$

14. $c - a$

15. $8 - c$

Use mental math, paper and pencil, or a calculator for each.

16. If $5\frac{1}{2}$ is added to a number, the sum is 10. What is the number?

17. If 4 is subtracted from a number, the difference is $4\frac{1}{2}$. What is the number?

18. If $5\frac{1}{4} + 5\frac{1}{4}$ is added to a number, the sum is $11\frac{1}{2}$. What is the number?

19. If $\frac{3}{4}$ is subtracted from a number, the difference is $\frac{3}{4}$. What is the number?

Think and Apply

20. In February, Rita's dog weighed $4\frac{3}{8}$ lb. In September it weighed $5\frac{3}{4}$ lb. How much weight did it gain?

21. **What if** Rita's dog gains another $1\frac{1}{2}$ lb? How much will it weigh?

22. In May, José's dog weighed $15\frac{7}{8}$ lb. It gained $1\frac{3}{4}$ lb in June. Pedro's dog weighed $16\frac{1}{4}$ lb in May and gained $1\frac{5}{8}$ lb in June. Whose dog weighed more in June? How much more?

Find the missing numbers in each sequence.
$\frac{1}{4}$, $\frac{3}{4}$, $1\frac{1}{4}$, ☐, ☐ $8\frac{1}{2}$, 7, $5\frac{1}{2}$, ☐, ☐

1. $48.521 + 9.308$

2. $6.005 - 4.12$

3. 5.7×4.3

4. $8.1 \div 0.9$

Find n.

5. $3n = 18$

6. $5 + n = 20$

Write each, using exponents.

7. $8 \times 8 \times 8$

8. $9 \times 9 \times 9 \times 9$

Evaluate each expression.

9. $8 \times (5 + 4)$

10. $8 \times 5 + 4$

11. $8 + 5 \times 4$

12. $(8 + 5) \times 4$

Solve.

13. What is the LCM of 2, 8, and 9?

14. What is the GCF of 16, 24, 28?

15. Write a prime number that is greater than 30 and less than 35.

16. Write a prime number that is greater than 50 and less than 55.

SUMMING UP

195

> Explain how to find *n* in each equation.
> **a.** $n + 9 = 17$ **b.** $n - 7 = 12$

Solving Fraction Equations

Scott works a maximum of 12 hours a week. This week he has already worked $7\frac{1}{2}$ hours. How many more hours can he work this week?

You can write an equation to solve the problem.

Let *n* be the number of hours he has left to work.

Then $n + 7\frac{1}{2} = 12$.

Solve equations with fractions and mixed numbers the same way you solve equations with whole numbers.

$$n + 7\frac{1}{2} = 12 \qquad \text{What is the inverse of adding } 7\frac{1}{2}?$$

$$n + 7\frac{1}{2} - 7\frac{1}{2} = 12 - 7\frac{1}{2} \qquad \text{Subtract } 7\frac{1}{2} \text{ from both sides.}$$

$$n = 4\frac{1}{2} \qquad \text{Solution}$$

Check $\quad 4\frac{1}{2} + 7\frac{1}{2} = 12 \qquad$ Replace *n* with $4\frac{1}{2}$ in the original equation.

More Examples

a. $\quad n - \frac{5}{8} = 1\frac{3}{8} \qquad$ Use the inverse of subtracting $\frac{5}{8}$.

$n - \frac{5}{8} + \frac{5}{8} = 1\frac{3}{8} + \frac{5}{8} \qquad$ Add $\frac{5}{8}$ to both sides.

$n = 1\frac{8}{8}$, or 2 $\quad$ Solution

Check $2 - \frac{5}{8} = 1\frac{3}{8} \qquad$ What does 2 replace in the original equation?

b. $\quad \frac{3}{5} + n = 1\frac{4}{5} \qquad$ Use the inverse of adding $\frac{3}{5}$.

$\frac{3}{5} - \frac{3}{5} + n = 1\frac{4}{5} - \frac{3}{5} \qquad$ Subtract $\frac{3}{5}$ from both sides.

$n = 1\frac{1}{5} \qquad$ Solution

Check $\quad \frac{3}{5} + 1\frac{1}{5} = 1\frac{4}{5} \qquad$ What replaces *n* in the original equation?

Solve and check.

1. $n + \frac{7}{8} = 3\frac{1}{8}$

2. $n - \frac{3}{4} = 5\frac{1}{2}$

3. $1\frac{5}{8} + n = 6$

4. $n - 4\frac{2}{3} = 7\frac{5}{6}$

Share Your Ideas 8 ounces are on one side of a scale. 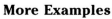 $2\frac{3}{4}$ ounces are on the other side. Describe two ways the scale can be balanced.

Solve and check.

5. $1\frac{3}{5} + n = 5$ **6.** $4\frac{1}{2} + n = 5\frac{1}{4}$ **7.** $n + 5\frac{1}{8} = 7\frac{1}{4}$ **8.** $n + 5\frac{3}{7} = 6$

9. $n - 8 = 1\frac{3}{4}$ **10.** $n - 7\frac{1}{2} = 5$ **11.** $n - 5\frac{1}{3} = 7\frac{1}{6}$ **12.** $n - 7\frac{3}{5} = 11\frac{1}{10}$

13. $8\frac{1}{5} + n = 9\frac{3}{10}$ **14.** $n - 5 = 7\frac{3}{4}$ **15.** $7\frac{3}{8} + n = 8\frac{1}{4}$ **16.** $4 + n = 12\frac{3}{4}$

17. $7\frac{3}{5} + n = 8\frac{1}{4}$ **18.** $n - 7\frac{1}{2} = 2\frac{1}{8}$ **19.** $1\frac{3}{4} + n = 3\frac{5}{8}$ **20.** $9\frac{1}{8} + n = 10\frac{1}{4}$

21. $n - 1 = 3\frac{1}{2}$ **22.** $n - 1\frac{5}{6} = 2\frac{1}{2}$ **23.** $n + 4\frac{1}{3} = 15\frac{5}{6}$ **24.** $n - 12\frac{3}{7} = 35\frac{1}{4}$

Select an equation for each sentence.

25. $8\frac{1}{2}$ plus a number n equals 12.   **a.** $n - 8\frac{1}{2} = 12$

26. A number n plus $8\frac{1}{2}$ equals 12.   **b.** $8\frac{1}{2} + n = 12$

27. A number n minus $8\frac{1}{2}$ equals 12.   **c.** $8\frac{1}{2} - n = 12$

28. $8\frac{1}{2}$ minus a number n equals 12.   **d.** $n + 8\frac{1}{2} = 12$

Think and Apply

Choose the equation that can be used to solve each problem.

29. Marissa drives $9\frac{3}{4}$ mi to her job at the college each day. On the way, she eats breakfast at a restaurant $1\frac{9}{10}$ mi from the college. How far is the restaurant from Marissa's house?

a. $n + 1\frac{9}{10} = 9\frac{3}{4}$

b. $n - 1\frac{9}{10} = 9\frac{3}{4}$

30. Professor Su works $9\frac{1}{2}$ hours each day. She spends $5\frac{3}{4}$ hours in her research lab and the rest of her time teaching. How much time does she spend teaching?

a. $5\frac{3}{4} - n = 9\frac{1}{2}$

b. $5\frac{3}{4} + n = 9\frac{1}{2}$

31. Peter worked $5\frac{1}{2}$ hours on Monday. How many hours must he work during the rest of the week in order to put in a 20-hour work week?

a. $n + 5\frac{1}{2} = 20$

b. $n - 5\frac{1}{2} = 20$

32. If Gregg spends another $3\frac{1}{2}$ hours at the office, he will complete an 8-hour work day. How many hours has he worked so far today?

a. $n - 3\frac{1}{2} = 8$

b. $n + 3\frac{1}{2} = 8$

Explain why you can add or subtract the same number from both sides of an equation to solve it.

SUMMING UP

Using Problem Solving

Planning Intersections

The intersection of Route 202 and Main Street is controlled by a traffic light with arrows. At each corner there is a No Right Turn on Red sign. Each numbered lane has a green arrow for 30 seconds. At that time all the other lanes have a red light. Citizens have complained that they must wait too long at the light. What should the city do to improve this very impractical situation?

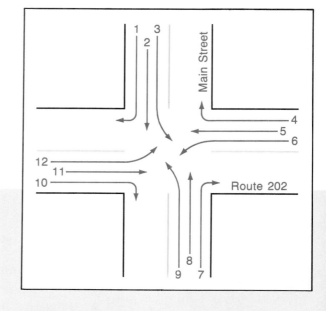

Working together

A. What is the greatest length of time a driver would have to wait at the light? Explain.

B. Which lanes of traffic could safely have a green light at the same time? What is a good way to record this information so it can be used to solve the problem?

C. What would you do to make the traffic flow better at the intersection? Make a plan for improving the traffic flow.

Sharing Your Ideas

1. Share your methods of recording which lanes of traffic can flow at the same time. What are the benefits and drawbacks of each method?

2. Compare the plans, developed in **C**, for dealing with the traffic problem at the intersection. How much time does each plan save drivers? How safe are the plans? Which plan do you prefer?

Extending Your Thinking

3. Information from a traffic survey reveals that few drivers turn left from Main Street onto Route 202. How would you change your plan for the intersection?

4. What if you decided to remove the No Right Turn on Red signs? Would that cause you to change your plan for the intersection? Explain.

5. A new office building is being put at the corner of Main Street and Route 202. The owners want a one-way exit as shown. How would you plan a traffic light now? Would you recommend that this new street be added here?

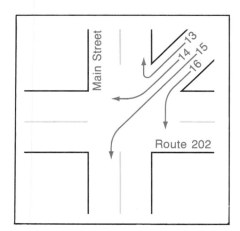

Summing Up

6. Would you recommend that there be a No Right Turn on Red sign at the intersection? Explain.

7. What other information would you like from a traffic survey to help you make a plan for the intersection?

8. Which of the three situations, **3**, **4**, or **5**, altered your original plan the most? Which altered it the least? Explain.

THINK
EXPLORE
SOLVE
LOOK BACK

199

Chapter Review

Write a fraction or mixed number for each. pages 172–173

1. ☐ ⊞

2. $8 \div 9$

3. $13 \div 4$

4. denominator: 6
   numerator: 5

Write an equivalent fraction and decimal for each. pages 174–175

5. $\frac{2}{3}$ 6. $\frac{1}{8}$ 7. $\frac{4}{9}$ 8. $\frac{11}{15}$ 9. $\frac{49}{50}$ 10. $\frac{4}{25}$

Find the value of n. pages 172–175; 178–181

11. $5\frac{1}{3} = \frac{n}{3}$

12. $0.4 = \frac{n}{5}$

13. $\frac{22}{7} = 3\frac{1}{n}$

14. $\frac{132}{213} = \frac{n}{71}$

15. $\frac{45}{72} = \frac{n}{8}$

16. $6\frac{1}{8} = \frac{49}{n}$

17. $1.3 = 1\frac{3}{n}$

18. $0.025 = \frac{1}{n}$

Compare. Use >, <, or = for each ⬤. pages 176–181

19. $8\frac{1}{4}$ ⬤ $8\frac{1}{3}$

20. 0.16 ⬤ $\frac{1}{5}$

21. $\frac{36}{72}$ ⬤ $\frac{4}{8}$

22. $\frac{6}{7}$ ⬤ $\frac{15}{16}$

23. $\frac{1}{4}$ ⬤ $\frac{1}{5}$

24. $\frac{19}{20}$ ⬤ $\frac{11}{12}$

25. $\frac{5}{11}$ ⬤ 0.5

26. $\frac{2}{3}$ ⬤ $0.\overline{6}$

Estimate. Then add or subtract. Write each answer in lowest terms. pages 186–195

27. $\frac{3}{5} + \frac{4}{5}$

28. $\frac{1}{2} + \frac{2}{3} + \frac{1}{4}$

29. $6\frac{1}{8} + 7\frac{2}{3}$

30. $20\frac{7}{9} - 1\frac{1}{4}$

31. $\frac{9}{10} - \frac{8}{10}$

32. $8 - 1\frac{4}{7}$

33. $38\frac{1}{2} + 2\frac{3}{4} + 1\frac{9}{20}$

34. $\frac{9}{16} - \frac{3}{8}$

Solve for n. Write each answer in lowest terms. pages 196–197

35. $n + \frac{1}{2} = \frac{7}{8}$

36. $n - 2\frac{3}{4} = \frac{1}{6}$

37. $\frac{5}{7} + n = 38$

Complete each statement. pages 172; 174

38. A fraction in which the numerator is less than the denominator is a _____ fraction.

39. If the GCF of the numerator and denominator is 1, then the fraction is in _____.

Solve. pages 183–185, 198–199

40. Carol spends $\frac{3}{4}$ hour each day delivering newspapers. Her brother spends $1\frac{1}{3}$ hours a day delivering papers. How much more time does Carol's brother spend each day delivering papers?

41. Cathy and Carlos started a trainee program. On the first day, Cathy worked 4 hours and Carlos worked 5 hours. If Cathy increases her time by $\frac{1}{2}$ hour per day and Carlos increases his time by $\frac{1}{4}$ hour per day, on what day will both be working the same number of hours? Use a table to help you solve the problem.

Chapter Test

Write a fraction or mixed number for each.

1. $8 \div 7$

2. denominator: 5; numerator: 4

Write an equivalent fraction and decimal for each.

3. $\frac{1}{6}$

4. $\frac{3}{4}$

5. $\frac{37}{50}$

Find the value of n.

6. $8\frac{2}{3} = \frac{n}{3}$

7. $0.\overline{3} = \frac{1}{n}$

8. $\frac{62}{6} = 10\frac{1}{n}$

9. $1.6 = 1\frac{n}{5}$

10. $\frac{27}{4} = n\frac{3}{4}$

11. $2\frac{3}{8} = \frac{19}{n}$

Compare. Use >, <, or = for each ⬤.

12. $3\frac{2}{7}$ ⬤ $3\frac{3}{8}$

13. $\frac{2}{3}$ ⬤ $0.\overline{6}$

14. 0.94 ⬤ $\frac{15}{16}$

15. $\frac{7}{8}$ ⬤ $\frac{3}{4}$

16. $\frac{3}{5}$ ⬤ $\frac{60}{100}$

17. $\frac{5}{6}$ ⬤ $\frac{11}{12}$

Add or subtract. Write each answer in lowest terms.

18. $1\frac{9}{10} + 8\frac{2}{7}$

19. $\frac{3}{8} + \frac{1}{4} + \frac{5}{12}$

20. $68\frac{5}{9} - 21\frac{2}{3}$

Solve for n. Write each answer in lowest terms.

21. $1\frac{12}{13} + n = 18$

22. $n - 321\frac{3}{4} = 202\frac{1}{2}$

23. $n - \frac{9}{10} = 3\frac{4}{5}$

Solve. Express each answer in lowest terms.

24. A newspaper reporter spent $12\frac{1}{2}$ hours at the scene of a fire and another $3\frac{1}{4}$ hours writing the article for the paper. How many hours did it take the reporter to cover the fire?

25. A systems analyst worked 52 hours in one week. He worked $37\frac{1}{2}$ hours from Monday to Friday. He worked $4\frac{1}{2}$ more hours on Saturday than he did on Sunday. How many hours did he work on Sunday?

THINK   A new employee at Cooper Print Shop works 5 days a week and receives 2 weeks vacation in addition to 6 holidays. What part of the calendar year (365 days) does he work? Express your answer as a fraction and as a decimal rounded to the nearest hundredth. Which expression is easier to understand? Why?

EXTENSION

Repeating Decimals

Here is a way to write a repeating decimal as a fraction. Study the two examples.

a. Write $0.\overline{7}$ as a fraction.

Let $1n = 0.777\ldots$

Then $10n = 7.777\ldots$

How many digits repeat? What power of 10 is multiplied times n?

Subtract.

$$\begin{aligned} 10n &= 7.777\ldots \\ -\ 1n &= 0.777\ldots \\ \hline 9n &= 7.000\ldots \end{aligned}$$

Solve for n.

$$\frac{9n}{9} = \frac{7}{9}$$

$$n = \frac{7}{9}$$

b. Write $0.\overline{27}$ as a fraction.

Let $1n = 0.272727\ldots$

Then $100n = 27.272727\ldots$

How many digits repeat? What power of 10 is multiplied times n?

Subtract.

$$\begin{aligned} 100n &= 27.272727\ldots \\ -\ 1n &= \ \ 0.272727\ldots \\ \hline 99n &= 27.000000\ldots \end{aligned}$$

Solve for n.

$$\frac{99n}{99} = \frac{27}{99}$$

$$n = \frac{3}{11}$$

1. Verify each result by writing $\frac{7}{9}$ and $\frac{3}{11}$ as decimals.

2. Use the pattern you see between the number of digits that repeat in each decimal and the power of 10 that is multiplied times n. Explain what power of 10 you would multiply times n to write $0.\overline{432}$ as a fraction. What power of 10 would you use to write $0.\overline{3411}$ as a fraction?

Use the method shown above to write each repeating decimal as a fraction.

3. $0.\overline{8}$ **4.** $0.\overline{09}$ **5.** $0.\overline{12}$ **6.** $0.\overline{25}$ **7.** $0.\overline{432}$

Maintaining Skills

Choose the correct answers. Write A, B, C, or D.

1. What is the value of 9^1?

   A 81   **C** 0

   B 9   **D** not given

2. What is 2,630,000 written in scientific notation?

   A 2.63×10^5 **C** 2.63×10^6

   B 26.3×10^5 **D** not given

3. Evaluate. Let $a = 4$. $a^2 + 14$

   A 30   **C** 24

   B 22   **D** not given

4. What is the inverse of multiplying by 10?

   A subtracting 10   **C** adding 10

   B dividing by 10   **D** not given

5. Solve. $a + 17 = 29$

   A 46   **C** 17

   B 22   **D** not given

6. What kind of angle is $\angle MNO$?

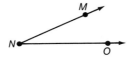

   A right angle   **C** acute angle

   B obtuse angle   **D** not given

7. $\overleftrightarrow{MN} \parallel \overleftrightarrow{RS}$ and $m\angle 2 = 115°$. What is $m\angle 5$?

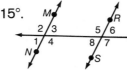

   A 115°   **C** 65°

   B 180°   **D** not given

8. What kind of triangle is $\triangle ABC$?

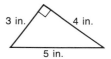

   A acute scalene   **C** right isosceles

   B right scalene   **D** not given

9. What is $4\frac{1}{3}$ as an improper fraction?

   A $\frac{13}{4}$ **C** $\frac{13}{3}$

   B $\frac{12}{4}$ **D** not given

10. $2\frac{1}{3} + 4\frac{3}{4}$

   A $7\frac{1}{12}$ **C** $6\frac{5}{12}$

   B $6\frac{5}{7}$ **D** not given

11. Solve for n. $n - 2\frac{2}{3} = 3$

   A $5\frac{1}{3}$ **C** $\frac{1}{3}$

   B $5\frac{2}{3}$ **D** not given

Solve.

12. Ann, Paula, Gary, and Steve are in line. Paula is between Gary and Steve. Steve is not first in line, but Ann is last. List the order in which the four are standing.

   A A, P, G, S   **C** A, G, P, S

   B G, P, S, A   **D** not given

13. There are 25 students working on the school newspaper and 36 working on the yearbook. Of these students, 12 work on both. How many students are there altogether?

   A 49   **C** 73

   B 37   **D** not given

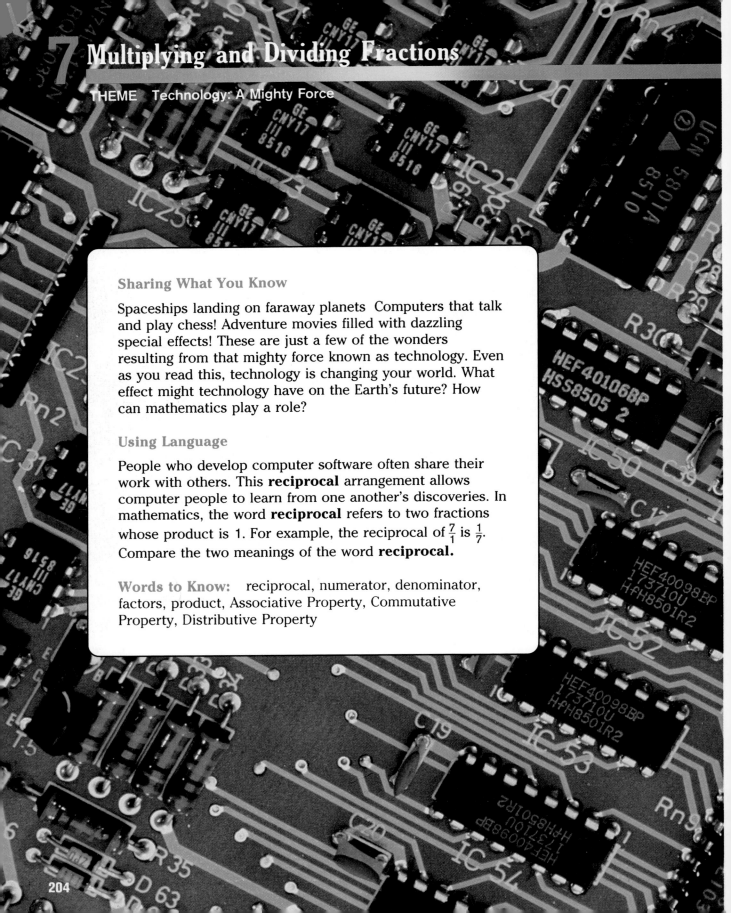

Sharing What You Know

Spaceships landing on faraway planets Computers that talk
and play chess! Adventure movies filled with dazzling
special effects! These are just a few of the wonders
resulting from that mighty force known as technology. Even
as you read this, technology is changing your world. What
effect might technology have on the Earth's future? How
can mathematics play a role?

Using Language

People who develop computer software often share their
work with others. This **reciprocal** arrangement allows
computer people to learn from one another's discoveries. In
mathematics, the word **reciprocal** refers to two fractions
whose product is 1. For example, the reciprocal of $\frac{7}{1}$ is $\frac{1}{7}$.
Compare the two meanings of the word **reciprocal.**

Words to Know: reciprocal, numerator, denominator,
factors, product, Associative Property, Commutative
Property, Distributive Property

Be a Problem Solver

Four families bought a video camera and cassette recorder at a total cost of $1,440. The Smythes will use the equipment for 2 months of the year, the James family 4 months, the Bensons $2\frac{1}{2}$ months, and the Franks $3\frac{1}{2}$ months. What are some of the ways that the 4 families could share the cost?

Write about the fairest way you found for the 4 families to share the cost of the equipment. Explain your choice.

How would you estimate the sum of $3\frac{7}{8}$ and $8\frac{1}{6}$?

Estimating with Fractions

Because of reduced costs, better service, and improved quality, in one company the number of international calls this year is $2\frac{3}{4}$ times what it was a year ago. On average, 7 calls a day were made a year ago. About how many calls a day are made now?

You can estimate by rounding.

$$\begin{array}{r} 2\frac{3}{4} \\ \times\ 7 \\ \hline \end{array}$$
Think $2\frac{3}{4}$ is closer to 3 than to 2.
$$\begin{array}{r} 3 \\ \times\ 7 \\ \hline 21 \end{array}$$
Why is the actual answer less than 21?

About 21 calls a day are made now.

You can also estimate with fractions by using compatible numbers.

Estimate $9\frac{3}{4} \div 3\frac{1}{8}$.

$$9\frac{3}{4} \div 3\frac{1}{8} \longrightarrow 9 \div 3 = 3$$

How would you estimate $22\frac{1}{4} \times 4\frac{1}{3}$, using compatible numbers?

Check Your Understanding

Estimate each product or quotient.

1. $5\frac{3}{8} \times 8$ **2.** $2\frac{1}{4} \times 5\frac{9}{10}$ **3.** $6\frac{1}{7} \div 1\frac{4}{5}$ **4.** $12\frac{3}{5} \div 4\frac{3}{8}$

5. $2\frac{1}{2} \times 2\frac{1}{2}$ **6.** $18\frac{1}{3} \div 3\frac{5}{9}$ **7.** $3\frac{2}{3} \times 26$ **8.** $7\frac{5}{8} \times 6\frac{1}{2}$

Share Your Ideas How did you estimate the product for **5**? Describe another way you could estimate it. Is rounding the numbers in **5** to 2×3 a way to estimate? Explain how you could use this method for other problems in **1–8** above.

Estimate each product or quotient.

9. $2\frac{1}{3} \times 7$ **10.** $8 \times 5\frac{7}{8}$ **11.** $8\frac{1}{2} \times 9\frac{1}{2}$ **12.** $18\frac{1}{2} \div 6$

13. $5\frac{2}{5} \times 4\frac{4}{5}$ **14.** $7\frac{3}{10} \times 5$ **15.** $6 \times 2\frac{1}{4}$ **16.** $12\frac{4}{5} \div 5$

17. $23\frac{1}{8} \div 4\frac{1}{2}$ **18.** $4\frac{1}{8} \times 7\frac{1}{5}$ **19.** $34 \div 4\frac{2}{3}$ **20.** $16 \div \frac{9}{10}$

21. $5\frac{3}{8} \times 6\frac{1}{2}$ **22.** $14\frac{3}{5} \div 5\frac{1}{8}$ **23.** $12\frac{5}{6} \times 8\frac{1}{4}$ **24.** $19 \times \frac{8}{9}$

25. $9\frac{3}{4} \div 1\frac{9}{10}$ **26.** $32\frac{3}{5} \times \frac{11}{12}$ **27.** $5\frac{1}{2} \div 10\frac{1}{4}$ **28.** $6\frac{7}{8} \div 14\frac{1}{5}$

29. Look back at **11**, **16**, **17**, and **21**. Find another way to estimate each.

Without multiplying, answer the following questions about examples a–e. Explain your reasoning.

a. $\frac{3}{5} \times \frac{1}{2}$ **b.** $8 \times 3\frac{1}{2}$ **c.** $2\frac{1}{2} \times 7\frac{1}{2}$ **d.** $\frac{1}{2} \times 5$ **e.** $\frac{3}{5} \times \frac{3}{4}$

30. Which example has a product greater than 24?

31. Which examples have products less than 1?

32. Which example has a product greater than 1 but less than 5?

33. Which example has the least product?

Without dividing, answer the following questions about examples f–j. Explain your reasoning.

f. $\frac{1}{2} \div \frac{1}{2}$ **g.** $2\frac{1}{2} \div 2\frac{1}{4}$ **h.** $1\frac{1}{2} \div 4\frac{3}{4}$ **i.** $5 \div \frac{1}{2}$ **j.** $3\frac{1}{8} \div 6\frac{3}{8}$

34. Which examples have quotients less than 1?

35. Which examples have quotients greater than 1?

36. Which example has a quotient of 1?

37. Which example has the greatest quotient?

Estimate and solve.

38. About how long will it take to make 8 calls, each $2\frac{1}{4}$ minutes long?

39. American Exporters, Inc., provides a recorded message of daily price quotes. It lasts $4\frac{1}{3}$ minutes. Can it be played 5 times in 20 minutes?

Is this statement always, sometimes, or never true?
* A mixed number times a mixed number is less than 1.

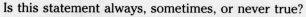

SUMMING UP

Write each number as a fraction.
a. 2   **b.** 5   **c.** 12

Multiplying Fractions

Five sixths of the monitors that are on are displaying graphics. What part of *all* the monitors are displaying graphics?

To visualize the answer, you can draw a picture.

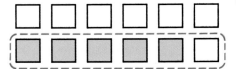

Think $\frac{1}{2}$ are on.

$\frac{5}{6}$ of those that are on are displaying graphics.

$\frac{5}{12}$ of all the monitors are displaying graphics.

To calculate the answer, you can multiply.

▶ To multiply two fractions, multiply the numerators and multiply the denominators.

$$\frac{1}{2} \times \frac{5}{6} = \frac{1 \times 5}{2 \times 6} = \frac{5}{12}$$

Three fourths of the 12 display models will be sold at a special discount price.

To find the number to be sold at the discount price, you can multiply. Explain why.

▶ To find the product of a fraction and a whole number, first write the whole number as a fraction. Then multiply.

$$\frac{3}{4} \times 12 = \frac{3}{4} \times \frac{12}{1} = \frac{3 \times 12}{4 \times 1} = \frac{36}{4} = \frac{9}{1} = 9$$

9 display models will be sold at discount.

Check Your Understanding

Multiply. Write each product in lowest terms.

1. $\frac{3}{4} \times \frac{1}{5}$

2. $\frac{5}{8} \times \frac{1}{2}$

3. $\frac{3}{5} \times 10$

4. $\frac{2}{3} \times 5$

5. $\frac{7}{8} \times \frac{5}{6}$

6. $\frac{5}{3} \times \frac{3}{5}$

Share Your Ideas   Look back at **1** and **4**. Describe how you would make a drawing to answer each.

Multiply. Write each product in lowest terms.

7. $\frac{5}{8} \times \frac{1}{3}$

8. $\frac{4}{5} \times \frac{1}{2}$

9. $\frac{3}{4} \times \frac{2}{5}$

10. $\frac{2}{3} \times \frac{2}{7}$

11. $\frac{5}{9} \times \frac{1}{9}$

12. $\frac{3}{7} \times \frac{1}{3}$

13. $\frac{1}{2} \times \frac{1}{4}$

14. $\frac{1}{2} \times \frac{1}{2}$

15. $\frac{3}{8} \times \frac{1}{5}$

16. $\frac{3}{4} \times \frac{3}{4}$

17. $\frac{2}{3} \times \frac{3}{2}$

18. $\frac{3}{7} \times \frac{1}{2}$

19. $\frac{2}{3} \times 9$

20. $\frac{1}{5} \times 12$

21. $\frac{3}{4} \times 9$

22. $\frac{7}{8} \times 16$

23. $\frac{3}{10} \times 10$

24. $\frac{3}{5} \times 20$

25. $\frac{1}{3} \times \$21$

26. $\frac{3}{4} \times \$100$

27. $\frac{1}{6} \times \frac{3}{5} \times \frac{1}{2}$

28. $\frac{2}{5} \times 8 \times \frac{7}{6}$

29. $\frac{3}{4} \times \frac{7}{8} \times 24$

30. $\frac{2}{3} \times \frac{4}{5} \times \frac{1}{4}$

Solve.

31. What is $\frac{2}{3}$ of 9?

32. What is $\frac{3}{4}$ of $20?

33. What is $\frac{1}{2}$ of $\frac{1}{3}$?

34. What is $\frac{2}{3}$ of $\frac{5}{6}$?

35. What is $\frac{1}{3}$ of $\frac{1}{2}$?

36. What is $\frac{3}{10}$ of 75?

Compare without multiplying. Explain your thinking.

37. $\frac{2}{3} \times \frac{7}{8}$ ● 1

38. 1 ● $\frac{3}{4} \times \frac{5}{6}$

39. $\frac{1}{2} \times 37$ ● $\frac{1}{2} \times 49$

40. $\frac{5}{8} \times 10$ ● 2

41. $\frac{11}{15} \times \frac{5}{8}$ ● $\frac{11}{15} \times \frac{3}{5}$

42. $\frac{5}{9} \times 34$ ● 17

Write *always*, *sometimes*, or *never* for each. Explain.

43. The Commutative Property of Multiplication is true for fractions.

44. The product of an improper fraction and a whole number is less than the whole number.

45. Computer City is selling a printer at $\frac{1}{4}$ off the regular price. How much would you get off on a printer that regularly sells for $280?

46. The stock clerk at Computer City reported the following data about the matrix printers in stock: $\frac{1}{4}$ are blue, $\frac{2}{3}$ are gray, $\frac{1}{4}$ are green. What is wrong with this information?

Logical Thinking

Write +, −, or × to make each sentence true. Use parentheses where necessary.

47. $\frac{1}{3}$ ● $\frac{1}{3}$ ● $\frac{1}{3} = 0$

48. $\frac{1}{3}$ ● $\frac{1}{3}$ ● $\frac{1}{3}$ ● $\frac{1}{3} = \frac{1}{3}$

Look back at **8, 9, 20,** and **21.** Rewrite each, using only decimals. Find the products. Why are they equal to the fraction products?

SUMMING UP

What is the GCF of 8 and 12? How did you find it?

Simplifying Factors

Three fifths of the 45 scientists at R & D Laboratories must be assigned to a superconductor project. How many scientists must be assigned to this project?

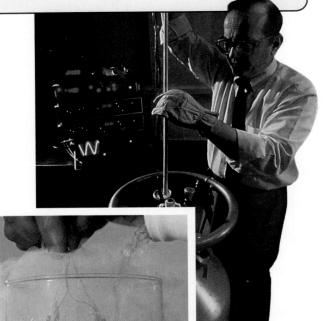

To find the answer, you can multiply $\frac{3}{5} \times 45$. You have a choice of ways to simplify.

a. You can multiply first and then simplify the product.

$$\frac{3}{5} \times 45 = \frac{3}{5} \times \frac{45}{1} = \frac{3 \times 45}{5 \times 1} = \frac{135}{5} = 27$$

b. You can simplify the factors first and then multiply.

Find a common factor of any numerator and any denominator.

$\frac{3}{5} \times 45$ 5 is the GCF of 5 and 45, so divide by 5.

Divide by the common factor.

$\frac{3}{\underset{1}{\cancel{5}}} \times \frac{\overset{9}{\cancel{45}}}{1}$

Multiply.

$\frac{3}{\underset{1}{\cancel{5}}} \times \frac{\overset{9}{\cancel{45}}}{1} = \frac{27}{1} = 27$

27 scientists must be assigned to the superconductor project.

Another Example

$\frac{5}{6} \times \frac{9}{10} = \frac{\overset{1}{\cancel{5}}}{\underset{2}{\cancel{6}}} \times \frac{\overset{3}{\cancel{9}}}{\underset{2}{\cancel{10}}} = \frac{3}{4}$

The GCF of 5 and 10 is 5. Divide by 5.
The GCF of 6 and 9 is 3. Divide by 3.

Why is it easier to divide by the GCF than by any other factor?

Check Your Understanding

Multiply. Write each product in lowest terms.

1. $\frac{3}{8} \times \frac{4}{5}$

2. $\frac{5}{6} \times \frac{3}{10}$

3. $\frac{3}{7} \times 28$

4. $\frac{4}{5} \times \$35$

5. $\frac{7}{8} \times \frac{8}{7}$

Share Your Ideas Explain why it is often easier to simplify before multiplying.

Multiply. Write each product in lowest terms.

6. $\frac{5}{8} \times \frac{4}{5}$

7. $\frac{7}{12} \times \frac{2}{7}$

8. $\frac{3}{8} \times 24$

9. $20 \times \frac{7}{10}$

10. $\frac{3}{4} \times \frac{1}{6}$

11. $\frac{3}{5} \times \frac{3}{4}$

12. $\frac{9}{10} \times \frac{2}{3}$

13. $\frac{5}{9} \times \frac{1}{2}$

14. $\frac{4}{7} \times 21$

15. $\frac{4}{5} \times \frac{3}{10}$

16. $36 \times \frac{8}{9}$

17. $\frac{3}{4} \times 72$

18. $\frac{10}{7} \times \frac{7}{8}$

19. $\frac{5}{6} \times 33$

20. $\frac{9}{5} \times \$95$

21. $\frac{6}{7} \times 84 \times \frac{1}{2}$

22. $\frac{5}{6} \times \frac{3}{5} \times \frac{2}{3}$

23. $\frac{3}{16} \times \frac{5}{9} \times \frac{8}{5}$

Follow the rule to find each missing number.

Rule: The output is $\frac{3}{8}$ of the input.

	Input	Output
24.	$\frac{4}{9}$	
25.	12	
26.	32	
27.	$\frac{16}{5}$	

Rule: The output is 3 less than $\frac{4}{5}$ of the input.

	Input	Output
28.	45	
29.	15	
30.	$\frac{25}{4}$	
31.	$\frac{31}{8}$	

Think and Apply

32. How many eggs are in $\frac{3}{4}$ dozen?

33. How many hours are in $\frac{2}{3}$ of a day?

34. How many minutes are in $\frac{1}{3}$ hour?

35. How many donuts are in $\frac{5}{2}$ dozen?

36. How many seconds are in $\frac{5}{6}$ of a minute?

37. Two thirds of the scientists at R & D Laboratories have worked on laser projects. Of these, $\frac{1}{2}$ have worked with fiber optics. What part of the staff has worked on both projects? How many scientists is this?

Explain why simplifying before multiplying does not change the product.

Mixed Review

1. $5.83 + 19.25$

2. $73.8 + 91.9$

3. $4.13 - 3.97$

4. $8.1 - 2.75$

5. 32×2.58

6. 9.4×1.5

7. 0.002×0.003

8. $3.5 \div 0.07$

9. $0.426 \div 0.6$

10. $2,406 \div 0.25$

11. $1,002 \div 0.75$

12. $5\frac{3}{4} - 3\frac{2}{3}$

13. $8\frac{2}{5} - 5\frac{7}{10}$

14. $2\frac{1}{2} + 3\frac{1}{3}$

15. $9\frac{3}{5} + 5\frac{3}{4}$

16. $8\frac{2}{7} + 1\frac{1}{2}$

Compare. Use <, >, or =.

17. $\frac{3}{8}$ ⬤ $\frac{6}{7}$

18. $\frac{15}{20}$ ⬤ $\frac{3}{4}$

19. 2.25 ⬤ 2.250

20. 9.06 ⬤ 9.1

21. 6 ⬤ 5.37

SUMMING UP

211

Multiplying Mixed Numbers

Before starting on their vacation, the Mendez family programmed their VCR to record $1\frac{1}{2}$ hours of programs a night for 4 nights. Will a 6-hour tape be adequate?

You have a choice of ways to find the answer. Describe how you might find the answer. Then compare your way with the two shown below.

(1) You can draw a number line.

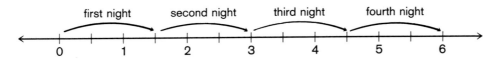

(2) You can multiply $4 \times 1\frac{1}{2}$ and compare the product with 6.   *Why do you multiply rather than divide?*

Write the whole number and   Simplify.   Multiply.
mixed number as fractions.

$4 \times 1\frac{1}{2} = \frac{4}{1} \times \frac{3}{2}$ $\frac{\cancel{4}^{2}}{1} \times \frac{3}{\cancel{2}_{1}}$ $\frac{\cancel{4}^{2}}{1} \times \frac{3}{\cancel{2}_{1}} = \frac{\cancel{4} \times 3}{1 \times \cancel{2}} = \frac{6}{1} = 6$

The 6-hour tape will be adequate because there are 6 hours of programs.

More Examples

a. $1\frac{3}{4} \times 1\frac{3}{7} = \frac{7}{4} \times \frac{10}{7}$

$= \frac{\cancel{7}^{1}}{\cancel{4}_{2}} \times \frac{\cancel{10}^{5}}{\cancel{7}_{1}}$

$= \frac{5}{2},$ or $2\frac{1}{2}$

b. $\frac{2}{3} \times 6\frac{1}{2} = \left(\frac{2}{3} \times 6\right) + \left(\frac{2}{3} \times \frac{1}{2}\right)$

$= \left(\frac{2}{\cancel{3}_{1}} \times \frac{\cancel{6}^{2}}{1}\right) + \left(\frac{\cancel{2}^{1}}{3} \times \frac{1}{\cancel{2}_{1}}\right)$

$= 4 + \frac{1}{3} = 4\frac{1}{3}$

Sometimes the Distributive Property can be used to multiply mentally.

Check Your Understanding

Estimate. Then multiply. Write each product in lowest terms.

1. $8 \times 1\frac{1}{2}$ **2.** $2\frac{2}{5} \times 5$ **3.** $1\frac{1}{8} \times \frac{8}{9}$ **4.** $3\frac{1}{9} \times \frac{3}{7}$

5. $2\frac{1}{3} \times 1\frac{1}{8}$ **6.** $4\frac{3}{4} \times 1\frac{2}{5}$ **7.** $6\frac{2}{3} \times 3\frac{3}{5}$ **8.** $\frac{7}{8} \times 3\frac{3}{7}$

Share Your Ideas   Explain how you would use the Distributive Property to multiply $8 \times 2\frac{1}{2}$, using mental math.

Estimate. Then multiply. Use mental math or paper and pencil. Write each product in lowest terms.

9. $\frac{6}{7} \times 9\frac{1}{3}$

10. $\frac{5}{9} \times 3\frac{3}{5}$

11. $4\frac{1}{2} \times \frac{2}{3}$

12. $3\frac{1}{8} \times \frac{4}{5}$

13. $\frac{3}{4} \times 2\frac{6}{7}$

14. $5 \times 1\frac{1}{10}$

15. $8 \times 1\frac{5}{12}$

16. $1\frac{5}{8} \times 4$

17. $1\frac{3}{7} \times 2$

18. $6 \times 1\frac{5}{6}$

19. $1\frac{1}{2} \times 2\frac{1}{3}$

20. $5\frac{3}{8} \times 1\frac{3}{5}$

21. $7\frac{1}{3} \times 1\frac{1}{3}$

22. $3\frac{3}{4} \times 1\frac{3}{10}$

23. $2\frac{1}{2} \times 1\frac{2}{3}$

24. $3\frac{5}{6} \times 1\frac{1}{3}$

25. $9\frac{1}{2} \times 1\frac{1}{5}$

26. $7\frac{1}{2} \times 3\frac{1}{5}$

27. $3\frac{3}{5} \times 1\frac{1}{9}$

28. $8\frac{2}{3} \times 2\frac{1}{6}$

29. $7\frac{1}{5} \times 4\frac{1}{6}$

30. $2\frac{5}{8} \times 1\frac{5}{7}$

31. $3\frac{3}{10} \times 2\frac{2}{9}$

32. $3\frac{1}{4} \times 2\frac{1}{5}$

33. $2\frac{4}{5} \times 1\frac{3}{5}$

34. $2\frac{2}{5} \times \frac{8}{9} \times 2\frac{3}{4}$

35. $2\frac{1}{2} \times 1\frac{1}{3} \times 4$

36. $4\frac{1}{6} \times 5 \times \frac{3}{10}$

37. $3\frac{3}{7} \times 2\frac{2}{3} \times 2\frac{5}{8}$

Compare without multiplying. Explain your thinking.

38. $1\frac{2}{3} \times 1\frac{1}{5}$ ● 1

39. $1\frac{2}{5} \times 3\frac{1}{8}$ ● 8

40. $3\frac{1}{7} \times 2\frac{4}{5}$ ● $3\frac{1}{7} \times 2$

41. $2\frac{2}{3} \times \frac{7}{8}$ ● $2\frac{2}{3}$

42. $10\frac{3}{5} \times 1\frac{1}{3}$ ● $10\frac{3}{5}$

43. $\frac{7}{8} \times \frac{4}{5}$ ● 1

Evaluate. Let $a = 1\frac{1}{2}$, $b = 2\frac{3}{4}$, and $c = \frac{4}{5}$.

44. $4 \times a + 3 \times b$

45. $a + b \times c$

46. $3 \times a + b - 2 \times c$

Think and Apply

Solve. Decide whether an estimate is sufficient or an exact answer is necessary.

At the right is a schedule for a current-events program. Time slots **A**, **B**, and **C** are for commercial advertising.

47. Can three $\frac{3}{4}$-minute commercials be shown during ad slot **A**?

48. How many $\frac{1}{2}$-minute commercials can be shown during ad slot **B**?

49. The program director must fit the commercials at the right in time slots **A**, **B**, and **C**. Schedule the commercials so that each will run.

KWOW	Channel 6			11:30–12:00 NOON		
O P E N 7 min China story	3 min **A**	6 min Interview	$2\frac{1}{2}$ min **B**	$6\frac{1}{4}$ min Hollywood story	$1\frac{3}{4}$ min **C**	C L O S E

Commercial	Time (min)	Commercial	Time (min)
soap	$1\frac{1}{4}$	athletic shoes	$\frac{7}{8}$
vitamins	$\frac{3}{4}$	salad dressing	$\frac{7}{8}$
cereal	$\frac{1}{2}$	orange juice	$\frac{1}{2}$
movie	$1\frac{1}{4}$	automobile	$1\frac{1}{4}$

Look back at **11**, **14**, and **16–18**. Explain how you could solve each, using mental math.

SUMMING UP

Which is greater—$\frac{2}{3} \times 15$ or $1\frac{1}{2} \times 6\frac{2}{3}$?

Multiplying Fractions and Mixed Numbers

A rocket must travel 40,000 km/h to put a satellite into orbit around the earth. To stay in orbit, the satellite must travel at $\frac{7}{10}$ this speed. How fast must a satellite travel to remain in orbit?

To find the answer, you can multiply $\frac{7}{10} \times 40,000$.

$$\frac{7}{10} \times 40,000 = \frac{7}{\underset{1}{\cancel{10}}} \times \frac{\overset{4,000}{\cancel{40,000}}}{1} = \frac{28,000}{1} = 28,000$$

To stay in orbit, a satellite must maintain a speed of at least 28,000 km/h.

More Examples

a. What is $\frac{2}{3}$ of $3\frac{3}{4}$?

$$\frac{2}{3} \times 3\frac{3}{4} = \frac{2}{3} \times \frac{15}{4}$$

$$= \frac{\overset{1}{\cancel{2}}}{\underset{1}{\cancel{3}}} \times \frac{\overset{5}{\cancel{15}}}{\underset{2}{\cancel{4}}}$$

$$= \frac{5}{2}, \text{ or } 2\frac{1}{2}$$

b. What number is $2\frac{1}{2}$ times as great as $2\frac{4}{5}$?

$$2\frac{1}{2} \times 2\frac{4}{5} = \frac{5}{2} \times \frac{14}{5}$$

$$= \frac{\overset{1}{\cancel{5}}}{\underset{1}{\cancel{2}}} \times \frac{\overset{7}{\cancel{14}}}{\underset{1}{\cancel{5}}}$$

$$= \frac{7}{1}, \text{ or } 7$$

How could you find the product in **a**, using mental math?

Check Your Understanding

Estimate. Then multiply. Write each product in lowest terms.

1. $\frac{3}{4} \times \frac{8}{9}$ **2.** $\frac{5}{6} \times 12$ **3.** $8 \times 2\frac{1}{4}$

4. $2\frac{2}{5} \times 1\frac{7}{8}$ **5.** $3\frac{5}{9} \times \frac{7}{8}$ **6.** $2\frac{1}{3} \times 1\frac{3}{8}$

7. $\frac{3}{5} \times 1\frac{2}{3}$ **8.** $\frac{7}{12} \times \frac{12}{7}$ **9.** $3\frac{1}{3} \times 9$

Share Your Ideas Look back at **2** and **3**. Create a problem for which each expression is a solution.

Practice

Estimate. Then multiply. Choose mental math or paper and pencil. Write each product in lowest terms.

10. $\frac{3}{4} \times \frac{5}{8}$

11. $\frac{3}{5} \times 15$

12. $\frac{2}{3} \times 4\frac{1}{2}$

13. $9 \times 2\frac{1}{3}$

14. $4\frac{2}{3} \times 1\frac{2}{7}$

15. $2\frac{2}{5} \times 2\frac{2}{3}$

16. $7 \times 2\frac{1}{2}$

17. $\frac{5}{12} \times 2\frac{2}{5}$

18. $\frac{8}{9} \times 9$

19. $\frac{7}{10} \times \frac{5}{7}$

20. $\frac{3}{5} \times \frac{5}{9}$

21. $12 \times \frac{2}{3}$

22. $\frac{5}{8} \times 3\frac{1}{5}$

23. $3\frac{1}{8} \times 4$

24. $1\frac{1}{3} \times 1\frac{2}{3}$

25. $7 \times \frac{2}{3}$

26. $1\frac{1}{3} \times \frac{4}{7}$

27. $\frac{9}{10} \times \frac{2}{3}$

28. $3 \times 5\frac{2}{3}$

29. $2\frac{3}{5} \times 1\frac{1}{9}$

30. $1\frac{1}{4} \times \frac{4}{5}$

31. $6 \times \frac{5}{6}$

32. $2\frac{1}{8} \times 3\frac{3}{7}$

33. $2 \times 2\frac{1}{4}$

34. $1\frac{3}{5} \times \frac{7}{8}$

35. $\frac{1}{4} \times 2\frac{1}{2} \times 16$

36. $\frac{3}{5} \times 1\frac{2}{3} \times 3\frac{1}{8}$

37. $\frac{4}{9} \times \frac{5}{8} \times 2\frac{1}{4}$

38. $7 \times 3\frac{1}{3} \times 6\frac{2}{7}$

39. **Look back** at **10–38.** Identify five problems for which you used mental math. Explain your solutions.

Solve.

40. What is $\frac{5}{6}$ of 32?

41. What is $\frac{1}{4}$ of $2\frac{1}{2}$?

42. What is $\frac{3}{8}$ of 6?

43. What number is 10 times as great as $6\frac{2}{3}$?

44. What number is $1\frac{5}{8}$ times as great as 16?

45. What number is $3\frac{1}{3}$ times as great as 10?

Think and Apply

Without multiplying, answer the following questions about examples a–e. Explain your reasoning.

a. $\frac{3}{8} \times 8\frac{1}{3}$

b. $\frac{1}{2} \times 2\frac{1}{2}$

c. $\frac{1}{4} \times 2\frac{1}{2}$

d. $8\frac{2}{6} \times \frac{3}{8}$

e. $\frac{1}{4} \times \frac{1}{4}$

46. Which has the least product?

47. Which two examples have equal products?

48. Which has a product that is half the product of **b**?

49. Which has a product greater than 1 but less than 2?

Solve. Decide whether an estimate is sufficient or an exact answer is necessary.

50. When U.S. astronauts were on the moon, they were able to jump much higher than on Earth because they weighed $\frac{1}{6}$ as much as on Earth. How much would a 78-kg person weigh on the moon?

51. Marlon is in training to become an astronaut. He can lift $1\frac{1}{3}$ times his own weight. He weighs 75 kg. Can he lift 150 kg?

Make a drawing to illustrate $\frac{3}{5}$ of 10. Use a number line to illustrate $10 \times \frac{3}{5}$.

SUMMING UP

Midchapter Review

Choose the best estimate. pages 206–207

1. $6\frac{1}{4} \times 7\frac{7}{8}$

   a. 24
   b. 36
   c. 48

2. $18\frac{1}{2} \div 5\frac{5}{6}$

   a. 3
   b. 6
   c. $\frac{1}{3}$

3. $\frac{9}{10} \times \frac{19}{20}$

   a. 0
   b. $\frac{1}{2}$
   c. 1

Estimate. Then multiply. Write each answer in lowest terms. pages 208–215

4. $\frac{1}{2} \times \frac{4}{5}$

5. $2\frac{1}{8} \times 3\frac{1}{4}$

6. $\frac{6}{11} \times \frac{2}{3}$

7. $3 \times \frac{1}{2} \times 4$

8. $1\frac{2}{3} \times 5\frac{4}{7}$

9. $\frac{2}{3} \times \frac{1}{8}$

10. $18 \times \frac{2}{9}$

11. $\frac{2}{3} \times 5 \times \frac{4}{5}$

12. $\frac{6}{7} \times \frac{49}{50}$

13. $4 \times 1\frac{3}{8}$

14. $2\frac{1}{7} \times 3\frac{1}{7}$

15. $1\frac{1}{8} \times \frac{4}{9} \times 0$

16. $16 \times 3\frac{1}{2}$

17. $\frac{3}{4} \times 1\frac{1}{3}$

18. $\frac{1}{2} \times \frac{1}{3}$

19. $1\frac{3}{8} \times \frac{2}{3}$

20. $2\frac{4}{5} \times 5$

21. $16\frac{1}{4} \times 2$

22. $\frac{1}{3} \times 3$

23. $\frac{1}{8} \times 1\frac{4}{5} \times 8$

24. $\frac{5}{9} \times \frac{9}{10}$

25. $12\frac{1}{4} \times 1\frac{3}{7}$

26. $15 \times 2\frac{3}{5}$

27. $\frac{7}{8} \times 6 \times 1\frac{1}{7}$

Complete each sentence with the correct word.

28. $\frac{1}{2} \times \frac{3}{4} = \frac{3}{4} \times \frac{1}{2}$ is an example of the _____ Property.

29. In the sentence $3\frac{1}{2} \times \frac{4}{5} = 2\frac{4}{5}$, $3\frac{1}{2}$ and $\frac{4}{5}$ are the _____ and $2\frac{4}{5}$ is the _____.

30. $\frac{3}{4}\left(2\frac{2}{3} + 1\frac{5}{6}\right) = \frac{3}{4} \times 2\frac{2}{3} + \frac{3}{4} \times 1\frac{5}{6}$ is an example of the _____ Property.

31. In $\frac{7}{8}$, 7 is the _____.

32. The product of $\frac{5}{8}$ and $\left(\frac{3}{4} - \frac{6}{8}\right)$ is _____.

Words to Know
numerator
denominator
Associative
Commutative
Distributive
zero
factors
multiples
product

Solve.

33. A laser printer can be purchased at Computer City for $750. A dot matrix printer can be purchased for $\frac{2}{5}$ the cost of the laser printer. How much does the dot matrix printer cost?

34. Software Sales is selling floppy disks at $\frac{1}{3}$ off the regular price of 10 for $18. How much will 30 disks cost?

Exploring Problem Solving

Computing Computers

Russell Middle School has bought 26 computers. They need to be divided among the grade levels. This table shows the enrollment in each grade.

Grade	Number of Students
5	102
6	124
7	105
8	85
9	104

Thinking Critically

How many of the 26 computers would you give to each grade level? Work in a group to develop a plan.

Analyzing and Making Decisions

Use a calculator where appropriate.

1. How many students are in the five grades? How many students are there for each computer? What fraction of a computer is this per student?

2. If $\frac{1}{20}$ of a computer is allotted for each student, how many computers should each grade level receive? What would happen if you rounded up to determine the number each grade should receive? What would happen if you rounded down?

3. If $\frac{1}{21}$ of a computer is allotted for each student, how many computers would each grade receive? Will this method allow for a fair distribution of all the computers?

4. How would you distribute the computers? Explain your thinking.

Look Back Does your answer make sense? On what did you base your decision on how to distribute the computers? Were all the computers distributed in your plan?

Compare your method of distribution and your plan with those of your classmates.

217

Problem Solving Strategies

Working Backwards

Electricians were installing outlets in a new office building. Each day they completed half a floor more than the day before. On Friday they finished the twenty-third floor, having completed $4\frac{1}{2}$ floors that day. On Monday they found out that the outlets they had used last Tuesday were defective. On what floors do they need to replace the defective outlets?

Sometimes you know what happened at the end of a problem. To solve it, you must work backwards to find out what was happening at the beginning.

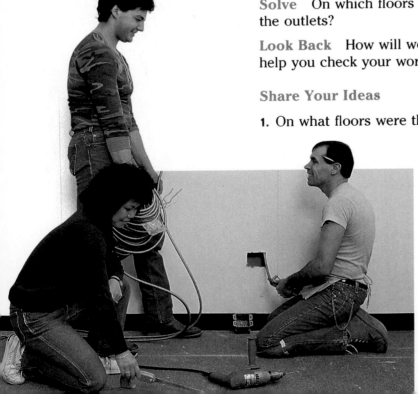

Solving the Problem

Think   What is the question?

Explore   On what floor did the electricians finish on Friday? How many floors did they complete that day? How much more did the crew do each day?

How many floors did they complete on Thursday? What floor did they start on and end on that day? How can you find out what floors they completed on Tuesday?

Solve   On which floors do the electricians need to replace the outlets?

Look Back   How will working forward from your answer help you check your work?

Share Your Ideas

1. On what floors were the electricians working on Monday?

Practice

 CHOICES **Solve. Use a calculator where appropriate.**

2. One morning the cashier at Audio and Video Mart took in $35.00, $17.50, $2.86, $241.50, and $216.75. He gave out $2.50, $15.00, and $8.50. At noon, $697.45 was in the cash register. How much money was in the cash register at the start of the business day?

3. To determine the selling price of a new compact disc (CD) player, the manager adds $10 to the price that she paid. Then she doubles this amount to obtain the selling price. With $6 tax, the total cost to the customer is $126. How much did the manager pay for the player?

4. Kathy is programming a CD player for a customer. The customer wants to hear the first four songs, skip half of the songs that are left, hear the next two songs, and then skip the last song. How many songs are on the CD?

Mixed Strategy Review

5. Members of a manufacturer's training team instructed sales people in how to use a camcorder. Each trainer trained 4 people in the morning and 6 people in the afternoon. That evening, the last 6 people of the entire 36-member sales staff were trained. How many trainers were there?

6. Bernie's answering machine has a 30-minute tape to record messages. He has programmed his machine so that a message can be no longer than $1\frac{1}{2}$ minutes. If the tape is full, what is the least number of messages that can be on the tape?

7. **Look back** at **6**. If the tape is full, what is the greatest number of messages that can be on the tape?

8. The Stines have programmed their thermostat for the temperatures shown on the table. How many hours of the week is the thermostat on 70°? on 65°?

THINK
EXPLORE
SOLVE
LOOK BACK

Create **Your Own**

Write a problem that must be worked backwards to solve.

Time	Monday–Friday	Saturday–Sunday
6:00 A.M.	70°	70°
7:45 A.M.	65°	70°
3:45 P.M.	70°	70°
10:30 P.M.	65°	65°

Activity

Exploring Division

You can make drawings to find quotients of whole numbers. This drawing illustrates $12 \div 4$. It shows how many groups of 4 there are in 12.

Can you make drawings to find quotients of fractions and mixed numbers?

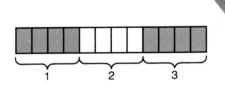

Working together

Materials: fraction strips in halves, thirds, fourths, fifths, sixths, and eighths

A. This drawing shows 1 divided into fourths. How many groups of $\frac{1}{4}$ are there in 1? This question can be written as a division sentence: $1 \div \frac{1}{4} = n$. Use your answer to find $2 \div \frac{1}{4}$ and $3 \div \frac{1}{4}$.

B. Use the drawing in **A** to find $\frac{3}{4} \div \frac{1}{4}$. That is, find the number of groups of $\frac{1}{4}$ there are in $\frac{3}{4}$. Are there more or fewer groups than in 1? Why?

C. Use fraction strips to show $2\frac{4}{5}$. How many groups of $\frac{2}{5}$ are there in $2\frac{4}{5}$? What is $2\frac{4}{5} \div \frac{2}{5}$?

D. Explain what each division example means. Then use fraction strips or create a drawing to find each quotient.

  (1) $6 \div 1\frac{1}{2}$ **(2)** $\frac{2}{3} \div \frac{1}{6}$ **(3)** $6\frac{3}{4} \div 1\frac{1}{8}$

Sharing Your Results

1. Describe how you found the number of groups of $\frac{1}{4}$ in $\frac{3}{4}$; the number of groups of $\frac{2}{5}$ in $2\frac{4}{5}$.

2. Compare your solutions to the division examples in **D** with those of other classmates. How are they alike? How are they different?

3. Explain how you represented 1 (a whole unit) in each example in **D**.

4. What are the quotients for **(1)**, **(2)**, and **(3)** in **D**?

Extending the Activity

This drawing shows $1 \div \frac{2}{5}$. There are $2\frac{1}{2}$ groups of $\frac{2}{5}$ in 1.

This drawing shows $\frac{1}{2} \div \frac{3}{4}$. It shows how many groups of $\frac{3}{4}$ there are in $\frac{1}{2}$. There is $\frac{2}{3}$ of a group.

Work with a partner.

5. Copy this drawing. Use it to find $1 \div \frac{3}{8}$. How many groups of $\frac{3}{8}$ are there in 1? Explain.

6. Copy this drawing. Use it to find $2\frac{1}{2} \div 1\frac{1}{2}$. How many groups of $1\frac{1}{2}$ are there in $2\frac{1}{2}$? Explain.

7. Explain what each division example means. Then create a drawing or use fraction strips to find each quotient.

   a. $1\frac{3}{8} \div \frac{1}{2}$ b. $3 \div \frac{4}{5}$ c. $\frac{1}{4} \div \frac{3}{8}$

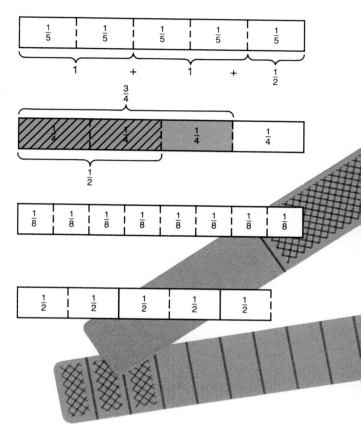

Summing Up

8. Explain how you represented 1 (a whole unit) in each example in **7**.

9. Compare your solutions to the division examples in **7** with your solutions to the examples in **D** on page 220. How are they alike? How are they different?

10. **Look back** at the quotients in **7** and the quotients in **D** on page 220. How do they compare?

11. Write a multiplication sentence to check each quotient in **D** and in **7**. Create a drawing or use fraction strips to illustrate each product.

12. In your own words describe what $\frac{3}{4} \div \frac{1}{2}$ means. Describe how you would find the quotient.

How would you write each as a fraction?

a. $5\overline{)10}$ **b.** $4 \div 9$ **c.** $a \div b$

Dividing Fractions

What if it takes $\frac{1}{10}$ of a min for this robot to fasten a bolt? How many bolts could the robot fasten in $\frac{1}{2}$ min?

You can divide to find the answer: $\frac{1}{2} \div \frac{1}{10}$. Explain why.

Study these steps for dividing.

(1) Write the division example as a fraction. $\frac{1}{2} \div \frac{1}{10} = \dfrac{\frac{1}{2}}{\frac{1}{10}}$

(2) Rename the fraction so the denominator is 1. To do this, multiply by the reciprocal.

Two numbers whose product is 1 are **reciprocals**.

a. $\frac{5}{8} \times \frac{8}{5} = 1$ **b.** $6 \times \frac{1}{6} = 1$ **c.** $2\frac{1}{4} \times \frac{4}{9} = \frac{9}{4} \times \frac{4}{9} = 1$

Name the reciprocals in **a**, in **b**, and in **c**.

Multiply the numerator and the denominator of the fraction by the reciprocal of the denominator, and simplify.

$$\dfrac{\frac{1}{2}}{\frac{1}{10}} \times \frac{10}{10} = \dfrac{\frac{1}{2} \times 10}{\frac{1}{10} \times 10} = \dfrac{\frac{1}{2} \times 10}{1} = \frac{1}{2} \times \overset{5}{\cancel{10}} = 5$$

The robot can fasten 5 bolts in $\frac{1}{2}$ min.

How do you know that $\dfrac{\frac{1}{2}}{\frac{1}{10}}$ and $\dfrac{\frac{1}{2} \times 10}{\frac{1}{10} \times 10}$ are equal?

Another Example

$$\frac{1}{10} \div \frac{3}{5} = \dfrac{\frac{1}{10}}{\frac{3}{5}} = \dfrac{\frac{1}{10}}{\frac{3}{5}} \times \dfrac{\frac{5}{3}}{\frac{5}{3}} = \dfrac{\frac{1}{10} \times \frac{5}{3}}{\frac{3}{5} \times \frac{5}{3}} = \dfrac{\frac{1}{10} \times \frac{5}{3}}{1} = \frac{1}{\underset{2}{\cancel{10}}} \times \frac{\cancel{5}}{3} = \frac{1}{6}$$

reciprocals

Write the reciprocal of each.

1. 8   **2.** $\frac{1}{10}$ **3.** $\frac{2}{5}$ **4.** $\frac{7}{2}$ **5.** 4

Divide. Write each quotient in lowest terms.

6. $\frac{5}{8} \div \frac{1}{4}$ **7.** $\frac{1}{6} \div \frac{2}{3}$ **8.** $\frac{4}{7} \div \frac{5}{7}$ **9.** $\frac{3}{8} \div \frac{2}{3}$ **10.** $\frac{5}{6} \div \frac{1}{4}$

Share Your Ideas Look back at the step in red in each example above. In your own words, describe how you could use multiplication and reciprocals to divide fractions.

Practice

Write the reciprocal of each.

11. 7   **12.** $\frac{1}{2}$ **13.** $\frac{3}{4}$ **14.** $\frac{7}{4}$ **15.** 12

Name the divisor and dividend in each.

16. $\frac{8}{12}$ **17.** $9\overline{)3}$ **18.** $17 \div 4$ **19.** $\frac{2}{5}$ **20.** $5 \div 6$

CHOICES   **Divide. Choose paper and pencil or mental math. Write each quotient in lowest terms.**

21. $\frac{4}{9} \div \frac{1}{3}$ **22.** $\frac{7}{8} \div \frac{1}{4}$ **23.** $\frac{1}{4} \div \frac{5}{8}$ **24.** $\frac{9}{10} \div \frac{2}{5}$ **25.** $\frac{3}{7} \div \frac{1}{3}$

26. $\frac{5}{9} \div \frac{2}{3}$ **27.** $\frac{3}{5} \div \frac{3}{10}$ **28.** $\frac{3}{4} \div \frac{1}{8}$ **29.** $\frac{1}{2} \div \frac{7}{10}$ **30.** $\frac{3}{4} \div \frac{7}{8}$

31. $\frac{3}{4} \div \frac{2}{3}$ **32.** $\frac{5}{9} \div \frac{5}{6}$ **33.** $\frac{1}{5} \div \frac{3}{5}$ **34.** $\frac{6}{7} \div \frac{5}{7}$ **35.** $\frac{5}{8} \div \frac{3}{4}$

36. $\frac{1}{2} \div \frac{3}{4}$ **37.** $\frac{3}{5} \div \frac{3}{4}$ **38.** $\frac{3}{4} \div \frac{5}{8}$ **39.** $\frac{2}{3} \div \frac{3}{4}$ **40.** $\frac{1}{8} \div \frac{1}{2}$

41. $4 \div \frac{1}{3}$ **42.** $\frac{5}{6} \div 3$ **43.** $6 \div 10$ **44.** $10 \div \frac{2}{3}$ **45.** $\frac{3}{4} \div 6$

Find each missing factor.

46. $\frac{3}{5} \times n = 1$ **47.** $n \times \frac{1}{3} = \frac{1}{3}$ **48.** $n \times 1 = \frac{1}{2}$ **49.** $n \times \frac{1}{6} = 1$

50. $\frac{1}{2} \times n \times \frac{2}{3} = \frac{1}{2}$ **51.** $5 \times n \times \frac{1}{5} = 1$ **52.** $n \times \frac{3}{5} \times 2 = 1\frac{1}{5}$ **53.** $n \times \frac{3}{4} \times \frac{1}{2} = 1$

Think and Apply

54. How many bolts can the robot on page 222 fasten in 5 min?

55. **What if** the time it takes the robot to fasten a bolt is cut in half? How many bolts can it fasten in $\frac{1}{2}$ min? in 5 min?

Test Taker

Sometimes you can use estimation to help you select the correct answer on a test. Estimate each answer. Then use your estimate to determine the correct answer.

56. $\frac{1}{4} \div \frac{5}{6}$

   a. $3\frac{1}{3}$ **b.** $1\frac{1}{2}$ **c.** $\frac{3}{10}$

57. $\frac{3}{5} \times 72$

   a. $\frac{8}{15}$ **b.** $10\frac{2}{5}$ **c.** $43\frac{1}{5}$

58. 65×74

   a. 4,810   **b.** 440   **c.** 48

Is this statement sometimes, always, or never true? Explain.
- The quotient of two fractions is greater than 1.

SUMMING UP

Dividing Mixed Numbers

Before laser optical scanners were installed at Nielson's Super Market, an average of 6 customers could be checked out in 30 minutes. The average sale is now totalled in $3\frac{1}{3}$ minutes. How many customers can be checked out in 30 minutes now?

To solve, you can divide: $30 \div 3\frac{1}{3}$.

Write the whole number and the mixed number as fractions.

$30 \div 3\frac{1}{3} = \frac{30}{1} \div \frac{10}{3}$

Divide as with fractions.

$\frac{30}{1} \div \frac{10}{3} = \frac{30}{1} \times \frac{3}{10} = \frac{\overset{3}{\cancel{30}}}{1} \times \frac{3}{\underset{1}{\cancel{10}}} = \frac{9}{1} = 9$

In 30 minutes, 9 customers can be checked out.

More Examples

a. $3\frac{3}{4} \div 1\frac{7}{8} = \frac{15}{4} \div \frac{15}{8}$

$= \frac{\overset{1}{\cancel{15}}}{\underset{1}{\cancel{4}}} \times \frac{\overset{2}{\cancel{8}}}{\underset{1}{\cancel{15}}}$

$= 2$

b. $5\frac{1}{4} \div 3\frac{1}{2} = \frac{21}{4} \div \frac{7}{2}$

$= \frac{\overset{3}{\cancel{21}}}{\underset{2}{\cancel{4}}} \times \frac{\overset{1}{\cancel{2}}}{\underset{1}{\cancel{7}}}$

$= \frac{3}{2}$, or $1\frac{1}{2}$

c. $\frac{7}{8} \div 1\frac{3}{4} = \frac{7}{8} \div \frac{7}{4}$

$= \frac{\overset{1}{\cancel{7}}}{\underset{2}{\cancel{8}}} \times \frac{\overset{1}{\cancel{4}}}{\underset{1}{\cancel{7}}}$

$= \frac{1}{2}$

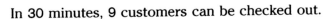

Check Your Understanding

Write the reciprocal of each.

1. $1\frac{1}{2}$
2. 11
3. $3\frac{3}{4}$
4. $2\frac{3}{5}$
5. $4\frac{5}{8}$

Divide. Write each quotient in lowest terms.

6. $2\frac{1}{3} \div 1\frac{1}{6}$
7. $5\frac{1}{4} \div 2\frac{1}{2}$
8. $1\frac{2}{3} \div \frac{5}{6}$
9. $1\frac{3}{10} \div 5$
10. $16 \div 2\frac{2}{3}$

Share Your Ideas   Look back at example **b.** How do you know that $\frac{21}{4} \div \frac{7}{2}$ equals $\frac{21}{4} \times \frac{2}{7}$?

Write the reciprocal of each.

11. $4\frac{2}{3}$ **12.** 18 **13.** $\frac{5}{8}$ **14.** $5\frac{1}{6}$ **15.** $3\frac{7}{10}$

Divide. Write each quotient in lowest terms.

16. $10 \div 2\frac{1}{4}$ **17.** $7 \div 2\frac{1}{3}$ **18.** $5 \div 1\frac{3}{5}$ **19.** $85 \div 3$ **20.** $92 \div 16$

21. $3\frac{5}{6} \div 2$ **22.** $4\frac{3}{4} \div 2$ **23.** $5\frac{3}{5} \div \frac{1}{5}$ **24.** $8\frac{1}{2} \div 4$ **25.** $9\frac{1}{5} \div 6$

26. $3\frac{3}{4} \div 1\frac{1}{2}$ **27.** $7\frac{1}{2} \div 3\frac{3}{4}$ **28.** $9\frac{1}{4} \div 4\frac{5}{8}$ **29.** $3\frac{1}{2} \div 10\frac{1}{2}$ **30.** $9\frac{1}{5} \div 4\frac{3}{5}$

31. $6\frac{3}{4} \div \frac{1}{8}$ **32.** $4\frac{2}{3} \div 9\frac{2}{3}$ **33.** $6\frac{5}{6} \div 2\frac{1}{3}$ **34.** $5\frac{1}{4} \div \frac{7}{8}$ **35.** $\frac{5}{9} \div 2\frac{2}{9}$

36. $4\frac{3}{5} \div 6\frac{9}{10}$ **37.** $5\frac{3}{8} \div 7\frac{1}{4}$ **38.** $8\frac{7}{8} \div 2\frac{3}{4}$ **39.** $4\frac{3}{4} \div 5\frac{1}{10}$ **40.** $6\frac{1}{8} \div 3\frac{7}{10}$

Use your number sense. Without multiplying or dividing, replace each ⬤ with <, >, or =. Explain your thinking.

41. $3\frac{1}{2} \div 1\frac{3}{4}$ ⬤ $1\frac{3}{4} \div 3\frac{1}{2}$

42. $5\frac{1}{3} \div 1\frac{1}{4}$ ⬤ $5\frac{1}{3} \times 1\frac{1}{4}$

43. $6 \div 2\frac{1}{2}$ ⬤ $3 \div 1\frac{1}{4}$

44. $12\frac{3}{4} \div 12\frac{3}{4}$ ⬤ $2\frac{1}{2} \times \frac{2}{5}$

45. In minutes and seconds, how long does the average sale at Nielson's now take?

46. Visit a supermarket. Count the number of customers served in 10 min in a regular lane and in an express lane. Compute the average waiting time in each lane.

47. Combine the data your class has collected. Would the combined data give a better estimate of the average waiting time? Explain your reasoning.

GROCERY LIST

1 box rice
1 gal milk
1 loaf bread
2 lb apples
1 box soap
1 bottle grape juice
1 box spaghetti
1 gal frozen yogurt
1 can green beans
1 can tomato soup
1 box cornflakes

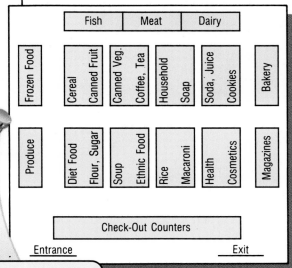

Visual Thinking

48. Describe the shortest route through Nielson's Super Market to get the items on the grocery list below.

| Fish | Meat | Dairy |

Frozen Food — Cereal | Canned Fruit | Canned Veg. | Coffee, Tea | Household | Soap | Soda, Juice | Cookies | Bakery

Produce — Diet Food | Flour, Sugar | Soup | Ethnic Food | Rice | Macaroni | Health | Cosmetics | Magazines

Check-Out Counters

Entrance   Exit

Explain the difference between $4\frac{1}{2} \times 1\frac{1}{2}$ and $4\frac{1}{2} \div 1\frac{1}{2}$.

SUMMING UP

Describe how you would solve each equation.

a. $\frac{n}{9} = 22$ **b.** $5n = 12.5$

Solving Fraction Equations

You can solve equations with fractions and mixed numbers
the same way you solve equations with whole numbers.

a. $\frac{1}{10} \times n = \frac{3}{5}$

$\frac{1}{10} \div \frac{1}{10} \times n = \frac{3}{5} \div \frac{1}{10}$ ⟵ Use the inverse of multiplication.

$n = \frac{3}{5} \div \frac{1}{10} = \frac{3}{5} \times \frac{\overset{2}{\cancel{10}}}{1} = 6$

Check $\frac{1}{10} \times 6 = \frac{3}{5}$ ⟵ Replace n with 6.

b. $x \div \frac{1}{3} = 1\frac{1}{2}$

$x \div \frac{1}{3} \times \frac{1}{3} = 1\frac{1}{2} \times \frac{1}{3}$ ⟵ Use the inverse of division.

$x = \frac{3}{2} \times \frac{1}{\underset{1}{\cancel{3}}} = \frac{1}{2}$

Check $\frac{1}{2} \div \frac{1}{3} = \frac{1}{2} \times \frac{3}{1} = \frac{3}{2}$, or $1\frac{1}{2}$ ⟵ Replace x with $\frac{1}{2}$.

c. $n \times 1\frac{3}{4} = 7$

$n \times 1\frac{3}{4} \div 1\frac{3}{4} = 7 \div 1\frac{3}{4}$

$n = 7 \div \frac{7}{4} = \overset{1}{\cancel{7}} \times \frac{4}{\underset{1}{\cancel{7}}} = 4$

d. $n \div \frac{1}{2} = 5$

$n \div \frac{1}{2} \times \frac{1}{2} = 5 \times \frac{1}{2}$

$n = \frac{5}{1} \times \frac{1}{2} = \frac{5}{2}$, or $2\frac{1}{2}$

Explain how inverses were used to solve **c** and **d**. How
would you check **c** and **d**?

Solve and check.

1. $5 \times n = 1\frac{1}{4}$ **2.** $n \div \frac{3}{8} = 3$ **3.** $n \div 5 = 1\frac{1}{2}$ **4.** $n \times 8 = 2\frac{1}{2}$

Share Your Ideas Look back at example **a**. Explain why
$\frac{1}{10} \div \frac{1}{10} \times n = n$. Look back at example **b**. Explain why $x \div \frac{1}{3} \times \frac{1}{3} = x$.

226

Solve and check.

5. $\frac{2}{3} \times n = 6$

6. $\frac{5}{8} \times n = 15$

7. $n \times \frac{4}{5} = 8$

8. $n \times 9 = 6$

9. $n \div \frac{1}{2} = 3\frac{1}{4}$

10. $n \div \frac{2}{3} = 5$

11. $n \div 1\frac{3}{5} = 5$

12. $n \times 5 = 12\frac{1}{2}$

13. $3\frac{1}{4} \times n = 8$

14. $\frac{5}{8} \times n = 1$

15. $n \div 2\frac{1}{3} = 1$

16. $7\frac{1}{5} \times n = 3\frac{3}{5}$

17. $n \div 4 = 1\frac{7}{8}$

18. $n \div 3\frac{1}{5} = \frac{1}{3}$

19. $n \times \frac{5}{8} = 1\frac{1}{2}$

20. $n \times 3 = \frac{1}{2} \times \frac{3}{4}$

21. $n \div \frac{2}{3} = 2\frac{1}{2} \times 3$

22. $\frac{2}{5} \times n = 2\frac{1}{2} \times 1$

Write an equation for each sentence. Then solve it.

23. The product of a number n and 3 is 2.

24. Three fourths of a number n is $4\frac{1}{2}$.

25. A number n divided by $1\frac{1}{4}$ is 10.

26. The product of a number n and $\frac{2}{3}$ equals $\frac{2}{5}$ times 5.

Think and Apply

Choose the appropriate equation(s). Then solve.

27. The Sicomac School Parents' Association raised $800 to purchase a software program. This was $1\frac{1}{3}$ times the cost of the program. How much did the program cost?

   a. $n \times 1\frac{1}{3} = \$800$ **b.** $n \div 1\frac{1}{3} = \$800$

28. The school board gave Sicomac School $30,000 to spend on the computer lab. The principal said $\frac{3}{5}$ could be spent on computers, $\frac{1}{3}$ on software, and the rest on printers. How much will be spent for each?

   a. $\frac{3}{5} \times c = \$30,000$ **b.** $\frac{3}{5} \times \$30,000 = c$

      $\frac{1}{3} \times s = \$30,000$ $\frac{1}{3} \times \$30,000 = s$

      $\frac{1}{15} \times p = \$30,000$ $\frac{1}{15} \times \$30,000 = p$

Draw a number line to solve this equation: $n \times \frac{2}{3} = 6$.

Mixed Review

1. $23.8 + 19.5$

2. $17.261 + 29.584$

3. $23.5 - 18.96$

4. $7.201 - 5.059$

5. 8.3×9.54

6. 7.5×23.7

7. $6.2 \div 3.1$

8. $2.35 \div 0.05$

9. $5\frac{3}{4} + 1\frac{1}{4}$

10. $8\frac{2}{3} - 4\frac{1}{3}$

11. $9\frac{3}{5} - 8$

12. $9\frac{1}{8} - 4\frac{5}{8}$

13. $8\frac{1}{2} + 4\frac{3}{5}$

14. $6\frac{2}{3} - 5\frac{1}{4}$

15. $8\frac{1}{4} - 5\frac{3}{8}$

16. $9\frac{7}{8} - 2\frac{9}{10}$

Solve for n.

17. $5 + n = 91$

18. $n - 17 = 14$

19. $\frac{5}{8} + n = 1\frac{1}{2}$

20. $\frac{3}{4} - n = \frac{1}{8}$

SUMMING UP

Activity

Exploring Fraction Patterns

Each storage box is half the size of the one below it.

Each term in the sequence below is half the number before it.

16, 8, 4, 2, 1, . . .

Can you continue the pattern?

Working together

A. Compare these two sequences. How are they alike? How are they different? Write a rule for each. Then write the next four terms.

- 1, 2, 4, 8, 16, _____ , _____ , _____ , _____ , . . .

- 16, 8, 4, 2, 1, _____ , _____ , _____ , _____ , . . .

B. Compare these two sequences. How are they alike? How are they different? Write the next three terms for each. Then simplify each term. Write a rule for each sequence.

- 16×1, $16 \times \frac{1}{2}$, $16 \times \frac{1}{4}$, $16 \times \frac{1}{8}$, $16 \times \frac{1}{16}$, _____ , _____ , _____ , . . .

- $16 \div 1$, $16 \div \frac{1}{2}$, $16 \div \frac{1}{4}$, $16 \div \frac{1}{8}$, $16 \div \frac{1}{16}$, _____ , _____ , _____ , . . .

C. Create a sequence. Use the rule *multiply by $\frac{1}{3}$*. Start with 1. Write the first six terms. Then create another sequence. Use the rule *divide by $\frac{1}{3}$*. Start with 1 and write the first six terms.

Sharing Your Results

1. Compare the two sequences in **A** with the two in **B**. How are they alike? How are they different?

2. How do the rules you wrote for the sequences in **A** compare with those you wrote for the sequences in **B**?

3. **Look back** at the two sequences in **C**. How are they alike? How are they different? Write a few sentences that describe the difference between multiplying by $\frac{1}{3}$ and dividing by $\frac{1}{3}$. Compare your answer with those of your classmates.

Extending the Activity

Work with a partner. Investigate these patterns. Use a calculator if possible.

Find each product.

4. 256×125

5. 340×179

6. $1,308 \times 685$

7. $256 \times \frac{1}{16}$

8. $340 \times \frac{13}{20}$

9. $1,308 \times \frac{5}{12}$

Find each quotient.

10. $256 \div 64$

11. $340 \div 8$

12. $1,308 \div 1,962$

13. $256 \div \frac{2}{3}$

14. $340 \div \frac{5}{16}$

15. $1,308 \div \frac{1}{5}$

Analyze.

16. Describe the numbers in **4–6.** In each case, is the product greater than either factor?

17. Describe the numbers in **7–9.** In each case, is the product greater than the whole number?

18. Describe the numbers in **10–12.** In each case, is the quotient greater than the dividend?

19. Describe the numbers in **13–15.** In each case, is the quotient greater than the dividend?

Summing Up

Write *always, sometimes,* or *never.*

20. The quotient of two fractions, each less than 1, is _____ less than the dividend.

21. The quotient of two whole numbers is _____ greater than the dividend.

22. The product of a whole number and a fraction less than 1 is _____ less than or equal to the whole number.

23. The quotient of a whole number divided by a fraction less than 1 is _____ greater than or equal to the dividend.

24. The product of two whole numbers is _____ greater than or equal to either factor.

25. A sequence with the rule *multiply by* $\frac{2}{3}$ _____ decreases. A sequence with the rule *divide by* $\frac{2}{3}$ _____ decreases.

26. The product of two fractions is _____ less than 1.

Express each fraction as a decimal.

a. $\frac{1}{2}$ **b.** $\frac{3}{4}$ **c.** $\frac{5}{8}$

Using a Calculator: Expressing Quotients

Jennifer and Rob need storage boxes for their compact disc collection. They have 38 compact discs. Each box will hold 12 discs. How many boxes do they need?

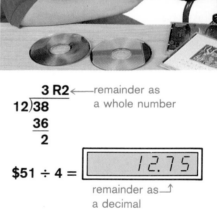

To find the answer, they divided on their calculator.

$$38 \div 12 = \boxed{3.1666666}$$

Rob said, "We can fill 3 boxes."

"Yes, but we need 4 boxes," replied Jennifer.

Explain each person's reasoning.

▶ To give a reasonable answer to a division problem, you may need to ignore the remainder or increase the quotient. In other division problems, you may have to express the remainder in one of the following three ways.

a. How many compact discs will be in the fourth storage box?

There will be 2 discs in the fourth box.

$$\begin{array}{r} 3\ \text{R2} \longleftarrow \\ 12\overline{)38} \\ \underline{36} \\ 2 \end{array}$$
remainder as a whole number

b. Rob and Jennifer's mother bought 4 compact discs for $51. On the average, how much did each disc cost?

The average cost was $12.75.

$$\$51 \div 4 = \boxed{12.75}$$
remainder as ⤴ a decimal

c. Jennifer's favorite compact disc album has 20 songs on it. It is 130 min long. On the average, how long is each song?

Each song averages $6\frac{1}{2}$ min.

$$6\frac{10}{20} = 6\frac{1}{2}$$
$$\begin{array}{r} 20\overline{)130} \\ \underline{120} \\ 10 \end{array}$$
remainder as a fraction

Check Your Understanding

Divide. Write each quotient in three ways.

1. $12 \div 5$

2. $4\overline{)85}$

3. $69 \div 15$

4. $\frac{36}{20}$

5. $25\overline{)260}$

Share Your Ideas Look back at **2.** Explain how to check each of the three quotients.

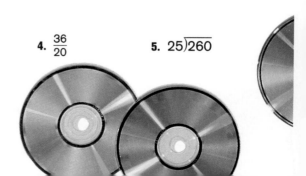

Practice

Divide. Write each quotient in three ways. Choose paper and pencil, mental math, or a calculator.

6. $5\overline{)82}$ **7.** $6\overline{)75}$ **8.** $4\overline{)95}$ **9.** $2\overline{)133}$ **10.** $8\overline{)125}$

11. $10\overline{)275}$ **12.** $12\overline{)150}$ **13.** $20\overline{)245}$ **14.** $14\overline{)133}$ **15.** $25\overline{)210}$

16. $155 \div 20$ **17.** $94 \div 16$ **18.** $390 \div 40$ **19.** $201 \div 24$ **20.** $810 \div 50$

21. $895 \div 80$ **22.** $265 \div 25$ **23.** $627 \div 22$ **24.** $942 \div 50$ **25.** $609 \div 28$

26. $\frac{29}{4}$ **27.** $\frac{15}{2}$ **28.** $\frac{83}{5}$ **29.** $\frac{110}{25}$ **30.** $\frac{57}{12}$

31. $1,020 \div 50$ **32.** $4,235 \div 25$ **33.** $280\overline{)4,270}$ **34.** $\frac{19,260}{540}$ **35.** $\frac{90,480}{360}$

Use a calculator to find each quotient. Then, using the displayed quotient, use subtraction and multiplication to find the remainder. Explain your method. Finally, write the quotient, using the remainder.

36. $279 \div 8$ **37.** $1,251 \div 6$ **38.** $794 \div 5$

39. $3,376 \div 64$ **40.** $8,007 \div 12$ **41.** $1,836 \div 32$

Think and Apply

Select the reasonable answer for each.

a. $2   **b.** $17.50   **c.** 17.5   **d.** 17

42. Cassettes cost $4 each. How many can you buy for $70?

43. Look back at **42.** How much change will you receive?

44. Rob bought 4 compact discs for $70. What was the average cost of each?

45. Rob's mother paid $4 per gram for perfume. How many grams did she buy if she paid $70 for a bottle?

Solve. Decide whether an estimate is sufficient or an exact answer is necessary.

46. How many classical albums can you buy for $80?

47. Look back at **46.** How much change will you receive?

48. Which costs more, a classical album or 2 rock albums?

49. What if you paid $101.70 for 6 albums? What albums did you buy?

Complete.
Dividend: 765. Remainder: R15. Quotient: $30\frac{3}{5}$. Divisor:?

SUMMING UP

Name some items you would measure in terms of each.
a. length   **b.** weight   **c.** capacity

Fractions and Measurement

Ms. Card wanted to buy a lap computer that weighs less than 4 pounds. She purchased one that weighs 60 ounces. Does her new computer weigh less than 4 pounds?

Use the facts below to change from one unit to another.

▶ To change to a larger unit, divide.

$$60 \text{ oz} = \underline{\hphantom{xx}} \text{ lb}$$

$$60 \div 16 = 3\frac{12}{16}, \text{ or } 3\frac{3}{4} \qquad \text{Why is 60 divided by 16?}$$

$$60 \text{ oz} = 3\frac{3}{4} \text{ lb}$$

Ms. Card's new computer weighs less than 4 pounds.

Weight	
16 ounces (oz) = 1 pound (lb)	
2,000 lb = 1 ton (T)	
Capacity	
8 fluid ounces (fl oz) = 1 cup (c)	
2 c = 1 pint (pt)	
2 pt = 1 quart (qt)	
4 qt = 1 gallon (gal)	
Length	
12 inches (in.) = 1 foot (ft)	
3 ft = 1 yard (yd)	
5,280 ft = 1 mile (mi)	

▶ To change to a smaller unit, multiply.

$$2\frac{1}{2} \text{ gal} = \underline{\hphantom{xx}} \text{ qt}$$

$$2\frac{1}{2} \times 4 = \frac{5}{\underset{1}{\cancel{2}}} \times \frac{\overset{2}{\cancel{4}}}{1} = 10 \qquad \text{Why is } 2\frac{1}{2} \text{ multiplied by 4?}$$

$$2\frac{1}{2} \text{ gal} = 10 \text{ qt}$$

More Examples

a. $9\frac{1}{2} \text{ pt} = \underline{\hphantom{xxxx}} \text{ qt}$

$9\frac{1}{2} \div 2 = \frac{19}{2} \times \frac{1}{2}$

$\qquad = \frac{19}{4} = 4\frac{3}{4}$

$9\frac{1}{2} \text{ pt} = 4\frac{3}{4} \text{ qt}$

b. $3 \text{ yd} = \underline{\hphantom{xxxx}} \text{ in.}$

$3 \times 3 = 9$

$3 \text{ yd} = 9 \text{ ft}$

$9 \times 12 = 108$

$3 \text{ yd} = 9 \text{ ft} = 108 \text{ in.}$

Check Your Understanding

Complete.

1. 7 T = _____ lb

2. 3 c = _____ pt

3. 13 ft = _____ in.

4. $5\frac{3}{8}$ lb = _____ oz

5. 14 pt = _____ gal

6. $5\frac{2}{3}$ yd = _____ ft

Share Your Ideas   Why do you multiply to change from a larger to a smaller unit? Why do you divide to change from a smaller to a larger unit?

Practice

Complete.

7. 5 lb = _____ oz

8. 9 T = _____ lb

9. 34 ft = _____ yd _____ ft

10. 8 gal = _____ pt

11. 10 c = _____ pt

12. 20 in. = _____ ft _____ in.

13. 64 in. = _____ ft

14. 144 in. = _____ yd

15. 24 oz = _____ lb

16. 45 qt = _____ pt

17. $8\frac{1}{2}$ gal = _____ qt

18. $5\frac{1}{2}$ pt = _____ c

19. $9\frac{2}{3}$ yd = _____ ft

20. $5\frac{1}{4}$ lb = _____ oz

21. 2 mi = _____ ft

22. $5\frac{1}{3}$ yd = _____ in.

23. $8\frac{3}{4}$ gal = _____ pt

24. $17\frac{1}{2}$ ft = _____ yd

Add or subtract.

25.
```
   3 ft 9 in.
 + 2 ft 6 in.
```

26.
```
   5 gal 3 qt
 - 2 gal 2 qt
```

27.
```
   10 lb
 -  4 lb 8 oz
```

28.
```
   6 qt 1 pt
 + 7 qt 1 pt
```

29.
```
   5 yd 1 ft
 - 2 yd 2 ft
```

30.
```
   8 lb  5 oz
 + 3 lb 12 oz
```

31.
```
   4 c 5 fl oz
 + 3 c 3 fl oz
```

32.
```
   6 T
 - 3 T 1,500 lb
```

Compare. Replace each ● with <, =, or >.

33. 15 lb ● 240 oz

34. 19 yd ● 54 ft

35. 73 in. ● $6\frac{1}{4}$ ft

36. 432 in. ● $11\frac{3}{4}$ yd

37. $7\frac{3}{4}$ T ● 225,000 oz

38. $6\frac{3}{4}$ mi ● 11,880 yd

Think and Apply

Change the unit of measure in each statement to a more appropriate one.

39. John's mother weighs 2,056 oz.

40. John's father is $2\frac{1}{18}$ yd tall.

41. The recipe called for $\frac{1}{8}$ qt of raisins.

42. Marla drank $\frac{1}{16}$ gal of water.

 43. Find the size of the containers of ten liquid products your family uses. Express the size of each container as a fraction of a pint or a fraction of a quart.

CHOICES Solve. Use paper and pencil or a calculator.

44. Light travels at 186,000 mi per second. How far will a beam of light travel in 1 minute?

45. Sound travels at 1,085 ft per second. What is its speed in mi per second? in mi per hour? Round to the nearest tenth.

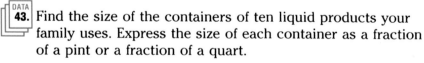

Find your weight in ounces. Find your height in yards. Estimate how far you walk each day in miles, yards, and feet.

SUMMING UP

Using Problem Solving

Who Is the Leading Character?

George Bernard Shaw's play *Major Barbara* has three acts. Acts 2 and 3, which are about the same length, are each twice as long as Act 1. The table shows the fraction of each act that each of the six main characters is on stage.

Character	Act 1	Act 2	Act 3
Lady Britomart	all of it	0	$\frac{9}{10}$
Mr. Undershaft	$\frac{2}{5}$	$\frac{2}{3}$	$\frac{3}{4}$
Barbara	$\frac{3}{5}$	$\frac{3}{4}$	$\frac{3}{4}$
Sarah	$\frac{3}{5}$	0	$\frac{3}{5}$
Stephen	all of it	0	$\frac{4}{5}$
Cusins	$\frac{3}{5}$	$\frac{2}{5}$	$\frac{3}{4}$

Rank the characters in order of the amount of time they spend on stage. You may find grid paper helpful.

Working together

A. Make a quick estimate of the time each character is on stage. Then rank the characters. How did you make your estimates?

B. Simulate the problem: Make a rectangle for each character in Act 1. Shade a fractional part of each rectangle to show the amount of time each character spends on stage. How should you represent Acts 2 and 3? How can you use this method to rank the characters?

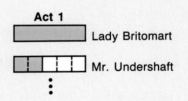

C. Do you see another method for finding out who is on stage the most? If so, try it. Explain your method.

Sharing Your Ideas

1. Rank the characters by the time spent on stage.

2. When you simulated the problem, how did you represent the time in Acts 2 and 3? Did you find another way to solve the problem? What was your method?

Extending Your Thinking

3. Major speeches are also important to a character. The following chart shows the number of major speeches for each character. Rank the characters in order of importance in terms of their major speeches.

Character	Act 1	Act 2	Act 3
Lady Britomart	2	0	0
Mr. Undershaft	1	2	5
Barbara	0	2	4
Sarah	0	0	0
Stephen	1	0	1
Cusins	0	1	1

4. Use both the time on stage and major speeches to rank the characters in order of their importance in the play. Be prepared to explain how you arrived at your decision.

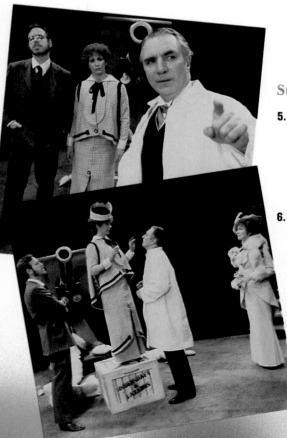

Summing Up

5. Who was the most important character, based upon major speeches? Who was the least important character? When rating by major speeches, does it matter that Act 2 and Act 3 are each twice as long as Act 1?

6. What was your order when you considered both major speeches and amount of time on stage? Compare the different methods of combining the two criteria. Which method did you prefer?

Chapter Review

Choose the best estimate. pages 206–207

1. $2\frac{1}{2} \div \frac{3}{4}$
   a. 1
   b. 2
   c. 3

2. $6\frac{1}{3} \times 2\frac{4}{5}$
   a. 12
   b. 18
   c. 21

3. $\frac{5}{8} \div \frac{1}{10}$
   a. 0
   b. 1
   c. 5

Estimate. Then multiply or divide. Write each answer in lowest terms. pages 208–215, 220–225

4. $\frac{1}{2} \div \frac{2}{3}$

5. $8\frac{1}{3} \times 1\frac{1}{5}$

6. $\frac{7}{9} \div \frac{1}{3}$

7. $6\frac{1}{3} \times 2$

8. $4\frac{1}{8} \times \frac{7}{8}$

9. $16 \times 1\frac{1}{3}$

10. $\frac{4}{9} \times 18$

11. $1\frac{1}{4} \times 6$

12. $\frac{2}{3} \times \frac{3}{4}$

13. $\frac{1}{8} \div \frac{1}{7}$

14. $2\frac{1}{3} \div 1\frac{3}{4}$

15. $2\frac{1}{3} \times 1\frac{3}{4}$

16. $6\frac{2}{5} \times \frac{5}{8}$

17. $6\frac{2}{5} \div \frac{5}{8}$

18. $\frac{4}{5} \times \frac{1}{2}$

19. $\frac{4}{5} \div \frac{1}{2}$

20. $4 \div 1\frac{1}{8}$

21. $\frac{3}{5} \div 6$

22. $\frac{3}{4} \div 1\frac{1}{3}$

23. $\frac{3}{4} \times 1\frac{1}{3}$

24. $20 \div \frac{4}{5}$

25. $8 \div 2\frac{1}{4}$

26. $12\frac{1}{2} \div 5$

27. $3\frac{2}{3} \div 5\frac{1}{2}$

Solve. pages 226–227

28. $x \times \frac{3}{4} = 1\frac{1}{2}$

29. $n \div \frac{1}{3} = 6$

30. $\frac{x}{6} = 1\frac{1}{3}$

31. $n \times 2\frac{1}{2} = 8$

32. $5 = n \div 3\frac{2}{3}$

33. $\frac{5}{6}x = 1$

34. $n \div \frac{2}{5} = 7\frac{1}{2}$

35. $3\frac{1}{3} \times y = 3\frac{1}{3}$

Divide. Write each quotient in three ways. pages 230–231

36. $16 \div 3$

37. $134 \div 4$

38. $1,805 \div 25$

39. $48\overline{)1,746}$

Complete. pages 232–233

40. 4 lb = _____ oz

41. 35 in. = _____ ft _____ in.

42. 19 ft = _____ yd

43. 28 oz = _____ lb _____ oz

44. 6 c = _____ qt

45. 4 gal = _____ pt

46. 18 fl oz = _____ c

47. 13,200 ft = _____ mi

48. $4\frac{1}{2}$ T = _____ lb

Solve. pages 217–219, 234–235

49. Each day Richard uses $\frac{1}{8}$ of the original length of his pencil. He took a new pencil on Monday. By Friday morning it was $3\frac{3}{4}$ in. long. How long was the pencil when it was new?

50. Patti has $25.75 to spend on paper for her computer. The paper costs $5.50 per pack. How many packs can she buy?

Chapter Test

Choose the best estimate.

1. $\frac{7}{8} \div \frac{1}{4}$

   a. 0

   b. $\frac{7}{8}$

   c. 4

2. $\frac{3}{5} \times \frac{7}{8}$

   a. 0

   b. $\frac{1}{2}$

   c. 1

3. $3\frac{2}{3} \times 1\frac{1}{6}$

   a. 4

   b. 6

   c. 8

Estimate. Then multiply or divide. Write each answer in lowest terms.

4. $\frac{1}{8} \times \frac{4}{5}$

5. $6\frac{2}{7} \div \frac{2}{7}$

6. $1\frac{2}{3} \times 2\frac{3}{5}$

7. $2\frac{1}{4} \div 1\frac{2}{3}$

8. $\frac{7}{8} \div \frac{1}{4}$

9. $12 \times 2\frac{1}{3}$

10. $\frac{5}{6} \div 10$

11. $10 \div \frac{5}{6}$

12. $\frac{3}{8} \times 2\frac{2}{3}$

Solve for n.

13. $\frac{3}{5}n = 8$

14. $n \div \frac{3}{4} = \frac{4}{5}$

15. $10n = 5$

16. $n \div 1\frac{3}{5} = \frac{5}{8}$

Divide. Write each quotient in three different ways.

17. $12 \div 5$

18. $380 \div 24$

19. $36\overline{)8,730}$

Complete.

20. 36 oz = _____ lb

21. $2\frac{1}{3}$ ft = _____ in.

22. $5\frac{1}{2}$ gal = _____ qt

23. 10 ft = _____ yd

Solve.

24. Carlos visited the library one day each week for four weeks. Each week his visit lasted $1\frac{1}{2}$ times as long as his preceding visit. The last week Carlos spent $2\frac{1}{4}$ hours at the library. How long was his visit during the first week?

25. The counter on Consuelo's VCR showed 8180 Friday morning. On Wednesday and Thursday nights she had taped a two-part show. Each part was the same length. Thursday morning the number on the counter was 6820. What number was on the counter Wednesday morning?

THINK   Evaluate. Let $a = \frac{1}{2}$, $b = \frac{3}{4}$, $c = 1\frac{1}{3}$, $d = 2\frac{1}{6}$.

$a \div b \times 2d + b \times c$

Fraction Estimation Game

Play this game in a group of 4 students.

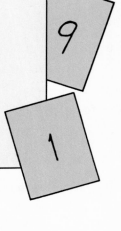

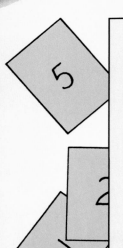

Instructions

1. Write each of the digits from 1 to 9 on nine cards.

2. Mix the cards well. Place them face down.

3. Each player, in turn, chooses one card. As the number is shown, all 4 players must record it in one of the four places below.

$$\frac{a}{b} \div \frac{c}{d}$$

4. The student with a quotient closest to 1 wins the game.

Play the game ten times. How did you decide which quotient was closest to 1?

Now try these. Choose the winner for each game.

1. Player A: $\frac{3}{2} \div \frac{1}{6}$

   Player B: $\frac{1}{3} \div \frac{6}{2}$

   Player C: $\frac{3}{6} \div \frac{1}{2}$

   Player D: $\frac{1}{6} \div \frac{3}{2}$

2. Player A: $\frac{4}{8} \div \frac{3}{7}$

   Player B: $\frac{4}{7} \div \frac{3}{8}$

   Player C: $\frac{4}{3} \div \frac{8}{7}$

   Player D: $\frac{3}{4} \div \frac{8}{7}$

3. Player A: $\frac{2}{9} \div \frac{6}{8}$

   Player B: $\frac{2}{8} \div \frac{6}{9}$

   Player C: $\frac{8}{9} \div \frac{2}{6}$

   Player D: $\frac{8}{2} \div \frac{6}{9}$

4. Which of these strategies would help you win the game?

   a. putting smaller numbers in the numerators

   b. building 2 fractions that are approximately equal

   c. trying to form reciprocals

5. Change the division sign to a multiplication sign. Play the game five more times. Find a strategy to help you win the game.

In chapters 4 through 6 we studied equations, geometry, and fractions.

Chef of the Day

List some occupations in which people add and subtract fractions. Did you include a carpenter, who must measure lengths of wood? Did you include a chef, who uses fractions when following a recipe?

The recipe below makes 9 muffins. What if your family were having guests for dinner, and you wanted to make 18 muffins instead of 9? How would you increase the recipe? Complete the index card below to make 18 muffins.

Raisin and Carrot Muffins

2 carrots, peeled and grated   ¾ c whole wheat flour
1 egg   1 tsp baking powder
¼ c honey   ½ tsp ground cinnamon
¼ c safflower oil or other oil   ¼ c raisins

Preheat oven to 350° F Grease and flour 9 muffin cups. Put carrots in bowl. Add the egg, honey, and oil and mix them together with a fork. In another bowl, combine the flour, baking powder, and cinnamon. Using a wooden spoon, beat the flour mixture and raisins with the other ingredients.

Fill the muffin cups about three-quarters full with the mixture. Bake the muffins for 20 minutes, until the centers spring back when pressed. Loosen the muffins with a knife and put them on a rack to cool.   Makes 9 muffins.

Why not try cooking this recipe. Or, if you have a favorite recipe you would rather make, discuss how you would make more or less of the amount shown on the recipe. For example, change your recipe to serve fewer people than the number shown on the recipe. Enjoy!

To make 18 muffins
   carrots
   eggs
   c honey
   c safflower oil
   c whole wheat flour
   tsp baking powder
   tsp ground cinnamon
   c raisins

Cumulative Review

Choose the correct answers. Write A, B, C, or D.

1. Evaluate. $(9 - 4) \times 3^2$

    A 27   **C** 45

    B 30   **D** not given

2. What is the value of $48 \div 4m$ for $m = 2$?

    A 6   **C** 4

    B 12   **D** not given

3. Choose the equation.
8 less than a number y is 15.

    A $y - 8 = 15$ **C** $y + 8 = 15$

    B $8 - y = 15$ **D** not given

4. What is the inverse of subtracting 4?

    A multiplying by 4   **C** subtracting 4

    B dividing by 4   **D** not given

5. Solve for n. $n + 19 = 24$

    A 5   **C** 15

    B 43   **D** not given

6. Solve for n. $\frac{n}{6} = 12$

    A 37   **C** 13

    B 72   **D** not given

7. Which statement is true?

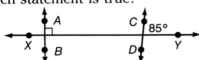

    A $\overline{AB} \parallel \overline{XY}$ **C** $\overline{AB} \parallel \overline{CD}$

    B $\overline{AB} \perp \overline{XY}$ **D** not given

8. What is the complement of $32°$?

    A $148°$ **C** $122°$

    B $58°$ **D** not given

9. What is x?

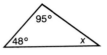

    A $85°$ **C** $37°$

    B $217°$ **D** not given

10. The sides of $\triangle ABC$ measure 4 cm, 5 cm, and 4 cm. What kind of triangle is ABC?

    A obtuse   **C** scalene

    B isosceles   **D** not given

11. $\overline{LM} \parallel \overline{ON}$. What kind of quadrilateral is $LMNO$?

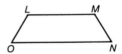

    A trapezoid   **C** parallelogram

    B square   **D** not given

12. Solve for n. $\frac{14}{35} = \frac{n}{5}$

    A 2   **C** 5

    B 7   **D** not given

13. Compare. $\frac{3}{8}$ ⬤ $\frac{11}{24}$

    A $<$ **C** $=$

    B $>$ **D** not given

14. Which fraction is equivalent to 0.85?

    A $\frac{3}{5}$ **C** $\frac{17}{20}$

    B $\frac{20}{85}$ **D** not given

15. $\frac{1}{6} + \frac{3}{4}$

    A $\frac{1}{3}$ **C** $\frac{11}{12}$

    B $\frac{7}{8}$ **D** not given

Choose the correct answers. Write A, B, C, or D.

16. $5\frac{2}{6} + 2\frac{2}{3}$

    A $2\frac{4}{6}$ C 8

    B $7\frac{1}{6}$ D not given

17. $3\frac{5}{9} - 1\frac{2}{3}$

    A $1\frac{8}{9}$ C $3\frac{2}{9}$

    B $2\frac{1}{9}$ D not given

18. Solve for n. $11\frac{1}{4} + n = 14\frac{5}{8}$

    A 4   C $3\frac{7}{8}$

    B $3\frac{3}{8}$ D not given

19. $\frac{2}{3} \times \frac{5}{6} \times \frac{3}{4}$

    A $\frac{10}{13}$ C $\frac{5}{12}$

    B $\frac{30}{84}$ D not given

20. $1\frac{2}{3} \times 2\frac{1}{5}$

    A $2\frac{1}{3}$ C $2\frac{1}{5}$

    B $3\frac{2}{3}$ D not given

21. $\frac{3}{7} \div \frac{2}{5}$

    A $1\frac{1}{14}$ C $\frac{14}{15}$

    B $\frac{6}{35}$ D not given

22. $4\frac{1}{4} \div \frac{3}{8}$

    A $11\frac{1}{3}$ C $\frac{3}{32}$

    B $4\frac{2}{3}$ D not given

23. What is the next term in the sequence?
    0, 3, 6, 9, 12, _____

    A 13   C 15

    B 14   D not given

Solve.

24. Mr. Jones bought 3 boxes of nails with 50 nails in each box and 2 boxes of nails with 30 nails in each. After completing his project, he was left with 15 nails. How many did he use?

    A 225   C 195

    B 210   D not given

25. Charlene reads stories to pre-school children twice a week. She can read 3 books each time. How many weeks will it take to read all 78 books in the pre-school section?

    A 13 weeks   C 6 weeks

    B 26 weeks   D not given

26. Larry sent a total of 40 postcards and letters. It cost him $.15 to mail each postcard and $.25 to mail each letter. His cost for postage was $7.40. How many letters did he send?

    A 20   C 22

    B 16   D not given

27. Jason has 81 green, black, and white marbles. He has twice as many white marbles as green, and three times as many black marbles as white. How many white marbles are there?

    A 10   C 9

    B 18   D not given

241

8 Using Graphs and Statistics

Sharing What You Know

Providing for a family is a large responsibility. Three basic needs are food, clothing, and shelter. What other items might be included in a family's budget? What kind of graph would best show the spending needs of a family?

Using Language

You know that many students ride a bus to school. This **mode,** or method, of transportation is used in both rural and urban areas. In statistics, the word **mode** refers to the number that occurs most often in a collection of data. Compare the two uses of the word **mode.**

Words to Know: average, range, mode, median, mean

Be a Problem Solver

Two hundred families live in the town of Otisville. The town has 100 children and 300 pets. How many children and pets does the average family have? How many "average" families are there in Otisville?

List ways in which the word "average" is used in school, in sports, when we talk about the weather, and so on.

Activity

Exploring Ways to Collect and Report Data

A supermarket asked customers to take part in a survey.
Customers were asked to complete this questionnaire.

Please take time to answer these questions. Your responses will help us serve you better.

1. How often do you shop here?
   a. more than twice a week   b. twice a week   c. once a week   d. less than once a week

2. About how many items do you usually buy?
   a. less than 10   b. 10-20   c. 50   d. more than 100

3. About how many items did you buy the last time you shopped here?
   a. less than 10   b. 10-20   c. 50   d. more than 100

4. About how long do you usually wait when checking out?
   a. no wait   b. 5 minutes   c. 10 minutes   d. longer than 10 minutes

5. How often do you use the express check-out lanes?
   a. every time you shop   b. every other time you shop   c. less than once a month

---

Working together

Materials: Workmat 4

A. Answer the questions on the survey, thinking of the last time you went to the supermarket.

B. Tally your results in a class table like this.

Questions	Tally			
	a	b	c	d
1				
2				
3				
4				
5				

Sharing Your Results

Use the data recorded in the table to answer these questions.

1. On the average, how many items do the students in your class usually buy?

2. On the average, how long do the students usually wait when checking out?

3. Name three items of information the supermarket can obtain from the answers to the questionnaire.

4. What do you think is the purpose of the survey?

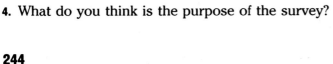

Extending the Activity

Work in a group. Each person should select a random sample of people and present the questionnaire on page 244.

Materials: Workmat 4

A. Discuss several ways to select a random sample of people.

B. Select 5 people from outside your class according to the method you think is most likely to be random.

C. Present the questionnaire to the sample population you have chosen. Ask them to answer the questions, thinking of the supermarket where they regularly shop.

D. Record the results for the 5 people you selected along with the results of the other people in your group.

5. Describe your method of selecting a random sample. Why, do you think, is it valid?

6. Are you confident that your results are truly representative of the local population? Would you change your method of sampling? Why or why not?

Summing Up

Work in your group.

7. Summarize your group's results of the questionnaire.
   a. How will you summarize the numerical data?
   b. How will you summarize the data that are not numerical?

8. Write a report of the results. Present the report to the class. Compare your group's report with the other reports.
   a. Did any groups summarize the data in the same way? If so, how did they do it?
   b. Which ways of summarizing the data were clearest? Why?

9. What if the results for all the groups were combined? Which data would be more reliable—that for your group or that for the whole class? Why?

10. What if the purpose of the survey was to evaluate the checkout system with the intent to possibly change it? The supermarket has 8 checkout lanes, 2 of which are express lanes. What would be your recommendations based on your results of the survey?

> Look up the words *median* and *mode* in the dictionary. Which word means "popular"? Which word means "middle"?

Median, Mode, and Range

For a project on family income, students at North Middle School surveyed 30 families to find how many members there were in each family. The data they collected appear at the right.

NUMBER OF MEMBERS IN 30 FAMILIES					
4	5	3	2	11	3
4	8	3	5	6	2
5	4	9	6	7	4
8	13	11	2	7	6
1	6	3	3	4	4

To see the **distribution** of the data, you can make a **line plot**.

- Draw a number line that includes all the numbers in the distribution.
- Mark an X above the number line for each number in the data.

```
                    x
              x   x
              x   x
              x   x
          x   x   x   x       x
      x   x   x   x   x   x   x
  x   x   x   x   x   x   x   x   x       x           x
──┼───┼───┼───┼───┼───┼───┼───┼───┼───┼───┼───┼───┼───┼──
  1   2   3   4   5   6   7   8   9  10  11  12  13
```

Statistics is the science of collecting, organizing, and analyzing data. Three statistical measures can be easily found, using a line plot.

▶ The **mode** is the number that occurs most often. A set of data may have more than one mode. It may have no mode if no number appears more than once. To find the mode on a line plot, locate the tallest column of X's. What is the mode for the data above?

▶ The **range** is the difference between the greatest and the least numbers. The greatest number on the line plot above is 13. What is the least? What is the range?

▶ The **median** is the middle of the distribution. If there is an even number of data, find the average of the two middle numbers. Thirty numbers are displayed on the line plot. What are the middle two? What is their average?

Check Your Understanding

Use the table of miles driven each day for 30 days.

1. Make a line plot of the data in the table.

2. Find the mode, the median, and the range.

3. Circle the mode and the median on the line plot.

Share Your Ideas Look back at the line plot shown above. **What if** the greatest value had not been included? How would that affect the median, the mode, and the range?

MILES DRIVEN EACH DAY					
57	53	42	37	48	60
53	64	34	48	35	57
53	37	30	48	64	35
65	34	37	53	36	42
35	64	48	57	48	53

Make a line plot for each set of data. Then find the mode, the median, and the range. Circle the mode and the median on the line plot.

4. 14, 20, 11, 16, 15, 19, 17, 15, 13, 14, 22, 14, 16, 14, 17, 12, 14, 13

5. 325, 350, 500, 475, 450, 400, 425, 400, 325, 350, 475, 450, 400, 375

6. 50, 63, 59, 53, 50, 51, 60, 57, 55, 50, 51, 53, 61, 50, 55, 59, 55, 53, 50, 51, 51, 57, 50, 51

7. 1,216; 1,219; 1,210; 1,219; 1,215; 1,214; 1,218; 1,219; 1,215; 1,214; 1,210; 1,211; 1,217; 1,213; 1,214; 1,216; 1,215; 1,217; 1,216; 1,213; 1,215; 1,218; 1,211; 1,213

8. 0.2, 0.4, 0.5, 0.8, 0.7, 0.6, 0.4, 0.6, 0.7, 0.8, 0.6, 0.5, 0.2, 0.4, 0.5, 0.6, 0.6, 0.8

Think and Apply

The table at the right shows the weekly family income for 20 families. The data have been rounded to the nearest $10.

9. Make a line plot.

10. Find the mode, the median, and the range.

WEEKLY FAMILY INCOME			
$350	$430	$290	$680
$380	$410	$510	$360
$410	$520	$370	$400
$490	$390	$410	$480
$420	$460	$420	$390

Copy the line plot below.

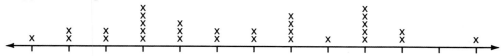

11. On the line plot, mark the median and the mode.

12. Label the points on the line plot with the numbers 10, 20, . . . up to 130. Using those numbers, find the median, the mode, and the range.

13. **What if** the points on the line plot were labeled with the numbers 1,000; 2,000; . . . up to 13,000? Using those numbers, find the median, the mode, and the range.

Which measure tells you about the most popular or most frequent responses? Which measures tell you about the whole set of data? Explain.

SUMMING UP

For lunch, John spent $2.03, Marsha spent $1.95, and Alice spent $2.87. What number would be "typical" of the amount spent for lunch? Explain.

Mean

The data in this table are the cost of food for one week for 20 families. The data range from a low of $19 to a high of $83. One way to find a typical cost of food is to find the **mean** of these numbers.

To find the mean of a set of data, add all the numbers and divide by the number of data.

The sum of the 20 numbers is $910.

$910 \div 20 = 45.5$

The mean is $45.50.

The mean, the mode, and the median are numbers that are typical of a set of data. Each is a type of average.

COST OF FOOD FOR ONE WEEK*				
$35	$29	$62	$41	$37
$19	$83	$43	$39	$51
$31	$45	$58	$36	$77
$24	$33	$48	$54	$65

*Data rounded to the nearest dollar

What if the lowest cost of food was not included? How would this affect the mean?

Check Your Understanding

Use the data in the table above.

1. Arrange the data in order from least to greatest. Find the median of the distribution. How does the median compare to the mean?

2. Describe the mode.

Find the mean of each set of numbers. Use a calculator.

3. 19, 59, 48, 25, 31, 12, 36, 67, 33, 8, 78, 99, 95, 72, 32, 63, 53, 56, 25

4. 520, 651, 357, 238, 274, 590, 993, 874, 802, 338, 764, 631, 461, 846, 953

5. 3.5, 6.4, 1.6, 1.3, 4.6, 8.3, 2.0, 4.7, 3.9, 0.9, 4.7, 8.3, 7.5, 1.5, 3.2

Share Your Ideas Is this statement sometimes, always, or never true? Explain.

• The median of a set of data is close to the mean.

Find the mean of each set of data. Choose a calculator, paper and pencil, or mental math. Explain your choices.

6. 18, 22, 19, 21, 20

7. 350, 250, 300, 400, 200

8. 1, 8, 7, 6, 9, 3, 2, 5, 4, 5

9. 40, 51, 68, 40, 51, 29, 38, 31, 15, 50

10. 3.2, 4.2, 3.9, 5.7, 3.5, 1.3, 0.1, 1.1, 3.6, 8.4, 5.3, 1.8, 0.4, 4.4, 9.7, 1.3, 9.8, 4.5

11. 0.34, 0.02, 0.48, 0.56, 0.71, 0.8, 0.65, 0.86, 0.85, 0.06, 0.23, 0.48, 0.09

Use the two sets of data below to answer 12–13.

a. 3, 5, 1, 7, 9, 4, 8, 6, 2, 9, 6, 7, 4, 6
b. 3, 5, 1, 7, 9, 4, 8, 6, 2, 9, 6, 7, 4, 6, 35, 64

12. Find the mean and the median of each set of data.

13. How are the mean and the median affected by the addition of 35 and 64 to the set of data in **a**?

The mean of each set of numbers is 56. What is the third number?

14. 54, 58, ☐   **15.** 42, 60, ☐   **16.** 42, 40, ☐   **17.** 16, 27, ☐

Think and Apply

Use a calculator.

18. The average of a set of 41 numbers is 37.2. What is the sum of the 41 numbers?

19. The average of a set of numbers is 54. The sum of the numbers is 1,350. How many numbers are in the set?

20. Last year the Meza family spent an average of $47.95 each week for food. How much did they spend for food for the year?

21. Alex's mathematics test grades are 87, 88, 89, and 88. What grade must he get on the last test to get a 90 average (mean) for the term?

Logical Thinking

You can estimate a mean and then adjust to find the actual mean. To find the mean of 82, 65, 74, 68, 79, and 76, do the following.

- Estimate the mean to be 70. Find the difference between each number and the estimated mean.

	+	−
82 − 70 →	12	
70 − 65 →		5
74 − 70 →	4	
70 − 68 →		2
79 − 70 →	9	
76 − 70 →	6	
	31	7

- Find the total difference.   31 − 7 = 24

- Divide by the number of data. Use the result to adjust your estimate.

24 ÷ 6 = 4
The mean is
70 + 4 = 74.

22. Explain how to use this method to find the mean of 35, 38, 22, 25, 29, 26, 31, 24, 30, and 37.

What do you need to know to calculate the mean of a set of data? If you know the mean and the number of data, can you find the sum of the data? Explain.

SUMMING UP

> Describe how to find the mean, the median, and the mode of a set of data.

Stem and Leaf Plots

Sally works part time on weekends. She uses her earnings to buy her own clothes, and she saves the rest. Sally rounded her earnings to the nearest dollar and recorded them each week for 6 months.

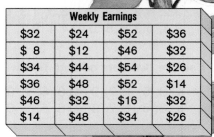

Weekly Earnings			
$32	$24	$52	$36
$ 8	$12	$46	$32
$34	$44	$54	$26
$36	$48	$52	$14
$46	$32	$16	$32
$14	$48	$34	$26

You can make a **stem and leaf plot** to show her results.

- Make a column of the tens digits of her data in order from least to greatest. This is the stem.

- Beside each tens digit record the ones digits that go with it in order from least to greatest. These are the leaves.

```
0 | 8
1 | 2 4 4 6
2 | 4 6 6          ──── mode
3 | 2 2 2 2 4 4 6 6
4 | 4 6 6 8 8      median
5 | 2 2 4
```
stem leaves

From a stem and leaf plot you can easily read the median, the mode, and the range.

a. The mode is the number that occurs most often. The mode is 32.
b. The median is the middle of the distribution. The middle numbers are 32 and 34. What is the median?
c. The range is the difference between the greatest and the least numbers. What is the greatest number? the least number? the range?

On a stem and leaf plot, where is the least number located? the greatest number?

Make a stem and leaf plot for each set of data. Find the mode, the median, and the range of each.

1. 30 48 31 50 41 31
   53 60 50 41 81 64
   79 46 46 69 47 71
   41 84 62 59 33 62
   33 81 42 78 57 68

2. 223 235 255 243 229
   251 249 234 236 240
   236 241 226 243 238
   238 223 240 246 236
   223 236 241 230 224

Share Your Ideas Look back at **2**. What numbers appear on the stem of your plot? How are the plots in **1** and **2** alike? How are they different?

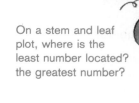

Practice

Make a stem and leaf plot for each set of data. Find the mode, the median, and the range of each.

3. 36 25 37 42 18 33 46 18 14 15
   26 33 45 26 48 14 13 14 45 13
   17 24 46 14 14 47 28 35 34 43

4. 9.7 6.4 5.4 9.6 7.4 6.7 8.3 6.8 7.4 8.7
   8.5 6.6 7.6 6.4 6.8 9.6 5.3 8.4 6.3 5.5
   9.8 7.6 9.5 8.3 7.6 5.9 7.5 8.6 6.4 8.1

5. 0.51 0.49 0.34 0.36 0.40 0.16 0.41 0.26
   0.43 0.38 0.23 0.35 0.55 0.09 0.39 0.38
   0.23 0.20 0.46 0.36 0.43 0.36 0.41 0.30

6. 25   37   186   43   95   177   62   85   164
   55   140 137   71   114   128   152   165   109

7. **Look back** at **6**. How is that stem and leaf plot like the one in **5**? How is it different? Is it useful to make a plot from the data? Why or why not?

8. Find the mean of the data in this stem and leaf plot.

4	0117
5	34669
6	237789
7	01123
8	1159

Think and Apply

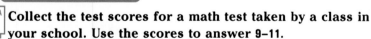

Collect the test scores for a math test taken by a class in your school. Use the scores to answer 9–11.

9. Find the median, the mode, and the range.

10. Find the mean of the students' scores.

11. How would you grade the test scores? That is, to which scores would you assign an A, a B, a C, a D, or a failing grade?

What are the advantages and disadvantages of displaying data in a stem and leaf plot? What does a stem and leaf plot show most clearly?

Mixed Review

1. $4{,}003 - 259$

2. $3{,}449 + 2{,}347$

3. 236×68

4. $10{,}857 \div 47$

5. $3.08 - 0.49$

6. $0.097 + 0.148$

7. 2.39×0.047

8. $15.998 \div 0.019$

9. $4\frac{5}{6} + 7\frac{2}{3}$

10. $12 - 5\frac{3}{8}$

11. $\frac{4}{5} \times 3\frac{1}{3}$

12. $12\frac{1}{2} \div 5$

Write *prime* or *composite*. Show the prime factorization of the composite numbers.

13. 91

14. 67

15. 210

16. 131

Evaluate. Let $n = 5$ and $x = 3.1$

17. $2n + 6$

18. $31 - 6x$

19. $n^2 - 5$

20. $3n + 5x$

SUMMING UP

GETTING STARTED

How are a line plot and a stem and leaf plot alike?
How are they different?

Box and Whisker Plots

A supermarket manager compared the number of items bought by women shoppers with the number bought by men shoppers. The data she recorded for 24 women and 24 men shoppers appear here and on page 253.

NUMBER OF ITEMS PURCHASED BY WOMEN SHOPPERS							
53	38	32	50	53	48	55	45
53	52	48	52	58	55	58	44
57	52	53	52	50	60	57	44

To display the data, you can make a **box and whisker plot.**

- Order the data from least to greatest. Find and mark the median to divide the data into two parts.

      32   38   44   44   45   48   48   50
      50   52   52   52   52   53   53   53
      53   55   55   57   57   58   58   60

- Divide the data into four **quartiles** by finding the median of each of the two parts.

- Draw the part of the number line needed to display the data. Mark the number line with the quartile measures you have found.

- Draw a **box** around the second and third quartiles. Mark the median of the data with a line through the box.

- What are the least and the greatest values in the set of data? Draw the **whiskers,** using these values.

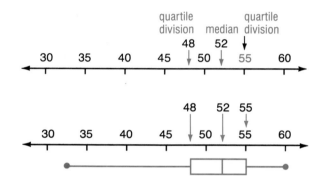

Check Your Understanding

1. Why is it helpful to order the data when making a box and whisker plot?

2. Make a box and whisker plot for the data below.

      45   58   54   48   45   46   55   52
      50   45   46   48   56   45   50   54
      50   48   45   46   46   52   45   46

Share Your Ideas   Compare a line plot and a box and whisker plot. How are they alike? How are they different?

Make a box and whisker plot for each set of data.

3. 80, 85, 110, 100, 96, 124, 89, 104, 106, 117, 85, 117, 94, 106, 89, 117, 100, 96, 117, 106, 110

4. 15, 16, 19, 18, 24, 26, 24, 18, 22, 17, 22, 17, 11, 25, 13, 19, 13, 15, 16, 14, 17, 14, 10, 18, 19, 23, 15, 12, 26, 18, 15, 22, 24, 19, 20, 24, 18, 22

5. **Look back** at 3. Make a stem and leaf plot for the data. How are the stem and leaf plot and the box and whisker plot alike? How are they different?

Make a box and whisker plot for each of the two sets of data. Use the same number line for both.

6. Points scored in 14 games by two basketball players:
Player A: 28, 6, 13, 9, 14, 29, 8, 13, 30, 6, 8, 14, 8, 9
Player B: 20, 17, 10, 12, 15, 18, 10, 19, 20, 17, 9, 20, 18, 19

7. Positions of two football teams ranked in the top 20 for 12 weeks:
Team 1—20, 20, 17, 15, 7, 2, 2, 2, 13, 15, 15, 18
Team 2—11, 12, 12, 10, 9, 9, 9, 10, 9, 10, 11, 10

Think and Apply

8. Draw your own box and whisker plot for the data on page 252 about women shoppers. On the same number line, make a box and whisker plot for the data about men shoppers, shown here.

9. Use the box and whisker plots to compare the two sets of data. What conclusions can you draw about the differences between women and men shoppers in a supermarket?

10. **Look back** at 6.
   a. Find the mean, the median, the mode, and the range for each set of data.
   b. What conclusions can you draw by comparing the boxes? the whiskers?

11. Describe the data displayed in this box and whisker plot. Consider the median, the mode, the mean, and the range. Are the data grouped tightly or spread out?

NUMBER OF ITEMS PURCHASED BY MEN SHOPPERS					
30	28	29	33	24	26
27	26	29	25	28	29
33	27	28	24	27	25
26	30	29	24	27	33

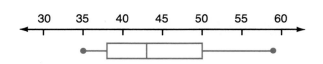

Describe a set of data that has short whiskers and a long box. How does that set differ from a set of data that has long whiskers and a short box?

SUMMING UP

GETTING STARTED

What if the grades on your math tests are 64, 73, 82, 65, 87, 54, 78, 87, 87? Which would you rather your teacher use—the mean, the median, or the mode? Why?

Using Measures of Data

Data can be analyzed in many ways, depending on whether you use the mean, the median, the mode, or the range.

This table shows the salaries of the employees of Best Department Store. The president found the mean of the data. He claimed, "The average salary in my store is $30,000!"

The sales people found the mode. They declared, "Most people in this store earn $20,000. The average salary is $20,000!"

Were they both right? Explain.

Position	Number of People	Salary
President	1	$105,000
Vice President	2	$ 72,000
Manager	4	$ 43,000
Salesperson	23	$ 20,000

The store manager said, "More than half our employees earn less than $21,000 a year." Which measure was she using? Which do you think best describes the salaries—the mean, the median, or the mode? Why?

The following statements were made using the range.

• The salaries range from $20,000 to $105,000.
• The lowest salary is $85,000 less than the highest one.

Check Your Understanding

1. Find the mean, the median, the mode, and the range of this data. Then describe the data, using each measure.

   57, 73, 99, 102, 90, 94, 62, 65, 94,
   91, 99, 94, 71, 88, 84, 59, 94, 63

Tell which measure was used to analyze the data.

2. More people use Clean Hair shampoo than any other shampoo.

3. The average age of children at the day care center is $2\frac{1}{2}$.

4. More than half the people in the world live in Asia.

Share Your Ideas Look back at 1. **What if** the data were the class scores on a math test? Describe the scores, using each measure. Did the class as a whole do well? Explain.

Find the mean, the median, the mode, and the range of each set of data. Then describe the data, using each measure.

5. 115, 131, 157, 159, 148, 152, 120, 123, 152, 149, 157, 152, 127, 146, 142, 117, 152, 121

6. 4, 13, 18, 10, 16, 15, 4, 9, 0, 22, 13, 5, 13, 4, 2, 8, 5, 4, 12, 22

7. 147, 151, 144, 143, 139, 158, 136, 147, 158, 163, 154, 155, 162, 136, 136, 132, 155, 143, 139, 136, 139, 144, 147, 147, 155

8. **Look back** at 5. Which measure do you think best represents the data? Why?

9. **Look back** at 6. **What if** you added the number 587 to the data? Which measures would change significantly? Which would change very little, if at all? What conclusions can you draw?

Tell which measure was used to analyze the data.

10. More people like baseball than any other sport.

11. The average monthly rainfall for last year was 4.2 inches.

12. There was a 38°F difference between the highest and the lowest temperatures for the month.

13. More poodles are registered with the American Kennel Club than any other type of dog.

14. Half the students in Ms. Jennings' class are 5 ft 4 in. or taller.

15. Last season 19.6 million more viewers watched the first-ranked TV series than watched the last-ranked series.

These are the test grades for three students in Mr. Nguyen's class.

Which measure is each student using to make the claim?

16. Billie Jo: "My average is about 81."

17. Samantha: "Half of my grades are 81.5 or greater. My average is 81.5."

18. Wayne: "I scored 86 more often than any other grade. My average is 86."

19. Which students do you think will receive the averages they claimed as final grades?

Samantha	30	51	52	74	78	81
	82	83	84	85	86	87
Billie Jo	70	72	74	74	74	77
	78	89	89	92	93	94
Wayne	15	32	34	71	77	78
	80	81	86	86	86	87

Visual Thinking

20. Which two are alike?

a. b. c.

d. e. f.

What is the purpose of calculating a statistical average?

SUMMING UP

Midchapter Review

Use the two sets of data below for 1–4. pages 246–253

a. 38, 46, 62, 57, 38, 42, 55, 38, 41, 46, 53, 52, 42, 45, 37, 32, 38, 43, 62, 36

b. 92, 89, 88, 79, 93, 89, 91, 95, 98, 90, 93, 89, 93, 94, 95

1. Make a line plot for each set of data. Find the mode, the median, and the range.

2. Find the mean of each set of data. Use a calculator.

3. Make a stem and leaf plot for each set of data.

4. Make a box and whisker plot for each set of data.

Which measure was used to analyze the data? pages 254–255

5. The Klincks averaged about 50 mph on their trip.

6. The most popular hobby of the students in Ms. Defazio's class is raising pets.

7. Half of the students in Mr. Fox's class scored 85 or better on the last test.

8. Last week the temperature went from a low of 28°F to a high of 51°F.

9. Camonica's final grade for this marking period was a 91.

10. The favorite color of the people in the survey was blue.

Find the word in column B that best completes each sentence in column A.

A	B
11. The number that occurs most often in a set of data is the _____.	**a.** range
	b. median
12. _____ is the science of collecting, organizing, and analyzing data.	**c.** mean
	d. mode
13. The _____ of a set of data is the sum of all the data divided by the number of data.	**e.** statistics
	f. line plot
14. You can read the mode, median, and range from a _____.	

Solve. pages 250–251

15. Mr. Cunningham made this stem and leaf plot for his class's attendance one month. Find the mode, the median, and the range.

```
1 | 8 9 9
2 | 0 1 1 2 3 3 4 5 5 5 7 8 8 8
3 | 0 0
```

Exploring Problem Solving

What Is the Grade?

Professor Amundsen teaches a class on economics. He gave a test that has a perfect score of 50 points. The scores appear at the right. He will assign a letter grade (A, B, C, D, or F) to each score.

Thinking Critically

What grades would you assign to the scores? Your group will need grid paper to help solve this problem.

NAME	GRADE	NAME	GRADE	NAME	GRADE
Alexander	30	Gewaise	43	Ronnie	24
Allport	24	Gooden	39	Russell	35
Ansmith	20	Haller	45	Shapiro	22
Burston	19	Harmen	45	Smith	6
Blake	30	Kora	28	Simons	5
Colby	41	Lang	38	Spector	37
Doley	35	McCormack	29	Turner	43
Ellsworth	30	Maisel	36	Undrus	38
Feltz	46	Nevelson	34		
Friedberg	34	Parkowki	33		

Analyzing and Making Decisions

1. Order the scores from the highest to the lowest. (Keep this information to help you make your graphs.) What was the highest score? What was the lowest score? What was the range of the scores?

2. What was the median score?

3. List the scores of the top $\frac{1}{4}$ of the class. List the scores of the lowest $\frac{1}{4}$ of the class.

4. How many students scored from 0 to 10? from 11 to 20? from 21 to 30? 31 to 40? from 41 to 50? Group the scores as follows: 0–5, 6–10, and so on. Graph this grouped data.

5. Examine all your data. What scores should receive an A; a B; a C; a D; an F? How many of each did you give?

Look Back Professor Amundsen would like to make it easier to grade the tests next time. Write suggestions for him to follow.

Problem Solving Strategies

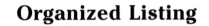

Organized Listing

Susan had been given the task of finding the median salary of the workers at their branch office. All the salaries but one were available. She knew, however, that the mean salary was $36,000. What was the median salary?

$23,000	$53,000	$75,000
$26,500	$21,000	$21,000
$34,350	$39,300	$37,000
$22,000	$37,350	$31,500
$26,000	$66,000	$28,650
$46,000	$39,000	

Sometimes using an organized list is an excellent way to study data and to solve a problem.

Solving the Problem

Use a calculator where appropriate.

CHOICES

Think   What do you need to find out? What information do you have?

Explore   Since you know the mean salary, how can you find the total amount of salaries? How can you use the total amount of salaries to find the missing salary? Once you know the missing salary, how can you use organized listing to find the median salary?

Solve   What is the median salary?

Look Back   Does your answer make sense? How can you tell?

Share Your Ideas

1. Does the mean or the median better represent the average salary of a worker at the office?

2. Look at the problem above and the problem on page 257. Why is it important that you do not leave any information out of your list?

258

Practice

Solve. Use a calculator where appropriate.
Use the information below to solve 3–4.

The Lopez family rented a boat. The fee was $10 for the first day, $9 for the second day, and $8 for the third day. The rate dropped $1 each day until it reached $5. The Lopez family paid $45.

3. How many days did they rent the boat?

4. There is a special weekly rate of $42 for 7 days. How much cheaper is this rate than the daily rate?

5. How many different rectangles can you find in drawing A?

6. How many different rectangles can you find in drawing B?

A.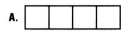

B.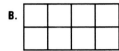

Mixed Strategy Review

Use the information in the sign to solve 7–8.

7. Mr. and Mrs. Lopez paid $10.25 for themselves and their 3 children (all aged 13 and under) to visit the museum. What are the age ranges of the children?

8. **What if** two adults and their children (all aged 13 and under) paid $12.00? How many children from each age range might have been in the family?

ROCKVILLE BOAT MUSEUM
ADULTS $3.00
CHILDREN: 11–13 $1.75
                6–10 $1.25
UNDER 6   NO CHARGE

Use the information below to solve 9–10.

The Lopezes have changed the oil every 3,000 miles and the filter every 6,000 miles ever since they bought their new car. The car odometer now reads 63,216.

9. What will the odometer read when the car needs a new oil filter?

10. If the Lopezes drive about 250 miles a week, in how many weeks will the car need a new oil filter?

Create Your Own

Use the information about the Lopezes' car to write a problem.

259

Name one advantage of displaying data in a graph as opposed to a table. Name a disadvantage.

Comparing Graphs

Data can be graphed in many different ways. The best way depends on the relationship you wish to show. The data shown here is displayed in the three graphs below.

Circle graphs can show the relationship of parts to a whole. They can also be used to compare the parts. Which American manufacturer accounts for about $\frac{1}{3}$ of the total sales?

Line graphs can show changes over time. They can show trends. The double-line graph displays the data in the table above. What trends does the graph show?

Bar graphs are useful for comparing quantities. The double-bar graph compares the median household income with the cost of an average car for two of the years in the table. How does the graph make it easy to compare values? How would you compare the items for each year?

Year	Median Household Income	Cost of an Average Car
1983	$23,976	$5,846
1984	$24,526	$6,135
1985	$24,952	$5,825
1986	$25,807	$6,541
1987	$25,986	$7,163

CAR SALES FOR 1986	
Manufacturer	**Sales**
Chrysler	962,057
Ford	2,019,783
General Motors	3,555,538
Other American-Made Cars	543,884
Imports	3,145,326

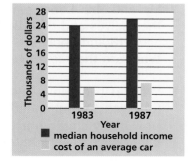

Check Your Understanding

Would you use a bar, a line, or a circle graph to display each of these? Why?

1. the population of the United States in 1900, 1910, . . . , 1980, 1990

2. the fraction of the total school population in each grade

3. the average high and low temperatures each month for a year

4. the number of male and female students in each seventh-grade class in your school

Share Your Ideas How would data that is best displayed in a circle graph differ from data that is best displayed in a line graph? a bar graph?

Make a bar, a line, or a circle graph for each set of data.
Explain your choice.

5.

AVERAGE WEEKLY EARNINGS OF CONSTRUCTION WORKERS			
1976	$283	1982	$427
1977	$296	1983	$443
1978	$319	1984	$459
1979	$343	1985	$464
1980	$368	1986	$467
1981	$399	1987	$480

6.

SPORTS PREFERENCE OF 500 STUDENTS		
Sport	Boys	Girls
Baseball	50	50
Basketball	30	50
Hockey	40	10
Soccer	20	40
Swimming	10	20
Track	40	40
Football	60	40

7.

U.S. POPULATION DISTRIBUTION (PERCENT OF POPULATION)		
	Urban	Rural
1790	5	95
1810	7	93
1830	9	91
1850	15	85
1870	26	74

8.

THE SMITHS' MONTHLY CAR EXPENSES	
Car payment	$120
Repairs	$60
Fuel	$60
Insurance	$120

Think and Apply

Use the graphs you made above to answer 9–14.

9. In which year did the average weekly earnings for construction workers increase the most? the least?

10. Which sport is the most popular among the boys? the least popular among the girls?

11. a. Which sports are preferred by more girls than boys?
   b. Which sports are equally preferred by boys and girls?

12. a. Did the percent of rural population increase or decrease from 1790 to 1870?
   b. What was the trend of the population in the United States from 1790 to 1870?

13. In which year was the ratio of urban to rural inhabitants nearly 1 to 3?

14. Which two expenses are two thirds of the Smiths' total expenses for their car?

DATA Find the data for one of these problems. Then graph the data in two different ways. Compare the graphs. Tell which is more appropriate. Explain your thinking.

15. the students in your class with brown eyes, blue eyes, hazel eyes, and so on

16. the number of students in the seventh grade in your school for each of the past 10 years

What kind of graph would you use to show each? Explain.
• changes over a 20-year period
• the win and loss records for the teams in a league

SUMMING UP

Activity

Analyzing Graphs

The seventh-grade students at Robert Sevey Junior High are studying about small businesses. The graphs on the bulletin board show three different patterns of growth in sales.

Working together

Materials: grid paper, rulers

A. Use the data at the right to make three line graphs. Use axes like the sample shown here.

B. You can use a graph to estimate values between two known values. Read the values on the graphs for the weekly sales for the fifth month for Elaine's Eatery and for Barbara's Boutique.

C. You can use a graph to estimate values beyond known values. Analyze the trend of each graph and table. Then extend each graph and table to the twelfth month.

AVERAGE WEEKLY SALES FOR 8 MONTHS		
Elaine's Eatery	Barbara's Boutique	Gary's Sports Shop
$150	$10	$400
$300	$20	$1,200
$450	$40	$1,600
$600	$80	$1,800
?	?	$1,900
$900	$320	$1,950
$1,050	$640	$1,975
$1,200	$1,280	$1,987.50

Sharing Your Results

1. What did you do to find the values for the fifth month for each graph? the twelfth month? What values did you find?

2. Write a few sentences describing the trend of each graph.

3. **What if** you were the owner of each business? What conditions might cause your business to grow as Elaine's Eatery has? as Barbara's Boutique has? as Gary's Sport Shop has?

4. Which business would you choose for investing your money? Explain your choice.

5. Present your group's graphs and conclusions to the class. Compare your graphs and conclusions with other groups'. How are they alike? How are they different?

Extending the Activity

Choose appropriate axes and graph the data in each table. Then do the following.

6. Estimate missing data.

7. Describe the trend of each graph.

8. Describe the rate of increase or decrease of each graph. Write a rule.

PRICE OF APPLES	
Number	**Cost**
2	$ .34
3	$ .51
4	?
6	$1.02
7	?
12	$2.04
15	?
16	?

PRICE OF BULK OAT BRAN	
Weight	**Cost**
4 oz	$ .45
8 oz	$ .90
12 oz	?
1 lb	?
1 lb 4 oz	$2.25
$1\frac{1}{2}$ lb	?
2 lb	$3.60
$2\frac{1}{2}$ lb	?
64 oz	?

Use the step-function graph below to answer 9–13.

9. How much does it cost to ride $\frac{1}{2}$ mi or less?

10. How much does it cost for every $\frac{1}{2}$ mile or less beyond the first $\frac{1}{2}$ mi?

11. How much does it cost to ride $\frac{3}{4}$ mi?

12. How much does it cost to ride $2\frac{1}{2}$ mi? 2.6 mi?

13. **Look back** at the graph. What is the difference between an open dot and a closed dot?

14. Why, do you think, is this kind of graph called a step function? Why is the graph of a taxi ride not a smooth line?

Summing Up

15. How does a table enable you to find missing data? How does a graph do this? Name one advantage of each method of finding missing data.

This graph shows the cost of a taxi ride with Melissa's Taxi Service. This type of graph is called a **step function.**

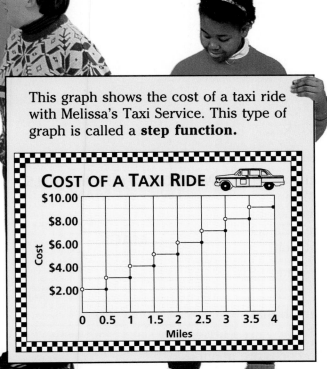

COST OF A TAXI RIDE

263

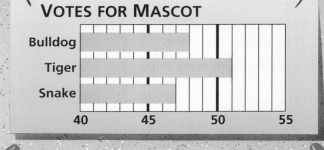

Does Brand A cost twice as much as Brand B? Why or why not?

$25 $30 $35

Brand A
Brand B

Using Data to Persuade

The students at Snellville Middle School are selecting a mascot for their teams. There were 48 votes for the bulldog, 51 votes for the tiger, and 47 votes for the snake. Three students made graphs to show the results.

Coach Snively wanted the snake as the mascot. "Snively's Snellville Snakes," he gloated. Which graph did Coach Snively like best? How does that graph distort the data?

How do the other graphs distort the data? Which graph makes it look as though the votes were practically tied? Which makes it look like the tiger got more than two times as many votes as the snake?

VOTES FOR MASCOT

Bulldog
Tiger
Snake

40   45   50   55

VOTES FOR MASCOT

Each Animal = 10 Votes

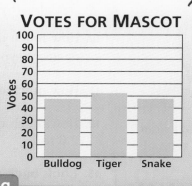

VOTES FOR MASCOT

Votes

100
90
80
70
60
50
40
30
20
10
0

Bulldog   Tiger   Snake

Check Your Understanding

1. This bar-pictograph is supposed to show quantity as a bar graph does—by the height of the picture. Magic Muffler installs nearly twice as many mufflers as the other company. In what way does this graph accurately depict this fact? In what way does it distort the information?

2. Draw a bar graph that shows the Magic Muffler data without distortion.

Share Your Ideas   Explain how to make a bar graph that distorts information in each of the following ways.

- Small differences are magnified.
- Large differences are minimized.

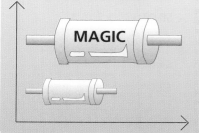

MAGIC MUFFLER INSTALLS TWICE AS MANY!

MAGIC

For each of the graphs below, answer these questions.
a. How does the graph distort the data?
b. What wrong conclusion could be drawn from the distorted data?

3.

CRAZY SAM'S USED CARS –
WE SELL MORE!

New Car Dealers

Other Used Car Dealers

Crazy Sam's

4.

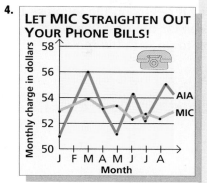

LET MIC STRAIGHTEN OUT
YOUR PHONE BILLS!

5.

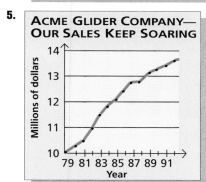

ACME GLIDER COMPANY—
OUR SALES KEEP SOARING

6.

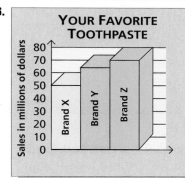

YOUR FAVORITE
TOOTHPASTE

Use each set of data to make two graphs. On the first, show that the data vary a great deal. On the second, show that the data are all practically the same.

7.

Year	Automobiles Sold	Year	Automobiles Sold
1981	6.26 million	1985	8.00 million
1982	5.05 million	1986	7.52 million
1983	6.74 million	1987	7.09 million
1984	7.62 million		

8.

Company	Mufflers Installed
Magic Muffler	154,296
Competitor A	146,983
Competitor B	141,337
Competitor C	139,225

How are graphs distorted to convey a false impression of the data? What should you look for in a graph to be sure the graph presents the data honestly?

Mixed Review

1. $803 - 177$

2. $4{,}656 + 4{,}769$

3. 462×37

4. $40{,}077 \div 73$

5. $26.04 - 9.79$

6. $3.0078 + 0.095$

7. 0.037×0.02

8. $501.368 \div 0.056$

9. $5\frac{2}{5} \times 4\frac{1}{2}$

10. $\frac{7}{8} \div 1\frac{3}{4}$

11. $6\frac{1}{3} - 4\frac{5}{6}$

12. $\frac{3}{5} \times \frac{5}{6} \times \frac{1}{4}$

Solve.

13. $n - 13 = 8$

14. $18 + x = 35$

15. $8y = 64$

16. $\frac{n}{3} = 25$

17. $5.3 + y = 12$

18. $x - 3.6 = 14.2$

19. $15n = 4.5$

20. $\frac{n}{0.7} = 9$

Using Problem Solving

Can Graphs Shape Opinions?

Paul and Manuel each prepared a report on the increase in food prices at the grocery stores for the past five years. Each student prepared a graph to go with his report.

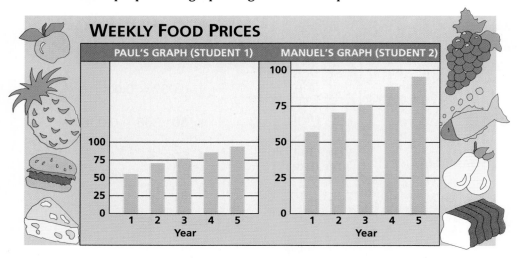

WEEKLY FOOD PRICES

PAUL'S GRAPH (STUDENT 1)

MANUEL'S GRAPH (STUDENT 2)

A. One student concluded that grocery prices had been increasing by a great amount. The other student said that there had been a small but steady increase. Look at the graphs. Which student do you think came to each conclusion? Why do you think so?

B. Study the graphs carefully. Do they show the same or different information? Do they look the same or different? Why do you think so? What are the differences? What are the similarities?

C. Make a different graph, using the same information. Does your graph support Paul's findings or Manuel's?

Sharing Your Ideas

1. Why might someone use a graph to show this data?

2. Is it possible for graphs to use the same information and yet present a different picture? Why or why not?

3. Which graph do you think better illustrates the information? Explain.

4. In what ways could someone change the appearance of a graph yet still keep the graph accurate?

Practice

5. One member of a family thought that the family should go to the movies more often. Another member felt that the family went to the movies often enough. They both made graphs to prove their points.

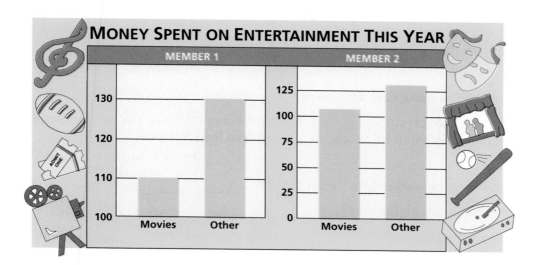

MONEY SPENT ON ENTERTAINMENT THIS YEAR

MEMBER 1

MEMBER 2

Which graph gives the impression that few movies are seen by the family? Do the graphs show the same information? Why do they look different?

6. What if it costs $1.10 for lunch in your school, and it costs about $.95 to make your own lunch? Make two graphs—one that could be used to show why you want to have your lunch made, and the other to show that you would rather buy your lunch.

Summing Up

7. How did you make your graph to show that you wanted to bring your lunch? that you wanted to buy your lunch?

8. What suggestions do you have to help people interpret graphs that are designed to convince or persuade? Write a short paragraph on this topic.

Chapter Review

Use the sets of data below to answer 1–3. pages 246–253

a. 34, 20, 31, 25, 25, 18, 30, 32, 25, 31, 25, 41

b. 11, 14, 17, 11, 9, 9, 8, 8, 11, 11, 8, 12, 14

1. Make a stem and leaf plot for the data in **a.** Name the mode and the range.

2. Make a box and whisker plot for the data in **b.** Name the median and the range.

3. Use a calculator. Find the mean of the data in **a**; in **b**.

Which measure was used to make each statement? pages 254–255

4. The average age of a U.S. president when first inaugurated is about 55 years.

5. Half the employees at Cooper Industries earn less than $10,000.

Use the graphs at the right to answer 6–11. pages 260–263

6. Which family spends more on housing?

7. Which family saves the greater part of their income?

8. How much do the Usyks spend monthly on food and household goods?

9. What fraction of their income do the Schultes spend on clothing?

10. For which graph is it easier to find the amount of money spent monthly on each item? Why?

11. For which graph is it easier to find the part of the monthly budget spent on each item? Why?

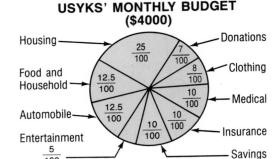

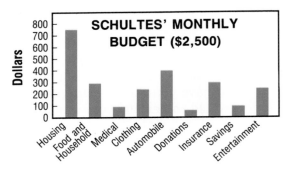

Solve. pages 257–259, 264–267

12. Bob and Chow both work Monday through Thursday at a toy store. Bob is off every fifth day. Chow is off every sixth day. They both were off this Monday. What is the next day they will both be off?

13. **a.** How does the graph at the right distort the data?
    b. What wrong conclusion could be drawn?

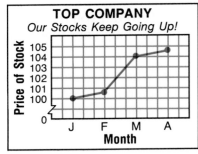

Chapter Test

Use the data in a for 1–4 and the data in b for 5–8.

a. 25, 25, 33, 21, 42, 22, 30, 26, 34, 43

b. 3, 5, 4, 8, 3, 4, 5, 8, 10, 11, 10, 5, 4, 3, 3

1. Make a stem and leaf plot for the data.

5. Make a box and whisker plot for the data.

2. Name the range of the data.

6. Name the range of the data.

3. Name the mode of the data.

7. Name the median of the data.

4. Name the mean of the data.

8. Name the mode of the data.

Which measure was used to make each statement?

9. Marty's bowling average is 136.

10. Marty's team voted to call themselves The King Pins.

11. In half of the games this season Marty has scored 130 or higher.

12. There is a 55-point difference between Marty's highest and lowest scores.

Use the graphs at the right to answer 13–18.

13. What fraction of her allowance does Sue save?

14. How much money does Ann spend on snacks each week?

15. What fraction of her allowance does each girl donate and save?

16. How much money does each girl use for entertainment in 4 weeks?

17. For which graph is it easier to find the amount of money spent on each item? Why?

18. For which graph is it easier to find the part of the allowance used for each item? Why?

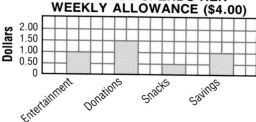

HOW ANN SPENDS HER WEEKLY ALLOWANCE ($5.00)

Snacks $\frac{25}{100}$ Savings $\frac{25}{100}$

Donations $\frac{20}{100}$ Entertainment $\frac{30}{100}$

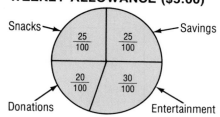

HOW SUE SPENDS HER WEEKLY ALLOWANCE ($4.00)

Solve.

19. Sara pays 50¢ to park for 2 hours. The parking meter takes quarters, dimes, and nickels. List the ways Sara can pay for parking.

20. a. How does the graph at the right distort the data?
    b. What wrong conclusion could be drawn?

THINK   Develop a set of data that has a mean of 30, a range of 28, a mode of 35, and a median of 34.

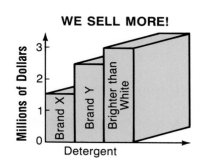

WE SELL MORE!

269

Histograms

A **histogram** is another way of showing data. A histogram looks like a bar graph. However, bars are always adjacent to each other. The width of a bar represents an interval of the data. The height of a bar represents the frequency of data in that interval.

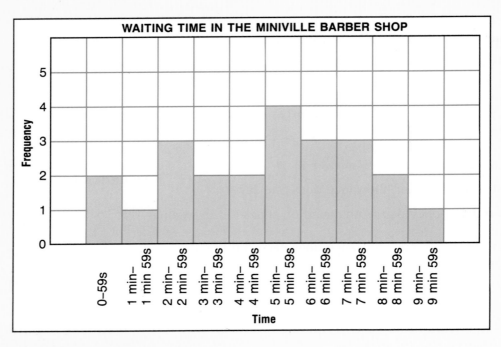

Examine the histogram above.

1. What is the interval represented by each bar?

2. Find the frequency for the following waiting times.

  a. less than 1 minute

  b. between 4 min and 4 min 59 s

  c. between 7 min and 7 min 59 s

  d. 6 min or more

3. In which interval would a person who waited $6\frac{1}{2}$ minutes be recorded on the histogram? In which interval would a person who did not wait at all be recorded?

4. How can you identify the mode from the histogram?

5. How many people are represented in the histogram?

Maintaining Skills

Choose the correct answers. Write A, B, C, or D.

1. What is the supplement of 45°?

  A 45°   **C** 135°

  B 225°   **D** not given

2. What type of triangle is $\triangle PQR$?

  A isosceles   **C** obtuse

  B scalene   **D** not given

3. Which is equivalent to $\frac{5}{8}$?

  A $\frac{15}{24}$ **C** $\frac{15}{32}$

  B $\frac{10}{24}$ **D** not given

4. Compare. $\frac{1}{8}$ ⬤ $\frac{1}{7}$

  A $<$ **C** $=$

  B $>$ **D** not given

5.
$$\begin{array}{r} \frac{5}{7} \\ + \frac{3}{14} \\ \hline \end{array}$$

  A $\frac{8}{21}$ **C** $\frac{1}{2}$

  B $\frac{13}{14}$ **D** not given

6. $1\frac{3}{4} - \frac{7}{8}$

  A $1\frac{1}{8}$ **C** $\frac{7}{8}$

  B $\frac{5}{8}$ **D** not given

7. $3\frac{3}{5} \times 2\frac{7}{9}$

  A 10   **C** $9\frac{3}{5}$

  B $6\frac{21}{45}$ **D** not given

8. $\frac{4}{5} \div \frac{2}{3}$

  A 1   **C** $\frac{5}{6}$

  B $\frac{6}{5}$ **D** not given

9. $1\frac{2}{3} \div 1\frac{1}{9}$

  A 3   **C** $1\frac{1}{3}$

  B $\frac{2}{3}$ **D** not given

10. What is the range?
63.4, 28.5, 15, and 89.2

  A 48.4   **C** 74.2

  B 87.7   **D** not given

11. Which group has a mean of 20?

  A 10, 15, 20, 25   **C** 20, 30, 40

  B 10, 20, 20, 40   **D** 10, 20, 20, 30

Solve.

12. An elevator stops on the 15th floor of an office building. It had gone up 3 floors, down 2, up 4, and down 1 floor. On what floor did it begin?

  A 15   **C** 11

  B 19   **D** not given

13. Sara bowled a 40 today. She wants to bowl a score $1\frac{1}{2}$ times each previous week's score. If she does this each week, what will her score be for each of the next 3 weeks?

  A 60, 90, 135   **C** 50, 80, 125

  B 40, 60, 90   **D** not given

9 Ratio, Proportion, Percent

THEME Photography: "Say Cheese!"

Sharing What You Know

What's wrong with these pictures? You are probably smiling because when things are out of proportion they look silly. Are you looking at giant crayons or at tiny people? How could you use mathematics to describe the distortions in these photographs?

Using Language

When something is in **proportion,** it appears in balance and in harmony with its surroundings. In mathematics, a **proportion** is a statement that two ratios are equal. You can enlarge a 4-in. by 5-in. photograph into an 8-in. by 10-in. one because the ratio of 4 to 5 is equal to the ratio of 8 to 10. Name some other examples of proportion that you see in everyday life.

Words to Know: proportion, ratio, scale, rate, unit price, cross products, terms

Be a Problem Solver

Marcia brings an envelope containing her best work to the photography club meeting. Inside the envelope there are 3 times as many color photographs as black-and-white photographs. There are 2 times as many slides as color photographs. How many times as many slides as black-and-white photographs are there?

Write about how you can tell which objects in a photograph are close and which objects are far away.

How would you compare the lengths of a 3-hour videotape and a 1-hour videotape? Is there more than one way to make the comparison?

Ratios and Equal Ratios

A professional photographer will take numerous shots to get a few that are good enough to publish.

What if a photographer took 36 pictures and 2 were published? What is the ratio of unpublished pictures to published pictures?

▶ A **ratio** is a pair of numbers that compares two quantities.

The ratio of unpublished pictures to published pictures is 34 to 2.

write   34 to 2, 34:2, or $\frac{34}{2}$ The **terms** of the ratio are 34 and 2.

read   thirty-four to two

Equal ratios make the same comparison. Multiplying or dividing each term by the same nonzero number gives an equal ratio.

$$\overset{\div\ 2}{34:2 = 17:1} \qquad \overset{\times\ 2}{34:2 = 68:4}$$
$$\underset{\div\ 2}{} \qquad\qquad \underset{\times\ 2}{}$$

What is the ratio of published pictures to all pictures?

Find two ratios that are equal to 2:36.

Check Your Understanding

Write each ratio in another form.

1. 9:6   **2.** 3 to 5   **3.** 7:11   **4.** $\frac{4}{3}$

Give two equal ratios for each.

5. 3 to 9   **6.** 6 to 15   **7.** 4 to 6   **8.** 9 to 2

Share Your Ideas How can you tell whether two ratios are equal?

Practice

Use the drawing to write each ratio.

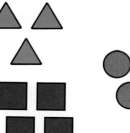

9. triangles to squares

10. triangles to all figures

11. squares to triangles

12. squares to not squares

13. circles to squares

14. circles to not circles

15. squares to all figures

16. triangles to circles

Write each ratio in another form.

17. 1 to 7

18. $\frac{3}{9}$

19. 4:36

20. $\frac{16}{5}$

21. 6 to 18

22. 18:1

23. $\frac{3}{14}$

24. 7:5

25. 11:37

26. 5:2

27. 21 to 3

28. $\frac{2}{11}$

Write two equal ratios for each.

29. 5:30

30. 6:3

31. 8:10

32. 7:2

33. 26:13

34. 9:15

35. 72:4

36. 3:26

37. 12:36

38. 44:6

39. 2:50

40. 17:5

Think and Apply

41. Shannon developed a roll of 36 prints. Twenty-seven turned out well. What is the ratio of good prints to bad prints?

42. For a fall foliage photo exhibit, Carrie shot 4 rolls of 36-print film. Fifty-four shots were used in this exhibit. What is the ratio of photos used to those not used?

43. Bruce videotaped a basketball game that was 1 hour 40 minutes long. He used a 3-hour videocassette. Write the ratio of used tape to total tape.

Logical Thinking

Use the numbers given to write equal ratios for each.

44. $\frac{a}{b} = \frac{c}{d}$
3, 15, 9, 5

45. $\frac{a}{b} = \frac{c}{d}$
4, 3, 15, 20

46. $a : b = c : d$
5, 10, 10, 20

47. $a : b = c : d$
3, 27, 54, 6

3:4 = 6:8   Does 3:4 equal 0.75:1?
Use your calculator to find out. Use division to find two other ratios that are equal to 3:4.

SUMMING UP

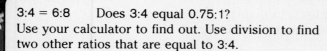

Rates

A **rate** is a ratio that compares different kinds of units.

12 prints for $3.60 compares prints to cost.

write   12 to $3.60,   12:$3.60, $\frac{12}{\$3.60}$

read   12 to $3.60

What is being compared in each of the rates described in Getting Started? Write a ratio for each.

Unit price is a rate that compares price to unit of measure.

You can find an equal ratio to find the unit price, or price per print, in a 12-print roll.

$\frac{12}{\$3.60} = \frac{1}{n}$ $\frac{12 \div 12}{\$3.60 \div 12} = \frac{1}{\$.30}$

What is another method for finding unit price?

The unit price, or price per print, is $.30.

FILM PROCESSING
12 prints $3.60
24 prints $6.00
36 prints $7.92

More Examples

Find the unit rate.

a. 150 miles in 3 hours

$\frac{150 \div 3}{3 \div 3} = \frac{50}{1}$

50 miles per hour

b. 1,240 calories in 4 servings

$\frac{1,240 \div 4}{4 \div 4} = \frac{310}{1}$

310 calories in 1 serving

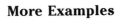 Check Your Understanding

Write each rate as a quantity per unit.

1. 105 words in 3 minutes   **2.** 240 students in 5 buses   **3.** 77 songs on 7 records

Find the unit price. Use mental math, a calculator, or pencil and paper.

4. 6 books for $10.50   **5.** 10 tickets for $100   **6.** $9.60 for 4 rides

Share Your Ideas Supermarkets are required to display labels showing the price per unit. How does this help you shop?

CHOICES **Write each rate as a quantity per unit. Use mental math, paper and pencil, or a calculator.**

7. 16 columns on 4 pages
8. 192 prints in 8 rolls
9. 245 cars washed in 7 days

10. 90 letters on 2 lines
11. 240 minutes in 4 classes
12. 500 bottles in 10 minutes

CHOICES **Solve for *n*. Use mental math, paper and pencil, or a calculator.**

13. 120 miles in 3 hours = *n* miles per hour
14. 30 lessons in 5 days = *n* lessons per day

15. 36 games in 4 weeks = *n* games per week
16. 574 ounces in 7 boxes = *n* ounces per box

Find the unit price. Round to the nearest cent.

17. 6 plays for $39.00
18. 3 cameras for $74.25
19. 1 dozen apples for $3.12

20. 7 pens for $6.93
21. $6 for 4 hours parking
22. 3 dozen bulbs for $6.48

Think and Apply

Determine the best buy. Use your calculator.

23.
SHAMPOO — 8 oz $2.69   12 oz $3.75

24.
FLASH BULBS — 3 for $1.77   6 for $3.60

25.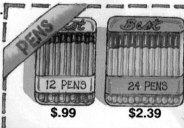
PENS — 12 PENS $.99   24 PENS $2.39

26.
TAPES — 2 for $5.50   3 for $8.50

27.
MILK — 1 gal $2.27   2 qt $1.53

28.
MARGARINE — 10 oz $.89   1 lb $1.29

DATA **29.** Select two supermarket ads from a newspaper. Compare the prices. Which store seems to have better buys? Justify your answer.

DATA **30.** Is the largest size of an item always the least expensive per unit? Find an item in a store or ad that shows this is not always true.

The sign reads 3 pens for $1.00. Tyler bought 1 pen and paid $.34. Explain.

SUMMING UP

What does the word *proportional* mean? Check the dictionary. Find or sketch two proportional shapes.

Proportions

Joe is a portrait photographer. Yesterday he took 360 color prints and 72 black and white prints. This means he took 5 color prints for every 1 black and white print.

The ratio 360:72 is equal to 5:1. How do you know this is true?

A **proportion** is a statement that two ratios are equal.

write $\frac{360}{72} = \frac{5}{1}$ or 360:72 = 5:1

read 360 is to 72 as 5 is to 1.

If two ratios are equal, the **cross products** of the ratios are equal.

$\frac{360}{72} \diagup\!\!\!\!\diagdown \frac{5}{1}$ ← cross products

$360 \times 1 = 72 \times 5$
$360 = 360$

To test whether two ratios are equal, you can either multiply or divide to find equal ratios or you can use cross products.

a. 3:5 ⬤ 21:75

Find the cross products.

$\frac{3}{5} \diagup\!\!\!\!\diagdown \frac{21}{75}$

3 × 75 ⬤ 5 × 21
about 240 ⬤ about 100   Use estimation.

3:5 ≠ 21:75

b. 21:28 ⬤ 9:12

Divide to find equal ratios.

$\frac{21 \div 7}{28 \div 7} = \frac{3}{4}$ **What if** you found the cross products?

$\frac{9 \div 3}{12 \div 3} = \frac{3}{4}$ What would you expect?

21:28 = 9:12

Check Your Understanding

 CHOICES

Use = or ≠ for each ⬤. Use mental math, a calculator, or paper and pencil.

1. $\frac{1}{8}$ ⬤ $\frac{3}{24}$ **2.** $\frac{12}{20}$ ⬤ $\frac{27}{45}$ **3.** 3:12 ⬤ 25:100   **4.** $\frac{2}{7}$ ⬤ $\frac{18}{49}$ **5.** 1.5:7 ⬤ 12:55

Share Your Ideas   Use the digits 2, 3, 6, and 9 to write as many different proportions as you can.

Practice

Use = or ≠ for each ⬤. Use mental math, paper and pencil, or a calculator.

6. $\frac{3}{10}$ ⬤ $\frac{4}{40}$ **7.** $\frac{3}{5}$ ⬤ $\frac{3}{7}$ **8.** $\frac{24}{36}$ ⬤ $\frac{2}{3}$ **9.** $\frac{12}{18}$ ⬤ $\frac{56}{84}$ **10.** $\frac{20}{5}$ ⬤ $\frac{4}{1}$

11. $\frac{2}{4}$ ⬤ $\frac{4}{8}$ **12.** $\frac{5}{7}$ ⬤ $\frac{55}{77}$ **13.** $\frac{0.3}{0.7}$ ⬤ $\frac{3}{70}$ **14.** $\frac{15}{19}$ ⬤ $\frac{180}{228}$ **15.** $\frac{9}{4}$ ⬤ $\frac{108}{56}$

16. $\frac{7}{10}$ ⬤ $\frac{21}{30}$ **17.** $\frac{3}{4}$ ⬤ $\frac{16}{24}$ **18.** $\frac{40}{30}$ ⬤ $\frac{3}{4}$ **19.** $\frac{2}{3}$ ⬤ $\frac{22}{33}$ **20.** $\frac{5}{7}$ ⬤ $\frac{6}{8}$

21. 4.2:6.7 ⬤ 42:67   **22.** 4:5 ⬤ 28:36   **23.** 9:0.6 ⬤ 36:24   **24.** $\frac{0.1}{1.3}$ ⬤ $\frac{2.2}{28.6}$

25. 5:6 ⬤ 10:11   **26.** 9:72 ⬤ 3:24   **27.** $\frac{0.9}{3}$ ⬤ $\frac{5.4}{18}$ **28.** $\frac{1.5}{6.5}$ ⬤ $\frac{5}{1.3}$

Write a proportion for each.

29. 6 for 78¢
9 for how much?

30. 7 to 8
How many to 5?

31. 6 to 17
12 to how many?

32. 5 for $1.87
How many for $5?

33. How much for 8
if $3 for 5?

34. 14 to 30
How many to 3?

Think and Apply

35. One photography store offered a roll of 24 prints for $9. Another store advertised 36 for $13.50. Which store has the better buy?

36. Lori counted 26 photographs in a 60-page magazine. She said that that was the same as 2 photographs for every 5 pages. Is Lori correct? Explain.

37. Dan has his own darkroom. To make developer solution he must mix 1 part concentrate to 4 parts water. He mixed 60 mL of concentrate and 240 mL of water. Did he use the correct proportion?

38. **What if** a photographer averaged 2 good prints per roll of 36-print film? If 5 rolls of film were used, how would you express the ratio of good prints to all prints?

Describe two methods you can use to decide if two ratios are equal.

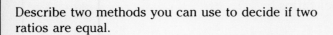
SUMMING UP

Write four different proportions for these cross products: $12 \times 6 = 8 \times 9$.

Solving Proportions

Sara is an interior decorator. She takes 2 "before" pictures and 5 "after" pictures for each job. This month she took 180 "before" pictures. How many "after" pictures does she have?

Write a proportion. Let n represent the number of "after" pictures.

"before" pictures ⟶
"after" pictures ⟶ $\dfrac{2}{5} = \dfrac{180}{n}$

Find an equal ratio or cross products to solve the proportion.

equal ratios

$\dfrac{2 \times 90}{5 \times 90} = \dfrac{180}{n}$ ⟵ Which method seems easier? Why? ⟶

$5 \times 90 = n$

$450 = n$ ⟵ Did you expect equal answers? ⟶

cross products

$\dfrac{2}{5} = \dfrac{180}{n}$

$2 \times n = 5 \times 180$

$2n = 900$

$n = 450$

Sara has 450 "after" pictures.

More Examples

a. $\dfrac{2}{0.7} = \dfrac{7}{n}$

$2 \times n = 0.7 \times 7$

$2n = 4.9$

$n = 2.45$

Explain why it is easier to use cross products in this example.

b. $\dfrac{8}{60} = \dfrac{2}{n}$

$\dfrac{8 \div 4}{60 \div 4} = \dfrac{2}{n}$

$60 \div 4 = n$

$15 = n$

Why is it easier to find an equal ratio in this example?

Solve each proportion. Explain which method you used.

1. $\dfrac{7}{9} = \dfrac{n}{54}$

2. $\dfrac{n}{9} = \dfrac{32}{144}$

3. $\dfrac{8}{32} = \dfrac{n}{20}$

4. $\dfrac{6}{15} = \dfrac{2.4}{n}$

5. $\dfrac{3}{n} = \dfrac{14}{2.8}$

Write a proportion. Then solve.

6. 3 radios per household
   How many radios in 100 households?

7. 390 calories in 3 servings
   How many servings for 260 calories?

Share Your Ideas How can you tell which proportions can be solved more easily by finding equal ratios?

Solve each proportion. Explain the method you used.

8. $\frac{25}{40} = \frac{n}{8}$ **9.** $\frac{n}{3} = \frac{3}{9}$ **10.** $\frac{20}{n} = \frac{45}{9}$ **11.** $\frac{3}{4} = \frac{21}{n}$ **12.** $\frac{n}{21} = \frac{15}{9}$

13. $\frac{1.4}{3.5} = \frac{2}{n}$ **14.** $\frac{0.7}{n} = \frac{28}{8}$ **15.** $\frac{13}{5} = \frac{n}{2.5}$ **16.** $\frac{24}{9} = \frac{10}{n}$ **17.** $7 : n = 8 : 40$

18. $2.4 : n = 2 : 3$ **19.** $n : 0.8 = 10 : 16$ **20.** $2 : 8 = 3 : n$ **21.** $n : 4 = 15 : 2$

Write a proportion. Then solve.

22. 16 revolutions per second
How many revolutions in 30 seconds?

23. 36 players on 2 teams
How many players on 5 teams?

24. 110 people per train
How many trains for 550 people?

25. 42 ounces in 3 boxes
How many ounces in 7 boxes?

Use a calculator to solve each proportion.

26. $n : 5.6 = 0.5 : 14$ **27.** $1.1 : 6 = 5.5 : n$ **28.** $5.2 : n = 1.3 : 1.6$

Solve.

29. Each of the cross products of a proportion is 48. One ratio is $6 : 16$. What is the other ratio?

30. Each of the cross products of a proportion is 36.8. One ratio is $2.3 : 4$. What is the other ratio?

Think and Apply

Write and solve a proportion for each.

31. A film processor can develop 100 negatives in 5 minutes. How many minutes will it take to develop 1,200 negatives?

32. Two film processors work at the same time but at different rates. One processes 100 prints in 5 minutes. The other processes 150 prints in 5 minutes. How many prints do they process together in 25 minutes?

33. Sara's "before" and "after" photographs are in the ratio of 2 to 5. She took 21 photographs. How many were "before" photographs? How many were "after" photographs?

Test Taker

Don't waste time using paper and pencil when estimation is faster!

$\frac{2}{5} = \frac{n}{21}$ **THINK** $\frac{2 \times 4}{5 \times 4} = \frac{n}{20}$

n is about 8.

Use estimation to select the answer.

34. $3 : 8 = n : 25$
   a. 1.78   **c.** 9.375
   b. 3.8   **d.** 19.5

35. $5 : 6 = 32 : n$
   a. 38.4   **c.** 50.75
   b. 42   **d.** 61.3

Is this statement always, sometimes, or never true? Explain.

- If $\frac{a}{b} = \frac{c}{d}$, then $\frac{a}{c} = \frac{b}{d}$.

SUMMING UP

Name three items for which scale drawings are used. Explain what the scale tells you about a map or drawing.

Maps and Scale Drawings

Aerial photography is used to make maps. A map is a type of scale drawing. A **scale drawing** is an enlarged or reduced drawing of an actual object.

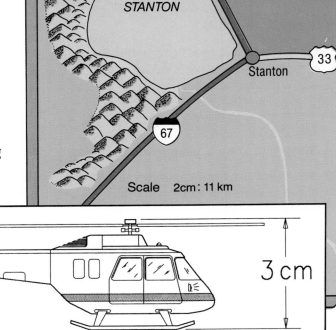

The scale for this map is 2 cm : 11 km. Every 2 cm on the map represents 11 km on land. The distance from Stanton to Hopewell measures 6 cm. How far apart are the towns?

$$\frac{\text{drawing} \rightarrow}{\text{actual} \rightarrow} \frac{2}{11} = \frac{6}{n}$$

$$2 \times n = 11 \times 6$$
$$2n = 66$$
$$n = 33$$

The towns are 33 kilometers apart.

The helicopter used to take aerial photographs is drawn to scale. The height of the helicopter is 21 m high. The drawing is 3 cm high. Find the scale.

$$\frac{\text{drawing} \rightarrow}{\text{actual} \rightarrow} \frac{3 \text{ cm}}{21 \text{ m}} = n$$

$$\frac{3 \div 3}{21 \div 3} = n$$

$$\frac{1}{7} = n$$

The scale is 1 cm : 7 m.

Scale   2cm : 11 km

3 cm

Check Your Understanding

Complete.

1. **Scale** 1 cm : 20 m
   Drawing is 17 cm.
   Find the actual length.

2. **Drawing** 4.5 cm
   Actual length is 9 m.
   Find the scale.

3. **Scale** 1 cm : 2 m
   Actual length is 11 m.
   Find the length of the drawing.

Share Your Ideas   What factors should be considered in choosing an appropriate scale for a scale drawing?

Use a proportion to find each actual dimension.

4. scale   1 cm : 5 km
     drawing   9 cm
     actual   _____

5. scale   1 cm : 25 m
     drawing   5 cm
     actual   _____

6. scale   4 cm : 3 m
     drawing   12 cm
     actual   _____

7. scale   9 cm : 2 m
     drawing   19 cm
     actual   _____

8. scale   5 cm : 13 km
     drawing   25 cm
     actual   _____

9. scale   1 mm : 6 m
     drawing   8 mm
     actual   _____

Find the scale for each drawing.

10. actual   15 km
      drawing   3 cm

11. actual   5 m
      drawing   5 cm

12. actual   100 m
      drawing   4 cm

Think and Apply

13. Make a scale drawing of one of the following. Choose an appropriate scale. Use a calculator or paper and pencil to determine the dimensions of the drawing.

   a. your classroom   **b.** your school
   c. a sports field   **d.** your home

Use the area map of Texas to answer the following questions.

14. Hector lives in Waxahachie and works in Dallas. About how many kilometers does he drive on the round trip each day?

15. After work on Mondays, Hector goes to classes at the University of Texas at Arlington. How far does he travel round trip on Mondays?

16. On Friday, Hector must be in Arlington on business. After work he will drive to Waco for a University of Texas/Baylor football game. What would be the shortest route?

17. Obtain a state map. Plan a vacation by car in your state. Mark the route on the map. Then find the total mileage of the trip.

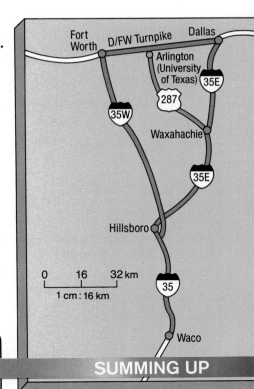

A map has a scale of 1 cm : 1 m. **What if** the scale is changed to 1 cm : 2 m? Will the map be larger? Explain.

SUMMING UP

Distance, Rate, and Time

Blurring in a photograph is used to convey motion. This car traveled 385 miles at 55 mph. How many hours did it take?

$$\textbf{rate } (r) = \textbf{miles per hour} = \frac{\textbf{miles} \longrightarrow}{\textbf{hours} \longrightarrow} \frac{55}{1} = \frac{385}{t} \longleftarrow \frac{\textbf{distance } (d)}{\textbf{time } (t)}$$

$$55 = \frac{385}{t}$$

$$55 \times t = 385$$

$$t = 7$$

It took 7 hours.

More Examples

a. **What if** you drove the car 250 mi for 5 h? What is the rate?

$$r = \frac{d}{t} = \frac{250}{5} = 50$$

You drove 50 mph.

b. **What if** you drove the car 60 mph for 4 h? How many miles were driven?

$$r = \frac{d}{t}$$

$$d = rt = 60 \times 4 = 240$$

You drove 240 mi.

Check Your Understanding

Solve.

1. 35 mph for 7 h
   Find the distance.

2. 1,125 mi at 125 mph
   Find the time.

3. 1,600 ft in 8 s
   Find the rate.

Share Your Ideas The formula $r = \frac{d}{t}$ is solved for r. Rewrite it solved for d. Rewrite it solved for t.

Complete the chart.

	Rate	Distance	Time
4.	66 mph	330 mi	t
5.	70 mph	d	3.7 h
6.	r	148 mi	18.5 min
7.	34 ft per s	d	12 s
8.	25 mph	47.5 mi	t
9.	r	160 mi	8 s
10.	10 yd per min	d	33 min
11.	r	1,170 mi	3 h 15 min
12.	72 ft per s	d	1 h

Write the unit for the missing part.

Example: distance in yards
              time in seconds
              rate in <u>yards per second</u>

13. distance in miles
    time in minutes
    rate in _____

14. distance in feet
    rate in feet per hour
    time in _____

15. rate in feet per second
    time in seconds
    distance in _____

16. time in minutes and
    seconds
    distance in yards
    rate in _____

Think and Apply

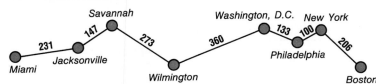

17. The Clark family will drive from Boston to Miami. They plan to average 50 mph and drive 7 hours each day. How many days will it take?

18. **What if** highway construction causes their average speed to be reduced to 40 mph? How many extra hours are needed?

19. Mr. Clark drove from Philadelphia to Wilmington in 9 hours. Find his approximate rate.

Martin flew 360 miles in $1\frac{1}{2}$ hours. He averaged 250 mph. Is this possible? Explain why or why not.

Mixed Review

Find the median and mode of each group of numbers.

1. 30, 60, 90

2. 88, 100, 92, 85

3. $15, $12, $12, $20, $17, $25

4. $6\frac{1}{2}$, 7, $7\frac{1}{2}$, 7, 8

5. 1.15, 2.2, 4.5, 5.3, 3.45

Name the quadrilateral described.

6. 4 equal sides

7. 4 equal sides, 4 right angles

8. only 2 sides parallel

9. 2 pairs of sides parallel

10. perpendicular diagonals

11. sides of 6 ft, 10 ft, 6 ft, and 10 ft

Give the prime factorization.

12. 188

13. 592

14. 1,001

15. 1,449

SUMMING UP

Many copy machines reduce or enlarge pictures. How are the copy and the original alike? How are they different?

Similar Figures

The nature photographer often interprets nature's power and beauty. This dramatic photograph was enlarged to poster size. Find the length of the poster.

These rectangles are **similar** because they have the same shape.

10 in.

8 in.

► When two figures are similar, the ratios of the lengths of corresponding sides are equal. That is, the corresponding sides are in proportion.

$$\frac{\text{length} \longrightarrow 10}{\text{width} \longrightarrow 8} = \frac{n}{24}$$

$$10 \times 24 = 8 \times n$$

$$240 = 8n$$

$$30 = n$$

The length of the poster is 30 in.

24 in.

$\triangle ABC$ is similar to $\triangle DEF$.
Find the length of $\overline{AC}$.

$$\frac{AB}{DE} = \frac{AC}{DF}$$

$$\frac{5}{2} = \frac{n}{4}$$

$$5 \times 4 = 2 \times n$$

$$20 = 2n$$

$$10 = n \qquad \text{The length of } \overline{AC} \text{ is 10 in.}$$

A

5 in.

C   B

F   E
4 in.   2 in.
   D

$\overline{AB}$ corresponds to $\overline{DE}$.
$\overline{BC}$ corresponds to $\overline{EF}$.
$\overline{AC}$ corresponds to $\overline{DF}$.

Check Your Understanding

SCAT is similar to TWIG. Complete.

1. Name three pairs of corresponding sides.

2. Find the lengths of $\overline{AT}$ and $\overline{TW}$.

C   A

15 in.   T

24 in.

S

2 in.
G   I
8 in.
T   W

Share Your Ideas Use a protractor to measure the angles of the two similar triangles above. Compare. Measure the angles of quadrilaterals *SCAT* and *TWIG*. Compare. Draw a conclusion.

SPOT is similar to JUMP. Complete.

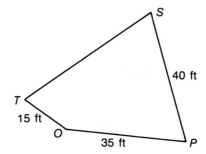

3. $\overline{SP}$ corresponds to _____.

4. $\overline{ST}$ corresponds to _____.

5. $\overline{MP}$ corresponds to _____.

6. The length of $\overline{MP}$ is _____.

7. The length of $\overline{TS}$ is _____.

Find the missing length for each pair of similar figures.

8.
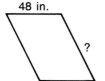
48 in.
8 in.
? 17 in.

9.
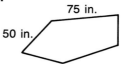
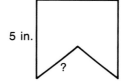
75 in. 90 in.
50 in. ?

10.
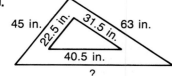
45 in. 31.5 in. 63 in.
22.5 in.
40.5 in.
?

11.
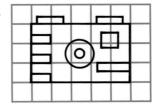
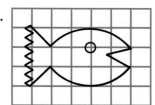
5 in. 2 in.
? 3 in.

Use paper with larger or smaller grids to draw a similar figure.

12.

13.

14.

15. Describe what would happen if you tried to make a drawing by using a grid of rectangles instead of squares. Justify your answer.

16. A flag stands 25 ft high. Its shadow is 10 ft long. The shadow of a pine tree is 23 ft. Draw a picture. Then estimate the height of the tree.

17. A copy machine will reduce a copy to 0.9 of the original. If a photograph measuring 8 in. by 12 in. is reduced, what are the dimensions of the copy?

True or *false*? Justify your answers.
- All rectangles are similar.
- All squares are similar.

SUMMING UP

Midchapter Review

Write two equal ratios for each. pages 274-275

1. 10:14
2. $\frac{8}{9}$
3. 7 to 16
4. 50:175
5. $\frac{99}{100}$

Find the unit price. pages 276-277

6. 8 tickets for $256
7. 2 dozen pens for $10.80
8. 72 records for $646.56

Use = or ≠ for each ●. pages 278–279

9. $\frac{5}{6}$ ● $\frac{8}{9}$
10. $\frac{6}{9}$ ● $\frac{10}{15}$
11. $\frac{20}{26}$ ● $\frac{10}{13}$
12. $\frac{27}{36}$ ● $\frac{21}{27}$
13. 17:3 ● 68:12

Solve each proportion. pages 280-281

14. $\frac{n}{7} = \frac{15}{35}$
15. $\frac{8}{n} = \frac{2}{9}$
16. $\frac{7}{16.8} = \frac{n}{6}$
17. $\frac{4}{11} = \frac{8}{n}$
18. 12:5 = n:7

Find the actual length for each. pages 282-283

19. scale: 1 in.:5 ft
    drawing: 7 in.
    actual: _____

20. scale: 2 in. to 15 ft
    drawing: 19 in.
    actual: _____

21. scale: 3 in.:70 mi
    drawing: 8 in.
    actual: _____

Solve. pages 284-285

22. 53 mph for 5 h
    Find the distance.

23. 810 mi at 40 mph
    Find the time.

24. 40.5 mi in 3 min
    Find the rate.

Find the missing length for each pair of similar figures. pages 286-287

25.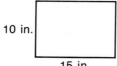

26.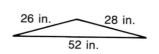

For each exercise, unscramble the letters to make a vocabulary word used in this chapter.

27. atori
28. laces
29. tear
30. tropropino

Solve.

31. There are cherries and grapes in a bag. The ratio of cherries to grapes is 8 to 19. How many pieces of fruit are in the bag if there are 40 cherries?

32. Yesterday Mr. Clark drove 225 mi at 50 mph. Today he drove 275 mi at 55 mph. Which day did he drive longer?

Exploring Problem Solving

How Fast Is She Running?

"Grandpa, that's the fourth time Mrs. Alvarez has jogged past us while we have walked once around the reservoir. Is she going four times as fast as we are?" asked Tony.

Thinking Critically

All three are traveling in the same direction and going at a constant pace. How much faster was Mrs. Alvarez jogging?

Analyzing and Making Decisions

1. **What if** Mrs. Alvarez started running just before Tony and his grandfather started walking? How many times would she go around the reservoir while Tony and his grandfather went once?

2. **What if** Mrs. Alvarez started running a fraction of a second behind them? How many times would Mrs. Alvarez go around the reservoir while they went once?

3. Since they are both going at a constant pace, about where would Mrs. Alvarez have passed them in question **1**? in question **2**?

4. How many times as fast as Tony and his grandfather is Mrs. Alvarez going?

Look Back   What if Mrs. Alvarez started jogging after Tony and his grandfather had been walking for a while? She might pass them for the first time when they were halfway around the reservoir. Where would Mrs. Alvarez pass them each of the next three times? About how many times as fast would she be going?

Problem Solving Strategies

Solve a Simpler Problem

The 10 members of the photography club took a trip. They decided to take a picture of every possible pair of students in the club. How many different ways can the 10 members be paired?

Often you can help solve a problem by solving a simpler problem.

Solving the Problem

Think What is the question?

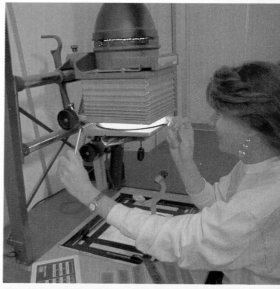

Explore If there were only 2 members, how many different pairs of students could there be? How many pairs could there be for 3 members? for 4 members? for 5 members? What pattern do you see developing? How can you use that pattern to tell how many pairs there are for 10 people?

Solve How many pairs are there?

Look Back How many terms do you think you need to find to discover the pattern?

Share Your Ideas

1. How could you find the number of pairs there are for 15 people?

Practice

 Solve. Use a calculator where appropriate.

2. The ten members of the photography club each gave one picture to each of the other members of the club. How many pictures were exchanged?

3. Maria is taking pictures of her 4 friends in the park. In how many different ways can she arrange them in a line?

4. The director of transportation in Martinsville is putting traffic lights at each intersection in the city. There are 89 east-west streets and 74 north-south streets that intersect. How many traffic lights will be needed?

5. Harold read from page 181 through page 210 of his photography book. How many pages did he read?

Mixed Strategy Review

6. Karen wants to enlarge a 4-in. by 6-in. photo so that the longer side will be 15 in. What should the length of the shorter side be?

7. Michael has made a portfolio of his best photographs. He has three black and white photos for every two color photos. If there are 45 photos in the portfolio, how many are black and white photos? How many are color photos?

8. Bernie cuts mats for a photo store. He receives $1.50 per mat. Yesterday he cut 30 mats, and tomorrow he needs to cut 50. Today he and Phil working together cut 20 mats. Bernie and Phil divided the money for the mats they cut today. How much did each boy receive for today's work?

9. Eugene put some of his photos in a show. Two thirds of his black and white shots were portraits of friends. The other 5 black and white photos were landscapes. How many black and white pictures did he have in the show?

Create Your Own

Make up a problem about enlarging a photo.

Activity

Exploring Percent

What is the most frequently used letter of our alphabet? the second most frequently used letter? Make a guess. Then experiment to find out.

Working together

Materials: grid paper, newspaper or magazine article

A. On grid paper, mark a 10 × 10 square. Have your partner read an article from a newspaper or magazine. As the words are read, record them on the grid, one letter to each box, until the entire grid is filled in.

B. Make another 10 × 10 square. Exchange roles and repeat the activity, using a different part of the same article.

C. For each grid, make a table like the one at the right. Record the number of times each letter was used. Then find the most frequently used letter.

D. Shade the boxes of the letter used most frequently.

E. Write a ratio and a decimal to represent the amount of the grid used for each letter.

F. *Percent* means "out of 100." Instead of writing $\frac{7}{100}$ or 0.7, you can write 7%. Rewrite each ratio as a percent.

Letter	A	B	C	D	E
Tally					
Number					
Ratio					
Decimal					
Percent					

Sharing Your Results

1. Compare your results with your partner's results. Are there differences? Why or why not?

2. Compare your results with those of another group. Do you expect differences? Why or why not?

3. Devise a way to combine the data of the entire class. With your teacher's help, make one class table.

4. What do you think is the most frequently used letter of the alphabet? the second most frequently used letter? Can you tell what the least frequently used letter is? If so, what is it?

Extending the Activity

This chart was developed by scientists and was based on a large number of samples.

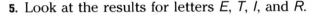

LETTER	E	T	A,O	N	I,R	S,H	D	L	C,U,M	F,P,Y	W,G,B	V	K,X,J	Q,Z
RATIO	$\frac{13}{100}$	$\frac{9}{100}$	$\frac{8}{100}$	$\frac{7}{100}$	$\frac{65}{1,000}$			$\frac{35}{1,000}$			$\frac{15}{1,000}$	$\frac{1}{100}$	$\frac{5}{1,000}$	
DECIMAL	0.13	0.09			0.065			0.035	0.03	0.02				0.002
PERCENT	13%	9%			6.5%	6%	4%				1.5%		0.5%	0.2%

5. Look at the results for letters *E*, *T*, *I*, and *R*.

   a. How can you change a ratio with a denominator of 100 to a percent?

   b. How can you change a decimal to a percent? Why does this work?

   c. How can you change a percent to a decimal?

   d. How can you change a percent to a ratio?

6. Copy and complete the table.

7. What is the most frequently used letter? Does this agree with your results? with the class results? Explain.

8. **What if** you analyzed an article about quails in Quebec? Would your results be close to those in the table above? Why or why not?

9. The ratio, the decimal, and the percent under each letter are all equivalent. Which would you prefer to use? Why?

Summing Up

10. Look up *percent* in a reference book. Where did the word *percent* come from? Where did the percent symbol come from?

11. Make a grid that is 10 by 10. Use colored pencils to make a design. Use at least 4 colors. Then find the percent of the grid used for each color.

Activity

Exploring Ratios, Decimals, and Percents

What percent of your basketball throws make baskets?
Play this game to find out.

Working together

Work as a class. All students, in turn, should do **C-F**.

Materials: wastebasket, 10 ping-pong balls, a bag

A. On each of four pieces of paper, write 2, 4, 5, or 10.
Use each number once. Put the papers into a bag.

B. Place a wastebasket in an aisle about 12 feet long.

C. Select a number from the bag. This is the number of
attempts allowed. Return the number to the bag.

D. Using that number of ping-pong balls, make as many
baskets as possible.

E. Record the number of attempts and the number of
baskets made.

F. Find the ratio of the number of baskets to the number of
attempts. Change the ratio to a decimal.

Sharing Your Results

1. Is it better to have two or ten attempts?
Explain your answer.

2. What different decimals are possible in
the game? Justify your answer.

3. How could you change the rules to allow
other decimals?

4. Did anyone get a decimal greater than 1?
Why or why not?

Extending the Activity

Work on your own. Study the examples.

$\frac{3}{100} = 3\%$	$\frac{17}{100} = 17\%$	$\frac{123}{100} = 123\%$

Change each ratio to a percent.

5. $\frac{37}{100}$ **6.** $\frac{7}{100}$ **7.** $\frac{11}{100}$ **8.** $\frac{71}{100}$ **9.** $\frac{17}{100}$

$0.07 = 7\%$	$0.13 = 13\%$	$1.5 = 150\%$

Change each decimal to a percent.

10. 0.02   **11.** 0.2   **12.** 0.22   **13.** 2.2   **14.** 2

$9\% = \frac{9}{100}$	$25\% = \frac{25}{100} = \frac{1}{4}$	$110\% = \frac{110}{100} = \frac{11}{10}$

Change each percent to a ratio.

15. 8%   **16.** 35%   **17.** 120%   **18.** 60%   **19.** 75%

$7\% = 0.07$	$17\% = 0.17$	$127\% = 1.27$

Change each percent to a decimal.

20. 50%   **21.** 5%   **22.** 8%   **23.** 15%   **24.** 155%

Find the one that does not belong.

25. 0.3, 3%, $\frac{30}{100}$ **26.** 90%, $\frac{9}{10}$, 0.09   **27.** $\frac{3}{4}$, 0.7, 70%

28. 0.8, $\frac{4}{5}$, 8%   **29.** $\frac{109}{100}$, 10.9%, 1.09   **30.** $1\frac{1}{2}$, 125%, 1.25

Summing Up

31. Explain what this sentence means: A percent is always a comparison.

32. Write directions to a sixth-grader on how to do each.

   a. Change a decimal to a percent.   **b.** Change a percent to a decimal.

   c. Change a percent to a ratio.   **d.** Change a ratio with a denominator of 100 to a percent

33. Change each decimal you found in **2** on page 294 to a percent.

Why is "out of 100" used instead of "out of 1,000" or "out of a dozen"?

Ratios, Decimals, and Percents

Do these sentences mean the same thing? Which is easiest for you to understand? Describe the differences and similarities.

75% of the underwater photographs are in focus.

3 out of 4 of the underwater photographs are in focus.

0.75 of the underwater photographs are in focus.

Here are three ways to write a ratio as a percent.

Use equal ratios.	Write a proportion. Use cross products.	Use division. Write the ratio as a decimal.
Find an equal ratio with a second term of 100.	$\frac{3}{8} = \frac{n}{100}$	$\frac{1}{3} = 3\overline{)1.000}^{\,0.333...}$
$\frac{3 \times 20}{5 \times 20} = \frac{60}{100} = 60\%$	$300 = 8n$ $37.5 = n$ $\frac{3}{8} = \frac{37.5}{100} = 37.5\%$	$\frac{1}{3} = 0.33\overline{3} = 33.\overline{3}\%$ $\frac{1}{3} = 0.33\frac{1}{3} = 33\frac{1}{3}\%$

Study the examples below. Then discuss which ratios work best for each method.

a. Write 3% as a ratio and as a decimal.

$3\% = \frac{3}{100}$

$3\% = 0.03$

b. Write 16.3% as a ratio and as a decimal.

$16.3\% = \frac{16.3}{100} \times \frac{10}{10} = \frac{163}{1,000}$

$16.3\% = 0.163$

c. Write $\frac{3}{12}$ as a percent.

$\frac{3}{12} = \frac{n}{100}$

$300 = 12n$

$25 = n$

$\frac{3}{12} = \frac{25}{100} = 25\%$

Write each as a percent. Explain the method you used.

1. $\frac{5}{8}$ 2. $\frac{4}{9}$ 3. $\frac{7}{5}$ 4. $\frac{19}{20}$ 5. $\frac{3}{125}$

Write each as a ratio in lowest terms and as a decimal.

6. 6% 7. 6.6% 8. 66% 9. 666% 10. 0.6%

Share Your Ideas Can all ratios be changed to percents? Can all percents be changed to ratios? Justify your answers.

Practice

Write each as a percent.

11. $\frac{4}{5}$ 12. $\frac{2}{11}$ 13. $\frac{3}{25}$

14. $\frac{17}{1,000}$ 15. $\frac{7}{8}$ 16. $\frac{2}{3}$

17. $\frac{29}{50}$ 18. $\frac{5}{9}$ 19. $\frac{11}{200}$

Write each as a ratio in lowest terms and as a decimal.

20. 60%   21. 85%   22. 15%

23. 8%   24. 10.5%   25. 2%

26. 71%   27. 6.5%   28. 8.9%

Write each number as a percent.

29. The human body is 0.47 muscle tissue.

30. Cara had 5 out of 6 problems correct.

31. The weight of the brain is 0.025 of total body weight.

32. There is a $\frac{3}{4}$ chance of rain.

Compare. Use >, <, or = for each ⬤.

33. 3% ⬤ 3   34. 1% ⬤ 0.001   35. $\frac{3}{4}$ ⬤ 65%

36. $\frac{9}{10}$ ⬤ 99%   37. $\frac{1}{2}$ ⬤ 51%   38. 0.175 ⬤ 17.5%

Think and Apply

DATA

39. **What if** your school was publishing a yearbook with individual photographs of each student and teacher? Find the number of students and teachers in your school. Determine an appropriate size for each photograph. At least 20% of each 8-in. by 10-in. page must be used for captions and margins. Plan a layout for each page. How many pages will be needed to picture every student and teacher?

Use 10-by-10 grids to model these numbers: $\frac{1}{3}$, 0.7, 42%, and $\frac{3}{4}$.

1. $3\frac{1}{2} + 1\frac{3}{4}$

2. $9 - 2\frac{7}{9}$

3. $4\frac{1}{2} \times \frac{3}{8}$

4. $3\frac{3}{4} \div \frac{3}{4}$

5. $\left(\frac{7}{8}\right)^2$

6. $\frac{1}{2} + \frac{4}{5} \times 2$

Evaluate for $n = 3$.

7. $6n^2$

8. $5n - 9$

9. $80 - 4n$

10. $(n - 1) \times 3n$

Is each number prime or composite?

11. 23

12. 47

13. 111

14. 307

15. 561

Write the prime factorization for each.

16. 32

17. 80

18. 100

19. 144

20. 285

SUMMING UP

Draw a circle and shade 100% of it. Divide the circle into 4 equal parts. What percent is 1 part? 2 parts? 3 parts?

Mental Math: Percent

Mr. Clark owns this camera shop. He feels the sign is too confusing. Use percents to make the sign more understandable.

SUPER SALE

MONDAY : PAY ½ OF THE TICKET PRICE

TUESDAY: PAY ½ OF YESTERDAY'S PRICE

WEDNESDAY: PAY ½ OF YESTERDAY'S PRICE

Monday	Tuesday	Wednesday
"Pay $\frac{1}{2}$" means "Pay 50%".	$\frac{1}{2}$ of 50% = $\frac{1}{2} \times \frac{1}{2}$ 25% = $\frac{1}{4}$ Pay 25%, or $\frac{1}{4}$, of the original price.	$\frac{1}{2}$ of 25% = $\frac{1}{2} \times \frac{1}{4}$ 12.5% = $\frac{1}{8}$ Pay 12.5%, or $\frac{1}{8}$, of the original price.

Use these percents to rewrite Mr. Clark's sign. Then use ratios to rewrite the sign. Which way is easier? Why?

What if you know $\frac{1}{10}$ = 10%, $\frac{1}{5}$ = 20%, and $\frac{1}{8}$ = 12.5%? How can you find percents for $\frac{3}{10}$, $\frac{5}{8}$, and $\frac{3}{5}$?

$$\frac{1}{10} = 10\% \qquad \frac{1}{8} = 12.5\% \qquad \frac{1}{5} = 20\%$$

$$\frac{3}{10} = 3 \times \frac{1}{10} \qquad \frac{5}{8} = 5 \times \frac{1}{8} \qquad \frac{3}{5} = 3 \times \frac{1}{5}$$

$$= 3 \times 10\% \qquad = 5 \times 12.5\% \qquad = 3 \times 20\%$$

$$= 30\% \qquad \qquad = 62.5\% \qquad \quad = 60\%$$

Check Your Understanding

Use mental math to write each ratio as a percent.
Use $\frac{1}{3} = 33\frac{1}{3}\%$, $\frac{1}{4} = 25\%$, and the equivalents above.
Explain your method.

1. $\frac{1}{6}$ 2. $\frac{3}{4}$ 3. $\frac{2}{3}$ 4. $\frac{1}{16}$ 5. $\frac{4}{5}$ 6. $\frac{2}{5}$

Share Your Ideas   If $\frac{1}{2}$ = 50%, how many other percents can you find by using mental math? List them.

Use mental math to write each ratio as a percent.

7. $\frac{1}{8} = 12.5\%$, so $\frac{3}{8} = n$.

8. $\frac{1}{5} = 20\%$, so $\frac{4}{5} = n$.

9. $\frac{1}{20} = 5\%$, so $\frac{11}{20} = n$.

10. $\frac{1}{25} = 4\%$, so $\frac{7}{25} = n$.

11. $\frac{1}{10} = 10\%$, so $\frac{9}{10} = n$.

12. $\frac{3}{5} = 60\%$, so $\frac{1}{5} = n$.

13. $\frac{3}{4} = 75\%$, so $\frac{1}{4} = n$.

14. $\frac{7}{10} = 70\%$, so $\frac{1}{10} = n$.

15. $\frac{2}{3} = 66\frac{2}{3}\%$, so $\frac{1}{3} = n$.

16. $\frac{9}{10} = 90\%$, so $\frac{3}{10} = n$.

Use mental math to choose the one that does not belong.

17. $\frac{3}{4}$, 70%, 0.75

18. 0.25, $\frac{1}{3}$, 25%

19. 1%, 0.01, $\frac{1}{1,000}$

20. 65%, $\frac{3}{5}$, 0.6

21. 5%, 0.5, $\frac{1}{20}$

22. $33\frac{1}{3}\%$, $\frac{1}{3}$, 0.3

Use mental math to choose the one closest to 50%.

23. 38.9%, 41%, 52.2%

24. 0.48, 0.3, 0.56

25. $\frac{2}{3}$, $\frac{4}{7}$, $\frac{3}{4}$

26. $\frac{5}{9}$, 0.456, 59%

27. The week before Mr. Clark's big sale, his sign read "Save $\frac{1}{4}$!" What percent did a customer save? What percent did a customer pay?

28. On Monday, Mr. Clark sold 30% of his inventory. On Tuesday he sold 42%, and on Wednesday he sold 17%. What percent of his inventory was left to sell?

29. Cassette tapes are on sale for 50% off the regular price. Compact discs are on sale for 25% off the regular price. What fraction of the regular price will you pay for a tape and for a compact disc?

Visual Thinking

Find the percent shaded. Explain your method.

30.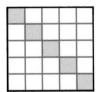

31.

32.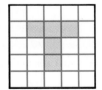

Explain two ways to use mental math to find the percent for $\frac{4}{5}$.

SUMMING UP

GETTING STARTED

Give decimals for 1% and 100%. Find three decimals less than 1% and three decimals greater than 100%.

Percents Less Than 1 and Greater Than 100

The Elite Photograph Gallery is featuring a display on flight. About $\frac{1}{2}$% of the photographs depict hot air balloons. What decimal and ratio represent $\frac{1}{2}$%?

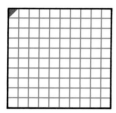

$$\frac{1}{2}\% = 0.5\%$$
$$= 0.005$$

$$\frac{1}{2}\% = \frac{\frac{1}{2} \times 2}{100 \times 2}$$

Are these equivalent? Why?

$$= \frac{1}{200}$$

About $\frac{1}{200}$ or 0.005 of the photographs depict hot air balloons.

What if attendance at the gallery increased 150%?

Find the decimal and ratio for 150%.

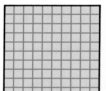 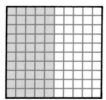

$$150\% = 1.50 = 1.5$$

$$150\% = \frac{150}{100} = 1\frac{50}{100} = 1\frac{1}{2}$$

Are these equivalent? Why?

In working with percents less than 1 or greater than 100, follow the rules used for percents between 1 and 100.

More Examples

a. 9 cases in 1,000

$$\frac{9}{1,000} = 0.009 = 0.9\%$$

b. Write 2.13 as a percent.

$$2.13 = 213\%$$

c. Write $\frac{2}{5}$% as a decimal.

$$\frac{2}{5}\% = 0.4\% = 0.004$$

Check Your Understanding

Write each percent as a decimal and as a ratio.

1. 0.1%   **2.** $\frac{3}{4}$%   **3.** $\frac{4}{5}$%   **4.** 220%   **5.** 185%   **6.** 525%

Share Your Ideas "Percents can be less than 1, between 1 and 100, or greater than 100." Rewrite this statement for decimals, using the decimal equivalents for 1% and 100%.

Practice

Write each percent as a decimal and as a ratio.

7. 180% **8.** $233\frac{1}{3}\%$ **9.** 315%

10. $\frac{1}{4}\%$ **11.** $\frac{3}{5}\%$ **12.** $\frac{7}{8}\%$

13. 111% **14.** 300% **15.** $\frac{1}{10}\%$

Write each as a percent.

16. $\frac{5}{4}$ **17.** $\frac{8}{3}$ **18.** $\frac{9}{8}$

19. 2.1 **20.** 3.45 **21.** 2

22. $\frac{7}{1,000}$ **23.** $\frac{7}{500}$ **24.** $\frac{3}{800}$

25. 0.0072 **26.** 0.006 **27.** 0.002

Explain what is wrong with each statement.

28. These books are on sale for 100% off. **29.** The new law decreased crime by 300%.

30. The skirt is 125% wool. **31.** They drank 223% of the juice.

Use mental math to write each as a percent.

Example: $1\frac{1}{4} = 1 + \frac{1}{4} = 100\% + 25\% = 125\%$

32. $2\frac{3}{4}$ **33.** $5\frac{1}{2}$ **34.** $1\frac{9}{10}$ **35.** $2\frac{4}{5}$ **36.** $3\frac{1}{3}$

Compare. Use >, <, or = for each ●.

37. $\frac{1}{2}\%$ ● $\frac{1}{2}$ **38.** $\frac{3}{4}$ ● 75% **39.** 0.75 ● $\frac{3}{4}\%$

40. 1% ● 0.1 **41.** 0.1% ● 0.001 **42.** 400% ● 4.0

Think and Apply

43. What if the gallery added your 10 best photographs to its collection of 1,990 photographs? Give the ratio, decimal, and percent of your photographs to the total.

44. What if admission to the gallery is 200% of last year's admission? How many times greater is this year's admission?

How can you tell by looking at a decimal if its equivalent percent will be less than 1 or greater than 100?

Using Problem Solving

Should Lucy Join the Book Club?

Lucy is considering joining the Fine Arts Book Club. She received the following information.

You agree to buy 6 or more books in the first year. Most books cost from $15 to $25 each before the discount.

There is a $2.50 postage and handling charge for each book purchased (free books are shipped free.)

Fine Arts Book Club

6 free books

All our books are
30% OFF
the publisher's list price.

We send you an order coupon with each month's selection. If you do not want the selection, return the coupon. Otherwise, the selection will be sent to you.

just for joining.

A. At least how many books will Lucy receive in the first year with the club?

B. At 30% off, the books cost from $10.50 to $17.50 each. About how much might Lucy pay for these books by purchasing them through the club?

C. About how much might she pay for them if she purchased them in a bookstore?

D. How can you compare joining the book club to buying books in the store?

E. How much might she spend for books in other years if she joined the club?

Sharing Your Ideas

1. What are some reasons for joining the club?

2. What are some reasons for not joining the club?

3. If Lucy asked your advice, would you tell her to join the club? Explain.

Practice

Before Lucy had decided whether or not to join the Fine Arts Book Club, she saw this advertisement for the Camera Book Club.

4. At least how many books will Lucy receive from this book club in the first year?

5. At 20% off, the books cost from $12 to $20 each. About how much will she pay for the books?

6. How does the cost of buying books from this club compare with the cost of buying these books in a bookstore?

7. Do you think it would be a good idea for Lucy to join this club? Explain.

8. Which club do you think has the best membership offer? Explain.

6 FREE BOOKS JUST FOR JOINING

Camera Book Club

You must agree to buy 3 books during the first year. Most books cost $15 to $25 each before the discount.

ALL BOOKS ARE 20%OFF LIST PRICE.

There is a $2 postage and handling charge for each book. (Free books are shipped free.) There is no monthly coupon to return. You receive a catalog every two months, and you order the books you want.

Summing Up

9. What are some reasons why a person might want to join a book club?

10. Why might a person prefer to buy books in a bookstore instead of through a book club?

11. Write a checklist of questions a person should consider when deciding whether to join a book club.

Chapter Review

Write two equal ratios for each. pages 274–275

1. $\frac{3}{5}$ **2.** $\frac{4}{9}$ **3.** $\frac{3}{10}$ **4.** $\frac{2}{3}$ **5.** $\frac{1}{8}$

Write the unit price. pages 276–277

6. 24 prints for $3.60   **7.** 6 combs for 66¢   **8.** 15 pens for $11.85

Use = or ≠ for each ⬤. pages 278–279

9. $\frac{3}{6}$ ⬤ $\frac{1}{2}$ **10.** $\frac{3}{5}$ ⬤ $\frac{9}{14}$ **11.** $\frac{5}{15}$ ⬤ $\frac{2}{6}$ **12.** $\frac{12}{16}$ ⬤ $\frac{27}{36}$ **13.** $\frac{6}{14}$ ⬤ $\frac{18}{41}$

Solve each proportion. pages 280–281

14. $\frac{3}{11} = \frac{n}{55}$ **15.** $\frac{4}{n} = \frac{2}{7}$ **16.** $\frac{2}{3} = \frac{8}{n}$ **17.** $\frac{n}{6} = \frac{7}{2}$ **18.** $\frac{25}{3} = \frac{7}{n}$

Complete. The scale on a map is 2 cm to 13 m. pages 282–283

19. The drawing is 6 cm. Find the actual length.

20. The drawing is 9 cm. Find the actual length.

21. The actual length is 91 m. Find the length of the drawing.

Solve. Use the formula $r = \frac{d}{t}$. pages 284–285

22. distance: 315 km
rate: 35 km per h
Find the time.

23. distance: 210 m
time: 5 s
Find the rate.

24. rate: 62 km per h
time: 3 h
Find the distance.

△ABC is similar to △HIJ. Complete. pages 286–287

25. $\overline{AB}$ corresponds to _____.

26. The length of $\overline{AB}$ is _____.

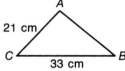
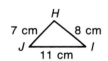

Write a percent for each. Use mental math, paper and pencil, or a calculator. pages 292–299

27. 0.7   **28.** 0.23   **29.** $\frac{3}{25}$ **30.** $\frac{17}{20}$ **31.** $\frac{7}{9}$

Write a ratio and a decimal for each. pages 296–297, 300–301

32. 65%   **33.** 8%   **34.** 13%   **35.** 0.5%   **36.** 200%

Solve. pages 289–291, 302–303

37. A triangle has no diagonals. A square has two. How many diagonals does an octagon have?

38. Richard is making a scale drawing of a road that is 2,700 km long. The drawing must fit in a 10 cm space. What scale should he use? Using the scale you have chosen, how long will the road be on the drawing?

Chapter Test

Write two equal ratios for each.

1. $3:5$

2. $\dfrac{5}{7}$

3. 6 to 40

Write the unit rate.

4. 18 ounces in 6 boxes

5. 216 beats in 3 minutes

Solve each proportion.

6. $\dfrac{3}{n} = \dfrac{4}{8}$

7. $\dfrac{10}{4} = \dfrac{n}{10}$

8. $\dfrac{8}{9} = \dfrac{16.8}{n}$

Solve. Use the formula $r = \dfrac{d}{t}$.

9. distance: 95 m
time: 5 s
Find the rate.

10. distance: 660 m
rate: 55 m per h
Find the time.

11. rate: 125 km per h
time: 6 h
Find the distance.

These figures are similar. Complete.

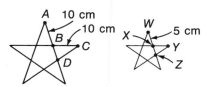

12. $\overline{BC}$ corresponds to _____.

13. The length of $\overline{XY}$ is _____.

Write each as a percent.

14. $\dfrac{3}{8}$

15. $\dfrac{3}{4}$

16. 0.7

17. $1\dfrac{3}{5}$

18. $\dfrac{1}{400}$

Write each as a ratio and as a decimal.

19. 0.2%

20. 2%

21. 20%

22. 20.5%

23. 200%

Solve.

24. Seven people are in a room. Each person shakes hands with every other person. How many handshakes are made?

25. A map of Greenfield Park shows the path through the park to be 2.4 in. long. The scale is given as 1 in.:0.2 mi. How long is the path?

THINK   Evaluate. Express the answer as a percent.

$$\dfrac{\frac{1}{2} \times \frac{1}{3} \times 0.06}{100}$$

Computer Link

Similar Figures

Two figures are similar if they have exactly the same shape. They do not have to be the same size.

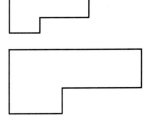

AT THE COMPUTER

Materials: Logo

A. Define each procedure shown. Enter T1 to call the first procedure. Then call T2 and T3. Compare the three triangles drawn. How are they related?

B. How are the commands for the triangles the same? How are they different?

```
TO T1
FD 30
RT 90
FD 40
RT 143
FD 50
RT 127
END
```

```
TO T2
FD 60
RT 90
FD 80
RT 143
FD 100
RT 127
END
```

```
TO T3
FD 15
RT 90
FD 20
RT 143
FD 25
RT 127
END
```

C. Complete the procedure T4 so that a triangle is drawn similar to the one drawn for T1.

```
TO T4
FD 90
RT ___
FD ___
RT ___
FD ___
RT ___
END
```

D. How did you figure out the lengths of the sides?

Sharing Your Results

1. How are the angles of similar triangles related? How are the sides related?

2. Complete the following statement:

   Two procedures produce similar triangles if _____
   _____

Extending the Activity

Is what you know about similar triangles true for other polygons?

3. Define the procedure PENT. It takes a whole number, decimal, or fraction as input. Then call PENT using each command. Record what is drawn.

   a. PENT 1

   b. PENT 2

   c. PENT 3

   d. PENT 1/2

```
TO PENT :S
FD :S * 18
RT 53
FD :S * 25
RT 74
FD :S * 25
RT 53
FD :S * 18
RT 90
FD :S * 40
RT 90
END
```

4. **a.** How is the figure created by PENT 2 related to the figure created by PENT 1?

   b. How is the figure created by PENT 3 related to the figure created by PENT 1?

   c. How is the figure created by PENT 1/2 related to the figure created by PENT 1?

5. **a.** Entering the command PENT 1 is equivalent to entering the sequence of commands at the right. Why?

   b. What sequence of commands is equivalent to entering PENT 2?

   c. Compare the commands you wrote for PENT 2 to the commands shown for PENT 1. How are the FD and RT commands related? Are the figures similar?

```
FD 18
RT 53
FD 25
RT 74
FD 25
RT 53
FD 18
RT 90
FD 40
RT 90
```

Summing Up

6. Explain why all figures created by PENT are similar.

7. Explain why it makes sense to call S in PENT the **scale factor.**

8. Give a definition for similar polygons that explains how the sides and angles of similar figures are related.

Use mental math to play this game. Two or three people can play. Make triples by matching an equivalent ratio, decimal, and percent.

First write an equivalent ratio and decimal for each percent below.

5%	$33\frac{1}{3}\%$	50%	125%
10%	$66\frac{2}{3}\%$	60%	150%
20%	30%	75%	0.5%
25%	40%	100%	1%

Make a deck of 48 cards—one for each percent, and one for each equivalent ratio and decimal.

- Shuffle the cards and deal the entire deck to all the players. Players place their matching percent, ratio, and decimal cards face up, as a triple, on the table. The remaining cards are held by the players and the game begins.

- One player chooses a single unknown card from the player on his or her left. If this card completes a triple, the triple is placed face up on the table. If no triple can be made, the card is added to the player's hand.

- Play proceeds to the left.

- Players take turns choosing cards until all triples have been made.

- The player with the most triples is the winner.

Maintaining Skills

Choose the correct answers. Write A, B, C, or D.

1. Which decimal is equivalent to $\frac{1}{25}$?

   A 0.05   **C** 0.25

   B 0.04   **D** not given

2. $5\frac{3}{5} + 2\frac{1}{3}$

   A $7\frac{1}{2}$ **C** $7\frac{14}{15}$

   B $7\frac{13}{15}$ **D** not given

3. Estimate. $2\frac{2}{3} \times 4\frac{7}{8}$

   A 5   **C** 8

   B 6   **D** 15

4. $\frac{3}{5} \times \frac{2}{3} \times \frac{5}{6}$

   A $\frac{1}{3}$ **C** $\frac{2}{5}$

   B $\frac{3}{5}$ **D** not given

5. $5\frac{1}{3} \div 2\frac{2}{3}$

   A $14\frac{2}{9}$ **C** 2

   B $\frac{1}{2}$ **D** not given

6. Find n. $\frac{1}{4} \times n = \frac{1}{5}$

   A $\frac{1}{20}$ **C** $1\frac{1}{4}$

   B $\frac{4}{5}$ **D** not given

7. What is the mode of 6.04, 5.3, 7.05, and 18.6?

   A 13.3   **C** 5.3

   B 9.2   **D** not given

8. Which has a range of 15?

   A 3, 14, 8, 1   **C** 5, 19, 17, 20

   B 20, 10, 15   **D** not given

9. Find the mean. 80, 50, 90, 100, 60

   A 76   **C** 380

   B 50   **D** not given

10. What is the rate per hour?
174 miles in 3 hours

   A 56 miles   **C** 522 miles

   B 58 miles   **D** not given

11. Solve the proportion. $\frac{3}{5} = \frac{n}{25}$

   A 18   **C** 15

   B 12   **D** not given

12. Find the time.   rate = 55 mph
distance = 247.5 miles

   A 4 h   **C** 5.5 h

   B 4.5 h   **D** not given

13. 9% = _____

   A $\frac{9}{100}$ **C** 0.19

   B $\frac{9}{10}$ **D** not given

Solve.

14. Sid paid the toll on the bridge in coins only. If he only had nickels and quarters, in how many ways could he have paid his toll?

   | Toll $1.00 |

   A 5   **C** 6

   B 2   **D** not given

15. There are only white and blue socks in a drawer. If you close your eyes and choose socks, what is the least number you must choose to be sure you have two of the same color?

   A 2   **C** 10

   B 8   **D** not given

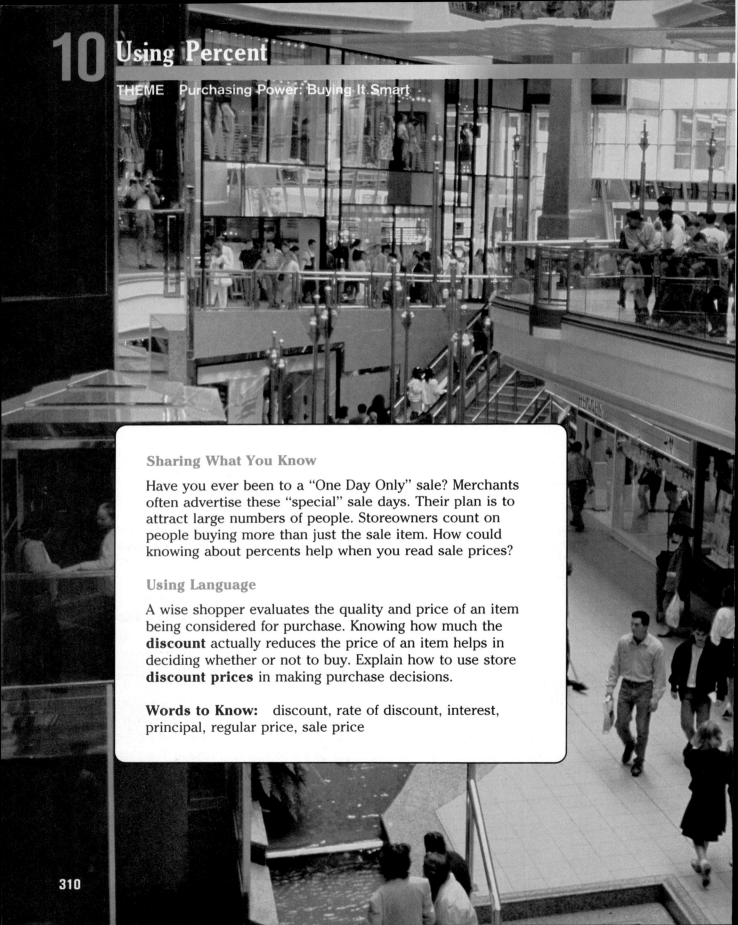

Sharing What You Know

Have you ever been to a "One Day Only" sale? Merchants often advertise these "special" sale days. Their plan is to attract large numbers of people. Storeowners count on people buying more than just the sale item. How could knowing about percents help when you read sale prices?

Using Language

A wise shopper evaluates the quality and price of an item being considered for purchase. Knowing how much the **discount** actually reduces the price of an item helps in deciding whether or not to buy. Explain how to use store **discount prices** in making purchase decisions.

Words to Know: discount, rate of discount, interest, principal, regular price, sale price

Be a Problem Solver

Read the following advertisement.

PRICES *SLASHED*

50%!

Buy today and take another 50% off!

How much would an item that originally sold for $100 cost if it were bought today?

Design a sale advertisement for your favorite record album. Decide which information you need to emphasize.

How would you find $\frac{1}{10}$ of $8? of $80? of $800?

Mental Math: Using Common Percents

Juanita phones home from college at least once a week. A sixty-minute call costs $10 on weekdays. Juanita can save 20% if she calls on a weekend. How much money does she save on a one-hour call made on Saturday?

You can use mental math to find the answer.

Think

10% of $\$10 = \frac{1}{10} \times \$10 = \$1$

Explain how you would find 40% of $10.

20% of $\$10 = 2\left(\frac{1}{10} \times \$10\right) = \$2$

Juanita saves $2 on a one-hour call if she calls on Saturday.

More Examples

a. Find 25% of 20.
Think
25% of $20 = \frac{1}{4} \times 20 = 5$

b. Find $33\frac{1}{3}\%$ of 30.
Think
$33\frac{1}{3}\%$ of $30 = \frac{1}{3} \times 30 = 10$

c. Find 15% of 80.
Think
15% of $80 = (10\%$ of $80) + (5\%$ of $80)$
$= \left(\frac{1}{10} \times 80\right) + \left(\frac{1}{20} \times 80\right)$
$= 8 + 4 = 12$

d. Find $62\frac{1}{2}\%$ of 80.
Think
$62\frac{1}{2}\%$ of $80 = \frac{5}{8} \times 80 = 50$

What property was used in **c** to find 15% of 80?

Use mental math to find each answer.

1. 10% of 10   **2.** 30% of 30   **3.** 75% of 80   **4.** $33\frac{1}{3}\%$ of 90

5. 60% of 60   **6.** 50% of 46   **7.** 15% of 60   **8.** 80% of $20

Share Your Ideas   Look back at example **b.** Explain how you would find $66\frac{2}{3}\%$ of 30.

Use mental math to find each answer.

9. 25% of 60

10. 10% of 70

11. 50% of 42

12. 75% of 40

13. $33\frac{1}{3}$% of 120

14. 60% of 110

15. 50% of 14

16. $66\frac{2}{3}$% of 18

17. 50% of 66

18. 75% of 48

19. 40% of 20

20. 100% of 111

21. 20% of 40

22. 50% of 90

23. 25% of 44

24. $37\frac{1}{2}$% of 80

25. 90% of 200

26. 200% of 90

27. 70% of 30

28. 300% of 50

29. $87\frac{1}{2}$% of 40

30. $33\frac{1}{3}$% of 48

31. 1% of 80

32. 500% of 20

Copy and complete the table. Use mental math. Use the Distributive Property where appropriate.

	Number	Percent of Number							
		5%	10%	15%	25%	35%	65%	75%	95%
33.	40								
34.	100								
35.	200								
36.	60								
37.	30								
38.	500								

39. Look back at **33.** Explain how you used mental math to find each percent of 40.

Juanita had $1,200 to spend to get ready for college. This circle graph shows how she spent the money. Use mental math to find each answer.

40. How much did Juanita spend for clothes?

41. How much did Juanita spend for bed and bath linens?

42. How much more did she spend on luggage and a backpack than on a microwave oven?

43. What if Juanita had spent only 35% of her money on clothes? How much money would she have saved?

Explain why you might want to find 20% of 50, using mental math, but would probably want to use a calculator to find 23% of 83.

COLLEGE EXPENSES

Clothes 40%

Bed/bath linens 25%

Luggage/backpack 15%

10%   10%

School and personal supplies   Microwave oven

SUMMING UP

Activity

Exploring Proportion and Percent

Working together

Materials: grid paper, a red and a blue pencil

10 out of 25 squares are blue. What percent are blue?

A. Cut out a 5-by-5 grid.
- Color 10 squares blue.
- Devise a different way to divide the 5-by-5 grid so that there are 100 squares in all. Use a red pencil to mark your new grid.
- How many squares are blue on your new grid?

80% of 25 squares are blue. How many squares are blue?

B. Cut out a 10-by-10 grid.
- Color 80% of the squares blue.
- Devise a different way to divide the 10-by-10 grid so that there are only 25 squares in all. Use a red pencil to mark your new grid.
- How many squares are blue on your new grid?

60%, or 15, of the squares are blue. How many squares are there in all?

C. Cut out a 10-by-10 grid.
- Color 60% of the squares blue.
- Devise a different way to divide the 10-by-10 grid so that only 15 squares are blue. Use a red pencil to mark your new grid.
- How many squares are there in all on your new grid?

Sharing Your Results

1. Write a ratio to show the number of blue squares compared to the total number of squares for both grids in **A**, in **B**, and in **C**.

2. Write a proportion, using each pair of ratios in **1**. How do you know that the ratios in each proportion are equal?

3. **What if** one of the terms in the proportion in **A** was missing? Explain how you would find it.

Extending the Activity

You can use the proportion

$$\frac{P}{100} = \frac{N}{W}$$

to solve many problems involving percent. *P* represents the value of the percent. *W* represents the whole. *N* represents a part of the whole. Study these examples.

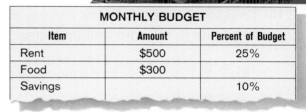

The table below shows part of the Johnsons' monthly budget.

a. How much money in all do they budget each month?

25%, or $500, of the Johnson's total budget is allotted for rent.

$$\frac{25}{100} = \frac{500}{W}$$
$$25W = 50,000$$
$$W = 2,000$$

The Johnsons budget $2,000 each month.

MONTHLY BUDGET		
Item	Amount	Percent of Budget
Rent	$500	25%
Food	$300	
Savings		10%

b. What percent are they budgeting for food?

$$\frac{P}{100} = \frac{300}{2,000}$$
$$2,000P = 30,000$$
$$P = 15$$

They are budgeting 15% for food.

c. How much are they budgeting for savings?

$$\frac{10}{100} = \frac{N}{2,000}$$
$$20,000 = 100N$$
$$200 = N$$

They are budgeting $200 for savings.

Here is more of the Johnsons' budget. Use the proportion $\frac{P}{100} = \frac{N}{W}$ to complete the table.

	Item	Amount	Percent of Budget
4.	Clothing		5%
5.	Utilities	$75	
6.	Recreation		$7\frac{1}{2}\%$
7.	Taxes	$400	

8. What percent of the Johnsons' income has not been budgeted?

Summing Up

9. What if you earned $2,000 a month? Make up a monthly budget. Decide what percent and how much of your income you will spend on each item in your budget. Compare your budget with those of your classmates.

GETTING STARTED

Find each, using mental math. Explain your method.
a. 30% of 30 **b.** 25% of 40

Percent: Using Ratios or Decimals

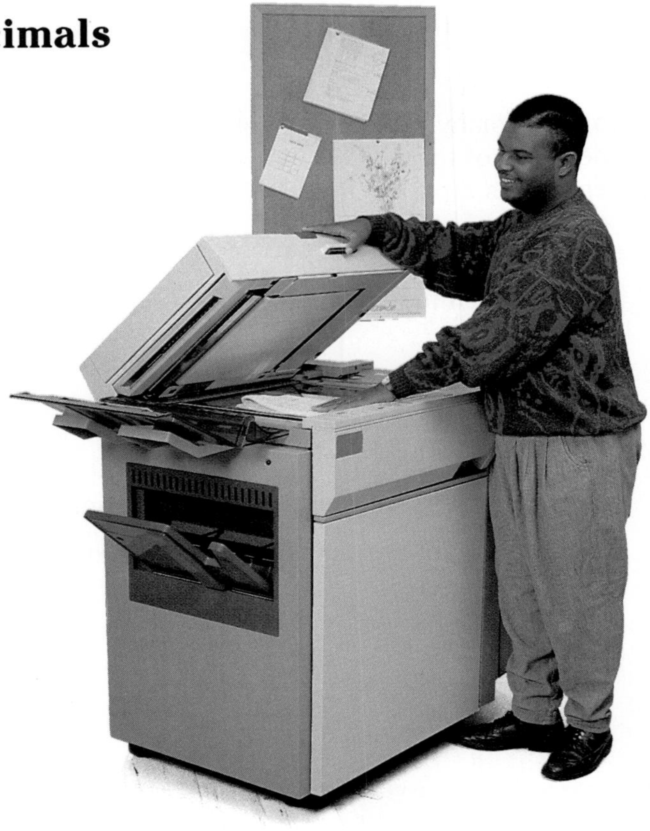

Ted will be given a 9% raise for excellent performance of his part-time job. He earns $90 a week. How much more money will he earn the week after the raise?

To solve this problem, you can use the proportion $\frac{P}{100} = \frac{N}{W}$. You can also rewrite the proportion as shown below and use the new equation to solve percent problems.

$$\frac{P}{100} \times W = \frac{N}{W} \times W$$ ← Multiply both sides of the equation by *W*.

$$\frac{P}{100} \times W = \frac{N}{\cancel{W}_1} \times \cancel{W}^1$$

$$\frac{P}{100} \times W = N$$ ← New equation

To find the amount of Ted's raise, let $P = 9$ and $W = 90$.

$$\frac{9}{100} \times 90 = N$$

Multiply, using the ratio $\frac{9}{100}$ or using the decimal 0.09.

Ratio

$$\frac{9}{100} \times 90 = \frac{9}{\cancel{100}_{10}} \times \cancel{90}^{9} = \frac{81}{10} = 8.1$$

Decimal

$$0.09 \times 90 = 8.1$$

Why can you use either $\frac{9}{100}$ or 0.09?

Ted will earn $8.10 more a week after the raise.

Check Your Understanding

Find the percent of each number. Use a ratio or a decimal.

1. 25% of 48 **2.** 17% of 98 **3.** $33\frac{1}{3}$% of 120 **4.** 27% of 325

5. 40% of 25 **6.** 29% of 180 **7.** 75% of 160 **8.** $66\frac{2}{3}$% of 360

Share Your Ideas What if Ted received an 11% raise? How would you use mental math to find the amount of his raise?

Practice

Find the percent of each number. Use mental math, a calculator, or paper and pencil.

9. 20% of 220   **10.** 28% of 95   **11.** 25% of 88   **12.** 63% of 300

13. 44% of 280   **14.** 98% of 550   **15.** $37\frac{1}{2}$% of 480   **16.** 60% of 450

17. $1\frac{1}{2}$% of 912   **18.** $33\frac{1}{3}$% of 390   **19.** 22% of 420   **20.** 35% of 510

21. 54% of 950   **22.** $66\frac{2}{3}$% of 750   **23.** 92% of $1,100   **24.** 46% of $825

25. $\frac{1}{2}$% of 200   **26.** 150% of 50   **27.** 19.6% of 85   **28.** $24\frac{3}{4}$% of 75

29. Look back at **9–28.** For which did you use mental math? Explain your method.

Without multiplying, decide which is greater. Explain your thinking.

30. a. 20% of 475   **31. a.** 10% of 500   **32. a.** $66\frac{2}{3}$% of 99   **33. a.** 25% of 404

b. 25% of 250   **b.** 20% of 251   **b.** $99\frac{1}{3}$% of 66   **b.** 75% of 103

Think and Apply

Many states tax the income of residents. Below is the state income-tax table Ted's father uses.

Schedule S			
Taxable Income		**Your tax is**	**Of the amount over**
Over	**But not over**		
$0	$10,000	2%	
$10,000	$50,000	$200 + 2.5%	$10,000

Last year his father's taxable income was $28,000.
$200 + 2.5% of ($28,000 − $10,000) =
$200 + (0.025 × $18,000) = $200 + $450 = $650
He paid $650 in taxes.

Use Schedule S to find the state income tax for each amount of taxable income. Use your calculator.

34. $7,500   **35.** $12,750   **36.** $5,200

37. $24,050   **38.** $19,800   **39.** $31,125

Look back at **9–16.** For which did you use ratios? For which did you use decimals? Explain your reasoning.

Visual Thinking

Estimate the percent of each circle that is red, blue, green, or yellow.

40.

41.

42.

SUMMING UP

Which is greater— $\frac{1}{3}$ off or $33\frac{1}{3}\%$ off? 50% off or $\frac{1}{2}$ off?

Discount and Sale Price

Abe has been waiting for the spring sale so that he could buy soccer shoes. The shoes he wants regularly sell for $49. What is the discount on the shoes? What is the sale price of the shoes?

▶ The **rate of discount** is the percent that the regular price is reduced. The **discount** is the amount that the regular price is reduced.

**SPORTS SAVER
SPRING SALE**

20% Discount
All Items

To find the discount, find the percent of the regular price.

discount = regular price × rate of discount
$$= \quad \$49 \quad \times \quad 0.2 \quad \text{20\% = 0.2}$$
$$= \quad \$9.80$$

To find the sale price, subtract.

sale price = regular price − discount
$$= \quad \$49 \quad - \quad \$9.80$$
$$= \quad \$39.20$$

What percent of the regular price is the sale price? Explain your thinking.

The discount on the shoes is $9.80. The sale price is $39.20.

Another Example

The regular price is $99. The rate of discount is $33\frac{1}{3}\%$. Find the sale price.

discount = $99 × $\frac{1}{3}$ = $33

sale price = $99 − $33 = $66

Check Your Understanding

Find the discount and sale price for each. Round to the nearest cent.

1. regular price: $120
   rate of discount: 10%

2. regular price: $150
   rate of discount: $66\frac{2}{3}\%$

3. regular price: $8.95
   rate of discount: 25%

Share Your Ideas Look back at 1. **What if** store employees receive an additional 10% discount on the sale price? Would their total discount be greater than, equal to, or less than a 20% discount on the regular price? Explain.

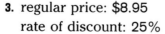

Find the discount and sale price for each. Round to the nearest cent.

4. regular price: $78
   rate of discount: $33\frac{1}{3}\%$

5. regular price: $44.95
   rate of discount: 25%

6. regular price: $29
   rate of discount: 20%

7. regular price: $50
   rate of discount: 40%

8. regular price: $125
   rate of discount: 35%

9. regular price: $45
   rate of discount: 15%

10. regular price: $120
    rate of discount: $37\frac{1}{2}\%$

11. regular price: $39.95
    rate of discount: $62\frac{1}{2}\%$

Solve.

12. The regular price is $25. The sale price is $20. What is the rate of discount?

13. The regular price is $49.95. The sale price is $39.96. What is the rate of discount?

Think and Apply

Which shop has the better sale price?

	Item	Sports Saver	Sport Stop
14.		regular price: $39.95 rate of discount: 10%	regular price: $42.95 rate of discount: 15%
15.		regular price: $36.50 rate of discount: 20%	regular price: $35.00 rate of discount: 15%
16.		regular price: $19.95 rate of discount: 20%	regular price: $17.95 rate of discount: 15%

17. Janet has saved $40 to buy a tennis racket that regularly sells for $59.99. She read an ad that announced a 25% discount on the racket. Has she saved enough money to buy it? If so, how much will she have left over? If not, how much more does she need?

18. Kendale paid $27.50 for a catcher's mask that was on sale. The regular price was $36.90. What was the discount?

Write *always, sometimes,* or *never.* Explain.
● A store offering 25% off _____ has lower prices than a similar store offering 20% off.

Mixed Review

1. $5.25 + 7.19$

2. $18.05 - 9.78$

3. 2.5×8.05

4. 63.5×0.011

5. $5\frac{3}{5} + 6\frac{3}{4}$

6. $7 - 2\frac{7}{9}$

7. $5\frac{1}{4} \times 2\frac{3}{7}$

8. $8\frac{3}{8} \div 1\frac{1}{4}$

Compare.

9. $\frac{5}{8}$ ⬤ $\frac{2}{3}$

10. $\frac{7}{8}$ ⬤ $\frac{9}{10}$

11. 3.5 ⬤ 3.055

12. 8.6 ⬤ 8.16

13. 3^2 ⬤ 2^3

14. 5^3 ⬤ 2^5

Solve for n.

15. $7n = 161$

16. $\frac{125}{n} = 10$

17. $0.5n = 25$

18. $\frac{3}{8} + n = 1\frac{1}{8}$

19. $n - \frac{3}{5} = \frac{3}{5}$

20. $n + 6.3 = 9$

SUMMING UP

Describe how you would solve for *n*.
$$n \times 72 = 8$$

Percent: Solving Equations

Mr. Paulino uses coupons when he shops. He
once saved $8 on a $50 order at the supermarket.
What percent of the total did he save?

Think What percent of 50 is 8?

You can write an equation to find the answer.
Use the formula $\frac{P}{100} \times W = N$. Let $W = 50$ and $N = 8$.

$$\frac{P}{100} \times 50 = 8$$

$$\frac{P}{2} = 8 \longleftarrow \text{What number would you multiply}$$

What does *P*
represent? $\longrightarrow P = 16$ both sides of this equation by to
get $P = 16$? Why?

Mr. Paulino saved 16% of his total bill.

What if Mr. Paulino saved $15, using coupons, and he
figured that $15 was 20% of his total bill? What would
his total bill have been before using the coupons?

Think 20% of what number is 15?

Use $\frac{P}{100} \times W = N$. Let $P = 20$ and $N = 15$.

$$\frac{20}{100} \times W = 15 \longleftarrow \text{How would you rewrite this equation,}$$
using a decimal instead of a ratio?

$$\frac{1}{5} \times W = 15$$

$$W = 75$$

Mr. Paulino's total bill would be $75. How much would he
actually spend, using the coupons?

Check Your Understanding

Solve.

1. What percent of 25 is 10?

2. 480 is what percent of 320?

3. 56% of what number is 224?

4. 75% of what number is 225?

Share Your Ideas What do *P*, *W*, and *N* represent in the
equation $\frac{P}{100} \times W = N$? **Look back** at the two problems at the
top of the page. Explain why $W = 50$ and $N = 8$ in the first
problem and why $P = 20$ and $N = 15$ in the second problem.

Solve. Choose mental math, paper and pencil, or a calculator.

5. What percent of 10 is 7?

6. What percent of 60 is 20?

7. 52% of what number is 31.2?

8. 200 is what percent of 80?

9. 25% of what number is 120?

10. $33\frac{1}{3}$% of what number is 62?

11. 150% of what number is 99?

12. 1% of what number is 100?

13. What is 300% of 25?

14. What percent of 90 is 75?

15. $37\frac{1}{2}$% of what number is 45?

16. What is $\frac{1}{2}$% of 400?

17. 4.5 is what percent of 90?

18. 400% of what number is 16?

19. What percent of 50 is $\frac{1}{2}$?

20. What percent of 25 is 0.15?

Use your number sense to select the correct answer. Explain your thinking.

21. 25% of n is 36.
What does n equal?

    a. 9 **b.** 50 **c.** 144

22. 40% of n is 30.
What is 20% of n?

    a. 15 **b.** 20 **c.** 75

23. 3 is $\frac{1}{2}$% of n.
What is 2% of n?

    a. 6 **b.** 12 **c.** 1,200

P.J.'s RESTAURANT

COUPON

All Dinners Served

2:00–4:00 P.M. 15% off
4:00–5:30 P.M. 10% off

Good Mar. 6 to Apr. 3   Unlimited use

SENIOR CITIZENS

Think and Apply

Use the information from this coupon for P.J.'s Restaurant to solve each problem.

24. Mr. and Mrs. Ramirez are senior citizens. They ate at P.J.'s on March 10. They were served dinner at 2:15 P.M. Their dinner cost $35 before the discount. How much did they pay for the dinner?

25. The following week, Mr. and Mrs. Ramirez ate dinner at P.J.'s at 2:45 P.M. They got $5.85 off. How much did their dinner cost before the discount? How much did they pay for dinner?

26. The next day, Mr. Ramirez ate at P.J.'s. He got a discount of $1.45 and paid $13.05 for his dinner. When was the dinner served? Explain your reasoning.

Explain how you can find the rate of discount if you know the regular price and the sale price.

SUMMING UP

Midchapter Review

Write a proportion for each. Then solve it. pages 314–315

1. 20% of 65
2. 35% of 80
3. 75% of 72
4. 16 is what percent of 8?
5. 32% of what number is 80?
6. What percent of 84 is 21?
7. 150% of what number is 120?

Choose mental math, paper and pencil, or a calculator to find each. pages 312–313, 316–317

8. 10% of 20
9. 71% of 300
10. 300% of 2
11. 75% of 40
12. $33\frac{1}{3}$% of 45
13. 50% of 75
14. 3% of 1
15. $\frac{1}{2}$% of 80
16. 63% of 500
17. 18% of 100
18. $66\frac{2}{3}$% of 48
19. 250% of 78

Find the discount and sale price for each. pages 318–319

20. regular price: $200
    rate of discount: 25%

21. regular price: $78
    rate of discount: $33\frac{1}{3}$%

22. regular price: $7.50
    rate of discount: 20%

23. regular price: $12.40
    rate of discount: 30%

24. regular price: $65
    rate of discount: 40%

25. regular price: $1,250
    rate of discount: 15%

Find the percent or the number. pages 320–321

26. What percent of 300 is 200?
27. 25% of what number is 5?
28. 38% of what number is 76?
29. What percent of 80 is 16?
30. What percent of 15 is 45?
31. 2% of what number is 5?
32. 400% of what number is 484?
33. What percent of 33 is 11?

Solve. pages 316–321

34. A package of 10 cassette tapes, originally $29.95, is on sale for 20% off. How much does 1 package cost on sale?

35. Mr. Lightfeather had 150 new cars on his lot. He has sold 102 of them. What percent has he sold?

Exploring Problem Solving

How Much Does it Cost?

The Neff family kept track of the money that they spent in June of Year A and in June of Year B. They also made a chart that showed how much it cost in June of Year B to buy exactly what they had bought in June of Year A.

Category	Amount Spent in June of Year A	What Year A Items Cost in Year B	Amount Spent in June of Year B
Groceries	$415	$445	$470
Clothing	150	161	83
Transportation	107	110	129
Personal Care	60	52	70
Entertainment	210	231	304
Housing	605	650	650
Other	112	153	180

Thinking Critically

How much did prices rise in one year? How did the Neffs' spending patterns change? In what category did they increase their spending the most?

Analyzing and Making Decisions

1. The Neffs' groceries cost $415 in June of Year A. Those same items in June of Year B cost $445. The cost of groceries in Year B is what percent of the cost of the same groceries in Year A? Which category of costs increased the most? Which category decreased the most?

2. Estimate the total cost of the items in Year A and the total cost of those same items in Year B. The total cost for Year B is what percent of the total cost for Year A? Estimate first. Then find the actual percent.

3. What percent of Year A spending is Year B spending when the actual Year B costs are used? (Column 4 shows the actual costs in Year B.) In which category was the percent the greatest?

Look Back   In June of Year C, the Neffs expect to have $2,200 a month to spend. How would you budget their money in each of the categories?

Problem Solving Strategies

Alternate Solutions

The Discount Houseware Store is having a sale. Here are the prices for the appliances that they have on sale.

If a customer bought one of each item on sale, how much money would be saved?

Often there are several methods for solving a problem. Use the method that works best for you.

ITEM	REGULAR PRICE	SALE PRICE
Toaster	$23.50	$21.00
Blender	$25.98	$23.48
Lamp	$29.99	$27.49
Iron	$12.99	$10.49
Telephone	$49.99	$47.49

Solving the Problem

Think   What is the question? What are the facts?

Explore   What is the total for all the items, using the regular prices? How can you find out how much is saved?

To find another method to solve the problem, look carefully at the prices. How much did Discount Houseware reduce each price? Is there a pattern? How can you use this information to solve the problem?

Solve   How much would customers save if they bought one of each item?

Look Back   Which method do you prefer? Explain.

Share Your Ideas

1. How are the two methods for solving this problem alike? How are they different?

2. Write a response to this statement: There is always one best method for solving a problem.

Practice

 Name two methods you could use to solve each problem. Then use one to solve. Use a calculator where appropriate.

3. Lisa is collecting boxes so she can prepare to move. She has 5 large boxes. Inside each large box are 2 medium-sized boxes. Inside each of the medium-sized boxes are 2 smaller boxes. How many boxes are there in all?

4. Ann and Sid are saving money for a camera. Ann has saved $100 and can save $8 a week. Sid has saved $60 and can save $12 a week. In how many weeks will they have the same amount of money?

5. Kim paid the taxi driver $27.00. This included a $4.00 tip. The taxi charges $1.75 for the first mile and $.25 for each additional $\frac{1}{5}$ of a mile. How many miles did she ride in the taxi?

6. Marvin is counting his dimes so that he can take them to the bank. When he puts them in piles of 2, 3, or 4 dimes each, he has one dime left over. If he puts them in stacks of 7 dimes each, he has none left over. He has fewer than 50 dimes. What is their total value?

Mixed Strategy Review

7. Kathy's salary at the dress shop is $210 each week. She also earns 12% commission on each item that she sells. In one week she sells items that total $550. What does she earn for that week?

8. A stereo is marked 30% off and costs $378. What was the original price of the stereo?

9. Berta, Lei, Dennis, and Trishna are giving a party. Berta spends $14 on food, and Lei spends $9 for invitations. Dennis spends $12 for decorations. How can the four people share the expenses equally?

10. Ten people are buying a gift for a friend who is moving. To pay for the gift each person needs to contribute $6. Later, 2 other people decide to contribute. Now, how much should each person contribute?

Create Your Own

Write a problem that can be solved in two different ways.

325

Which is greater—$\frac{1}{4}$ of 40 or $\frac{1}{3}$ of 48? Explain.

Estimating Percent

Ms. Shao and Ms. Kawahara's bill for lunch is $19.35. They should tip the waiter about 15% for good service. How much should they leave as a tip?

A tip is not usually computed exactly. Estimate to find the amount. Here are two ways to estimate.

Think $19.35 is about $20.

- **15% of 20 = 0.15 × 20 = 3**

- **15% of 20 = (10% of 20) + (5% of 20)**
  = (0.1 × 20) + (0.05 × 20)
  = 2 + 1 = 3

Ms. Shao and Ms. Kawahara should leave about $3 as a tip.

More Examples

a. What percent of 51 is 32?

    Think 51 is about 50.   ←⎯ Look for
           32 is about 30.   ←⎯ compatible
                          numbers.

$$\frac{P}{100} \times 50 = 30$$
$$P = 60$$

32 is about 60% of 51.

b. 64% of what number is 58?

    Think 64% is about $66\frac{2}{3}$%.
            58 is about 60.

$$\frac{2}{3} \times W = 60$$
$$W = 90$$

58 is 64% of about 90.

Check Your Understanding

Estimate.

1. 23% of 80

2. 53% of 48

3. 19% of 104

4. 65% of what number is 80?

5. 50 is what percent of 148?

6. 97 is what percent of 205?

7. $32\frac{1}{2}$% of what number is 71?

Share Your Ideas Which of the methods shown above do you prefer for finding a tip? Why?

Practice

Estimate.

8. 38.7% of 60

9. What percent of 180 is 62?

10. 76% of 101

11. What percent of 28 is 3?

12. 66% of 210

13. What percent of 52 is 10?

14. 60% of 42

15. What percent of 19 is 59?

16. 34% of 62

17. $63\frac{1}{2}$% of what number is 50?

18. $4\frac{1}{2}$% of 59

19. 34% of what number is 60?

20. $87\frac{1}{2}$% of 158

21. 83% of what number is 163?

22. 195% of 31

23. 71% of what number is 68?

Choose the best estimate. Explain your thinking.

24. 62% of 151 is n.

   a. 90   **b.** 140

25. 73.5% of 63 is n.

   a. 25   **b.** 45

26. 11% of n is 4.

   a. 40   **b.** 60

27. What percent of 175 is 89?

   a. 25%   **b.** 50%

28. $248\frac{1}{2}$% of n is 198.

   a. 500   **b.** 80

29. What percent of 184 is 957?

   a. 50%   **b.** 500%

Think and Apply

Find the total bill for each meal and estimate the tip.

30.

Dansbury Depot

Salad	$1	85
Turkey Sandwich	4	50
Milk		85
Melon Cups	2	25
Subtotal		
Tax		52
Total		

31.

Dansbury Depot

Soup	$2	25
Quiche	5	75
Cranberry juice		
float	1	85
Bananas Supreme	2	95
Subtotal		
Tax		62
Total		

Name two situations when it is useful to estimate percent.

1. 14.865 + 81.929

2. 8.71 − 3.97

3. 8.2 × 5.7

4. 0.06 × 0.005

5. 2.412 ÷ 0.24

6. 37.5 ÷ 0.025

7. $5\frac{3}{8} + 2\frac{3}{5}$

8. $6\frac{3}{4} - 5\frac{1}{2}$

9. $9\frac{7}{10} - 5\frac{4}{5}$

10. $\frac{5}{8} \div \frac{1}{4}$

11. $3\frac{1}{5} \times 1\frac{7}{8}$

12. $3\frac{2}{3} \div 1\frac{5}{6}$

13. $12 \times \frac{1}{12}$

Find the unknown measure for each pair of similar triangles.

14.

15.

16.

SUMMING UP

327

What is sales tax?

Using a Calculator: Finding Sales Tax

Most states have sales tax. An advertised price usually does not include the sales tax. If the state sales tax is 6%, what is the amount of tax for the television?

COLOR
★ TV ★

21 inch screen

$429.99
(TAX NOT INCLUDED)
SALE ENDS
• SATURDAY •
Space Age Electronics
San Antonio, TX

Write an equation to solve.

$\frac{6}{100} \times 429.99 = N$

$0.06 \times 429.99 = N$

The state sales tax is $25.80.

Use a calculator to multiply.

25.7994

Think 25.7994 rounds to 25.80.

Some *cities* have a sales tax in addition to a state sales tax. San Antonio collects $1\frac{1}{2}\%$ tax, and the state of Texas collects 6% tax.

To find the total tax on the television, you can add the percents, using mental math. Then multiply, using a calculator.

$6\% + 1\frac{1}{2}\% = 7\frac{1}{2}\%$

$0.075 \times 429.99 = N$

Why is 429.99 multiplied by 0.075?

32.24925

The total sales tax is $32.25. What is the total cost of the television, including state and city sales tax?

Check Your Understanding

**Find the sales tax for each purchase. Use a calculator.
Round to the nearest cent.**

1. purchase: $1,048
   tax: 4%

2. purchase: $28.50
   tax: $6\frac{1}{2}\%$

3. purchase: $9.95
   tax: 5%

Share Your Ideas How would you use mental math to find the sales tax on any item if the tax rate is 5%?

Use a calculator to find the sales tax on each item. Round to the nearest cent.

4. sneakers
   cost: $39.98
   sales tax: 5%

5. new car
   cost: $15,380
   sales tax: $6\frac{1}{2}$%

6. record album
   cost: $8.95
   sales tax: 8.2%

7. stereo
   cost: $599
   sales tax: 7%

8. gym equipment
   cost: $249.39
   sales tax: 6%

9. jacket
   cost: $72.99
   sales tax: 8%

Find each tax and the total amount of the taxes collected in each city.

10. Dallas

    state tax: 6%
    city tax: 2%
    purchase: $104

11. Denver

    state tax: 3%
    city tax: 4.1%
    purchase: $12,600

12. St. Louis

    state tax: 4.225%
    city tax: 1.875%
    purchase: $460

13. **Look back** at **4–9.** Find the cost of each item, including tax. Use a calculator.

Think and Apply

In many states the sales tax is not applied to all items. At Sloan's Super Market, taxable items are identified on the cash-register receipt. The sales tax is $6\frac{3}{4}$%.

Find each total, including tax.

14.

Sloan's
Supermarket
3. 49 tax
4. 20 tax
1.19 tax
.79 tax
1.42
5.29
6.19
2.29 tax
.15
.25
1.09 tax
Total

15.

Sloan's
Supermarket
2.89 tax
.98
1.55
3.65 tax
.29
6.39 tax
.87
1.59 tax
2.10
.99 tax
Total

Logical Thinking

16. A plane flies from Los Angeles to New York, making a stop at Detroit. Leaving Los Angeles, its passenger seats are $66\frac{2}{3}$% filled. In Detroit, 50% of the passengers on board from Los Angeles depart, but others board the plane. Leaving Detroit, 75% of the seats are filled. In New York, 90 people depart. How many passengers were on the plane from Los Angeles to Detroit?

What if you are purchasing an item that costs $1,000? Why is it important to consider the sales tax when planning for the purchase of the item?

SUMMING UP

Using Problem Solving

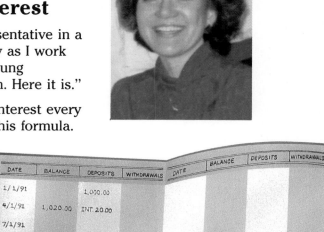

Interview: Calculators and Interest

Nina Sawon works as a customer service representative in a bank. Nina said, "I use my calculator constantly as I work with our customers. One day I had to help a young customer named Steve with an interest problem. Here it is."

Steve deposited $1,000. His account will earn interest every three months. The interest is computed using this formula.

Interest = principal × rate × time

How much interest will Steve earn after three months?

$$3 \text{ months} = \frac{1}{4} \text{ year}$$

Think **$1,000 × 0.08 × 0.25 = $20** ← interest earned

Examine Steve's passbook. The interest was added to the balance. When will the balance on Steve's account equal $2,000, if he does not deposit or withdraw money?

Working together

Materials: paper and pencil, ruler, a calculator

A. Make a passbook savings book similar to the one shown above.

B. Find the interest and the new balance on Steve's account for each quarter until the balance on Steve's account is equal to or greater than $2,000.

C. In the passbook, record the interest earned and the balances.

Sharing Your Ideas

1. How did you compute the interest and the new balance for each quarter?

2. When will the balance be double the original deposit?

3. If Steve does not deposit or withdraw money from his account, when will the balance be at least $4,000?

Practice

MILLER SAVINGS

PASSBOOK SAVINGS

$7\frac{1}{2}\%$

Annual Rate

Compounded Semiannually

County Savings

Passbook Savings

$7\frac{3}{4}\%$ Annual rate

Compounded Annually

SUBURBAN SAVINGS

Passbook Savings

Compounded Quarterly $7\frac{2}{5}\%$ Annual Rate

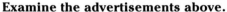

Examine the advertisements above.

4. **What if** you were going to deposit $1,000 in a bank for only six months? Which bank would pay the greatest amount of interest?

5. **What if** you were going to deposit $10,000 for one year? In which bank would you deposit the money?

6. **What if** each of the three banks changes its interest rate to 8% annually? You deposit $10,000 in each bank. How much money will you have in each bank at the end of one year?

Summing Up

7. How did you determine which bank paid the greatest amount of interest for a six-month deposit?

8. How did you determine in which bank you would deposit $10,000 for the one-year?

9. What factors do you think determine the amount of interest that a bank will pay on your savings?

How many degrees are in a circle? in half a circle? in a quarter of a circle?

Using a Calculator: Making Circle Graphs

Sarah keeps track of how she spends and saves the earnings from her part-time job. She made a circle graph of the data, which she included in a report she wrote on consumer spending. She used a calculator to compute the data for the graph.

Monthly Expenditures (Earnings: $200)			
Item	Amount	Percent of Total	Degrees
School lunches	$35	17.5%	63°
Transportation	25		
Clothes	40		
Recreation	30		
Savings	60		
Other	10		

● She found the percent of her total earnings that each item represents.

Item: School lunches—$35

$$\frac{P}{100} \times 200 = 35$$

$$P = 17.5$$

17.5% of Sarah's income is spent for school lunches.

● She found the number of degrees that each percent represents.

$$17.5\% \text{ of } 360° =$$

$$0.175 \times 360° = N$$

63

17.5% of 360° is 63°.

● With a compass, she drew a circle. Then, for each item, she drew a central angle. She labeled each part of the circle.

1. Copy the chart that Sarah made. Use a calculator to complete the chart. Check your results.

2. Use the data in your chart to draw a circle graph. Label each section. Compare your graph with those of your classmates.

Share Your Ideas Look back at 1. Explain how you checked your results after completing the chart.

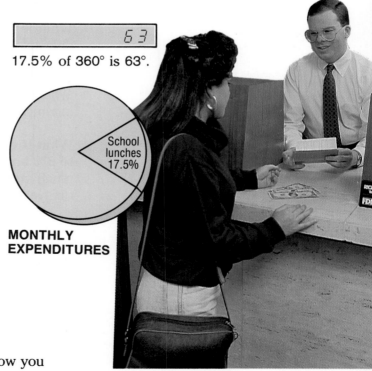

School lunches 17.5%

MONTHLY EXPENDITURES

Find the measure of the central angle represented by each percent of a circle graph. Round each to the nearest degree.

3. 25%   **4.** 20%   **5.** 80%   **6.** 90%   **7.** 55%

8. 75%   **9.** $66\frac{2}{3}$%   **10.** 48%   **11.** 37%   **12.** 68%

This circle graph shows the money budgeted for sports equipment at a high school. Use the graph to answer 13–15.

13. What is the total amount budgeted for sports equipment?

14. Find the percent budgeted for each sport. Then find the degree measure represented by each percent.

15. Draw a circle graph, using the percents and degree measures you found in **14**. Label each section of your graph with the type of sport and the percent budgeted. Compare your graph with the one at the right.

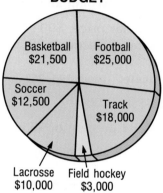

WASHINGTON HIGH SCHOOL SPORTS EQUIPMENT BUDGET

For each table below, draw a circle graph. Use a calculator to compute the data for each graph. Round to the nearest degree.

16. Land Use—
    Russel Farm

Category	Acres
Fruit groves	20
Strawberries	6
Vegetables	15
Fallow fields	12
Pond	4
Buildings	3

17. Population by Age—
    Waldo County

Age	Number
0–18	3,600
19–35	6,400
36–50	4,000
51–65	3,200
66–80	2,400
81 +	400

18. Adult Employment—
    Waldo County

Category	Number
Factory	2,000
Farming	2,200
Forestry	800
Government	200
Professional	400
Office	1,000
Retail	800
Self-employed	600

Think and Apply

19. Take a survey of ten students to collect data about how they spend their weekdays. Some categories might be school, eating, sleeping, studying, recreation, reading, practicing a musical instrument or a sport. Use your data to make a circle graph that shows how a typical student spends a weekday.

Pat computed the following data to make a circle graph: 45%—162°, 23%—86°, 21%—76°, 10%—36°. What is wrong?

SUMMING UP

Chapter Review

Choose mental math, paper and pencil, or a calculator to find each. pages 312–317, 320–321

1. 75% of 36

2. $66\frac{2}{3}\%$ of 54

3. 250% of 28

4. 25% of what number is 18?

5. What percent of 198 is 99?

6. What percent of 37 is 18.5?

7. What percent of 240 is 2.4?

Find the discount and sale price. pages 318–319

8. regular price: $99
rate of discount: $33\frac{1}{3}\%$

9. regular price: $7.99
rate of discount: 25%

Estimate. pages 326–327

10. 48% of 250

11. 25% of 395

12. 34% of 149

13. What percent of 98 is 18?

14. What percent of 74 is 111?

15. 9% of what number is 3.1?

16. 246% of what number is 48?

Find the sales tax for each purchase. Round to the nearest cent. pages 328–329

17. purchase: $84
sales tax: 5%

18. purchase: $16.99
sales tax: 6%

19. purchase: $1,485
sales tax: $4\frac{1}{2}\%$

Find the interest for each. Use a calculator. pages 330–331

20. principal: $500
rate: 8%
time: 6 months,
compounded quarterly

21. principal: $1,200
rate: $6\frac{1}{2}\%$
time: 3 years, compounded
every 6 months

22. principal: $5,500
rate: $7\frac{1}{2}\%$
time: 2 years, compounded
quarterly

Make a circle graph, using the following information. pages 332–333

23. Ticket sales totaled $560. The people collected the following amounts: Joe—$168, Chico—$140, Pia—$112, Tina—$84, Cesar—$56. Label the circle graph, using names and percents collected.

Solve. pages 324–325, 330–331

24. Judith Chan paid $38.95 when she took her family out to dinner. She left a $6 tip. Was her tip reasonable? Explain.

25. Emma has $2,000 in her savings account. How much interest will she earn in one year at $6\frac{3}{4}\%$ if the interest is compounded every 3 months? What will be her year-end balance?

Chapter Test

Find each number or percent.

1. 300% of 18

2. What percent of 15 is 6?

3. $87\frac{1}{2}$% of 64

4. What percent of 8 is 3?

5. 1% of 150

6. What percent of 14 is 35?

7. 100% of what number is 16?

8. 5% of what number is 20?

Choose the best estimate.

9. 66% of 89
    a. 40 **b.** 60 **c.** 80

10. What percent of 158 is 82?
    a. 50% **b.** 75% **c.** 150%

11. 23% of what number is 28?
    a. 60 **b.** 90 **c.** 120

12. 153% of 119
    a. 120 **b.** 150 **c.** 180

Find each missing number.

13. regular price: $440
rate of discount: 25%
discount: _____
sale price: _____

14. purchase: $50
rate of sales tax: 5%
sales tax: _____
total cost: _____

15. purchase: $21.95
rate of sales tax: 6%
sales tax: _____
total cost: _____

16. principal: $500
rate of interest: 6%
time: 6 months,
compounded quarterly
interest: _____

17. regular price: $6.95
rate of discount: 10%
discount: _____
sale price: _____

18. principal: $1,800
rate of interest: 8%
time: 3 years, compounded
every 6 months
interest: _____

Solve.

19. Circle Shoe Store took in the following amounts for shoes sold during the month of August: men's dress shoes—$750, women's dress shoes—$1,500, children's shoes—$750, adult athletic shoes—$2,000. This circle graph was made using this information. Was it made correctly? Explain.

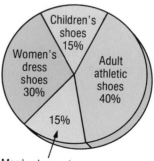

Men's dress shoes

20. Barney spent $11.34. He bought a wall calendar for $6.85 and pocket calendars for $.79 each. He paid $.54 in sales tax. How many pocket calendars did he buy?

THINK   Which is the better buy for this $50 sweater—on sale at 50% off or reduced 20% each week for 3 weeks?

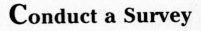

Conduct a Survey

Conduct this survey.

- Ask 60 people the following question: "About how many books have you read in the past year?" Include adults and students in your sample.

- Record each result, identifying the person as an adult or student and listing the number of books read.

1. Find the mean, mode, median, and range of your survey. Analyze these results. Which measure best describes the survey?

2. Separate the data into two groups: data from adults and data from students. Compare the data from these two groups.

3. What percent of the people in your sample read fewer than 5 books? Do you feel that this is an accurate prediction for the population of the U.S.? Justify your answer.

4. Decide which type of graph (bar, line, or circle) would best display the results of your survey. Explain your choice. Then graph the results.

5. Write a paragraph describing the results of your survey.

Maintaining Skills

Choose the correct answers. Write A, B, C, or D.

1. $4\frac{1}{3} \times 1\frac{5}{7}$

   A $4\frac{5}{21}$ C $5\frac{3}{5}$

   B $7\frac{3}{7}$ D not given

2. $3\frac{2}{3} \div 2\frac{2}{3}$

   A $1\frac{3}{8}$ C 1

   B $\frac{8}{11}$ D not given

3. Solve for n. $\frac{2}{3} \times n = \frac{1}{2}$

   A $\frac{1}{3}$ C $1\frac{1}{6}$

   B $1\frac{1}{3}$ D not given

4. What is the range of 82.4, 16.03, 15.01, and 14.2?

   A 1.83   C 31.91

   B 68.2   D not given

5. What is the mode? 56, 82, 91, 82, 77

   A 35   C 77.6

   B 82   D not given

6. Which ratio is equal to 5:7?

   A 5 to 6   C 5 to 7

   B 7 to 5   D not given

7. What is the scale for the drawing?
   actual = 80.8 cm   drawing = 20.2 cm

   A $\frac{1}{8}$ C $\frac{1}{5}$

   B $\frac{3}{4}$ D not given

8. $\frac{7}{9} = $ _____

   A $77\frac{7}{9}\%$ C 77%

   B 79%   D not given

9. 0.1% = _____

   A 0.10   C 0.001

   B 0.01   D not given

10. $66\frac{2}{3}\%$ of 906

    A 64   C 604

    B 302   D not given

11. The regular price is $86. The rate of discount is 25%. Find the sale price.

    A $8.60   C $21.50

    B $64.50   D not given

12. 8% of what number is 8?

    A 10   C 64

    B 100   D not given

Solve.

13. Bea wanted to buy a poster in Quebec. It cost $10.25 in Canadian money. At that time 100 Canadian dollars were equal to 87 United States dollars. How much did the poster cost in United States dollars?

    A $8.92   C $8.20

    B $11.78   D not given

14. Shelly and Amy shared the driving on a 252-mile trip. Shelly drove twice as many miles as Amy did. How many miles did Amy drive?

    A 74 miles   C 126 miles

    B 168 miles   D not given

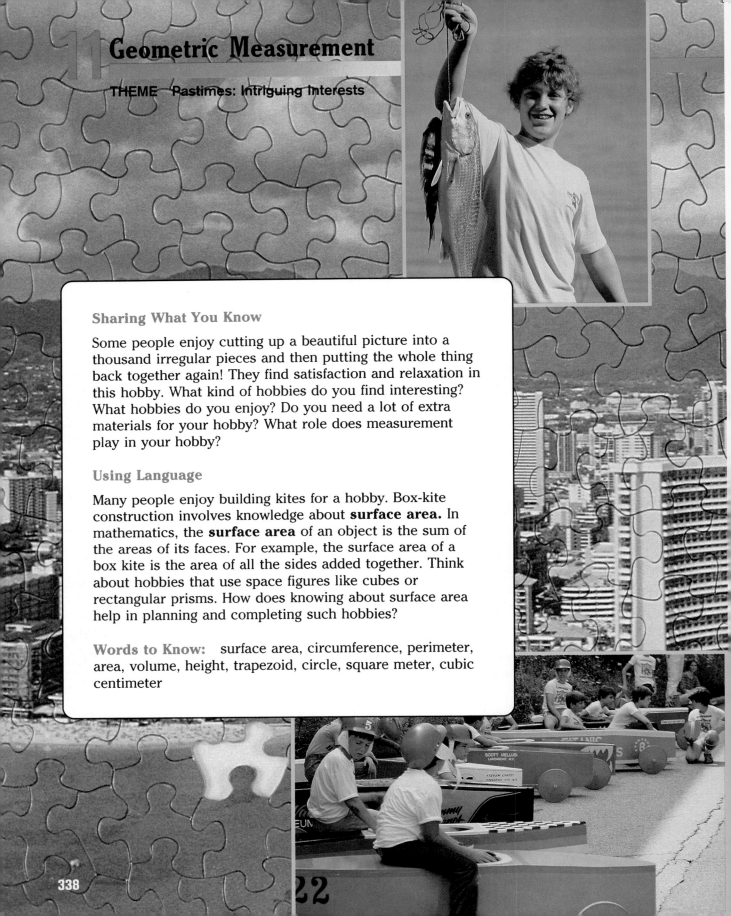

Geometric Measurement

Sharing What You Know

Some people enjoy cutting up a beautiful picture into a thousand irregular pieces and then putting the whole thing back together again! They find satisfaction and relaxation in this hobby. What kind of hobbies do you find interesting? What hobbies do you enjoy? Do you need a lot of extra materials for your hobby? What role does measurement play in your hobby?

Using Language

Many people enjoy building kites for a hobby. Box-kite construction involves knowledge about **surface area.** In mathematics, the **surface area** of an object is the sum of the areas of its faces. For example, the surface area of a box kite is the area of all the sides added together. Think about hobbies that use space figures like cubes or rectangular prisms. How does knowing about surface area help in planning and completing such hobbies?

Words to Know: surface area, circumference, perimeter, area, volume, height, trapezoid, circle, square meter, cubic centimeter

Be a Problem Solver

Darryl has constructed the following cube using 64 small cubes. If he paints all six sides of the large cube, how many small cubes will not have any paint on them?

Interview someone who has an interesting hobby. Write about what you learned in your interview.

Relating Perimeter and Area

What if a square and a rectangle that is not square have the same area? Which has the greater perimeter? **What if** they have the same perimeter? Which has the greater area?

Working together

Materials: geoboard or grid paper

A. On a geoboard or grid paper, make as many rectangles as you can that have the same area as a square 6 units on a side. The dimensions should be whole numbers. Record your findings in a table like this.

6 units by 6 units grid

Rectangle	Length	Width	Perimeter
1 2 3	6	6	24

B. On a geoboard or grid paper, make as many rectangles as you can that have the same perimeter as a square 6 units on a side. Record your findings in a table like this.

Rectangle	Length	Width	Area
1 2 3	6	6	36 square units

Sharing Your Results

Look back at the data you recorded above.

1. Which rectangle that you made in **A** has the greatest perimeter?

2. Which rectangle has the least perimeter?

3. Which rectangle that you made in **B** has the greatest area?

4. Which rectangle has the least area?

Extending the Activity

Perform this experiment. Record your findings in a table like this.

Rectangle	Length	Width	Perimeter	Area
1				
2				

C. On a geoboard or grid paper, make any rectangle. Record its length, width, perimeter, and area.

D. Make a new rectangle by doubling the length. Do not change the width. Record your findings.

E. Make a new rectangle by doubling the length and the width of the rectangle in **C**. Record your findings.

Use the data you recorded to answer these questions.

5. How did the perimeter change when the length was doubled?

6. How did the area change?

7. How did the perimeter change when both the length and the width were doubled?

8. How did the area change?

Summing Up

Make predictions.

9. Given any area, predict the shape of the rectangle with the greatest perimeter. Predict the shape of the rectangle with the least perimeter. Explain your reasoning.

10. Given any perimeter, predict the shape of the rectangle with the greatest area. Predict the shape of the rectangle with the least area. Explain your reasoning.

11. What if you and your friends are going to make a vegetable garden on a vacant lot near your home? You have $100 to spend on fencing for the garden. The fencing costs $2.50 per foot. What is the largest garden you could make?

12. Given any rectangle, predict how the perimeter and the area will change when both the length and the width are doubled. Illustrate your prediction with three examples.

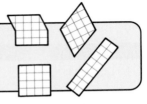

Predict which has the greatest area. Then count to verify your answer.

Area of Rectangles and Parallelograms

Renée is in charge of planning the booths for the annual Red River Craft Show. Each dealer is allowed 12 m^2 of floor space. Renée must mark the outline of each booth with masking tape. To use the least amount of tape, she decides to make the booth 3 m by 4 m.

What shape booth would require the least amount of tape? If the sides of the booth must have whole-number lengths, did Renée make the right choice? Explain your reasoning.

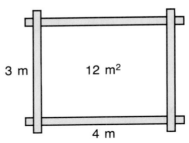

3 m   12 m²   4 m

The formula for the area of a rectangle can be used to find the area of a parallelogram. Draw this rectangle on grid paper. Show how it can be cut and rearranged to form the parallelogram.

What is the area of the parallelogram?

 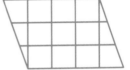

To find the area of a rectangle or a parallelogram, multiply the base times the height.

$$A = b \times h = bh$$

Check Your Understanding

Find the area of each quadrilateral.

1.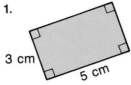
3 cm   5 cm

2.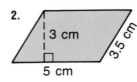
3 cm   5 cm   3.5 cm

3.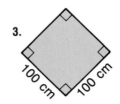
100 cm   100 cm

4.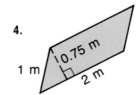
1 m   0.75 m   2 m

Share Your Ideas Look back at **3**. Find the area in square meters. Remember that 100 cm = 1 m. Explain your thinking.

Find the area of each quadrilateral. Choose a calculator, paper and pencil, or mental math.

5. 4 cm / 2 cm

6. 12 m / 12 m

7. 9.5 m / 11 m / 11 m

8. 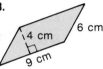 6 cm / 4 cm / 9 cm

9. 6 m / 2.5 m

10. 3 cm / 5 cm

11. 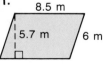 8.5 m / 5.7 m / 6 m

12. 25 cm / 40 cm / 30 cm

13. Look back at **9–12.** Which did you solve using mental math? Explain your strategies.

Evaluate each formula for the given values.

14.

s	$A = s^2$
7 m	
5.6 m	
20 m	

15.

l	w	$A = lw$
10 m	7.3 m	
32 cm	17 cm	
20 m	8.2 m	

16.

b	h	$A = bh$
9 cm	6 cm	
4 m	2.5 m	
6.8 m	5.5 m	

Solve.

17. The area of a rectangle is 900 m². Its length is 36 m. Find its width.

18. The area of a parallelogram is 42 cm². Its height is 3.5 cm. Find its base.

19. The area of a square is 196 cm². Find the length of a side.

20. The perimeter of a square is 36 m. Find its area.

Think and Apply

21. The room where the Red River Craft Show is held is 20 m by 36 m. Renée must allow at least 2 m along a side for an entrance and at least 2 m for an exit. They do not have to be on the same side. According to fire laws, any aisles must be at least 2 m wide. Renée would like to allow as many exhibitors as possible. Use grid paper to show your plan for the craft show booths. Explain your reasoning.

22. Find the area of the shaded region. Describe your method.

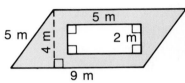

5 m / 5 m / 4 m / 5 m / 2 m / 9 m

Describe the similarities and the differences between finding the area of a rectangle and finding the area of a parallelogram.

SUMMING UP

Exploring the Area of Triangles and Trapezoids

The area of a triangle is half the area of a parallelogram with the same base and height.

$$A = \frac{1}{2} bh$$

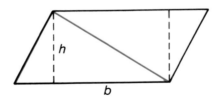

How can you use a parallelogram to find the area of a trapezoid?

Working together

Materials: grid paper 4 squares to an inch, scissors, Workmat 5

A. Copy these trapezoids on grid paper. Draw two more congruent trapezoids of any size. Cut out the trapezoids.

B. Use each pair of trapezoids to form a parallelogram. Record your findings in a table like this. (b = base, h = height, A = area)

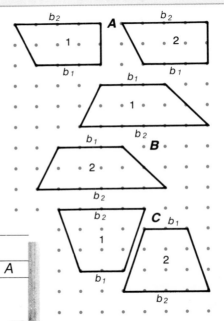

Trapezoid					Parallelogram		
	b_1	b_2	h	A		$b_1 + b_2$	h	A
1					Pair			
2					A			

Sharing Your Results

Look back at the data you recorded.

1. How is the area of each trapezoid related to the area of the parallelogram it was used to form?

2. What measurements do you need to find the area of a trapezoid?

3. Write a rule for finding the area of a trapezoid.

Extending the Activity

The kite is named after a bird of prey. Over the centuries, kites have been used for many things—for fishing, for signaling, for collecting weather data, and, of course, for recreation. How many square inches of cloth are needed to make this kite?

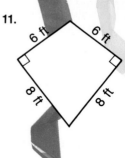

Work with a partner.

4. Devise a method to find the area of this kite.

5. Compare your method with those of other classmates. How are the methods alike? How are they different?

6. Write a rule for finding the area of a kite.

7. Extend the dashed perpendicular lines 2 in. at either end to show the extra cloth needed to fold over the frame of the kite. How much cloth is needed to make the kite?

Work on your own. Use your rules to find the area of each figure.

8.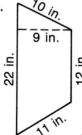

9.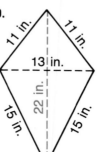

10.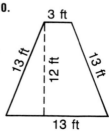

11.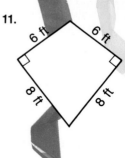

Summing Up

12. Describe how you could divide a trapezoid into two triangles to find its area. Show an example.

13. Write a formula for finding the area of a trapezoid. Use A for area, h for height, and b_1 and b_2 for the lengths of the two parallel sides.

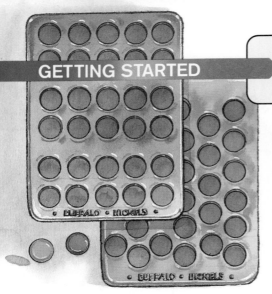

GETTING STARTED

Trace a jar lid on grid paper. Estimate the area by counting squares.

Circumference and Area of Circles

Susan Felter designed these coin collection books. The cardboard from the holes is discarded when the books are manufactured. Susan is comparing the amounts of cardboard that will be discarded from these two books.

How would you solve this problem? What strategy would you use? Explain your method.

First Susan must find the amount of cardboard discarded from one hole. You can use a model.

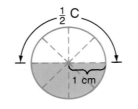

- Draw a circle. Divide the circle into sections. Shade half the circle.
- Cut out the circle. Cut along the dotted lines. Arrange the pieces to form a "parallelogram."
- The height of the "parallelogram" is the radius of the circle. The base is half the circumference of the circle.
- The "parallelogram" and the circle have the same area.

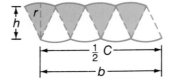

$A = bh = \frac{1}{2}Cr$ $\boxed{C = \pi d = 2\pi r}$ ←—Explain how you know that this sentence is true.

$= \frac{1}{2} \times 2\pi r \times r = \pi r \times r = \pi r^2$

The diameter of a nickel is 2 cm. The circumference of a nickel is $C = \pi d \approx 3.14 \times 2$ cm $= 6.28$ cm ≈ 6 cm.
└ approximately equal to

The area of a nickel is $A = \pi r^2 \approx 3.14 \times (1 \text{ cm})^2 = 3.14 \times 1 \text{ cm}^2 = 3.14 \text{ cm}^2 \approx 3 \text{ cm}^2$.

3 cm^2 of cardboard is discarded for each nickel.

Check Your Understanding

Find the circumference and the area of each circle. Use 3.14 for π. Round to the nearest one.

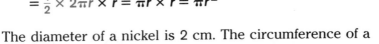

1. $r = 4$ cm   **2.** $d = 4$ cm   **3.** $d = 10$ m   **4.** $r = 2.5$ m

Share Your Ideas What does the ratio of the circumference of a nickel to its diameter equal? Is this ratio the same for *every* circle? Explain your reasoning.

Find the circumference and the area of each circle. Choose
paper and pencil, mental math, or a calculator. Use 3.14
for π. Round to the nearest one.

5.

6.

7.

8.

9. $r = 5$ m

10. $d = 8$ m

11. $r = 8$ cm

12. $d = 12$ cm

13. $d = 15$ m

14. $r = 3.5$ m

15. $r = 4.2$ cm

16. $d = 100$ cm

17. Look back at **16**. Find the circumference in meters and
the area in square meters. Round to the nearest tenth.

Find the area of the shaded region. Use 3.14 for π. Round to
the nearest one. Use a calculator to help you.

18.

19.
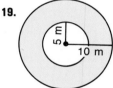

20.
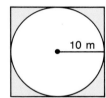

21.
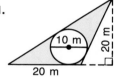

22. Compare the amount of cardboard
discarded from the two nickel books
on page 346. Which book has more
waste? How much more? Round to
the nearest square centimeter.

Visual Thinking

23. In each circle, is there more red or
more black?

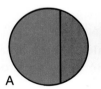

A

B

C

D

E

F

Explain the difference between the area and the
circumference of a circle; between calculating the
area and calculating the circumference.

SUMMING UP

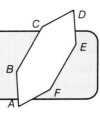

How many ways can you find to divide this polygon into two triangles and a parallelogram, using two straight lines?

Area of Irregular Figures

Some members of the Oakdale Senior Citizens Club make stained-glass panels. The panels are donated to Oakdale Hospital for sale in the gift shop. How much ruby glass was used to make this panel?

How would *you* solve this problem? What strategies would you use? One way to solve it is to use *divide and conquer*.

The ruby region can be divided into five smaller regions.

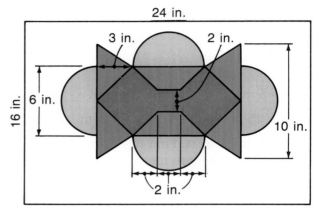

1 square	2 trapezoids	2 triangles

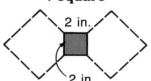 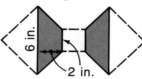 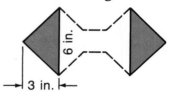

$A = s^2 = 2^2 = 4$
area = 4 in.^{2}

$A = \frac{1}{2}(2 + 6)(2) + \frac{1}{2}(2 + 6)(2) = 16$
area = 16 in.^{2}

$A = \frac{1}{2}(3)(6) + \frac{1}{2}(3)(6) = 18$
area = 18 in.^{2}

4 in.^{2} + 16 in.^{2} + 18 in.^{2} = 38 in.^{2}
To make the panel, 38 in.^{2} of ruby glass was used.

Describe a way to find the amount of cobalt-blue glass used to make the panel above. Compare your method with those of your classmates.

Check Your Understanding

First describe how you would find the area of each shaded region. Then find the area. Round to the nearest one if necessary.

1.
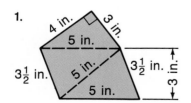

2.
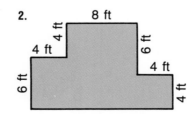

3.
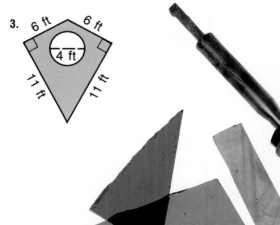

Share Your Ideas Look back at **1–3**. Compare your methods with those of your classmates. For each region, was there more than one way to find the area? Explain.

Choose pencil and paper, a calculator, or mental math.
CHOICES Find the area of each shaded region. Round to the nearest one if necessary.

4.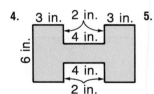

5.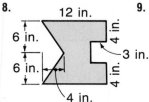

6.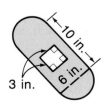

7.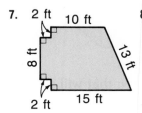

8.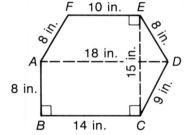

9.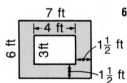

Choose the best estimate for each.

10. the area of *ADEF*
   a. 100 in.²   **b.** 200 in.²

11. the area of *ABCD*
   a. 75 in.²   **b.** 125 in.²

12. the area of *ABCDF*
   a. 200 in.²   **b.** 250 in.²

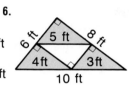

Think and Apply

Decide whether an exact answer is necessary or an estimate is sufficient. Then answer the question.

13. Mr. Mendez bought the glass for the panel on page 348. It comes in 12-in. squares. How many pieces of amber glass did he have to buy?

What if you were a designer of stained glass? The Oakdale Senior Citizens Club has asked you to design a window for their center. The window is 24 in. by 12 in.

14. Design a window, using all of a 6-in. by 6-in. piece of ruby glass. You may use any other colors you wish, in any amount.

Look back at **7.** How many different ways can you find to compute the area? Describe them.

Solve.

1. 30% of 60

2. What percent of 8 is 24?

3. 20 is 40% of what number?

4. 55% of 80

5. What percent of 15 is 5?

6. 75% of 32

7. 150 is 150% of what number?

8. What percent of 100 is $12\frac{1}{2}$?

9. $37\frac{1}{2}$% of 48

10. $3\frac{1}{2}$% of 200

Solve for *x*.

11. $x + 7 = 14$

12. $3x = 36$

13. $\frac{x}{8} = 9$

14. $x - 18 = 6$

15. $5x = 5$

16. $6x = 2$

17. $x - 37 = 28$

18. $x - 72 = 0$

19. $13 = \frac{x}{13}$

20. $17 = x - 82$

Activity

Exploring Surface Area

Can you make a pattern that will fold to form
this prism? Experiment! The dimensions are given.

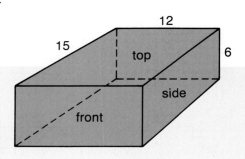

Working together

Materials: grid paper 4 squares to an inch, scissors,
cardboard, tape

A. Use grid paper. Experiment to draw a pattern that will
fold to form the prism shown above.

B. Cut out the pattern. Fold and tape the edges to form the
prism. If you wish, you may glue cardboard to the grid
paper before folding.

C. Repeat **A** and **B**, this time making a different pattern that
will fold to form the prism.

D. Calculate the amount of grid paper needed to make each
pattern. Give your answer in square units, or grids.

E. Cut each prism open and flatten the pattern.

Sharing Your Results

1. Compare your patterns with those of your classmates.
How are they alike? How are they different?

2. How many different patterns were made?

3. Did all the patterns require the same amount of paper?
If not, which ones required more or less than others?

4. What is the area of the top of the prism? What is the area
of the front? What is the area of one side?

5. What is the total area of the surface of the prism?

6. Describe how to find the surface area of the prism.

Extending the Activity

Work in your group.

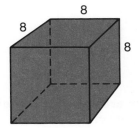

7. Use grid paper. Make three different patterns for this cube. Cut out the patterns. Fold and tape the edges to form the cube. Then cut each cube open and flatten the pattern.

8. Compare your three patterns. How are they alike? How are they different?

9. Did all three patterns require the same amount of paper? If not, which one required the most paper? the least?

10. What is the area of each face of the cube? What is the total area of the surface of the cube?

11. Describe how to find the surface area of the cube.

Summing Up

12. Describe the similarities and the differences between finding the surface area of the prism on page 350 and finding the surface area of the cube above.

13. Use your answers to **6** and **11** to find the surface area of each prism.

a.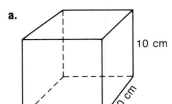
10 cm
10 cm
10 cm

b.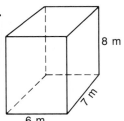
8 m
6 m
7 m

This cube was made up of 27 white cubes, each measuring 1 dm on a side. The outside was painted red.

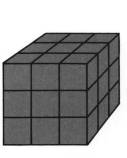

14. What is the area of the surface that was painted?

15. How many cubes have paint on three sides? on two sides? on one side? on no sides?

Midchapter Review

Find the circumference of the circle in 4. Use 3.14 for π. Find the area of each figure. Round to the nearest one for 1 and 4. pages 342–347

1.
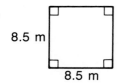
8.5 m
8.5 m

2.
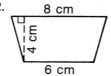
8 cm
4 cm
6 cm

3.
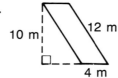
10 m
12 m
4 m

4.

16 cm

Find the area of each shaded region. Use 3.14 for π. pages 348–349

5.
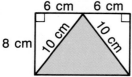
6 cm 6 cm
8 cm
10 cm 10 cm

6.
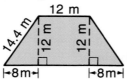
12 m
14.4 m
12 m
12 m
8m 8m

7.
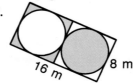
16 m
8 m

8.
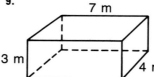
10 cm
3 cm
4 cm
5 cm
18 cm

Find the surface area of each figure. pages 350–351

9.
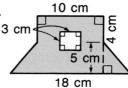
7 m
3 m
4 m

10.
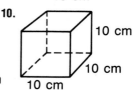
10 cm
10 cm
10 cm

Fill in the blanks.

11. The distance around a circle is its _____.

12. The _____ of a region is the number of square units needed to cover the region.

13. A _____ is a unit of area.

14. The _____ of a parallelogram is a segment that joins opposite sides and is perpendicular to the base.

15. The distance around a polygon is its _____.

16. The _____ of a figure is the sum of the areas of all its faces.

Words to Know
circumference
perimeter
area
surface area
parallelogram
height
trapezoid
circle
square meter
cubic centimeter

Solve. pages 342–343

17. Ms. Proudfoot is painting the walls of her bedroom. The room is 4 m wide, 5 m long, and 2.5 m high. A 4-liter container of the paint she wants will cover 32 m². How many 4-liter containers should she buy?

18. Two of the walls each have 2 windows 1 m by 1.5 m. The other two walls each have 1 door 1 m by 2 m. The windows and doors will not be painted. From the leftover paint, does Ms. Proudfoot have enough to paint the ceiling?

352

Exploring Problem Solving

Designing Packages

Ted is designing a box for a skateboard. The dimensions of the skateboard are slightly less than the following: length—24 in., width—6 in., height—4 in.

Thinking Critically

How would you construct the box? How would you lay it out so that you could cut the greatest number of boxes from a sheet of cardboard?

Analyzing and Making Decisions

1. What would a cardboard box look like if it were taken apart carefully and laid flat?

2. What shape might the box for the skateboard have? What shape might each side of the box have? How can you make the box stay together? How would you position the skateboard in the box?

3. Draw two different sketches for the skateboard box. Be sure to allow for the overlap for fastening the edges together. Label each part. Give the measurements of each part.

4. Make a final drawing of your skateboard box laid out flat. Give the dimensions for each part of the box. Cut out and fold it into a box. Does your box look useable? Explain.

Look Back What if cardboard comes in sheets 6 ft by 5 ft? How many of your flattened boxes could you fit on a sheet? Explain.

How did you make sure that your box stayed together? Did this increase the amount of cardboard you used?

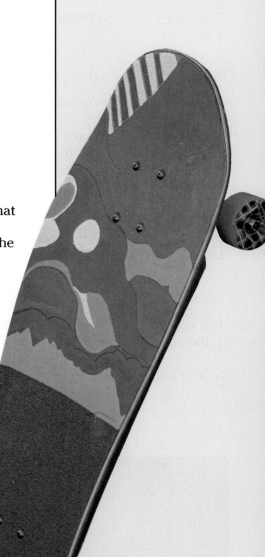

Problem Solving Strategies

Making and Using Drawings

Sam must set up a fence in a straight line that is 45 feet long. He must put a stake in the ground at the start of the fence and another one every 3 feet. How many stakes will he need?

Sometimes you can better understand a problem by making a drawing.

Solving the Problem

Think   What is the question? What information do you have?

Explore   Draw a simple map of the line to be staked. Where should Sam put the first stake? Where should he put the next? How can he keep track of how many stakes to put in the ground?

Solve   How many stakes did he need?

Look Back   How can he make sure he has enough stakes?

Share Your Ideas

1. If you divide 45 feet by 3 feet you get 15 spaces between the stakes. Is this the number of stakes you need? Explain.

2. Why might a drawing be important in solving this problem?

Practice

CHOICES **Solve. Use a calculator where appropriate.**

Use the information below to solve 3–6.

Myra is building a circular garden that is 36 feet across. Around the outside she is making a 3-foot-wide path. She wants to cover the garden while the work is being done.

3. Myra plans to buy a circular tarpaulin to cover just the garden. About how large an area does she need to cover?

4. She wants to put wood chips three inches deep on the path. How many cubic feet of wood chips does she need?

5. Each bag contains 6 cubic feet of chips. How many bags will she need?

6. On the outside of the path, she wants to plant ferns about every four feet. How many ferns will she need?

Mixed Strategy Review

7. Myra pays $10 for 6 plants plus soil and planters. She pots them and sells them at flower shops. She charges $10 for 4 plants. How many plants must she sell to make a profit of $50?

Use the information below to solve 8–9.

Using colored foil, Myra covered the sides and bottom of a planter that is 8 in. tall and has a base 20 in. by 6 in.

8. How many square inches of foil did she need to cover the planter? Explain.

9. Could she use a 20-in. by 30-in. piece of foil to cover the planter? Explain.

Create Your Own

Write a problem for which a drawing might be used to find the solution.

Name as many things in your classroom as you can that are prisms. Estimate which one has the greatest volume.

Volume of Prisms

Hector raises tropical fish. His fish tank will hold 24 neon tetras. How much water does Hector need to fill the tank?

To find the amount of water needed to fill the tank, Hector must find the volume of the tank to the water-level mark.

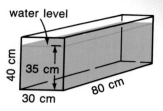

water level

40 cm
35 cm
30 cm
80 cm

▶ The volume of a prism is the area of the base times the height.

$$V = Bh$$

Explain why the formula for the volume of a rectangular prism could also be written $V = lwh$.

The area of the base of the tank is 80 cm × 30 cm = 2,400 cm². The volume of water is 35 cm × 2,400 cm² = 84,000 cm³.

1,000 cm³ equals 1 dm³. How many cubic decimeters of water does Hector need?

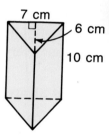

7 cm
6 cm
10 cm

The formula $V = Bh$ can be used to find the volume of any prism.

$$B = \frac{1}{2} \times 7 \times 6$$
$$h = 10$$
$$V = \frac{1}{2} \times 7 \times 6 \times 10 = 210$$

The volume of this triangular prism is 140 cm³.

Write the formula for the volume of a triangular prism in another way.

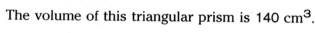

Check Your Understanding

Estimate the volume of each prism. Then compute the volume.

1.
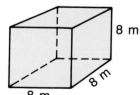
8 m
8 m
8 m

2.
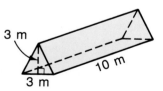
3 m
3 m
10 m

3.
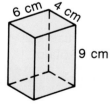
6 cm 4 cm
9 cm

Share Your Ideas Describe the relationship between the volume of prism **A** and the volume of prism **B**. Explain your reasoning.

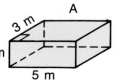
3 m
2 m
5 m
A

3 m
2 m
5 m
B

Estimate the volume of each prism. Then compute the volume. Choose mental math, paper and pencil, or a calculator.

4.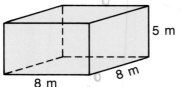

5 m
8 m
8 m

5.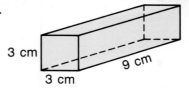

3 cm
3 cm
9 cm

6.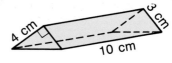

4 cm
3 cm
10 cm

7.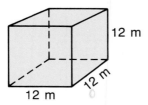

12 m
12 m
12 m

8.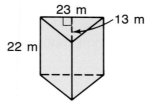

23 m
13 m
22 m

9.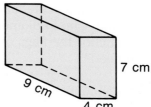

7 cm
9 cm
4 cm

10. The volume of a rectangular prism is 540 m³. The height of the prism is 9 m. What is the area of the base?

11. The area of the base of a triangular prism is 56 cm². The volume of the prism is 224 cm³. What is its height?

12. Which has the greater volume—a rectangular prism 9 cm long, 3 cm wide, and 8 cm high, or a cube 6 cm on a side?

13. Which has the greater volume—a triangular prism 15 cm high with base 27 cm², or a cube 8 cm on a side?

14. The volume of a rectangular prism is 175 m³. The prism is 5 m high and 5 m wide. What is the length of the base?

15. The volume of a rectangular prism is 600 cm³. The prism is 10 cm long and 5 cm wide. How high is the prism?

Think and Apply

16. 1,000 cm³ = 1 L. How many liters of water does Hector need to fill the fish tank shown on page 356?

17. How many cubic decimeters are there in 1 liter?

18. Neon tetras are about 5 cm long. Swordtails are about 7.5 cm long. For every centimeter a fish is long, there must be 20 cm² of water surface at the top of a fish tank. If Hector had 12 neon tetras, how many swordtails could he have in his tank?

Write a few sentences describing the differences between the surface area of a prism and the volume of a prism.

SUMMING UP

Solve this riddle: Exactly how much dirt is there in a hole 1 foot deep and 2 feet in diameter?

Volume of Cylinders

Ben is setting up a skateboard course. He has 10 cans, each 6 in. high and 4 in. in diameter, that he must fill with sand. They will anchor the flags on his course. How much sand does Ben need?

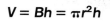

4 in. 6 in.

To find the volume of a cylinder, use the same formula you used to find the volume of a prism.

▶ The volume of a cylinder is the area of the base times the height.

$$V = Bh = \pi r^2 h$$

The area of the base of the can is $\pi \times (2 \text{ in.})^2$ $\approx 3.14 \times 4 \text{ in.}^2 = 12.56 \text{ in.}^2$

The volume of the can is $12.56 \text{ in.}^2 \times 6 \text{ in.} = 75.36 \text{ in.}^3$

Ben needs 76 in.^3 of sand to fill 1 can. How much sand will Ben need to fill all 10 cans?

Why was 75.36 rounded up to 76 instead of down to 75?

Estimate the volume of each cylinder. Then compute the volume. Use a calculator. Use 3.14 for π. Round to the nearest one.

1.
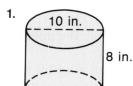
10 in.
8 in.

2.
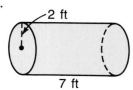
2 ft
7 ft

3.
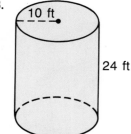
10 ft
24 ft

Share Your Ideas Explain why the formula for the volume of a cylinder, $V = Bh$, can be rewritten as $V = \pi r^2 h$.

Estimate the volume of each cylinder. Then compute the volume. Use a calculator. Use 3.14 for π. Round to the nearest one.

4.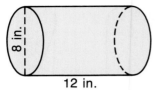

12 in.

5.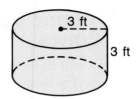

6.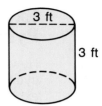

7.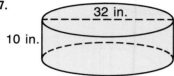

8.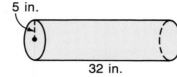

9.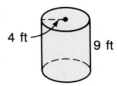

10. The volume of a cylinder is 1,570 in.³ The area of its base is 314 in.² Find its height.

11. The volume of a cylinder is 612 ft³. The height of the cylinder is 12 ft. What is the area of its base?

12. Which has the greater volume—a cube 5 ft on a side or a cylinder 5 ft high and 5 ft in diameter?

13. Which cylinder has the greater volume— one 12 in. high and 4 in. in diameter or one 4 in. high and 12 in. in diameter?

14. The volume of a cylinder is about 2,512 ft³. The diameter of its base is 20 ft. Find the height of the cylinder.

15. The radius of one cylinder is twice the radius of another. How many times as great is the volume of the first cylinder?

Find the volume of the shaded part of each cylinder. Use a calculator. Use 3.14 for π. Round to the nearest one.

16.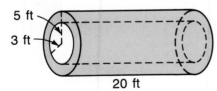

17.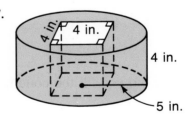

Logical Thinking

18. Would 1 million nickels fit in your classroom? How would you figure out if they would? Work with a partner to find a way.

Compare finding the volume of a cylinder and finding the volume of a prism. How are they alike? How are they different?

SUMMING UP

Activity

Exploring the Volume of Pyramids and Cones

How much more popcorn will fit in the cylinder than in the cone? Try this experiment to find out.

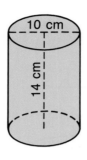

Working together

Materials: 1 small coffee can (1 lb), tagboard, scissors, compass, cm ruler, stapler, enough popping corn to fill the coffee can

15 cm

A. On tagboard, draw a semicircle with a radius of 15 cm. Cut out the semicircle. Roll it to form a cone with a base that matches that of the coffee can. The height of the cone will be approximately the same as that of the coffee can. Staple the edge of the cone.

B. Fill the cone with popping corn. Pour the corn into the coffee can. Repeat until the coffee can is full. Record the number of times you filled the cone.

Sharing Your Results

1. How many times did you fill the cone before the coffee can was full?

2. How would you find the volume of the coffee can?

3. Explain how you would use the volume of a cylinder and the results of your experiment to find the volume of a cone.

4. What is the volume of the coffee can?

5. **Look Back** at 3 and 4. What, do you think, is the volume of the cone?

Extending the Activity

How many times as great is the volume of this prism than the volume of this pyramid? Predict and then experiment to verify.

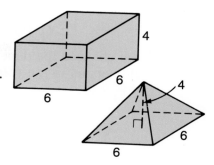

Work in your group.

Materials: grid paper 4 squares to an inch, tagboard, glue, scissors, tape, enough popping corn to fill the prism

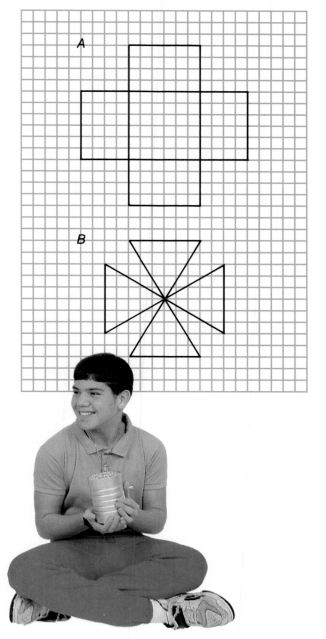

A. Glue a piece of grid paper to the tagboard. Copy each of the patterns at the left on the grid paper.

B. Cut out the patterns. Fold and tape the edges of pattern **A** to form a prism. Fold and tape the edges of pattern **B** to form a pyramid. They will each have the same base and height.

C. Fill the pyramid with popping corn. Pour the corn into the prism. Repeat until the prism is full. Record the number of times you filled the pyramid.

Use the results of your experiment to answer 6–8.

6. How many times did you fill the pyramid before the prism was full?

7. How many times as great is the volume of a prism than the volume of a pyramid with the same base and height?

8. Find the volume of the prism and the volume of the pyramid used in your experiment.

Summing Up

9. Use the results of your experiment and the formulas for the volume of a cylinder and the volume of a prism. Write formulas for the volume of a cone and the volume of a pyramid.

Activity

Exploring Volume: Changing Dimensions

What if you changed the dimensions of this box?
What would happen to the volume of the box?

7 cm

5 cm

2 cm

Working together

Materials: centimeter cubes

A. Use centimeter cubes to construct a model of the box above.

B. Combine your cubes with those of other groups to form these rectangular prisms, each related to the one in **A**.

(1) a prism twice as high
(2) a prism twice as long
(3) a prism twice as long and twice as wide
(4) a prism twice as high and twice as long
(5) a prism twice as high, twice as long, and twice as wide

C. Record your results in a table like this.

Length	Width	Height	Volume
5 cm	2 cm	7 cm	

Sharing Your Results

Look back at the numbers you recorded.

1. What happened to the volume in each case above?

2. Use your results to predict what would happen to the volume if you tripled one dimension. What would happen if you tripled two dimensions? three dimensions?

3. Verify your predictions in **2** by finding the volume.

4. What would happen to the volume if you took half of each dimension?

362

Extending the Activity

What happens to the surface area of a prism when the dimensions are changed?

Work in your group.

5. Extend the table on page 362 to include surface area. Find the surface area of each prism.

Length	Width	Height	Volume	Surface area
5 cm	2 cm	7 cm		

6. What happened to the surface area when all three dimensions were doubled? Explain why.

7. Predict what would happen to the surface area if all three dimensions were tripled. Verify your prediction by finding the surface area.

Summing Up

Generalize. Write a rule for each.

8. How does the volume of a rectangular prism change if one dimension is made *n* times as long?

9. How does the volume of a rectangular prism change if two dimensions are each made *n* times as long?

10. If the three dimensions of a rectangular prism are each made *n* times as long, how does the volume of the prism change? How does the surface area change?

11. Write a formula for finding the volume of a cube with side *s*. Then write a formula for the volume of a cube when all dimensions are multiplied by *n*.

Using Problem Solving

Decorating the House

Mr. and Mrs. Chin are redecorating their house. They have just finished painting the walls and ceiling of a room that is 18 ft long, 16 ft wide, and 8 ft high. They used a little less than 2 gallons of paint. (A gallon of paint covers about 400 sq ft.)

"We need to paint the smaller room. It is 9 ft wide, 16 ft long, and 8 ft high," said Mrs. Chin.

"That's half the size of the one we just painted. We will need only half the amount of paint, or a little less than a gallon," said Mr. Chin.

A. About how much surface area did they cover in the larger room that they painted? Does it seem reasonable that they would have used two gallons of paint? Explain.

B. About how much surface area will they need to paint in the smaller room? How much paint will they need?

Sharing Your Ideas

1. Do you agree that the smaller room is half the size of the larger one? Explain.

2. What fractional part of 2 gallons of paint would it take to paint the smaller room? Do you agree with what Mr. Chin said? Explain.

Practice

3. Mr. and Mrs. Chin are looking for some decorative mirrors to hang over the fireplace in the library and in the hall. Which of these shapes of mirrors do you like?

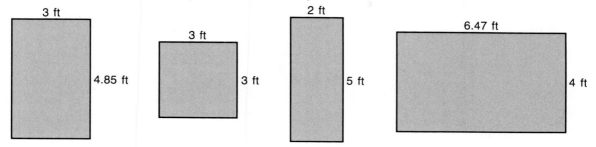

4. A golden rectangle is one in which the ratio of the lengths of adjacent sides is 1 to 0.618. Many people think that this rectangle is the most pleasing to the human eye. Which of the rectangles in **3** are golden rectangles? Did you choose any of them?

5. The golden ratio is a ratio of 1 to 0.618. The human body has several parts that are in such a ratio. Examine the ratios below and see if they are close to the golden ratio.

   a. The ratio of your height to the measure from your waist to the floor.

   b. The ratio of the distance from your waist to the floor to the distance from your waist to your knees.

   c. Can you find any other examples of golden ratios from either the human body or objects in your room? Make a list.

Summing Up

6. Where did you find examples of the golden ratio or a golden rectangle?

7. Name three ways in which mathematics can help you when you are redecorating your home.

Chapter Review

Find the circumference of the circles in 4 and 6. Use 3.14 for π.
Find the area of each figure. Round to the nearest one in 4–6. pages 342–347

1.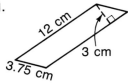

2.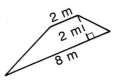

3.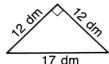

4.

5.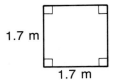

6.

7.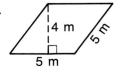

8.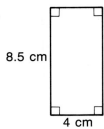

Find the area of each shaded region. Use 3.14 for π. Round to the nearest one in 9. pages 348–349

9.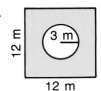

10.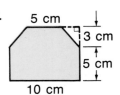

11.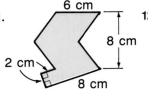

12.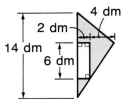

Find the surface area in 13. Find the volume of each figure.
Use 3.14 for π. Round to the nearest one. pages 350–351, 356–361

13.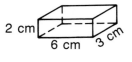

14.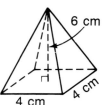

15.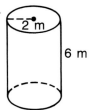

16.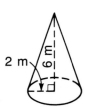

Solve. pages 340–341, 353–355, 362–365

17. Look back at the rectangle in **8.** What would the area be if the length and width were doubled?

18. Look back at the prism in **13.** What would the volume be if the length, width, and height were doubled?

19. Atlas Rug Company is installing wall-to-wall carpeting in a lobby 30 m square. In the center is a circular fountain 6 m in diameter. To the nearest square meter, how much carpeting will be used?

20. The carpeting costs $17.50 a square meter. It will take 4 people 3 hours to install the carpeting. They each earn $18 an hour. How much will the new carpeting cost to buy and install?

Chapter Test

Find the area of each figure. Find the circumference of the circle in 1. Use 3.14 for π. Round to the nearest one.

1.
9 cm

2.
7 cm
7 cm
9 cm

3.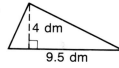
4 dm
9.5 dm

4.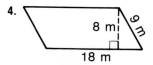
8 m
9 m
18 m

Find the area of each shaded region. Use 3.14 for π. Round to the nearest one.

5.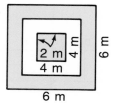
2 m
4 m
4 m
6 m
6 m

6.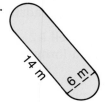
14 m
6 m

7.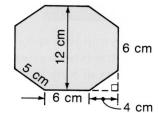
12 cm
5 cm
6 cm
6 cm
4 cm

Find the surface area of each prism.

8.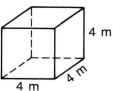
3 cm
10 cm
5 cm

9.
4 m
4 m
4 m

Find the volume of each figure. Use 3.14 for π. Round to the nearest one.

10.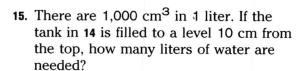
3 cm
10 cm
5 cm

11.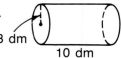
3 dm
10 dm

12.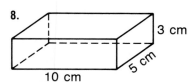
3 m
6 m
5 m

13.
6 m
8 m

Solve.

14. The average length of a neon tetra is 5 cm. For every centimeter a fish is long, there must be 20 cm² of surface water. How many fish will fit in this tank?

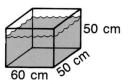
50 cm
60 cm
50 cm

15. There are 1,000 cm³ in 1 liter. If the tank in **14** is filled to a level 10 cm from the top, how many liters of water are needed?

16. Salita is wallpapering a wall in her kitchen that is 4 m long and 2.5 m high. One roll of wallpaper covers about 3 m². How many rolls of paper does Salita need?

THINK The volume of a cube is 216 m³. What are its dimensions?

Computer Link

Area and Perimeter

You can use a computer spreadsheet to explore how area and perimeter are related.

AT THE COMPUTER

Materials: computer spreadsheet

The basic unit of a spreadsheet is called a cell. Cell A2 contains the label height. What cell contains a formula for the area of a rectangle?

A. Enter the data shown on the right in your spreadsheet. The value of cell B4 is found by multiplying the base in cell B1 by the height in cell B2. Explain how the perimeter is calculated.

B. Enter different values for the base and height. Notice that the values for the area and perimeter update automatically.

C. Use the spreadsheet to find the perimeter of five different rectangles that have area of 36 square units. Which rectangle has the least perimeter?

D. Find ten different rectangles that have perimeter of 30 units. Which rectangle has the greatest area?

SPREADSHEET DEFINITION

	A	B
1	base	5
2	height	8
3		
4	area	B1*B2
5	perimeter	(2*B1)+(2*B2)

SPREADSHEET DISPLAY

	A	B
1	base	5
2	height	8
3		
4	area	40
5	perimeter	26

Sharing Your Results

1. Look back at **D**. Did you find the greatest possible area? Explain.

2. Is it possible for the numbers in cells B4 and B5 of the spreadsheet display above to be equal? If so, give an example.

Extending the Activity

Use the spreadsheet to solve each problem.

3. Find the greatest rectangular area than can be enclosed by a fence that is 40 feet long.

4. Is there a least rectangular area that can be enclosed by a forty foot fence? Why or why not?

5. If you want a garden to be 100 square feet what is the least fencing needed to enclose it?

6. Find the greatest possible perimeter for a rectangle that is 100 square units. Explain.

7. Try this challenge. Use a spreadsheet to find the volume and surface area of a rectangular prism given its length, width, and height. Describe the shape of a prism that has the greatest volume for a given surface area.

Summing Up

8. What can you conclude about the shape of a rectangle that has the greatest area for a given perimeter?

9. Explain how you found the least perimeter for a rectangle with a given area.

Tangram Math

Use grid paper to make this figure. Use the given dimensions. Cut the 7 pieces apart.

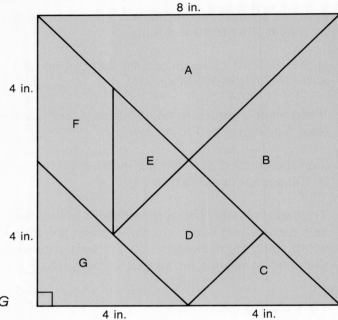

8 in.

4 in.

A

F

E

B

4 in.

D

G

C

4 in.   4 in.

Find the area of each.

1. A   2. C   3. D   4. F   5. G

Use the given pieces to make each shape.

6. Use *C*, *D*, and *E* to make a rectangle.

7. Use *C*, *F*, and *E* to make a rectangle.

8. Use *C*, *D*, and *E* to make a trapezoid.

9. Use *C*, *D*, and *E* to make a triangle.

Rearrange the 7 pieces to make each shape.

10.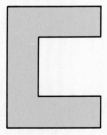

11.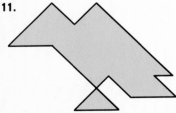

12.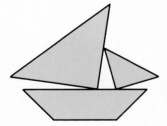

Show that the following statement is true.

13. The sum of the areas of all the pieces equals the area of the large square.

Fractions, graphs and statistics, ratio, proportion, percent, and geometric measurement have been covered in the previous five chapters of our mathematics book.

Where Does the Time Go?

How much time do you spend sleeping in one year? shopping? travelling to and from school? watching television, reading, or doing other activities?

Have each member of your family keep a record of the time spent on an activity for one week. Then make an estimate of the time spent on this activity for one year.

For example, below is a record of the hours Corey spends sleeping and the calculations of the time for one year.

Mon.	Tues.	Wed.	Thurs.	Fri.	Sat.	Sun.
7 h	$6\frac{1}{2}$ h	8 h	$7\frac{1}{4}$ h	$5\frac{1}{2}$ h	$7\frac{3}{4}$ h	9 h

1. Total time for one week: 51 hours

2. Estimate for one year: About 50 hours per week × 52 weeks = 2,600 hours

3. About how many 24-hour days are there in 2,600 hours?
   Estimate: About 2,400 hours ÷ 24 hours = 100 days

In one year, Corey will sleep about 100 days out of 365!

The ratio $\frac{100}{365}$ can be used to estimate the percent of time in one year that is spent sleeping. How can you convert the ratio to a percent? Use a calculator to find the percent. Did you get an answer of 27.4%? That leaves about 70% of Corey's time for other activities.

Now it's your turn to calculate how much time you spend on one activity. Try it for other activities also. You might discover some interesting facts about where your time goes.

Cumulative Review

Choose the correct answers. Write A, B, C, or D.

1. What is the mode? 18, 14, 13, 14, 16

    A 15   **C** 14

    B 5   **D** not given

2. What is the mean of 21.55, 14.25, 14.25, and 10.75?

    A 10.8   **C** 15.2

    B 15.4   **D** not given

3. What is the median of 8.6, 3.21, 5.09, 3.5, and 2.1?

    A 6.5   **C** 4.5

    B 3.5   **D** not given

4. Which ratio is equal to 5:7?

    A 15:14   **C** 35:49

    B 20:35   **D** not given

5. Which ratio is equal to 4 to 21?

    A 1:5   **C** 4:21

    B 21:4   **D** not given

6. Find the unit rate.
64 oz for $5.12

    A $.08 per ounce   **C** $1.32 per ounce

    B $.80 per ounce   **D** not given

7. Solve for n. $\frac{n}{8} = \frac{6}{48}$

    A 6   **C** 1

    B 8   **D** not given

8. What is the scale?
actual = 91.2 cm
drawing = 15.2 cm

    A 1:8   **C** 2:7

    B 1:6   **D** not given

9. What is 0.35 written as a percent?

    A 15%   **C** 3.5%

    B 35%   **D** not given

10. What is 62.5% written as a ratio?

    A $\frac{5}{8}$ **C** $\frac{6}{7}$

    B $\frac{7}{8}$ **D** not given

11. If $\frac{1}{50} = 2\%$, then $\frac{13}{50} = $ _____.

    A 4%   **C** 26%

    B 13%   **D** not given

12. What is 75% of 40?

    A 10   **C** 30

    B 20   **D** not given

13. Which is the greatest amount?

    A 10% of 500   **C** $33\frac{1}{3}\%$ of 90

    B 20% of 200   **D** 50% of 50

14. Find the discount if the regular price is $55 and the rate of discount is 10%.

    A $0.55   **C** $5.50

    B $1.55   **D** not given

15. What percent of 40 is 35?

    A 40%   **C** 75%

    B 50%   **D** not given

16. 12% of what number is 18?

    A 150   **C** 2.16

    B 216   **D** not given

Choose the correct answers. Write A, B, C, or D.

17. Estimate. 15% of $48.79

    A $2.50   **C** $5.00

    B $12.00   **D** $7.50

---

18. An item costs $52. The sales tax rate is 5%. Find the tax.

    A $0.52   **C** $5.20

    B $2.60   **D** not given

---

19. Find the area of the rectangle.
$l = 1.6$ m $w = 2.4$ m

    A 3.84 m^2 **C** 8 m^2

    B 4 m^2 **D** not given

---

20. Find the area.

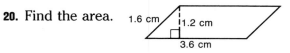

    A 6.4 cm^2 **C** 4.32 cm^2

    B 5.76 cm^2 **D** not given

---

21. Find the area.

    A 13.5 m^2 **C** 6.75 m^2

    B 7.7 m^2 **D** not given

---

22. Find the area of a circle with radius 6 cm. Use 3.14 for π.

    A 18.84 cm^2 **C** 113.04 cm^2

    B 59.1576 cm^2 **D** not given

---

23. Find the volume of the prism.

    A 28 m^3 **C** 48 m^3

    B 576 m^3 **D** not given

Solve.

24. A submarine landed at the surface of the water after rising 15 m, diving 5 m, diving 4 m more, and rising 14 m. How far below the surface was the submarine at the start?

    A 8 m   **C** 15 m

    B 20 m   **D** not given

25. Debi won $128 in a contest. The amount of winnings doubled each day until there was a winner. Debi won on the fifth day. What would have been the amount of the prize if it had been won on the first day?

    A $10.00   **C** $2.00

    B $8.00   **D** not given

26. Apples cost $.25 each, peaches cost $.15 each, and bananas cost $.20 each. If each fruit is bought, what is the maximum number of pieces of fruit that can be bought for $1.25?

    A 6   **C** 9

    B 5   **D** not given

27. Peg called her mother long distance from camp. The cost of the call was $1.45 for the first minute and $.37 for each additional minute. How long did the call last if the total cost was $5.89?

    A 13   **C** 12

    B 11   **D** not given

12 Pre-Algebra: Integers and Graphing

Sharing What You Know

Your family is planning a vacation. Where will you go? To the mountains? To the seashore? Perhaps on an archaeological dig? Wherever you choose, there are many things to consider. How will you get there? Where will you stay? How long will your trip last? How much money will you spend? A well-planned trip is often the best kind. How might planning a vacation involve mathematics?

Using Language

When you **coordinate** or arrange a trip, you will probably want to select some special sites to visit. You can locate these points of interest on a map. Maps which include grids make the locating of points easier. In mathematics, points can be located on a **coordinate plane.** How is coordinating a trip like plotting points on a coordinate plane? How are they different?

Words to Know: function, integer, absolute value, opposites, coordinate plane, *x*- and *y*-axes, origin, ordered pair

Be a Problem Solver

A tour guide says, "Last year my age was the square of a whole number. Next year my age will be the cube of another whole number. How old am I?"

Draw a map on graph paper. Plot two points, A and B, on the map. Then write a set of directions from Point A to Point B.

Activity

Exploring Integers

The Santa Rosa Ocean Pier will be completed in 1995. At high tide it is 10 meters above sea level. There are workers at many different levels. At 10 m below sea level, the workers found schools of fish.

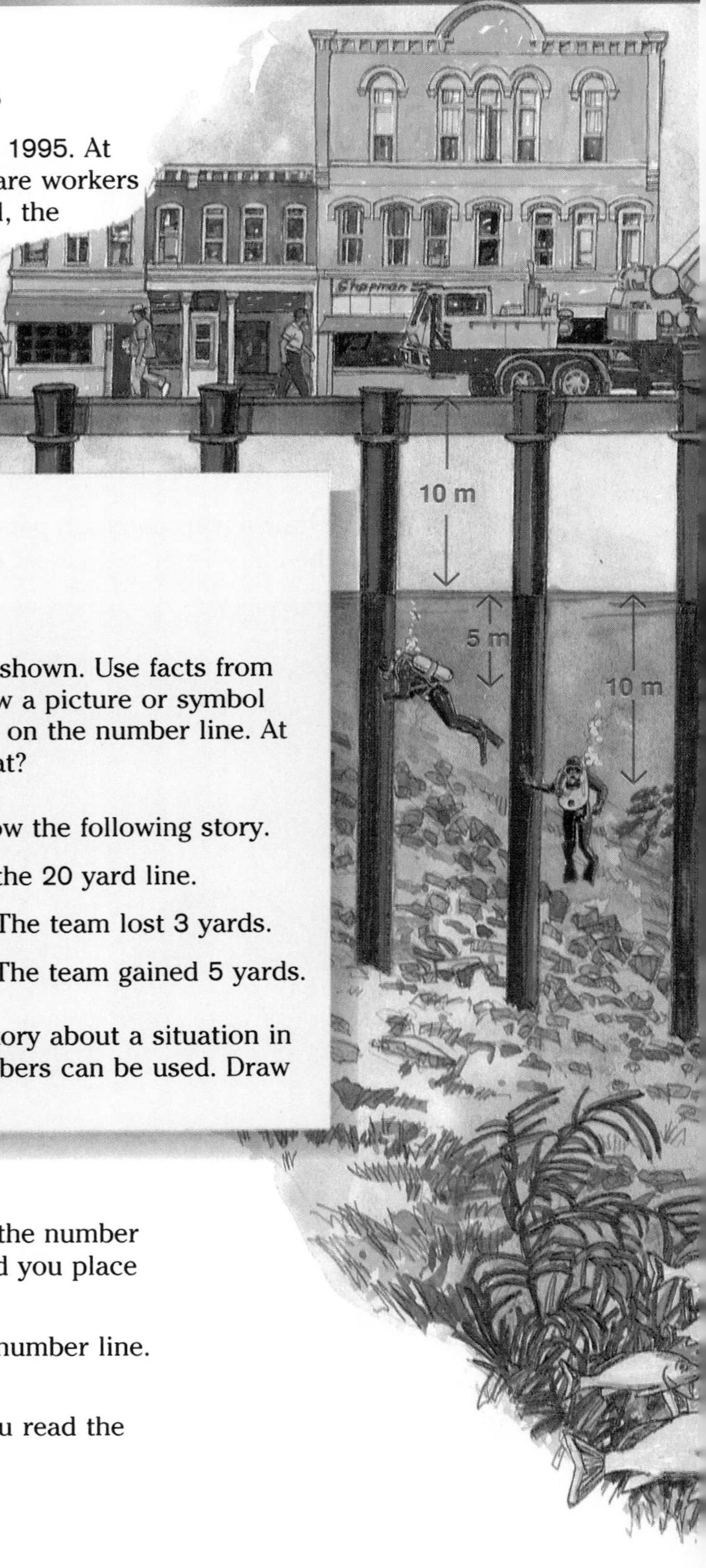

10 m

5 m

10 m

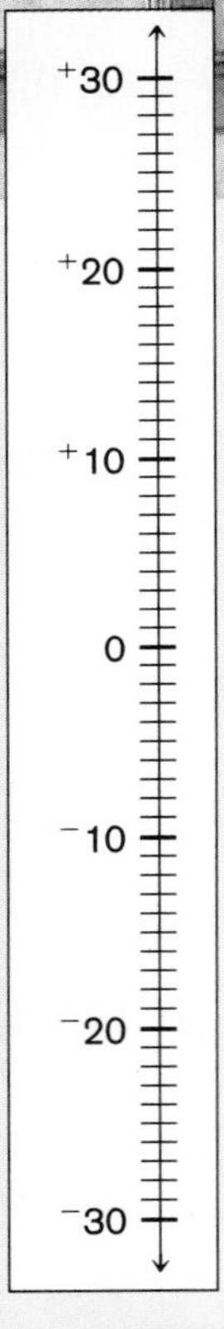

Working together

Materials: number lines

A. Draw a number line like the one shown. Use facts from the story and picture above. Draw a picture or symbol for each fact at the correct place on the number line. At what point will you place the boat?

B. Draw another number line to show the following story.

The play began with the ball on the 20 yard line.

a. The team gained 5 yards.   b. The team lost 3 yards.

c. The team lost 7 yards.   d. The team gained 5 yards.

C. Work together to write a short story about a situation in which positive and negative numbers can be used. Draw a number line for the story.

Sharing Your Results

1. Where did you place the top of the crane on the number line for the Santa Rosa Ocean Pier? Where did you place the workers? the boat?

2. Tell the story of the football game. Use your number line. What was the net gain or loss?

3. Read the short story your group wrote. As you read the story, point to the facts on the number line.

25 m

25 m

Extending the Activity

**Work with a partner. Draw a number line.
Use it to model each situation.**

4. Darryl saved $4.

5. Gary owes $5.

6. The stock fell 3 points.

7. The stock rose 2 points and then fell 1 point.

8. Maria took 2 steps forward and then 4 steps back.

9. Juanita took 5 steps back and then 3 steps forward.

Use a number line to find the location of each elevator listed below. The elevators are in a building that has a lobby at ground level (0), seven floors above the lobby, a basement, and 3 sub-basements. All elevators start at the lobby.

10. Elevator A: Down 1, Up 3, Down 4, Down 2, Up 2

11. Elevator B: Up 3, Down 4, Up 6, Down 2, Down 1

12. Elevator C: Down 4, Up 5, Down 1, Up 3, Down 4

13. Elevator D: Up 6, Up 1, Down 8, Up 5, Up 2, Up 1

14. Elevator E: Down 1, Down 2, Down 1, Up 4, Up 4, Down 4

15. Use a number line to model each situation.

Bob	Ted
Savings: $2	Savings: $0
Earns: $5	Earns: $3
Spends: $8	Earns: $2
Earns: $2	Spends: $3
Earns: $3	Spends: $2
Spends: $5	Earns: $2

Summing Up

16. Who has more money, Bob or Ted? Explain.

17. Explain how you can use positive and negative numbers to model Bob and Ted's situations.

18. Name some other situations in which positive and negative numbers can be used.

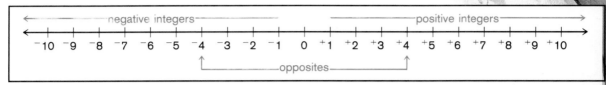

Order these numbers from least to greatest.
9   8.5   7.011   8.51   7.1

Comparing and Ordering Integers

The numbers . . . ⁻3, ⁻2, ⁻1, 0, ⁺1, ⁺2, ⁺3, . . . are **integers**.

Two integers that are the same distance from 0 in opposite directions are **opposites.**

⁻4 and ⁺4 are each 4 units from 0.

⁻4 and ⁺4 are opposites.

▶ The **absolute value** of an integer is its distance from zero on the number line.

Opposite integers have equal absolute values. Explain why.

⁺4 and ⁻4 are each 4 units from 0.

$|{}^+4| = 4$ The absolute value of ⁺4 is 4.

$|{}^-4| = 4$ The absolute value of ⁻4 is 4.

You can use the number line to compare integers.

▶ The greater of two integers is the integer that is farther to the right on the number line.

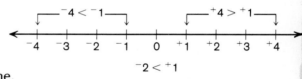

Name the least integer whose value is greater than all negative integers.

Check Your Understanding

Write an integer for each. Then write its opposite.

1. negative 23   **2.** positive 8   **3.** negative 75

Compare. Use >, <, or = for each ●.

4. ⁻4 ● ⁺1   **5.** ⁺3 ● ⁻8   **6.** 0 ● ⁻9   **7.** ⁻5 ● ⁻4   **8.** ⁻10 ● ⁻15

Write the absolute value of each integer.

9. $|{}^-7|$ **10.** $|{}^+30|$ **11.** $|{}^-8|$ **12.** $|{}^-19|$ **13.** $|{}^+7|$ **14.** $|{}^-31|$

Share Your Ideas   *True* or *false*? All integers are either positive or negative. Explain.

Write the absolute value of each integer.

15. $|^-5|$ **16.** $|^+15|$ **17.** $|^+8|$ **18.** $|^+9|$ **19.** $|^-4|$ **20.** $|^-17|$

21. $|^-101|$ **22.** $|^+52|$ **23.** $|^-33|$ **24.** $|^-8|$ **25.** $|^-9|$ **26.** $|^+500|$

Compare. Use >, <, or = for each ●

27. $^+18$ ● $^+15$ **28.** $^+19$ ● $^-23$ **29.** $|^-4|$ ● $|^+4|$ **30.** $^-2$ ● 0

31. $^-11$ ● $^-7$ **32.** $^-1$ ● $^-6$ **33.** $|^-2|$ ● $|^+2|$ **34.** $^-4$ ● $^-5$

35. $^+2$ ● $^-2$ **36.** $^-5$ ● $^+1$ **37.** $^+100$ ● $^-100$ **38.** $|^-3|$ ● $|^+3|$

Write the integers in order from least to greatest.

39. $^+2,\ ^-4,\ ^+8,\ ^-3,\ ^-7,\ 0$ **40.** $^+18,\ ^+2,\ ^-6,\ ^-5,\ ^+4,\ ^-1$

41. $^-5,\ ^-2,\ ^-8,\ ^-9,\ ^-14,\ ^-1$ **42.** $^-102,\ ^-58,\ ^-105,\ ^-15,\ ^-73,\ 0$

Solve.

43. What is the greatest negative integer?

44. What is the least positive integer?

45. Can you name the least negative integer? Explain your answer.

46. Can you name the greatest positive integer? Explain your answer.

Think and Apply

To pass the time while riding in the car, Adam and Anna play number games. Here is one of them:

Adam: I'm thinking of a number between $^-30$ and $^+10$.
Anna: Is it greater than $^-10$?
Adam: No.
Anna: Is it greater than $^-15$?
Adam: Yes.
Anna: Is it less than $^-10$?
Adam: No.
Anna: The number is $^-10$.

47. Explain how Anna knew that the integer was $^-10$.

48. Choose a partner. Play the game. Take turns.

Using a number line, explain how you would compare $^-6$ and $^+1$.

SUMMING UP

Activity

Exploring Addition of Integers

You can use checkers to model integers. Let black checkers represent positive integers and red checkers represent negative integers.

A pair of black and red checkers represents 0.

How can you use the checkers to model addition of integers?

Working together

Materials: sets of checkers or counters in 2 colors

A. Use checkers to model each integer.

B. Show $^+4 + ^-5$ with checkers. Make pairs of black and red checkers. How many pairs can you make? What is the value of each pair? How many checkers remain unpaired? What integer does the remaining checker represent?

$^+4$ $^-5$

C. Take a handful of red and black checkers. Find the sum.

D. Find each sum. Write an addition sentence for each.

[1]   [2]   [3]

Sharing Your Results

1. Compare your method for integer addition with the method used by other groups.

2. How can you tell without calculating whether a sum is positive, negative, or zero?

Extending the Activity

Work in a group.

**Use checkers to model each example.
Record your results.**

3. $^+7 + {}^+4$

4. $^-2 + {}^-5$

5. $^+7 + {}^-7$

6. $^+5 + {}^-2$

7. $^-4 + {}^+8$

8. $^+9 + {}^-10$

9. $^+2 + {}^-8$

10. $^-2 + {}^-2$

11. $^-6 + {}^+10$

12. $^-4 + 0$

13. $^-3 + {}^+1$

14. $0 + {}^-5$

15. Make up 5 addition examples. Then make a checker model to find each sum. Record your results.

**Can you use a checker model to find the sum of three integers?
Experiment to find each sum. Record your results.**

16. $^+3 + {}^-4 + {}^+5$

17. $^+6 + {}^-6 + {}^+3$

18. $^-7 + {}^-2 + {}^-2$

19. $^+3 + {}^+2 + {}^-6$

20. $^-2 + {}^+4 + {}^-3$

21. $^-3 + {}^+2 + {}^-6$

Summing Up

22. How does pairing red and black checkers help you find the sum?

23. Explain how you found the sum of three integers with a checker model.

24. Write an example whose sum is 0. Write another example whose sum is $^-1$.

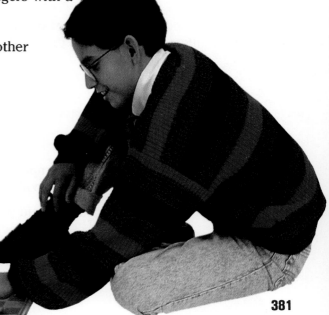

Activity

Exploring Subtraction of Integers

What integer is modeled?

What if you add a pair of red and black checkers?
Does the value change?

In how many ways can you model $^+1$?

Working together

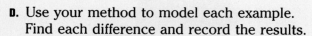

Materials: sets of checkers or counters in 2 colors

A. Use checkers or counters to model each subtraction.
Find each difference and record the results.

$$^+5 - {}^+2 \qquad {}^+6 - {}^+4 \qquad {}^+3 - {}^+1$$

$$^-4 - {}^-1 \qquad {}^-5 - {}^-2 \qquad {}^-3 - {}^-2$$

B. Make three different models, each showing $^+2$.
Draw each model you make.

C. Devise a way to model this subtraction.

$$^+5 - {}^+7$$

How can you use the models you made of $^+2$ to help?

How many pairs of red and black checkers must you add
so that you can subtract $^+7$?

D. Use your method to model each example.
Find each difference and record the results.

$$^+3 - {}^+5 \qquad {}^+2 - {}^+8 \qquad {}^-1 - {}^-5 \qquad {}^+4 - {}^+5$$

$$^-3 - {}^-6 \qquad {}^-5 - {}^-6 \qquad {}^+5 - {}^-6 \qquad {}^-5 - {}^+6$$

Sharing Your Results

1. Compare your method for subtracting integers with the
method used by other groups.

2. Explain why you add pairs of red and black checkers
to subtract.

Extending the Activity

Work in groups to solve the subtraction and addition examples below. Model each example and record in a chart.

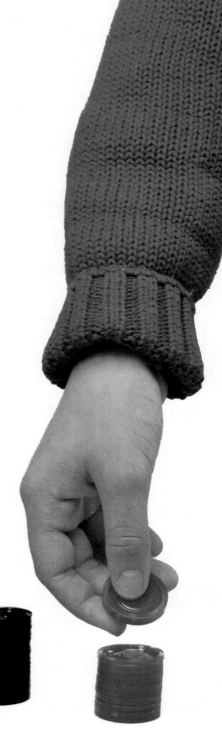

	Subtraction	Addition
3.	$^+7 - {}^+2 = $ _____	$^+7 + {}^-2 = $ _____
4.	$^-5 - {}^+3 = $ _____	$^-5 + {}^-3 = $ _____
5.	$^+3 - {}^-2 = $ _____	$^+3 + {}^+2 = $ _____
6.	$0 - {}^+4 = $ _____	$0 + {}^-4 = $ _____
7.	$^-2 - {}^+5 = $ _____	$^-2 + {}^-5 = $ _____

8. Make a model to show $^-2 - {}^-6$. Describe the model.

   Is subtracting 6 red checkers the same as adding 6 black checkers? Explain.

Summing Up

9. Why is it possible to subtract a greater number from a lesser number?

10. How can you tell before subtracting whether the answer will be positive, negative, or zero?

11. Look at the chart you made. Describe a way to subtract integers without using the checker model.

Explain how you would find the sum of the absolute values of ⁻7 and ⁻4.

Adding Integers

Ramon is exploring 4 meters below sea level. He descends 3 meters to join his sister. How far above or below sea level are Ramon and his sister?

Find ⁻4 + ⁻3.

You can use a number line to add integers.

Start at 0.
Move 4 units to the left. (⁻4)
Then move 3 units to the left. (⁻3)

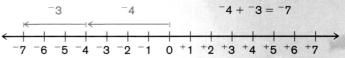

⁻4 + ⁻3 = ⁻7

Ramon and his sister are 7 meters below sea level.

Use a number line to show ⁺4 + ⁺2.

▶ The sum of two positive integers is a positive integer.
The sum of two negative integers is a negative integer.

Find ⁻7 + ⁺5.

Start at 0.
Move 7 units to the left. (⁻7)
Move 5 units to the right. (⁺5)

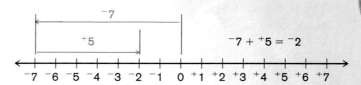

⁻7 + ⁺5 = ⁻2

▶ The sum of a positive integer and a negative integer has the same sign as the integer that is farther from 0, that is, the integer with the greater absolute value.

▶ The sum of an integer and its opposite is 0.

$$^+2 + ^-2 = 0$$
$$^-7 + ^+7 = 0$$

Opposites are called **additive inverses** of each other because their sum is 0.

Check Your Understanding

Add. Use a number line if needed.

1. ⁺4 + ⁺7
2. ⁻3 + ⁻8
3. ⁺5 + ⁻7
4. ⁻7 + ⁻10
5. ⁺2 + ⁻2
6. ⁻6 + ⁺8
7. ⁺5 + ⁻1
8. ⁻9 + ⁻2

Share Your Ideas Describe how you would add integers without a number line.

Practice

Add. Use a number line if needed.

9. $^+4 + {}^+8$

10. $0 + {}^+6$

11. $^+9 + {}^+3$

12. $^+1 + {}^+7$

13. $^-9 + {}^-2$

14. $^-6 + {}^-5$

15. $^-4 + {}^-1$

16. $^-7 + 0$

17. $0 + {}^-8$

18. $^-5 + {}^-1$

19. $^-1 + {}^-1$

20. $^-2 + {}^-2$

21. $^-8 + {}^+6$

22. $^-4 + {}^+5$

23. $^+5 + {}^-8$

24. $^-7 + {}^+6$

25. $^+6 + {}^-7$

26. $^-9 + {}^+6$

27. $^-4 + {}^+8$

28. $^+8 + {}^-3$

29. $^+4 + {}^+9 + {}^-7$

30. $^-3 + {}^-6 + {}^+2$

31. $^+2 + {}^-8 + {}^+3$

32. **Look back** at **29-31**. Explain how you used the associative property to find the sums.

Examine examples a-d. Then, without calculating, answer the questions below. Explain your thinking.

a. $^+5 + {}^+9$ **b.** $^-5 + {}^-9$ **c.** $^-5 + {}^+9$ **d.** $^+5 + {}^-9$

33. Which example has the greatest sum?

34. Which example has the least sum?

35. Which sums will be positive?

36. Which sums will be negative?

37. Which example has the greater sum, **c** or **d**?

38. Which examples have sums that are opposites of each other?

Think and Apply

Use the map for each problem.

39. Ramon's family drove 8 miles from the hotel to the Scuba Shop. Then they drove 3 miles to the Sweet Surf. How far is the Sweet Surf from the hotel?

40. How far is Coral Beach from the hotel?

Explain how to find the sum of $^-8 + {}^+2$, using the number-line model; using the checker model.

Name the opposite of each integer.

$^+9$ $^-5$ $^-7$ $^+4$ $^-8$

Subtracting Integers

On February 10, the Lee family went skiing in Steamboat Springs, Colorado. How much did the temperature change from early morning to midday?

You can use mental math to find the difference.

At 6:00 A.M. the temperature was $^-5°$ F.
To get to 0°, the temperature rose 5°.
To get to $^+10°$, the temperature rose another 10°.
The total rise was 15°.

You can subtract to find the difference.

$$^+10 - {}^-5 = {}^+10 + {}^+5 = {}^+15$$

opposites

▶To subtract an integer, add its opposite.

Between early morning and midday the temperature rose 15° F.

How much did the temperature change from midday to evening?

$$0 - {}^+10 = 0 + {}^-10 = {}^-10$$

opposites

Between 12:00 P.M. and 6:00 P.M. the temperature fell 10° F.

Find each difference. Then describe a rule for subtracting 0 from any integer.

a. $^+5 - 0$ **b.** $^-5 - 0$

Check Your Understanding

Find each missing integer.

1. $^+5 - {}^-4 = {}^+5 + n$ **2.** $^-7 - {}^-4 = {}^-7 + n$ **3.** $^+6 - {}^+9 = {}^+6 + n$

Subtract.

4. $^+5 - {}^+2$ **5.** $^+7 - {}^-4$ **6.** $^+8 - {}^-12$ **7.** $^+2 - {}^+7$

8. $^-3 - {}^-2$ **9.** $^-4 - {}^+3$ **10.** $^-6 - {}^-9$ **11.** $^-5 - {}^+8$

Share Your Ideas Explain how you would check the answers for **4**, **6**, and **8**.

Find each missing integer.

12. $^+4 - ^-4 = ^+4 + n$

13. $^-7 - ^-6 = ^-7 + n$

14. $^-2 - ^-6 = ^-2 + n$

15. $^-9 - ^-10 = ^-9 + n$

16. $0 - ^-1 = 0 + n$

17. $^-7 - 0 = ^-7 + n$

Subtract.

18. $^+5 - ^+1$

19. $^+8 - 0$

20. $^+4 - ^+10$

21. $^-5 - ^-1$

22. $^-9 - 0$

23. $^-9 - ^-10$

24. $^+5 - ^-3$

25. $^-5 - ^+3$

26. $^-4 - ^-6$

27. $^+8 - ^+11$

28. $^-6 - ^-5$

29. $^+2 - ^-7$

30. $^+28 - ^-14$

31. $^+82 - ^-15$

32. $^-35 - ^-35$

Think and Apply

Examine examples a–d. Then, without calculating, answer the questions below. Explain your thinking.

a. $^-7 - 0$

b. $0 - ^-7$

c. $^+5 - ^+5$

d. $^-9 - ^-9$

33. Which two examples will have the same answer?

34. Which two examples will have opposites as answers?

35. Which example will have the greatest difference?

36. Which example will have the least difference?

Write a number sentence, using integers for each. Solve.

37. The temperature in the morning was $^-4°$ F. The temperature has dropped $2°$ F. What is the temperature now?

38. According to Kevin's bank statement, he has $10 in the bank. If he deposits $50 and then withdraws $20, what is his new balance?

> **Look back** at **24–26.** Write each as an addition example. Then draw a number line to model each addition.

Mixed Review

1. 2.3×7.8

2. 5.9×0.002

3. $2.36 \div 0.04$

4. $0.025 \div 0.005$

5. $8\frac{1}{2} + 3\frac{2}{3}$

6. $2\frac{1}{3} - 1\frac{7}{8}$

7. $2\frac{1}{2} \times 1\frac{3}{5}$

8. $4\frac{1}{8} \div \frac{1}{8}$

9. $2 \div 9$

Find n.

10. 20% of $80 is n.

11. 14% of $25 is n.

12. 8 is 4% of n.

13. 5% of n is 10.

Find the perimeter of each rectangle.

14. $l = 5$ km; $w = 6$ km

15. $l = 2.3$ m; $w = 7$ m

16. $l = 6.5$ cm; $w = 2.1$ cm

Find the area of each triangle.

17. $b = 3$ cm; $h = 5$ cm

18. $b = 13$ cm; $h = 9$ cm

19. $b = 1.2$ m; $h = 6.1$ m

SUMMING UP

Midchapter Review

Write an integer for each. pages 376–377

1. a rise in stock of 4 points
2. 5° C below 0
3. a gain of 6 pounds
4. a loss of 9 yards

Write the absolute value of each. pages 378–379

5. $|^-1|$
6. $|^+5|$
7. $|^+8|$
8. $|^-8|$
9. $|^-6|$
10. $|^+6|$

Compare. Use >, <, or = for each ⬤. pages 378–379

11. $^+5$ ⬤ $^-4$
12. $^-3$ ⬤ $^-2$
13. $^-8$ ⬤ $^+7$
14. $|^+2|$ ⬤ $|^-2|$
15. $^-2$ ⬤ 0
16. $|^-1|$ ⬤ $|^+1|$
17. $^+14$ ⬤ $^+13$
18. $^-7$ ⬤ $^-8$

Write the integers in order from least to greatest. pages 378–379

19. $^-8, ^+8, ^+1, ^-7$
20. $^-4, ^-3, ^+2, ^-1$
21. $^-9, 0, ^+7$

Add or subtract. pages 384–387

22. $^-2 + ^+5$
23. $^+1 - ^-2$
24. $^-3 - ^+2$
25. $^+6 + ^-7$
26. $^+3 + ^+2$
27. $^-6 - ^-4$
28. $^-6 + ^-4$
29. $^+10 - ^+8$
30. $^-1 + ^+1$
31. $^-5 + ^-4$
32. $^-6 - ^-8$
33. $^+1 - ^-1$

Complete.

34. $\dots ^-3, ^-2, ^-1, 0, ^+1, ^+2, ^+3 \dots$ are called _____.

35. The distance that an integer is from 0 on the number line is called the _____ of the integer.

36. _____ have the same absolute value but different signs.

Words to Know
positive integers
absolute value
integers
opposite integers

Solve.

37. The Saiga antelope from the great Steppes of Central Asia was perfectly adapted to the climate. Temperatures ranged from $^+22°C$, to $^+28°C$ in summer while winter temperatures ranged from $^-6°C$ to $^-16°C$. What was the range in temperature for summer? for winter?

38. The temperature dropped 2° each hour between 4:00 P.M. and midnight. The temperature at 4:00 P.M. was $^+9°C$. What was the temperature at midnight? Make a table to find out.

Exploring Problem Solving

When Was the Pharaoh Born?

Andrea went on an archaeological dig for her vacation. She learned the following:

A. Queen Amneris's father became pharaoh of Egypt when he was only 18 years old.

B. An ancient clay tablet from Nineveh, in Mesopotamia, indicates that a solar eclipse took place in the 21st year of the Mesopotamian king's reign.

C. Another Mesopotamian tablet lists the gifts that the king received when he was crowned. These include a golden sword from Queen Amneris of Egypt.

D. In the tomb of Queen Amneris is a papyrus that dates from the time the sword was made. It states that her father gave her the sword to give to the king. He had it made 48 years earlier, when he became pharaoh.

E. Astronomers today have calculated that there was a total eclipse of the sun in Nineveh, in 763 B.C., while Nineveh was the capital of the region.

Thinking Critically

When was the pharaoh born? When was the king of Mesopotamia crowned? When did Queen Amneris's father become pharaoh? Use what you know about integers as you work in groups.

Analyzing and Making Decisions

1. For what one event do you know the date? What other event can you identify from that date? Which date is 21 years before 763 B.C.—742 B.C. or 784 B.C.? Explain.

2. When was the king of Mesopotamia crowned? Explain.

3. When was the pharaoh crowned? When was he born? Explain.

Look Back—To check the date of the eclipse, carbon-14 dating could be used. Scientists use material that was originally living at that time. What evidence mentioned in this lesson could they test?

Problem Solving Strategies

Logic

Tony's class took a survey of where they like to go on vacation. Tony knows that his four friends each went to a different place for vacation last summer. He cannot remember where Andy, Sally, Lester, and Marian went. He does remember that the four vacation spots were a famous city, an amusement park, the lake, and the seashore. He also knows these things:

- Andy did not go to the city.
- Lester and Sally went boating.
- Lester collected seashells.

Where did each of his friends go on vacation?

When solving logic problems, a table can help you sort out the information.

Solving the Problem

Think What is the question? How could the table help you solve the problem? Copy the table and complete it as you organize the clues.

Explore Did any of the children vacation at the same place? What does the first clue tell you? How can you show it on your table? Read the rest of the clues. What do they tell you?

Solve Where did each person go?

Look Back There were no clues about Marian. How did you know where she went?

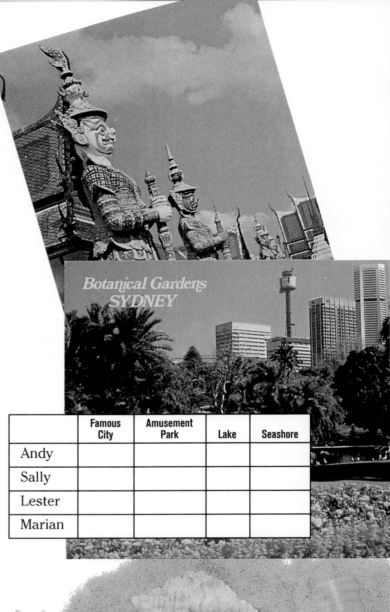

	Famous City	Amusement Park	Lake	Seashore
Andy				
Sally				
Lester				
Marian				

Share Your Ideas

1. **Look back** at the problem on page 389 and the one on this page. Would you agree or disagree with this statement: Careful reading is a very important part of solving logic problems. Explain.

Practice

CHOICES **Solve. Make a table where appropriate.**

2. Linda, Marcy, Reuben, and Jane went to the museum. There was a special exhibit with four different galleries: Aztec, Inca, Maya, and North America. Each person went to a different gallery.

   a. Linda saw Jane go to the Maya Gallery.
   b. Reuben did not go to the North America Gallery.
   c. Marcy and Reuben did not go to the Inca Gallery.

   Which gallery did each person visit?

3. Tim, Shirley, Ed, and Jim each took different vacations. They went to either Kenya, Thailand, Australia, or Norway.

   a. Tim's best friend went to Thailand.
   b. Neither Ed nor Jim went to Norway.
   c. Shirley went to Australia.
   d. Jim went to Kenya last year, but not this year.

   Where did each person go on vacation?

4. Claire, Dona, Eric, and Frank each traveled by plane to different sites in Egypt. They took either the Desert Duster or the Flying Camel.

   a. The Desert Duster landed at Aswan, Faiyum Basin, and Thebes.
   b. The Flying Camel landed at Faiyum Basin, Giza, and Thebes.
   c. Dona and Eric were on the same plane.
   d. Neither Dona nor Frank went to Aswan or Thebes.
   e. Eric flew on the Flying Camel.
   f. Claire was on a plane with one other member of the group.

   Who went to which site?

Mixed Strategy Review

5. The 10 members of the Harris family paid $101 to get into the amusement park. Tickets for children under 12 were $8 each. Tickets for everyone else were $15 each. How many children in the Harris family are under 12?

Create **Your Own**

Write a logic problem that can be solved by using a chart.

Activity

Exploring Multiplication and Division of Integers

Many calculators have a change-of-sign key for integers. $\boxed{+\!\circlearrowleft\!-}$

Here is how to enter a negative number.

To enter $^-6$, press $\boxed{6}$ $\boxed{+\!\circlearrowleft\!-}$ ⟶ $\boxed{ -6}$

To find $^-1 \cdot {}^+3$, press $\boxed{1}$ $\boxed{+\!\circlearrowleft\!-}$ $\boxed{\times}$ $\boxed{3}$ $\boxed{=}$ ⟶ $\boxed{ -3}$

Use your calculator to explore multiplication of integers.

Working together

Materials: calculators

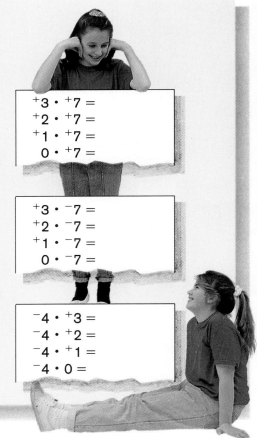

A. Copy the charts at the right. Extend each pattern to include three more factor pairs.

Use your calculator to find each product.
Look for patterns in the factors and in the products.

$^+3 \cdot {}^+7 =$
$^+2 \cdot {}^+7 =$
$^+1 \cdot {}^+7 =$
$0 \cdot {}^+7 =$

B. Make a similar chart, using your own factors.
Use the patterns you found to predict the products.
Then use a calculator to verify your predictions.

$^+3 \cdot {}^-7 =$
$^+2 \cdot {}^-7 =$
$^+1 \cdot {}^-7 =$
$0 \cdot {}^-7 =$

C. Based on your discoveries, predict each product below.
Then use a calculator to verify your predictions.

$^+4 \cdot {}^+8 \qquad {}^+4 \cdot {}^-8 \qquad {}^-4 \cdot {}^+8 \qquad {}^-4 \cdot {}^-8$

D. Discuss the sign of the product when you multiply each.

- two positive integers
- two negative integers
- a positive and a negative integer

$^-4 \cdot {}^+3 =$
$^-4 \cdot {}^+2 =$
$^-4 \cdot {}^+1 =$
$^-4 \cdot 0 =$

Sharing Your Results

1. Compare your conclusions about multiplying integers with the conclusions of other groups.

2. Discuss how the signs of the factors affect the sign of the product.

Extending the Activity

Use your calculator to explore division with integers. Work with a partner.

3. Copy the charts at the right. Extend each to include two more division facts. Make a third chart, using your own division facts.

4. Use a calculator to find each quotient. Study the patterns and analyze the results.

$$^+21 \div {}^+7$$
$$^+14 \div {}^+7$$
$$^+7 \div {}^+7$$
$$0 \div {}^+7$$
$$^-7 \div {}^+7$$

$$^+21 \div {}^-7$$
$$^+14 \div {}^-7$$
$$^+7 \div {}^-7$$
$$0 \div {}^-7$$
$$^-7 \div {}^-7$$

Based on your discoveries, predict each quotient. Then use a calculator to verify your predictions.

5. $^+42 \div {}^+6$ 6. $^+42 \div {}^-6$ 7. $^-42 \div {}^+6$ 8. $^-42 \div {}^-6$

9. $^+81 \div {}^+9$ 10. $^+81 \div {}^-9$ 11. $^-81 \div {}^+9$ 12. $^-81 \div {}^-9$

Copy and complete the table with the words *positive* and *negative*.

	dividend	divisor	quotient
13.	positive	positive	
14.		negative	positive
15.	positive	negative	
16.	negative		negative

Summing Up

17. What similarities do you see when you compare the multiplication and division charts?

18. If a product is a positive integer, what do you know about both factors?

19. If a quotient is a positive integer, what do you know about the divisor and the dividend?

20. Write your own rules for multiplying and dividing integers.

Explain how you would find each sum.

$^-4 + {}^-4 + {}^-4 + {}^-4$ $^+7 + {}^+7 + {}^+7$

Multiplying Integers

A National Park Service guide at the Cape Cod National Seashore said that many American beaches lose sand due to natural erosion. The ocean at one seaside resort has been churning away 3 feet of beach a year. How many feet of beach will be eroded in 4 years?

To find the answer, you can draw a picture.

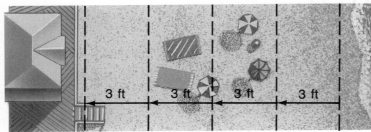

3 ft   3 ft   3 ft   3 ft

You can add.

$^-3 + {}^-3 + {}^-3 + {}^-3 = {}^-12$

You can multiply.

$^+4 \cdot {}^-3 = {}^-12$

The ocean will cause the beach to erode 12 feet in 4 years.

Write an equation to show where the beach was 10 years ago.

▶ The product of a positive integer and a negative integer is a negative integer.

$^+8 \cdot {}^-9 = {}^-72$ $^-6 \cdot {}^+6 = {}^-36$

▶ The product of two negative integers or two positive integers is a positive integer.

$^-5 \cdot {}^-5 = {}^+25$ $^+8 \cdot {}^+4 = {}^+32$

Check Your Understanding

Multiply.

1. $^+2 \cdot {}^+3$ 2. $^-4 \cdot {}^-4$ 3. $^+6 \cdot {}^-3$ 4. $^-4 \cdot {}^+9$

5. $^-2 \cdot {}^-2$ 6. $^+4 \cdot {}^-1$ 7. $^-8 \cdot 0$ 8. $^+7 \cdot {}^+5$

Share Your Ideas   Explain why the product of three negative integers is a negative integer.

Multiply.

9. $^+5 \cdot {}^+7$
10. $^+5 \cdot {}^-7$
11. $^-5 \cdot {}^-7$
12. $^-4 \cdot {}^-3$

13. $^+8 \cdot {}^+9$
14. $^-7 \cdot {}^+1$
15. $^-9 \cdot 0$
16. $^+9 \cdot 0$

17. $^-1 \cdot {}^-1$
18. $^+1 \cdot {}^+1$
19. $^+6 \cdot {}^-5$
20. $^-7 \cdot {}^-9$

21. $^-8 \cdot {}^-6$
22. $^+9 \cdot {}^-9$
23. $^+8 \cdot {}^+8$
24. $^-5 \cdot {}^-6$

25. $^-3 \cdot {}^+2 \cdot {}^+5$
26. $^+5 \cdot {}^+5 \cdot {}^+1$
27. $^-3 \cdot {}^-3 \cdot {}^-4$

Erosion
Control Area
Please-Keep Off

Think and Apply

28. Will the product of an odd number of negative integers be a negative integer? Experiment. Use a calculator. Multiply 5 negative integers; 7 negative integers; 9 negative integers. Record and then analyze your results. Write your conclusion.

29. Will the product of an even number of negative integers be a positive integer? Conduct an experiment similar to the one above.

30. The temperature on the beach has been dropping 3° F per hour since 6:00 P.M. How much will the temperature change in 5 hours?

31. **Look back** at **30.** If the temperature was 80° F at 6:00 P.M., what will the temperature be at 11:00 P.M.?

Test Taker

Select the correct answer. Use your number sense and estimation skills to eliminate illogical and extreme answers.

32. $^-43 \times {}^+48$
   a. $^-212$
   b. $^-2,064$
   c. $^+264,000$
   d. $^+20,640$

33. $^+21 \times {}^+293$
   a. $^+6,153$
   b. $^-62,533$
   c. $^+48,263$
   d. $^-6,453$

Explain how you can tell without multiplying which of these examples has the greater product.
$^-250 \cdot {}^-200$ $^+250 \cdot {}^-200$

SUMMING UP

Explain how you would find each product.

$^-5 \cdot {}^+4$ $^+7 \cdot {}^+8$ $^-4 \cdot {}^-6$

Dividing Integers

On a mountain tour the plane descends 25 meters in 5 seconds. On the average, how many meters per second does the plane drop in altitude?

Find $^-25 \div {}^+5$.

▶ The quotient of a positive and a negative integer is negative.

$^-25 \div {}^+5 = {}^-5$

Explain why $^-25$ is used as the dividend.

The plane descends 5 meters per second.

On another ride the plane descended at the rate of 8 meters per second until it dropped 240 meters. How many seconds did this descent take?

Find $^-240 \div {}^-8$.

▶ The quotient of two positive or two negative integers is positive.

$^-240 \div {}^-8 = {}^+30$

Explain why a negative number is used for both the divisor and the dividend.

It took 30 seconds for the plane to descend 240 m.

More Examples

a. $^+45 \div {}^+9 = {}^+5$ **b.** $^+18 \div {}^-3 = {}^-6$ **c.** $^-36 \div {}^-9 = {}^+4$

Check Your Understanding

Divide.

1. $^+81 \div {}^+9$ **2.** $^-81 \div {}^+9$ **3.** $^-81 \div {}^-9$ **4.** $^+5 \div {}^-1$

5. $0 \div {}^+5$ **6.** $^-72 \div {}^-8$ **7.** $^+63 \div {}^-7$ **8.** $^+42 \div {}^+6$

Share Your Ideas   Explain how you would check your answers for **1**, **2**, and **3**.

CHO-OYU
26,750 ft
8,153 m

PUMORI
23,442 ft
7,145 m

Divide. Use mental math to check your answers.

9. $^+54 \div {^+6}$

10. $^-35 \div {^-5}$

11. $^+42 \div {^-6}$

12. $^-63 \div {^+9}$

13. $^-72 \div {^-8}$

14. $^-81 \div {^-9}$

15. $^+21 \div {^-3}$

16. $^+27 \div {^+3}$

17. $^-30 \div {^+5}$

18. $^+20 \div {^-4}$

19. $^-27 \div {^-9}$

20. $^+24 \div {^+8}$

21. $^-18 \div {^-9}$

22. $^-36 \div {^-9}$

23. $^+24 \div {^+3}$

24. $^-48 \div {^+8}$

25. $^+18 \div {^-3}$

26. $^-27 \div {^+9}$

27. $^-24 \div {^-6}$

28. $^-32 \div {^+8}$

29. $\dfrac{^-25}{^-5}$

30. $\dfrac{^+49}{^-7}$

31. $\dfrac{^+56}{^-8}$

32. $\dfrac{^-64}{^-8}$

33. $\dfrac{^+9}{^-9}$

34. $\dfrac{^-72}{^-8}$

35. $\dfrac{^-81}{^-9}$

36. $\dfrac{^+64}{^-8}$

37. $\dfrac{^-45}{^-5}$

38. $\dfrac{^-42}{^+6}$

39. $\dfrac{^-630}{^-7}$

40. $\dfrac{^+640}{^-80}$

Think and Apply

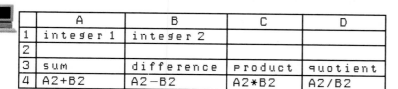

	A	B	C	D
1	integer 1	integer 2		
2				
3	sum	difference	product	quotient
4	A2+B2	A2−B2	A2*B2	A2/B2

Use a computer spreadsheet to find the sum, the difference, the product, and the quotient of pairs of integers. First enter the formulas shown on the spreadsheet above. Then, in cells A2 and B2, enter each pair of integers below. Finally, enter any ten pairs of integers you choose.

41. $^+3$ and $^-6$

42. $^-10$ and $^+5$

43. $^-1$ and $^-3$

44. $^-55$ and $^-99$

45. $^-31$ and $^+248$

46. $^+51$ and $^-187$

EVEREST
29,028 ft
8,848 m

Logical Thinking

Write *always, sometimes,* or *never.*

47. The sum of two negative integers is _____ a negative integer.

48. The product of two negative integers is _____ greater than the product of two positive integers.

49. The product of two opposites is _____ a negative number.

50. If the quotient is $^-1$, the divisor and dividend are _____ opposites.

MAKALU
27,807 ft
8,475 m

Describe five situations in which numbers decrease in value. Example: The temperature fell 8 degrees.

SUMMING UP

Describe how you would solve for *n*.

$$n - 23 = 35$$

Using Integers: Solving Equations

You can solve equations with integers by using the inverse operation. Examine how each equation is solved for *n*.

a. $n + {}^+6 = {}^-2$ Use the inverse of adding $^+6$.

$n + {}^+6 - {}^+6 = {}^-2 - {}^+6$ Subtract $^+6$ from both sides.

$n = {}^-2 + {}^-6$

$n = {}^-8$ Solution

Check ${}^-8 + {}^+6 = {}^-2$ Replace *n* with $^-8$.

Explain why $n + {}^+6 - {}^+6 = n$.

---

b. $n - {}^-5 = {}^+13$ Use the inverse of subtracting $^-5$.

$n - {}^-5 + {}^-5 = {}^+13 + {}^-5$ Add $^-5$ to both sides.

$n = {}^+13 + {}^-5$

$n = {}^+8$ Solution

Check ${}^+8 - {}^-5 = {}^+13$ Replace *n* with $^+8$.

---

c. ${}^-3n = {}^+27$ Use the inverse of multiplying by $^-3$.

$\dfrac{{}^-3n}{{}^-3} = \dfrac{{}^+27}{{}^-3}$ Divide both sides by $^-3$.

$n = {}^-9$ Solution

Check ${}^-3 \cdot {}^-9 = {}^+27$ Replace *n* with $^-9$.

---

d. $\dfrac{n}{{}^-8} = {}^+6$ Use the inverse of dividing by $^-8$.

$\dfrac{n}{{}^-8} \cdot {}^-8 = {}^+6 \cdot {}^-8$ Multiply both sides by $^-8$.

$n = {}^-48$ Solution

Check $\dfrac{{}^-48}{{}^-8} = {}^+6$ Replace *n* with $^-48$.

Explain why $\dfrac{n}{{}^-8} \cdot {}^-8 = n$.

Solve and check.

1. $n + {}^+7 = {}^-20$ **2.** $n - {}^-2 = {}^+17$ **3.** ${}^-4n = {}^+24$ **4.** $\dfrac{n}{{}^-3} = {}^+3$

Share Your Ideas   Look back at **b**. Explain why
$n - {}^-5 + {}^-5 = n$. Look back at **c**. Explain why $\dfrac{{}^-3n}{{}^-3} = n$.

Solve and check.

5. $^-6n = {}^-42$ 6. $\frac{n}{-9} = {}^-8$ 7. $^+5 + n = {}^-15$ 8. $n + {}^+8 = {}^+7$

9. $n + {}^-12 = {}^+4$ 10. $^-9 + n = {}^-6$ 11. $^+4n = {}^-28$ 12. $n - {}^+4 = {}^-7$

13. $\frac{n}{-8} = {}^-24$ 14. $^-8n = {}^+56$ 15. $^+15 + n = {}^-12$ 16. $^+7n = {}^-49$

17. $^-6 + n = {}^+8$ 18. $\frac{n}{+9} = {}^+1$ 19. $n + {}^-7 = {}^+7$ 20. $^+6 = \frac{n}{-7}$

21. $^-4n = {}^-28$ 22. $n - {}^+6 = {}^-7$ 23. $n + {}^+8 = {}^-9$ 24. $\frac{n}{-11} = {}^-5$

25. $^+3n - {}^+2 = 10$ 26. $^-5n + {}^-1 = 24$ 27. $^+4n - {}^-6 = {}^-30$ 28. $^-2n + {}^-3 = {}^+7$

Choose the equation that describes each sentence.

29. A number n increased by $^+3$ is $^-4$.

    a. $^+3n = {}^-4$ **b.** $n + {}^-4 = {}^+3$

    c. $n + {}^+3 = {}^-4$ **d.** $n + {}^-3 = {}^+4$

30. $^+5$ more than a number n is 0.

    a. $n + 0 = {}^+5$ **b.** $n + {}^+5 = 0$

    c. $n - {}^+5 = 0$ **d.** $n + {}^-5 = 0$

31. A number n decreased by $^+5$ is $^+14$.

    a. $n - {}^+5 = {}^+14$ **b.** $n - {}^+14 = {}^-5$

    c. $\frac{n}{+5} = {}^+14$ **d.** $^-5 - n = {}^+14$

32. A number n divided by $^-5$ is $^+7$.

    a. $\frac{n}{+7} = {}^-5$ **b.** $\frac{-5}{n} = {}^+7$

    c. $\frac{n}{-5} = {}^+7$ **d.** $\frac{+7}{-5} = n$

Write an equation for each sentence. Then solve.

33. $^+5$ times a number n is $^-15$.

34. A number n divided by $^-6$ is $^-9$.

35. The product of a number n and $^-7$ is $^-49$.

36. The sum of a number n and $^-15$ is $^-18$.

Select the appropriate equation for each. Then solve.

37. At 9:00 A.M., the visibility from the mountain tramway was 3 km. At 3:00 P.M., the visibility was 21 km. What was the change in visibility?

    a. $^+3 + n = {}^+21$
    b. $^+3 + {}^+21 = n$

38. From a mountain lookout, tourists can view the Serpentine River 1,500 m below and the snow-covered mountain peaks 3,500 m above. How far above the river are the mountain peaks?

    a. $^+3,500 - {}^+1,500 = n$
    b. $^+3,500 + {}^+1,500 = n$

Create a drawing for **38.** Show the mountain peaks, the river, and the lookout. Label the distances.

SUMMING UP

If $n > {}^-10$, tell which of the following integers cannot be n.

$$^-4 \qquad ^-12 \qquad ^+5 \qquad 0 \qquad ^-15$$

1989 CALENDAR OF EVENTS AND LODGING GUIDE

VISITOR GUIDE AND MAP

Checking into where to stay. Checking out when to play.

Using Integers: Solving Inequalities

An **inequality** is a mathematical sentence that uses one of the symbols below.

$<$ is less than

$>$ is greater than

$\leq$ is less than or equal to

$\geq$ is greater than or equal to

The solutions of an inequality are all the values that make the inequality true.

You can solve inequalities in the same way you solve equations.

Solve

$$n + {}^+5 > {}^+9$$
$$n + {}^+5 - {}^+5 > {}^+9 - {}^+5$$
$$n > {}^+4 \longleftarrow \text{solution: all numbers greater than } {}^+4$$

List of integer solutions: $^+5, {}^+6, {}^+7, \ldots$

Check Try any integer greater than $^+4$.

Try $^+5$.

$$^+5 + {}^+5 > {}^+9 \longleftarrow \text{Replace } n \text{ with } {}^+5.$$
$$^+10 > {}^+9$$

Another Example

Solve

$$\frac{n}{+3} \leq {}^-2$$
$$\frac{n}{+3} \cdot {}^+3 \leq {}^-2 \cdot {}^+3$$
$$n \leq {}^-6 \longleftarrow \text{solution: all numbers less than } {}^-6$$

List of integer solutions: $\ldots, {}^-8, {}^-7, {}^-6$

Check Try any integer less than or equal to $^-6$.

Try $^-9$.

$$\frac{^-9}{+3} \leq {}^-2 \longleftarrow \text{Replace } n \text{ with } {}^-9.$$
$$^-3 \leq {}^-2$$

SAN ANTONIO

Solve each inequality. Then list the integer solutions.

1. $n + {}^-2 > {}^+3$

2. $n - {}^+6 \leq {}^+2$

3. $\frac{n}{+5} > {}^+4$

4. $^+2n < {}^+10$

Share Your Ideas What similarities and differences do you see between solving equations and solving inequalities?

Solve each inequality. Then list the integer solutions.

5. $n + {}^-9 > {}^+5$

6. $n - {}^-2 > {}^-4$

7. ${}^+6n \geq {}^-36$

8. ${}^+9n < {}^+81$

9. ${}^-7 + n < {}^-4$

10. ${}^+5 + n > {}^-4$

11. ${}^+4n \leq {}^+8$

12. $n + 0 > {}^-5$

13. $n - {}^+3 \geq {}^-8$

14. ${}^-3 + n < {}^+5$

15. ${}^+\frac{n}{5} > {}^+9$

16. ${}^+\frac{n}{7} \leq {}^-8$

17. $n + {}^-3 > {}^-5 + {}^-3$

18. ${}^+6 + n \geq {}^-2 - {}^-6$

19. $n - {}^+9 \leq {}^-8 + {}^-5$

20. ${}^-5 + n > {}^+4 - {}^-7$

Write an inequality for each. Then solve.

21. A number n minus ${}^-6$ is greater than ${}^+3$.

22. A number n minus ${}^+7$ is greater than or equal to 0.

23. The sum of n and ${}^+2$ is less than or equal to ${}^-8$.

Find each n.

24. n is an integer.
$n - {}^-3 > {}^-14$, and
$n + {}^+5 < {}^-10$

25. n is an integer.
$n + {}^-3 > {}^+2$, and
$n - {}^-2 < 9$

Think and Apply

Choose the inequality to solve each problem. Then solve.

26. Becky made a $100 down payment on her plane ticket to Dallas. The travel agent told her that the total airfare would be no more than $375. How much more does she need to pay?

a. $375 - n < $100
b. $375 + n \leq $100
c. $n + $100 \leq $375
d. $n + $100 < $375

27. In addition to Dallas, Becky plans to visit the River Walk in San Antonio, and the university at Austin. If her vacation budget is $800, what is the minimum she will have available to spend after airfare?

a. $n + 375 \geq 800$
b. $n - 375 > 800$
c. $375 - n > 800$
d. $800 - n \geq 375$

Solve each inequality. Then explain the differences in the solutions.
$$x + 1 < 9 \qquad x + 1 \leq 9$$

Mixed Review

1. $2.7 + 3.8 + 9.9$

2. $6.41 + 2.83 + 1.09$

3. $7.1 - 7.08$

4. $6.009 - 5.8$

5. 0.02×0.005

6. 1.8×0.09

7. $0.4 \div 8$

8. $5.4 \div 0.06$

9. $0.8 \div 0.008$

10. $9.27 \div 0.09$

Find each n.

11. 15% of $60 is n.

12. n is 20% of $5.

13. 30% of n is $60.

14. $40 is 25% of n.

Find the area of each. Use 3.14 for π.

15. Circle: $r = 2$ cm

16. Circle: $d = 5$ m

17. Square: $s = 5\frac{1}{2}$ cm

18. Square: $s = 6.2$ cm

19. Rectangle: $l = 4$ m;
$w = 6$ m

20. Rectangle: $l = 7.1$ m,
$w = 5$ m

SUMMING UP

Describe how you would solve each.

$$^-5 + n = ^-7 \qquad n - {}^+4 > {}^+5$$

Graphing on the Number Line

You can graph the solution for an equation or an inequality.

Solve the equation $n + {}^-3 = {}^+4$.

$$n + {}^-3 = {}^+4$$
$$n + {}^-3 - {}^-3 = {}^+4 - {}^-3$$
$$n = {}^+7$$

Graph the solution.

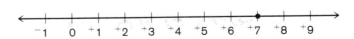

Solve the inequality $n - {}^-8 \leq {}^+6$.

$$n - {}^-8 \leq {}^+6$$
$$n - {}^-8 + {}^-8 \leq {}^+6 + {}^-8$$
$$n \leq {}^-2$$

Graph the integer solutions.

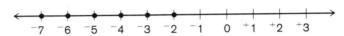

The solution includes all
integers less than or equal to $^-2$.

Another Example

Solve the inequality $^+4n > {}^-12$.

$$^+4n > {}^-12$$
$$\frac{^+4n}{^+4} > \frac{^-12}{^+4}$$
$$n > {}^-3$$

Graph the integer solutions.

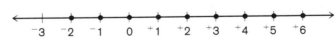

The solution includes all integers
greater than $^-3$.

Write an inequality for each graph.

1.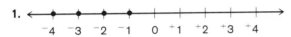

2.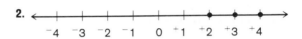

Solve each. Then graph its integer solutions.

3. $n + {}^-8 = 0$

4. $n - {}^+4 \geq {}^-2$

5. $^+6n < {}^-30$

Share Your Ideas Look back at 1. Explain why the graph
shows the solutions for two inequalities.

Write an equation or inequality for each graph.

6.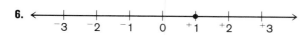

$-3 \quad -2 \quad -1 \quad 0 \quad +1 \quad +2 \quad +3$

7.

$-5 \quad -4 \quad -3 \quad -2 \quad -1 \quad 0 \quad +1$

8.

$-15 \quad -14 \quad -13 \quad -12 \quad -11 \quad -10 \quad -9$

9.

$-1 \quad 0 \quad +1 \quad +2 \quad +3 \quad +4 \quad +5$

10.

$-5 \quad -4 \quad -3 \quad -2 \quad -1 \quad 0 \quad +1$

11.

$-30 \quad -29 \quad -28 \quad -27 \quad -26 \quad -25 \quad -24$

Solve each. Then graph the integer solutions.

12. $n + {}^-9 = {}^+8$

13. ${}^+3n > {}^-15$

14. ${}^-6 + n < {}^+6$

15. $n - {}^+5 \leq {}^-7$

16. $n - {}^-2 \geq 0$

17. ${}^+4n \leq {}^-16$

18. $n + {}^-12 \geq {}^-8$

19. $n + {}^+8 \leq {}^-3$

20. $n - 0 \geq {}^-2$

21. ${}^+7n > {}^-35$

22. $n - {}^-3 > {}^+2 - {}^+8$

23. $n + {}^-27 \geq {}^-3 + {}^-8$

24. ${}^-4 + n = {}^+4 - {}^-1$

25. $n - {}^-7 \geq {}^-2 - {}^-7$

Think and Apply

Solve. Then graph the integer solutions.

26. A number n plus ${}^-3$ is less than ${}^+8$.

27. Five more than a number n is greater than or equal to 0.

28. A number n multiplied by ${}^+4$ is greater than ${}^-28$.

29. A number n minus ${}^+7$ is less than or equal to ${}^-5$.

30. A number n divided by ${}^+8$ is greater than ${}^-5$.

31. When the sum of ${}^+9$ and ${}^-3$ is subtracted from a number n, the result is greater than or equal to ${}^-6$.

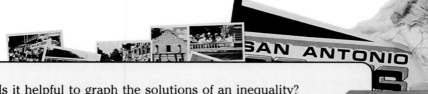

Is it helpful to graph the solutions of an inequality? Why or why not?

SUMMING UP

Name two different ways to describe locations on a map.

Graphing Ordered Pairs

Linda included a map in the report she wrote about her vacation in New Hampshire. To help the reader locate points of interest, Linda drew a pair of perpendicular axes on the map to create a **coordinate plane**.

In a coordinate plane the horizontal axis is called the **x-axis,** and the vertical axis is called the **y-axis**. The axes intersect at a point called the **origin.**

The x-axis and the y-axis separate the coordinate plane into four quadrants.

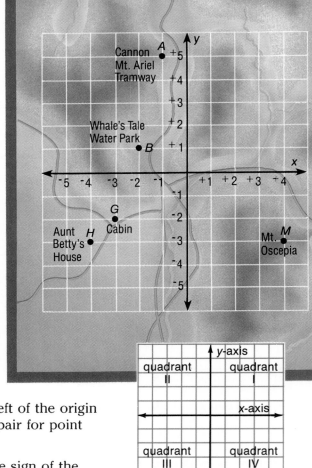

You can use an **ordered pair (x,y)** to locate any point on the coordinate plane. The first coordinate, x, tells the number of units left or right of the origin. The second coordinate, y, tells the number of units above or below the origin. The coordinates of the origin are (0,0).

The cabin is located at point G, 3 units to the left of the origin and 2 units down from the origin. The ordered pair for point G is (⁻3, ⁻2).

In what quadrant is point G located? What is the sign of the x- and y-coordinates for all points in quadrant III?

Write the ordered pair that locates each point of interest on the map.

1. Whale's Tale Water Park
2. Cannon Mount Ariel Tramway
3. Aunt Betty's House
4. Mount Oscepia

Use graph paper. Graph and label each point.

5. A (⁻3, ⁺5)   6. B (⁺5, ⁺2)   7. C (⁻4, ⁻2)   8. D (⁺4, ⁻2)   9. E (0, ⁻1)

Share Your Ideas   What is the y-coordinate for any point on the x-axis? What is the x-coordinate for any point on the y-axis? Explain.

Write the ordered pair for each point.

10. A
11. B
12. C
13. D
14. E
15. F
16. G
17. H
18. I
19. J
20. K
21. L

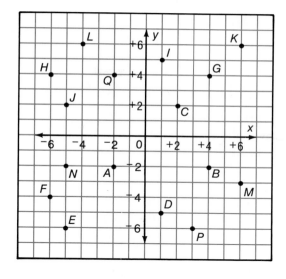

Write the letter of the point named by each ordered pair.

22. ($^-5$, $^-2$)
23. ($^+2$, $^+2$)
24. ($^-4$, $^+6$)
25. ($^+3$, $^-6$)
26. ($^-2$, $^+4$)
27. ($^+6$, $^-3$)

Think and Apply

Use graph paper for 28–33.

28. Graph each ordered pair. Connect these points in order: ($^-1$, $^-3$), ($^+6$, $^+1$), ($^+5$, $^+6$), ($^-2$, $^+2$), ($^-1$, $^-3$). What figure is formed?

29. Graph each ordered pair. Connect these points in order: ($^-3$, $^-4$), ($^+3$, $^-4$), ($^+3$, $^+2$), ($^-3$, $^+2$), ($^-3$, $^-4$). What figure is formed?

30. Graph each ordered pair. Connect these points in order: ($^-5$, $^-2$), ($^-4$, $^-5$), ($^-3$, $^-2$), ($^-2$, $^-5$), ($^-1$, $^-2$). What letter is formed?

31. Graph each ordered pair. Connect these points in order: ($^+2$, $^-3$), ($^+2$, $^+4$), ($^+5$, $^+4$), ($^+5$, $^+1$), ($^+2$, $^+1$). What letter is formed?

32. Create an isosceles triangle. Place vertices at (0, $^+5$) and ($^-2$, $^-5$). Where did you place the third vertex?

33. The midpoint of a line segment is ($^-4$, $^+4$). An endpoint is (0, 0). What ordered pair names the other endpoint?

$\mathbf{M}$athematics and History

34. The French mathematician René Descartes (1596–1650) is credited with developing coordinate geometry. It is said the idea came to him as he lay on his bed, watching a fly on the tiled ceiling. He described the fly's position by locating its distance from two intersecting lines (axes). This insight was the basis of the coordinate plane.

    How would you describe the location of the fly?

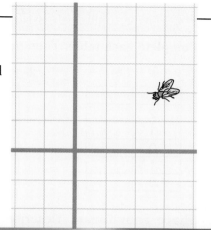

Use graph paper to graph each point.
  A($^-4$, $^-2$), B($^-2$, $^+1$), C(0, $^+4$), D($^+2$, $^+1$), E($^+4$, $^-2$)

SUMMING UP

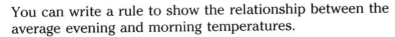

If $y = x - {}^+2$ and $x = {}^+5$, explain how you would find the value of y.

Graphing from a Rule

In February, the average 6:00-P.M. temperature at Eagle Lake is about 5° warmer than the average 6:00-A.M. temperature.

You can write a rule to show the relationship between the average evening and morning temperatures.

6:00-P.M. temperature = 6:00-A.M. temperature + 5°

Let y represent the 6:00-P.M. temperature and x the 6:00-A.M. temperature.

$$y = x + {}^+5$$

You can use the rule $y = x + {}^+5$ to make a table of values The values in the table can be shown as ordered pairs. $({}^-3, {}^+2)$, $({}^-2, {}^+3)$, $({}^-1, {}^+4)$, $(0, {}^+5)$, $({}^+1, {}^+6)$ are some of the solutions for the equation $y = x + {}^+5$.

Which ordered pair shows the value of y when $x = {}^-1$?

You can graph the ordered pairs on a coordinate plane. Draw a line through the points. The line shows all the solutions to $y = x + {}^+5$. The line is the graph of the equation.

Name another pair that satisfies the rule $y = x + {}^+5$.

x	y
$^-3$	$^+2$
$^-2$	$^+3$
$^-1$	$^+4$
0	$^+5$
$^+1$	$^+6$

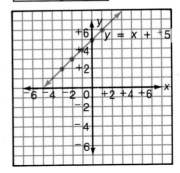

Check Your Understanding

Complete each table. Then graph each equation.

1. $y = x - {}^+5$

x	y
$^+2$	
$^+1$	
0	
$^-1$	
$^-2$	

2. $y = x + {}^-4$

x	y
$^+4$	
$^+2$	
0	
$^-2$	
$^-4$	

3. $y = {}^-2x$

x	y
$^+1$	
0	
$^-1$	
$^-2$	
$^-3$	

4. $y = \dfrac{x}{{}^+2}$

x	y
$^+2$	
0	
$^-2$	
$^-4$	
$^-6$	

Share Your Ideas Describe how you would graph the equation $y = x$.

Complete each table. Graph each equation.

5. $y = x - {}^+2$

x	y
$^+3$	
$^+1$	
$^-1$	
$^-3$	
$^-5$	

6. $y = x + {}^-3$

x	y
$^+7$	
$^+4$	
$^+1$	
$^-2$	
$^-5$	

7. $y = {}^-3x$

x	y
$^+4$	
$^+3$	
$^+2$	
$^+1$	
0	

8. $y = \frac{x}{^+3}$

x	y
$^+9$	
$^+6$	
$^+3$	
0	
$^-3$	

Make a table of values for each equation. Then graph the equation.

9. $y = x - {}^+7$

10. $y = x + {}^-5$

11. $y = x + {}^+1$

12. $y = x + {}^+4$

13. $y = {}^+3x$

14. $y = \frac{x}{^-2}$

15. $y = x + {}^+2 - {}^-1$

16. $y = {}^+2x + {}^+5$

Look back at 9. Then answer the questions.

17. What is the value of y when x is 0?

18. What is the value of x when y is $^-2$?

19. What is the value of y when x is $^+3$?

20. Can any solutions for this equation be graphed in quadrant II? Explain.

Think and Apply

Eagle Lake Noon Temperatures (° Celsius)							
Day	Sun	Mon	Tue	Wed	Thu	Fri	Sat
Air Temperature	32°	34°	36°	36°	35°	35°	33°
Water Surface Temperature	16°	17°	18°	19°	20°	21°	22°

Mr. Anderson has been fishing at Eagle Lake since he was a young boy. He told the Chen family that in July, the water temperature at 15 m below the surface of the lake is 3°C colder than the surface temperature.

21. Write an equation that shows the relationship between the surface temperatures and the temperatures 15 m below the surface of Eagle Lake. Use x for the surface temperature. Use y for the temperature 15 m below the surface.

22. Look back at **21.** Use your equation to write ordered pairs. Use a water-surface temperature in the chart for each x.

Look back at **22.** Graph the ordered pairs on a coordinate plane.

SUMMING UP

Using Problem Solving

Planning a Vacation

The Brewsters and their two children are planning a trip to a tropical island. They plan to spend no more than $3,000. The cost of the airfare for the family is $700. Their hotel will cost $100 a night, and they think that food will cost about $30 a day, per person.

A. How much will the Brewsters spend per day to stay in the hotel and to eat?

B. What other expenses might the Brewsters have on their trip?

C. What do you think is the greatest number of days that the Brewsters can spend on their vacation?

Sharing Your Ideas

1. To obtain the $700 airfare and the $100 per night hotel charge, the Brewsters must make reservations. For how many days do you think they should have reservations? Explain.

2. **What if** the Brewsters could reduce their airfare to $500 and their hotel costs to $80 a night by making reservations for 10 days or more? Would you recommend that they do this? Explain.

Practice

3. Next year, while the Brewster children are visiting their grandparents, Mr. and Mrs. Brewster are planning to go to Mexico. They have saved $3,500. The chart below shows Mr. and Mrs. Brewster's estimated expenses.

Expenses	1 Week or Less	1 to 2 Weeks	More than 2 Weeks
Airfare	$1,400	$1,100	$800
Hotel (per night)	$ 90	$ 80	$ 70
Food (per day, per person)	$ 40	$ 40	$ 40
Gifts	$ 200	$ 300	$350
Entertainment	$ 200	$ 250	$250
Clothing for Trip	$ 300	$ 300	$350

Make up three different trip plans for Mr. and Mrs. Brewster that show projected total expenses for different lengths of stay.

4. If you were Mr. and Mrs. Brewster, how long would you stay?

Summing Up

5. Which length of stay do you think is the best for the Brewsters? Explain.

6. Why might someone charge you less per day for staying somewhere longer?

Chapter Review

Write an integer for each. pages 376–377

1. 2°C below zero

2. a gain of 5 yards

3. stock falling 4 points

Compare. Use >, <, or = for each ●. pages 378–379

4. $^-5$ ● $^-2$

5. $^-8$ ● $^+8$

6. $^+4$ ● $^+3$

7. $|^-6|$ ● $|^-7|$

Add, subtract, multiply, or divide. pages 384–387, 394–397

8. $^-2 \cdot ^-6$

9. $^-10 \div ^+5$

10. $^+6 - ^-5$

11. $^-1 + ^+1$

12. $^-5 + ^-7$

13. $^+6 \cdot ^-3$

14. $^-18 \div ^-2$

15. $^-2 - ^-5$

Solve for n. Then graph the solution on the number line. pages 398–403

16. $^-2n = ^+12$

17. $n + ^+5 = ^-10$

18. $n - ^-4 = ^+10$

19. $^+5 + n \geq ^+7$

20. $^+3n > ^-15$

21. $\frac{n}{^+4} \leq ^-2$

22. $n - ^-5 < ^+12$

23. $\frac{n}{^-5} = ^-8$

Write the ordered pair that locates each point. pages 404–405

24. *A*

25. *B*

26. *C*

27. *D*

28. *E*

29. *F*

On graph paper, draw an x-axis and a y-axis and graph each point. pages 404–405

30. $R\,(^-3, 0)$

31. $S\,(^+2, ^+3)$

32. $T\,(^+1, ^-2)$

33. $M\,(0, ^+2)$

34. $N\,(^-1, ^-4)$

35. $P\,(^+3, ^-1)$

Make a table of values. Then graph each equation. pages 406–407

36. $y = x + ^-6$

37. $y = x - ^-1$

38. $y = ^+4x$

Solve.

39. Dr. Spade and his three students, Carol, Kai, and Chris, found a pot, a vase, a spoon, and a knife. Who found each item?

   - Kai and Dr. Spade worked alone.
   - Kai discovered the most artifacts.
   - Dr. Spade discovered the first one.
   - The vase was found before the pot and the knife by 2 people working together.
   - The spoon was found before the vase.

40. The kingdom of Meroë in Sudan flourished from 395 B.C. to A.D. 350. How many years is that?

395 B.C.   0   350 A.D.

Chapter Test

Compare. Use >, <, or = for each ●.

1. $^-6$ ● $^-7$

2. $|^-2|$ ● $|^+2|$

3. $^+4$ ● $^-4$

4. $|^-8|$ ● $|^+7|$

Add, subtract, multiply, or divide.

5. $^-3 \cdot {^-8}$

6. $^-6 + {^-7}$

7. $^+8 - {^-2}$

8. $^-12 \div {^+4}$

Solve for *n*. Then graph.

9. $^-3n = {^+9}$

10. $^-4 + n = {^-8}$

11. $\frac{n}{^+6} = {^-12}$

12. $n - {^-2} = {^-4}$

13. $^+4n > {^-8}$

14. $n - {^+5} \le {^-10}$

15. $^-2 + n \ge {^+4}$

16. $\frac{n}{^+2} < {^+5}$

Write the ordered pair that locates each point.

17. *A*

18. *B*

19. *C*

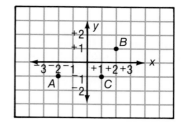

On graph paper, mark the *x*-axis and the *y*-axis and graph each point.

20. $J(^-1, {^-2})$

21. $K(^+4, {^+2})$

22. $L(^-3, {^+2})$

Solve.

23. Richard, Ann, Bonnie, and Bill are preparing for an archeological dig. Research must be done, travel planned, tools gathered, and storage materials found. Who does which task?

- Bonnie is the sister of the man who gathers the tools.
- Bill, an only child, owns a travel agency.
- Research is done by Richard's daughter.

24. Wrought ironwork was developed under the Han dynasty (206 B.C to A.D. 220). How many years did the dynasty span?

25. The Battersea Shield, found in the Thames River at Battersea, London, could have been made during a 200-year period. The dates are from A.D. 100 to what year B.C.?

THINK   Evaluate.

$$\frac{^-3(^+2 \cdot {^-3} - {^-6}) \div {^-4} + {^-1} \cdot {^+2}}{^-2}$$

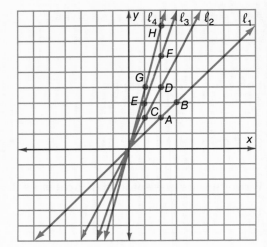

1. Examine lines l_1, l_2, l_3, and l_4. How are they different?

2. List the ordered pairs that locate each pair of points.

a. A, B **b.** C, D **c.** E, F **d.** G, H

3. Look back at the ordered pairs in **2**. How much does the y value increase when the x value increases by 1?

For any two points on a line, the ratio of the change in the y value to the change in the x value is called the **slope of the line.**

$$\text{slope of } l_4 = \frac{4}{1}$$

4. What is the slope of l_1? l_2? l_3?

5. What do you think happens to the slope of a line as the line approaches the position of the y-axis?

6. What do you think happens to the slope of a line as the line approaches the position of the x-axis?

Maintaining Skills

Choose the correct answers. Write A, B, C, or D.

1. What is the rate?
66 players for 6 teams

  A 10 per team   **C** 6 per team

  B 11 per team   **D** not given

2. Find the rate.
distance = 189.75 m   time = 8.25 h

  A 22 mph   **C** 23 mph

  B 21 mph   **D** not given

3. What is 1.03 as a percent?

  A 10.3%   **C** 13%

  B 103%   **D** not given

4. What is $\frac{3}{4}$% as a decimal?

  A 0.0075   **C** 0.075

  B 0.75   **D** not given

5. What is the discount if the regular price is $82 and the rate of discount is 15%?

  A $1.23   **C** $12.30

  B $8.20   **D** not given

6. Find n. 40% of n is 25.

  A 10   **C** 62.5

  B 1,000   **D** not given

7. What percent of 63 is 42?

  A $66\frac{2}{3}$%   **C** $33\frac{1}{3}$%

  B 15%   **D** 150%

8. What is the area of a triangle with $b = 8$ cm and $h = 16$ cm?

  A 64 cm^2 **C** 62 cm^2

  B 128 cm^2 **D** not given

9. What is the volume of a rectangular prism with $B = 120$ m^2 and $h = 3$ m?

  A 120 m^3 **C** 340 m^3

  B 40 m^3 **D** not given

10. Compare. $^-2$ ● $^-6$

  A <   **C** =

  B >   **D** not given

11. $4 + {}^-7$

  A 3   **C** $^-3$

  B $^-11$ **d** not given

12. $^-4 - {}^-8$

  A $^+4$ **C** $^-4$

  B $^-12$ **D** not given

13. $^-72 \div {}^-9$

  A $^-8$ **C** 8

  B 9   **D** not given

Make a drawing to solve 14 and 15.

14. Bryan puts fence posts around a circular field 90 ft in circumference. He places the posts 3 ft apart. How many posts does he use?

  A 31   **C** 29

  B 30   **D** not given

15. Monica puts fencing around the circular field in **14**. The fence is 5 ft high. She attaches the fence to each post in three places. To the nearest foot, what is the length of the fence?

  A 283 ft   **C** 270 ft

  B 450 ft   **D** not given

13 Probability

THEME   What's Probable?

Sharing What You Know

Pets communicate with their owners, but not by using words! It is likely that your dog will communicate with you by barking or nudging you with its nose. What other behaviors of pets are likely? How might your pet's predictability help you to care for it?

Using Language

What is the probability that you might ride in a car this weekend? If you ride in a car frequently, it is likely you will ride in a car this weekend. The word **frequent** means occurring often. When studying mathematics, you use a **frequency table** to make a list of data together with the number of times that data occur. Why, do you think, is **frequency table** a good name for this kind of data listing?

Words to Know: frequency table, sample space, outcome, probability, compound event, independent event, impossible event, equally likely outcomes, relative frequency

Be a Problem Solver

Jan has flipped a penny 3 times and it has come up heads each time. Is it more probable that the penny will come up heads or tails on the fourth toss? Explain.

Create a chart in which you list events that are *Highly Likely, Somewhat Likely,* or *Unlikely* to occur during one school day.

Activity

Devising Experiments: Making Predictions

What if you choose two 3-digit numbers at random? What are the chances their product is even? Make a prediction. Then perform the experiment below to test your prediction.

Working together

Materials: a paper bag containing 10 cards, each printed with a different number from 0 to 9; a calculator

A. Pick a card from the bag, record the number, and replace the card. Do this 3 times to form a 3-digit number. Then repeat to form another 3-digit number. If you choose a zero for the hundreds digit, replace it and choose again.

B. Use a calculator to multiply the two 3-digit numbers. Record whether the product is even or odd.

C. Repeat **A** and **B** for nine more pairs of 3-digit numbers.

D. Record your results, together with those of the other groups, in a table like this.

Total Number of Products Found	Number of Even Products	Ratio of Even Products to Total Products

Sharing Your Results

Use the information in the table to answer these questions.

1. What was the ratio of even products to total products for the class? How does the ratio for the class compare with the ratio for your group?

2. How does your prediction compare with the ratio for your group? with the ratio for the class?

3. When is the product of two numbers even? When is it odd? How would this information help you make a prediction about the experiment above?

Extending the Activity

Each time you perform an experiment, it is called a *trial*. The **relative frequency** of a result of an experiment is the ratio at right.

$$\frac{\text{number of times the desired result occurs}}{\text{total number of trials}}$$

The greater the number of trials, the more reliable the relative frequency is.

4. For the experiment on page 416, what is the relative frequency of an even product for your group? for the class?

Work in your group. Choose two of the problems below.

Materials: pencil, number cube, bottle cap, paper cup

Make a prediction about the relative frequency of each. Then devise an experiment to test your prediction. Record your results.

5. When a 6-sided pencil is rolled on a flat surface, what are the chances it will land with the brand name face up?

6. When a number cube is tossed, what are the chances a 6 will land face up?

7. When a bottle cap is tossed, what are the chances the cap will land with the brand name face up?

8. When a paper cup is tossed, what are the chances the cup will land on its side?

Summing Up

9. Compare your group's results with those of other groups. Do the relative frequencies agree? If not, explain why you think they do not.

10. Combine the results for **5–8** for the class. How do the relative frequencies for your group compare with those for the class? Which relative frequency seems more consistent with your prediction?

11. Did any of the relative frequencies computed for your group or for the class vary greatly from your prediction? If so, explain why you think they did.

How many ways can a 6-sided number cube land when tossed? How many ways can a coin land when tossed?

Probability

A number cube with sides numbered 1, 2, 3, 4, 5, and 6 is tossed. What is the probability of tossing a 3?

- In an experiment, such as tossing a number cube, each possible result is an **outcome.** If each result is as likely to occur as every other, they are *equally likely* outcomes.

- The **sample space** of an experiment is the set of all possible outcomes.

- Any part of a sample space is called an **event.** There may be one outcome, more than one outcome, or even no outcomes in an event.

▶ The probability that an event, *P(E),* will occur is the ratio of the number of favorable outcomes to the number of possible outcomes in the sample space.

$$P(E) = \frac{\text{number of favorable outcomes}}{\text{number of possible outcomes}}$$

$P(\text{tossing a 3}) = \dfrac{1}{6}$ ← number of favorable outcomes of tossing a 3
← number of possible outcomes of tossing a number cube

The probability of an *impossible* event is 0. What, do you think, is the probability of an event that is *certain* to occur?

▶ The sum of the probabilities of all the outcomes in a sample space is always 1.

Listed below are the probabilities for tossing the number cube.

$P(1) + P(2) + P(3) + P(4) + P(5) + P(6) = 1$

$\dfrac{1}{6} + \dfrac{1}{6} + \dfrac{1}{6} + \dfrac{1}{6} + \dfrac{1}{6} + \dfrac{1}{6} = 1$

Check Your Understanding

List the favorable outcomes and find the probability of each event for the experiment *tossing a number cube*. Classify each event as impossible, certain, or neither.

1. Toss a 5 or a 6. **2.** Toss an even number. **3.** Toss an 8. **4.** Toss a number < 7.

Share Your Ideas What, do you think, are the least and the greatest values for the probability of an event? Explain.

Use the spinner, cards, and cubes at the right.
Give the sample space for each experiment.

5. Flip a coin.

6. Pick a number from 1 to 10.

7. Toss a cube lettered from G to L.

8. Spin the spinner.

9. Pick a card from the deck.

10. Draw a cube from the bag.

List the favorable outcomes and find the probability of each
event. Classify each event as impossible, certain, or neither.

11. Spin a vowel on the spinner.

12. Flip a head on a coin.

13. Draw a blue cube from the bag.

14. Spin a W on the spinner.

15. Pick a multiple of 10 from the deck of cards.

16. Toss an odd number on the number cube at the top of page 418.

17. Pick a 17 from the deck of cards.

18. Spin a consonant on the spinner.

19. Pick a prime number from the deck of cards.

20. Pick a factor of 60 from the deck of cards.

21. Draw a purple cube from the bag.

22. Flip a tail or a head on a coin.

23. Spin a letter in your first name on the spinner.

24. Pick a card from the deck that shows a multiple of 5 and 12.

Think and Apply

25. Craig says, "I'm thinking of an even number between 1 and 21." Omar says, "I'm thinking of an odd number between 1 and 21." If you try to guess the numbers, are the probabilities of guessing correctly in both cases equal?

What is the sample space for the experiment *picking a letter in your full name?* Are the outcomes equally likely? Explain.

Test Taker

What if you are not sure of the answer to a problem? You can guess the answer. Here is a way to increase your chances of guessing the correct one: Eliminate answers that are obviously incorrect.

Eliminate the impossible answers.
Explain your choices. Then select the
correct answer if you can.

26. *P*(tossing tails twice)

   a. 1   **b.** $\frac{1}{2}$ **c.** $\frac{1}{4}$ **d.** 0

27. It takes 2 men 2 days to do a job. It takes 4 men _____ day(s) to do the same job.

   a. 1   **b.** 2   **c.** 3   **d.** 4

SUMMING UP

What is the sample space for this spinner?

The Counting Principle

The seventh graders at Wilmot Junior High are planning a class trip. They have a choice of going to Seashore Wildlife Refuge or Whitewater Falls State Park. For dinner they can choose El Coyote Mexican Restaurant, The Black Angus Steak House, or Cerchiara's Italian Ristorante. How many possible combinations of choices for recreational area and restaurant are there?

One way to solve this problem is to list the outcomes, or choices. Use a tree diagram.

There are 6 possible choices. One is to go to the Seashore Wildlife Refuge and eat dinner at El Coyote Mexican Restaurant. What are the other five choices?

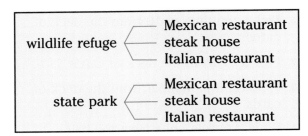

You can also use the **Counting Principle** to solve the problem.

▶ If there are *m* choices for a first decision and *n* choices for a second decision, then there are $m \times n$ choices for the first decision followed by the second.

choices of recreational areas × choices of restaurants = total possible combinations

$$2 \qquad \times \qquad 3 \qquad = \qquad 6$$

The combination for Jeremy's hall locker is 9–15–9. How many three-number combinations are possible on a locker with numbers from 0 to 19?

$$20 \qquad \times \qquad 20 \qquad \times \qquad 20 \qquad = \qquad 8,000$$

choices for first number   choices for second number   choices for third number

Would it be practical to make a tree diagram for this situation? Explain.

Check Your Understanding

Find the number of possible choices or outcomes.

1. There are 5 shirts and 3 pairs of jeans. Choose 1 shirt and 1 pair of jeans.

2. A number cube is tossed and a coin is flipped.

Share Your Ideas Look back at **2**. What are the outcomes? **What if** the spinner in Getting Started were spun as well? Could you quickly list the possible outcomes? Explain.

Practice

List the outcomes for each.

3. The spinner in Getting Started is spun and a coin is flipped.

4. A vowel is chosen and a card is drawn from those above.

5. A pair of socks is chosen from 1 green pair, 1 blue pair, and 1 striped pair. A pair of shoes is chosen from a pair of sneakers, a pair of loafers, and a pair of sandals.

6. A guitar, a flute, a banjo, or a piano is chosen to play jazz or country-western music.

Find the number of possible choices or outcomes.

7. A menu has 8 appetizers and 6 entrees. Choose 1 appetizer and 1 entree.

8. Janine has 4 blouses and 5 scarves that match. Choose 1 blouse and 1 scarf.

9. The spinner in Getting Started is spun and a number cube is tossed.

10. A three-number combination is chosen for a lock with numbers from 0 to 39.

Think and Apply

11. How many different combinations of juice and cereal can you choose for breakfast?

12. How many ways are there to travel from Blue County to Green Pastures by way of Yellow Town?

13. What if Route 9A is closed for repairs? How many ways are there to make the trip?

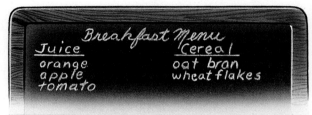

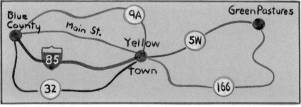

A community center offers summer programs for preschoolers.

14. How many different programs are possible?

15. If Gina's father wants her to take swimming, how many different programs can she take?

16. If Yani leaves each day at 12:30, how many different programs can she take?

A president and vice-president must be elected from a class of 100. Can you use the Counting Principle to find how many choices there are? Explain.

SUMMING UP

When you toss a number cube twice, does the outcome of the first toss affect the outcome of the second toss? Explain.

Independent Events

In your dresser drawer, you have 1 pair of socks of each color—blue, brown, white, red, and black. You reach into the drawer without looking. The first pair you pull out is red, the wrong color! You replace it and pull out another pair. What is the probability that you will choose the red pair twice?

Choosing two pairs of socks is a **compound event.** It is made up of more than one event. The events are **independent.** That is, the events have no effect on one another, since the first pair was replaced. Under what circumstances would the choice of the second pair be affected by the choice of the first?

▶ If A and B are independent events, the probability that both events will occur, written P(A, B), is as follows.

$$P(A, B) = P(A) \cdot P(B)$$

The probability of choosing a red pair of socks is $\frac{1}{5}$. How do you know?

The probability of choosing the red pair twice is

$$P(\text{red, red}) = P(\text{red}) \cdot P(\text{red}) = \frac{1}{5} \cdot \frac{1}{5} = \frac{1}{25}.$$

Another Example

A number cube is tossed twice. What is the probability of tossing an even number and then a number less than 3?

P(even number, number < 3) =

$P(\text{even number}) \cdot P(\text{number} < 3) = \frac{3}{6} \cdot \frac{2}{6} = \frac{6}{36} = \frac{1}{6}$

Check Your Understanding

A coin is flipped twice. Find each probability.

1. P(heads, heads)

2. P(heads, tails)

3. P(tails, heads)

4. P(tails, tails)

Share Your Ideas   Look back at **1–4.** Use a tree diagram to justify each answer.

Find each probability.

Experiment: Spin this spinner and flip a coin.

5. P(3, heads)

6. P(odd number, heads)

7. P(prime number, tails)

8. P(number $<$ 7, tails)

Experiment: Flip a coin and toss a number cube.

9. P(heads, 2)

10. P(tails, prime number)

11. P(tails, number $<$ 5)

12. P(heads, 7)

Find the probability of each compound event.

Experiment: Pick one marble without looking. Replace it. Pick another marble.

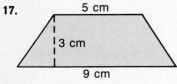

13. Event: Pick two red marbles.

14. Event: Pick a red marble followed by a blue one.

15. Event: Pick a blue marble followed by a yellow one.

Experiment: A number cube is tossed twice.

16. Event: Toss a 6 and a 4.

17. Event: Toss an even number and an odd number.

18. Event: Toss two matching numbers.

19. Event: Toss a 3 and a 7.

20. **Look back** at 5 and 11. Use a tree diagram to justify each answer.

Think and Apply

21. Make up an experiment for which there are independent events. Make up a compound event consisting of two of the independent events. Find the probability of the compound event.

22. Mr. James needs 2 students to help him set up the science lab. There are 12 girls and 8 boys in his class. He chooses 2 names from a hat. If he replaces the first name, what is the probability he will choose the same name twice?

Explain how you could use the Counting Principle to find the probability of a compound event.

Mixed Review

1. $^-16 + ^-8$

2. $^-12 + 10$

3. $3 - ^-7$

4. $^-9 - 6$

5. $3 \times ^-8$

6. $^-12 \times ^-5$

7. $^-48 \div ^-8$

8. $^-100 \div 5$

9. $36 - 45$

10. $^-11 \times 10$

Solve.

11. $33\frac{1}{3}\%$ of 36

12. 55% of 100

13. What percent of 50 is 35?

14. 24 is 30% of what number?

15. 125% of 200

16. What percent of 16 is 80?

Find the area of each shaded region.

17.

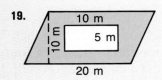

5 cm

3 cm

9 cm

18.

20 m

19.

10 m

5 m

10 m

20 m

SUMMING UP

423

Midchapter Review

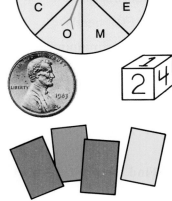

Give the sample space for each experiment. Then list the favorable outcomes and find the probability of each event. Use the cards, spinner, number cube, and coin shown. pages 418–419

Experiment: Draw a card.

1. Event: Draw a red card.

2. Event: Draw a purple card.

Experiment: Flip the coin.

3. Event: Flip a head.

4. Event: Flip a head or a tail.

Experiment: Toss the number cube.

5. Event: Toss an even number.

6. Event: Toss a number > 5.

Experiment: Spin the spinner.

7. Event: Spin a consonant.

8. Event: Spin an O.

Use a tree diagram to show the sample space of each experiment. Then find the probability of each compound event. Use the cards, spinner, and number cube shown above. pages 422–423

Experiment: Spin the spinner and toss the cube.

9. $P(T, 2)$

10. $P(O,$ even number$)$

11. $P($vowel, 3$)$

12. $P(M, 7)$

Experiment: Pick a card without looking. Replace it. Pick another card.

13. $P($blue, red$)$

14. $P($red, yellow$)$

15. $P($red, white$)$

16. $P($purple, green$)$

Fill in each blank. Select the correct word(s) from the list at the right.

17. A(n) _____ is the set of all outcomes of an experiment.

18. Each possible result of an experiment is a(n) _____.

19. If all the outcomes are just as likely to occur, they are _____.

20. Events that have no effect on one another are _____.

21. A(n) _____ event is made up of more than one event.

Words to Know
probability
outcome
sample space
independent
equally likely
impossible
compound
relative frequency

Solve. pages 420–421

22. Richard orders his lunch from this menu: appetizers—salad or soup; entrees—sandwich, pasta, or chili. He will choose one appetizer and one entree. How many choices does he have? List them.

23. How many ways are there to go from the school to the recycling center by way of the town hall?

Exploring Problem Solving

THINK
EXPLORE
SOLVE
LOOK BACK

Which Car Has the Best Chance to Win?

You are playing a car-race game. Each car in the game has two or more numbers assigned to it. You use two number cubes, each with the digits 1 through 6 on it. The two cubes are tossed, and the digits are added. Each time a car's number comes up, the car moves a space. The race track is 10 spaces long.

Thinking Critically

Which car do you think has the best chance of winning? Work together in a small group. You may wish to use two number cubes to experiment.

Car	Car Moves When These Numbers Are Tossed
Blue	5, 2, and 3
Yellow	6 and 10
Red	4 and 7
White	9 and 11
Green	8 and 12

Analyzing and Making Decisions

1. What are the different numbers you can toss on one cube? If you toss a 1 on the first cube, can you toss a total of 6 with both cubes? How? What if you toss a 2, 3, 4, 5, or 6 on the first cube? List all the ways you can toss a total of 6 with both cubes.

2. Name all the sums you can get by tossing two cubes. How many different ways are there to get each sum? How many different ways are there to get all the possible sums?

3. Which sum do you think is the most likely to be tossed? Put the sums in order from the most likely to the least likely.

4. Which car do you think has the best chance of winning? Explain.

Look Back   Change the numbers that go with each car. Try to make the chances of winning the game as even as possible. What numbers would you put with each car?

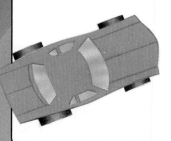

Problem Solving Strategies

Simulation

Sam and Dave have created a game with a unique method of moving from space to space. In a box there are 9 counters, each with a different number from 1 to 9 on it. A player picks a counter, records the number shown on it, and then puts it back into the box. The player then picks another counter. The player multiplies the two numbers and then moves the number of spaces shown by the left-most digit in the product. For a single-digit number, the player moves that number of spaces. What is the most likely number of spaces that a player will move?

Sometimes you can solve a problem by simulating the action with a drawing or a chart rather than acting it out.

Solving the Problem

Think   What is the question? What are the facts?

Explore   How many possible products are there? Complete the multiplication table. Record only the left-most digit of each product. What should you look for in the table?

×	1	2	3	4	5	6	7	8	9
1	1	2	3						
2			6						
3				1					
4				1		2			
5				2					
6									
7									
8									
9									8

Solve   What is the most likely number of spaces that a player will move? Explain.

Look Back   Was it necessary to count the number of occurrences of each digit? Explain.

Share Your Ideas

1. **What if** a player who gets the number 1 can take another turn? What is the probability that a player will get two 1's in a row?

Practice

 Solve. Use a calculator where appropriate.

2. Knockout is played with 6 black marbles numbered 1 to 6 and one white marble numbered 7. The marbles are arranged clockwise in consecutive order in a circle. One player going in numerical order knocks out every second marble until only one marble is left. To have the white marble left, where should a player start?

3. Fred tosses a cube with the numbers 1 through 6 on it. Jay tosses the same cube. They multiply the pair of numbers. If the product is even, Fred wins. If the product is odd, Jay wins. What is the probability that each will win?

4. To play Toss a Prime you use two cubes, each numbered from 1 to 6. You may toss one cube, or you may toss two cubes and add the numbers on them, to try to get a prime number. You take ten turns and then total the number of primes that you toss. Should you toss one or two cubes?

5. A bag contains 8 white, 7 red, and 5 blue marbles. Without looking, how many marbles can you remove and be sure there are 4 marbles of at least one color in the bag?

Mixed Strategy Review

6. There are three boxes of golf balls. One box contains only white balls, another contains only orange balls, and the third contains both white and orange balls. The boxes are labeled "white", "orange", and "white and orange", but each box is labeled incorrectly. You can determine the proper labeling for the boxes by choosing only one ball from one box. Which box is that? Explain.

7. Tanya opened a puzzle book. The first page said, "Open this book to the first two facing pages whose numbers when multiplied have a product greater than 1,000." To which pages should she open the book?

8. Six girls ran in a race. Edna finished before Carol and Fran. Barbara beat Carol. Fran was next after Barbara. Donna came in last and Agnes first. In what order did they finish?

Create **Your Own**

Write a question about a game for which the action can be simulated.

Activity

Exploring Permutations

In how many ways can you arrange these cards?

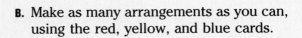

Working together

Materials: 4 cards—1 red, 1 yellow, 1 blue, 1 green

List the arrangements you make for **A–C**.

A. Make as many arrangements as you can, using the red card and the yellow card.

B. Make as many arrangements as you can, using the red, yellow, and blue cards.

C. Use the red, yellow, blue, and green cards. How many arrangements can you make?

D. Show the number of arrangements you made in a table like the one below.

Cards Used	Number of Cards Used	Number of Arrangements Made
red and yellow	2	

Sharing Your Results

1. Compare your list of arrangements with those of other groups. Do your lists agree? Are there any arrangements you found that other groups did not find? Are there any arrangements other groups found that you did not find?

2. What methods did you use to record all the arrangements?

3. How many ways are there to arrange 1 card? 2 cards? 3 cards? 4 cards?

4. What pattern is there between the number of cards and the number of arrangements of the cards?

5. Use the pattern in **4** to predict the number of ways there are to arrange 5 cards and then 6 cards. Would it be easy to verify your predictions? Explain.

Extending the Activity

▶ A **permutation** is an arrangement of items in a specific order.

You can use the Counting Principle to find the number of permutations for a given number of items. Study this example to find the number of permutations for the 4 cards on page 428.

$$4 \quad \times \quad 3 \quad \times \quad 2 \quad \times \quad 1 \quad = \quad 24$$

| choices for first card | choices for second card | choices for third card | choices for fourth card |

There are 24 ways to arrange the cards. Why are there 3 choices for the second card? 2 choices for the third card? 1 choice for the fourth card?

Work with a partner.

6. Use the Counting Principle to find the number of permutations of 6 cards and of 7 cards.

7. **What if** you wanted to find the number of permutations of the 4 cards, using only 2 at a time? Use the Counting Principle. How many permutations are there?

8. List the permutations of the 4 cards, using 2 at a time.

Use the Counting Principle to find the number of permutations for each. Use a calculator if you wish.

9. 3 cards, using 2 at a time
10. 5 cards, using 2 at a time
11. 4 cards, using 3 at a time
12. 6 cards, using 3 at a time
13. 6 cards, using 4 at a time
14. 5 cards, using 4 at a time

Summing Up

Work on your own. Use a calculator to solve. Apply what you have learned about permutations.

15. Ten runners are competing in a marathon. In how many ways can the first and second prizes be awarded?

16. Eight people are to stand in a line at the front of the classroom. In how many ways can they do this?

17. There are 7 possible commercials to be used in 3 time slots. How many possible arrangements are there?

18. Make up a problem involving permutations. Exchange problems with your partner and solve.

Exploring Combinations

How many groups of 2 cards can you make from these 4 cards?

Working together

Materials: 4 cards—1 red, 1 yellow, 1 blue, 1 green

List the cards in each group you make for **A–C**.

A. Use the red and yellow cards. Make as many groups of 1 card and of 2 cards as you can.

B. Use the red, yellow, and blue cards. Make as many groups of 1 card, of 2 cards, and of 3 cards as you can.

C. Use all four cards. Make as many groups of 1 card, of 2 cards, of 3 cards, and of 4 cards as you can.

D. Use a table like this to show the number of groups for each number of cards.

		Number of cards in each group		
		1 card	2 cards	3 cards	4 cards
Number of cards in all	2				
	3				
	4				

Sharing Your Results

1. Compare the cards in your groups with those of other classmates. Do your lists of cards agree? Explain.

2. What methods did you use to determine the cards in each group?

3. How many groups are there for each selection from 2 cards? from 3 cards? from 4 cards?

4. There is exactly 1 group of 0 cards for any number of cards. Add a column for 0 cards to the left of the one for 1 card in the table in **D**. What pattern do you see in the entries in the table? What is the sum of each row of the table?

430

Extending the Activity

▶ A **combination** is a selection of items without regard to order.

Work with a partner.

5. Use the pattern you found in **4** to predict the number of combinations for 5 cards, using only 3 at a time.

6. Add a white card to the 4 cards you used on page 430. Use the red, yellow, blue, green, and white cards to verify your prediction for **5**. List the cards in each combination.

Use the pattern from 4 to find the number of combinations.

7. 5 cards, using 2 at a time   **8.** 6 cards, using 3 at a time

9. 6 cards, using 4 at a time   **10.** 5 cards, using 4 at a time

Summing Up

Look back at the combinations you found above and the permutations you found on page 429. Compare the number of permutations with the number of combinations for each.

11. 4 cards, using 2 at a time   **12.** 4 cards, using 3 at a time

13. 5 cards, using 2 at a time   **14.** 6 cards, using 4 at a time

15. Which would you expect to be greater—the number of permutations or the number of combinations of 10 things, using 3 at a time? Why?

Work on your own. Apply what you have learned about combinations and permutations.

16. You have 6 sweaters. You are packing 2 of them to take on vacation. How many different choices do you have?

17. How many different selections of 3 posters can you buy from 4 posters that are for sale? In how many ways can you arrange the 3 posters across a wall in your room?

18. How many different groups of 5 singers can be chosen from 8 people auditioning for the parts?

19. Make up a problem involving combinations or permutations. Exchange problems with your partner and solve.

Using Problem Solving

Is It Wise to Guess?

A question from a multiple choice test appears below. On this test, a student receives 1 point for each correct response, 0 points for no response, and loses $\frac{1}{4}$ point for each incorrect response.

The American Revolution lasted how many years?

a. 4 years **b.** 10 years **c.** 8 years **d.** 1 year **e.** not given

A. If there are 5 possible answers, and you take a random guess, what is the probability that you will guess the correct answer? What is the probability that you will answer the question incorrectly?

B. What if there are 5 questions that you do not know? You take a random guess on each question. On the average, about how many will you get right? How many will you get wrong? What score will you get on these 5 questions?

C. What if you guessed randomly at 100 questions like the one above? On the average, about how many questions would you probably answer correctly? On the average, about how many would you guess incorrectly? What would your score be? **What if** there were no penalty for incorrect responses? What would your score be?

Sharing Your Ideas

1. Why, do you think, would a testmaker penalize a student $\frac{1}{4}$ point for each incorrect response? Why would they not penalize a student for not answering a question?

2. **What if** on a 100-question test you knew the answers for 75 questions and did not know the answers for 25 questions? Would it make sense to guess on the 25? Explain.

3. How long did the American Revolution last? What do you think the probability is that you are correct?

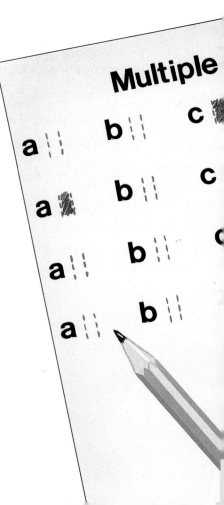

Extending Your Thinking

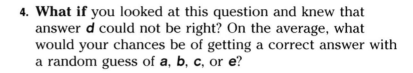

Where was the Battle of Bunker Hill fought?

a. Bunker Hill   **b.** Breed's Hill   **c.** Revolutionary Hill

d. Mt. Everest   **e.** not given

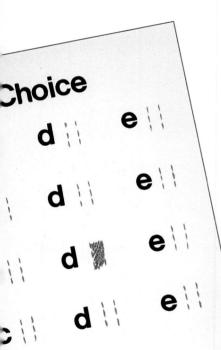

4. **What if** you looked at this question and knew that answer **d** could not be right? On the average, what would your chances be of getting a correct answer with a random guess of **a**, **b**, **c**, or **e**?

5. **What if** you took a 100-question test and could eliminate one possible answer as not correct? On the average, how many questions would you probably answer correctly? What would your score be? How does that compare with your score when you selected from 5 possible choices?

6. **What if** you could eliminate 1 more answer, **c**, leaving only 3 choices? On the average, how would you score on the 100-question test now?

7. **What if** you knew the answer was between only 2 choices, **a** and **b**? On the average, how would you score on the 100-question test now?

8. Where do you think the Battle of Bunker Hill was fought? What is the probability that you are correct?

Summing Up

9. If you were teaching a class on how to improve scores on multiple choice tests, what would you tell your students about guessing? Explain.

10. Why, do you think, do testmakers include the response "not given"?

11. **What if** you made a test for which each question had only 4 possible answers? How many points would you take off for an incorrect guess?

Chapter Review

Find the probability of each event. Use the cards, spinner, and marbles shown here. pages 418–419, 422–423

Experiment: Draw a card.

1. Event: Draw a 3.

2. Event: Draw an even number.

Experiment: Spin the spinner.

3. Event: Spin a number.

4. Event: Spin an F.

Experiment: Spin the spinner and pick a marble.

5. P(number, red)   6. P(letter, orange)   7. P(vowel, green)   8. P(S, yellow)

Experiment: Draw a card. Replace it. Draw another card.

9. $P(1, 1)$ 10. $P(2, 4)$ 11. $P(0, 5)$ 12. P(two numbers < 5)

How many different choices or outcomes are possible? pages 420–421

13. The spinner above is spun and then a number cube is tossed.

14. Jack chooses 1 shirt and 1 tie from 5 shirts and 4 ties that match.

15. A letter from the alphabet is chosen and a coin is flipped.

16. Kesha chooses 1 ring and 1 necklace from 5 rings and 3 necklaces.

Use the Counting Principle to find the number of permutations for each number of cards, each a different color. pages 428–429

17. 3 cards   18. 4 cards   19. 5 cards   20. 6 cards

21. 3 cards, using 2 at a time   22. 5 cards, using 3 at a time

Find the number of combinations for each. pages 430–431

23. 3 cards, using 2 at a time   24. 5 cards, using 3 at a time

25. 4 cards, using 2 at a time   26. 6 cards, using 5 at a time

Solve. pages 425–427, 432–433

27. In seventh grade Bert can take painting or sculpture. In eighth grade he can take silk-screening, woodcutting, or jewelry making. How many different art programs can Bert choose for seventh and eighth grades?

28. Four cubes just fit in a row in a box. The green one is next to and at the right of the red one, which is farthest to the left. The blue one is at the right of the yellow one. List the cubes in order.

Chapter Test

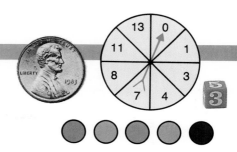

Give the sample space for each experiment. Use the spinner, marbles, coin, and cube at the right.

1. Roll a number cube.
2. Spin the spinner.
3. Pick a marble and flip a coin.
4. Flip a coin twice.

Find each probability. Use the spinner and marbles at the right.

Experiment: Draw a marble.
5. *P*(blue marble)

Experiment: Spin the spinner.
6. *P*(number < 15)

Experiment: Spin the spinner and flip a coin.
7. *P*(even number, heads)

8. *P*(number < 15, tails)

Experiment: Pick a marble and spin the spinner.
9. *P*(red marble, prime number)

10. *P*(yellow marble, 8)

How many different choices or outcomes are possible?

11. Choose 1 kind of bread and 1 kind of soup from rye, wheat, or brown bread, and chicken, tomato, or lentil soup.

12. Spin the spinner above and draw a card from a deck containing 1 red, 1 blue, 1 purple, 1 green, and 1 white card.

Find the number of permutations for each.

13. 4 people, chosen 3 at a time

14. 4 people, chosen 4 at a time

Find the number of combinations for each.

15. 4 people, chosen 3 at a time

16. 5 people, chosen 2 at a time

Solve.

17. Marianne is displaying 4 photos by pairs. How many different pairs can she display?

18. Two names are chosen from 5 placed in a hat. *Jane* is one of them. The first name is replaced. What is the probability of drawing *Jane* twice?

19. To raise money, Help for the Homeless is selling packages of 1 calendar and 1 roll of wrapping paper. There are 2 kinds of calendars and 7 kinds of wrapping paper. How many different packages are possible?

20. Annelie enters her father's office building on the ground floor. She goes down 1 floor to the bookstore, then goes up 12 floors before going down 3 floors to his office. On what floor is the office?

THINK   The police department is distributing bicycle tags. Each tag has a three-digit number. What is the probability that your number will end in 0 or 3?

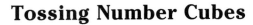

Computer Link

Tossing Number Cubes

When you toss a number cube, what is the probability of tossing 2? 5? a number less than 3? a number that is not 1?

AT THE COMPUTER

Materials: Logo

A. Define the TOSS procedure that outputs a random number from 1 to 6. Use it to simulate tossing a number cube by entering PR TOSS several times. Does one number print more often than another?

```
TO TOSS
OP 1 + RANDOM 6
END
```

B. Define the procedure COUNTIT. Enter COUNTIT 1 to find the number of times out of 120 that the outcome is 1.

```
TO COUNTIT :N
MAKE "COUNT O
REPEAT 120 [IF TOSS = :N [MAKE "COUNT :COUNT + 1]]
PRINT :COUNT
END
```

C. Use COUNTIT to find the number of times each outcome occurs out of 120 times. You may have to change = in the third line of the procedure to < or >.

- P(5)   • P(2)   • P(number less than 3)   • P(not 1)

D. Use the TOSS and COUNTIT procedures to simulate tossing a 6-sided pencil. Predict how many times the trademark will not land on top. Compare your prediction and your results.

Sharing Your Results

1. Explain how probability relates to your results in **B**.

2. Compare tossing a number cube with tossing a pencil. How are the experiments the same? How are they different?

Extending the Activity

What if you toss two number cubes? Do you get one sum more often than another? You can use Logo to find out.

3. Modify the procedure TOSS so that it simulates tossing 2 number cubes. What sums are possible? Enter PR TOSS several times. Do you get one sum more often than another?

```
TO TOSS
OP (1 + RANDOM 6) + (1 + RANDOM 6)
END
```

4. Choose any one of the possible sums and use the COUNTIT procedure to tally how many times that sum is tossed out of 144 tosses. Record your work.

5. Use the COUNTIT procedure to find the number of times each of the other possible sums is tossed out of 144 tosses. Compare the results for each sum.

6. What sum did you get the greatest number of times? Why do you think that happened?

7. What sum did you get the least number of times? Explain.

Summing Up

8. Complete the chart to list all possible outcomes when tossing two number cubes. Then find the probability of tossing each sum.

SUM OF TWO NUMBER CUBES						
	1	2	3	4	5	6
1						
2						
3						
4						
5						
6						

9. Use the probability of tossing each sum to predict how many times out of 144 tosses you might expect to toss each sum. Then compare your predictions to your results from **4** and **5**. What do you notice?

10. What is the total of the probabilities for all possible outcomes? Why?

Random Walks!

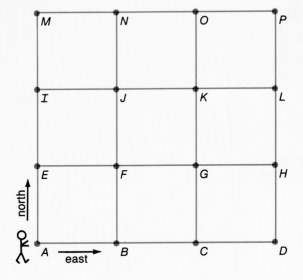

Ray takes his daily walk in the park pictured at the right. He likes to walk a different route each day. When he reaches an intersection, he randomly chooses to walk north or east.

List all the ways to reach each intersection if Ray starts at *A*. For example, here are the ways to go from *A* to *K*.

E N N E	N E E N
E N E N	N E N E
E E N N	N N E E

1. How many ways did you find to walk from *A* to *M*? to *N*? to *P*?

It takes Ray 1 minute to walk from intersection to intersection.

2. How long does it take Ray to walk from *A* to *P*?

3. Which intersections can he reach in exactly 3 minutes?

4. What is the probability that a 3-minute walk will end at *J*? at *M*?

5. After walking for 4 minutes, what is the probability that Ray arrives at *N*? at *L*?

Maintaining Skills

Choose the correct answers. Write A, B, C, or D.

1. What is 25% of 85?

　A 3.4　　　　　　　**C** 63.75

　B 21.25　　　　　　**D** not given

2. 630 is what percent of 210?

　A $33\frac{1}{3}\%$　　　　　　**C** 300%

　B $66\frac{2}{3}\%$　　　　　　**D** not given

3. 92% of what number is 138?

　A 150　　　　　　　**C** 126.96

　B 46　　　　　　　　**D** not given

4. What is the area?

　4.5 cm

　8.1 cm

　A 12.6 cm^2　　　　**C** 25.2 cm^2

　B 36.45 cm^2　　　**D** not given

5. What is the area of a circle with $d = 8.4$ ft? Use $\pi \approx 3.14$. Round to the nearest tenth.

　A 55.4 ft^2　　　　**C** 26.4 ft^2

　B 13.2 ft^2　　　　**D** not given

6. What is the volume of a cylinder with $r = 4$ in. and $h = 10$ in.? Use $\pi \approx 3.14$. Round to the nearest tenth.

　A 1,256 in.^{3}　　　**C** 502.4 in.^{3}

　B 125.6 in.^{3}　　　**D** not given

7. Compare. $^-15$ ⬤ $^-10$

　A <　　　　　　　　**C** =

　B >　　　　　　　　**D** not given

8. $^-4 - 9$

　A 4　　　　　　　　**C** $^-5$

　B $^-13$　　　　　　**D** not given

9. $^-3 \cdot {}^-10$

　A $^-13$　　　　　　**C** $^-3$

　B 30　　　　　　　　**D** not given

10. Solve for n. $8 + n = {}^-12$

　A 4　　　　　　　　**C** $^-20$

　B $^-4$　　　　　　　**D** not given

11. How many possible outcomes are there for tossing 2 coins?

　A 2　　　　　　　　**C** 8

　B 4　　　　　　　　**D** not given

12. If you toss two number cubes, what is $P(\text{sum of } 3)$?

　A $\frac{1}{12}$　　　　　　　**C** $\frac{1}{18}$

　B $\frac{1}{36}$　　　　　　　**D** not given

Solve.

Sue, Betty, Carolyn, and Allyse are sisters. Their ages are 16, 15, 12, and 10. Betty is older than Allyse. Sue is one year older than Betty. The sum of Allyse's and Sue's ages is 26.

13. How old is Carolyn?

　A 16　　　　　　　**C** 15

　B 10　　　　　　　**D** not given

14. Marci places fence posts in a line, one every 3 feet. The distance from the first fence post to the last is 90 feet. How many fence posts does she use?

　A 31　　　　　　　**C** 29

　B 30　　　　　　　**D** not given

14 Geometry • Construction

Sharing What You Know

What kind of art interests you? Do you like art that stands still, or do you like art that moves? Alexander Calder created both types of art. Look at the photographs of Calder's mobile. Which part of this moving sculpture is the most interesting to you? Discuss how works of art such as these use geometry.

Using Language

You might like one segment of Calder's mobile, and your friend may prefer a different part. A **segment** is one part of a whole. In the study of mathematics, a **line segment** is a part of a line. It has two endpoints. How is a segment of a work of art like a line segment? How is it different?

Words to Know: line segment, bisect, perpendicular, congruent, angle, perpendicular bisector, Pythagorean Rule

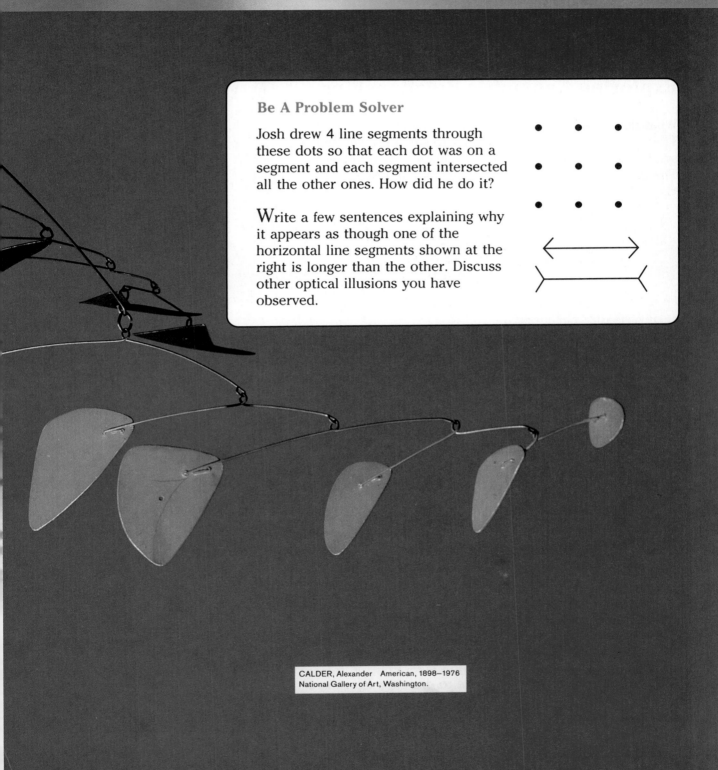

Be A Problem Solver

Josh drew 4 line segments through these dots so that each dot was on a segment and each segment intersected all the other ones. How did he do it?

Write a few sentences explaining why it appears as though one of the horizontal line segments shown at the right is longer than the other. Discuss other optical illusions you have observed.

CALDER, Alexander   American, 1898–1976
National Gallery of Art, Washington.

441

Activity

Exploring Geometric Relationships

What do you see when you look at this picture? Be careful! There are two ladies here! In order to see both, you must see the parts of the picture in two different relationships. The ability to see many relationships is important in visualizing geometric figures.

Working together

First try to visualize each figure. Then make the drawing.

Materials: ruler, compass

A. Copy points *P* and *Q*. Then draw the shortest path from *P* to *Q*.

B. Copy point *R* and line *ST*. Then draw the shortest path from *R* to $\overleftrightarrow{ST}$.

C. Copy point *V*. Draw all points 1 cm from *V*.

D. Write a sentence describing each figure you drew in **A–C**.

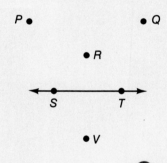

Sharing Your Results

1. Compare your drawings with those of other groups. Did everyone sketch the same figures? If not, how are the drawings different?

2. **Look back** at **B**. Label the point *W* where the path intersects $\overleftrightarrow{ST}$. What is the relationship between $\overleftrightarrow{RW}$ and $\overleftrightarrow{ST}$?

3. What instrument would you use to draw the figure in **C**?

4. Exchange descriptions from **D** with another group. Use the descriptions to draw the three figures. If you cannot draw a figure, explain why. Compare your drawings with those of the other groups.

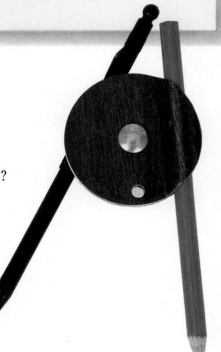

Extending the Activity

Work in a group. One person should do E, one F, and one G. First try to visualize each figure. Then make the drawing.

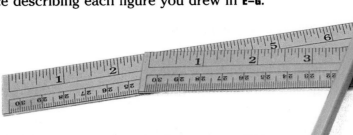

E. This is the shortest path from *L* to *M*. Draw all points that are 1 cm from segment *LM*.

F. This is all points 1 cm from point *K*. Draw all points 1 cm from circle *K*.

G. Copy points *X* and *Y*. The distance from *X* to *Y* is 2 cm. Draw all points that are both 2 cm from *X* and 3 cm from *Y*.

H. Write a sentence describing each figure you drew in **E–G**.

5. Compare your drawings with those of other groups. Did everyone draw the same figures? If not, how are the drawings different?

6. Look back at **F**. How would your drawing differ if circle *K* had a radius of 0.75 cm?

7. Look back at **G**. **What if** $\overline{XY}$ was 1 cm long? How would your drawing of the points 2 cm from *X* and 3 cm from *Y* differ? First try to visualize. Then make a drawing.

8. What if $\overline{XY}$ was 2 cm, as shown in **G**, but you drew the points that were both 2 cm from *X* and 5 cm from *Y*? How would your drawing differ from the one in **G**? First try to visualize. Then make a drawing.

Summing Up

9. In each of **A–C** and **E–G** was the figure you visualized the same as the one you drew? How were they alike? How were they different?

10. Look back at **7–8**. Were you able to visualize each figure before you drew it? Why or why not?

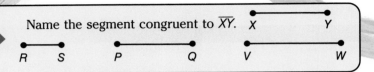

Constructing Congruent Segments and Angles

You use a compass and a straightedge to construct figures—for example, a segment congruent to a given segment, such as $\overline{JH}$.

J ●————————● H

Draw any segment, $\overline{MS}$, longer than $\overline{JH}$.	Place the compass tip on J and draw an arc through H.	Use the same compass opening. Place the compass tip on M. Draw an arc intersecting $\overline{MS}$. Label N. $\overline{MN} \cong \overline{JH}$
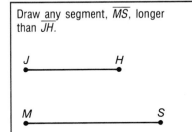		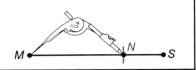

How do you know that segment MN is congruent to segment JH?

You can also construct an angle congruent to a given angle, for example, $\angle POR$, using only a compass and a straightedge.

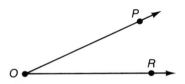

Draw any ray, $\overrightarrow{FG}$. Place the compass tip on F and draw an arc intersecting $\overrightarrow{FG}$. Label C.	Using the same compass opening, place the tip on O and draw an arc intersecting both rays. Label X and Y. Place the tip on Y. Adjust the compass to draw an arc through X.	Using the same compass opening, place the tip on C and draw a second arc intersecting the first. Label B. Draw $\overrightarrow{FB}$. $\angle POR \cong \angle BFC$
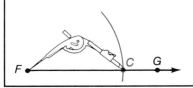	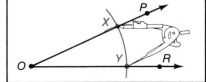	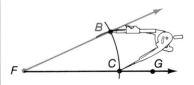

How do you know that $\angle POR$ is congruent to $\angle BFC$?

Check Your Understanding

Trace each figure. Then construct a figure congruent to each.

1.

2.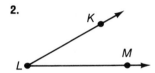

3.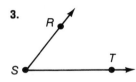

4.

Share Your Ideas Can the method described above be used to copy any angle—acute, right, obtuse, straight, reflex?

444

Trace each figure. Then construct a figure congruent to each.

5.

6.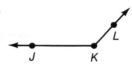

7.

8.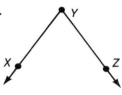

Use a ruler to draw a segment with the given length. Then construct a segment congruent to each.

9. 5 cm

10. 6 cm

11. 7 cm

12. 8.5 cm

13. 78 mm

Use a protractor to draw an angle with the given measure. Then construct an angle congruent to each.

14. 40°

15. 22°

16. 90°

17. 146°

18. 268°

Think and Apply

Use a compass and a straightedge to construct each triangle congruent to △RST.

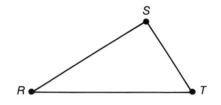

19. Construct each of the following.

- ∠C congruent to ∠R
- $\overline{CE}$ congruent to $\overline{RT}$
- ∠E congruent to ∠T

Label vertex D where $\overrightarrow{CD}$ intersects $\overrightarrow{ED}$.
Is △CDE ≅ △RST? How do you know?

20. Construct each of the following.

- $\overline{GF}$ congruent to $\overline{SR}$
- ∠F congruent to ∠R
- $\overline{FH}$ congruent to $\overline{RT}$

Draw $\overline{GH}$. Is △FGH ≅ △RST? How do you know?

21. Construct each of the following.

- $\overline{JK}$ congruent to $\overline{RS}$
- With the tip of your compass on R, draw an arc through T. Using the same setting, place the tip on J and draw an arc.
- With the tip of your compass on S, draw an arc through T. Using the same setting, place the tip on K and draw an arc that passes through the first arc.

Label the point of intersection L.
Is △JKL ≅ △RST? How do you know?

Describe the difference between drawing or sketching a figure and constructing a figure.

SUMMING UP

Bisecting Segments and Angles

Copy $\overline{XY}$ and $\angle TUV$ on a piece of paper.

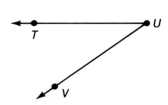

- Fold the paper so that X and Y touch. Unfold the paper. Label the point on $\overline{XY}$ at the fold Z. Describe the relationship between $\overline{XZ}$ and $\overline{ZY}$.
- Fold the paper so that $\overrightarrow{UT}$ lies on $\overrightarrow{UV}$. Unfold the paper. Draw $\overrightarrow{US}$ along the fold between $\overrightarrow{UT}$ and $\overrightarrow{UV}$. Describe the relationship between $\angle TUS$ and $\angle VUS$.

You can use a compass and a straightedge to bisect a segment or an angle. A **bisector** divides a figure into two congruent parts.

A.		
Open the compass to slightly more than half the length of $\overline{RQ}$. With the tip on R, draw an arc intersecting $\overline{RQ}$.	Use the same compass opening. With the tip on Q, draw an arc intersecting $\overline{RQ}$. Label D and S.	Draw $\overrightarrow{DS}$. Label T. T is the midpoint of $\overline{RQ}$. $\overrightarrow{DS}$ is the **perpendicular bisector** of $\overline{RQ}$.
B.		
With the compass tip on Y, draw an arc intersecting both rays. Label B and E. 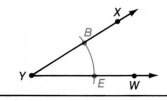	With the compass tip on B, draw a second arc as shown. 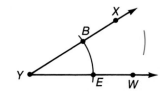	Use the same compass opening. Place the tip on E. Draw a third arc as shown. Label D. Draw $\overrightarrow{YD}$. $\overrightarrow{YD}$ is the **angle bisector** of $\angle XYW$. 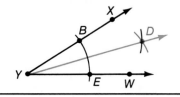

Check Your Understanding

Trace each figure. Then construct the bisector.

1.
2.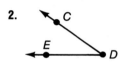
3.
4.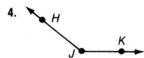

Share Your Ideas Look back at **A**. How is $\overline{RT}$ related to $\overline{TQ}$? How do you know? Look back at **B**. How is $\angle XYD$ related to $\angle WYD$? How do you know?

Trace each figure. Then construct the bisector.

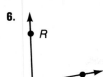

5. P Q   6. R N T   7. U V   8. S R T

Each construction has been done incorrectly. What is wrong?

9.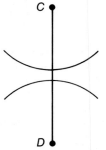
C
D

10.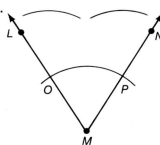
L N O P M

11.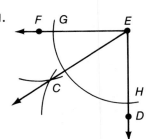
F G E C H D

12.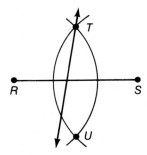
T R S U

13. Draw a segment 6 cm long. Label the endpoints A and B. Bisect the segment. Locate any point on the perpendicular bisector but not on $\overline{AB}$. Label it C. Draw $\overline{AC}$ and $\overline{BC}$. What kind of triangle is △ACB?

14. Draw a segment 4 cm long. Label the endpoints F and G. Open your compass to 4 cm. Use this opening to bisect $\overline{FG}$. Label H, one of the points where the two arcs intersect. Draw $\overline{FH}$ and $\overline{GH}$. What kind of triangle is △FHG?

How could you construct the perpendicular bisector of a segment or the bisector of an angle without a compass and straightedge?

Mixed Review

1. 9,976.4 − 103.47

2. $11\frac{4}{7} - 9\frac{6}{7}$

3. $7\frac{3}{8} \times 4\frac{1}{4}$

4. 104.3 × 9.72

5. 10.327 + 46.99

6. $4.32\overline{)9.6552}$

7. $26\frac{7}{8} \div 8\frac{3}{4}$

8. $82\frac{7}{11} + 103\frac{10}{11}$

9. 11% of 92

10. 19 is what percent of 40?

11. 45 is 27% of what number?

12. 83% of 1,700

13. 9 is what percent of 2?

Compare. Use >, <, or =.

14. $\frac{2}{3}$ ● $\frac{1}{2}$

15. 0.456 ● 0.45

16. $4\frac{2}{6}$ ● $4\frac{1}{3}$

17. $\frac{7}{18}$ ● $\frac{1}{2}$

18. $\frac{5}{9}$ ● $\frac{5}{6}$

SUMMING UP

447

Identify all perpendicular lines in this figure.

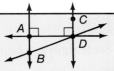

Constructing Perpendicular Lines

This painting, *New York City (1940–41),* by the twentieth-century Dutch painter Piet Mondrian, has many perpendicular lines, which he had to construct to make the painting.

Giraudon/Art Resource

You can construct perpendicular lines, using a compass and a straightedge. To construct a line perpendicular to a given line through a point on the line, follow these steps.

Place the compass tip on *P*. Draw two arcs that intersect the line, using the same compass opening. Label *H* and *N*. 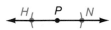	Bisect $\overline{HN}$. Label *R*. $\overleftrightarrow{RP} \perp \overleftrightarrow{HN}$ $\overleftrightarrow{RP}$ is the **perpendicular bisector** of $\overline{HN}$. 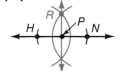

How do you know that $\overleftrightarrow{RP} \perp \overleftrightarrow{HN}$?

You can also construct a line perpendicular to a given line through a point not on the line.

Open the compass to slightly more than the distance from *B* to the line. With the tip on *B*, draw an arc intersecting the line at two points. Label *S* and *T*.	With the compass tip on *S*, draw a second arc on the same side of the line. Using the same opening, place the tip on *T* and draw a third arc as shown. Label *X*.	Draw $\overleftrightarrow{BX}$. $\overleftrightarrow{BX} \perp \overleftrightarrow{ST}$

Trace each figure.

1. Construct a line perpendicular to $\overleftrightarrow{CD}$ through *Q*.

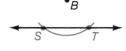

2. Construct a line perpendicular to $\overleftrightarrow{GH}$ through *P*.

Share Your Ideas Look back at the construction of the line perpendicular to $\overleftrightarrow{ST}$ through point *B*. How do you know that $\overleftrightarrow{BX} \perp \overleftrightarrow{ST}$?

448

Trace each figure.

3. Construct a line perpendicular to $\overleftrightarrow{PT}$ through A.

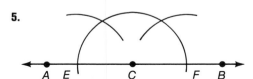

4. Construct a line perpendicular to $\overleftrightarrow{MR}$ through M.

Each construction has been done incorrectly. What is wrong?

5.

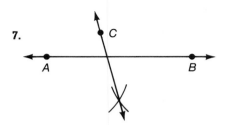

6.

7.

8.

Trace the figure.

9. Construct $\overleftrightarrow{CD}$ perpendicular to $\overleftrightarrow{AC}$.

10. Construct $\overleftrightarrow{BE}$ perpendicular to $\overleftrightarrow{AC}$.

11. What is the relationship between $\overleftrightarrow{CD}$ and $\overleftrightarrow{BE}$?

Think and Apply

12. Copy $\overline{AB}$. Then proceed as follows.

- Construct a line perpendicular to $\overline{AB}$ at A. On the line, mark off $\overline{AF}$ the same length as $\overline{CD}$.
- Construct a line perpendicular to $\overline{AB}$ at B. On the line, mark off $\overline{BG}$ the same length as $\overline{CD}$, on the same side of $\overline{AB}$ as $\overline{AF}$.
- Draw $\overline{FG}$.
  Name the figure you have constructed. What is the measure of each angle?

Visual Thinking

Find the point that is the same distance from each of the two given points.

13. A and B   **14.** P and B

15. B and S   **16.** A and M

How could you construct a line perpendicular to a given line and through a given point without a compass and straightedge?

Midchapter Review

Trace each segment or angle. Then construct a congruent figure. pages 444–445

1.

2.

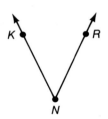

3.

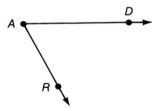

Trace each segment or angle. Then use a straightedge and compass to bisect it. pages 446–447

4.

5.

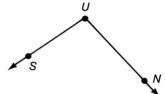

6.

Trace each figure. pages 448–449

7. Construct a line perpendicular to $\overleftrightarrow{DF}$ through *M*.

8. Construct a line perpendicular to $\overleftrightarrow{VX}$ through *P*.

Match each word in column A with its definition in column B.

A

9. bisect

10. perpendicular

11. congruent

12. angle

13. perpendicular bisector

B

a. a line that divides a segment into two congruent parts and is perpendicular to the segment

b. two rays with a common endpoint

c. to divide into two congruent parts

d. intersecting to form right angles

e. having the same size and shape

Solve. pages 442–443

14. Copy this figure. Then construct the shortest path from *P* to $\overleftrightarrow{QR}$.

15. Copy this figure of Red and his 3-m leash. Then construct the boundary of Red's "run."

Exploring Problem Solving

Reductions and Expansions

This map is being made into a poster. On the poster, the map will have a diameter twice as long as the one here.

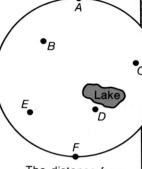

The distance from A to F is $1\frac{3}{4}$ in.

Thinking Critically

Make a map that has a diameter that is twice as long as the original. Make sure that all the cities appear in the same relative position. A ruler, a protractor, a compass, and unlined paper or Workmat 6 will be useful.

Analyzing and Making Decisions

1. If you make a new circle with a diameter twice as long as the one on this page, how long will the diameter be? How long will the radius be? Would it help if you knew that a line from City A to City F would pass through the center of the circle? Explain. Make a new map that has a diameter that is twice as long as this one.

2. What difficulties could you experience in trying to put the cities in their same relative positions? How can you put them in their positions on the new map?

3. Explain how to place cities A and F on the map. Then place them.

4. Trace the smaller map or use Workmat 6. Draw a line between City A and City F. Connect point B to points A and F. What figure did you make? How can you reproduce that figure on the larger map so you can place City B?

5. Place all the cities in their same relative positions on your map. How did you determine where to place them?

Look Back How can you accurately place the lake on the new map? Try it.

Problem Solving Strategies

Solving a Simpler Problem

An artist has been asked to make a model of an ancient ruin for a museum. She will use 4 wooden blocks for each column. To form an arch, she puts 1 block at the top of 2 columns.

How many blocks will she need to make 46 arches?

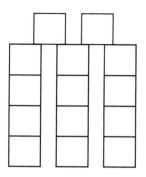

When a problem appears too difficult to solve immediately, sometimes you can solve a simpler problem. This may help you see a pattern or a formula.

Solving the Problem

Think   What do you need to find out? What are the facts?

Explore   How many blocks are needed to form one arch? two arches? three arches? Make a table. Continue the table for at least 5 arches. What pattern do you see?

Solve   How many blocks does she need?

Look Back   Write a rule so that you can find the number of blocks needed for any number of arches.

Share Your Ideas

1. **What if** you needed 3 blocks at the top of two columns? How would that change your rule?

Practice

CHOICES **Solve. Use a calculator where appropriate.**

2. An artist is sketching a stained glass window. He has sketched three sections, showing the pieces of glass needed. If there are 10 sections, how many pieces of stained glass are needed?

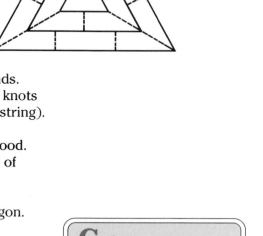

3. An artist was making a sculpture, using odds and ends. She tied 136 pieces of string end to end. How many knots did she need to tie? (Hint: Try 2, 3, and 4 pieces of string).

4. An artist made an 8-sided polygon, using pieces of wood. Wire was strung for each diagonal. How many pieces of wire were needed to make the diagonals?

5. The same artist made 14 diagonals for another polygon. This polygon had how many sides?

Mixed Strategy Review

6. On a vacation to the Southwest, the Thompsons visited four ancient Zuni Indian sites. They found four types of pottery. They learned that when one settlement is found on top of another, it was built later than the one beneath it. They saw the following sites.

Site 1   One settlement with both Type A and Type B pottery

Site 2   One settlement with both Type B and Type C pottery

Site 3   Two settlements were found. The bottom settlement contained Type C pottery. The top settlement contained Type A pottery.

Site 4   One settlement with both Type A and Type D pottery

List the pottery types from oldest to newest.

Create Your Own

Use the information in the drawing to write a problem.

Use these drawings to solve 7 and 8.

7. Select one figure that does not belong and explain why.

8. Look at all the figures again. Select a different figure that does not belong. Explain why.

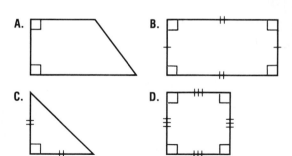

453

Activity

Exploring Squares and Square Roots

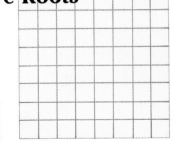

What is the area of this square?
What is the length of each side?

If you know the length of a side of a square, how can you find its area?

What if you know the area of a square? How can you find the length of a side of the square?

Working together

Work in a group of three. One person should build the square. One person should sketch the square on grid paper. One person should record the results. Change roles occasionally so that each person has a chance to build, sketch, and record.

Materials: base-ten blocks (hundreds, tens, and ones), grid paper

A. Using base-ten blocks, build a square with each of the following sides.
    (1) 9 units   **(2)** 12 units   **(3)** 15 units

B. Use each number of blocks to build the largest possible square.
    (1) 121   **(2)** 156   **(3)** 196   **(4)** 260

C. Record your results in a table like this.

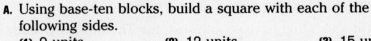

Length of side of square	Area of square

Sharing Your Results

1. Look back at **B.** Did you use *all* the blocks to build each square?

2. Did you ever have any blocks left over?

3. Given any number of blocks, can you always build a square, using *all* the blocks? Why or why not?

4. What relationship do you see between the length of each side of a square and the area of the square?

Extending the Activity

The **square** of a number n, written n^2, is that number multiplied by itself.

> The square of 8 is 64. $8^2 = 64$

Perfect squares are squares of whole numbers.

> 1, 4, 9, 16, 25, 36, 49, 64, 81, 100, . . . are perfect squares.

The **square root** of a number n, written $\sqrt{n}$, is a number that when multiplied by itself equals n.

> The square root of 64 is 8. $\sqrt{64} = 8$

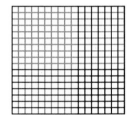

Work in your group.

5. This model shows 289.

   a. What is $\sqrt{289}$? How do you know?
   b. What is 17^2? Explain how the model shows this.

Give the number and the square root of the number shown by each model of base-ten blocks below.

6.

7.

8.

Find each. Use a model to verify each answer.

9. $\sqrt{169}$ **10.** 14^2 **11.** 16^2 **12.** $\sqrt{324}$ **13.** 20^2

Summing Up

A table of squares and square roots appears on page 520. To find the square or square root of a number, you might use this table, mental math, or a calculator.

Choose the best way to find each of the following. Explain your choices.

14. 48^2 **15.** $\sqrt{49}$ **16.** $\sqrt{8,281}$ **17.** 265^2 **18.** $\sqrt{30,625}$ **19.** 11^2

Activity

Exploring the Pythagorean Rule

This 3,000-year-old mural shows some of the tools ancient Egyptians used. One is a rope with 12 equidistant knots. A surveyor could mark off a piece of land by pulling the rope into a triangle with sides measuring 3, 4, and 5 units. What kind of triangle would this form?

Egyptian Expedition of the Metropolitan Museum of Art, Rogers Fund, 1930. (30.4.44)

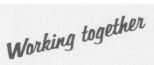

Materials: base-ten blocks, Workmat 7

A. Construct two perpendicular rays. Using base-ten blocks, arrange 9 blocks and 16 blocks each in a square as shown. Draw the triangle formed by these squares.

B. Rearrange the blocks in the two squares to form a square along the third side of the triangle. Is a side of the square the same length as the side of the triangle?

C. Repeat the procedure in **A** and **B** for the following numbers of blocks.

(1) 25 and 144 **(2)** 36 and 64 **(3)** 64 and 225

D. Record your results in a table like this.

Length of each side			Area of the square along each side		
a	b	c	a	b	c

Sharing Your Results

1. Were you always able to form a square on the third side of each triangle? What kind of triangle did you form?

2. What is the relationship between each side measure and the area of the square along that side?

3. What is the relationship between the area of the squares along both shorter sides and the area of the square along the longest side?

Extending the Activity

In the sixth century B.C., Pythagoras proved that for any right triangle, the sum of the square of the measures of the two legs equals the square of the measure of the hypotenuse. The **hypotenuse** is the side opposite the right angle.

Let a and b be the measures of the legs and c be the measure of the hypotenuse.

$$a^2 + b^2 = c^2$$

This is called the **Pythagorean Rule.**

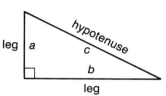

If the sides of a triangle satisfy the Pythagorean Rule, then the triangle is a right triangle.

$$a^2 + b^2 = c^2$$

$$3^2 + 4^2 \bullet 5^2$$

$9 + 16 = 25$, so $3^2 + 4^2 = 5^2$.

$\triangle ABC$ is a right triangle.

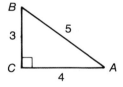

Work with a partner to find whether each triangle is a right triangle. Explain your reasoning.

4.

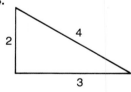

5.

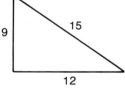

6.

7.

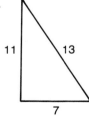

Summing Up

8. Explain how your models in **A–C** on page 456 show the Pythagorean Rule.

9. Explain how you could use the Pythagorean Rule to find the missing measure of right triangle PQR. What is the length of the hypotenuse?

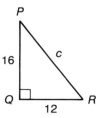

10. Explain how you could use the Pythagorean Rule to find the missing measure of right triangle XYZ. What is the length of $\overline{XZ}$?

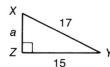

457

Using Problem Solving

Interview: Calculators and Art

Maryann Hancock is the art director for juvenile books at a publishing house. "In designing a book, it is important to lay out the pages so that they are both attractive and informative. Pictures and text must work together to create a unified page that communicates well to the reader," Maryann said to a visitor.

Pictures can be enlarged or reduced to fit in a space. To decide whether a picture will fit well in the space. Maryann draws a diagonal through the space. She then puts the picture in the corner of the space. The closer the opposite corner of the picture comes to the diagonal, the better the fit.

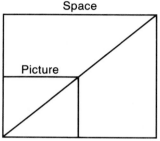

Use a ruler and the method above to solve.

A. Maryann has a picture that is 8 in. by 5 in. She has arranged the page in three different ways. One arrangement gives her a space that is 7 in. by 2 in., another, space that is 5 in. by 2.5 in., and another, space that is 4 in. by 4 in. Which space has the best proportion for the picture?

B. Maryann has the following pictures and available spaces for them.

Picture Size	Available Space
6 in. × 5 in.	3 in. × 3 in.
9 in. × 6 in.	6 in. × 4 in.
4 in. × 3 in.	5 in. × 4 in.

Which picture would you put in which space? Explain.

Sharing Your Ideas

1. Why does drawing a diagonal through the space make it possible to determine whether a picture will fit?

Practice

Once it has been decided where a picture will be placed, the photographer must be told how much to enlarge or reduce the photo. If a 9–in. × 6–in. picture is being put into a 4–in. × 3–in. space, the designer determines how much the photo needs to be reduced.

Maryann said, "We formerly used a proportion wheel. Now we use a calculator to do these calculations. I will divide 4 by 9 and find that I need to reduce the picture to about 44% of its original size. Then I will find 44% of 6 in., which is 2.64 in. So the picture will fit. I tell the photographer to reduce the photo to 44% of its original size. The photo that goes into the book will be about 4 in. × 2.6 in."

Solve. Use a calculator.

What directions would you give the photographer for reducing or enlarging these pictures? What will be the measurements of the reduced or enlarged pictures?

Picture Size	Space Size
2. 11 in. × 6 in.	6 in. × 4 in.
3. 14.5 in. × 11.75 in.	8 in. × 6 in.
4. 5 in. × 3 in.	8 in. × 6 in.
5. 9 in. × 6 in.	5 in. × 3 in.

6. Sometimes one or both sides of a picture can be cropped, or cut, to fit in a space. The designer has a 10-in. × 8-in. picture. At least 2 inches can be cut from the top to make the picture fit. How would you cut and reduce the photo to fit in a 6-in. × 4-in. space? Find the amount to be cut off and the percent of reduction.

Summing Up

7. Why is it important that a designer make sure that a picture is enlarged or reduced properly for a book?

8. How does the designer use knowledge of geometry and a calculator to find an appropriate size for pictures?

Chapter Review

Construct congruent figures. pages 444–445

1. Use a ruler to draw a segment 7 cm long. Use a straightedge and compass to construct a congruent segment.

2. Use a protractor to draw an angle with measure 80°. Use a straightedge and compass to construct a congruent angle.

Trace each figure. Use a straightedge and compass to bisect it. pages 446–447

3.
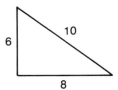

4.

5.

Trace the figure at the right. Then construct the following. pages 448–449

6. a line perpendicular to $\overleftrightarrow{MP}$ through M

7. a line perpendicular to $\overleftrightarrow{MP}$ through S

Find each square or square root. Use mental math or the table on page 520. pages 454–455

8. $\sqrt{144}$ 9. 5^2 10. 15^2 11. $\sqrt{100}$ 12. 20^2

Use the Pythagorean Rule to decide whether each triangle is a right triangle. pages 456–457

13.

6, 10, 8

14.

10, 26, 24

15.

3, 6, 5

Solve. pages 451–453, 458–459

16. **What if** this pattern is continued until there are 28 dots in 7 rows? Then line segments are drawn to connect all the dots horizontally and diagonally. How many triangles would there be in each row? How many triangles would there be congruent to △ABC?

17. **Look back** at 16. How many lines must be constructed to form the perpendicular bisectors of every side of △ABC and all triangles congruent to it?

Chapter Test

Trace each figure. Then construct a figure congruent to it.

1.

2.

Trace each figure. Use a straightedge and compass to bisect it.

3.

4.

Trace the figure at the right. Then construct the following.

5. a line perpendicular to $\overleftrightarrow{AB}$ through Q

6. a line perpendicular to $\overleftrightarrow{AB}$ through A

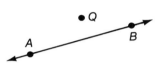

Find each square or square root. Use mental math or the table on page 520.

7. 10^2

8. $\sqrt{81}$

9. $\sqrt{289}$

10. 14^2

Use the Pythagorean Rule to decide if each triangle is a right triangle.

11.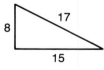

12.

Solve.

13. How many nonoverlapping polygons are formed by the perpendicular bisectors of the sides of a regular 16-sided polygon? of a regular 15-sided polygon?

14. Draw $\overline{XY}$ 2 cm long. Use a straightedge and compass to construct all points that are both 1 cm from X and 1 cm from Y.

15. Marvin sets up his camera tripod as shown at the right. What is the length of the shortest path from his tripod to his car?

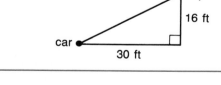

THINK   Complete rows 3 and 5.

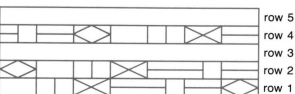

Regular Polygons and Spirals

Can you use Logo to draw a regular polygon with 5 sides?
10 sides? 20 sides? The answer may surprise you.

Materials: Logo

A. Define the procedure POLY, which inputs the number of
sides and the length of each side of a regular polygon.
How is the value of TURN determined?

```
TO POLY :N :LENGTH
MAKE "TURN 360 / :N
REPEAT :N [FORWARD :LENGTH RIGHT :TURN]
END
```

B. Use each command to call POLY. Record what is drawn.

- POLY 5 30   • POLY 8 30   • POLY 12 30   • POLY 25 30

C. Experiment. What values of N could you use to draw
figures that are not polygons? What values of N could
you use to draw figures that do not look like polygons
on the screen?

D. **What if** you change line 2 of POLY to MAKE "TURN 120.
What is drawn for N = 3, N = 4, and N = 5?

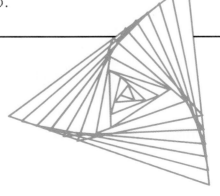

Sharing Your Results

1. Explain how each figure in **B** is drawn.

2. **What if** TURN equals 45. What values of N could
you use to draw a regular polygon? Explain.

Extending the Activity

What if you decrease the length of the side of a polygon each time you draw a side?

3. Define the procedure CHANGEPOLY. How does the value of DISTANCE change each time the procedure is called?

```
TO CHANGEPOLY :DISTANCE :TURN
IF :DISTANCE < 0 [STOP]
FD :DISTANCE
RT :TURN
CHANGEPOLY :DISTANCE - 3 :TURN
END
```

4. Predict what the result of each command will be. Then enter each command and describe your results. Are the results what you expected? Why or why not?

a. CHANGEPOLY 100 120   **b.** CHANGEPOLY 80 72

c. CHANGEPOLY 80 60   **d.** CHANGEPOLY 60 45

e. CHANGEPOLY 90 150   **f.** CHANGEPOLY 80 144

5. Enter CHANGEPOLY 90 120 and CHANGEPOLY 90 119. Then experiment using inputs for TURN that are close to those in **4**. Describe how the drawings change.

6. Use any numbers you choose to create an original design.

Summing Up

7. What regular polygon is drawn for each value of TURN? Why?

a. 30   **b.** 45   **c.** 60   **d.** 72

8. Describe how you created an original design.

Pretzel Math Constructions

You can construct a pentagon, a hexagon, and a heptagon by tying strips of paper into knots.

- To make a pentagon, use one long strip of paper. Make an overhand knot as shown. Tighten the knot and press flat. Cut the extra paper from the ends.

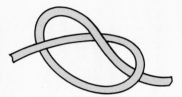
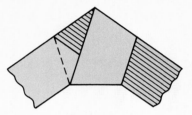

- To make a hexagon, use 2 long strips of paper. Make a square knot as shown. Tighten the knot and press flat. Cut the ends.

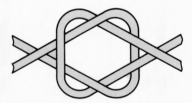
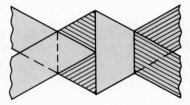

- To make a heptagon, use one long strip of paper. Loop it as shown. Tighten and press flat. Cut the ends.

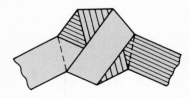

Family Math

The last three chapters of our mathematics book covered pre-algebra, probability, and geometric constructions.

It's Greek to Me!

A cube is a space, or solid, figure with six congruent square sides. There are only four other space figures for which all faces are congruent. These figures are called **regular polyhedrons.**

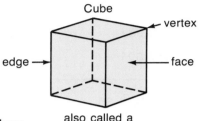

Cube
vertex
edge
face

also called a
Hexahedron

Tetrahedron
(4 triangles)

Octahedron
(8 triangles)

Icosahedron
(20 triangles)

Dodecahedron
(12 pentagons)

Make at least one of the space figures shown above. Use cardboard and glue or tape to make the figures. Trace each pattern below on a sheet of paper. Cut out the pattern and use it to make a pattern on cardboard. To construct all of the space figures, you will need 32 triangles, 6 squares, and 12 pentagons.

triangle

square

pentagon

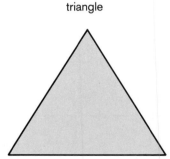  

How many faces are in the space figure you constructed?
How many edges?
How many angles?

Look around the house. Can you find any of these polyhedrons?

Final Review

Choose the correct answers. Write A, B, C, or D.

1. Estimate. $12.18 + $2.98 + $41.35

   A $150.00   **C** $5.00

   B $100.00   **D** $55.00

---

2. 16,352 − 12,371

   A 3,981   **C** 4,081

   B 4,021   **D** not given

---

3. 6,340 × 35

   A 50,720   **C** 220,900

   B 221,900   **D** not given

---

4. 191.16 ÷ 81

   A 0.4237   **C** 2.36

   B 23.6   **D** not given

---

5. What is the prime factorization of 80?

   A $2^4 \times 5$ **C** $2^3 \times 5^2$

   B $2^5 \times 5$ **D** not given

---

6. What is the LCM of 7 and 21?

   A 7   **C** 42

   B 12   **D** not given

---

7. What is an expression for 2 more than 5 times a number y?

   A $2y + 5$ **B** $5 + 2y$

   B $5y + 2$ **D** not given

---

8. What is the value of $5x^2 \div 9$ for $x = 3$?

   A 5   **C** 7

   B 25   **D** not given

---

9. What is the m∠2 if $\overleftrightarrow{AB} \parallel \overleftrightarrow{CD}$ and m∠7 = 125°?

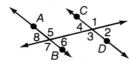

   A 125°   **C** 180°

   B 55°   **D** not given

---

10. What is an 8-sided polygon called?

   A octagon   **C** hexagon

   B nonagon   **D** not given

---

11. What is another name for $\frac{14}{5}$?

   A $3\frac{1}{5}$ **C** $2\frac{4}{5}$

   B $2\frac{3}{5}$ **D** not given

---

12. $1\frac{3}{4} - \frac{5}{8}$

   A $1\frac{1}{8}$ **C** $\frac{6}{8}$

   B $\frac{1}{6}$ **D** not given

---

13. $\frac{5}{6} \times \frac{2}{3}$

   A $\frac{6}{9}$ **C** $\frac{5}{9}$

   B $\frac{5}{6}$ **D** not given

---

14. $3\frac{2}{3} \div 2\frac{2}{3}$

   A $9\frac{7}{9}$ **C** $1\frac{1}{3}$

   B $1\frac{3}{8}$ **D** not given

---

15. Solve the proportion. $\frac{20.8}{n} = \frac{5.2}{11.2}$

   A 44.8   **C** 5.6

   B 22.4   **D** not given

Choose the correct answers. Write A, B, C, or D.

16. What is 525% as a decimal?

   A 525   **C** 0.0525

   B 52.5   **D** not given

17. What is 25% of 16?

   A 16.4   **C** 4

   B 8   **D** not given

18. $33\frac{1}{3}\%$ of what number is 12?

   A 4   **C** 12

   B 36   **D** not given

19. What is the area of a square with $s = 7.4$ m?

   A 54.76 m^2 **C** 27.38 m^2

   B 29.6 m^2 **D** not given

20. What is the area of a triangle with $b = 15.2$ in. and $h = 7$ in.?

   A 106.4 in.^{2} **C** 22.2 in.^{2}

   B 53.2 in.^{2} **D** not given

21. $4 \cdot {}^-6$

   A $^-10$ **C** 24

   B $^-24$ **D** not given

22. Solve for n. $4n = {}^-16$

   A 4   **C** $^-4$

   B $^-8$ **D** not given

23. What is $\sqrt{36}$?

   A 6   **C** 9

   B 13   **D** not given

Solve.

24. Deidre won $270 on the 4th day of a contest. The amount had tripled each day until there was a winner. How much was the prize worth on the first day of the contest?

   A $10   **C** $2

   B $8   **D** not given

25. Pedro paid cash for his bicycle. It cost $117.00. What is the greatest number of 5-dollar bills he needed if he paid with only 5-dollar bills and four 20-dollar bills?

   A 3   **C** 8

   B 4   **D** not given

26. Rita took a taxi to her hotel from the airport. It cost $5.25 for the first half mile and $1.25 for each additional $\frac{1}{8}$ mile. The bill was $11.50. How far did she travel?

   A $1\frac{1}{8}$ mi   **C** 1 mi

   B $\frac{5}{8}$ mi   **D** not given

27. Tami wants to cut a piece of wood into 25 equal pieces. How many cuts should she make?

   A 25   **C** 24

   B 26   **D** not given

Extra Practice

Write each number in expanded form. pages 2–7

1. 56,320,000
2. 11,090,000,408
3. 6 billion, 485 million, 30 thousand
4. 23.7804
5. 0.003578
6. 900.0614

Write each number in standard form.

7. $(9 \times 100,000,000) + (3 \times 1,000,000) + (2 \times 100,000) + (4 \times 10,000) + (6 \times 10) + (5 \times 1)$

8. ten billion, fifty-three million, nine hundred

9. $\left(7 \times \frac{1}{10}\right) + \left(1 \times \frac{1}{1,000}\right) + \left(6 \times \frac{1}{10,000}\right) + \left(4 \times \frac{1}{1,000,000}\right)$

10. 2 and 67 millionths

Set B

Compare. Use <, >, or = for each ●. pages 8–9

1. 9,973 ● 9,937
2. 4.69 ● 4.96
3. 250 ● 205
4. 37.063 ● 3.7063
5. 15,301 ● 1,530
6. 7.64 ● 7.640

Write in order from least to greatest.

7. 53,482; 53,842; 56,324
8. 492,924; 492,249; 492,429
9. 8.4; 8.04; 8.104; 8.004
10. 1.7; 1.78; 1.7008; 1.8

Set C

Estimate, then add or subtract. pages 18–25

1. $14,265 + 8,598$
2. $\$134.97 + 23.75$
3. $365.15 + 67.19$
4. $2.11 + 54.07$
5. $840.2 + 76.013$

6. $41.725 + 76.342 + 15.59$
7. $18,446 + 993 + 3,255$
8. $12.236 + 3.87 + 5.409$
9. $\$287.36 + 122.88 + 49.10$
10. $\$14.63 + 2.85 + 26.71$

11. $8.59 + 36 + 14.5$
12. $80 - 7.65$
13. $1.8206 - 0.79$
14. $\$55 - \$2.99$

15. $32,608 - 7,035$
16. $\$63.58 - 6.74$
17. $182.5 - 97.62$
18. $63 - 2.395$
19. $624,383 - 53,540$

20. $308.9 - 41.58$
21. $37,483 - 9,078$
22. $8.97 - 0.6364$
23. $643.709 - 58.8$
24. $5,600 - 29.01$

Set A

Estimate, then multiply. pages 38–45

1. 4.6 × 9	2. 0.61 × 33	3. 7.7 × 65	4. 342 × 5.3	5. 2,134 × 42
6. 8.1 × 5.9	7. 34.7 × 6.48	8. 0.89 × 7.5	9. 26.2 × 630	10. 5.73 × 2.23
11. 5.635 × 0.004	12. 0.796 × 0.03	13. 0.564 × 0.09	14. 63.8 × 4.37	15. 3.9 × 9.6

16. 34.2 × 40 × 0.05   17. 2.76 × 0.601 × 70   18. 30 × 0.684 × 3.5

19. 3.78 × 6.4 × 0.8   20. (2.9 × 0.46) + (7.1 × 0.46)   21. 0.35 × 4.92 × 7

Set B

Estimate, then divide. Round the quotients in 5–20 to the nearest hundredth. pages 50–57

1. 4)20.8   2. 7)56.42   3. 8.4)15.12   4. 0.05)11.8

5. 26)$37.84   6. 0.007)5.9   7. 0.53)4,306   8. 0.19)$18.39

9. 9 ÷ 7   10. $8 ÷ 3.4   11. 7.1 ÷ 2.8   12. 6,352.08 ÷ 7.3

13. 16.84 ÷ 3.8   14. 230.9 ÷ 8.4   15. 12.879 ÷ 5.1   16. 54 ÷ 2.6

17. 30.64 ÷ 35   18. 11.08 ÷ 0.79   19. 6 ÷ 19   20. 261.864 ÷ 4.9

Set C

Complete. pages 58–59

1. 8 cm = _____ mm   2. 5 _____ = 5,000 g   3. 30,000 m = 30 _____

4. 53 dL = 530 _____   5. _____ cm = 9.3 dm   6. 500 cg = 5 _____

7. 0.08 L = _____ cL   8. _____ m = 438 cm   9. 87.6 m = _____ km

10. 39.1 _____ = 3.91 g   11. 0.79 cL = 7.9 _____   12. _____ m = 0.09 km

13. 8,000 _____ = 8 g   14. 900 L = 9 _____   15. _____ km = 2,900 m

16. 0.315 kL = _____ L   17. _____ mm = 12 cm   18. 38 _____ = 0.38 m

Compare. Replace each ● with <, >, or =.

19. 500 mL ● 5 L   20. 600 g ● 0.6 kg   21. 280 cm ● 2.75 m

Extra Practice

──────── Set A ────────

Write using exponents. pages 72–73

1. $9 \times 9 \times 9 \times 9 \times 9$ 2. $4 \times 4 \times 4 \times 4$

3. $6 \times 6 \times 6$ 4. $1 \times 1 \times 1 \times 1 \times 1 \times 1 \times 1$

Write as a product of factors. Then write in standard form.

5. 8^3 6. 10^6 7. 6^0 8. 3^5 9. 15^1 10. 5^4

──────── Set B ────────

Write in standard form. pages 74–75

1. 3.5041×10^6 2. 4.8×10^{10} 3. 6.789×10^3

4. 4.7102×10^8 5. 5.634×10^2 6. 3.54×10^7

Write in scientific notation.

7. 96,000   8. 342 million   9. 829,400,000

10. 47 billion   11. 651.9   12. 3,450.6

──────── Set C ────────

Write the prime factorization, using exponents. pages 84–85

1. 60   2. 72   3. 75   4. 82   5. 250

6. 43   7. 280   8. 132   9. 243   10. 128

Write the composite number named by each prime factorization. Use a calculator to help.

11. $3^2 \times 5^2$ 12. $2^3 \times 5 \times 13$ 13. $2^3 \times 11$ 14. $2^2 \times 3^3 \times 5^2$

15. 8^3 16. $2^2 \times 13^2$ 17. $2^5 \times 3 \times 5^2$ 18. $2^3 \times 7^2 \times 13$

──────── Set D ────────

Find the GCF. pages 86–89

1. 12, 21   2. 8, 36   3. 10, 28   4. 21, 28

5. 12, 24   6. 30, 50   7. 35, 48   8. 12, 15, 24

Find the LCM.

9. 6, 9   10. 5, 15   11. 4, 9   12. 8, 10

13. 12, 15   14. 15, 27   15. 20, 35   16. 4, 5, 6

Set A

Write an expression for each. Use *x* as the variable. pages 102–107

1. six more than five times a number

2. twelve less than a number

3. four more than twice a number

4. a number divided by 18

Write each expression in words.

5. $3x - 5$

6. $\frac{4a}{5}$

7. $b + 9$

8. $y - 6$

Find the value of each expression.

9. $8 + 54 \div 9$

10. $15 - 3 \times 4$

11. $7 + 6 \times 8$

12. $42 \div 6 - 4$

13. $5 \times 8 - 8 \times 4$

14. $\frac{12 + 6}{3} - 6$

15. $4^2 + 3^3$

16. $(50 - 5) \div 3^2$

Evaluate each expression. Let *x* = 4 and *y* = 8.

17. $3x - 8$

18. $y^2 + 2$

19. $2xy$

20. $\frac{y}{x}$

21. x^2y

Set B

Write an equation for each. pages 108–109, 122–123

1. Five times a number *a* is 65.

2. Ten is three less than a number *n*.

3. Tracey is *b* years old. In 12 years she will be 21 years old.

Evaluate each formula for the given values.

4. $d = r \cdot t$; $r = 24$; $t = 1.6$

5. $s = \$18h$; $h = 60$

6. $2x + 9 = y$; $x = 7$

Set C

Solve and check. pages 114–121, 124–125

1. $a - 12 = 4$

2. $b + 6 = 15$

3. $34 = c - 29$

4. $114 = d + 18$

5. $x - 3.4 = 16$

6. $6.4 + y = 13.3$

7. $50 = g - 17$

8. $46 = p - 49$

9. $6a = 48$

10. $7.5b = 75$

11. $c \div 4 = 18$

12. $13 = \frac{m}{5}$

13. $\frac{n}{16} = 7$

14. $p \div 8 = 8$

15. $g \times 14 = 70$

16. $15 = \frac{t}{6}$

17. $2y + 7 = 29$

18. $3n - 12 = 0$

19. $18 + 4m = 38$

20. $64 = 8x - 16$

21. $5a + 4 = 39$

22. $12b + 8 = 80$

23. $24 = 6y - 6$

24. $100 = 9p - 8$

Extra Practice

Complete. Use Figure 1. $\overleftrightarrow{AB} \| \overleftrightarrow{CD}$. $\overleftrightarrow{EF} \perp \overleftrightarrow{CD}$. $m\angle 1 = 65°$ pages 134–139

1. $\overleftrightarrow{EF} \perp$ _____.

2. $\angle 14$ is a(n) _____ angle.

3. $\overleftrightarrow{EF}$ and $\overleftrightarrow{HI}$ intersect at _____.

4. $\angle 4$ is a(n) _____ angle.

5. $\angle$_____ and $\angle$_____ are complementary angles.

6. $\angle 12$ and $\angle$_____ are adjacent angles.

7. $\angle 2$ and $\angle$_____ are vertical angles.

8. $\angle 1$ and $\angle$_____ are corresponding angles.

9. $m\angle 12 =$ _____   10. $m\angle HGD =$ _____

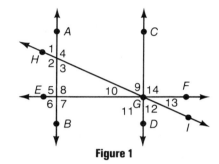

Figure 1

Find the missing measures. The polygon in 1 is regular. pages 140–147

1.

2.

3.

4.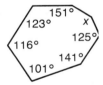

Write true or false.

5. The measure of an angle of a regular pentagon is 72°.

6. Polygon *ABCDEFGH* is an octagon.

7. The sum of the angle measures of a hexagon is 720°.

8. In quadrilateral *JKLM*, side $\overline{JK}$ is adjacent to side $\overline{LM}$.

Complete. Use Figure 2. Quadrilateral *WXYZ* ≅ quadrilateral *ABCD*.

9. $\overline{WX}$ corresponds to _____.

10. $\angle Z \cong \angle$_____

11. $WZ = 15$ cm; _____ $= 15$ cm

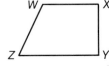 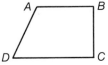

Figure 2

Set A

Complete. Use figure 1. pages 152–153

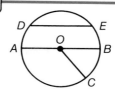

Figure 1

1. A chord of circle O is _____.

2. A radius of circle O is _____.

3. If AO = 10 cm, then AB = _____ cm.

4. If the central angle AOC measures 130°, then arc AC measures _____.

Set B

Use figure 2. Identify each image of A. C is the center of rotation. pages 154–159

1. reflection image

2. rotation image

3. translation image

Figure 2

Set C

Sketch a figure that would have these directional views. pages 160–161

1.

front   side   top

2.

front   side   top

3.

side   top

Set D

Write each as an improper fraction. pages 172–173

1. $4\frac{7}{8}$ **2.** $5\frac{2}{3}$ **3.** $10\frac{3}{5}$ **4.** $2\frac{6}{7}$ **5.** $7\frac{5}{6}$

6. $3\frac{4}{9}$ **7.** $8\frac{3}{10}$ **8.** $1\frac{15}{16}$ **9.** $6\frac{1}{2}$ **10.** $9\frac{3}{4}$

Write as a mixed number.

11. $\frac{18}{7}$ **12.** $\frac{21}{10}$ **13.** $\frac{8}{5}$ **14.** $\frac{29}{21}$ **15.** $\frac{15}{4}$

16. $\frac{4}{3}$ **17.** $\frac{100}{65}$ **18.** $\frac{33}{19}$ **19.** $\frac{163}{140}$ **20.** $\frac{301}{100}$

Set E

Write an equivalent fraction for each. pages 174–175

1. $\frac{3}{4}$ **2.** $\frac{2}{7}$ **3.** $\frac{9}{10}$ **4.** $\frac{6}{15}$ **5.** $\frac{8}{21}$

Write in lowest terms.

6. $\frac{12}{18}$ **7.** $\frac{10}{25}$ **8.** $\frac{17}{34}$ **9.** $\frac{22}{33}$ **10.** $\frac{60}{72}$

Set A

Compare. Use >, <, or = for each ⬭. pages 176–177

1. $\frac{4}{8}$ ⬭ $\frac{1}{2}$ 2. $\frac{13}{4}$ ⬭ $\frac{13}{5}$ 3. $\frac{2}{7}$ ⬭ $\frac{2}{5}$ 4. $\frac{7}{8}$ ⬭ $\frac{3}{4}$ 5. $\frac{13}{25}$ ⬭ $\frac{14}{25}$

6. $1\frac{4}{5}$ ⬭ $1\frac{5}{6}$ 7. $3\frac{2}{3}$ ⬭ $3\frac{4}{6}$ 8. $5\frac{8}{10}$ ⬭ $5\frac{3}{4}$ 9. $7\frac{2}{9}$ ⬭ $7\frac{1}{3}$ 10. $\frac{9}{9}$ ⬭ $\frac{20}{20}$

List in order from least to greatest.

11. $\frac{1}{4}, \frac{1}{9}, \frac{1}{5}$ 12. $\frac{5}{10}, \frac{3}{10}, \frac{8}{10}$ 13. $\frac{7}{12}, 3, \frac{1}{4}$ 14. $3\frac{2}{3}, 3\frac{3}{5}, 3\frac{7}{10}$

Set B

Write each fraction or mixed number as a decimal. Write each decimal as a fraction or mixed number in lowest terms. pages 178–181

1. $\frac{7}{9}$ 2. 0.28 3. 4.175 4. $\frac{5}{8}$ 5. 0.06

6. $\frac{31}{100}$ 7. 0.375 8. $2\frac{4}{5}$ 9. $\frac{9}{50}$ 10. 2.35

Compare. Use <, >, or = for each ⬭.

11. 2.4 ⬭ $2\frac{2}{5}$ 12. $\frac{3}{4}$ ⬭ 0.75 13. $1\frac{2}{3}$ ⬭ 1.6 14. $\frac{3}{8}$ ⬭ 0.33

Set C

Tell whether each fraction is less than, equal to, or greater than $\frac{1}{2}$. pages 186–187

1. $\frac{2}{5}$ 2. $\frac{5}{8}$ 3. $\frac{6}{12}$ 4. $\frac{5}{9}$ 5. $\frac{11}{21}$ 6. $\frac{2}{6}$

Estimate each sum or difference.

7. $\begin{array}{r} \frac{2}{7} \\ + \frac{7}{10} \\ \hline \end{array}$ 8. $\begin{array}{r} 3\frac{1}{4} \\ + 4\frac{4}{5} \\ \hline \end{array}$ 9. $\begin{array}{r} 6\frac{3}{4} \\ - 3\frac{2}{3} \\ \hline \end{array}$ 10. $\begin{array}{r} 9\frac{5}{6} \\ - 4\frac{8}{9} \\ \hline \end{array}$ 11. $\begin{array}{r} 15\frac{3}{8} \\ + 6\frac{3}{5} \\ \hline \end{array}$

Set D

Add or subtract. Write each sum or difference in lowest terms. pages 188–195

1. $\begin{array}{r} \frac{5}{8} \\ + \frac{1}{4} \\ \hline \end{array}$ 2. $\begin{array}{r} \frac{2}{3} \\ + \frac{3}{5} \\ \hline \end{array}$ 3. $\begin{array}{r} 4\frac{7}{9} \\ + 3\frac{1}{5} \\ \hline \end{array}$ 4. $\begin{array}{r} 6\frac{9}{10} \\ + 7\frac{1}{5} \\ \hline \end{array}$ 5. $2\frac{5}{12} + 6\frac{1}{3} + 5\frac{5}{8}$

6. $\frac{5}{9} - \frac{1}{2}$ 7. $\frac{7}{8} - \frac{1}{5}$ 8. $8\frac{7}{12} - 2\frac{1}{4}$ 9. $7\frac{5}{6} - 3\frac{1}{5}$

10. $16 - 4\frac{7}{10}$ 11. $9\frac{1}{3} - 3\frac{3}{4}$ 12. $5\frac{7}{12} - 2\frac{2}{3}$ 13. $6\frac{1}{5} - \frac{2}{3}$

Set E

Solve and check. pages 196–197

1. $1\frac{2}{3} + n = 7$ 2. $3\frac{1}{3} + n = 6\frac{1}{6}$ 3. $n + 4\frac{1}{9} = 8\frac{1}{3}$ 4. $n + 3\frac{4}{9} = 8$

5. $n - \frac{1}{4} = 2\frac{7}{8}$ 6. $n - 1\frac{2}{3} = 4$ 7. $n - 5\frac{5}{6} = 12\frac{1}{12}$ 8. $6\frac{4}{5} + n = 9\frac{1}{6}$

Set A

Estimate, then multiply. Write each product in lowest terms. pages 206–215

1. $\frac{5}{6} \times \frac{1}{4}$
2. $\frac{4}{5} \times \frac{1}{8}$
3. $\frac{5}{7} \times \frac{2}{3}$
4. $\frac{5}{8} \times \frac{1}{8}$
5. $\frac{4}{7} \times \frac{1}{4}$

6. $\frac{2}{3} \times 15$
7. $\frac{3}{5} \times 8$
8. $\frac{1}{5} \times \$45$
9. $\frac{3}{4} \times 6 \times \frac{7}{5}$
10. $\frac{1}{3} \times \frac{2}{5} \times \frac{7}{8}$

11. $\frac{4}{7} \times 8\frac{2}{5}$
12. $3\frac{1}{3} \times \frac{4}{5}$
13. $2\frac{1}{2} \times 3\frac{2}{5}$
14. $4\frac{2}{3} \times 1\frac{3}{4}$
15. $3\frac{1}{4} \times \frac{5}{6} \times 2\frac{2}{3}$

Set B

Estimate, then divide. Write each quotient in lowest terms. pages 220–225, 230–231

1. $\frac{5}{8} \div \frac{1}{4}$
2. $\frac{7}{10} \div \frac{3}{5}$
3. $\frac{4}{9} \div \frac{9}{10}$
4. $\frac{5}{7} \div \frac{3}{4}$
5. $\frac{1}{6} \div \frac{3}{10}$

6. $\frac{2}{3} \div 8$
7. $\frac{1}{2} \div \frac{5}{6}$
8. $3 \div \frac{1}{5}$
9. $\frac{1}{8} \div \frac{5}{8}$
10. $\frac{4}{5} \div \frac{7}{10}$

11. $4 \div 2\frac{2}{3}$
12. $4\frac{5}{7} \div 2\frac{3}{4}$
13. $\frac{4}{9} \div 3\frac{3}{5}$
14. $5\frac{1}{2} \div \frac{5}{6}$
15. $5\frac{3}{8} \div 4\frac{3}{10}$

Divide. Write each quotient in three ways.

16. $4\overline{)78}$
17. $82 \div 8$
18. $\frac{115}{20}$
19. $12\overline{)92}$
20. $183 \div 24$

Set C

Solve and check. pages 226–227

1. $\frac{3}{4} \times n = 12$
2. $\frac{5}{6} \times n = 35$
3. $n \times \frac{3}{8} = 9$
4. $n \times 8 = 6$

5. $n \div 3 = 2\frac{5}{6}$
6. $n \times 4 = 6\frac{2}{5}$
7. $n \div 2\frac{3}{4} = \frac{1}{8}$
8. $2\frac{1}{3} \times n = 7$

Set D

Complete. pages 232–233

1. 4 lb = _____ oz
2. 7 T = _____ lb
3. 29 ft = _____ yd _____ ft

4. 14 c = _____ pt
5. $6\frac{1}{2}$ gal = _____ pt
6. 87 in. = _____ ft

7. 288 in. = _____ yd
8. 28 oz = _____ pt
9. 32 qt = _____ pt

Add or subtract.

10. 4 ft 5 in.
  + 3 ft 9 in.
11. 6 gal
  − 2 gal 3 qt
12. 9 lb 6 oz
  + 4 lb 10 oz
13. 8 yd 1 ft
  − 3 yd 2 ft

Set A

Make a line plot and find the mode, median, and range for each. Use a calculator to find the mean for each. pages 246–249

1. 21, 27, 19, 23, 22, 26, 25, 22, 20, 21, 28, 21, 23, 21, 25, 17, 21, 20

2. 160, 180, 300, 240, 220, 200, 260, 200, 160, 180, 240, 220, 200, 340

3. 1,524; 1,521; 1,518; 1,521; 1,520; 1,522; 1,525; 1,528; 1,520; 1,522; 1,518; 1,515; 1,516; 1,514; 1,522; 1,524; 1,520; 1,516; 1,524; 1,514; 1,520; 1,525; 1,515; 1,514

Set B

Make a stem and leaf plot for each set of data. Find the mode, median, and range for each. pages 250–253

1. 31, 17, 32, 46, 8, 28, 44, 8, 12, 18, 19, 27, 38, 19, 45, 12, 10, 12, 38, 10, 15, 20, 44, 12, 12, 35, 22, 27, 26, 29

2. 5.3, 2.8, 1.6, 5.1, 3.4, 2.9, 4.6, 2.4, 3.4, 4.3, 4.5, 2.3, 3.1, 2.8, 2.4, 5.1, 1.8, 4.8, 2.7, 1.4, 5.6, 3.2, 5.5, 4.6, 3.2, 1.9, 3.6, 4.7, 2.8, 4.1

Make a box and whisker plot for this set of data.

3. 15, 9, 12, 10, 11, 18, 6, 12, 20, 9, 6, 11, 6, 10, 18, 14, 12, 15, 19, 13, 12, 16, 18, 14, 11, 18, 13, 16

Set C

Make a bar, line, or circle graph for each set of data. Explain your choice. pages 260–261

1.

AVERAGE DAILY TEMPERATURE	
Sunday, 61°	Thursday, 61°
Monday, 58°	Friday, 62°
Tuesday, 64°	Saturday, 65°
Wednesday, 60°	

2.

INSTRUMENT PREFERENCES OF 600 STUDENTS		
	Boys	Girls
Piano	40	100
Drums	120	40
Violin	60	90
Guitar	80	70

Use the graphs you made above to answer 3–6.

3. On which day did the temperature increase the most?

4. What was the trend of the temperature from Wednesday to Saturday?

5. Which instrument is most popular among the boys? Among the girls?

6. Which instruments are preferred by more girls than boys?

Set A

Write two equal ratios for each. pages 274–277

1. 4:24   **2.** 15:5   **3.** 12:15   **4.** 9:4   **5.** 22:11

6. 12:18   **7.** 54:3   **8.** 5:12   **9.** 15:45   **10.** 3:75

Write each rate as a quantity per unit.

11. 420 minutes in 4 movies   **12.** 540 words in 36 lines   **13.** 20 classes in 5 days

Find the unit price. Round to the nearest cent.

14. 6 pads for $5.32   **15.** 3 rackets for $89.85   **16.** 2 dozen balls for $9.98

Set B

Use = or ≠ for each ⬤. pages 278–281

1. $\dfrac{3}{6}$ ⬤ $\dfrac{10}{20}$ **2.** $\dfrac{4}{9}$ ⬤ $\dfrac{36}{81}$ **3.** $\dfrac{0.2}{0.5}$ ⬤ $\dfrac{2}{50}$ **4.** $\dfrac{15}{16}$ ⬤ $\dfrac{195}{208}$ **5.** $\dfrac{7}{3}$ ⬤ $\dfrac{84}{48}$

Solve each proportion.

6. $\dfrac{15}{20} = \dfrac{n}{4}$ **7.** $\dfrac{27}{n} = \dfrac{36}{4}$ **8.** $\dfrac{n}{9} = \dfrac{14}{6}$ **9.** $\dfrac{2.1}{3.5} = \dfrac{3}{n}$ **10.** 9:n = 7:42

11. $\dfrac{7}{n} = \dfrac{35}{25}$ **12.** 2:6 = 3:n   **13.** 1.8:n = 3:4   **14.** $\dfrac{n}{4} = \dfrac{14}{3}$ **15.** $\dfrac{8}{3} = \dfrac{n}{1.8}$

Set C

Use a proportion to find each actual dimension. pages 282–285

1. scale 1 cm: 50 m
    drawing 8 cm

2. scale 4 cm: 8 km
    drawing 12 cm

3. scale 1 mm: 15 m
    drawing 9 mm

4. scale 4 cm: 5 m
    drawing 18 cm

Find the scale for each drawing.

5. actual 20 km
    drawing 4 cm

6. actual 8 m
    drawing 8 cm

7. actual 50 m
    drawing 2 cm

Set D

Write each as a percent. pages 292–299

1. $\dfrac{3}{5}$ **2.** $\dfrac{4}{9}$ **3.** $\dfrac{7}{20}$ **4.** $\dfrac{5}{8}$ **5.** $\dfrac{9}{200}$ **6.** $\dfrac{17}{50}$

Write each as a ratio in lowest terms and as a decimal.

7. 40%   **8.** 65%   **9.** 18%   **10.** 4%   **11.** 63%   **12.** 5.1%

Extra Practice

Estimate. pages 326–327

1. 27.9% of 50

2. What percent of 39 is 4?

3. 84% of 103

4. What percent of 150 is 53?

5. 68% of 180

6. What percent of 49 is 20?

Solve. pages 314–317, 320–321

1. What is 32% of 84?

2. What percent of 24 is 8?

3. 48% of what number is 38.4?

4. What percent of 84 is 70?

5. What is 45% of $180?

6. 120% of what number is 90?

7. What is 57% of 250?

8. 3.5 is what percent of 50?

9. What is $2\frac{1}{2}$% of 624?

Find the discount and sale price. Round to the nearest cent. pages 318–319, 328–331

1. regular price: $87
   rate of discount: $33\frac{1}{3}$%

2. regular price: $39.95
   rate of discount: 25%

3. regular price: $42
   rate of discount: 30%

Find the sales tax on each item. Round to the nearest cent.

4. tennis racket
   cost: $59.98;
   sales tax: 6%

5. television
   cost: $2,150;
   sales tax: $5\frac{1}{2}$%

6. compact disc
   cost: $14.95;
   sales tax: 7.6%

Find the interest.

7. $2,000 at $8\frac{1}{2}$% for 4 years, compounded annually

8. $30,000 at $7\frac{3}{4}$% for 21 months, compounded quarterly

9. $20,000 at $7\frac{4}{10}$% for 24 months, compounded semiannually

10. $800 at 6.7% for 2 years, compounded quarterly

This circle graph shows how many students played each instrument. Use the graph to answer questions 1–3. pages 332–333

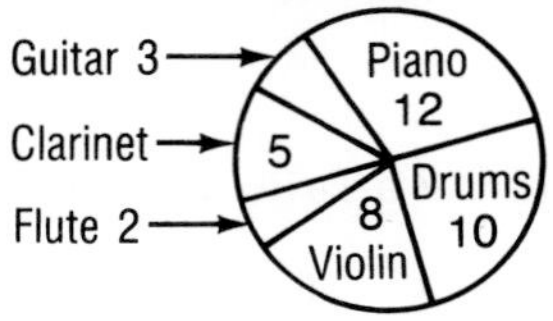

1. What is the total number of students?

2. Find the percent that played each instrument.

3. Find the degree measures represented by each percent.

NUMBER OF STUDENTS PLAYING INSTRUMENTS

Guitar 3
Clarinet — 5
Flute 2
Piano 12
Drums 10
Violin 8

Set A

Complete. pages 340–341

1. If you double the length and width of a rectangle, what happens to the area? What happens to the perimeter?

2. If you double the length of a rectangle and the width is unchanged, what happens to the area? What happens to the perimeter?

Set B

Find the area of each figure. Use 3.14 for π. pages 342–349

1.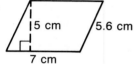
5 cm 5.6 cm
7 cm

2.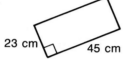
23 cm 45 cm

3.
7.4 m 7.4 cm

4.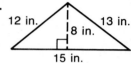
12 in. 13 in.
8 in.
15 in.

5.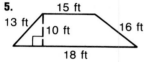
15 ft
13 ft 10 ft 16 ft
18 ft

6.
9 cm

7.
6.2 m

8.
8 m
8 m
(shaded region)

Set C

Find the surface area of each figure. pages 350–351

1.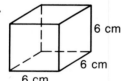
6 cm
6 cm
6 cm

2.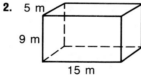
5 m
9 m
15 m

3.
20 cm
7 cm
14 cm

Set D

Find the volume of each figure. Use 3.14 for π. pages 356–361

1.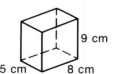
9 cm
5 cm 8 cm

2.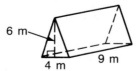
6 m
4 m 9 m

3.
8 ft
6 ft

4.
9 m
6 m

5.
8 m
6 m
6 m

Extra Practice

Set A

Compare. Use >, <, or = for each ●. pages 378–379

1. $^+15$ ● $^-19$ 2. $^-11$ ● $^+5$ 3. $^-3$ ● 0 4. $^-13$ ● $^-8$ 5. $^-2$ ● $^-7$

Write the integers in order from least to greatest.

6. $^+3, ^-5, ^+6, ^-2, ^-8, 0$

7. $^+12, ^+5, ^-7, ^-2, ^+6, ^-1$

Set B

Add, subtract, multiply, or divide. pages 380–387, 392–397

1. $^+3 + ^+9$ 2. $0 + ^+8$ 3. $^-7 + ^-4$ 4. $^-6 + 0$ 5. $^-5 + ^+2$

6. $^+7 + ^-2$ 7. $^-9 + ^+4$ 8. $^-8 + ^+7$ 9. $^+5 + ^-8$ 10. $^-4 + ^-4$

11. $^+6 - ^+2$ 12. $^+5 - 0$ 13. $^+3 - ^+11$ 14. $^-4 - ^-3$ 15. $^-8 - ^-9$

16. $^+7 - ^-5$ 17. $^-6 - ^-4$ 18. $^+6 - ^+10$ 19. $^-9 - ^-8$ 20. $^+1 - ^-7$

21. $^+6 \cdot ^+8$ 22. $^+4 \cdot ^-9$ 23. $^-5 \cdot ^-7$ 24. $^-3 \cdot ^+6$ 25. $^-8 \cdot ^-9$

26. $^+5 \cdot ^-4$ 27. $^-6 \cdot ^-7$ 28. $^+9 \cdot ^+9$ 29. $^-4 \cdot 0$ 30. $^-7 \cdot ^+1$

31. $^+63 \div ^+7$ 32. $^-45 \div ^-9$ 33. $^-54 \div ^+6$ 34. $^+24 \div ^-3$ 35. $^-21 \div ^-7$

36. $^+20 \div ^-5$ 37. $^-32 \div ^-8$ 38. $^+49 \div ^+7$ 39. $\dfrac{^+48}{-6}$ 40. $\dfrac{^-56}{-8}$

Set C

Solve and check. pages 398–403

1. $^-8n = ^-48$ 2. $\dfrac{n}{-7} = ^-6$ 3. $^+4 + n = ^-12$ 4. $^-6 - n = ^-4$

5. $n + ^-14 = ^+8$ 6. $^-16 + n = ^-9$ 7. $^+3n = ^-27$ 8. $^+5 - n = ^-9$

Solve each inequality. Then graph the integer solutions.

9. $n + ^-6 > ^+3$ 10. $n - ^-5 < ^-2$ 11. $^+4n > ^-36$ 12. $\dfrac{n}{+3} < ^+2$

13. $^-4 + n < ^-8$ 14. $^+3 + n \geq ^-6$ 15. $^+6n < ^+48$ 16. $\dfrac{n}{+2} \leq ^-4$

Set D

Write the ordered pair for each point. pages 404–405

1. A 2. B 3. C

4. D 5. E 6. F

Write the letter of the point named by each ordered pair.

7. $(^-4, ^-1)$ 8. $(^+3, ^+3)$ 9. $(^-2, ^+5)$

10. $(^+4, ^-5)$ 11. $(^-3, ^+6)$ 12. $(0, ^+4)$

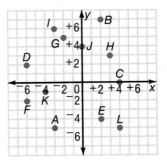

Set A

List the favorable outcomes and find the probability of each event. Use the spinner and cards in Figures 1 and 2. pages 418–419

1. Spin a vowel on the spinner.

2. Pick an even number from the deck of cards.

3. Pick an odd number from the deck of cards.

4. Spin a consonant on the spinner.

5. Pick a factor of 20 from the deck of cards.

6. Spin a C on the spinner.

Figure 1

| 2 | 4 | 6 | 8 | 10 | 12 | 14 | 16 | 18 | 20 |

Figure 2

Set B

Find each probability. pages 422–423

Experiment: Spin this spinner and toss a number cube.

1. P(B, 3)　　2. P(consonant, even number)　　3. P(vowel, prime number)

Find the probability of each compound event.

Experiment: Pick one card without looking. Replace it. Pick another card.

4. Event: Pick a white card followed by a red one.

5. Event: Pick two blue cards.

| R | W | R | W | R |
| B | W | B | R | R |

Set C

Find the number of possible choices or outcomes. pages 420–421

1. Daniel has 5 sweaters and 3 pairs of pants. Choose 1 sweater and 1 pair of pants.

2. The spinner in **Set A** is spun and a coin is tossed.

3. A four-number combination is chosen for a lock with numbers from 0 to 19.

4. A menu has 6 appetizers, 4 entrees, and 3 desserts. Choose 1 appetizer, 1 entree, and 1 dessert.

Set D

Find the number of permutations for each. pages 428–431

1. Four pictures are on a wall. In how many ways can they be arranged?

2. How many possible arrangements are there for license plates using 4 different letters?

Find the number of combinations for each.

3. 5 cards, using 3 at a time

4. 6 cards, using 5 at a time.

Extra Practice

Set A

Trace each figure. Then construct a bisector for each. pages 446–447

1. E

2.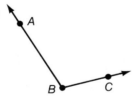

3.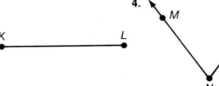

4.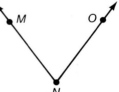

Set B

Trace each figure. Then complete the construction. pages 448–449

1. Construct a line perpendicular to $\overleftrightarrow{DE}$ through F.

2. Construct a line perpendicular to $\overleftrightarrow{XY}$ through X.

1.

2.

Set C

Find each. pages 454–455

1. 17^2

2. $\sqrt{144}$

3. 30^2

4. $\sqrt{225}$

5. 24^2

Set D

Tell whether each triangle is a right triangle. pages 456–457

1.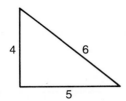

2.

3.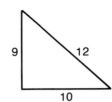

4.

Find the missing measure of each right triangle.

5.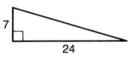

6.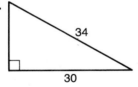

7.

8.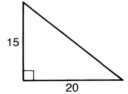

Set A

Solve. Use a calculator where appropriate. pages 11–13, 26–27

In professional football, a safety is 2 points, a field goal is 3 points, a touchdown is 6 points, and an extra point (only possible after a touchdown) is 1 point.

1. The Packers won 14–0. How might they have scored? Assume that there is no more than one safety.

2. The Rams were losing 17 to 13. Then they scored and won by 2 points. How might they have scored?

3. Miguel Flores kicks field goals and extra points. He scored 10 points in today's game. How could he have scored them?

4. The federal holiday, Washington's Birthday, is celebrated the third Monday in February. What are the possible dates for the holiday?

In a basketball game the players scored some field goals worth 3 points and some worth 2 points.

5. Tina scored 9 points. How could she have scored them?

6. Fred scored 11 points. How could he have scored them?

Set B

Solve. Use a calculator where appropriate. pages 47–49, 62–63

1. It is estimated that a car gets 28.2 miles per gallon of gas on the highway. If the gas tank holds 16.3 gallons, how far can the car go on a tankful of gas?

2. At speeds over 40 miles per hour, air resistance causes fuel economy to drop. A car getting 19.7 miles per gallon at 40 mph delivers 18.3 at 50 mph and 16.2 at 60 mph. How many fewer miles can you go on 12 gallons of gas at 60 mph than at 40 mph?

3. A certain car can go an average of 21 miles per gallon in the city. It can go an average of 29 miles per gallon on the highway. The gas tank holds 13 gallons. What is the difference in miles between the ratings on a tankful of gas?

4. Mr. Branson started with a full tank of gas, drove 338 miles, and filled his tank with 14.7 gallons of gas. His car is rated to get 24 miles per gallon. Did his car perform better or worse than the rating?

5. The Carsons are taking a trip that is 355 miles. Their car gets 29 miles to the gallon. Will they need to stop for gas on the trip?

6. The Smiths are driving 451 miles. They usually average 55 miles per hour. At that rate, how long should it take to drive the distance?

Extra Practice

──────────────────────────────── Set A ────────────────────────────────

Solve. Use a calculator where appropriate. pages 81–83, 90–91

1. The dots at the right show the first three triangular numbers: 1, 3, and 6. What are the next three?

2. What is the tenth triangular number?

3. The dots at the right show the first three square numbers. What are the next three?

4. What is the tenth square number?

5. The dots at the right show the first three rectangular numbers. What are the next three?

6. What is the tenth rectangular number?

7. Make a Venn diagram for the multiples of 4 from 1 to 36 and the multiples of 6 from 1 to 36.

8. Make a Venn diagram for the factors of 48 and the factors of 40.

──────────────────────────────── Set B ────────────────────────────────

Solve. Use a calculator where appropriate. pages 111–113, 126–127

1. The Ecology Club had a bake sale to raise money for a project. They sold 8 dozen brownies at $.20 each and 6 dozen cookies at $.15 each. How much money did they raise?

2. A name brand box of crackers costs $1.39 for 9 ounces. The store brand costs $1.79 for 12 ounces. Which costs less per ounce?

3. Brian paid $4.39 each for 4 rolls of film. He paid $8.59 for developing and printing each roll. How much did Brian spend in all for his pictures?

4. The PTA is selling school sweatshirts for $18.50 as a fundraiser. They paid $10.25 for each shirt. How many shirts do they have to sell to raise $400?

5. Harry worked for 25 hours last week. Mike worked 19 hours. Who made more money?

6. Luisa went to work on Monday the 1st. She works every 3rd day. Her friend stops in to see her at work on the 2nd Tuesday of the month. Would Luisa be working that day?

Set A

Solve. Use a calculator where appropriate. pages 149–151, 162–163

1. A clock ticks 6 times in 5 seconds. How many times will it tick in 10 seconds?

2. Mr. Swenson wants to cut a log into 8 equal pieces. How many cuts must he make?

3. Mrs. Allison bought some stock for $500 and sold it for $600. Then she bought it again for $700 and sold it for $800. How much money did she make or lose in the series of transactions?

4. Beth's watch is 10 minutes fast, but she thinks that it is 5 minutes slow. Brian's watch is 5 minutes slow, but he thinks it is 10 minutes fast. If they both allow just enough time to catch a train, who will miss the train?

5. Sharon makes a down payment of $50 on a television set. She then pays $30 a month for the next year. How much did she pay for the television?

6. A boat travels 58 miles in 4 hours. If it continues at this rate how far should it travel in the next five hours?

Set B

Solve. Use a calculator where appropriate. pages 183–185, 198–199

1. Mr. Stanek sells 17 different models of ceiling fans. Some have 4 blades, and the others have 5 blades. The models have a total of 74 blades. How many of each kind are there?

2. Donna was hired along with 3 other people to work the 5-hour evening shift. Each worker was paid $3.55 an hour. Donna worked two evenings a week. How much did she earn each week?

3. Josh and Sal made $45 shoveling snow. Sal made $\frac{2}{3}$ as much as Josh. How much did Josh make?

4. Mrs. Garcia spent $5.00 on 25-cent and 15-cent stamps. If she bought 26 stamps, how many of each kind did she buy?

5. Thirty-one students are members of the debating club and 42 students are in the play. Of these students, 12 are in both. How many different students are there in the two groups?

6. On Saturday, Randy worked 2 more hours than Alicia. Together they worked 14 hours. How many hours did Alicia work?

Extra Practice

Solve. Use a calculator where appropriate. pages 217–219, 234–235

1. Mrs. Zinn used $\frac{1}{2}$ of the quarters in her purse to pay the first toll. She used $\frac{2}{3}$ of the remaining quarters to pay the second toll. She then had only 1 quarter. How many quarters did she have when she started?

2. Montville has had the following snowstorms this month: 8 in., 12 in., 5 in., 18 in. and 9 in. How much more snow needs to fall this month to break the old record of 72 inches in a month?

3. Jenny picked a basket of apples at an orchard. On the way home, she gave $\frac{1}{3}$ of the apples to her uncle and $\frac{1}{3}$ of what was left to her grandmother. She ended up with 12 apples. How many did she pick?

4. Elise added $12 to her savings account in June. At the end of the month she withdrew $\frac{1}{2}$ of the money. In July, she added $12 and withdrew $\frac{1}{2}$ of the balance at the end. On August 1 she had $11 in her account. How much was in the account on June 1?

5. Barbara and her brother delivered 36 newspapers. Her brother only delivered half as many as Barbara did. How many did he deliver?

6. Mr. Webb rented a car for $39 a day and $.35 per mile. He drove the car 600 miles, and his total bill was $366. How many days did he rent the car?

Solve. Use a calculator where appropriate. pages 257–259, 266–267

Three television stations are polling some of the first 30 voters who leave a polling place. WABS polls every fifth voter. WCBC polls every third voter. WNBS polls every second voter.

1. How many people are polled by WABS?

2. How many people are polled by exactly 2 of the stations?

3. How many are polled by all 3 stations?

4. How many of the 30 people were not polled at all?

5. Ana, Cathy, Denise, and Felicia are playing in a round-robin tennis tournament. Each player must play a match with every other player. How many matches will be played?

6. High school basketball uniforms can have any number from 3 through 55 provided that only the digits 0 through 5 are used. How many different uniform numbers are possible?

7. To find the selling price of a new stereo, the manager doubles the price that he paid for it. He then adds $10 for shipping and $16.20 for a tax to obtain a selling price of $286.20. How much did the stereo cost the store manager?

8. There are 15 red marbles and 15 blue marbles in a bag. How many marbles must you pull out of the bag to be sure that you have at least one red and one blue marble?

Set A

Solve. Use a calculator where appropriate. pages 289–291, 302–303

1. The Nguyens garden is square and 60 feet long on each side. Mr. Nguyen wants to fence three sides–putting posts every 6 feet. How many posts does he need?

2. Carrie has a piece of posterboard 18 in. by 29 in. She wants to mount photographs that measure 3 in. by 4 in. on the posterboard. If she puts them as close together as possible, how many photos can she fit on the posterboard?

3. The Big Baseball League has 12 teams in 12 different cities. To conduct business, teams in each city need a direct telephone connection to each of the other cities. How many connections are needed?

4. Mark has 5 different books on the shelf of his school locker. In how many different ways can he arrange the books on the shelf?

5. Rodney has 10 coins worth 94 cents. He could not make 75 cents in change. What coins did he have?

6. Amy, Bob, Carmen, and Dena are standing in line. In how many different ways can they stand in order?

Set B

Solve. Use a calculator where appropriate. pages 323–325, 330–331

1. When Paula telephones her grandparents long distance, it costs $.75 for the first minute and $.20 for each additional minute. If Paula has $2.95 to spend, how long can the call be?

2. Arnold picked up some slides and some prints. Three-fourths of these were prints and 12 were slides. How many slides and prints did he pick up altogether?

3. Mr. Kim has less than 50 action figures on display in his store. Louis bought $\frac{1}{3}$ of them. Karina bought $\frac{1}{4}$ of the remaining figures. Then Carmen bought $\frac{1}{2}$ of what was left. If 12 figures are still on display, how many were in the original display?

4. To send a package overnight to Tulsa costs $9.25 for 1 lb and $15.75 for any amount up to 2 lb. Each additional pound up to a 10-lb limit costs $4.00. If the charge is $31.75, how much did the package weigh?

5. The Strollers Walking Club bought 17 pairs of walking shoes for 80% of the regular price of $35 a pair. How much did they pay for the 17 pairs of shoes?

6. Sandy wants to enlarge an 8 in. by 10 in. photo so that the longer side is 12.5 in. How long should the shorter side be when it is enlarged?

Set A

Solve. Use a calculator where appropriate. pages 353–355, 364–365

1. Mr. Young is planning to put a walkway around his garden. He will use flagstone that is 2 feet square. The garden is now a 10 ft by 14 ft rectangle. If he puts the walkway just inside the boundary, how many flagstones will he need?

2. Another alternative for Mr. Young is to remove some of the lawn around the garden. Then he will put the walkway just outside the garden boundary. How many flagstones will he need for this walkway?

3. The flagstones cost $15.00 each. What is the cost for each of the walkways?

4. Which walkway would you build? Explain.

5. Myran made a 25% down payment on his new car. If he now owes $10,893, how much was the down payment?

6. Cindy is programming a CD player. She wants to hear the first 3 songs, then skip $\frac{1}{3}$ of the songs that are left, and then play the last four songs. How many songs are on the CD?

Set B

Solve. Use a calculator where appropriate. pages 389–391, 408–409

1. In the talent show at summer camp, Rob, Joan, Lena, and Victor performed as a comedian, a singer, a guitar player, and a piano player. Rob and Lena finished their acts before the comedian and the piano player. Joan laughed at the comedian's jokes. The guitar player asked Lena to help set up the equipment. What talent did each person have?

2. There were 5 girls at a party. Ana wore a red sweater and Iris wore a white sweater. Leona did not wear yellow. Beth and the girl in green defeated Ana and the girl in yellow in a game. Jennifer and the girl in the pink sweater had to leave early. What color did each girl wear?

3. Ms. Russo, Ms. Palmer, and Ms. Thatcher work as banker, teacher, and engineer. Ms. Palmer lives next door to the banker. The teacher has never met Ms. Thatcher. Ms. Thatcher and Ms. Palmer were roommates in college. Who works at each job?

4. Cindy, Chris, and Carol went to Florida, Colorado, or Wisconsin on vacation. Carol was not in a state that borders Canada. Cindy swam in the ocean while on vacation. In which state did each girl spend her vacation?

Set A

Solve. Use a calculator where appropriate. pages 425–427, 432–433

1. Anna, Bill, Carla, and David each live in a different house. Bill does not live in a red or a green house. Carla does not live in a red or yellow house. David lives in a blue house. In what color house does each person live?

2. Randy is standing beside his desk. He will toss a coin 4 times. For each head, he takes one step forward. For each tail, he takes one step backward. The first toss is heads. What is the probability that he ends up where he started after 4 tosses?

3. Ann is hanging balloons on a fence. She hangs a blue, a red, and a white balloon, in that order, and repeats the pattern one time. She adds a yellow balloon after the last white balloon. Now what is the pattern?

4. Ann puts 2 green balloons between each red and white balloon. She has put up a total of 32 balloons. How many balloons of each color are there?

5. Louise and Meena each toss a number cube with the numbers 1 through 6 on it. They multiply the pair of numbers. If the product is less than 10, Louise wins. If the product is 10 or greater, Meena wins. What is the probability that each will win?

6. A television set is now marked 40% off and it costs $255. What was the original cost? **What if** the store sells the set at 50% off the original price? What will the new selling price be?

Set B

Solve. Use a calculator where appropriate. pages 451–453, 458–459

1. What is the greatest number of diagonals that can be drawn in a 9-sided figure? (Hint: Try a 4- and a 5-sided figure.)

2. What is the greatest number of diagonals that can be drawn in a 10-sided figure?

3. An artist built a square with 21 sections of stained glass. If another row of sections is added, how many sections in all will be needed?

4. Look at the picture of the stained glass. **What if** you added 4 more rows? How many sections would you have now?

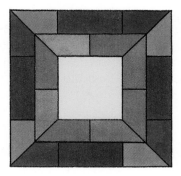

5. A bag contains 12 white marbles, 8 red marbles, and 9 blue marbles. Without looking, what is the greatest number of marbles that can be removed so that there are at least 5 marbles of each color in the bag?

6. What are the first two consecutive positive whole numbers whose product is greater than 300? whose product is greater than 500?

1 Adding and Subtracting Whole Numbers and Decimals

Page 5
5. 4 hundred thousand; (2×10^{10}) + $(9 \times 10^9) + (4 \times 10^5) + (6 \times 10^3)$
9. 3,002,537 **11.** 326,512,708
13. one hundred twenty-seven million, seven hundred seventy thousand
17. 2,300; 2,400; 2,500; 2,600

Page 7
5. 0.6 **9.** 0.000034 **17.** 50.207
21. $(1 \times \frac{1}{100}) + (2 \times \frac{1}{1,000})$ + $(3 \times \frac{1}{10,000})$ **25.** four hundred sixty-two hundred-thousandths

Page 9
5. < **7.** = **9.** > **13.** =
17. < **19.** 18,175; 18,350; 19,175

Pages 12–13
3. 5, 6, 7, or 8 runs

Page 15
7. 92 **11.** 8 **13.** 0.43 **17.** 665
25. 2.7, Commutative **29.** 39, Associative

Page 19
7. $97.04 **13.** > **17.** exact

Page 21
7. $422.45 **11.** 49.74 **17.** 19.432
19. 91.075 **23.** 15.406 **29.** 55.96

Page 23
5. 13,818 **21.** > **27.** a, b, c

Page 25
5. 6,416 **11.** $16.95 **15.** 33.05

2 Multiplying and Dividing Whole Numbers and Decimals

Page 35
7. 72 **13.** 900
23. 1; Identity Property of Multiplication
29. 0; Zero Property of Multiplication
35. true; Distributive Property

Page 37
7. 835 **9.** 0.902 **15.** 158.21
19. 15,620,000 **27.** 10 **31.** 1,000,000

Page 39
9. 1,166 **13.** 540 to 700; 625.6
31. 258.1

Page 41
7. 387 **9.** 462.8 **17.** 110,000
19. 17.22 **21.** 232.4 **25.** 75.166

Page 43
9. 671 **13.** 8,557 **17.** 89.1
21. 2,150 **25.** 34,930 **31.** 0.3046

Page 45
9. 55.912 **15.** 0.4 **33.** 25.389

Pages 48–49
1. David; $60.35 **5.** 4,140 spark plugs
7. once or twice

Page 51 Estimates will vary.
9. $30\overline{)270}$; 27 ÷ 3 = 9 **17.** 250
29. $40

Page 53
7. $.79 **11.** 163 **21.** 0.625
25. 2.5; 0.25; 0.025

Page 55
5. 0.4 **11.** $.51 **19.** 0.3
25. 12.79 **29.** b; it is the only one less than $1.

Selected Answers

7. 1.1   **9.** 0.01   **23.** 698.1
31. False; the quotient has been rounded.

Page 59
7. 100   **13.** 1   **17.** g   **21.** L
25. 3.27   **31.** =   **37.** =

Page 61
7. $.80   **9.** $3.90   **15.** $37.50
23. b   **27.** b

3 Number Patterns and Number Theory

Page 71
5. yes, yes, no, yes, no, no   **13.** 0, 10, 20, 30, 40, 50, 60, 70, 80, 90; 2, 5, 10

Page 73
11. 11^2 **19.** 25,125   **23.** $3 \times 3 \times 3 \times 3 \times 3$; 243   **29.** 11×11; 121   **33.** 1

Page 75
7. 4   **13.** 790,000   **17.** 303,050
23. 4×10^3 **33.** 8.4067×10^3

Pages 82–83
3. 26 people

Page 85
7. $2^2 \times 3^2$ **13.** $2 \times 3 \times 5 \times 7$
21. 196   **29.** true   **35.** false

Page 87
7. 3   **13.** 5   **17.** 25   **19.** 5
25. true

Page 89
7. 12   **11.** 60   **19.** 120   **23.** 4;48
27. 12;144

Pages 90–91
1. Draw circles as shown in diagram; odd numbers: 1, 3, 5, 7, 9; prime numbers: 2, 3, 5, 7; odd and prime: 3, 5, 7

4 Pre-Algebra: Expressions and Equations

Page 103
9. $10x$ **17.** 3 times a number a, divided by 4

Page 105
7. 14   **13.** 3
19. $(9 + 6) \div 3 + 2^3 = 13$ **25.** 24.596

Page 107
7. 82   **11.** 12   **15.** 0   **19.** $2t - 9;7$

Page 109
5. $3t = 83$ **11.** A number increased by 19 is 70.   **15.** no   **19.** yes

Pages 112–113
1. They would gain $151.
7. 3 Sundays

Page 115
9. subtract 15   **13.** divide by 2
23. 37   **27.** 133

Page 119
5. add 10, $n = 13$ **17.** subtract 3 from both sides   **21.** $x - 5 = 58$, $x = 63$

Page 121
5. divide by 7; $x = 7$ **17.** 37

Page 123
7. $9 - 5$; 4   **13.** $2 \cdot 3 + 7$; 13   **19.** 45

Pages 126–127
1. Look at the given pairs of inputs and outputs and find the relationship between the numbers in the pair. Find the numbers that follow the pattern.

5 Geometry

Page 135
9. b   **19.** False. $\overleftrightarrow{AB}$ intersects $\overleftrightarrow{FC}$ at C.
27. False. A line has no endpoints.

Page 137   Estimates may vary.
7. acute; $30°$ **11.** straight; $180°$

Page 139
9. $58°$ **13.** true; adjacent to $\angle 1$
25. true; $\overline{PQ} \perp \overline{RS}$

Pages 150–151
3. 1 blue marble, 99 red marbles
5. 50 students   **7.** 290 miles

Page 155
13. yes; $\frac{1}{2}$ turn cw or ccw   **15.** line, 3;
rotational, 3

Pages 162–163
1. They are identical. The figure at 3 is a
translation image of the figure at 1.

6 Adding and Subtracting Fractions

Page 173
13. $\frac{7}{2}$ **21.** $\frac{11}{4}$ **25.** 2   **33.** $3\frac{2}{3}$
37. $n = 2$ **43.** $n = 9$

Page 175
11. $\frac{2}{10}, \frac{3}{15}, \frac{4}{20}$ are possible answers.
17. $n = 3$ **27.** yes   **39.** $\frac{3}{4}$

Page 177
7. $>$ **13.** $=$ **17.** $=$ **21.** $\frac{1}{7}, \frac{1}{3}, \frac{1}{2}$
25. $3\frac{1}{4}, 3\frac{3}{10}, 3\frac{2}{5}$ **27.** $n = 3$

Page 181
7. $0.\overline{4}$ **9.** $5\frac{1}{40}$ **15.** 0.23 **19.** $5\frac{7}{8}$
23. $=$ **33.** $0.\overline{2}$

Pages 184–185
1. 11 slices of pizza, 10 hamburgers
3. Sandy sold 12 air conditioners. Richard
sold 4.   **7.** The red one, owned by the
mechanic

Page 187
9. $>$ **13.** $<$ **21.** 1 or $1\frac{1}{2}$ **27.** 1
31. $1\frac{1}{2}$ **35.** $7\frac{11}{24}$

Page 189
7. 1   **15.** $\frac{3}{2}$ **21.** $\frac{5}{12}$ **27.** $\frac{1}{10}$ **35.** $\frac{13}{18}$

Page 191   Estimates may vary.
7. $12\frac{1}{2}$; $12\frac{7}{10}$ **13.** 19; $18\frac{7}{10}$
17. 20; $19\frac{17}{24}$ **25.** $15\frac{1}{2}$; $15\frac{3}{5}$ **27.** c

Page 193
7. 4; $4\frac{1}{15}$ **15.** 10; $10\frac{1}{7}$ **19.** 4; $4\frac{7}{20}$
23. 5; $4\frac{11}{15}$ **27.** $\frac{5}{24}$ **33.** $4\frac{1}{2}$

Page 195
7. $17\frac{2}{3}$ **13.** $\frac{5}{12}$

Page 197
7. $n = 2\frac{1}{8}$ **11.** $n = 12\frac{1}{2}$ **13.** $n = 1\frac{1}{10}$
21. $n = 4\frac{1}{2}$ **27.** a

7 Multiplying and Dividing Fractions
Page 207   Estimates may vary.
9. 14; $16\frac{1}{3}$ **15.** 12; $13\frac{1}{2}$ **17.** 6; $5\frac{5}{36}$
25. 5; $5\frac{5}{38}$

Page 209
7. $\frac{5}{24}$ **19.** 6   **27.** $\frac{1}{20}$ **37.** $<$

Page 211
7. $\frac{1}{6}$ **9.** 14   **25.** $\frac{9}{2}$, or $4\frac{1}{2}$

Selected Answers

Page 213

9. 8   **15.** $11\frac{1}{3}$ **21.** $9\frac{7}{9}$ **27.** 4

31. $7\frac{1}{3}$ **35.** $13\frac{1}{3}$ **39.** $<$

Page 215

11. 9   **13.** 21   **17.** 1   **21.** 8

23. $12\frac{1}{2}$ **35.** 10   **41.** $\frac{5}{8}$

Pages 218–219

3. $50   **7.** cannot tell

Page 223

11. $\frac{1}{7}$ **17.** divisor: 9, divided: 3

21. $1\frac{1}{3}$ **29.** $\frac{5}{7}$ **43.** $\frac{3}{5}$ **47.** $n = 1$

Page 225

11. $\frac{3}{14}$ **13.** $\frac{8}{5}$ **17.** 3   **21.** $1\frac{11}{12}$

23. 28   **25.** $1\frac{8}{15}$ **29.** $\frac{1}{3}$ **33.** $2\frac{13}{14}$

Page 227

5. $n = 9$ **7.** $n = 10$ **11.** $n = 8$

13. $n = 2\frac{6}{13}$ **17.** $n = 7\frac{1}{2}$

25. $\frac{n}{1\frac{1}{4}} = 10$, $n = 12\frac{1}{2}$

Page 231

7. 12 R3, 12.5, $12\frac{1}{2}$ **19.** 8 R9, 8.375,

$8\frac{3}{8}$ **27.** 7 R1, 7.5, $7\frac{1}{2}$

Page 233

11. 5   **15.** $1\frac{1}{2}$ **19.** 29

25. 6 ft 3 in.   **31.** 8 c

8. Using Graphs and Statistics

Page 247

5. mode: 400; median: 400; range: 175

7. mode: 1,215; median: 1,215; range: 9

Page 249

7. 300   **9.** 41.3   **11.** about 0.47

13. The mean doubles, while the median remains unchanged.

Page 251

3. mode: 14; median: 27; range: 35

Page 255

5. median: 147; mean: 140; mode: 152; range: 44   **7.** median: 147; mean: 146.64; modes: 136 and 147; range: 31

11. mean

Pages 258–259

3. 6 days   **5.** 10 rectangles   **7.** 2 children aged 6–10, 1 child aged 11–13

9. 66,000 miles

Page 261

7. double-bar graph   **11. a** basketball, soccer, swimming   **b.** baseball and track

9 Ratio, Proportion, Percent

Page 275

9. $3:4$, or 3 to 4, or $\frac{3}{4}$ **17.** $1:7$ or $\frac{1}{7}$

21. $6:18$ or $\frac{6}{18}$ **27.** $21:3$ or $\frac{21}{3}$

Page 277

7. 4 columns per page or $4:1$

13. $n = 40$ **17.** $6.50

Page 279

7. $\neq$ **11.** $=$ **17.** $\neq$ **25.** $\neq$

33. $\frac{n}{8} = \frac{3}{5}$

Page 281

9. $n = 1$ **11.** $n = 28$ **13.** $n = 5$

19. $n = 0.5$ **25.** $42:3 = n:7$; $n = 98$

27. $n = 30$

Page 283

5. 125 m   **7.** $4.\overline{2}$ m

Page 285
5. 259 mi   11. 6 mi per min or 360 mph
13. mi per min

Page 287
3. $\overline{JU}$ 9. 60 in.

Pages 290–291
3. 24 ways   7. 27 black and white, 18
color   9. 15 pictures

Page 297
11. 80%   13. 12%   15. 87.5%
19. 5.5%   21. $\frac{17}{20}$, 0.85
25. $\frac{1}{50}$, 0.02   27. $\frac{13}{200}$, 0.065
29. 47%   33. $<$

Page 299
13. 25%   17. 70%   21. 0.5
23. 52.2%

Page 301
7. 1.8, $\frac{9}{5}$ 9. 3.15, $\frac{63}{20}$ 17. $266\frac{2}{3}$%
23. 1.4%   33. 550%   37. $<$

10 Using Percent

Page 313
9. 15   11. 21   13. 40   19. 8
23. 11   27. 21   29. 35

Page 317
9. 44   17. 13.68   21. 513   25. 1
27. 16.66

Page 319
5. $11.24; $33.71   11. $24.97; $14.98

Page 321
5. 70%   7. 60%   9. 480   11. 66
17. 5%

Pages 324–325
3. $276   5. 18 miles   9. Each should
pay $8.75. Trishna pays Berta $5.25,
Dennis $3.25, and Lei $.25

Page 327   Estimates may vary.
9. $33\frac{1}{3}$%   11. 10%   15. 300%
17. 75 or 80   25. b; $\frac{3}{4}$ of 60 is 45.

Page 329
5. $999.70   11. $378; $516.60; $894.60

Pages 330–331
1. interest = new balance $\times$ 0.08 $\times$ 0.25;
next balance = previous balance + interest
5. County Savings

Page 333
3. 90°   5. 288°   13. $90,000

11 Geometric Measurement

Page 343
5. 8 cm^2 9. 15 m^2 15. 73 m^2;
544 cm^2; 164 m^2 17. 25 m

Page 347
5. C = 13 m; A = 13 m^2 9. C = 31 m;
A = 79 m^2 19. 236 m^2

Page 349
5. 30 ft^2 7. 166 ft^2 11. b. 125 in.^{2}

Pages 354–355
1. No. You have one more stake because
you start the line with a stake.
5. 16 bags   7. 60 plants

Page 357
5. 81 cm^3 9. 252 cm^3

12 Pre-Algebra: Integers and Graphing

Page 379
15. 5   17. 8   21. 101   23. 33
27. $>$ 31. $<$ 35. $>$ 37. $>$

495

Selected Answers

39. $^-7$, $^-4$, $^-3$, 0, $^+2$, $^+8$

Page 385
9. $^+12$ **13.** $^-11$ **17.** $^-8$ **19.** $^-2$
23. $^-3$ **27.** $^+4$ **33. a.** $^+5 + {}^+9$
37. c. $^-5 + {}^+9$

Page 387
13. $n = {}^+6$ **15.** $n = {}^+10$ **19.** $^+8$
21. $^-4$ **25.** $^-8$ **27.** $^-3$

Pages 390–391
3. Tim, Norway; Shirley, Australia; Ed, Kenya; Jim, Thailand **5.** 7 children

Page 395
9. $^+35$ **11.** $^+35$ **13.** $^+72$ **15.** 0
17. $^+1$ **19.** $^-30$ **21.** $^+48$

Page 397
9. $^+9$ **11.** $^-7$ **13.** $^+9$ **15.** $^-7$
17. $^-6$ **21.** $^+2$ **23.** $^+8$ **25.** $^-6$
29. $^+5$ **31.** $^-7$ **39.** $^+90$

Page 399
5. $n = {}^+7$ **7.** $n = {}^-20$ **15.** $n = {}^-27$
17. $n = {}^+14$ **19.** $n = {}^+14$ **21.** $n = {}^+7$
29. c. $n + {}^+3 = {}^-4$ **33.** $5n = {}^-15$; $n = {}^-3$

Page 401
5. $n > {}^+14$; $^+15$, $^+16$, $^+17$, . . .
9. $n < {}^+3$; . . . , 0, $^+1$, $^+2$
15. $n > {}^+45$; $^+46$, $^+47$, $^+48$, . . .

Page 403
7. $n < {}^-1$ or $n \le {}^-2$ **13.** $n > {}^-5$
17. $n \le {}^-4$ **23.** $n \ge {}^+16$ **27.** $n \ge {}^-5$

Page 405
11. $(^+4, {}^-2)$ **13.** $(^+1, {}^-5)$ **23.** C

Page 407
5. $^+1$, $^-1$, $^-3$, $^-5$, $^-7$ **17.** $^-7$

13 Probability

Page 419
5. H, T **9.** 10, 20, 30, 40, 50, 60, 70, 80, 90, 100 **11.** A, E, I; $\frac{3}{8}$; neither

17. none; 0; impossible **19.** none; 0; impossible

Page 421
3. Blue, Head; Blue, Tail; Yellow, Head; Yellow, Tail; Red, Head; Red, Tail; Green, Head; Green, Tail; Purple, Head; Purple, Tail; White, Head; White, Tail

Page 423
5. $\frac{1}{8}$ **7.** $\frac{1}{4}$ **9.** $\frac{1}{12}$ **11.** $\frac{1}{3}$
13. $\frac{1}{4}$ **17.** $\frac{1}{4}$

Pages 426–427
3. Fred, 3 in 4; Jay, 1 in 4
7. 32 and 33

14 Geometry ● Construction

Page 445
19. In each case, only one triangle is possible once the given elements are congruent.

Pages 452–453
3. 135 knots **5.** 7 sides

Page 455
7. 144, 12 **9.** 13 **11.** 256 **15.** 7

Pages 458–459
3. Reduce by 55%.

HINT To write a number in expanded form, find the place value of each nonzero digit.

$30,200,050$ = $(3 \times 10,000,000) + (2 \times 100,000) + (5 \times 10)$
= $(3 \times 10^7) + (2 \times 10^5) + (5 \times 10^1)$

Write each number in expanded form.

1. 240,700

2. 6,000,507

3. 8,080,000,000

4. 19,000,000

5. 300,200,000

6. 17,000,170,000

Write each number in standard form.

7. $(8 \times 10^6) + (5 \times 10^2) + (3 \times 1)$

8. $(9 \times 10^8) + (8 \times 10^6) + (3 \times 10^5) + (2 \times 10^1)$

9. 4 million, 28 thousand, 6

10. 108 billion, 2 million, 58 thousand, 3 hundred

Write each number in words.

11. 11,000,700

12. 2,000,000,020

13. 75,000,000,060

Write the value of the digit 7.

14. 70,000,815

15. 9,700,000

16. 700,000,000,000

17. 17,206,450

18. 146,753

19. 63,428,070

Give the next three numbers to continue each pattern.

20. 2, 20, 200, 2,000

21. 1,000, 1,010, 1,020

22. 16 million, 26 million, 36 million

23. 600 million, 60 million, 6 million

Skill Hints

To place the decimal point in a product, consider the number
of decimal places in each factor.

$$4.8 \rightarrow \text{tenths} (0.1)$$
$$\underline{\times 0.7} \rightarrow \underline{\times \text{tenths} (0.1)}$$
$$3.36 \rightarrow \text{hundredths} (0.01)$$

$$0.67 \rightarrow \text{hundredths} (0.01)$$
$$\underline{\times 0.4} \rightarrow \underline{\times \text{tenths} (0.1)}$$
$$0.268 \rightarrow \text{thousandths} (0.001)$$

Place the decimal point correctly in each product.

1. $6.47 \times 3.3 = 21351$

2. $53.92 \times 18.8 = 1013696$

3. $0.567 \times 8.9 = 50463$

4. $12.8 \times 75.361 = 9646208$

5. $22.4 \times 7.6 \times 0.3 = 51072$

6. $7.34 \times 1.13 \times 0.5 = 41471$

Estimate. Then multiply.

7. $\begin{array}{r} 1.2 \\ \times\, 7.3 \\ \hline \end{array}$

8. $\begin{array}{r} 4.7 \\ \times\, 0.5 \\ \hline \end{array}$

9. $\begin{array}{r} 11.3 \\ \times\, 0.8 \\ \hline \end{array}$

10. $\begin{array}{r} 0.37 \\ \times\, 1.7 \\ \hline \end{array}$

11. $\begin{array}{r} 5.6 \\ \times\, 5.6 \\ \hline \end{array}$

12. $\begin{array}{r} 0.09 \\ \times\, 0.08 \\ \hline \end{array}$

13. $\begin{array}{r} 5.15 \\ \times\, 0.31 \\ \hline \end{array}$

14. $\begin{array}{r} 8.26 \\ \times\, 0.7 \\ \hline \end{array}$

15. $\begin{array}{r} 0.345 \\ \times\, 0.61 \\ \hline \end{array}$

16. $\begin{array}{r} 586 \\ \times\, 92 \\ \hline \end{array}$

17. $6{,}424 \times 1{,}000$

18. $357 \times 10{,}000$

19. $8.8 \times 0.9 \times 10$

20. $1{,}000 \times 3.99$

21. 54.3×100

22. 0.003×100

23. 7.85×3.2

24. $8.7 \times 4.6 \times 2.1$

25. $11.2 \times 6.7 \times 8.4$

26. $0.789 \times 1{,}000$

27. 45.67×10

28. $0.0005 \times 1{,}000$

29. $0.6 \times 0.4 \times 100$

30. $1{,}000 \times 6.8 \times 0.5$

31. $2.5 \times 2.5 \times 100$

32. $704 \times 10{,}000$

33. $0.5 \times 750 \times 10$

34. $38 \times 6.2 \times 0.9$

H
I Be sure to place a zero in the quotient when the dividend is
N less than the divisor.
T

$$
\begin{array}{r}
106 \\
7\,\overline{)742} \\
\underline{7} \\
42 \\
\underline{42} \\
0
\end{array}
\qquad
\begin{array}{r}
10.8 \\
9\,\overline{)97.2} \\
\underline{9} \\
72 \\
\underline{72} \\
0
\end{array}
\qquad
\begin{array}{r}
3.04 \\
1.2\,\overline{)3.648} \\
\underline{3\,6} \\
48 \\
\underline{48} \\
0
\end{array}
$$

Estimate. Then divide.

1. $0.9\,\overline{)2.763}$ 2. $8\,\overline{)162.4}$ 3. $7.1\,\overline{)319.5}$ 4. $0.003\,\overline{)0.2418}$

5. $1.5\,\overline{)90.6}$ 6. $26\,\overline{)1,014}$ 7. $2.8\,\overline{)29.96}$ 8. $5.6\,\overline{)571.2}$

9. $825 \div 100$ 10. $789 \div 1,000$ 11. $86.1 \div 10$ 12. $4,600 \div 1,000$

13. $80.96 \div 1.6$ 14. $476.13 \div 59$ 15. $\$921.57 \div 13$ 16. $\$1,154.16 \div 24$

Divide. Round each quotient to the nearest hundredth.

17. $56 \div 0.9$ 18. $\$82.25 \div 4$ 19. $1,247 \div 14$ 20. $897 \div 45$

Find the unit price. Round to the next greater cent.

21. 7 for $1.00 22. 6 for $.89 23. 3 for 28¢ 24. 5 for 32¢

25. 16 for $4.50 26. 11 for $5.25 27. 19 for $6.78 28. 24 for $57

Estimate to help select the correct quotient.

29. $2.8\,\overline{)100.8}$
   a. 0.36
   b. 3.6
   c. 36
   d. 360

30. $9 \div 32$
   a. 0.28125
   b. 2.8125
   c. 28.125
   d. 281.25

31. $0.75\,\overline{)63.15}$
   a. 0.842
   b. 8.42
   c. 84.2
   d. 842

32. $39\,\overline{)25.35}$
   a. 0.065
   b. 0.65
   c. 6.5
   d. 65

Skill Hints

In writing a standard number in scientific notation, the number of places the decimal point is moved corresponds to the power of 10.

$$72{,}058. = 7.2058 \times 10^4$$

4 places

$$8{,}900{,}000. = 8.9 \times 10^6$$

6 places

Find each missing number.

1. $7 \times 10^{\square} = 7{,}000$

2. $8.1 \times 10^7 = \square$

3. $\square \times 10^4 = 93{,}000$

4. $6.91 \times 10^5 = \square$

5. $2.54 \times 10^{\square} = 254$

6. $3.09 \times 10^{\square} = 30{,}900$

7. $\square \times 10^6 = 6{,}500{,}000$

8. $\square \times 10^4 = 12{,}000$

9. $9.4 \times 10^8 = \square$

Write each in scientific notation.

10. $60{,}700$

11. $801{,}000$

12. $7{,}000{,}654$

13. $182{,}000{,}000$

14. $34{,}400{,}000$

15. $5{,}505{,}000$

Write each in standard form.

16. 7.1×10^3

17. 8.205×10^6

18. 1.75×10^3

19. 2.2×10^5

20. 6.04×10^4

21. 8×10^9

22. 3.74×10^4

23. 9.075×10^2

24. 6×10^7

25. $7 \times 7 \times 7 \times 7$

26. 6^5

27. 15^3

28. $8 \times 8 \times 8 \times 8 \times 8$

29. 64^0

30. 1^{25}

H
I
N
T
To write an equation from words, translate the words into mathematical symbols.

Three less than twice a number is ten. $2n - 3 = 10$

　　$- 3$　　　$2n$　　$=\ 10$

Five times a number, increased by one is sixteen. $5n + 1 = 16$

　　$5n$　　　　$+ 1$　　　$=\ 16$

Write an equation for each.

1. Sixteen divided by a number n is two.

2. Tim is t years old. In 5 years he will be 30 years old.

3. Five more than a number x is eighteen.

4. Each cup costs $.50. Sue buys t cups for $7.00.

5. Sam drove 536 mi Monday and n mi Tuesday for a total of 800 mi.

6. Sue read x books out of 25 and has 13 left to read.

Write each equation in words.

7. $7x + 9 = 23$

8. $n - 6 = 10$

9. $8y = 80$

10. $x \div 3 = 5x$

11. $7 + n = 20$

12. $3a - 5 = 13$

Tell if the given number is a solution of the equation.

13. $3y + 5 = 35$　　Let $y = 9$.

14. $6x - 9 = 39$　　Let $x = 8$.

15. $n + 36 = 72$　　Let $n = 36$.

16. $\frac{n}{8} = 9$　　Let $n = 64$.

17. $5x = 45$　　Let $x = 8$.

18. $8 - 3y = 2$　　Let $y = 2$.

19. $\frac{2x}{5} = 6$　　Let $x = 15$.

20. $10 - 6n = 3$　　Let $n = 2$.

21. $5m - 3m = 6$　　Let $m = 5$.

22. $4y - \frac{2y}{3} = 10$　　Let $y = 3$.

Skill Hints

> **HINT** To find the number of degrees in a polygon with 3 or more sides, multiply 180° by 2 less than the number of sides.

pentagon $(5 - 2) \times 180° = 3 \times 180° = 540°$
2 less than 5 sides

decagon $(10 - 2) \times 180° = 8 \times 180° = 1{,}440°$
2 less than 10 sides

Find the sum of the angle measures for each.

1. hexagon

2. octagon

3. quadrilateral

4. nonagon

5. dodecagon

6. 20-sided polygon

Find the missing angle measure for each.

7. pentagon with angles of 110°, 100°, 90°, and 80°

8. hexagon with 2 angles of 95° and 3 angles of 111°

9. quadrilateral with angles of 68°, 92°, and 45°

10. octagon with 3 angles of 147°, 3 angles of 108°, and 1 angle 82°

11. hexagon with 5 angles of 125°

12. heptagon with 3 angles of 120° and 3 angles of 150°

13. right triangle with an angle of 66°

14. triangle with 2 angles of 68°

Write *true* or *false*.

15. All hexagons have six angles.

16. Some rectangles are squares.

17. The sum of the angle measures of every decagon is 1,440°.

18. A quadrilateral can have angles that measure 154°, 62°, 107°, and 40°.

$\overset{\text{H}}{\underset{\text{T}}{\overset{\text{I}}{\text{N}}}}$ To subtract unlike mixed numbers, rename using the LCD.

$$\begin{array}{l} \quad\quad\quad\quad \overset{\lceil 5 = 4 + 1 \rceil\downarrow}{} \\ 5\frac{1}{3} \;=\; 5\frac{4}{12} \;=\; 4 + 1\frac{4}{12} \;=\; 4\frac{16}{12} \\ -1\frac{3}{4} \;=\; 1\frac{9}{12} \;=\; 1\frac{9}{12} \quad\quad\;=\; 1\frac{9}{12} \\ \hline 4 - 9 = ? \longrightarrow \quad\quad\quad\quad 3\frac{7}{12} \;\longleftarrow\; \text{difference} \end{array}$$

Estimate. Then subtract.

1. $\quad 2\frac{1}{2}$
 $\quad -1\frac{1}{4}$

2. $\quad 3\frac{1}{4}$
 $\quad -1\frac{1}{4}$

3. $\quad 4\frac{1}{8}$
 $\quad -1\frac{1}{4}$

4. $\quad 5\frac{1}{10}$
 $\quad -1\frac{1}{4}$

5. $\quad 6\frac{1}{3}$
 $\quad -1\frac{1}{4}$

6. $\quad 3\frac{2}{3}$
 $\quad -1\frac{1}{2}$

7. $\quad 4\frac{5}{8}$
 $\quad -2\frac{5}{6}$

8. $\quad 5$
 $\quad -3\frac{3}{7}$

9. $\quad 2\frac{7}{8}$
 $\quad -\;\frac{7}{8}$

10. $\quad 16\frac{1}{3}$
 $\quad -5\frac{3}{4}$

11. $8\frac{2}{5} - 3\frac{5}{6}$

12. $5\frac{2}{9} - 2\frac{1}{2}$

13. $6 - \frac{3}{4}$

14. $12\frac{2}{5} - 7$

Solve and check.

15. $3\frac{1}{2} + n = 5$

16. $2\frac{3}{5} + n = 4$

17. $9\frac{3}{8} + n = 12$

18. $5\frac{2}{3} + n = 15$

19. $2\frac{1}{4} + 4\frac{7}{8} = n$

20. $3\frac{2}{3} + 3\frac{2}{3} = n$

21. $1\frac{5}{7} + 2\frac{3}{7} = n$

22. $2 + 5\frac{7}{9} = n$

23. $n + 1\frac{3}{4} = 5\frac{1}{2}$

24. $n + 2\frac{1}{2} = 3\frac{1}{4}$

25. $n + 3\frac{4}{7} = 7$

26. $n + 8\frac{1}{3} = 12\frac{3}{4}$

H
I
N
T

To solve a fraction equation, be sure to do the same thing to both sides of the equation. Use inverse operations to solve fraction equations.

$$\frac{3}{5} \times n = 9$$

$$\frac{3}{5} \div \frac{3}{5} \times n = 9 \div \frac{3}{5}$$

$$n = \frac{\overset{3}{\cancel{9}}}{1} \times \frac{5}{\cancel{3}_1}$$

$$n = 15$$

← Use the inverse operation →

$$n \div \frac{3}{4} = 12$$

$$n \div \frac{3}{4} \times \frac{3}{4} = 12 \times \frac{3}{4}$$

$$n = \frac{\overset{3}{\cancel{12}}}{1} \times \frac{3}{\cancel{4}_1}$$

$$n = 9$$

Solve and check.

1. $\frac{4}{5} \times n = 16$

2. $\frac{2}{3} \times n = 20$

3. $\frac{5}{8} \times n = 30$

4. $n \div \frac{3}{7} = 63$

5. $n \div \frac{7}{8} = 32$

6. $n \div \frac{3}{10} = 80$

7. $n \times 3\frac{1}{2} = 14$

8. $n \times 2\frac{2}{3} = 24$

9. $n \times 1\frac{3}{4} = 21$

10. $n \div 1\frac{1}{3} = 3$

11. $n \div 5\frac{3}{5} = 10$

12. $n \div 3\frac{2}{3} = 12$

13. $n \times 1\frac{5}{6} = 2$

14. $n \div 4\frac{4}{5} = \frac{1}{3}$

15. $n \times 6 = 5\frac{1}{2}$

Write an equation. Then solve it.

16. The product of a number x and $2\frac{1}{2}$ is $5\frac{1}{2}$.

17. The product of a number x and $3\frac{3}{4}$ is $\frac{5}{6}$.

18. One half of a number x is $5\frac{2}{3}$.

19. A number x divided by $\frac{3}{5}$ is $3\frac{2}{3}$.

20. Three and a half times a number m equals $2\frac{1}{3}$.

21. The quotient of a number m and 8 equals $\frac{2}{5}$.

22. Ten times a number x equals the product of $\frac{2}{3}$ and $1\frac{1}{2}$.

23. A number n divided by $\frac{1}{4}$ equals the product of $2\frac{1}{4}$ and $\frac{1}{3}$.

^H
^I The mean and median of a set of data are not always numbers
^N in the data.
^T

Test scores: 90, 82, 80, 90

Arrange in order: 80, 82, 90, 90

Median: $\frac{82 + 90}{2} = 86$

Mean: $\frac{80 + 82 + 90 + 90}{4} = 85\frac{1}{2}$

Find the mean, mode, median, and range for each.

1. weekly salaries: $310, $455, $680, $425, $511

2. bowling scores: 210, 132, 109, 210, 151, 186

3. miles driven: 683, 513, 489, 555

4. glass jars recycled: 86, 92, 108, 111, 95

5. books read by class: 53, 53, 66, 88, 75

A stem and leaf plot is given for math test scores. Find each.

6. mean

7. mode

8. median

9. range

6	3
7	22259
8	1688
9	05

Tell which measure was used to analyze the data.

10. More than half the students in the class scored 85 or better on the last math test.

11. More people prefer the color blue than any other color.

12. The average monthly snowfall last winter was 5.5 in.

Skill Hints

H I N T Draw an X over a proportion to show the numbers to multiply for the cross products. Then solve the proportion.

$\frac{3}{4} \diagdown \frac{n}{22}$

$$3 \times 22 = 4 \times n$$
$$66 = 4 \times n$$
$$66 \div 4 = 4 \div 4 \times n$$
$$16.5 = n$$

Use = or ≠ for each ⬤.

1. $\frac{3}{2}$ ⬤ $\frac{9}{6}$

2. $\frac{2}{3}$ ⬤ $\frac{9}{18}$

3. $\frac{1}{3}$ ⬤ $\frac{5}{16}$

4. $\frac{2}{5}$ ⬤ $\frac{8}{20}$

5. $\frac{9}{8}$ ⬤ $\frac{10}{9}$

6. $\frac{9}{27}$ ⬤ $\frac{7}{21}$

7. $\frac{10}{12}$ ⬤ $\frac{15}{18}$

8. $\frac{8}{10}$ ⬤ $\frac{10}{8}$

9. $\frac{3}{5}$ ⬤ $\frac{35}{25}$

10. $\frac{6}{8}$ ⬤ $\frac{3.3}{4.4}$

Solve each proportion.

11. $\frac{n}{7} = \frac{12}{28}$

12. $\frac{3}{4} = \frac{n}{12.8}$

13. $\frac{n}{10} = \frac{3.5}{5}$

14. $\frac{12}{6} = \frac{n}{9}$

15. $\frac{3}{n} = \frac{30}{44}$

16. $\frac{12}{15} = \frac{16}{n}$

17. $\frac{24}{n} = \frac{32}{36}$

18. $\frac{6}{10} = \frac{16.2}{n}$

19. $n : 15 = 5 : 75$

20. $6 : n = 8 : 10$

21. $9 : 12 = n : 20$

22. $10 : 35 = 40 : n$

Write each as a percent.

23. $\frac{3}{10}$

24. $\frac{33}{100}$

25. $\frac{3}{500}$

26. $\frac{3}{1,000}$

27. $\frac{537}{100}$

28. $\frac{68}{10}$

29. $\frac{19}{1,000}$

30. $\frac{344}{10}$

Write each as a ratio.

31. 39%

32. 10%

33. 253%

34. 0.4%

35. 500%

36. $66\frac{2}{3}\%$

37. $\frac{1}{4}\%$

38. $1\frac{1}{2}\%$

H
I   Every percent equation has 3 parts: the percent, P,
N   the whole, W, and the part of the whole, N.
T
Remember: $\frac{P}{100} \times W = N$.

What percent of 50 is 20?	20% of 40 is what number?
$\frac{P}{100} \times 50 = 20$	$\frac{20}{100} \times 40 = N$
$\frac{P}{100} = \frac{20}{50}$	$\frac{1}{5} \times 40 = N$
$P = 40$	$8 = N$
40% of 50 is 20.	20% of 40 is 8.

20% of what number is 40?

$\frac{20}{100} \times W = 40$

$\frac{1}{5} \times W = 40$

$W = 200$

20% of 200 is 40.

Solve.

1. What percent of 20 is 9?

2. $33\frac{1}{3}\%$ of 180 is what number?

3. 15% of what number is 84?

4. What percent of 40 is 15?

5. 25% of 36 is what number?

6. 12% of what number is 60?

7. What percent of 40 is 36?

8. 85% of 48 is what number?

9. 2% of what number is 56?

10. What percent of 80 is 37.6?

11. 75% of 88 is what number?

12. 110% of what number is 99?

Find the sale price.

13. regular price: $56.00
    rate of discount: 20%

14. regular price: $125.00
    rate of discount: 32%

π (pi) is a number. An approximation of its value is 3.14.

Twice the radius of a circle is the diameter.

What if a circle has a radius of 3 cm?
Find the circumference and the area of the circle.

$C = \pi d$ $\qquad\qquad$ $A = \pi r^2$

$\approx 3.14 \times 6$ cm $\qquad\qquad$ $\approx 3.14 \times 3$ cm $\times$ 3 cm

≈ 18.84 cm $\qquad\qquad$ ≈ 28.26 cm^2

Find the circumference and the area of each circle.

1. radius = 7 mm

2. diameter = 8 m

3. radius = 9 m

4. diameter = 10 cm

5. radius = 3.2 mm

6. diameter = 11 cm

7. radius = 6.7 m

8. diameter = 8.2 km

9. radius = 1.4 m

Find the area of each figure.

10.

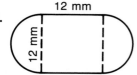

10 cm

8 cm

11.

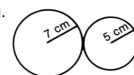

7 cm   5 cm

12.

12 mm

12 mm

13.

10 m   20 m

HINT

The sum of two positive integers is positive. $^+4 + {}^+5 = {}^+9$

The sum of two negative integers is negative. $^-8 + {}^-3 = {}^-11$

The sum of a positive integer and a negative integer has the same sign as the integer with the greater absolute value.

$^-8 + {}^+3 = {}^-5$
$^-2 + {}^+6 = {}^+4$

To subtract an integer, add its opposite.

$^+4 - {}^+5 = {}^+4 + {}^-5 = {}^-1$
$^+6 - {}^-3 = {}^+6 + {}^+3 = {}^+9$

Add or subtract.

1. $^-4 + {}^-7$

2. $^-4 + {}^+8$

3. $^-4 + {}^-13$

4. $^+4 + {}^+10$

5. $^+3 + {}^-5$

6. $^+5 + {}^-6$

7. $^+7 + {}^-7$

8. $^-8 + {}^-7$

9. $^+4 - {}^-6$

10. $^+5 - {}^+7$

11. $^+6 - {}^+4$

12. $^+5 - {}^+12$

13. $^-7 - {}^+5$

14. $^-8 - {}^-3$

15. $^-9 - {}^+1$

16. $^-6 - {}^-6$

Solve and check.

17. $^-4 + n = {}^+10$

18. $n - {}^+5 = {}^-10$

19. $^-6 + n = {}^-5$

20. $n - {}^+3 = {}^+12$

21. $n + {}^-7 = {}^-20$

22. $n - {}^+10 = {}^-3$

23. $n + {}^+6 = {}^-11$

24. $n - {}^-8 = {}^+18$

25. $^+6 - {}^-7 = n$

26. $^+4 - {}^+12 = n$

27. $^+10 + {}^-18 = n$

28. $^-36 + {}^+14 = n$

29. $n - {}^-10 = {}^+6$

30. $^+14 + n = {}^-7$

31. $^-13 + n = 0$

32. $^-42 + n = {}^-12$

H
I
N
T

The product and the quotient of two positive integers or two negative integers are positive.

$$-3 \cdot -8 = +24 \qquad -35 \div -7 = +5$$
$$+6 \cdot +5 = +30 \qquad +48 \div +6 = +8$$

The product and the quotient of a positive integer and a negative integer are negative.

$$-4 \cdot +7 = -28 \qquad -27 \div +3 = -9$$
$$+3 \cdot -6 = -18 \qquad +16 \div -2 = -8$$

Multiply.

1. $-7 \cdot -8$

2. $+5 \cdot -4$

3. $-3 \cdot +5$

4. $+6 \cdot +6$

5. $-9 \cdot +6$

6. $-8 \cdot -8$

7. $-9 \cdot +7 \cdot -1$

8. $-2 \cdot -3 \cdot -4$

9. $+5 \cdot -9$

10. $-7 \cdot +4 \cdot -2$

11. $+8 \cdot +7$

12. $-7 \cdot -7 \cdot -1$

Divide.

13. $-20 \div -2$

14. $-15 \div +3$

15. $+24 \div -4$

16. $+49 \div +7$

17. $-42 \div -6$

18. $+48 \div -6$

19. $-45 \div -5$

20. $-55 \div +11$

21. $-56 \div -7$

22. $+25 \div -5$

23. $-64 \div +8$

24. $+72 \div -8$

Solve and check.

25. $\frac{n}{+6} = -8$

26. $+4n = -36$

27. $-5n = -50$

28. $\frac{n}{-7} = +8$

29. $-81 = -9n$

30. $-60 = +6n$

31. $-5 = \frac{n}{-6}$

32. $-7 = \frac{n}{+3}$

33. $-49 = +7n$

34. $-63 = -9n$

35. $\frac{n}{-6} = +5$

36. $-11 = \frac{n}{-5}$

For a given number of items, to find the number of
permutations, multiply the number of choices for each
selection.

Find the number of permutations of 5 things, chosen 5 at a time.

$$5 \times 4 \times 3 \times 2 \times 1 = 120$$

Find the number of permutations for each.

1. 4 people, chosen 3 at a time

2. 5 people, chosen 2 at a time

3. 6 cards, chosen 6 at a time

4. 10 books, chosen 3 at a time

5. 26 letters, chosen 2 at a time

6. 10 digits, chosen 4 at a time

7. 15 volumes, chosen 1 at a time

8. 9 pens, chosen 2 at a time

Find the number of combinations for each.

9. 3 people, chosen 2 at a time

10. 4 people, chosen 2 at a time

11. 5 cards, chosen 2 at a time

12. 6 cards, chosen 2 at a time

13. 4 cards, chosen 3 at a time

14. 5 cards, chosen 4 at a time

15. 6 books, chosen 3 at a time

16. 6 books, chosen 5 at a time

Skill Hints

The square of a number n is that number multiplied by itself.

$$7^2 = 7 \times 7 = 49$$

The square root of a number n is a number that when multiplied by itself equals n.

$$\sqrt{49} = 7$$

Find the square of each number.

1. 1   **2.** 6   **3.** 13   **4.** 17   **5.** 22

6. 25   **7.** 31   **8.** 40   **9.** 18   **10.** 35

Find the square root of each number.

11. 1   **12.** 4   **13.** 25   **14.** 81   **15.** 144

16. 324   **17.** 729   **18.** 196   **19.** 900   **20.** 2,500

Let a and b be the measures of the legs and c be the measure of the hypotenuse of a right triangle. Then the Pythagorean Rule states that $a^2 + b^2 = c^2$. If the sides of a triangle satisfy the Pythagorean Rule, then the triangle is a right triangle.

$$6^2 + 8^2 = 10^2$$
$$36 + 64 = 100$$

Is each triangle a right triangle? Write *yes* or *no*.

21. 4 cm, 5 cm, 7 cm   **22.** 5 m, 12 m, 13 m   **23.** 5 m, 6 m, 8 m

24. 9 cm, 12 cm, 15 cm   **25.** 8 km, 10 km, 12 km   **26.** 34 m, 30 m, 16 m

absolute value The distance a number is from 0 on the number line. p. 378

acute angle An angle with a measure less than 90°. p. 136

acute triangle A triangle with three acute angles. p. 144

additive inverses Two numbers whose sum is 0. p. 384
Example: $^-3$ and $^+3$ are additive inverses.

adjacent angles Angles that have a common ray and a common vertex between them. p. 138

angle Two rays with a common endpoint called the vertex. p. 136

arc A part of the circumference of a circle. p. 152

area The number of square units needed to cover a region. p. 340

associative property of addition The way that addends are grouped does not change the sum. p. 14
Example: $(a + b) + c = a + (b + c)$

associative property of multiplication The way that factors are grouped does not change the product. p. 34
Example: $(a \times b) \times c = a \times (b \times c)$

base (of a polygon) p. 342
Example:
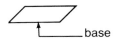
base

base (of a space figure) p. 356
Example:

base

bisect To divide into two congruent parts. p. 446

box and whisker plot A method of displaying the quartiles and the range of the data. p. 252
Example:

central angle An angle that has its vertex at the center of a circle. p. 153

chord A line segment with both endpoints on a circle. p. 152

circle A plane closed figure with all points the same distance from a point called the center. p. 152

circumference The distance around a circle. p. 346

combination A selection in which order is not important. p. 431

common factor A factor of two or more numbers. p. 86

common multiple A multiple of two or more numbers. p. 88

commutative property of addition The order of the addends does not change the sum. p. 14
Example: $a + b = b + a$

commutative property of multiplication The order of the factors does not change the product. p. 34
Example: $a \times b = b \times a$

complementary angles Two angles the sum of whose measures is 90°. p. 138
Example:
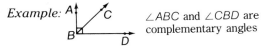
$\angle ABC$ and $\angle CBD$ are complementary angles

composite number A whole number greater than 1 with more than two factors. p. 78

compound event Two or more events considered together. p. 422

cone A space figure with a circular base and one vertex. p. 360

congruent figures Figures that have the same size and shape. p. 142

coordinate plane The plane determined by a horizontal number line, called the x-axis, and a vertical number line, called the y-axis, intersecting at a point called the origin. Each point of the plane corresponds to an ordered pair of numbers. p. 404

counting principle If a first event has *n* outcomes and a second event has *m* outcomes, then the first event followed by the second event has $n \times m$ outcomes. p. 420

Glossary

cross products Products obtained by multiplying the numerator of one fraction by the denominator of a second fraction and the denominator of the first fraction by the numerator of the second fraction.   p. 278

Example: $\frac{2}{3} = \frac{4}{6}$ $2 \times 6 = 3 \times 4$

cube A space figure with six square faces.   p. 351

cylinder A space figure with two parallel bases that are congruent circles.   p. 358

data Information that is gathered.   p. 246

decimal A number with one or more places to the right of a decimal point.   p. 6

degree (°) A unit for measuring angles.   p. 136

denominator The number below the fraction bar in a fraction.   p. 172

diagonal A segment joining any two nonadjacent vertices in a polygon.   p. 140

diameter A line segment that passes through the center of a circle and has both endpoints on the circle.   p. 152

discount The amount that a regular price is reduced.   p. 318

distributive property of multiplication over addition If one factor is a sum, multiplying before adding does not change the product.   p. 34
Example: $a \times (b + c) = (a \times b) + (a \times c)$

divisible A number is divisible by another number if, after dividing, the remainder is zero.   p. 70

edge The segment formed where two faces of a space figure meet.   p. 351
Example:

—edge

endpoint A point at the end of a segment or ray.   p. 135

equation A number sentence with an equals sign (=).   p. 108

equilateral triangle A triangle with all sides congruent.   p. 144

equivalent fractions Fractions that name the same number.   p. 174

estimate To give an approximate rather than an exact answer.   p. 18, 22, 38, 50, 186, 206

event One or more outcomes of an experiment.   p. 418

expanded form A number written as the sum of the values of its digits.   p. 4

exponent A number that tells how many times the base is used as a factor.   p. 72

expression A mathematical phrase made up of a variable or combination of variables and/or numbers and operations.   p. 102

Examples: $5n$, $4x - 7$, $(5 \times 2) - \frac{6}{3}$

face A flat surface of a space figure.   p. 351

factors Numbers that are multiplied to obtain a product.   p. 34, 76
Example: For $3 \times 8 = 24$, 3 and 8 are factors of 24.

formula An equation that states a fact or rule.   p. 122

fraction A number in the form $\frac{a}{b}$ that names part of a region or part of a group. The number below the fraction bar is the denominator. The number above the fraction bar is the numerator.   p. 172

frequency The number of times a given item occurs in a set of data.   p. 244, 414

frequency table A listing of data together with their frequencies.   p. 244

graph A drawing used to present data. Some types are bar graphs, line graphs, and circle graphs.   p. 260

greatest common factor (GCF) The greatest number that is a factor of each of two or more numbers.   p. 86

height (of a parallelogram) A segment that joins opposite sides and is perpendicular to the base.   p. 342
Example:

—height

514

height (of a triangle) A segment drawn perpendicular to a side of a triangle from the opposite vertex. p. 344

height

heptagon A polygon with seven sides. p. 140

hexagon A polygon with six sides. p. 140

histogram A bar graph that represents frequency data. p. 270

hypotenuse In a right triangle, the side opposite the right angle. p. 457

identity property of addition The sum of any number and 0 is that number. p. 14
Example: $0 + a = a$

identity property of multiplication The product of any number and 1 is that number. p. 34
Example: $1 \times a = a$

improper fraction A fraction in which the numerator is greater than or equal to the denominator. p. 172

independent events Two events in which the outcome of the second is not affected by the outcome of the first. p. 422

inequality A mathematical sentence that uses one of the symbols $<$, $\leq$, $>$, $\geq$, or $\neq$. p. 400

integer The numbers . . . $^-3, ^-2, ^-1, 0, ^+1, ^+2, . . .$ p. 376

interest The charge for borrowing money or the amount paid for the use of money. p. 330

intersecting lines Lines that have exactly one point in common. p. 134
Example:

$\overleftrightarrow{AB}$ intersects $\overleftrightarrow{CD}$ at point *F*.

inverse operations Two operations that are opposite in effect. Addition and subtraction are inverse operations. Multiplication and division are inverse operations. p. 114

isosceles triangle A triangle with two congruent sides. p. 144

least common denominator (LCD) The least common multiple of the denominators of two or more fractions. p. 188

least common multiple (LCM) The least nonzero number that is a multiple of each of two or more numbers. p. 88

line The collection of points along a straight path. A line has no endpoints. p. 134

line of symmetry A line that divides a figure into two congruent parts. p. 154

line plot A method of showing each item of data on a number line. p. 246

line segment A part of a line having two endpoints. p. 444

lowest terms A fraction is in lowest terms, or simplest form, when the GCF of the numerator and the denominator is 1. p. 174

mean In a collection of data, the sum of all the data divided by the number of data. p. 248

median The middle number or average of the two middle numbers in a collection of data when the data are arranged in order. p. 246

mixed number A number written as a whole number and a fraction. p. 172

mode The number or numbers that occur most often in a collection of data. p. 246

multiple of a number The product of that whole number and any other whole number. p. 70, 76

negative integer An integer less than 0. p. 378

numerator The number above the fraction bar in a fraction. p. 172

obtuse angle An angle with a measure greater than 90° but less than 180°. p. 136

obtuse triangle A triangle with one obtuse angle. p. 144

octagon A polygon with eight sides. p. 140

opposites Two numbers that are the same distance from 0 on the number line but in opposite directions. p. 378
Example: $^+3$ and $^-3$ are opposite integers.

ordered pair A pair of numbers used to locate a point in the coordinate plane. p. 404

origin The point of intersection of the *x*-axis and *y*-axis in a coordinate plane. p. 404

outcome A possible result of a probability experiment. p. 418

Glossary

parallel lines Lines in the same plane that never intersect. p. 134

parallelogram A quadrilateral with opposite sides parallel. Each pair of opposite sides and angles is congruent. p. 146

pentagon A polygon with five sides. p. 140

percent A ratio whose second term is 100. Percent means parts per hundred. The symbol % is used for percent. p. 292

perimeter The distance around a polygon. p. 340

permutation An arrangement of items in which order is important. p. 429

perpendicular lines Two lines that intersect to form right angles. p. 134

pi π The ratio of the circumference of a circle to its diameter. The ratio is the same for all circles. $\pi \approx .3.14$ or $\frac{22}{7}$ p. 346

plane A flat surface extending endlessly in all directions. p. 134

point A location in a plane or in space. p. 134

polygon A closed plane figure made up of line segments. p. 140

polyhedron A space figure whose surfaces or faces are all flat. p. 161

positive integer An integer greater than 0. p. 378

prime factorization Writing a number as the product of prime factors. p. 84
Example: $24 = 2 \times 2 \times 2 \times 3$

prime number A whole number greater than 1 with only two factors—itself and 1. p. 78

principal An amount of money borrowed or loaned. p. 330

prism A polyhedron with two parallel, congruent faces called bases. p. 356

probability The ratio of favorable outcomes to possible outcomes of an experiment. p. 418

product The answer in multiplication. p. 38

proper fraction A fraction in which the numerator is less than the denominator. p. 172

proportion A sentence that states that two ratios are equal. p. 278

Example: $\frac{3}{6} = \frac{8}{16}$

pyramid A space figure whose base is a polygon and whose faces are triangles with a common vertex. p. 361

Pythagorean rule In a right triangle the square of the measure of the hypotenuse (c) equals the sum of the squares of the measures of the legs (a and b). That is, $c^2 = a^2 + b^2$. p. 456

quadrilateral A polygon with four sides and four angles. p. 146

quotient The answer in division. p. 50

radius A line segment with one endpoint at the center of a circle and the other endpoint on the circle. p. 152

range The difference between the greatest and the least numbers in a collection of data. p. 246

rate A ratio that compares different kinds of units. p. 276

ratio A pair of numbers that compare two quantities or describe a rate. p. 274

ray A part of a line that has one endpoint and extends endlessly in one direction. p. 136

reciprocals Two fractions whose product is 1. p. 222

Example: $\frac{3}{4} \times \frac{4}{3} = 1$

rectangle A parallelogram with four right angles. p. 146

reflection The mirror image of a figure about a line of symmetry in a plane. p. 154

regular polygon A polygon with all sides congruent and all angles congruent. p. 141

relative frequency The ratio of the number of favorable outcomes to the total numbers of trials. p. 417

repeating decimal A decimal in which a digit or group of digits repeats endlessly. p. 180

rhombus A parallelogram with all sides congruent. p. 146

right angle An angle that measures 90°. p. 136

right triangle A triangle with one right angle. p. 144

rotation A transformation obtained by rotating a figure through a given angle about a point. p. 154

sample space All the possible results, or outcomes, for an experiment. p. 418

scale drawing A drawing that is a reduction or an enlargement of an actual object. p. 282

scalene triangle A triangle that has no congruent sides. p. 144

scientific notation Writing the number as the product of two factors. The first factor is a number from 1 to 10. The second factor is a power of 10 in exponent form. p. 74

sequence A list of numbers that follow a rule or a pattern. p. 70

similar figures Figures that are the same shape but not necessarily the same size. p. 286

skew lines Lines that do not intersect and are not in the same plane. p. 134

solution The value of a variable that makes a number sentence true. p. 108

solve To find all the solutions of an equation. p. 118

sphere A space figure with all points the same distance from a point called the center. p. 161

square (in geometry) A rectangle with all sides congruent. p. 146

square (in numeration) To multiply a number by itself. p. 455
Example: The square of 7 is $7 \times 7 = 7^2 = 49$

square root The square root of a, written $\sqrt{a}$, is the number whose square is a. p. 455
Example: The square root of 36, $\sqrt{36}$, is 6, since $6^2 = 36$. p. 455

statistics The science of collection, organizing, and analyzing data. p. 246

stem and leaf plot A method of organizing data for the purpose of comparison. p. 250
Example:

```
3 | 0 1 4
4 | 5 2 6
5 | 1 1 3     Key:
6 | 2          3|4 = 34
```

straight angle An angle that measures 180°. p. 136

supplementary angles Two angles the sum of whose measures is 180°. p. 136

Example:

∠ACB and ∠BCD are supplementary angles.

surface area The sum of the areas of all the faces of a space figure. p. 350

terminating decimal A decimal that ends or repeats only zeros. p. 180
Example: 0.75 is a terminating decimal.

tessellation A design in which congruent figures are arranged to fill the plane in such a way that no figures overlap and there are no gaps. p. 159, 162

transformation A change in the size, shape, or position of a figure. p. 158

translation A change in position resulting from a slide without any turn. p. 156

transversal A line that intersects two or more lines at different points. p. 138

trapezoid A quadrilateral with exactly one pair of parallel sides. p. 146

tree diagram A diagram used to show outcomes of an experiment. p. 420

triangle A polygon with three sides. p. 144

unit price The ratio: price per unit of measure. p. 60, 276

variable A letter used to stand for a number in an expression or equation. p. 102

Venn diagram A special diagram using overlapping circles to show the relationship between groups of objects. p. 90

vertex A point where two or more sides of a geometric figure meet. p. 136

vertical angles A pair of opposite angles formed by intersecting lines. p. 138

volume The number of cubic units needed to fill a space figure. p. 356

***x*- and *y*-axes** The horizontal and vertical number lines in a coordinate plane. p. 404

zero property of multiplication The product of any number and 0 is 0. p. 34
Example: $a \times 0 = 0$ and $0 \times a = 0$

Computer Terms

BACK *n* (BK *n*) Moves the turtle backward *n* turtle steps.

BASIC A computer language.

cell The smallest unit of a spreadsheet located by a column and a row.

CLEARSCREEN (CS) Clears the screen. In some versions, also homes the turtle.

DRAW or CG In some versions, clears the screen and homes the turtle.

FORWARD *n* (FD *n*) Moves the turtle forward *n* turtle steps.

HIDETURTLE (HT) Makes the turtle not visible on the screen.

HOME Positions the turtle in the middle of the screen, heading straight up.

IF condition [ ] [ ] If condition is true, executes command(s) in first [ ]. If false, executes command(s) in second [ ].

IF . . . THEN . . . ELSE Equivalent to IF condition in some versions of Logo.

ITEM *n* [ ] Returns the *n*th item in a list.

LEFT *n* (LT *n*) Turns the turtle left *n* degrees from its current heading.

Logo A computer language.

MAKE "X *n* Assigns the value *n* to the variable named.

OUTPUT (OP) In a procedure, returns a value.

PENDOWN (PD) Allows turtle to draw again.

PENERASE (PE) Allows turtle to erase a line segment. (Use command with PENDOWN).

PENUP (PU) Allows turtle to move without drawing.

PRINT (PR) A Logo command that shows information on the screen.

procedure Creates a new Logo command that can execute a specified set of commands. A procedure is called by entering its name.

RANDOM *n* Returns a whole number from 0 to $n - 1$.

REMAINDER *n*1 *n*2 Returns the remainder of $n1 \div n2$.

REPEAT *n*[ ] A Logo command that repeats commands within brackets *n* times. *Example:* REPEAT 4 [FD 10] moves the turtle 10 turtle steps forward four times.

RIGHT *n* (RT *n*) Turns the turtle right *n* degrees from its current heading.

SETPOS [*n*1 *n*2] Positions the turtle at a specified point (*n*1, *n*2). (Some versions of Logo)

SETXY *n*1 *n*2 Positions the turtle at (*n*1, *n*2). (Some versions of Logo)

SHOWTURTLE (ST) Makes the turtle visible on the screen.

spreadsheet Data consisting of rows and columns of numbers. A computer spreadsheet records data and performs calculations.

To procedure name, . . . END Defines a procedure.

turtle step A measure of turtle movement.

Squares and Square Roots

N	N²	√N
1	1	1.00
2	4	1.41
3	9	1.73
4	16	2.00
5	25	2.24
6	36	2.45
7	49	2.65
8	64	2.83
9	81	3.00
10	100	3.16
11	121	3.32
12	144	3.46
13	169	3.61
14	196	3.74
15	225	3.87
16	256	4.00
17	289	4.12
18	324	4.24
19	361	4.36
20	400	4.47
21	441	4.58
22	484	4.69
23	529	4.80
24	576	4.90
25	625	5.00
26	676	5.10
27	729	5.20
28	784	5.29
29	841	5.39
30	900	5.48
31	961	5.57
32	1,024	5.66
33	1,089	5.74
34	1,156	5.83
35	1,225	5.92
36	1,296	6.00
37	1,369	6.08
38	1,444	6.16
39	1,521	6.24
40	1,600	6.32
41	1,681	6.40
42	1,764	6.48
43	1,849	6.56
44	1,936	6.63
45	2,025	6.71
46	2,116	6.78
47	2,209	6.86
48	2,304	6.93
49	2,401	7.00
50	2,500	7.07

N	N²	√N
51	2,601	7.14
52	2,704	7.21
53	2,809	7.28
54	2,916	7.35
55	3,025	7.42
56	3,136	7.48
57	3,249	7.55
58	3,364	7.62
59	3,481	7.68
60	3,600	7.75
61	3,721	7.81
62	3,844	7.87
63	3,969	7.94
64	4,096	8.00
65	4,225	8.06
66	4,356	8.12
67	4,489	8.19
68	4,624	8.25
69	4,761	8.31
70	4,900	8.37
71	5,041	8.43
72	5,184	8.49
73	5,329	8.54
74	5,476	8.60
75	5,625	8.66
76	5,776	8.72
77	5,929	8.77
78	6,084	8.83
79	6,241	8.89
80	6,400	8.94
81	6,561	9.00
82	6,724	9.06
83	6,889	9.11
84	7,056	9.17
85	7,225	9.22
86	7,396	9.27
87	7,569	9.33
88	7,744	9.38
89	7,921	9.43
90	8,100	9.49
91	8,281	9.54
92	8,464	9.59
93	8,649	9.64
94	8,836	9.70
95	9,025	9.75
96	9,216	9.80
97	9,409	9.85
98	9,604	9.90
99	9,801	9.95
100	10,000	10.00

N	N²	√N
101	10,201	10.05
102	10,404	10.10
103	10,609	10.15
104	10,816	10.20
105	11,025	10.25
106	11,236	10.30
107	11,449	10.34
108	11,664	10.39
109	11,881	10.44
110	12,100	10.49
111	12,321	10.54
112	12,544	10.58
113	12,769	10.63
114	12,996	10.68
115	13,225	10.72
116	13,456	10.77
117	13,689	10.82
118	13,924	10.86
119	14,161	10.91
120	14,400	10.95
121	14,641	11.00
122	14,884	11.05
123	15,129	11.09
124	15,376	11.14
125	15,625	11.18
126	15,876	11.22
127	16,129	11.27
128	16,384	11.31
129	16,641	11.36
130	16,900	11.40
131	17,161	11.45
132	17,424	11.49
133	17,689	11.53
134	17,956	11.58
135	18,225	11.62
136	18,496	11.66
137	18,769	11.70
138	19,044	11.75
139	19,321	11.79
140	19,600	11.83
141	19,881	11.87
142	20,164	11.92
143	20,449	11.96
144	20,736	12.00
145	21,025	12.04
146	21,316	12.08
147	21,609	12.12
148	21,904	12.17
149	22,201	12.21
150	22,500	12.25

Measures

Metric

LENGTH
1 millimeter (mm) = 0.001 meter (m)
1 centimeter (cm) = 0.01 meter
1 decimeter (dm) = 0.1 meter
1 dekameter (dam) = 10 meters
1 hectometer (hm) = 100 meters
1 kilometer (km) = 1,000 meters

MASS/WEIGHT
1 milligram (mg) = 0.001 gram (g)
1 centigram (cg) = 0.01 gram
1 decigram (dg) = 0.1 gram
1 dekagram (dag) = 10 grams
1 hectogram (hg) = 100 grams
1 kilogram (kg) = 1,000 grams
1 metric ton (t) = 1,000 kilograms

CAPACITY
1 milliliter (mL) = 0.001 liter (L)
1 centiliter (cL) = 0.01 liter
1 deciliter (dL) = 0.1 liter
1 dekaliter (daL) = 10 liters
1 hectoliter (hL) = 100 liters
1 kiloliter (kL) = 1,000 liters

AREA
1 square centimeter (cm²) = 100 square millimeters (mm²)
1 square meter (m²) = 10,000 square centimeters
1 hectare (ha) = 10,000 square meters
1 square kilometer (km²) = 1,000,000 square meters

Customary

LENGTH
1 foot (ft) = 12 inches (in.)
1 yard (yd) = 36 inches
1 yard = 3 feet
1 mile (mi) = 5,280 feet
1 mile = 1,760 yards

WEIGHT
1 pound (lb) = 16 ounces (oz)
1 ton (T) = 2,000 pounds

CAPACITY
1 cup (c) = 8 fluid ounces (fl oz)
1 pint (pt) = 2 cups
1 quart (qt) = 2 pints
1 quart = 4 cups
1 gallon (gal) = 4 quarts

AREA
1 square foot (ft²) = 144 square inches (in.²)
1 square yard (yd²) = 9 square feet
1 acre = 43,560 square feet
1 square mile (mi²) = 640 acres

TIME
1 minute (min) = 60 seconds (s)
1 hour (h) = 60 minutes
1 day (d) = 24 hours
1 week (wk) = 7 days
1 year (yr) = 12 months (mo)
1 year = 52 weeks
1 year = 365 days
1 century (c) = 100 years

Formulas

$P = 2(l + w)$ — Perimeter of a rectangle
$P = 4s$ — Perimeter of a square
$P = ns$ — Perimeter of a regular polygon
n = number of sides
$A = lw$ — Area of a rectangle
$A = s^2$ — Area of a square
$A = bh$ — Area of a parallelogram
$A = \frac{1}{2}bh$ — Area of a triangle
$C = \pi d$ — Circumference of a circle
$A = \pi r^2$ — Area of a circle
$V = lwh$ — Volume of a rectangular prism
$V = Bh$ — Volume of any prism
B = area of base
$V = \pi r^2 h$ — Volume of a cylinder
$I = prt$ — Simple interest

Symbols

$=$ is equal to
$\neq$ is not equal to
$>$ is greater than
$<$ is less than
$\geq$ is greater than or equal to
$\leq$ is less than or equal to
$\approx$ is approximately equal to
$\cong$ is congruent to
$\sim$ is similar to
... continues without end
$1.\overline{3}$ repeating decimal 1.333 . . .
% percent
π pi (approximately 3.14)
° degree
°C degree Celsius
°F degree Fahrenheit

$\overleftrightarrow{AB}$ line AB
$\overline{AB}$ line segment AB
$\overrightarrow{AB}$ ray AB
$\angle ABC$ angle ABC
$m\angle ABC$ measure of angle ABC
$\triangle ABC$ triangle ABC
$\overarc{AB}$ arc AB
$\parallel$ is parallel to
$\perp$ is perpendicular to
2:5 ratio of 2 to 5
10^2 ten to the second power
$\sqrt{}$ square root
$^+4$ positive 4
$^-4$ negative 4
$|^-4|$ absolute value of $^-4$
$(3, ^-4)$ ordered pair 3, $^-4$
$P(E)$ probability of event E

Index

Index

Index

Index

Credits